W9-ACE-537

Sing
with the
Heart of a Bear

Sing
with the
Heart of a Bear

Fusions of
Native and American Poetry
1890–1999

Kenneth Lincoln

UNIVERSITY OF CALIFORNIA PRESS

Berkeley   Los Angeles   London

University of California Press
Berkeley and Los Angeles, California

University of California Press, Ltd.
London, England

© 2000 by the Regents of the University of California

Library of Congress Cataloging-in-Publication Data

Lincoln, Kenneth.
    Sing with the heart of a bear : fusions of native and American poetry, 1890–1999 /
Kenneth Lincoln.
        p.   cm.
    Includes bibliographical references.
    ISBN 0-520-21889-2 (alk. paper). — ISBN 0-520-21890-6 (pbk. : alk. paper)
    1. American poetry—Indian authors—History and criticism.   2. American poetry—
Indian influences.   3. Indians in Literature.   I. Title.
PS310.I52L56   1999
811.009'897—dc21   99-11519
                                                                                        CIP

Manufactured in the United States of America

08   07   06   05   04   03   02   01   00   99   10   9   8   7   6   5   4   3   2   1

The paper used in this publication meets the minimum requirements of ANSI/NISO
Z39.48-1992 (R 1997) (*Permanence of Paper*).

for my mother, Helen Graham (1921–1997),
who taught me to listen
with love for my daughter, Rachel,
who hears me now

This is an instance of the "sacred language" . . . *çanté mató keçaça,* also translated "with a heart that is different," but carrying the idea of the fierceness of a bear.

FRANCES DENSMORE, *Teton Sioux Music*

How can we get there from here, I wonder, to the center of the world, to the place where the universe carries down the song of night to our human lives? How can we listen or see to find our way by feel to the heart of every yes or no? How do we learn to trust ourselves enough to hear the chanting of the earth? To know what's alive or absent around us, and penetrate the void behind our eyes, the old, slow pulse of things, until a wild flying wakes up in us, a new mercy climbs out and takes wing in the sky?

LINDA HOGAN, *Dwellings*

CONTENTS

III • TRIBAL SIBYLS

'This may wel be rym dogerel,' quod he.
'Why so?' quod I, 'why wiltow lette me
Moore of my tale than another man,
Syn that it is the beste rym I kan?'
'By God,' quod he, 'for pleynly, at a word,
Thy drasty rymyng is nat worth a toord!
Thou doost noght elles but despendest tyme.
Sire, at o word, thou shalt no lenger ryme.
Lat se wher thou kanst tellen aught in geeste,
Or telle in prose somwhat, at the leeste,
In which ther be som murthe or som doctryne.'

The Canterbury Tales,
"HEERE THE HOOST STYNTETH CHAUCER"

I made you the gift of a small, brown stone,
And you described it with the tips of your fingers
And knew at once that it was beautiful—
At once, accordingly you knew,
As you knew the forms of the earth at Abiquiu:
That time involves them and they bear away,
Beautiful, various, remote,
In failing light, and the coming of cold.

N. SCOTT MOMADAY TO GEORGIA O'KEEFFE,
"FORMS OF THE EARTH AT ABIQUIU"

PREFACE

Cultural Fusions

Finding myself now surrounded by professors of hip-hop; by clones of Gallic-Germanic theory; by ideologues of gender and of various sexual persuasions; by multiculturalists unlimited, I realize that the Balkanization of literary studies is irreversible.

"ELEGIAC CONCLUSION," HAROLD BLOOM, *The Western Canon*

Sing with the Heart of a Bear cross-refers Anglo-American and American Indian literatures, as they have evolved over a century. Drawing coalitional ties across territorial boundaries, I am not trying to prove or disprove any Big Bang Theory, hyper-textual or otherwise, nor do I champion what Harold Bloom calls the School of Resentment in ethnic and feminist cultural studies. The focus raises a basic question: As critics hassle reconstructed historical polemics behind Euro-American texts, classical or emancipated, can readers address a native poetics? We need to locate textual benchmarks in this hybrid new land. Since the Harper, Norton, Oxford, Cambridge, and Heath revised anthologies of American literature are layered now with American Indian writings, why is there no whisper of ceremonial tradition or native literatures in Bloom's Western Canon? An ax is buried in the curriculum.

No doubt, to trace comparative aesthetics through our multicultural histories will intersect tangled thoroughfares. Why bother to conflate mainstream and so-called ethnic texts, when both sides vex the middle? Clearing a two-way path may serve to weed respected texts of canonical presumption; equally, this indigenous tracking can help to rescue ghettoized new writings from ethnocentric obscurity, dismissed as upstart or politically correct fads. All these issues turn on what we think, diversely, literature is. If *rymyng* and closed-field literary theory, since Chaucer's day to Derrida, seem suspect, or worse, *nat worth a toord!,* let's get back through literary history, postdeconstructively, to what Ezra Pound calls the A-B-C of reading: How and why writers think what they mean, as a social scientist might ask, when we hear, read, or say things said to be literary. New Critical *-ism* to post-colonial chasm, we need to know what separates writer from reader, audience from context, critic from common sense. How can we lessen the textual distance, the critical disturbance?

Scholars are welcome to this debate, but not granted house rule or given the last word. I'd like to stir the reader's interest in ethnic cultures, both migrant and aboriginal—particularly in how literary interactions from Old World to New, émigré to native, have fused into American literatures. Hybrid aesthetics have an honorable history. Chaucer's texts infused Norman French into Middle English literacy, blended continental inflections with island colonizations of Celts and Picts by northern European Angles and Saxons. Medieval English may seem distant in history and place, an odd dialect of our tongue in a different time-space, to be sure, but not so other translatively that we cannot savor Chaucer's verse tales, six hundred years seasoned. The same appreciation holds for Sappho, Homer, and the Bible in translation, or for Dante, Wyatt, Shakespeare, and Wordsworth in other inflections across the Big Water. Great writings are canonized for intrinsic reasons, both regionally and across tribes and tongues in translation.

The Americas are fusional cultures, complexly translative, and New World migrations have crossed from everywhere. Adventuring waves of Asians (two-way Bering Strait passages, over some forty or more thousand years), then émigré Europeans bringing enslaved Africans, finally newcomers from around the globe brought their languages and cultures with them to the Americas, and we are their descendants. Their talk is our tradition, their mixed cultures make up our textual canons.

What does it mean to be *A Nation of Immigrants,* as John F. Kennedy wrote of United States history, cross-hatching the tribal homelands of Native Americans? "The three ships which discovered America," President Kennedy noted, "sailed under a Spanish flag, were commanded by an Italian sea captain, and included in their crews an Englishman, an Irishman, a Jew and a Negro." At the shores of successive migratory waves, now for over five hundred years in the Lower Forty-Eight, have stood some five hundred tribal peoples, speaking as many separate tongues. As the English and Dutch were beaching New England four centuries ago, the French were circling into Canada. Already dividing South America with the Portuguese, the Spanish penetrated the Southwest along El Camino Real. "There goes the neighborhood," Natives quip today. Since 1607, over sixty million people (matching the hemisphere's pre-Columbian population) have immigrated to the United States, in Kennedy's words "the largest migration of people in all recorded history." Who are Americans, then? "Remember, remember always that all of us," Franklin D. Roosevelt told the Daughters of the American Revolution, "and you and I especially, are descended from immigrants and revolutionists." Today around the world, forty to eighty million peoples live in political exile from their birthlands. One million migrate legally each year, and sixty percent come to the United

States, where Native Americans number some two million, less than half their original population. If international exodus and cross-cultural relocation are still taking place, how can Americans reroot with the bedrock of Native America?

Cultural fusions are the rule. At the strictly Anglo-American level of exchange, the literary history of fourteenth-century England need be no less foreign to Americans, it strikes me, than native American homelands need be alien to F. O. Matthiessen's "American Renaissance." Stretching further, native writers such as Louise Erdrich, N. Scott Momaday, or James Welch do not have to be ethnically segregated from F. R. Leavis's "Great Tradition" of modern literature, Jane Austen through Henry James to D. H. Lawrence, crossing the Atlantic as English canon after the century's turn. Blending native traits from both sides of a mixed heritage, according to biologists, fuses hybrid genius. Indeed, in the 1890s the Cherokee writer John M. Oskison studied literature at Stanford and Harvard. The Fox anthropologist William Jones studied medicine at Harvard and took a doctorate under Franz Boas at Columbia in 1904. The elder Osage poet today, Carter Revard, specializes in Chaucer and medieval literature at Washington University, having studied at Yale and Oxford Universities, as did the Salish historian from Idaho D'Arcy McNickle. Also from Oklahoma Indian territory and schooled at Stanford under Yvor Winters, the Kiowa Nobel nominee N. Scott Momaday has taught in Moscow on a Fulbright and annually in Germany, received the top Italian prize in literature for his novel, *House Made of Dawn*, and lectures internationally as a creative critical writer on Emily Dickinson, syllabics, and postmodernist verse. "American Indian literature is becoming a very important, recognizably important, part of American literature as a whole," Professor Momaday told Laura Coltelli, an American Indian Studies scholar at the University of Pisa. "And we are just now rethinking the boundaries of American literature, and we are obliged, I think, to include oral tradition, elements of oral tradition, that we did not even think of including twenty-five years ago" (*Winged Words*).

Native and modern have fused as the world interconnects. Kith to kin, more of culture than genetics melds humans with analogous aesthetic traits. New generations evolve, separate, and marry out of their bloodlines. As peoples mix, ethnicity is not exempt from exogamy, nor does immigrant culture remain émigré forever, especially in this hybrid new land. Human biology has always been crossing territorial boundaries. The scientific term *heterosis* means that "pure" breeds are upgraded by mixing. This biological principle counters full-blood claims to racial purity as it warns of mutant inbreeding. In addition, cultural overlaps accompany biological fusions. Race, or what Robert Redfield calls "socially supposed races," becomes a social construct of time, exogamy, and region, anthropologists say, not a "pure" blood determinant. Less than one percent of the total gene pool differentiates any two races. Since "virtually all human beings are mongrels!" Clyde Kluckhohn reasons, we need to renew an old American premise, *e pluribus unum*, unity in diversity. This Harvard Navajo scholar wrote a classic study of ethnicity, *Mirror for Man: The Relation of Anthropology to Modern Life*, that turns on cultural hybridity. "For countless thousands of years human beings have been wandering over the surface of the globe," the ethnologist reminds us, "mating with whomever opportunity afforded or fancy dictated." Mixed connections, aesthetic and otherwise, outweigh perceived differences, though differing cultures trade on variations, to be sure.

Comparativist and mixed, no one motive drives the machinery of this book. Discussion of native poetics could reach a social scientist wondering about cultural fusions, a tribal chanter questioning if ceremonial song relates to textual talk, an Ivy League classicist uneasy with performance poetry, a native rapper interested in coastal Beats. As a White scholar in contemporary literature and Native American Studies, I've navigated this range of discussion over three decades, and much of my professional life keels on its swells and troughs. Whether in Europe, China, or the States, speaking on the literary differentials from margin to mainstream never fails to draw an audience or a debate. So *Sing with the Heart of a Bear* could pique an Old World critic curious about literary diversity or a New World writer of color wrestling with mainstream exclusions. The discourse might draw a southern formalist challenging midwestern plain style, a freeverse Californian contesting New England privilege, a young Indian rhymer seeking recognition as an American poet. The audience includes anyone interested in contemporary literatures, ethnic to canonical, free verse to formalist. Beyond history, culture, and hermetic text, some measure of imagination, even intuition, is necessary to read further: *caveat lector*.

My model for *Sing with the Heart of a Bear* comes from the literate, impassioned essay, Lawrence to Heaney, Kazin to Vendler. To "make glad" the reader's heart, Ezra Pound said in the *ABC of Reading*, the writer should try to see the world freshly and clearly. Setting the bar for modernism, Pound advocated "the direct examination of phenomena," getting to the "root" of matters with least interference. Pound's creative standards carried into the next generation. "He and I preferred critics who were writers to critics who were not writers," Robert Lowell remembers John Berryman. "We hated literary discussions animated by jealousy and pushed by caution." Learn of pine from the pine, Bashō said, of bamboo from bamboo.

Return to primary sources. In defense of so-called informants of culture, Clifford Geertz reminds social scientists that diverse people doing their work, in whatever corner of the world, know far more than any outsider could ever surmise about their lives (*Local Knowledge*). Just so, Paul Valéry localizes more insight into French poetics than any deconstructionist of late-nineteenth-century European art. Wallace Stevens, by way of Valéry, fires a reader's interest in the poetic imagination. So, too, Natives themselves are specialists in Native American Studies. Conversely, from the outside looking in, anthropology, history, and linguistics remain essential to non-Indians breaking cultural ground, no less than literary criticism, philosophy, or folklore. The personal fusions, crossovers, and obstinate exclusions are self-defining stories. Cultural bridgings have been historic. Archie Phinney (Nez Percé), Francis La Flesche (Omaha), Charles Eastman, M.D. or *Ohiyesa* (Lakota), Knud Rasmussen (Inuit), John Swanton (Creek), William Jones (Fox), Arthur C. Parker (Seneca), J. N. B. Hewitt (Tuscarora), and Ella Deloria (Lakota) rank brilliantly among the earliest native ethnologists. First Indian writers mixed fiction and social reality in literary fusions: Susette La Flesche (Omaha), Pauline Johnson (Mohawk), Mourning Dove or *Humishuma* (Salish), Gertrude Bonin (*Zitkala-Sa*, Lakota), Alexander Posey (Creek), John M. Oskison (Cherokee), John Joseph Mathews (Osage), Luther Standing Bear (Lakota). More recently, social historians like D'Arcy McNickle (Salish/Creek), Vine Deloria, Jr. (Lakota), and Alfonso Ortiz (San Juan Pueblo) have crossed not only anthropology, law, and literature, but cultural and racial boundaries. Collaborations are key. Keith Basso's conversations with "Slim Coyote," a.k.a. Nick Thompson, tell us more about the grounded Cibecue Apache "stalking with stories" than any Bureau of American Ethnology report, just as Richard Erdoes hanging out with John (Fire) Lame Deer gives us firsthand, if generalized, Lakota glimpses into Indian life this century.

On the American Indian side, *Sing with the Heart of a Bear* honors a long-time tribal way of talking matters over collectively. I learned this mode of communal dialogue early on, some thirty years ago now, with my Lakota brother, Mark Monroe, sitting around a kerosene stove with half a dozen or so Sioux, discussing things all day and night long. The attorney Allogan Slagle showed me the Cherokee side of this tradition on month-long treks through western reservations—the daily meditations and mediations essential to human, and spiritual, exchange. With his rolling baritone and profound good humor, the Tewa scholar Alfonso Ortiz was a master of tribal discourse—good talk. I dedicated my first book, *Native American Renaissance,* to our friendship. And for some thirty working years now, the UCLA American Indian Studies Center has been a lively matrix of tribal discourse. This straight-on tradition of speaking and treating, of speech-making and interactive dialogue, goes back from Wilma Mankiller and Paula Gunn Allen, through Lawrence Antoine and Dawson No Horse, Lakota *wicasa wakán* who taught me about good medicine. Dialogic oratory traces back through Sitting Bull and Geronimo, Wovoka and Seattle, Sacajawea and Jacataqua, Sequoyah and Handsome Lake. Contemporary poets and critics enter this tribal dialogue in our century, W. S. Merwin to N. Scott

Momaday, Denise Levertov to Linda Hogan, Calvin Bedient to Jarold Ramsey. Our exchange is the ongoing discourse of cross-cultural America, a tribal model less measured than meditated, less calculated than envisioned. In this regard, the mind turns not on a print cache or studied text, but on what a person can remember, believe deeply, and recount by heart. The talk seems more deeply felt than dazzling, in human concern finally over what matters most to the people.

Primal rooting holds just as firmly in formal Western literature, where technician trails the visionary who makes us *see*. "There is no wing," Stevens said, "like meaning." D. H. Lawrence on Lawrence, or the same poet-novelist on any other writer, Cooper to Whitman—the free verse "rose" as a "running flame," say, liberated from Hopkins's "terrible crystal"— tells us more about poetic revolutions than all the postmodernist machinery mustered in past decades. Ezra Pound on Gaudier-Brzeska's sculpture, on Fenollosa's Chinese ideogram, or on a reading list from Confucius to cummings stands above a gaggle of graduate programs. Marianne Moore on Pound's Cantos, William Carlos Williams on the particular universal thing, Theodore Roethke on humbling creative processes—these texts place us in the artists' minds and bodies, even at times down on our knees. The *Paris Review* interviews with writers this century are essential. Ted Hughes on the shamanic practice of hunting down poems or on the neo-primitive thrall of his wife, Sylvia Plath; Scott Momaday on Kiowa ways, Linda Hogan on the bear, wolf, or whale in her ecopoetic landscape, Luci Tapahonso on Four-Corners Dinetáh or Navajo culture; Carolyn Forché on working-class Detroit to Salvadoran war horrors, or Seamus Heaney on growing up in Derry—these primary voices speak in working witness of daily poetic lives. No wasted words, no making it up, no promotional fat or padding, but "speaking straight ahead about what concerns us," so Williams put it. This hands-on attitude works as well for textual parsing down to the syllable as it does for reenvisioning cultural history.

Known early as the Others, along with companion 1920s poets who did not weather the seasons (Kreymborg, Bynner, Lindsay, Sarett, even Sandburg), the verse iconoclasts we look back on as modernist—Stevens, Moore, Eliot, Stein, Pound, and Williams—were certainly not canonical then, as we have come to regard them. The so-called modernists were an original upheaval, a postwar protest against set verse forms (dating through Longfellow, Whittier, Bryant, Millay) in the belief that they, the Others, were radically American, naturally genuine, poetically true to their idiosyncratic visions of the New World. With characteristic brio Ezra Pound announced in 1918, "As for the nineteenth century, with all respect to its achievements, I think we shall look back upon it as a rather blurry, messy sort of a period, a rather sentimentalistic, mannerish sort of a period" ("A Retrospect" in *Pavannes and Divisions*). Pound called for a more *granite* poetics "nearer the bone," "harder and saner" than the "rhetorical din" or "luxurious riot" of the Victorian past. "At least for myself, I want it so, austere, direct, free from emotional slither." So these new American writers were no more conventional or mainstream than pioneering poets of the American or Native American renaissances (Poe, Melville, Emerson, Whitman in the 1850s to Momaday, Welch, Harjo, Hogan in the 1970s). Their margin is now in our mainstream, and culture keeps flowing.

FOREST EDGE DIALECTS

The phrase "a mind to obey nature" crystallized much of what I'd encountered in American Indian materials and linked with Chief Joseph's statement, "The earth and myself are of one mind."

ROGER DUNSMORE, *Earth's Mind*

What is a "mind" of the native earth? Roger Dunsmore asks, writing personal essays about teaching Native American literature. He poses a "native" American or chthonic consciousness balancing a world inhabited anciently by tribal peoples, now seen new by Euro-Americans. Gary Snyder's eco-poetic husbandry of an "earth household," chanted as a "house made of dawn" by Navajos, frames this native minding. And historically, Scott Momaday's "remembered earth" arcs back to Mary Austin's "American rhythm," through Lawrence's New Mexico poems and Williams's writing in eastern seaboard dialects. An *earth-minded* aesthetics roots culture in what the Lakota hear as "grandfather" stones, or *Tunkáshila*, speaking within a nourishing mother *Unçi*, or earth.

The first New World literatures "at the forest's edge," Constance Rourke notes of Indian-White history, grew out of seventeenth-century treaty pageants, beginning in Jamestown in 1607. Early on, a pilgrim Thanksgiving gave thanks across the Buckskin Curtain for native welfare, the gift of green corn to immigrants starving on foreign soil, as intercultural treaties set the first American stage. Four hundred years ago, witnessed by émigré pilgrims, frontier ceremonies were charged with ritual language: invocation, oratory, prayer, storytelling, ceremony, song, and dance struck a cross-cultural chord still resonating across the Americas. Today, a nation of immigrants, we are still treating among hybrid peoples, some here since time immemorial, as the Pueblos say, many more relocated from recent cultural dispersals around the globe, all intermixing, dark and light blending. In the millennial United States census, multiple racial identities will be options to the box checked "Other." We need to consider finally that we are all in this country together, reading one another's lives, writing across racial and cultural frontiers, even *singing with the hearts of bears*. None is purely one or the other.

In the wake of Quincentennial celebrations and cross-cultural *re*-discoveries of the Americas, what are the fusional native poetics of our American literatures? William Carlos Williams wrote in what he called *the American grain* and devoted a lifetime to catching, no less than Frost, Faulkner, Welty, or Sandburg, the mixed-blood, spoken aesthetics of local places. More recently, Frederick Turner traces a *spirit of place* across the literary terrain of this country, from Thoreau, Mari Sandoz, and William Carlos Williams to Leslie Silko: "a radically native art, a literature, arose from a Massachusetts pond, the upper Nebraska panhandle, a New Jersey mill town, a New Mexico Indian pueblo." Keith Basso's *Wisdom Sits in Places* anchors Apache narrative "wisdom" in Southwest placement and place-names, storytelling geography where "time takes on flesh" (as Mikhail Bakhtin has posited of *chronotopes*) "and becomes visible for human contemplation." This mountain or that stream or those cottonwoods tell Southwest Natives why and how they are Cibecue Apaches. "The land looks after us," Nick Thompson adds: no Apaches without rooted stories or grounded songs.

The conflation of time, space, ground, flesh, and story results in a native tribal ethic of "reciprocal appropriation," as seen by Scott Momaday, where natives give and take environmentally within the biosphere. "I believe that from the time the paleo-Indians, to use an anthropological term, set foot on the North American continent," Momaday told the German literary biographer Matthias Schubnell, "they began developing an aesthetics that is in keeping with and somehow related directly to the American landscape." Reciprocal tribalism among plant, animal, spirit, and human has been the critical factor triggering human social emergence, according to biological anthropology cited by Terrence Deacon in *The Symbolic Species: The Co-evolution of Language and the Brain* (1997). This delicate interdependence led to the evolution of culture and language some million to two million years ago, *Homo habilis* to *Homo erectus*.

Native Americans carry a "genetic experience of the landscape," Momaday says of continued evolution over some thirty to forty millennia, "a way of seeing that has been developed over a long period of time." This native way infuses regional native poetics. The Kiowa artist writes "out of the conviction of having lived, in my ancestors, for many thousands of years in North America," he told the Canadian native writer, Tom King (*MELUS* 1983, reprinted in *Conversations with N. Scott Momaday*). The acculturating exchanges of particular peoples and specific places keep Native Americans native and American, as writers cross cultures today.

RETELLING THE RHYTHMS

Where is a savage and luxuriant man?
WHITMAN TO EMERSON, *Leaves of Grass*, 1856

Native memory is carried in distinctive rhythms, a blend of speech and song. Maria Chona recalls her Papago father singing softly in cactus camp a hundred years ago: "That is how our people always talk to their children, so low and quiet, the child thinks he is dreaming. But he never forgets" (*The Autobiography of a Papago Woman*, 1936). Today, A. A. Hedge Coke, mixed-blood Tsalagi and Huron graduate of the University of California at Berkeley and the Santa Fe Institute of American Indian Arts, writes about her off-reservation childhood in Amarillo, Texas: "While busy with the beadwork, my father would tell us about our ancestors. His voice was gentle and strong and had a rhythm that made it easy to remember things he said. It was rhythmically patterned, like a song" ("Seeds" in Ortiz, *Speaking for the Generations*, 1997). Jeannette C. Armstrong, one of Canada's leading Native writers, feels that her Okanagan speech rhythms rise from a tribal earth inflection: "The land as language surrounds us completely, just like the physical reality of it surrounds us. Within that vast speaking, both externally and internally, we as human beings are an inextricable part—though a minute part—of the land language" ("Land Speaking" in Ortiz). Rather than making up art, this Salish speaker bears her ongoing tribal culture: "Through my language I understand I am being spoken to, I'm not the one speaking. The words are coming from many tongues and mouths of Okanagan people and the land around them. I am a listener to the language's stories, and when my words form I am merely retelling the same stories in different patterns."

What are the native verse patterns? Begin biologically: The nineteenth-century physician and poet Oliver Wendell Holmes heard accentual meter in binary heart rhythms, Alfred Kazin recalls in *An American Procession*. "To *be* or *not* to *be*," Hamlet paces iambically, or a gospel chorus chants, "A*maz*ing *grace* how *sweet* the *sound*." The San Juan Pueblo women's choir sang this spiritual in Tewa at Alfonso Ortiz's wake in January 1997. Could there be, at least intuitively, crossovers of what Mary Austin called an *American rhythm* buried anciently in the landscape, felt in local native dialects, resurfacing transculturally in the pulse, gait, and speech of westering migrants, still skirting indigenous cultures long settled in the land? How would modernists speak of this pace? "Rhythm is form cut into TIME," Pound insisted on space-time elements, "as a design is determined SPACE." What are the rhythmic designs of native space? Sioux tribes speak of a "four-winds" cardinal plains placement, spiritually grounded, and Navajo people honor their world's *hozhó* symmetry and harmony in the Southwest. Consider the timeless ceremonial chants of indigenous tribes, the seasonal winds and cycling waters of a "four corners" landscape. Newcomers are listening. From Yankee woodsmen mending walls and New England matriarchs quilting, to southern gentlefolk gossiping with Shakespearean inflections, to Navajo women clucking over mutton stew and Lakota high-plains tremolos, our American cadences vary, and, sadly, native tongues are dying.

Hundreds of indigenous native tongues have gone silent this century. Some six thousand global languages presently spoken are diminishing by several hundred each decade. Eighty percent of two hundred extant tribal languages north of the Rio Grande are no longer spoken fluently by anyone under fifty, according to Michael Krauss, director of the Alaska Native Language Center. Native Language Network, Fall 1997, reports that if the trend continues, only twenty indigenous languages will survive into the middle of the next century. Up to ninety percent of the world's six thousand languages may go moribund in the next century, only six hundred tongues "reasonably safe" by a minimum of one hundred thousand speakers (Steven Pinker, *The Language Instinct*). What are the reciprocal terms of language and cultural renewal in the four winds of the New World?

American peoples are grafted from other cultures around the world and redefined geographically. As indigenous and relocated natives, most Americans speak an English removed from hundreds of parent tongues across the Big Waters, Europe and Africa to Asia and Australia. Indigenous and dialectal rhythms are sculpted into our hybrid language and history. This study tracks the verbal landscape of our coevolutionary native space, New England farmers and southern gentry, Trail of Tears relocatees and Southwest migrants, midwestern pioneers and Sooner sodbusters, transcontinental explorers and Indian women guides. We need to parse the rhythms that root American speech patterns, from reservation relocatees now moving (over two-thirds of them) into urban areas, to West Coast transplants still digging for the good life in a land of promise.

Mary Austin thought there was a native American pulse in the rolling landscape and tribal dialect of each historical region. She turned, respectfully though perhaps at times naively, to American Indian cultures for grounding and guidance that might carry all of us through the land: "the whole instinctive movement of the American people," Austin prefaced in George Cronyn's *The Path on the Rainbow* in 1918, "is for a deeper footing in their native soil." Antonín Dvořák had earlier called for such native grounding in the *New York Herald*, May 28, 1893: "The new American music must strike its roots deeply into its own soil," as Brian Swann notes in his newest anthology of Native American song-poems, *Wearing the Morning Star*. Dvořák's Ninth Symphony, *From the New World*, borrowed themes from Longfellow's "The Song of Hiawatha," itself borrowed from Schoolcraft's Algon-

kian folklore and metered by way of the Finnish *Kalevala*. Not all translations
are so artificially cobbled. An appropriation that honors its sources, a trans-
lation by Washington Matthews or Frances Densmore, for example, is no
less than cultural borrowing and reinvention. Seen less defensively, this
acculturative process is the nativizing of newcomers, as some Indians note,
the "Americanizing" of the immigrant. "Acculturation means a two-way, a
reciprocal kind of thing in which there is a realization of one world that is
composed of both elements, or many for that matter," Momaday told the
Indian historian Rupert Costo: "we ought to educate the white man. We
ought to reconstruct the institutions within the dominant society, so that
the Indian values are available to the dominant society." Go "into the
enemies' camp," the native Pulitzer novelist advised the First Convocation
of American Indian Scholars in 1970. "The Indian, in order to discover who
he is, must do that on a comparative basis. It does him no good to know who
he is, so long as that knowledge isolates him . . . alienates and shuts him off
from the possibilities that are available to him in the world."

Americans walk and talk their land topically. The poets develop a distinct
sense of measured foot, felt and heard in updated native verse rhythms.
Wallace Stevens invented "a kind of walking poetry," Stanley Kunitz ob-
serves, "verse that reflects the energy of a man in stride." Stevens noted in
a letter, "I have to jot things down as I go along," and when the poet-
executive reached the insurance company office, his secretary wrote up the
lines. N. Scott Momaday rhymes epigrammatic "charms" as he swims laps
each morning in the Arizona desert ("like eating peanuts," he muses pub-
licly). Imagine for a moment: Wallace Stevens in dress Florsheims walking
two miles to work across Hartford, Emily Dickinson in lace-up, low-heel
shoes pacing her father's Amherst garden, Robert Frost out picking Ver-
mont apples in his Wellington boots. Just so, picture Native and American
poets today: Scott Momaday cadencing his lines to the pace of Southwest
desert landscapes, James Welch crossing the Montana prairie in Justin cow-
boy boots, Sherman Alexie shooting hoop in high-top Converse tennis
shoes somewhere in Seattle. Linda Hogan might put on black flats cleaning
cages for the Colorado Wildlife Rehabilitation Clinic, Joy Harjo sport Tony
Lama boots playing saxophone with Poetic Justice at an Albuquerque rock
concert, Sharon Olds wear soft-soled whites teaching a New York poetry
workshop at Goldwater Hospital. Imagine a booted Carolyn Forché stum-
bling down Salvadoran dirt roads, Linda Gregg barefoot in Greece. These
circumstances are local to the poet's stride, rooted in each writer's verse.

The native measures are compelling. A latter-day, relocated English pil-
grim in the 1920s, D. H. Lawrence struck deep into the taproot of native
blood-soil as he measured the downbeat of tribal dances. Pueblo chanters
drew the sun's buried heat up through their loins, remaking themselves
seasonally in Hopi dances: "how deep the men are in the mystery they are

practicing, how sunk deep below our world, to the world of snakes, and dark ways in the earth, where are the roots of corn, and where the little rivers of unchannelled, uncreated life-passion run like dark, trickling lightning, to the roots of the corn and to the feet and loins of men, from the earth's innermost dark sun" (*Mornings in Mexico*).

Conversely, Ezra Pound bootlegged Whitman's "barbaric yawp" across the Big Water to "make it new" within the context of Western classics. His college counterpart, William Carlos Williams, sidestepped the ambling metrics of Continental verse and discovered a "variable" foot in Jersey tribal speech. The good doctor hybridized a Renaissance mother tongue, as he saw the "pure products of America" gone "crazy" with the rush for freedom. "Unless it be that marriage / perhaps / with a dash of Indian blood," Williams held out, rebirths a large-hipped, domestic Elsie. This diminished Elizabeth, fallen-virgin queen poorly resurgent in the suburbs, hungers for golden beauty among mixed-blooded Americans, "until they eat filth" in an uncharted new land. "Somehow it seems to destroy" the classical sentiment of purity, Williams says. The strain leaves "broken brain" Americans witness to a new world freshly fallen, fragmented hands on the wheels of isolate cars. Out of broken Renaissance forms quicken mixed-blood, New World measures, what Williams heard in the springing contagion of "variable" feet.

No less than Lawrence, T. S. Eliot found the neolithic in the New Age of Euro-American modernism, as the wasting heroic couplet caved in to poetic bedrock: "What I call the 'auditory imagination' is the feeling for syllable and rhythm, penetrating far below the conscious levels of thought and feeling, invigorating every word; sinking to the most primitive and forgotten, returning to the origin and bringing something back, seeking the beginning and the end. It works through meanings, certainly, or not without meanings in the ordinary sense, and fuses the old and obliterated and the trite, the current, and the new and surprising, the most ancient and the most civilized mentality" (*The Use of Poetry and the Use of Criticism*). In an odd twist, Lawrence came to the New World, and Eliot went to the Old to rediscover ancient and classical rhythms. These poets acculturated across continents, old voices made new.

Still we ask: What distinguishes American verse, where do we mine the motherlode of New World voices? Which tales do our poets sing, and what inflections do we hear in the rhythms, pitches, and parsings of native lines? To complete the pilgrimage after five hundred years, how do American and Native American poetics cross-resonate today? Who are the tribal writers of the twentieth century?

Unto the woman he said, I will greatly multiply thy sorrow and thy conception; in sorrow thou shalt bring forth children; and thy desire *shall be* to thy husband, and he shall have rule over thee.

And unto Adam he said, because thou hast hearkened unto the voice of thy wife, and hast eaten of the tree, of which I commanded thee, saying, Thou shalt not eat of it: cursed *is* the ground for thy sake; in sorrow shalt thou eat *of* it all the days of thy life.

GENESIS 3:16–17

Sing with the Heart of a Bear tracks the Renaissance invention of the Wild Man, the recurrent Adamic myth of animist brothers and earth sisters lost from the Garden, contiguous with Native American cultures among us. This study discusses the first anthology of American Indian verse, *The Path on the Rainbow,* culled by George W. Cronyn from the Smithsonian Bureau of American Ethnology Reports and Anthropological Papers of the American Museum of Natural History, published at the end of World War I. Jorge Luis Borges began his university surveys of American literature with Cronyn's texts of tribal song-poems. Next to older transcriptions of oral traditions stand twenty-eight contemporary Indian poets, selected by Paula Gunn Allen and me. These pan-tribal poets speak to, with, and against American mainstream bards, from Whitman's freed verse, through the Greenwich Village Renaissance (sandwiched between Great Wars), to post-apocalyptic Beat incantations, to transglobal questions of tribe and verse at the century's close. As the California Wintu dreamed our late-night, post-modern crises many centuries ago:

> Where will you and I sleep?
> At the down-turned jagged rim of the sky you
> and I will sleep.

The second part of *Sing with the Heart of a Bear* takes a detailed look at contemporary poetry by way of native ethnicity and gender splits. From Dickinson through Plath, a century's span in Massachusetts, Marianne Moore's terms for an *interest in* imaginative poetry, *genuine* and *raw,* charge modern verse. Gender is no small wedge. "It is a very grave question," wrote Willa Cather, homeboy prairie muse in 1895, when my maternal plains grandmother was born, "whether women have any place in poetry." Frontier-canted, what "slant of light" has set women and ethnic poets apart from canonical verse this century? From Pound, through Williams and Stevens, to Roethke and new Indian poets Momaday, Welch, and Alexie, the American Adam may still "go savage" across the literary Buckskin Curtain, as scholars have documented, from Henry Nash Smith in *Virgin Land* to R. W. B. Lewis in *The American Adam,* from Leo Marx in *The Machine in the Garden* to Roy Harvey Pearce in *Savagism and Civilization.* Two books dominated American reading through the early twentieth century, the Bible and Milton's *Paradise Lost;* no ancestral Puritan parlor was complete without these neolapsarian texts as post-Columbian pillars. So the Edenic myths of lost native innocence and expulsion from the Garden survive two millennia of Old World expansion, "manifest" fallen destinies rerooted with a vengeance in the New World. What is the wild new freedom that sets the Americas apart from the rest of the world, what are its native continuities? The Adamic poet labors in the garden to till verse and still answer the counterpoint of feminist sisters.

> Therefore the LORD GOD sent him forth from the garden of Eden, to till the ground from whence he was taken.
> So he drove out the man; and he placed at the east of the garden of Eden cherubim, and a flaming sword which turned every way, to keep the way of the tree of life.
>
> GENESIS 3:23–24

There are alternative native stories. Across the great divides of race and gender rise darker sisters of Eve, daughters of Pocahontas and Tekakwitha and Sacajawea, setting ancient tribal rhythms in verse. TallMountain to Hogan and Harjo, McKay to Whiteman and Tapahonso, these Native American women listen when no one is left to speak, and speak beyond the gendered chasm of silence. What raw or genuine connection do these matrilineal descendants have with verse sisters in the current mainstreams of poetry, Graham, Gregg, or Olds? Finally, to locate the debate globally, *Sing with the Heart of a Bear* engages the intercultural politics and terrible innocence of a Slovak-Irish émigré granddaughter, Carolyn Forché, tracking the dispossessed through a world torn between greed and ennui:

> It is either the beginning or the end
> of the world, and the choice is ourselves
> or nothing.

Our poetics lie here on the line, the angel of history holding an apocalyptic sword over all of us.

ACKNOWLEDGMENTS

When I started thinking seriously about Native American Literature in 1970, there was no field, no graduate program, few writers, no scholars. Today, an intertribal council connects writers across the country—my thanks and respect to all for *helping out*, as they say in Sioux country. Native writers have been both inspirational and engaging—Scott Momaday, Bobbi Hill, Luci Tapahonso, Judith Volborth, Joseph Bruchac, Barney Bush, Mike Kabotie, Joy Harjo, Mary TallMountain, Linda Hogan, and Sherman Alexie. Thanks to Mark Monroe, Raymond J. DeMallie, Jr., and Wilbur Between Lodges for checking my Lakota translations. My UCLA colleagues have stood by these studies with clear minds and strong hearts, especially Mike Rose, Ephraín Crystál, Greg Sarris, Paula Gunn Allen, Hanay Geiogamah, Paul Kroskrity, Gary Nash, Johannes Wilbert, Carole Goldberg-Ambrose, Duane Champagne, Peter Nabokov, Paul Sheats, and Cal Bedient. I will miss showing this book to the late Alfonso Ortiz and hearing his chortled blessings. Thanks to Shiela Levine, director of the University of California Press, and Linda Norton, humanities editor, who backed this project when others backed away.

Sam and Kappy Wells give a home to rest my work. The Monroe *tiospaye* in northwest Nebraska draws me back to my place of origin. Old students and friends in the field keep the work lively and personable—Allogan Slagle, Rebecca Tsosie, David Smith, Lorenzo Baca, Margaret Archuleta, Carolyn Dunn, Deidre Evans-Pritchard, Bonnie Glaser-Coffin, Richard Keeling, Blanca Jensen, Betty Donahue, Diana Bahr, Paul Apodaca, Amy Ware, Bill Bright, Brian Swann, David Guss, Gretchen Bataille, James Ruppert, Susan Scarberry-Garcia, Raymond DeMallie, Jr., Ken Roemer, Laura Coltelli, Gaetano Prampolini, Annamaria Pinazzi, and countless others. *Dok-shá.*

As my mother was leaving this world, my daughter conceived a child, to be born the same year as this book. May the next century bless all our issue.

Kenneth Lincoln
LA CIENEGUILLA, NM

The preface and chapter one were published as "Native Poetics" in a Native American special issue of *Modern Fiction Studies* (Spring 1999). Portions of chapter two appeared as the new foreword to George W. Cronyn, *American Indian Poetry* (1918; Ballantine, 1991). Earlier parts of chapter three appeared in *The Jacaranda Review* Supplement, 1992—my deepest thanks to the Native American poets and their publishers for permissions to reprint. An unrevised version of chapter four appeared as "(Native) American Poetries" in *The Southwest Review*, 1978. Shorter sections on TallMountain, Tapahonso, and Whiteman appeared in Gretchen Bataille's *Native American Women*, Garland, 1993. Parts of the Graham section in chapter ten first appeared in *The Jacaranda Review*, 1986. A brief part of the Hogan material in chapter eleven appeared as the foreword to *Eclipse*, UCLA Native American Studies Series, 1984. Sincere appreciation for permission to revise, expand, and reprint from all these sources.

〔 I 〕

AT THE FOREST'S EDGE

ONE

Native Poetics

*As for native American individuality, though certain to come, and on a large scale,
the distinctive and ideal type of Western character . . . has not yet appear'd.*

WALT WHITMAN, *Leaves of Grass*, 1891

Native is generic for birthrights in a naturally given place. The noun *poetics*, originally "makings" in Greek, turns problematic in time—suspiciously "made up," or decorative, even delusional among late-twentieth-century arts. Given that human beings are *born-making* things the world over, this cross-cultural study tracks the *figure* a poem *makes* in our time. Whether that figure melts as Frost's ice on a hot stove, or disappears as Stevens's pheasant in the bush, today's canonical poem often seems elusively "made," relatively marginalized from society's workings, even oddly antiquated—perhaps only a construct of "som murthe or som doctryn."

Native American aesthetics, by contrast, still premises art as morally, kinetically, even spiritually engrained in the natural tribal world—a native *good*, not so much personally made or made up, as naturally given and passed through an artist. Traditionally Lakota, the artist can *sing with the heart of a bear.*

"When a man does a piece of work which is admired by all we say that it is wonderful," Chased-by-Bears told Frances Densmore (*Teton Sioux Music* 1918), "but when we see the changes of day and night, the sun, moon, and stars in the sky, and the changing seasons upon the earth, with their ripening fruits, anyone must realize that it is the work of some one more powerful than man." Bear Necklace, a *yuwipi* healer, gave Sitting Bull a "talking" stone worn in a bag around his neck until the day of his death and burial. Rounded *Tunkáshila* stones carry "grandfather" voices in Lakota. *Tunkan* fly through the darkness in all-night, healing *lowanpi* or "sings." Chased-by-Bears said to Densmore, "The sacred stone may appear in the form of a person who talks and sings many wonderful songs." Birds and beasts, trees and rocks chant this animist power, and sometimes men "understand the meaning of the songs of birds," even "the call and cry of the animals."

3

New World writers, native and canonical, polarize a transethnic dialogue, one that cuts acculturatively both ways: making and crafting, or receiving and bearing native arts. Can there be fusional crossovers? Early this century, D. H. Lawrence left England and caught the Pueblo drift of native poetics, as Georgia O'Keeffe was coming from New York to Abiquiu, "Not I, not I, but the wind that blows through me." Émigré to the Southwest after the First World War, Lawrence felt himself less the poet as maker than receptor of natural art.

> If only, most lovely of all, I yield myself and am borrowed
> By the fine, fine wind that takes its course through the chaos of the world
> Like a fine, an exquisite chisel, a wedge-blade inserted

"Admit them," Lawrence addressed "the three strange angels" knocking at midnight in the New World in his early modernist "Song of a Man Who Has Come Through."

How do we speak of these muses, native or Euro-American? It helps to be culture-specific and work from our own beginnings—in my own case, coming from Sioux country. "Sing with the heart of a bear," *çanté mató keçaça*, Two Shields chanted in "sacred language," recording Lakota songs for Frances Densmore about the time Lawrence and O'Keeffe were coming through. "Strangely human is this little melody," the ethnomusicologist notes of No. 93, "A Wind from the North." Recorded at Standing Rock, North Dakota, in 1914, the song is an old *wakán* or "sacred" lyric learned from White Shield out of the last century. *Çanté tókeça* connotes "a heart that is different," a fierce bear's heart, Two Shields said of chanting "used by medicine-men in which familiar words take on an occult meaning." This thickening and deepening of "ordinary" language through chant is what we otherwise call poetry. Two Shields ends his song, *wazíyata taté hiyó ma aü' we*, "a wind from the north comes for me." To sing with the *fiercely different heart of a bear,* the Lakota still feel today, summons the cleansing, healing north wind.

"The bear is the only animal," Two Shields explained, "which is dreamed of as offering to give herbs for the healing of man." *Siyáka,* or Teal Duck, agreed: given the bear's claws for digging roots, "if a man dreams of a bear he will be expert in the use of herbs for curing illness." The names of Densmore's medicine singers are litany to totemic kinship with Old Man *Mató:* Bear Eagle, Weasel Bear, Charging Bear, Chased-by-Bears, Bear Face, Bear Necklace, Bear Soldier, Crow Bear, Bear-with-White-Paw, Holy-Face Bear. Their Lakota songs, scored ethnomusicologically in bar staves, are even more strangely powerful. Eagle Shield sang a bone-doctoring bear song for Densmore in "all the tones of the octave except the sixth" (No. 86): *Kolá waná hiyúye / Mató omá kiyake / Kolá hiyúye / Lená wayánk hiyúye / Wayánk hiyúye / Mató omá kiyake.* Since the measures break into a 7/7/5   7/5/7 syllabic pattern, a singable translation might sound this way:

> Come toward me now my brother,
> A bear has told me how, so
> Friend come toward me now,
>
> Come and see all these healings,
> Come see these healings,
> Brother bear has told me how.

In using wild lettuce to treat kidney pain, Eagle Shield also sang this "Appeal to the Bear" (No. 87): *Até hóyeya / Até hóyeya / Iyótiye wákiye / Até hóyeya / Iyótiye wákiye.* Robert Higheagle translates "Appeal to the Bear" in lyric 5/5/7/5/7 syllabics,

> Father send a voice,
> Father send a voice,
> A hard task I am having.
> Father send a voice,
> A hard task I am having.

"The song is minor in tonality and melodic in structure," Densmore notes, "containing all the tones of the octave except the seventh and second." Finally, Eagle Shield explained the medicinal use of wild licorice root and sang "Song of the Bear" (No. 88) in two heroic couplets of eight syllables to each line: *Minápe kin wakán yeló / Pezíhuta óta yeló. // Minápe kin wakán yeló / Táku iyúha óta yeló.* If the couplets are to remain singable, their translation could be

> Oh these scraping claws are sacred!
> All-healing herbs lie everywhere!
>
> My scraping claws are sacred, ho!
> These all connect us everywhere!

When he doctored, Bear-with-White-Paw wore one side of his hair unbraided and a necklace of two medicine bags with a bear's claw. "The bear is very truthful," he said of his guardian mentor. "He has a soul like ours, and his soul talks to mine in my sleep and tells me what to do." Before each healing, the medicine man prayed to his ursine muse, "My friend, I am poor and needy. Listen well to me." Bear-with-White-Paw drummed and sang Densmore a single complex healing bear-song, scored in D minor: *Até hiyúye yo / Até hiyúye yo / Até hiyúye yo / Hunónpa makáta yunká cha / Piyáwakagé // Até hiyúye yo / Iná hiyúye yo / Iná hiyúye yo / Hunónpa makáta yunká cha / Piyáwakagé / Iná hiyúye yo.* In two stanzas of 6/6/6/9/5 and 6/6/6/9/5/6 syllabic measure, the song would translate,

Father healer come out!
Father healer come out!
Father healer come out!
Two-legged, won't you lie on the earth
To make me anew.

Father healer come out!
Mother healer come out!
Mother healer come out!
Two-legged, won't you lie on the earth,
I am made anew,
Mother healer come out.

Over a period of several weeks while Euro-Americans prepared to fight the First World War, Bear-with-White-Paw chanted and brought Frances Densmore specimens of healing herbs: western wallflower for cramps; alum root for diarrhea; puccoon for hemorrhaging lungs; "niggerhead" for toothache, bowel disorder, and tonsillitis; horsemint for fever; umbrellawort for broken bones. "These are the medicines which I use for the purposes I have told you," the Lakota healer explained, "and the song which I sing when I use them." Still today, these *wakán* or sacred lyrics help to doctor the Lakota in fierce-hearted, healing-bear songs.

Why a bear? Go to the beginnings: the genus *Ursus* appears when *Homo habilis* is first learning phonemes, some two million years back (Steven Pinker, *The Language Instinct*). Predominately Northern Hemispheric, twelve species of bears range north of Mexico. Native Americans claim their ursine kinship to the aboriginal past—*Grandfather, Grandmother, Old Man, Cousin.* The Cree call bear a "four-legged human." By 1607 Algonkians had long seen Ursa Major as the Great Bear, astrologically agreeing with the first English pilgrims in 1607. Across the thirty-six-mile Bering Strait, Ural Altaic natives honor the bear as *Worthy Old Man, Good Father,* and *Grandfather on the Hill.* Ursidae bears have migrated three times across the Siberian land bridge into the Americas. The Kurile Ainu of Japan declaim: "As for me, I am a child of the god of the mountains; I descended from the divine one who rules in the mountains."

Bears may be the oldest human *totems* or native guardian spirits. The Lakota see bears in terms of medicine, defense, and culture: as healers (digging for roots), warriors (defending kin with fierce strength), and teachers ("single-incident" learners, as with human intelligence). Bears pair, domesticate, suckle their infants, raise and teach their young for several years. They can be trained to walk, to ride a unicycle, and to dance. Like humans, bears are five-finger-and-toed, cub-raising, familial, territorial, omnivorous, reasoning, even bipedal. Their excrement looks human, only larger, and a skinned bear looks like an old man. Bears sing-song a kind of "musical rainbow" when pleased, biologists say, and cry when displeased. They hibernate through winter and resurrect in spring, magically, so that Orpheus is seen as a bear. Even the wily strategist, Odysseus, appears as a Homeric bear, the thinking warrior's hero. The title of the first recorded Old English epic, *Beowulf,* means "bear", literally "bee-wolf." The Finnish *Kalevala,* rhythmic source for Longfellow's "Song of Hiawatha," calls *Otso,* or bear, Illustrious, Pride, the Master, and Loved-one from the Glenwood. Carl Jung felt that a bear with glowing eyes hovered in the human unconscious. In *The Sacred Paw* Paul Shephard and Barry Sanders see the omnivorous bear as an "ideogram of man in the wilderness," so like humans, yet different, "the prototype of the wild animal" in all of us. Tribal seers would not disagree. To sing with a bear's heart that is different, *çanté mató keçaça,* is to connect with the native within, the oldest kinship of human, nature, and language. This deep song-poetry heals with the cleansing north wind.

During the postwar, modernist heyday, as Native Americans were becoming American citizens in 1924, Irving Hallowell completed research on human-bear history for a doctorate at the University of Pennsylvania. Two years later, he published a classic monograph, "Bear Ceremonialism in the Northern Hemisphere," in the 1926 *American Anthropologist* (accompanied by Elsie Clews Parsons on the Tewa ceremonial calendar and Jaime de Angulo on Pit River conjugations). This was a year after Fitzgerald published *The Great Gatsby,* Williams printed *In the American Grain,* and Hemingway released *In Our Time.* The zoological ethnographer found a cross-layered, intercontinental matrix sacralizing bears as guardian spirits with honorific kinship terms, *Great One, Elder Brother, Great-Grandfather, Uncle.* Tribal bear rituals proved globally homogeneous: hunted in early spring; called personally from the den and slain by hand with axe or spear; spoken to ceremonially with tobacco, food, and art; feasted on tribally; and finally respected by placing the bones in trees or returning them to the den.

Not only Native American, but European and Asian, Paleolithic bear ceremonies of an "ancient Boreal culture," Hallowell concluded, probably began in Eurasia and crossed the Bering Strait with migratory hunters. Whether bear honorings went one direction or the other, or possibly both, the rituals interconnected northern peoples around the globe. Biologically and mythologically, the bear is the grand old man of native totemic guardians. N. Scott Momaday's *The Ancient Child* (1989) tracks a mixed-blood artist, "Set" (Kiowa for bear), through the hibernation, death, and rebirth of modern Indian consciousness. The tribal myth of a brother bear, who chases his seven sisters into the stars of Ursa Major, draws Momaday's narrative through-line taut: "One hunter, a man with a withered neck, was so deeply enchanted by the bear's behavior that upon its approach he could do nothing but stand with his arms at his sides. The bear came upon him, breathed the scent of camas upon him, and laid its great flat head to the hunter's genitals. In a strange moment in which there was no fear on either side, there was recognition on both sides, the hunter said. The bear cried in a human voice."

Ceremonial chant, or "song-poetry," may be the world's oldest art form, grounded spiritually as traditional art. Eagle Shield doctored hemorrhaging with a bear claw and cone flower, Lakota *wináwazi hutkan,* literally a "female pine root" (figuratively a blood relationship), singing this chant in seven-syllabic lines, "Bear Told Me" (No. 89): *Kántuhuwa lúta wan / mató omákiyaka / táku sitómniyan / kolá omákiyaka / kántuhuwa lúta wan / mató omáyaka.* "Bear Told Me" translates in short:

> Red plum brush is blood ripe now,
> Old Man Bear has told me this.
> Something strong flows everywhere,
> A friend has told me this now.
> Red plum brush is now blood ripe,
> The bear has told me this.

Like bear honorings, the more ancient premise of a native aesthetics can intersect cross-lingually, circling the globe, what the Navajo call *hozhó* (goodness in beautiful balance), or the Chinese call *wei wu wei* ("not-to-go" against the natural grain), or in a different sense, what Plato simply called the Good. How do we accept, realize, or arrive at this ideal, and what is its specific relationship to the so-called *real*— from Wallace Stevens imagining a blackbird reality in language, to Galway Kinnell crawling inside his poem's bear carcass, to Scott Momaday tracking his four-legged brother, to Linda Hogan rescuing wounded raptors? "Two-legged" ceremonial notions, as the Sioux say, Native and American poetics range from bearing things to remaking the art of the real.

Why cross cultures? Granted, much may be lost in hyphenated translation, but imagine a homogenous world without others—no lingual and cultural correlatives, no international discourse with border neighbors, no forum to "unite" nations, for that matter, no talk outside our own town tongue. There would be no cultural curiosity, no exogamous mystery. Those who know only their own language, Goethe noted, do not even know that. Without translated languages, we risk missing the mystery within our own speech. Imagine no sacred words of our own, since poetry may be what (creatively) is lost in translation, as Frost said.

So decoding even our own given temporality and tongue, the deeper recesses and resources of native talk, may hinge on recognizing other ways of seeing and saying commonly shared things about our bearlike lives: what we are and are not, for starters. Since all Native American verse in English is, by definition, poetry in translation (and all poetry is native translation of an original or prevision), native American poetics may generate a doubly original tongue (in translation of inner translations) and emerge multiply creative for all of the Americas. What differing poetics are at stake here, and can we collaborate in bridging cultural terms?

STRANGERS ALIKE

We meet no Stranger but Ourself.
EMILY DICKINSON

"On the basis of the other," Julia Kristeva adds to the poet's Stranger, "I become reconciled with my own otherness-foreignness." The concept is a derivation of Freud's probing the "uncanny strangeness" or *unheimlich* of the "homely," the assumed familiar. Foreign is nowhere if not within, this East European analyst ventures in *Strangers to Ourselves,* all of us foreigners, to ourselves, to each other. And poetry often draws out a Stranger within, Heather McHugh argues of Emily Dickinson in *Broken English:* "the most profound other is very close to home: like Rilke, she is devoted to the otherness of a self. Like Marianne Moore's, her peculiarity is fashioned in assiduous craft, and her will to be peculiar saves her from conventional doings, from doing meaningless time." Foreign to ourselves and convention, then, we tolerate others, in effect, *mine other* as estranged kin or shadow double. "If I am a foreigner," Kristeva culturally closes the equation on itself, "there are no foreigners."

Calibrating the resistant distance between Others can be the rage or cliché of the day, as the banner of alterity waves from the flagpole of every other college English program; yet what does "otherness" really get down to? "Can the Subaltern speak?" feminists like Gayatri Spivack ask, rhetorically speaking. Do the "lit-crit-cult" labels take us anywhere, beneath the skin, to understand how others listen and speak across verbal frontiers? Strong crosswinds are blowing. Wendy Rose, Miwok-Hopi poet, chisels lines "For the Scholar Who Wrote a Book About an American Indian Literary Renaissance":

> Do you remember
> when you twisted the wax from your ears
> and shouted to me, 'You finally speak!'
> because now you
> could finally hear?
> The renaissance, you said, had begun
> and beads began to sprout
> around our necks, stones germinated
> from the backs of our fingers;
> the drum began in the middle of the night
> and you said 'The words have broken free
> from silent stoic throats'

and from the pain of forgetting
we almost agreed.

In xenophobic anger, we and others polarize differences. Suppression mutes common concerns in all corners. Separatism belies deeper cultural connections.

"I, too, dislike it," Marianne Moore teases readers with our equivocal attraction to poetry. This equivocation may be our native-émigré issue. Among the damning charges made against Euro-American interest in native cultures is that most Anglos would rather play Indian than know any, or know anything about Indians (see, among others, Raymond Stedman's *Shadows of the Indian* and Philip Deloria's recent *Playing Indian*). On the pejorative slope of Otherness, many tribal peoples blanketly distance outsiders as non-Indian. The term replicates xenophobic days when birth certificates or voter registrations were generically marked non-White. As recently as 1954 in a Santa Rosa, California, county hospital, the birth certificate for Gregory Sarris, "Baby Unnamed," listed his absent father (Emilio Hilario, Miwok-Filipino) as "Unknown Non-White." Times are curiously reversed. In the 1990s, Sarris has finessed that ethnic legitimacy into tribal chair of the Federated Coastal Miwok, a full professorship in literature at UCLA, and six-figure book and movie contracts. Contexts change. Make no mistake, some native margins have been academically mainstreamed, even if living standards for reservation Indians remain marginally desperate. *Indian* has become a label of privilege, as *Anglo* or worse, *white boy*, skid toward disrespect loaded with guilt. This labeling war is not without etymological torque. "Indian" referred exploratorally to the wrong continent, and "Anglo" came from the "neck-angle" of Northern Europe, "Angles," on which Pope Gregory, seeing blond Roman slaves, punned *angeli*, or angels.

We can do better across the Buckskin Curtain. Knowing cross-cultural specifics about American and Native American literacies, oral to written, spans differences across poetic conceptions. Perhaps a better understanding of others would help to locate common roots that connect us all as American, indeed, human in the Americas. Seeing Others as extended humans, distant kin rather than "non-Us," may heal schisms that have isolated and hamstrung tribal cultures since invasional conquests. If we are to be genuinely postcolonial in the twenty-first century, we all stand to be liberated cross-culturally.

The issue of margin and mainstream has come down to whose side we stand estranged on: male or female, dark or light, populist or elitist, colonial or postcolonialist, neoprimitivist or postmodernist. "Under the skin we are all colored, the color of blood," says the New Mexico Hispanic poet Sabine Ulibarri, where I live. Add to this the ninety-nine-plus percent of genetic overlap among all human beings. "There is no primitive verse,"

Helen Carr, the British critic, ventures in *Inventing the American Primitive;* "only other traditions."

The Other is struggling to come home in the New World. Sherwood Anderson elegized heartland America in *Poor White.* The historical novelist saw that dispossession came all too quickly, fallen white to reborn ethnic, when "the stumps had been cleared, the Indians driven away." We still sift the losses. Does America know its cultural roots yet? Alfred Kazin remarks in *On Native Grounds,* "perhaps too short a period elapsed between Sitting Bull and Henry James." In fact, James was writing *The American* the moment that Sitting Bull crushed Custer at the Little Big Horn, June 1876. The novelist was publishing *The Bostonians* ten years later in 1886, when Buffalo Bill Cody toured America with Sitting Bull. James was sketching plays in England as the great Sioux leader was assassinated December 15, 1890, at Standing Rock, North Dakota. Sitting Bull and Henry James, then, overlay in cultural history, so-called "civilized" and "savage." These Red-White doubles were each as sophisticated and cultured as the other, tribal icons of their times and people.

Art and science are inversely methodological, Clyde Kluckhohn reasons in *Mirror for Man;* they intersect trying to render cultural histories "intelligible." For the artist,

> Sitting Bull is the dramatic exemplification of the whole struggle of the Indians against the white man. For the anthropologist, Sitting Bull disappears in the mass of Plains Indian chieftains, to be understood in terms of all our knowledge of the role of the chief, of various situational factors at that time, as well as in terms of his own particular life history. The humanities approach generally questions through particular persons or incidents. Anthropology deals with particulars in the framework of universals.

By way of revisionist intercultural history, a reader catches echoes of Sitting Bull's song-poetry in the shadows of Henry James's study. In cross-comparativist poetics, Lawrence's search for the "free" verse line underlies Eliot's "dialect of the tribe" in a modernist wasteland. Where are the natives, who are women? Tribal poets in our own day—Linda Hogan and Joy Harjo to N. Scott Momaday and James Welch—write from the wreckage of an invaded aboriginal land. Blending the genius of migrant and indigenous cultures, fusing the genders, could lead readers through the wasteland into a genuine new loam and literary ground.

"I am neither thief nor stranger, but merely your neighbor, sir," Heathcliff says in *Wuthering Heights,* a novel cherished by Emily Dickinson. The poet herself has been beloved by Mary TallMountain, Scott Momaday, Joy Harjo, Linda Hogan, Denise Levertov, Linda Gregg, and Charles Wright, among many. "All poets are brothers and sisters under the skin of language," Stanley Kunitz offers in *A Kind of Order, A Kind of Folly.* "A poet is a man who yearns to swim in Lake Chauggogagogmanchauggagogchabuna-

gungamaugg, not in Lake Webster," Kunitz says, remembering the callow
fascination of "talking Indian" in his New England childhood. "He loves
a language that reaches all the way back to its primitive condition." Cultural
crossings, including religious and philosophical shifts, inform this reaching
back.

Imagine a contrast neoprimitively radical, alterity *in extremis,* Emily Dickinson contemporary with Sitting Bull. They were, in fact, born within
months of each other the winter of 1830–31. Of distinguished lineage,
visionary power, and early heroic courage, he was an Odysseus of Great
Plains tribes. Sitting Bull conducted reluctant warfare with outsiders,
achieved military victory at the Little Big Horn, and lived through foreign
exile in Canada. He was extradited by a hostile government and went
through a chastened homecoming, a decade of speeches, storytelling, and
elegy until his martyrdom in 1890. Through it all, Sitting Bull remained a
man of narrative cunning and lyric brilliance. Dickinson was the Sappho
of New England Puritanism. An iconic wit and lyric brilliance shaped her
own verse measure from Protestant hymnal. Spiritual independence and
feminist separatism gave her imaginative freedom. The passion and grace
of her own mind, the voluntary silence and privacy of her self-created voice
were resurrected as cartonage from mummified gender caches of literary
history. Once examined, the distances between Sitting Bull and Emily Dickinson may seem less estranging than engaging. These divergent icons, a
century later, mark native polarities in the New World and set up voices of
cultural convergence to come by the millennium's ending.

For the moment, this contrast is diagonal history, not literary exegesis.
I only wish to map the regional terrain and projected distances, which are
as much culturally oppositional as aesthetically appositional. Viewing texts
and cultural overlays from transverse perspectives, the method is neomodernist, not unlike Pound's Vorticist look at the sculpture of Gaudier-Brzeska
or Fenollosa's study of Chinese ideograms. The oblique angle from Lakota
warrior to Amherst poet sets up a critical vortex, more vector than parallel.
In a wartime London art movement, Pound advanced the diagonal Vorticist
fusion of neoprimitive and modernist art: the vortex is "a radiant node or
cluster . . . from which, and through which, and into which, ideas are constantly rushing" *(Gaudier-Brzeska).* Quoting Aquinas, Pound drew kinetic
lines from names to things, *"Nomina sunt consequentia rerum,"* and traced
Vorticist dynamics through tactile arts—tangible masses and "planes in
relation" with works by Wyndham Lewis, Jacob Epstein, and Henri Gaudier-
Brzeska, who forged tools from old steel spindles and "cut stone until its
edge was like metal."

Pound saw torqued kinetic intensity as "the language of exploration,"
he said in *Fortnightly Review,* September 1914. He invoked the projectile
slipstream of a sphere thrown through space, from military ballistics to the

earth's trajectory. The cover image for the 1917 Vorticist magazine, *Blast!*, was a solid cone (the geometry of Yeats's gyre) with an axial rod (the "spherical triangle," Pound felt, was key to modern sculpture). Like analytic calculus in solid geometry, Vorticist aesthetics turned on a dynamic physics—the image-in-motion, the conical field of energy as projective vortex. Pound wanted to hammer out a concrete poetics with the sculptor's "energy cut into stone," in and against the American grain, generating "points of departure, and lines along which the thought or the work may advance" *(Gaudier-Brzeska)*. Poets like H. D., Williams, and Pound himself were "feeling back along the ancient lines of advance" to the "primitive sap" of the ancients, in our analogue from Emily Dickinson to Sitting Bull.

"To be assisted of Reverse," Dickinson wrote, "One must Reverse have bore—." Alterity may be a matter of angled perception or essentialist insistence: "We can find no scar, / But internal difference, / Where the meanings, are—." Differences do set up convergences. Linguists still insist on a unified field of cultural languages, and anthropologists posit universal human paradigms. In relating Amherst poet to Plains warrior, begin with less than one percent genetic difference separating all races. We are all *Homo sapiens,* ninety-nine-plus percent alike more than unlike. Organ or blood donor recipients don't die of race, gender, or culture. We speak with one another, since *Homo erectus* over a million years back, and thus differ from other animals. The translative word, distinguishing humans from other life-forms, binds us to each other across dialects, tongues, histories, geologies, politics, and genders. So language and eventually writing, estranged as we may seem, define us as human. Linguistic distance is both bond and blade between us, definition and difference. Slant or no, the day's light falls on us all. "When it comes, the Landscape listens—/ Shadows—hold their breath—/ When it goes, 'tis like the Distance / On the look of Death—."

Emily Dickinson was born December 10, 1830, in her father's brick Homestead family house, built by his father in Amherst, Massachusetts. Three months later, roughly the same latitude only two thousand miles west, *Tatanka Iyotanke,* or Sitting Bull, first named Slow for his deliberate ways, was born in a buffalo-skin tepee at Many-Caches on the Ree (now Grand) River, near the present Bullhead, South Dakota. Emily Dickinson was three months old that Lakota Winter-when-Yellow-Eyes-Played-in-the-Snow, March 1831, Moon of the Red Grass Appearing. What separates these two by culture, gender, and terrain would appear to be less than one percent of the spiritual lexicon, song-poem to hymn text, connecting them as native poets who sing with bears' hearts.

Their cultures were at war. The winter of these two Americans' birth, 1830–31, Andrew Jackson initiated a thirty-year Removal Era, 1830–60, which dislocated hundreds of thousands of Native Americans, over seventy tribes dumped in Oklahoma. Between four thousand and eight thousand relocated Cherokee alone died along "The Trail of Tears" from Georgia to Oklahoma. In his second annual statement to the country, President Jackson said: "What good man would prefer a country covered with forests and ranged by a few thousand savages to our extensive Republic, studded with cities, towns, and prosperous farms, embellished with all the improvements which art can devise or industry execute, occupied by more than 12 million happy people, and filled with all the blessings of liberty, civilization and religion?" In 1831, Chief Justice John Marshall defied an Anglophilic President Jackson in *Cherokee Nation v. Georgia:* the United States Supreme Court recognized Indian tribes as "domestic dependent nations with an unquestionable right to the lands which they occupy. . . ." The next year, 1832, Jackson appointed a Commissioner of Indian Affairs under the War Department and continued removing natives west. By 1890, the frontier was rescinded and all Indians reserved, along with endangered wild animals in a newly conceived national parks system. We are still living with that reserve-and-salvage mentality.

The early-modernist bow was neoprimitively strung in 1890, the year of Sitting Bull's death on December 15, two weeks before the Wounded Knee massacre. That year, the United States Census Bureau declared the frontier closed. Eighteen ninety was the same year that Mabel Loomis Todd and T. W. Higginson published the woodenly edited *Poems of Emily Dickinson,* First Series. Dickinson's verse was "wayward and unconventional in the last degree," Thomas Higginson wrote peevishly in *The Christian Union,* September 25, 1890, "poetry plucked up by the roots; we have them with earth, stones, and dew adhering, and must accept them as they are." That year Adolph Bandelier released *The Delight Makers,* his historical novel about the Rio Grande Pueblo cultures, and Daniel G. Brinton published one of the first essays on the subject, "Native American Poetry," in *Essays of an Americanist.* April 1890, a young Robert Frost printed his first poem in the Lawrence High School Bulletin, "La Noche Triste," on Montezuma's death and Cortés retreating from Tenochtitlán, as described in Prescott's *Conquest of Mexico.*

In that year, 1890, Vincent Van Gogh, the failed seminarian, sketched black-and-white barren trees and Provençal field workers, painted a whorl of crows over a wheat field, then shot himself through the heart. In this year of early primitive modernism, W. B. Yeats elegized his Gaelic childhood in "The Lake Isle of Innisfree," first published October 1890 in *The London Observer.* "I will arise and go now," the Gaelic bard chanted, "for always night and day / I hear lake water lapping with low sounds by the shore; / While I stand on the roadway, or on the pavements grey, / I hear it in the deep heart's core." Spring of the same year, Joseph Conrad (Polish steamer captain, Józef Konrad Korzeniowski) ran into colonists and head-hunters up the Belgian Congo and immortalized them as deckhands to colonialism a decade later in *Heart of Darkness*. "The voice was gone," Marlow ends Kurtz's story. "What else was there? But I am of course aware that next day the pilgrims buried something in a muddy hole." The next spring, a mixed-blood Peruvian, Paul Gauguin, left France for Tahiti, wishing "to steep myself in virgin nature," he told *Echo de Paris*, "to see no one but savages," as Jack Weatherford records in *Savages and Civilization: Who Will Survive?* Early in the new century, Gauguin would die of alcoholism at fifty-three, having engendered several syphilitic children with three native brides.

We need to ask what led to this historical upheaval and crisis of tradition, for better or worse, the turn-of-a-century advent of neoprimitive modernism. In 1846, fifteen years old, Sitting Bull counted first coup, touching an enemy and getting away, while Emily Dickinson struggled against Christian conversion at Amherst revival meetings in the East.

> Wonder—is not precisely Knowing
> And not precisely Knowing not—
> A beautiful but bleak condition
> He has not lived who has not felt—
>
> Suspense—is his maturer Sister—
> Whether Adult Delight is Pain
> Or of itself a new misgiving—
> This is the Gnat that mangles men—

In 1847–48, as Dickinson entered Mount Holyoke Female Seminary, South Hadley, Massachusetts, western trails were leading toward gold discoveries in California, then Colorado, Montana, Oregon, the Southwest, and the Black Hills of South Dakota, squarely at the heart of Sioux country, in what was then called the *Great American Desert*. Jackson had removed the "Civilized Tribes" from Georgia and Alabama, God given for gold and good land for the taking. By 1850, Dickinson had chosen not to serve Congregationalist norms and stopped going to church. "The Dust like the Mosquito," she wrote, "buzzes round my faith." That year, the California slaughter of some one hundred thousand natives, their population reduced to sixteen thousand in thirty years, began with the Mariposa War against Miwoks and Yokuts. Militia and miner vigilantes, natives said, "shot Indians like rabbits."

In 1856 Sitting Bull, legendary as a stealer of Crow ponies, was wounded in the left foot. By the Civil War, 1861–65, he had become a Lakota sash bearer in the Strong Heart Society. He staked himself to the battleground and took on all comers. Sitting Bull killed his first white man in 1863, the year Kit Carson forced the Navajos on the Long Walk to Bosque Redondo, and the next year he was shot through the buttocks by a cavalry soldier.

Inheriting a visual malady from both parents, Emily Dickinson had her first serious eye treatment in Boston in 1862. That year she composed 366 unpublished poems. The next year she wrote, "It was not Death, for I stood up, / And all the Dead, lie down—/ It was not Night, for all the Bells / Put out their Tongues, for Noon."

> When everything that ticked—has stopped—
> And Space stares all around—
> Or Grisly frosts—first Autumn morns,
> Repeal the Beating Ground—
>
> But, most, like Chaos—Stopless—cool—
> Without a Chance, or Spar—
> Or even a Report of Land—
> To justify—Despair.

By 1868, the Civil War over, Lincoln dead, the Red Cloud Treaty was signed at Fort Laramie, guaranteeing the Sioux perpetual sovereignty in the Dakota Territory, as long as the grass and waters flowed. Dickinson wrote, "That odd old man is dead a year—/ We miss his stated Hat. / 'Twas such an evening bright and stiff / His faded lamp went out." At the same time, Dickinson was writing some of her most quoted lines: "Tell all the Truth but tell it slant—/ Success in Circuit lies / Too bright for our infirm Delight / The Truth's superb surprise." The next year, 1869, General Philip Sheridan, meeting a Comanche chief, said that "the only good Indians I ever saw were dead."

Emily Dickinson's father died June 16, 1874, within a month of Custer's discovering gold in the Black Hills, the year Robert Frost was born in San Francisco. From then on, Dickinson recused herself from public scrutiny and stayed mostly in her room, reading and writing letters and, as it turned out, almost two thousand poems, including epistolary verses. She took no part in church or community affairs. Foreshadowing Plath's suspect *Colossus* or *Daddy*, Dickinson referred to God as "Burglar, banker, father," eventually deferring to the generic "Master" of her last three letters, recipient unknown.

The Fort Laramie Red Cloud treaty was no sooner made than prospectors broke it. After fasting and receiving a vision during a Sun Dance, June 14, 1876, Sitting Bull was shown that his enemies would fall upside down, hats tumbling off, into his camp: "I give you these because they have no ears," the native spirits said of whites who would not listen. Two days later at Rosebud, Montana, Sitting Bull defeated "Three Stars," General George Crook, who commanded more than 1,000 cavalry soldiers and 260 Indian scouts. Nine days later, June 25, 1876, the Sioux "rubbed out" an impetuous Custer's Seventh at the Little Big Horn. Today there are counties and cities named after Custer in Montana, Idaho, South Dakota, Colorado,

Oklahoma, Kentucky, and Nebraska. With the Union a hundred years old in 1876, Helen Hunt Jackson, nativist author of *Ramona* in eight years, asked her reacquainted Amherst childhood friend, Emily Dickinson, to contribute to *A Masque for Poets*. "Success" was among Dickinson's handful of published poems.

A premodernist native poetics was in the making toward the end of the nineteenth century. Wallace Stevens was born in Reading, Pennsylvania, in 1879, while Sitting Bull was in Canadian exile, the year Captain Richard H. Pratt opened the Carlisle Indian School in a converted Pennsylvania army post. William Carlos Williams was born in Rutherford, New Jersey, in 1883, two years after the Hunkpapa chief was extradited from Canada to Standing Rock, North Dakota. Adopting Annie Oakley as his "little sure-shot" daughter, the Sioux warrior went with Buffalo Bill's Wild West in 1885, the year Ezra Pound was born in Hailey, Idaho, and D. H. Lawrence was born in Middlesex, England, "at the forest's edge" between the coal mines, where his father worked, and King Arthur's ancient Sherwood wilderness. Emily Dickinson died the next year, May 15, 1886.

> It was a Pit—with fathoms under it—
> Its Circuit just the same.
> Seed—summer—tomb—
> Whose Doom to whom?

Marianne Moore was born a year later, as was her Carlisle Indian student from Oklahoma, Jim Thorpe, the Sauk and Fox "greatest athlete in the world," according to King Gustav of Sweden when Thorpe won both the decathlon and pentathlon in the 1912 Olympics. T. S. Eliot was born the year after, 1888, in St. Louis, Missouri.

In the spring of 1889, Catherine Weldon, a rich Brooklyn widow and head of the National Indian Defense Association, moved in with Sitting Bull and his two wives on the Ree River. Washing dishes, sweeping floors, cooking, painting his portrait, Weldon was known as "Woman-Walking-Ahead," or more simply, "Sitting Bull's White Squaw." She painted his portrait, and he proposed marriage, but government agents forced her to leave the North Dakota reservation and return to New York.

The fall of 1890, a meadowlark warned the fifty-nine-year-old chief, "The Sioux will kill you!" In two months it was all over. Indian police from the Bullhead clan arrested and shot *Tatanka Iyotanke,* dragged naked from his bed at dawn. Fifteen Sioux died that morning in the crossfire. "We have killed each other on both sides," Eagle Man mourned December 15, 1890. Two weeks later at Pine Ridge, the dead Custer's ghostly Seventh staged the Wounded Knee Massacre, butchering Big Foot and three hundred more Sioux civilians.

"We are all related," the Lakota sing out, *Mitakuye oyasin!* So-called savage and civilized, male and female, Sitting Bull and Emily Dickinson stand for true alterity, it would seem, a formidable distance between West and East. Yet they are related internally by native spirits and poetic voices, "word senders" sui generis with singing bear hearts. He had five wives and she never married: a political man and a poetic woman, his Great Plains prairie was dotted with skin lodges, her father's Amherst garden was walled in. "His heart was pure and terrible," Dickinson elegized her father, "and I think no other like it exists." Samuel Dickinson was buried in the Amherst family plot where his daughter now lies.

Sitting Bull told his people in the 1880s, "I was born near where I stand. I want you to hold these lands. They will be worth far more. Value them at twenty dollars a foot." His was a semi-nomadic buffalo culture, following game from Canada to Kansas, and hers an obstinate New England Puritanism that she queried, patriarchal back through Cotton Mather to Calvin. "More than the Grave is closed to me—/ The Grave and that Eternity / To which the Grave adheres—".

Square-shouldered and deep-chested, limping from an early wound in his left sole, Sitting Bull looked straight at his listener when he talked. In 1882 he spoke directly in Lakota to a Select Congressional Committee from Washington (Senate Report 148 to 348), headed by Senator Henry L. Dawes from Massachusetts, where Dickinson still lived:

> *Sitting Bull:* Do you not know who I am, that you speak as you do?
> *Dawes:* I know that you are Sitting Bull, and if you have anything to say, we will be glad to hear you. . . .
> *Sitting Bull:* I am here by the will of the Great Spirit, and by His will I am a chief. My heart is red and sweet, and I know it is sweet, because whatever passes near me puts out its tongue to me; and yet you men have come here to talk with us, and you say you do not know who I am. I want to tell you that if the Great Spirit has chosen anyone to be the chief of this country, it is myself.

His was a pride that could not bow, a courage that would not budge. She was inwardly proud, outwardly coy and come-hither. Twenty years earlier, April 16, 1862, Emily Dickinson asked Thomas Higginson, "Are you too deeply occupied to say if my verse is alive?" She enclosed verses and her name, "asking you, if you please, sir, to tell me what is true? That you will not betray me it is needless to ask, since honor is its own pawn." In a self-depicting letter three months later: "I had no portrait, now, but am small, like the Wren; and my hair is bold like the Chestnut bur; and my eyes, like the Sherry in the Glass, that the Guest leaves. Would this do just as well?"

Sitting Bull was direct, personable, eloquent, wry in later years. "What does it matter how I pray," he tweaked Christian missionaries, "so long as my prayers are answered?" Of his lifelong resistance to White acculturation:

"Let it be recorded that I was the last man of my people to lay down my gun," he said when extradited from Canada in 1881. Living in Sitting Bull's camp, the Cheyenne Wooden Leg called his Lakota leader "the one old man chief of all the camps combined." By contrast, Emily Dickinson was oblique, gnomic, diffident: "All men say 'What?' to me," she teased Higginson, "but I thought it a fashion." Sitting Bull was honored an epic hero by some: "For he was surely a fighter, a thinker, a chief, and a gentleman," said Private J. F. Waggoner, the soldier who built the warrior's coffin and helped to bury him December 17, 1890. An army mule named Caesar pulled Sitting Bull's cart to the graveyard, where five gallons of quicklime were poured into his coffin and the lid nailed down. "We laid the noble old Chief away without a hymn or a prayer or a sprinkle of earth," Waggoner said, four years after Dickinson had died. Only the ignorant would quibble either poet's elegy. She draws a breathtaking strangeness from our common language, he translates natively across deep chasms the nobility of a Great Vision.

Dickinson prepared all her life for death, triggered by her 1861 eye disease and depressive crises. She held vigils for the dying and felt intimations of her own end, no Christian certainty about an afterlife. "I had a terror since September," she wrote Higginson in 1862, "I could tell to none; and so I sing, as the boy does by the burying ground, because I am afraid." Shortly before her death from Bright's disease at fifty-five, she wrote:

> Drowning is not so pitiful
>   As the attempt to rise.
> Three times, 'tis said, a sinking man
>   Comes up to face the skies,
> And then declines forever
>   To that abhorred abode
>
> Where hope and he part company,—
>   For he is grasped of God.
> The Maker's cordial visage,
>   However good to see,
> Is shunned, we must admit it,
>   Like an adversity.

The year following her death, 1887, Senator Dawes of Massachusetts brokered the General Allotment Act through Congress, massively reducing "surplus" Indian lands for White settlement and sale.

"I would rather die an Indian," Sitting Bull said, "than live a white man." The war chief knew every day, from pubescence to old age, that he was ready to go honorably as a Strong Heart. Vestal translates one of his early favorite songs: "No chance for me to live; / Mother, you might as well mourn." And toward the end, *Tatanka Iyotanke* was still singing, *Oyate kin taku yakapelo / Ikicize imatancan qon / Ehkales le han wani ye.* Robert Higheagle translates for Vestal: "You tribes, what are you saying? / A war-chief I have been, / All the same, I am still living." Or in the ten-nine-eight syllabic count, parallel to the Lakota phonemes, triadically spaced:

> What are you chewing on now, complainers?
> I wanted to be a warrior.
> Surely now, I am still alive.

Three days before his assassination, Sitting Bull was entreating peace, as roughly translated by Andrew Fox, his son-in-law, December 12, 1890, in a letter to Major James McLaughlin, the North Dakota Standing Rock agent: "I wish no one to come to in my pray with they gund or knife: so all Indians Pray to god for life & try to find out good road and do nothing wrong. in they life: This is what we want & Pray: . . . I want answer back soo. Sitting Bull." No answer came.

In 1883, three years before her death, Emily Dickinson wrote a friend, Maria Whitney: "You are like God. We pray to Him, and he answers 'No.' Then we pray to Him to rescind the 'no,' and He don't answer at all. . . ."

Analogues across continental, gender-specific, and cultural divides scratch the historical imagination; still these two song-poets connect by way of deeper thematic and spiritual resonance. The odd meaningful intersection may be most fertile. In their own iconographic ways, Emily Dickinson and Sitting Bull share the inner voices and incandescent images that make poets write and singers sing. Both were "word senders," spiritual seers— neither fools, nor proselytizers, nor party-liners—but worldly mystics who understood the power of the word to move people's daily lives.

What is the power of the word? The "language instinct," as Steven Pinker decodes biological linguistics, is shared by humans and song-learning birds, "an instinctive tendency to acquire an art" noted by Charles Darwin in *The Descent of Man* (1871). "He spoke like singing," says the Lakota visionary, Black Elk, remembering the "all-colors of light" Great Spirit. About the time of Black Elk's vision in the early 1870s, Dickinson wrote:

> This was a Poet—It is That
> Distills amazing sense
> From ordinary Meanings—
> And Attar so immense
>
> From the familiar spices
> That perished by the Door—
> We wonder it was not Ourselves
> Arrested it—before—

All "word senders," as the Sioux say, are moved by a *totem*ic world (Ojibwa, "my fellow clansmen") of animal guardians and spirit powers. "I knew a Bird that would sing as firm / in the centre of Dissolution, / as in it's Father's nest—," William Schurr ferrets the lines out of Dickinson's prose correspondence, "Phenix, or the Robin / . . . I leave you to guess."

> Many a phrase has the English language—
> I have heard but one—
> Low as the laughter of the Cricket,
> Loud, as the Thunder's Tongue—
>
> Murmuring, like old Caspian Choirs,
> When the Tide's a' lull—
> Saying itself a new inflection—
> Like a Whippoorwill

Sitting Bull's prophetic meadowlark and yellowhammer, Emily Dickinson's "plashless" bird-as-butterfly and buzzing fatal fly were winged messengers to these sibling visionaries—harbingers, muses, daemons, spirits, native gods.

Dickinson said the top of her head was taken off by a true poem, "so cold that no fire could ever warm me." This torqued ecstasy shows up in the ritual vision of a "death" song for Sitting Bull, sung as a call to the best of life: *Ikicize waonkon* he / *wana henala yelo* he / *iyotiye kiya waon.* Higheagle renders the song for Densmore:

> A warrior
> I have been.
> Now it is all over.
> A hard time I have.

This is the supplicant voice of a lyric warrior, an image quite different from murderous Sioux at the Little Big Horn, and there is more to say of this song-poem in the next chapter. Farther north, the Netsilik Inuit hunter and songmaker, Orpingalik, told Knud Rasmussen, dog sledding across the Arctic in the 1920s:

> Songs are thoughts, sung out with the breath when people are moved by great forces and ordinary speech no longer suffices. Man is moved just like the ice-floe sailing here and there out in the current. . . . Thoughts can wash over him like a flood, making his breath come in gasps and his heart throb. Something like an abatement in the weather will keep him thawed up. And then it will happen that we, who always think we are small, we feel still smaller. And we will fear to use words. But it will happen that the words we need will come of themselves. When the words we want to use shoot up of themselves—we get a new song. (In Astrov, *The Winged Serpent*)

The ecstatic dream, from Dante and Donne, to Keats and Coleridge, to Heaney and Hogan, calls the shaman's song through sacred tongues. These are dreamers spiritually "made of words," as N. Scott Momaday revised Wallace Stevens, who borrowed the phrase from Paul Valéry.

Dickinson and Sitting Bull, both "word senders," drew from natural voices and native visions. Amherst poet and Sioux singer were each word crafters, in scripted and oral traditions. Emily Dickinson left 1,775 hand-written poems, arcanely scribbled gems, over 900 in a small box of 49 sewn fascicles, locked away and discovered by her sister Lavinia at her death. Some 875 more surfaced, along with a full body of correspondence, over a thousand letters. "Best Things dwell out of Sight / The Pearl—the Just— Our Thought." William Shurr and Judith Farr mine verse buried in her prose correspondence, as in this letter describing an opera singer:

> The brow is that of Deity—
> the eyes, those of the lost,
> but the power lies in the throat—
> pleading, sovereign, savage—
> the panther and the dove!

In an unscripted oral tradition, Sitting Bull was a legendary speaker and singer with "a high, resonant, melodious voice," Stanley Vestal records from firsthand informants, among them White Bull, the chief's Lakota nephew. "The Sioux do not talk unless they have something to say," Vestal explains in Sitting Bull's biography. "They have songs for every situation in which a man can find himself: for courting, for feasting, for thanksgiving and mourning, for peace and for war, for welcome and farewell, for victory and defeat—even for the moment of death." Tribal prestige often turned on being "able to sing the right song at the right moment," and Sitting Bull, soldier-singer, was regarded as something of the Lakota poet laureate in his own day, no less than England's Renaissance warrior-king, Henry VIII. *Tatanka Iyotanke* scripted his own life as an imaged winter-count up to 1870, "Hieroglyphic Autobiography of Sitting Bull," forty picture-events of a warrior's life later published in a 1929 Bureau of American Ethnology report.

Frances Densmore recorded a number of Sitting Bull's songs, with musical score, in *Teton Sioux Music* (1918). Stanley Vestal collected several dozen more from White Bull (who adopted the biographer) and printed Robert Higheagle's translations in the 1934 *Southwest Review* as "The Works of Sitting Bull, Real and Imaginary": *Anpao kin imawani ye / Chanonpa wan hi omawani ye,* rendered by Higheagle for Vestal, "At daybreak I roam. / I seek a peace-pipe as I wander around." More consistent with the Lakota internal rhyme and syllabic count, the lines are meant to be sung:

> At daybreak I wander off from home
> seeking a medicine pipe as I roam.

After being wounded in battle and appointed head chief of the western Sioux, Sitting Bull sang, *Oyate kin, wama yankapi ye / Itanchan kin henapila yelo / Miye kakes blihe michiye.* Higheagle translates: "Ye tribes, behold me. / The chiefs of old are gone. / Myself, I shall take courage." A version of the ten-syllabic tercet, closer to the sung Lakota:

> All my lost relatives, here behold me!
> The leaders of olden days are all gone,
> I take heart freshly as rain on lakes.

Dickinson's hymnal measure, the four-three pulse of common meter taken from Protestant church services (Moody & Sankey hymnal), is no more or less "poetic" than Sitting Bull's syllabic-counted, meadowlark-inspired "spirit" songs to the Power-that-Moves-moves, *Takuskanskan.* Song-poetry is the median. Western prairie meadowlarks have at least twenty-six different original songs (a relative triadic cadence of the European lark begins Verdi's *La Traviata).* As the "Sioux bird," they are said to sing the truth, serving as oracles. In 1861 Dickinson wrote "Because I see—New Englandly—":

> The Robin's my Criterion for Tune—
> Because I grow—where Robins do
> But, were I Cuckoo born—
> I'd swear by him—
> The ode familiar—rules the Noon—
> The Buttercup's, my Whim for Bloom—

Sitting Bull always spoke of birds and was fond of stories about the Bird People. *Ate oyate tawe makiyin na, Tatanka Iyotanke* sang, *Yuha iyotiye wakiya.* Higheagle translates: "The Father (God) has given me the Bird People for mine, / And with them a hard time I am having." In English syllabics and imagery closer to the lyric original:

> My Father has given me his breasted wings,
> I shall rise up as the mourning dove.

Prophetically, a yellowhammer's song saved the young hunter from a grizzly bear near the Ree River, and he composed a song on the spot, as Vestal records: "Pretty bird, you saw me and took pity on me; / You wish me to survive among the people. / O Bird People, from this day always you shall be my relatives!"

Finally, Sitting Bull and Emily Dickinson knew verbal transformations, powerful metamorphoses: they lived through cataclysmic changes, inside and out, from dream visions to death conversions, from Civil War to Indian holocaust, from pastoral childhood to Gatling guns and mechanical gears uprooting the land. They were both mighty bear-heart dreamers. " 'Twas a Divine Insanity,'' Dickinson wrote:

> And whether it was noon at night—
> Or only Heaven—at Noon—
> For very Lunacy of Light
> I had not power to tell—
> . . . .
> I could not have defined the change—
> Conversion of the Mind
> Like Sanctifying in the Soul—
> Is witnessed—not explained—

Dickinson writes of bearing witness to miraculous changes, without trying to explain spiritual or imaginative metamorphosis. "Bear down, rise up; touch the earth,'' goes the native saying. Even today, as the Great Vision turns on grounded being, revitalized Native Americans turn to a people's tribal history, ancestors in the land, singing guardians and spirits all around. "Healthy feet can hear the very heart of Holy Earth,'' Sitting Bull would say. He was usually up before dawn, walking barefoot in the short-grass. After Canadian exile, he vowed: "The land I have under my feet is mine again. I never sold it, I never gave it to anyone.'' A poet's integrity is rooted in knowing the details of place and deeper being, not on trade or acclaim. Emily Dickinson wrote to her editor, Thomas Higginson, June 8, 1862: "If fame belonged to me, I could not escape her; if she did not, the longest day would pass me on the chase, and the approbation of my dog would forsake me then. My barefoot rank is better.'' So it was, for both seer-poets.

"Emily Dickinson, A Primitive,'' Edward Sapir titled his review of her newly published work in the May 1925 *Poetry* magazine, a year after Indians were made citizens. Her work held "a strange, unsought, and almost clairvoyant freshness.'' Allen Tate felt that Cotton Mather would have burned Dickinson as a witch. The "partially cracked poetess at Amherst,'' dressed in white and holding out two day-lilies as her "introduction,'' Higginson said, wrote verse "remarkable, though odd.'' He judged her lines "too delicate—not strong enough to publish.'' As with the life and shamanic songs of Sitting Bull, there's tonnage here that stops the casual reader, staggers the average critic. "I've got a Tomahawk / in my side but that / dont hurt me much.'' Dickinson's unforgivably mannerist and brilliant eccentricity was irksome to Yvor Winters, who wrote early *In Defense of Reason* (1938), "of all great poets, she is the most lacking in taste.'' Her meter, at worst, was "a kind of stiff sing-song,'' Winters carped, her diction "a kind of poetic nursery jargon." Though Dickinson stumbled through "a desert of crudities," Winters begrudgingly crowned her "one of the greatest lyric poets of all time," back to Sappho. Later in the Santa Fe magazine *Viva*, August 6, 1972, Winters's student, N. Scott Momaday, titled a column, "A Love Affair with Emily Dickinson."

Across Sapir's nativist praise, Winters's cranky admiration, and Momaday's love affair, a reader might pause to ask of Dickinson: does primitive mean a genuine, a native American poet? Emily Dickinson is the most "original" of all American poets, even Harold Bloom wagers in *The Western Canon*, "the best mind of all our poets," he holds, among Western poets in four centuries. Still, hers was a primitively gay nature, in a world "pure and terrible" as her father's heart. Her reality was consistently offbeat, shocking, delightful: her *is* unnerves the timid.

> But nature is a stranger yet;
> The ones that cite her most
> Have never passed her haunted house,
> Nor simplified her ghost.

Dickinson's originality strikes an American note. "In the beginning," John Locke declaimed of the primally free, New World natural order, "all the World was AMERICA" (1689 *Second Treatise of Government*). Native Enlightenment—the nobility of savagery, the genius of the free man—fired a New World break with old institutions. "Deep down, the US," Jean Baudrillard could drop cryptically in *America* (1988), "is the only remaining primitive society." Natural, genuine, freed, "America is the original version of modernity," Baudrillard waxes. Helen Carr sees this modernist light on the Americas as "poetic primitivism," an ongoing rage for freedom.

How does "Emily Dickinson, A Primitive" square with what we think to be modernism or, for that matter, a woman's poetics? Consider Robert Frost's opening salvo in his *Complete Poems*, the "Figure a Poem Makes," referenced at the beginning:

> If it is a *wild tune,* it is a poem. . . . Just as the *first mystery* was how a poem could have a tune in such a straightness as meter, so the second mystery is how a *poem can have wildness* and at the same time a subject that shall be fulfilled. . . . The line will have the more charm for not being mechanically straight. We enjoy the *straight crookedness of a good walking stick.* . . . It must be *more felt than seen ahead* like prophecy. It must be a *revelation,* or a series of revelations, as much for the poet as for the reader. . . . *the wild free ways of wit and art: from delight to wisdom.* The *figure* is the same as for *love. Like a piece of ice on a hot stove the poem must ride on its own melting.* (emphasis mine)

Good walking meter needs burls and crooks, Frost suggests—wild synapses and rightly twisted syntax—to counterbalance the straight metrical expectation, else the line sound artificial, fixed, mechanical. Break "the sound of sense with all their irregularity of accent across the regular beat of the metre," he wrote John Bartlett from England in July 1913: "I alone of English writers have consciously set myself to make music out of what I may call the sound of sense." The Vermont farmer glared back some years later: "They cannot scare me with their empty spaces / Between stars—on stars where no human race is, / I have it in me so much nearer home / To scare myself with my own desert places."

Frost's midlife career as a poet caught the public eye in the modernist 1920s, about the time of Emily Dickinson's literary resurrection. "Had I not seen the Sun / I could have borne the shade / But Light a newer Wilderness / My Wilderness has made—." No less than Sitting Bull's chants, poetry by both Frost and Dickinson is personal revelation, realistic prophecy, what Robert Lowell would call "the blazing out," or Mallarmé, "the flash of intellect." Like love, "from delight to wisdom," a poem rides on its own going, changing, revealing, and undoing, more an alchemical process than mechanical product, the audience warming to it stove side.

The Complete Poems of Emily Dickinson was published by Martha Dickinson Bianchi and Alfred Leete Hampson, June 2, 1924, three years after suffragettes won the vote and the year Native Americans were granted United States citizenship. An unusual number of women were working as linguistic anthropologists and writers in native ethnopoetics: Mary Austin, Ella Deloria, Natalie Curtis Burlin, Frances Densmore, Gertrude P. Kurath, Ruth Bunzel, Ruth Underhill, Elsie Clews Parsons, Mari Sandoz, Willa Cather, Dorothy Dematracapoulou. By 1932, both Vestal's *Sitting Bull* and John Neihardt's *Black Elk Speaks* were printed as modestly successful Plains Indian tales, followed a decade later by Mari Sandoz's fictional autobiography, *Crazy Horse, the Strange Man of the Oglalas.* Despite Vestal's biographical history or Neihardt's witnessing narrative, the public saw the Indian as a bygone relic, vanishing, crushed by Manifest Destiny. A painting of Custer's inglorious demise at the Little Big Horn hung in most every bar in America, a twisted beer-hall salute to Native genocide. It would be two more years, 1934, before John Collier engineered the Indian Reorganization Act, a move toward the original self-determination of over five hundred Native American tribes then accounted in the United States. Their sovereignty is still being contested.

It is critical to address our own vexing questions over a native poetics, to measure the overlapping distances from older mentors to present models, to find a "good road" into the next century interculturally. The last of Dickinson's 1775 collected verses reads:

> The earth has many keys.
> Where melody is not

Is the unknown peninsula.
Beauty is nature's fact.

But witness for her land,
And witness for her sea,
The cricket is her utmost
Of elegy to me.

How far have we come? What lines strike the cultural parameters among genders, politics, and peoples? Which are the poetics of America today? Listen. These voices have something to tell us.

TWO

≋(•)≋

Aboriginal American Texts

Oblique convergences of native song-poetry and hymnal verse measure, Sitting Bull to Emily Dickinson, were planted in the 1890s. Ethnographers were translating and inscribing tribal chants, while Lavinia Dickinson opened the cherry-wood box with her sister's verse fascicles and began transcribing the handwritten lines for publication. Whether Native or New England, the transcriptions were roughly redacted from truer originals— so much lost in translation, to be sure, but the seeds were drilled for a fusional poetics.

> There died a myriad,
> And of the best, among them,
> For an old bitch gone in the teeth,
> For a botched civilization . . .
>
> EZRA POUND,
> "HUGH SELWYN MAUBERLEY," 1918

The War was over. Eight and a half million men from the trenches lay dead. Buffalo Bill Cody died a drunken circus showman the year before, and the imperial West had scrapped itself to salvage. In this wasteland nadir of 1918, George W. Cronyn anthologized "Indian" transliterations from Smithsonian Bureau of American Ethnology reports and Anthropological Papers of the American Museum of Natural History, a collection first called *The Path on the Rainbow*. He borrowed the title from Navajo healing "night chants," originally translated by the Southwest cowboy-surgeon Washington Matthews:

> In Kininaéki.
> In the *house made of dawn.*

In the *story made of dawn.*
On the trail of dawn.
O, *Talking God!* . . .
From the *house made of mirage,*
From the *story made of mirage,*
From the doorway of rainbow,
The path out of which is the rainbow [italics mine]

The native concept of a spirit-who-speaks-with-us, Navajo *Talking God,* would show up fifty years later in the Pulitzer-winning novel *House Made of Dawn,* by a Kiowa "man-made-of-words," N. Scott Momaday.

Cronyn's 1918 sampler of Indian literary wares was the first collection to make headlines, the same year that Charles A. Eastman, M.D., otherwise known as the Lakota *Ohiyesa,* published *Indian Heroes and Great Chieftains* with Little, Brown and Company in Boston. Daniel Brinton's 1883 "Aboriginal American Authors and Their Productions" lay fallow among scholars, and Natalie Burlin Curtis's ethnomusicology, *The Indians' Book,* had gotten modest press. "Rough-Rider" Theodore Roosevelt wrote a frontispiece longhand from the White House in 1907: "These songs cast a wholly new light—on the depth and dignity of Indian thought, the simple beauty and strange charm—the dream of a vanished elder world—of Indian poetry." The myth of "elder" Indians vanishing was popularized by Edward Curtis in a scrimmed, shadowy photograph of four horseback Navajos disappearing into the distance.

Why Indian literature in 1918? Tens of thousands of *American* Indians had volunteered for the First World War, though they were not yet United States citizens. Ninety-seven percent of some four to six million ancestors in the States had been exterminated in the previous three centuries. In fact, the United States government waged the "Indian Wars" on many of these veterans' mothers and fathers from 1860 to 1890, when the Census Bureau declared the frontier closed and Indians were "reserved" behind barbed wire. So in 1924, Congress granted all "Indians," dubbed "American" in Buffalo Bill Cody's *Wild West* billing, dual citizenship out of their native loyalty, that is, war service. They could be ethnic aboriginals, among five hundred "domestic dependent nations," and "native" Americans, tax-paying veterans.

But what landed Cronyn's anthology at the eclectic threshold of Western literature? Indeed, *The Path on the Rainbow* eventually assumed the lead text in Jorgé Luis Borges's classes on the American canon. Why culturally include, rather than exclude in the vanishing frontier way, some sixty million pre-Columbian "Americans" in the Western Hemisphere? In the United States alone, they had been decimated to a quarter of a million political refugees by 1900, along with two hundred and fifty remaining Texas bison. Out west, xenophobia, racism, and genocide festered on the flip side of the buffalo-head nickel, the silhouette of a Sioux elder. The artist and cultural scion Frederic Remington could snarl, "Jews, Injuns, Chinamen, Italians, Huns," echoing Chivington and Custer, "the rubbish of the earth I hate." Indians had been made prisoners of war on reservations from the 1880s on—stripped of their clothing, culture, and spirits by grizzled Civil War colonels, hardpan pioneers, make-over missionaries, sleazy traders, and hardass bureaucrats. These patriots figured that the only "good" Indians left (better dead than Red) better get civilized, fast, before they disappeared. "The Indians must conform to 'the white man's ways,' " the Commissioner of Indian Affairs menaced in 1889, "peaceably if they will, forcibly if they must. This civilization may not be the best possible, but it is the best the Indian can get." *Listen up, pilgrims,* John Wayne would later say in the movies.

Sorely, to be sure, the West needed a revised myth to supersede New World carte blanche. In a curious turnabout, the mythographers reached into the present past and reinvented the Indian, the heart of this continent's humanity. The resurrected noble savage, reduced by a factor of sixteen since 1492, rose on literary wings above the anarchic pillars of Manifest Destiny.

"From *Poetry, a Magazine of Verse,*" Cronyn acknowledged, "came the inspiration for this anthology." These "genuine American classics," freely adapted not as translations but "interpretations" elsewhere (*McClure's, Scribner's, Sunset, Others*) by such as Carl Sandburg, Witter Bynner, Vachel Lindsay, Lew Sarett, and Amy Lowell, were nudged into rebirth by the February 1917 "Aboriginal" issue of the country's premier journal of verse, *Poetry* magazine. "Suspicion arises definitely that the Red Man and his children," Sandburg tweaked readers, "committed direct plagiarisms on the modern imagists and vorticists." Ezra Pound published three of his early Cantos and a review of T. S. Eliot's "The Love Song of J. Alfred Prufrock" in the August 1917 *Poetry,* opening salvos of neoprimitive modernism from Occident to Orient:

> Hang it all, Robert Browning,
> there can be but the one "Sordello."
> But Sordello, and my Sordello?
> Lo Sordels si fo di Mantovana.
> So-shu churned in the sea.
> Seal sports in the spray-whited circles of cliff-wash,
> Sleek head daughter of Lir,
>   eyes of Picasso
> Under black fur-hood, lithe daughter of Ocean . . .

Freshly married and toeing the margins of *The Waste Land,* T. S. Eliot was clerking in a London bank at the end of the Great War. He reviewed

Cronyn's anthology in *The Atheneum,* October 17, 1919, under the mock title, "War-Paint and Feathers." Starting tongue-in-cheek with Armenian, "vanishing" tribal song-poetry, lately rediscovered and reinterpreted vers libre, Eliot dryly notes that the translation manqué "is declared to be superior, in its subtle and mystical simplicity, to anything that can be bought secondhand on Charing Cross Road." The barbarians mill at the gates, Eliot fears, and now the "Chippeway has the last word in subtlety, simplicity, and poeticality" (though the native's continent stands "backing him," Mary Austin reflects in Cronyn's foreword). "The Red Man is here," Eliot surmises, "what are we to do with him, except to feed him on maple sugar?"

Then comes a curious reversal. "The maxim, Return to the sources, is a good one," the expatriot St. Louis reviewer says unblinking, to "revivify the contemporary activities" in the arts. The modern reader should know something of Freud and Fabre, Eliot argues, as now of "the medicine-man and his works." So, too, a modern poet should acknowledge all verse "accomplishments" since poetry's "beginnings—in order to know what he is doing himself." Eliot concludes neoprimitively: "And as it is certain that some study of primitive man furthers our understanding of civilized man, so it is certain that primitive art and poetry help our understanding of civilized art and poetry." Yet why so? wonders the Harvard doctorate in philosophy and literature, and then answers his question on native grounds. Most competent "to understand both civilized and savage," a modern poet will be "the most ready and the most able of men to *learn from the savage*" (italics mine).

Why Eliot's about-face? Across the page, reprinted under the heading "Ninety Years Ago," an 1829 British editor had challenged, "Is there such a thing as American literature?" Like asking "the nature of snakes in Ireland," the *Atheneum* reviewer had smirked in 1829, "when we try to discover whether the literature of America is independent, we are stopped by the preliminary doubt whether it has a literature, whether it has even the genius of one to come." Apart from Washington Irving, Dr. Channing, and Mr. Cooper of "The Last of the Mohicans," went the nineteenth-century continental bias, We-in-England find no literary merit on the New World plain.

To counter mossback Anglo-centrism, the transplanted Missouri native would bridge intercultural modernism. Uncultured by ethnocentric standards, his New World wilderness held poetic shards rare in Britain. Eliot writes of the modernist poet:

> But, as he is the first person to see the merits of the savage, the barbarian and the rustic, he is also the first person to see how the savage, the barbarian and the rustic can be improved upon; he is the last person to see the savage in a romantic light, or to yield to the weak credulity of crediting the savage with any gifts of mystical insight or artistic feeling that he does not possess himself.

Cronyn's retranslations serve as a start, though Eliot's Amerindian caveat turns on ethnological authenticity and human equivalencies, not out-of-culture epiphanies. The poet asks for accurate translations, not silly interpretations, real anthropological data, not born-again nativist impressions. "The poet and the artist and the anthropologist will be the last people to tolerate the whooping brave, with his tale of maple sugar, as a drawing-room phenomenon." And in less than three years Eliot, neoprimitive poet, Euro-American modernist, goes on to parse his own wasteland runes, "savagely still." Arid plain at his back, the Fisher-King concludes: "These fragments I have shored against my ruins."

Further inspired by Cronyn's *The Path on the Rainbow,* Harriet Monroe gathered another "aboriginal number" of *Poetry* in 1920, where Mary Austin and others re-revised native verse. Emma Hawkridge waxed neo-primitive in "The Painted Desert":

> Over the wasteland a strong wind goes;
> Like captured heat lies the cactus rose.
> The desert sings.

Whose paint, which rose, what desert, from Gertrude Stein, to Dylan Thomas, to T. S. Eliot? Wallace Stevens had printed an early version of "The Anecdote of the Jar" in the October 1919 *Poetry* issue (winning the Helen Haire Levinson Prize), under the mock heading, "Pecksniffiana," reference to a peck-and-sniff Victorian busybody in Dickens's *Martin Chuzzlewit.* An arrogant granduncle of Eliot's Prufrock (which Pound debuted five years earlier, as mentioned, in *Poetry* magazine), the cant hypocrite Pecksniff orders the world to his fickle liking and forces an unwilling woman to marry him. And so, that avuncular grey jar sits comically imperious in the New World:

> It made the slovenly wilderness
> Surround that hill.

> The wilderness rose up to it.
> And sprawled around, no longer wild.
> The jar was round upon the ground
> And tall and of a port of air.

> It took dominion everywhere.

The next year Pablo Picasso and Wyndham Lewis sketched petroglyphic abstractions in *The Dial* (July 1921), while D. H. Lawrence, newly relocating to the New World, confessed his fastidious bias in "Snake." Also in *The Dial,* W. C. Williams scratched American verse from what T. S. Eliot otherwise called, after Mallarmé on Poe, "the dialect of the tribe," and W. B. Yeats celebrated an Irish tribal renaissance in his *Autobiography.* Ethnographic reviews by Edward Sapir on Max Müller and by Mary Austin on

Frank Cushing underscored what Austin termed "the search for native sources of inspiration in the poetry and drama and design of Amerind art." With artists and ethnographers plumbing "deep-rooted aboriginal stock" and the very rhythms of the land itself in "Aboriginal American Literature," Austin would grouse that "it is still easier to know more of Beowulf than of the Red Score of the Delaware, more of Homer than of the Creation Myth of the Zuñi, more of Icelandic sagas than of the hero myths of Iroquois and Navajo." Her point still stands.

Cronyn's sources had been the field work of Daniel Brinton, Natalie Curtis Burlin, Frances Densmore, J. W. Fewkes, Alice Fletcher, John Peabody Harrington, James Mooney, Washington Matthews, Henry Rowe Schoolcraft, Stephen Riggs, John R. Swanton, and other pioneering linguistic anthropologists, godfathered by European-trained social scientists under Franz Boas. The next generation of Ruth Benedict, Ruth Bunzel, Pliny Goddard, A. L. Kroeber, Robert Lowie, Elsie Parsons, Paul Radin, Knud Rasmussen, Edward Sapir, Frank G. Speck, Herbert Spindon, Ruth Underhill, J. R. Walker, Clark Wissler, and scores of others would add their translative genius to American Indian Studies. Knud Rasmussen, Ella Deloria, Charles Eastman, William James, Francis La Flesche, and Archie Phinney grew into Native ethnographers of note, and the translation race was on.

Introducing Cronyn's *The Path on the Rainbow*, Mary Austin appealed to "the resident genius" of our native terrain as a kind of New World neoclassicism, grounded in the cultural bedrock of Native America. Half a century later, N. Scott Momaday still called for "an American land ethic": "We Americans need now more than ever before—and indeed more than we know—to imagine who and what we are with respect to the earth and sky." Here in the pre-Columbian literary landscape, Americans could dig down to find their own Homer in tribal epics, Plato in philosophic parables, Diogenes in trickster picaresques. Indian women traced their own Sappho in lyric romances, Dido in heroic tragedies, and Demeter in creation myths, among hundreds of diverse Native American cultures. Frances Densmore's translations stood foremost as recreative Western literature. From the Lakota:

> Soldiers,
>   you fled.
> Even the eagle dies.

From the Yuman:

> The bush is sitting
>   under a tree
>   and singing.

From the Yaqui:

> The water bug
> is drawing
> the shadows of the evening
> toward him on the water.

In *Papago Music* Densmore had recorded the shamanic healer's "Song of Owl Woman," or Juana Manuel, somewhat altered in *The Path on the Rainbow:*

> In the great night my heart will go out;
> Toward me the darkness comes rustling.
> In the great night my heart will go out.

Densmore later raised the ticklish issue of recreative translation: "The word 'rattling' was said to be a literal translation. To us the word means simply a noise, which darkness could scarcely make, but the sound of a rattle is associated with magic and mystery in the mind of the Indian. In quoting this poem, George Cronyn substitutes the word 'rustling' for 'rattling,' but this is not a synonym. It is gentle and soft in its implication, and there is no vigor in the corresponding verb. This is the song of a terrified spirit, facing the greatest mystery that the mind can conceive. The subject is worthy of Dante. In the 'great night' the spirit heard sounds of fearful and stupendous import. The darkness 'came rattling.' " What is the difference between darkness "rustling" and "rattling" (or Higginson substituting "weight" for "Heft," as truer rhyme in Dickinson's "There's a certain Slant of light")? Were she bilingually gifted with a poet's ear in both languages, which would Owl Woman hear, and what works better in English? What kind of medicine does the chant work in either culture? Which audience must a translation satisfy? If Densmore stays linguistically pure to the Papago and blunts the poem's generative English spark, the "Song of Owl Woman" fails as a translated poem. If she freely adapts to English poetics, the "poem" no longer speaks from or for its source, but plays Indian. Can there be an authentic crossing?

The translative art, Stanley Kunitz says of reworking Anna Akhmatova in English, is a form of rebuilding, better rearchitecting "a new city out of the ruins of the old" (*A Kind of Order, A Kind of Folly*). As a "sum of approximations," not all attempts are equal. The translative "object is to produce an analogous poem in English out of available signs and sounds, a new poem sprung from the matrix of the old, drenched in memories of its former existence, capable of reviving its singular pleasures." Most critically, "the purpose of poetical translation is the poetry," as Ernest Fenollosa wrote on the Chinese ideogram: "Failure or success in presenting any alien poetry in English must depend largely upon poetic workmanship in the chosen medium" (*The Chinese Written Character as Medium for Poetry*). From the King James Bible, to Chapman's *Homer*, to Fitzgerald's *Rubáiyát*, Kunitz adds, the real test is "how to restore the dignity and style that had been lost in transit." Creatively improvised equivalents arise, Kunitz argues, "for the sake of prosodic harmony, naturalness of diction, and brightness of tone," among other issues. Thus the "so-called literal version" cannot arrogate the creative original "at the expense of its secret life, its interconnecting psychic tissue, its complex harmonies."

"The poem's form is the sound it makes when spoken," H. S. McAllister suggests (in Swann, *Smoothing the Ground*). Does this hold true for literate as well as oral cultures? "I see no reason why an oral tradition and a written tradition shouldn't co-exist," Kunitz feels, "—they've done so for centuries. Historically the former have influenced the latter, as when the ballads entered into the stream of English Romanticism." Reasonable enough, so far. When the reader does not "speak" or sing in the original native voice, but silently scans a text in English, what "form" informs the sound of recognition? Recreative poetics come up in Densmore's retranslation of Sitting Bull's "last" song (No. 193), through Robert Higheagle. Chanting the song from memory, Used-as-a-Shield said of their 1889 camp at Standing Rock, "Sitting Bull used to go around the camp circle every evening just before sunset on his favorite horse, singing this song":

> A warrior
> I have been;
> now
> it is all over.
> A hard time
> I have.

What was the original "song"—singing for power, as Ruth Underhill put it—of *Tatanka Iyotanke* ("Bull Sitting" in Lakota, a mystic name from the four ages of human life)? Used-as-a-Shield told Densmore at Standing Rock in 1914, twenty-four years after the martyr's assassination, that he heard his Hunkpapa *wicasa wakán* or "man holy" chant this song through the 1880s. What did its "form" sound like? Densmore's Euro-American musicology scores the key in G-flat minor with a descending fourth and two cascading thirds—something like a prophetic meadowlark's song, a recurrent pattern in plains chants. (Sitting Bull's oracle bird, the western meadowlark, warned him of danger from childhood to his death.)

> *I-ki-ci-ze wa-on kon* he
> *wa-na he-ná-la ye-lo* he
> i-yo-ti-ye ki-ya wa-on

The first Lakota word means "head warrior" (confronting face-to-face) and the second "to know how," the third "to want." Occurring twice at the

No. 198. Song of Sitting Bull (a)   (Catalogue No. 612)

Sung by Used-as-a-Shield

Voice ♩ = 60
Drum ♩ = 60
Drum-rhythm similar to No. 6

I - ki - ći - ze   wa - oŋ   ḳoŋ   *he*   wa - na   he - na - la   ye - lo

he   i - yo - ti - ye   ki - ya wa - oŋ

WORDS

iki'ćize.....................	a warrior
waőŋ' ḳoŋ....................	I have been
wana'........................	now
hena'la yelo'................	it is all over
iyo'tiye kiya'...............	a hard time
waőŋ'........................	I have

Francis Densmore, *Teton Sioux Music* (1918), Bulletin no. 61, Bureau of American Ethnology, Smithsonian Institution, U.S. Government Printing Office.

ends of lines, "he" is an untranslatable vocable (more precisely, an imperative enclitic, as William Powers explains in "Translating the Untranslatable"). *Wa-na* is "now" and *he-ná-la* means "all gone," terminated with the stress particle *ye-lo*. The long verb with its auxiliary ("make to be") in the third line means "to suffer, to find it hard," literally "to crash against." The last word, *wa-on*, means again "to know how," as in the opening line—

and the mentor nickname for the teacher-healer-warrior bear, *waonze*, derives from *wa-on*.

So, how does Densmore retranslate all this from Higheagle? Literally. And what about form? Freely.

And what of the vocables? Ignored.

What patterns the original verse? Each line rides on eight syllables, so they could be syllabically chanted, that is, musical.

Most telling, can we sing Densmore's English translation in the original musicology, as transcribed? Hardly. The Sioux cedar flutist Kevin Locke opens his 1983 Featherstone cassette album, *Lakota Wiikijo Olowan,* with this same flute melody (here titled "The Lakota National Anthem," learned from Noah Has Horns in Bullhead, South Dakota, a century after Sitting Bull). A song still sung, the following eight-syllabic triad may work better than Densmore's free verse transcription; at least it can be sung in English, approximating the original form:

> So I have been a warrior,
> and now it is all over, so
> I know to bear against hard times.

As set down earlier, Sitting Bull was a military genius, great healer, compelling speaker, and visionary singer with a high tenor voice. Does his true character carry over into our cultural understanding by way of translation? As Dell Hymes argues (*"In Vain I Tried to Tell You"*), we may have to translate everything all over again, once the bilingual model is acknowledged, and social scientists learn, via verbal artists, how to distinguish a verse line from a stump.

By 1929, Dorothy Demetracapoulou was collecting Dream Dance songs among the California Wintu around Mount Lassen. "I recorded them intermittently," she wrote in *Anthropos* (1935), "chiefly as an expression of literary art, partly for their ethnographic value, partly for linguistic purposes. I secured them in text and translated them as literally as the discrepancy between Wintu and English would permit." Sadie Marsh lost her best friend, "who a little after came to her in a dream with a company of other female spirits, weeping, dancing and singing this song":

> Down west, down west we dance,
> We spirits dance,
> We spirits weeping dance.

And the traditional Anonymous Wintu sang,

> Where will you and I sleep?
> At the down-turned jagged rim of the sky you
> and I will sleep.

Hymes asked in 1981, "Do these texts, restored to something like their true form, have power to move us, as part of the first literature of our land?" Do they move us away from, or toward Native America, and do we catch anything of their original poetics, genuinely translated?

Something has been moving Westerners toward American Indians for a long time now. Since the Renaissance, Europeans have shared American fascinations with the "native" American as the newest and oldest, most "free" and worst "wild" peoples of the New World. Out of a Western wilderness, for better or worse, a native Adam and Eve reappeared for a second chance in the Garden. As mentioned, D. H. Lawrence quick-claimed the 1920s Southwest with his runaway German wife, Frieda, when they relocated among Pueblo Indians around Taos. Theirs was a postwar move emblematic of Euro-American migrations to the New World for three centuries. (Indeed, English pilgrims set the palisaded stage, but there were so many immigrant Germans that *Deutsch* was optioned as a working tongue of the Continental Congress.) Lawrence, godson of Walter Raleigh, re-turned to Italy, where Amerigo Vespucci had been commissioned by the Medici to sail west. In the wake of Cronyn's *The Path on the Rainbow,* Mabel Dodge Luhan's *Lorenzo* published *The Plumed Serpent* and *Mornings in Mexico* about "Indianizing" or Americanizing the White Man. After his "savage pilgrimage" around the postwar globe to New Mexico Pueblos, Lawrence died in southern France, while reading a biography of Columbus and be-fore he could complete his writings on the original Americans. His ashes lie next to Frieda's in the Sangre de Cristo mountains north of Taos today.

Thoreau died whispering "Indians" and "moose," they say, before he could finish his masterwork on American natives and their tongues. He left twelve cryptically coded notebooks. Walt Whitman worked in the Bureau of Indian Affairs in 1864, and Marianne Moore taught four years at Carlisle Indian School while Jim Thorpe was a student there. Isak Dineson's father lived in Wisconsin in 1872 among *"les sauvages,"* as he called them, and she moved to Africa to find a tribal home. As noted, Ezra Pound, Wallace Stevens, William Carlos Williams, H. D., Amy Lowell, and the Imagists re-imagined American Indian visual and verbal arts via *Poetry* magazine and *The Dial,* through the translative insistences of Mary Austin and compatriot anthropologists.

Modernist primitive thinking capped four centuries of Western organi-cism, as documented in Welsh's *Roots of Lyric,* Rothenberg's *Symposium of the Whole,* and Torgovnick's *Gone Primitive: Savage Intellects, Modern Lives.* Such neoprimitivism, in fact, was registered early this century among the Fauvists in France, the short-lived Vorticist movement of Pound and Wynd-ham Lewis in England, Picasso's prodigious wonder over native African masks (*Les Demoiselles D'Avignon* in 1907, for example, and cave paintings discovered to be eighteen thousand years old in southern France). T. S.

Eliot salvaged his *Waste Land* from these runes and ethnological models: to wit, Frazer's *The Golden Bough,* Weston's grail mythology within a regenerate Christianity, and the linguistic anthropology coming from Europe by way of Boas, Sapir, and others.

"Native" concerns of modernist rethinking, particularly in the arts and social sciences after the First World War, forefront the American Indian as cultured neoprimitive. The speeches and oratory of Peter Nabokov's *Native American Testimony* remind us that the first recorded "American chronicles," as Constance Rourke noted, took place in Red-White ceremonies, where New World pilgrims made treaties with resident native nations "at the forest's edge" in axed clearings. "By what names are they distinguished," Roger Williams catalogued in the 1643 *A Key into the Languages of America:* "First, those of the *English* giving: as *Natives, Salvages, Indians, Wild-men,* (so the *Dutch* call them *Wilden), Abergeny men, Pagans, Barbarians, Heathen.*" Caliban, a name Tzvetan Todorov hears corrupted from *Carib, Khan, Canis,* and "cannibal," has long been a symbol of native nobility and concomitant savagery. Mythographers of the West, led by Columbus, were tracking a dog-headed, aboriginal emperor feeding on human flesh, from Montaigne writing satirically on misconceived cannibals, to Shakespeare's Prospero as the shamanic artist-surrogate, to Rousseau's noble jungle savage, to Robert Penn Warren's American elegy, *Chief Joseph of the Nez Perce,* published in 1982, when he was appointed America's first poet laureate. A Renaissance Prospero adopts the wild man as his bestial son, "this thing of darkness I / acknowledge mine" (*The Tempest* 5.1.275–76), lowering cultural shades scrimmed by Columbus and Vespucci on the Brazilian Tupinamba, carried forward today. Can an Old World father acknowledge a New World son after five centuries of cataclysm, or will "this thing of darkness" further curse the patriarchal invasion of his island?

Rousseau and ensuing cultural romantics, Schiller, Schlegel, and Coleridge among them, godfathered native adoptees in America, from Cooper to Thoreau, Whitman to Sandburg, on to Hemingway, Hugo, Snyder, Merwin, Kinnell, Creeley, Waggoner, and Bly, among many others. The mix has not been unmitigated or without gender complexes. "The stark, loveless, wordless unison of two men who have come to the bottom of themselves," Lawrence concluded dispassionately of Cooper's Leatherstocking Tales, chary of "blood-mixing of the two races, white and red."

Beyond all this heart-beating stand the figures of Natty and Chingachgook: two childless, womanless men, of opposite races. They are the abiding thing. Each of them is alone, and final in his race. And they stand side by side, stark, abstract, beyond emotion, yet eternally together. All the other loves seem frivolous. This is the new great thing, the clue, the inception of a new humanity. (*Studies in Classic American Literature*)

What is this "new great thing" in Western humanity? Cross-cultural neo-primitives share artistic compatriots in Europe, from Gauguin in the riotous jungle, to Gaudier-Brzeska sculpting primal animal forms, to Stravinsky drumming the rites of spring, to Jawlensky painting Inuit and Hopi masks, to Miró's childlike play. Kafka sparked his "wish to become a Red Indian" in a prose fragment of 1927: "If one were only an Indian, instantly alert, and on a racing horse, leaning against the wind, kept on quivering briefly over the quivering ground." In 1970 at the University of California, Berkeley, recalls the Irish Nobel poet, Seamus Heaney, now holding a Harvard chair, "There was a strong sense of contemporary American poetry in the West with Robert Duncan and Bly and Gary Snyder rejecting the intellectual, ironical, sociological idiom of poetry and going for the mythological. I mean everyone wanted to be a Red Indian, basically" (interview, *Ploughshares* 1979).

"Know then," Johann Herder wrote a friend at the end of the eighteenth century, "the more alive and freedom-loving a people is . . . the more savage, that is, alive, free, sensuous, lyrically active, its songs must be." Cronyn caught the drift in Densmore's Chippewa translation:

> As my eyes
> search
> the prairie
> I feel the summer in the spring.

Puccini went so far as to write an opera with an Indian chorus in 1910, *La Fanciulla del West,* "The Golden Girl of the West," featuring two Indian soloists. A Prussian convict, Karl May, wrote arguably the most widely read "Indian" pseudo-fiction in the world—about the noble Indian Winnetou and his Caucasian sidekick, Old Shatterhand—and May's romances competed with Longfellow's *Hiawatha* and Cooper's Leatherstocking Tales. Karl May proved the favorite author of no less than Karl Marx, Bertolt Brecht, Adolf Hitler, and Albert Schweitzer, and thousands of young Germans today carry the middle name Winnetou. Finally, Dylan Thomas acted out the "Red Man" myth of the wild child at home in Wales, lost in "the Gorsehill jungle" of *Portrait of the Artist as a Young Dog:* "On my haunches, eager and alone, casting an ebony shadow, with the Gorsehill jungle swarming, the violent, impossible birds and fishes leaping, hidden under four-stemmed flowers the height of horses, in the early evening in a dingle near Carmarthen, my friend Jack Williams invisibly near me, I felt all my young body like an excited animal surrounding me. . . . There, playing Indians in the evening, I was aware of me myself in the exact middle of a living story, and my body was my adventure and my name."

The Path on the Rainbow would spawn Margot Astrov's *The Winged Serpent* at the end of the Second World War, poetry and prose further translated from BAE and American Anthropologist reports of the 1880s through the 1930s, with snippets of contextual notes and a serviceable introduction. Writing a Stanford dissertation published under the title *The Sky Clears* (1951), A. Grove Day collected even newer old materials under Yvor Winters, who then tutored N. Scott Momaday (one of the five best poets to craft a great American poem, Winters announced in *Forms of Discovery*). Day's monograph was a step toward an emerging bicultural appreciation of native poetics. By the end of the 1960s, Indian anthologies were popping up like wildflowers: Jerome Rothenberg's inventive *Shaking the Pumpkin,* William Brandon's a bit too freely reworked *The Magic World,* John Bierhorst's pellucid *In the Trail of the Wind,* Robert Dodge and Joseph McCullough's contemporary *Voices from Wah'Kon-Tah* and the newer Indian writers in Dick Lourie's *Come to Power,* Duane Niatum's *Carriers of the Dream Wheel,* and Shirley Hill Witt and Stan Steiner's *The Way.*

By 1983, Michael Castro in *Interpreting the Indian* had cross-referred American poets iconoclastically searching for Native *at-oneness* with holistic tribal issues—Mary Austin, Lew Sarett, Carl Sandburg, William Carlos Williams, Hart Crane, and John Neihardt in the 1920s and '30s, through Yvor Winters, Charles Olson, Jerome Rothenberg, and Gary Snyder in the 1950s and '60s. Circling canonical through-lines, Castro traced the margins of tribal and modernist crossovers. The groundswell of Native American verse, especially Harjo, Hogan, Tapahonso, TallMountain, Momaday, and Alexie in the last two decades, was still coming. In 1985 Brian Swann's *Song of the Sky* "re-expressed" native song-poems as open improvisations, "shadows of shadows," à la Mary Austin's *The American Rhythm,* and brought the translative cycle full circle. Geronimo, the Apache warrior in his seventies, told Nancy Curtis: "The song that I will sing is an old song, so old that none knows who made it. . . . The song tells how, as I sing, I go through the air to a holy place where Yusun (the Supreme Being) will give me power to do wonderful things. I am surrounded by little clouds, and as I go through the air I change, becoming spirit only." *Song of the Sky* reshapes Geronimo's spoken verse:

> through the air
> as I move
> changing
> I go to   a sacred place
> this is the way
> going up
> little cloud   me

In the last decade, Swann has continued to churn out scholarly and poetic collections, including *Wearing the Morning Star* (1996) and *Coming to Light* (1994), lauded by Alfonso Ortiz, the distinguished Tewa anthropologist:

"By far the best anthology on the subject ever assembled. It eclipses every-thing else."

If our *first* literatures are native, and our translations echo old worlds colliding with new ones, the native "power to move us" is still nascent in George W. Cronyn's *The Path on the Rainbow*. The anthology serves as an initial cornerstone to our multicultural diversity and ancient rootedness in this good land. Its intercultural rhythms and oblique rhymes, native meta-phors and tribal wisdoms, open the rainbow's path of national literary di-versity. Here a native poetics, still emerging from visionary tradition and historical disillusion, honeycombs American culture.

PARSING ETHNOPOETICS

With beauty before me, may I walk,
With beauty behind me, may I walk,
With beauty above me, may I walk,
With beauty under me, may I walk,
With beauty all around me, may I walk,
In old age wandering on a trail of beauty, lively, may I walk,
In old age wandering on a trail of beauty, living again, may I walk,
It is finished in beauty.

NAVAJO NIGHT CHANT,
TRANSLATED BY WASHINGTON MATTHEWS,
IN FRANZ BOAS, *Primitive Art*

"Given the facts of human migrations and casual crossbreeding," Clyde Kluckhohn argues, "*pure races* are strictly mythological." If the social con-struction of "races" is determined environmentally, for the most part (sun-light, habitat, diet, bodily functions, social activities, seasonal variations, historical events), personal genealogy is just as radically shifting a complex, parent to child. Out of a hundred and six chromosome variables, genes are inherited in pairs from mother and father, then reshuffled, and half are discarded to make a new person. Even siblings don't have identical genetic patterns, the Austrian monk, Gregor Mendel, found over a century ago. No two individuals the same, then, culture is more an act of consent than descent, according to Werner Sollors, more social construct than blood lineage. It follows that cultural poetics are more made than born, both within a social group or looking inversely out. "A lot has been said of how American culture is a miscegenated culture, how it is a product of a mixing and mingling of diverse races and cultures and languages, and I would agree with that," notes Harryette Mullen, the Black poet, in a 1996 *Callaloo* interview with Calvin Bedient. "I would say that, yes, my text is deliberately a multi-voiced text, a text that tries to express the actual diver-sity of my own experience living here, exposed to different cultures. 'Mongrel' comes from 'among.' Among others. We are among; we are not alone. We are all mongrels.''

Assuming to protect purity, essentialist groups have drawn lines globally in the sand a long time back. The word ethnic comes from Greek *ethnoi* for ''people'' or ''nation,'' distinct from neighbors. Athenians saw other *ethnoi* as *barbarians,* babbling ''bar-bar'' like cloven sheep. With the construction of the Roman Empire, itself an immigrant intrusion on Etruscan and other natives, Latin *ethnicus* came to mean ''pagan'' or ''heathen,'' the *others* out there. By 1470, ethnic meant neither Christian nor Jewish, but *gentile,* savage, the Other. The Renaissance, a set of cultural appropriations from southern to northern Europe (Wyatt importing Petrarch's hendecasyllabic sonnet to England as iambic pentameter, hence Shakespeare's blank verse), set off forays into still other cultures. The discovery of the New World brought mythical Others, an unknown hemispheric complex of cultures, within translating distance. So the term *ethnology* by 1851 applied to a branch of social sciences dealing with comparative cultures, the social constructs of others. More recently, ethnicity has turned on the ethics of alterity: who looks across boundaries at whom and why.

Franz Boas published *Primitive Art* in 1927 through the Oslo Institute for Comparative Research in Human Culture, the next year with Harvard University Press. ''The local culture determines what kind of experiences have a poetic value,'' Boas surmised after forty years' study, ''and the intensity with which they act.'' Yet across local differences, human nature seemed to Boas more constant than different, families more like than unlike. So cultures, Boas concluded, were more transculturally uniform than chaotic, clans more coherent than incoherent. So-called primitives are culturally relative to our own being and times:

> Anyone who has lived with primitive tribes, who has shared their joys and sorrows, their privations and their luxuries, who sees in them not solely subjects of study to be examined like a cell under the microscope, but feeling and thinking human beings, will agree that there is no such thing as a ''primitive mind,'' a ''magical'' or ''prelogical'' way of thinking, but that each individual in ''primitive'' society is a man, a woman, a child of the same kind, of the same way of thinking, feeling and acting as man, woman or child in our own society.

Such empathic pluralism from the godfather of anthropology!—the first American Indian ethnographer gone native, as Marianna Torgovnick snipes about ''a male-centered, canonical line of Western primitivism'' in *Gone Primitive,* ignoring women field workers from Ella Deloria to Frances Densmore. All too reflexively familiar, the German-American's Other served to legitimize his own Western interests, this Duke lit crit has decided of Boas, subtitling her study *Savage Intellects, Modern Lives,* a neat, neoprimitive, white-male-bashing paradigm. Ethnic wars become postcolonial gender battles. A year after *Gone Primitive* (1990), Eric Cheyfitz extended the critique to *The Poetics of Imperialism: Translations and Colonialization from "The Tempest" to "Tarzan."* No wonder Harold Bloom gets hysterical about the "Balkanization of literary studies."

Virginia Woolf seems to have set the modernist time line in "Modern Fiction" with the remark, "in or about December, 1910, human character changed." She referred to the London art exhibit, "Manet and the Post-Impressionists," curated by the Quaker Victorian of the Bloomsbury Group, Roger Fry. *Modern* was equated with *Primitive* throughout the exhibit, featuring new work by Manet, Cézanne, Gauguin, Van Gogh, and Matisse. Woolf also tagged the 1908 Cambridge freethinkers, gathering as nature worshippers around Rupert Brooke until his 1915 war death, the "Neo-pagans." Torgovnick notes in *Gone Primitive* that "primitive objects became, in England, high art." A modernist daisy chain laced from Franz Boas in Europe, to Mary Austin in New York, to D. H. Lawrence and Georgia O'Keeffe in New Mexico. These Euro-American connections linked Ezra Pound, T. S. Eliot, W. B. Yeats, Wyndham Lewis, John Galsworthy, E. M. Forster, and even the Kent cluster of Joseph Conrad, H. G. Wells, Stephen Crane, Ford Madox Ford, and Henry James, all in one way or another string-tied to Virginia and Leonard Woolf in Bloomsbury.

Roger Fry went on to publish *Vision and Design* in 1920, the advent of New York renaissances, Harlem to Greenwich. This leading art critic and curator spoke of formalist issues, *universals,* he felt, from African and Bushman art, to an essay on "Ancient American Art" among the Aztecs, to "Mohammedan Art" in Islam. "Fry conceived of his aesthetic theories," Torgovnick hazards, "educating the eye to appreciate masterpieces wherever it finds them—in museums and galleries, in the ateliers of neglected artists, or in African villages." Pound had done more or less just so, discovering the neoprimitive sculptor, Henri Gaudier-Brzeska, in a London gallery; proselytizing for the ethnopoetic high-to-low art of W. B. Yeats, T. S. Eliot, Robert Frost, and James Joyce; promoting the rediscovery of cross-cultural, multilinguistic classics from Dante, to Daniel, to Homer and Confucius. By the end of his life, Pound published an anthology of such salvaged literary anthropology, *Confucius to Cummings,* crossing primitive and modern. So, too, modernist writers such as Marianne Moore, William Carlos Williams, Mary Austin, Wallace Stevens, Amy Lowell, Carl Sandburg, and D. H. Lawrence served as voices in the New-Old World dialogue on aesthetics. Torgovnick carries neoprimitivism to our own times: "The primitive is in our museums and homes, in our closets and jewelry boxes, in our hearts and minds. The primitive is everywhere present in modernity and postmodernity, as impetus or subtext, just as modernity or postmodernity forms the subtext of much ethnological writing and thinking." The West has gone primitive, Torgovnik suspects, to validate not-so-secret fantasies, repressed desires, and cultural fears of what a wasteland industrial "civilization" has made of things. If so, what are the potential gains, not just the perceived losses, and where do we go from here?

Back to Boas and *our* alterity, biological universals may be finely edged by epistemological calipers. How do social scientists, or artists, know what they know, in any given time or place, about the Other? Was Franz Boas in New York City seeing overlapping native behavior at the frontier end of the American wilderness, "officially" in the year 1890, when George Custer's reconstituted Seventh Cavalry butchered Indian stragglers on the high plains at Wounded Knee? What native vision spurred Daniel Brinton, a trained physician and the first American professor of ethnology and archaeology at Philadelphia's Academy of Natural Sciences, to publish song translations of Inuit, Pawnee, Kiowa, and Ojibwa in his 1890 essay, "Native American Poetry"? How analogously savage in the Southwest was the Pueblo trickster in Adolph Bandelier's 1890 *The Delight Makers*? "The very constitution of their field of study," Hayden White contends of human science and subjectivity, seems "a *poetic* act, a genuine 'making' or 'invention' of a domain of inquiry."

Poetics, we know, has a tangled history. The word derives from Greek *poietikos* for "the art of making," shifting personally to Latin *poeta* or *vates* for "prophet-maker," to a Renaissance rebirthing of classical thought as premodernism, to Romantic self-creation by the revolutionary end of the eighteenth century, to early modernist erasures of the Self-as-god in the late nineteenth century, to the verbal icon of the 1920s, to postmodernist *decreations*. The word *art* itself, cognate with arm, artisan, artifice, and articulate, comes from the Indo-European root, **-ar*, meaning "to join," "to fit," and "to make." Lewis Hyde sees the global Trickster (Greek Hermes, Norse Loki, African Legba, Native American Coyote, Chinese Monkey King) as the archetypal artisan hinge maker, driven by appetite and exclusion to reinvent order through disorder (*Trickster Makes This World: Mischief, Myth, and Art*). Deviant from the tribal priest, parodic of the shaman, this crafty outsider improvises a self-legitimizing art. He rearticulates his own chronos from chaos, disjoining then rejoining arthritic social patterns. Born of a cave earth-mother, Maia, and the illicit promiscuity of Zeus, two-day-old Hermes cons turtle out of his shell and improvises a lyre with sheep gut, the first stringed instrument ("Homeric Hymn to Hermes," 420 B.C.). He steals his elder brother's cattle, then charms Apollo into exchanging the bright herding whip for his makeshift lyre, and finally seduces his father Zeus on Olympus with a clever lyric lie, stealing back into heaven's legitimacy as the rustic, reed-piping thresholder of purpose, the timeless messenger, the outsider admitted. Since Trickster is our ancient, now more than ever modern (Frederick Douglass, Marcel Duchamp, Allen Ginsberg,

John Cage, Maxine Hong Kingston, Hyde reasons variously) liminal artist of mixed blood, seductive song, and tales of guile, where has a decentered poetics landed today? From joiner to loner, creation to decreation, the Western artist limns the wings of alienated modern society. The native stranger must steal back what was stolen through exile and colonial appropriation—lineage, language, land, cultural love—never to be given up freely (if not by gift, then by theft, the go-between hazards). The New World fit is problematic, a stiff hinge, if armature at all. Apart from Native Americans, we are all émigrés in the wake of Columbus and Cortés. Yet we are all *ethnics* as well, still here, even if coming from elsewhere.

What, then, is the ethnic context of our aesthetics, and is it translatable? "The behavior of everybody, no matter to what culture he may belong," Boas counters 1920s ethnocentrism, "is determined by the traditional material he handles, and man, the world over, handles the material transmitted to him according to the same methods." In *The Invention of Ethnicity* Werner Sollors adds a fine point, half a century later: "The forces of modern life embodied by such terms as 'ethnicity,' 'nationalism,' or 'race' can indeed be meaningfully discussed as 'inventions.' " Well, then, is invented ethnicity but a crafted act of will, or more of Trickster's grafted accident, greasing the joints between history and personality? We do not invent DNA racial combinations, gender differentiations, intelligence quotients, inherited languages, social customs, or our historical age at the moment of creation, though people may work to readjust birth conditions and given mores as they grow older. The place we are born, and the places we move through, and the transcribed texts are influenced by climate and seasonal swings, by a biospheric complex far beyond our engineering, dependent on certain slants of light, soil and water, botany and biology, and, some would argue, a history of those gone before us, including the spirits. All human transactions affect us as history, the presence of the past working through us. These space-and-time junctures-in-process result in what Mikhail Bakhtin calls "time-taking-on-flesh," or symbolic cultural *chronotopes*. Think of the Golgotha crucifixion for a Christian, Gautama under the bo tree for a Buddhist, a Black Hills Lakota singing with the heart of a bear, or a Jewish Moses shouldering Yahweh's stone tablets on Mount Sinai. In the United States, consider the Founding Fathers signing the Declaration of Independence in Philadelphia, or more recently, the mushrooming atomic cloud at White Sands, New Mexico, 1944.

Symbolic chronotopes lead toward cultural constructions, worldviews of space-time as clusters of process. They continue to shape, to unshape, and to reshape our behaviors as groups of people, from families and friendships, to clans and villages, to local districts and geographical regions, to artificially boundaried states and countries: *ethnoi,* "people" or "nation." Each is continually revising a language or tribal dialect; an economics of getting on; markets of good goods; social structures of interaction; psycho-biologies of healing, bettering, and extending life; religious codes of gods; historical ancestors and spirit worship; ceremonial behaviors from Sun Dance to surfing; and the arts of the true and beautiful, for lack of better terms, what we like.

Outside to inside, how do we parse all this? For some thirty years now, Native American Studies has worked from a multidisciplinary paradigm. The social sciences ask contextual questions of human data. Anthropologists want to know how people think they think, from psychogenetics to symbolic reasoning. Sociologists look at daily behavior patterns that shape longer-range actions. Historians seek to know how memory shapes present consciousness, how bygone times are still with us. Linguists study the language drift of verbal signs, from etymology, that is, the archaeological history of language; to philology, or the philosophy of language, "love of logos"; to syntax and semantics, or the structures and uses of language; to semiology or cultural "signs," gestures spoken and unspoken, that convey meaning among people. Writers look and listen acutely to the world around them, process this information inwardly, and speak to what they witness. Discussing prewar Vorticism as the projected energy of art-in-motion, Ezra Pound wrote in the first issue of *Blast!*, "Every concept, every emotion presents itself to the vivid consciousness in some primary form. It belongs to the art of this form. If sound, to music; if formed words, to literature; the image, to poetry; form, to design; colour in position, to painting; form or design in three planes, to sculpture; movement, to the dance or to the rhythm of music or verses."

Art critics ponder formal shapings of texts, along with contextual questions of how truth and beauty come to be so called: for starters in language, how do sound, shape, tone, timber, pitch, interval, and texture determine the aesthetics of consensual meaning? How do we know what we mean to say, and does it mean the same when we say it to others? Listen with "the cave of the ear," Frost says in "Sentence Sounds," and catch the echoing drift of American speech patterns. "I aint a going [to] hurt you, so you needn't be scared," or "Never you say a thing like that to a man!" or "No fool like an old fool." In the acoustic arts, music for example, how do phonemics, beat, tone, tare, harmonics, and lyric phrasing please us, or not? Beginning with pitch and rhythm, there is a connection, ancient to modern, between African talking drums and Stravinsky. In the visual and plastic arts—rock carvings, to stereopticons, to mobile bronze sculptures, to laser shows—how do light, color, surface, texture, contrast, composition, or sequence determine our responses? From eighteen-thousand-year-old cave paintings of bison in southern France, to Native American winter counts on buffalo robes, to sportive canvases by Kandinsky and Miró, to computer-generated "virtual" reality, human beings express their imagined lives in sequenced visual space. How do we feel what we feel, mud bath to blown glass, snapshot to strobe-light rock concert? As far back as Varro, the Roman grammarian, there appear to have been 228 distinct meanings of *good*. Modern video or Pueblo ceremonial dance, what makes a good film good, a dance engaging or soothing or electrifying?

Oral performance, fixed verse, or virtual reality, what is literacy and literature, *singing with a bear's heart,* what words for what purpose? To repeat H. S. McAllister on Native American shamanic translations, "The poem's form is the sound it makes when spoken." So poetry may be the shape of the words spoken: but what is the *shape* of sound? Acoustically, a verse-line "sounded" or spoken in space may image a physical continuum with height, depth, width, and patches of thinness and thickness, even harmonic resonances, or overtones and undertones. A voice resonates at so many vibrations and decibels per second, no less than middle C on a piano, and a listener hears what could be called character, personality, or style, in a sequence of tones or syllables making words. Optically, a verse line may suggest a visual shape or structure, even ideogrammatically, an image with the interplay of ideas going on around it, through it, beyond it (which to prefer, "the blackbird whistling," Stevens muses, "Or just after"). Thus, ideationally, sounds strike into thickets of what we call meaning—the significance of sense, translated conceptually, and back again to the senses, perceiving and feeling what it all means. Ezra Pound termed these poetic tools *melopoeia,* or sound, *phanopoeia,* or sight, and *logopoeia,* or interplay of ideas: any good poet uses all three at once, usually leaning on one or the other at a time. Stevens has a fine ear at Key West, Williams a clear eye on the red wheel barrow, Pound a sharp mind in the Pisan Cantos, and all three are masters of combining sound, sight, and idea in the rhythmic or musical phrase, whether metrically formal or informally variable. The ancient Greek term *mousike,* according to James Winn on poetry and music, encompassed dance, melody, poetry, and elementary education. Over two millennia, we have subdivided the musical arts, while native cultures have unified them ceremonially. In *Primitive Art* Franz Boas found the hinge between oral formulaic traditions and silent printed texts to turn on musical cadence or rhythmic meter: "The two fundamental forms of literature, song and tale, are found universally and must be considered the primary form of literary activity. Poetry without music, that is to say forms of literary expression of fixed rhythmic form, are found only in civilized communities, except perhaps in chanted formulas. In simpler cultural forms the music of language alone does not seem to be felt as an artistic expression, while fixed rhythms that are sung occur everywhere." Discussing literature, music, and dance toward the end of *Primitive Art,* Boas concludes, "Two elements are common to all song: rhythm and fixed intervals," lines generally occurring in two- to seven-part measures. More recently, Donald E. Brown has argued that all cultures (a Universal People theory sparked by Chomsky's Universal Grammar) generate some forms of rhetoric, narrative, gossip, lying, humor, and poetry, the latter characterized by linguistic patterns of repetition and three-second lines separated by pauses (*Human Universals* 1991).

So how does this all add up to oral or written poetry, for starters, and to what end? "Primitive poetry is primarily lyric, in many cases dithyrambic," Boas writes. Among other performance variables, singers and storytellers use poetry mixed with prose, formal measures and informal idioms, to catch and engage their listeners' attentions. Love songs call to absent beloveds in parallel measure. Anaphoric prayers itemize personal needs and invoke the gods to help, inspire, or guide. Lullaby refrains engage and soothe children, put them to sleep. Rhythmic hunting or planting songs encourage growth and call to animals. War chants summon courage or humiliate the enemy with driving meters. Arrhythmic gaming songs focus and unfocus concentration, distract the opponent and beg luck. At the least, call-and-response storytelling gathers family and friends, educates the young, confers skills, passes the time, warns, wakes up, chastises, or mollifies an audience; telling our story reminds us of the past, or foretells the future. The result of aural amusement is to stave off boredom, to excite curiosity, to stimulate imagination. Words pull us out of ourselves into a larger world, to look more closely into our immediate world, to remind us we are not alone, or if alone, that others are lonely too. Social speech and communal song help us to accept, even to understand our own joy or suffering with others, or to take our minds off our complacency or pain.

How do we ground a discussion of cultural poetics, and where does this talk go? Ethnopoetics would embrace all this in the literatures, oral or otherwise, of other peoples, places, times, tongues, gods, goods, fears, desires, pasts, projected futures—as with Emily Dickinson, our own local poetries as voices of the *other*. Literary criticism, at its most basic, can be the useful little things we say about everything, craft to culture to cosmos, the significant details of language. We must find starting points. Not to put too fine a point on it, but Emily Dickinson's verse *turns* on a dash or comma. Marianne Moore's lines build on syllables, and Sylvia Plath's trade on the white spaces around words. Pound's metrics depend on "cut" and drilled diction in energy vortices, Williams's "variable foot" leans on the phoneme and phrase spaced visually, Stevens's "harmonium" rises lyrically on pitch and cadence. Emerging from oral traditions and entering higher education, Native American poets are no less originally attuned: N. Scott Momaday crafts the musical sequence, James Welch reaches for the torque in speech, and Sherman Alexie runs with the word-riff. Linda Hogan, in a more spiritually secular sense, listens for the soul's beat; Joy Harjo feels for hoof beat and heartache. Linda Gregg writes from the tip of the tongue,

Jorie Graham from the tangible abstraction, Sharon Olds from parodic commonplace. All these poets are moderns and postmoderns, ethnic, to émigré, to expatriate, which is to say they speak among and for us in our century, but where does this poetic talk begin as American literature?

INTERJECTIVE BREATH

Our search is not for primal sources but for basic structures of poetic language, whether they are found in a Bantu riddle or a poem by Donne, in a Cherokee charm or a song by Shakespeare. If the poetics of one leads us in some suggestive way to the poetics of the other, we will have discovered something about the language of poetry without involving ourselves in either genetic or psychological assumptions.

ANDREW WELSH, *Roots of Lyric*

"All in me is song," recalls the Netsilik Inuit, Orpingalik, telling Knud Rasmussen, "I sing as I draw breath." Some linguists posit that the "language instinct" could have evolved ritually two million years ago from interjections, phonemes with no fixed morphemic meaning, what English governed by Latin syntax calls the eighth part of speech, *Ah!* or *Ha!* These interjected exclamations carry the primal sense of language as emotionally charged ideas, syllable by syllable, *Eh?* to *Oh!* to *Aha!* As evolving *Homo habilis* began voicing experience and thought by way of breath, heartbeat, footstep, and feelings shared symbolically (rhythms of desire, hunger, fear, humor, pathos, labor), vowel-charged phonemes reified the hoots and howls of culturally common lives. Beyond hunting mastodons, the human brain took a quantum leap toward language (see the recent work of psycholinguist Steven Pinker, *The Language Instinct,* and biological anthropologist Terrence Deacon, *The Symbolic Species*). The first recorded Old English epic, *Beowulf,* begins with *Hwæt,* or "Lo!" my linguistic colleague, Donka Minkova, reminds me. Something in the nature of an interjective poetics, from *Beowulf* to *Beloved,* would reascribe significance to every syllable, recharge emotional gist to each word's sequential immediacy, so that the *blazing out,* as Lowell says of Roethke, might reaffirm the effect of a text, the book become Pound's *ball of light* felt in a reader's hands, *language charged with meaning.* The modernist charge overlays what Ruth Underhill, a Franz Boas field-worker from Columbia University, calls *Singing for Power,* subtitled *The Song Magic of the Papago Indians of Southern Arizona,* first published in 1938. This would be generatively, as the Lakota say, *to sing with the heart of a bear that is fiercely different.*

In this regard, consider the intersection of prose and poetry as a lingual axis where verse is vertical, stretching and rising up off the page in shaped line lengths. The lines *leap,* some say, with incantatory cadences and luminous images, as song and dance have long charged language rhythmically, tonally, and metaphorically ("with ah! bright wings," Hopkins says). The line breaks may even seem to project vertical columns of textual light, and the carved images italicize ideas that may indeed, as Linda Hogan writes, soar into "the thin blue tail of the galaxy." The stanzas are shaped, emblazoned on the page in designs that originally shadow older forms of experiential insight. The poet's diction minimizes, or tries to minimize, the distance between what-it-says-it-is and what-it-signifies, all the while calling on inner voices or echoes within the careworn sounds. "He spoke like singing," to repeat how Nick Black Elk recalls the "all-colors of light" vision-man of *Wakán Tanka*, the Great Mystery. The old word-visions "have remembered themselves all these years." N. Scott Momaday hears "Carriers of the Dream Wheel" across the heartland plains:

> They are old men, or men
> Who are old in their voices,
> And they carry the wheel among the camps,
> Saying: Come, come,
> Let us tell the old stories,
> Let us sing the sacred songs.

What differentiates song and story? Paul Valéry talked about poetry and prose as the difference between dancing and walking—that is, motion sufficient unto itself and movement to get somewhere ("Remarks on Poetry"). The dancer moves by patterned design *within* space and time, listening to an inner cadence in tune with an outer score; the walker passes *through* space-time, from one place to another. So prose is more horizontal than vertical, with a progressive stride that carries what Jorie Graham calls the *run run* of narrative pacing. Prose has someplace to go, a terrain to cover, characters to detail, a village to consider, ideas to be revealed. Prose is busy doing, not as an end in itself, but connecting a reader with a region, a report, a climate and history, lives unfolding. Prose diction tends to be more communicable, the metaphors more canted to relay ideas and information, the plot layering in social complexity. "Only connect," E. M. Forster asked. Here words are messengers that should not get in the way of the story's *character*, as inversely, ideology best not blunt a poem's musical *tone*. Pitch and timing are all. "I have come to know," Momaday begins *The Man Made of Words*, "that much of the power and magic and beauty of words consists not in meaning but in sound." Design in prose, so too, is less a texture of motion than a transparency into reality. Finally, the prose voice expresses "one of us," recognizable and true-to-lives lived, whether cockroach, king, or cuckold; the poetic voice is often "one of them" among us, an alterity discovered within ("internal difference," Dickinson says of slant despair, "Where the meanings, are"). The axial crossover would be whether we can *talk a poem,* as Frost often said, or sing a story, as Homer chanted Greek epics and Confucius set Chinese folk sayings to stringed lyrics. Pound revoiced the classical Odes of the *Shih-Ching,*

> No tool 'gainst tiger,
> no boat for river.
> That much, no more,
> and they know it;
> but above all to be precise
> at the gulf's edge
> or on thin ice.

Czeslaw Milosz, the Polish expatriot and poet, titles his modern anthology of translated world verse *A Book of Luminous Things* (1997). He seems to mean, by this title, the *lightening* effect of poetry among common objects, even at tragic moments where G. M. Hopkins finds the "terrible crystal" at the wretched heart of things, that glow-in-the-dark illumination Wallace Stevens otherwise found to be "bright, green wings" on Sunday morning, or "green green's apogee" in summer's credences. Milosz's global lines carry a leaping anima alive in and to the world around us, however shaded it seems, from Paul Celan verbally aghast after the Holocaust, to a visually surcharged Emily Dickinson, to a verbally buoyant William Blake, to the cindered heart of Seamus Heaney, who hears the Gaelic muses advise in ·"North":

> "Compose in darkness.
> Expect aurora borealis
> in the long foray
> but no cascade of light.
>
> Keep your eye clear
> as the bleb of the icicle,
> trust the feel of what nubbed treasure
> your hands have known."

Things hark back to preverbal being waking us to language—silence, darkness, pause, solid object—that lead toward words. There may be a disturbing, indescribable quality to modern poetry that moves readers beyond grief-stricken muteness, a restless space in silence that lights up the blank canvas with the desire to name things for what they are, or what they suggest. The Blackfeet poet, James Welch, runs on blank verse heartbeats "In My Lifetime":

> Desperate in my song,
> I run these woman hills, translate wind
> to mean a kind of life, the children of Speakthunder
> are never wrong and I am rhythm to strong medicine.

These lines touch the initial tenets of an interjective poetics, neoprimitive to modernist, back to the beginnings of evolutionary voicings.

Perhaps not so surprising, on further reflection, medicine people in Sitting Bull's Lakota traditions still speak of the luminous, ceremonial words and dance chants that enliven and bind their people tribally. A *wicasa wakán*, or "man holy," regards the surcharged language of healing rituals, from vision quest, to *yuwipi* "binding" rite, to Sun Dance chant, as *wakán*, transverbally charged with meaning. Strangely enough, tribal history is recorded in these ceremonial nodes. Black Thunder's pictographic calendar of the Teton Sioux, Densmore notes, begins in 1801 with an *olówanpi* or "sing for someone," ritually translated as "truthfully singing winter." The eighty-year-old Red Weasel said through Robert Higheagle's English, "In regard to the songs, Dreamer-of-the-Sun told me that I may pray with my mouth and the prayer will be heard, but if I sing the prayer it will be heard sooner by Wakántanka." These are the mysterious and musically italicized traditions of the *lowanpi* or "sing" that calls on a strange kinship of othering within the *tiospaye*, the extended clan "living in a circle." A disturbing charm, indeed an ecstatic charge haunts the transformative power of these ancient ceremonies. "Word senders," or what we could otherwise call poet-singers, call through dream visions (knowing with "the heart's eye," John Fire said); find voice in archaic languages (singing with "the heart of a bear," Two Shields chanted); see by luminous images ("wide as daylight and as starlight," Black Elk remembers his Great Vision grandfathers, "old like stars, like hills"); and dance with pulsing rhythms to the shamanic ways of ritual wisdom. ("It was so beautiful that nothing anywhere could keep from dancing," Black Elk recalls, "all danced together to the music of the stallion's song.") "Something sacred wears me," Siyáka sang for Densmore, "all behold me coming." How these Lakota oral traditions and hundreds of other tribal cultures evolve into a Native/American poetics, literally the verse-lines of Momaday and Welch, through Whiteman and Harjo, is the story of this study.

The sacred singing of Native North America rises along the vertical axis of poetry. The visionary path of "walking in a sacred manner," no less than the poet swaying to the great bear's primal cadence, leads toward Theodore Roethke's chant reclaiming him from fatal writer's block: "Is that dance slowing in the mind of man / That made him think the universe could hum?" And Momaday, timelessly, returns to the great bear:

> Seen, he does not come,
> move, but seems forever there,
> dimensionless, dumb,
> in the windless noon's hot glare.

"Yes, I was dancing-mad," Roethke concludes, "and how / That came to
be the bears and Yeats would know." Whether Orpingalik speaks of the
inner thaw of the great ice floe and words that "shoot up of themselves"
in song-poems; or Roethke recalls the visionary presence of Yeats bearing
his chant lines; or the masked Hopi *katcinas* enter the villages droning their
three-tone, pulse-step dances for rain; or Momaday is visited by the ancient
Kiowa bear-child of the sky; or a Lakota healer draws power through prayer-
ful "breath in the pipe"; or all-nations' powwow drums call the people
across urban Indian America—the vertical axis of leaping, ceremonial lan-
guage arcs from singer to poet, dancer to chanter in a sacred secularization
of native life, singing with the different heart of a bear. These words spark
the everyday catalyst to a deeper, more significant world, a life all the more
to be lived. "Part of the rainbow is visible in the clouds, and part disappears
in the ground," Siyáka told Frances Densmore of the Lakota "sacred
hoop": "What we see is in the shape of a hoop. This word is employed by
medicine-men and especially by dreamers of the elements of the air and
the earth." This sense of the native poetic is not other-worldly, or tran-
scendental, but rises up out of a spiritually concrete earth, a daily world
between earth and sky, a vision that lures the dead back to life, this life the
envy of angels, animals, and other beings. "They would have wept to step
barefoot into reality," Wallace Stevens, "Large Red Man Reading," senses
of ghosts gathering about his native life.

Can we parse these leaping, luminous lines? Try thinking about a cou-
plet, originally thirty lines, then cut to fifteen lines six months later by Ezra
Pound. Written just before and during the First World War, over a year the
poem was pared down to two lines: "Three years ago in Paris I got out of
a 'metro' train at La Concorde, and saw suddenly a beautiful face, and then
another and another, and then a beautiful child's face, and then another
beautiful woman," Pound says in the memoir *Gaudier-Brzeska*, "and I tried
all that day to find words for what this had meant to me, and I could not
find any words that seemed to me worthy, or as lovely as that sudden emo-
tion." That evening, walking home along the Rue Raynouard, Pound
sensed an "expression," not words themselves, but "an equation . . . not
in speech, but in little splotches of colour." The muse arrived as visual
tone, "a word, the beginning, for me, of a language in colour":

In a Station of the Metro

The apparition of these faces in the crowd;
Petals on a wet, black bough.

How do we think about this? The first step, after hearing the poem—seeing
and registering its lines—would be listening for the *syllable*, the opening
phoneme "In" joined with the following "a." We have some forty pho-

nemes or pure sounds to work with as English syllables—a scale of notes half the range of an ordinary piano—composed of consonants, vowels, and double vowels called diphthongs (nineteen English vowels in all, compared with seven in Italian). These are the building blocks of language, some languages using fewer than thirty phonemes (eleven in Polynesian), others more than eighty (141 in Khoisan or "Bushman").

With Pound's title, "In a Station of the Metro," the vowels hold sway. The inner sounds come forward along the roof of the mouth to peek: the first syllable seems to get more weight or stress, as we normally say "*In* a," so the phrase rocks down and forward, as might the rest of the title. This is not the way iambic English normally sways, but stress-slack trochaically, "In a Station of the Metro." Catchy as that close analysis may be, it's not poetic. Where's the dithyrambic variable? An alternative rhythm is set up through ordinary syntax in the sweep of the title—how we would normally phrase it, if asked directions, say, by an American tourist in Paris. "In a *Sta*tion of the *Me*tro," the vernacular cadence has it. Here *syntax* works through syllables gathered in sequence. These phrasings cadence minums, countering formal inclinations close-up with longer-range idiomatic patterns; and this cadencing leads quickly to a third variable, *structure,* in what versifiers call the poetic line (or sentence to a prose writer). Where the line ends is significant, at least where it seems to pause, visually, for beneath the voice the given course of the eye may be countered by the ear's vernacular norms. Syllable and syntax tense within structure, and a principle begins to emerge: stress and counterstress, form and usage, close look and perspective listening. This syncopation leads toward what we might call the periodicity of art, or patterned variation. Such internal sway makes it challenging and interesting and, for that matter, appealing.

So far we are still feeling for a drift in Pound's title, which seems to be approachable with at least two cadences: formally, a series of trochees falling in four beats, "*In* a *Sta*tion *of* the *Me*tro," and more informally, "In a *Sta*tion of the *Me*tro," two long anapestic phrasings that rise, cluster, and fall gracefully to the first line. The reverse cadences work with and against each other, creating a dynamic that makes for the tensile strength of the rhythmic line. As Boas speaks of literary style in all poetry, "repetition, particularly rhythmic repetition, is one of its fundamental, esthetic traits." Dithyrambic rhythm, stressed repetition with variation, holds sway, singing with a *different* heart.

Reversing metric tilt, the verse description thickens in the opening line: again, the syllables could group iambically in six-beat phrasings, "The *appa*rition *of* these *fac*es *in* the *crowd*," but this seems stiff, too formal. The idiomatic ear takes over to adjust the pattern to our liking, "The appa*ri*tion of these *fac*es in the *crowd*"—a lovely sprung rhythm, mysteriously cadenced, three extended anapestic phrasings with half the full stresses.

Is there an emerging fourth variable, one we could call *style*, everything from diction, to metrics, to shaped or formed structures, as well as the artist's personage in the wings? At first, with the title, the style seems neutral, even a bit flat: a place, underground, of public transport, in diction and rhythm no more elegant sounding than pedestrian directions. But as the title flows haiku-like into the first line, we come up, metrically and etymologically, against the Latinate "ap-par-*i*-tion," which seems to pick up the diction and rhythmic pace, to pop up phonemically with the double *p*s. The buried off rhyme between "*i*-tion" and "*fac*-es," set against the compact density of "crowd," complicates and gives texture to the lines, all the while remaining relatively ordinary in setting, language, and technique. So the style is normative, even vernacular, but capable of opening up, thickening, deepening, as long as style never calls attention to itself over the terms of the poem itself—its own being, apart from the maker.

So far, so good, perhaps, but halfway in the couplet blossoms: "Petals on a wet, black bough." The poem turns radically on the semicolon; the line pause, or break, seems to twist everything around and back on itself, structurally causing us to read the apparitional faces as an image or *sign*, a simile (faces like petals) or symbol (petals of faces). Here the sounds-as-syntactically-structured-signs begin to make *sense;* that is, they move toward meaning. "The image is itself the speech," Pound insists. "The image is the word beyond formulated language." If "faces" may suggest "petals," and a metro station in a French (not too foreign to Norman English) city may occasion a poetic vision, what does it all add up to? Be patient, test the ear and eye: Is the syntax of the first word iambic, as ordinarily spoken ("Pe*tals*"? never in a hundred years), or trochaic, "*Pet*als *on* a *wet*, black *bough*"? That's better, but seems still a bit too regular, too monotonous. The ear must override the routine mind's-eye and vary the stress, to adjust a formal mishmash, as so, "*Pet*als on a *wet*, black *bough*." That's at least more metrically engaging, with the trochee-become-dactyl giving way, somewhere in the cluster of unstressed syllables, to the reasserted iambs in the second and third phrases.

Something is still amiss, the pattern is not quite taut. What if the regular expectations of one pattern repeating another slough off, and we hear normative voice emphasis, against drilled image closure, weighting all three last syllables?—"*Pet*als on a *wet*, *black bough*." It's irregular, but arresting, powerfully sprung into place. The line seems to hang petal-like, about to fall; on a syllabic or phonemic level, the last vowels moan, "eh" "ae" "ow" and the dental *t* clangs off the labial *b* as the plosive *k* cuts off before the second labial *b*. This is the musical equivalent of thirds, fourths, fifths, and diminished sevenths chorded into an arrhythmic cadence. The last word, "bough," hangs there, suspended, no consonant to nail it down, unforgettable. All this is achieved by reversing the iambic expectation with a trochee, "*Pet*als," then reversing that with an anapest, "on a *wet*," trying to right the line's rhythm, then drilling the eidetic image to a close, "*black bough.*" The imploded spondee fairly crackles at the edges and vowels out woefully in the middle of words. The syllables pace sequentially together through space, measured in the time it takes to read them, and at the same time the sounds radiate larger and smaller fields of energy, three-dimensionally, like tiny fireworks shooting off in the sky. It feels like connecting the dots of a child's coloring book, only to find Van Gogh's *Starry Night* bursting off the page. Minus the closing dental, "bough" almost rhymes with "crowd," positionally above it. This creates a couplet effect, an attempt to couple, at least, against the dissonant tension working the lines. Pound tries to explain by analogy, "my experience in Paris should have gone into paint. If instead of colour I had perceived sound or planes in relation, I should have expressed it in music or in sculpture."

Beyond a native poetics, there's something Eastern behind the Western surface of all this. Structurally, a proportional metric cadences the lines, beginning with the title, syllabically 8–12–7, supra-metrically 4–6–4, and metrically normative as 2–3–3. Haiku syllables run 5–7–5, more or less proportionate to Pound's freer construction. So Confucius complements Homer, *The Analects* adds to *The Odyssey*, something deeper in the human psyche circles the globe. The near couplet draws all poetry closer, aesthetically, in a manner of speaking, ethnic or our own. Pound stands somewhere in the middle as global translator. A Westerner born in Hailey, Idaho, graduate of Penn with Williams and Hilda Doolittle, expatriate back to the European classics, highbrow to the art of London, Paris, and Venice; then in the middle of his life, an alleged war subversive, convicted of lowly treason, imprisoned for twelve years in a Maryland mental institution, released to return to Italy, where he lived out his life twenty more years, writing cantos in silence. Such is the man behind the near couplet.

What can we say about early-twentieth-century American verse, by way of Pound's example, and ethnopoetics? "I think these examples demonstrate," Boas admits, "that it is not easy to discover from published material the stylistic pattern of primitive narrative. Sometimes the rendering is bald and dry owing to the difficulties of expression that the interpreter cannot overcome; sometimes elaborated in a superimposed literary style that does not belong to the original." Yes, the crossover difficulty is immense, but let's hazard some provisional guidelines about modernism, as Boas does about oral translations into print. Rejecting a "rather smarmy" Victorian aesthetics, the new American poetry is microsyllabically concise, even minimalist—*cut* in Fenollosa's term for ideogrammatic diction, *sprung* in Hopkins's term for meter, even thrust past conventional rhythm, as Pound

argued the vortical trochee's *heave* against built-in iambic conventions—
but still patterned in its own native poetics. Modernist verse is sometimes
near-rhymed, as in Dickinson's "success in Circuit," slant telling; almost
pairing, the near verse remains startling, arresting, thoughtful, though shy
of "visionary" in the Romantic sense. Formally, Pound's two lines break
into a hexameter-tetrameter couplet, neither heroic nor coupling, but ap-
positional, the images of faces and petals working by analogy. "So we get
mimesis without the cosmic designs that once made it meaningful," Donald
Wesling concludes of modernist "organic vitalism" in *The Chances of Rhyme.*
"The artist imitates that which is within the thing, not, as in a copy, in the
spirit of idle rivalry, but, *natura naturans,* grasping the process of the thing
through sympathetic identification. Thus the writer will convey to us his
sense of order through the order of his syllables."

The six-four couplet structure tilts and rebalances, off and leaning back
into pattern, completing the ten-stressed meter of an older, evenly accented
and rhymed "heroic" couplet. Contrasts are key within the patterns. The
artist places a natural, even classical, image of blossoms against obdurate
urban modernity, a "station" of the "metro" (commuter station of the
secular cross). Still, an ancient nature blossoms from the dank roots and
rails of the city. The diction hovers in some middle range, not too fancy,
never overstated, echoing voices of the people, yet concentrated into ur-
gency, depth, intensity of feeling. Disillusion pitches against true illusion,
skepticism against belief. Communal transcends personal. The upright lyric
I is suspect: this is not the self-construct of Wordsworth, Emerson, Tenny-
son, or Hopkins, but dramatis personae or ironic mask (the dramatic
monologues of Browning, Poe, and Hardy anticipate early modernists
Frost, Eliot, and Stevens). The first-person eye dissolves into more inclusive
consideration, an indirect, hard-worn aye, back to the masses, back to the
common tribe.

"In a poem of this sort," Pound says, "one is trying to record the precise
instant when a thing outward and objective transforms itself, or darts into
a thing inward and subjective." What does the poet mean by this, what does
the poem signify, finally what's its sense? Perhaps something about the
ghosts of people in crowds, dim-lighted, massed in public transit, going
somewhere, but really nowhere, given the mortal condition. A minor epiph-
any springs back with nature's petals in season—set against the unseen
trunk of a massive, rooted blossomer whose rain-soaked limb, dark against
the darkness, backgrounds the lights of petaled faces, commuting to work,
on the brink of war, anonymously together, going home. The fine points
are crucial. "An epic diffusiveness," Boas discovers among swirling partic-
ulars, "an insistence on details is characteristic of most free primitive nar-
rative." As Two Shields sang with a bear's heart, "a wind from the north
comes for me."

Pound may have been thinking of Eurydice in hell, Kora underground (as was his rival-friend Williams at the time), and the Orphic mystery cults that sprang up around loss and recovery. Early Greeks saw the elegiac celebration of gain-in-loss through the stories of Orpheus, losing Eurydice looking back, torn apart by jealous would-be lovers and thrown into the river, where his head kept singing of his beloved and charmed all the plants and animals to come down to the waters. Perhaps. Pound may have been foreshadowing Yeats's "O chestnut-tree, great rooted blossomer, / Are you the leaf, the blossom or the bole?" in "Among School Children." Or his moment may have been simply a vision of color, a preverbal insight, a visitation. That's one of the secrets of good literature: there's always more to be considered beyond the parsing, assumptions to be revised, mysteries.

THREE

ई(•)ई

Indian Poetry in Our Time

Early- to late-twentieth-century American literature folds tribal literacies into modernist, then postmodernist translative forms. Diagonal crossings, from warriors through "word-senders" to Dickinson's "Soul *at the White Heat,*" mark the hybrid fusions, oral to written texts. Pound's syllabic attentions and folkloric global aesthetics, from Confucius to Homer, show up in Momaday's Southwest metrics, by way of Yvor Winters in the early 1960s, who was influenced by Southwest native poetics in the 1920s. Marianne Moore's naturalist care emerges in the Midwest eco-syllabics of Linda Hogan's taut lines, whose naturalist attentions have educated a generation of non-native women writers. Yeats's chant measures, by way of Theodore Roethke or Dylan Thomas, sway the blank verse visions and postwar tensions of James Welch and Roberta Hill, via Richard Hugo's tutelage in Montana. And poets like Hugo, Snyder, Creeley, Merwin, Kinnell, Hughes, and Heaney have clearly been schooled in Native American ethics and aesthetics. Cross-pollinations work both ways.

Certainly other than literary influences shaped the Native American renaissance—regional cultural depths and indigenous tongues, ceremonial song-lines, tribal histories, acculturative resistances, spiritual and religious complexes, daily prayers and curses, folkloric beliefs and tall tales, parables and jokes, lullabies and recipes—but Western literary history and Euro-American forms adaptively focus native literatures on the page, as published in the United States. Modern literary tools have stocked the quivers of native "word-senders" to write their differences, to transcribe tribal distinctions, to chant and tell America from ancient oral texts, speaking with bear hearts. Whitman singing America, seconded by Langston Hughes and later Allen Ginsberg, certainly cadence Joy Harjo's blues verse riffs down to the standup improvisations of Sherman Alexie. W. S. Merwin and Robert

Creeley's shadow syllables, registered in the darker minims of Williams or the late Pound Cantos (back through Poe), trace the pilgrim steps and warrior fears in Simon Ortiz, Paula Gunn Allen, and Ray Young Bear, students of American poets-at-large, New Mexico to Iowa and Black Mountain. And were there no Emily Dickinson, there would be less Mary TallMountain (who named her cat after a godmother poet), no D. H. Lawrence, little Luci Tapahonso, no Langston Hughes, less Joy Harjo. The song-lines and story-riffs distinctively loop, cross, subdivide, spiral, and recross, but Native and American literatures have interfaced and interlaced down through the century.

CRITICAL PASSAGES

I grew up listening to songs on the radio, poems in my house, music and storytelling. How people said things was crucial. I finally experienced poems in books when I went to public schools in Tulsa, Oklahoma, and read Emily Dickinson and fell in love with poetry—the soundscape of poems. This became as important as the poem in a trumpet or sax solo on the radio, the poem in Patsy Cline singing a song.

JOY HARJO, "THE LANGUAGE OF TRIBES," *Bloomsbury Review,*
NOVEMBER / DECEMBER 1997

Twenty-five years ago, trained in Victorian studies, I looked home and started thinking of a Native American renaissance, a tribal rebirth in this country. The term does not mean sudden or first emergence. The Medici court of fifteenth-century Florence turned to Ficcino's translations of ancestral Greek and Roman classics as their base for early modern thought; from this ground sprang the Renaissance masters, Leonardo, Michelangelo, Donatello, Botticelli, and Fra Lippo Lippi, among many others, a cultural renewal spreading north and west across Europe. Ezra Pound followed neoclassical suit in our own century's arts, looking to indigenous and interglobal literacy for an American model. Renaissance means *re*newing, making the word new again by bringing the past into the present, and everyone gets a say in this country.

Aside from British literature, I was teaching what scholars call modernism in Pound, Stevens, Moore, Bishop, Stein, Eliot, Fitzgerald, and Hemingway, for starters. "Make it new" was their byword. Meanwhile, a poet like Langston Hughes found blues originality in Black culture, and later writers such as Zora Neale Hurston mined storytelling genius from Black dialect, as Toni Morrison does today. Marcus Garvey and W. E. B. Du Bois drew on cultural pride and community organization in the Afro-American population. And in my own local origins were Willa Cather, John Neihardt, and Mari Sandoz, notable homestate writers, later inspirations in Wright Morris, Loren Eiseley, and Ron Hanson.

My father's and mother's pioneer Nebraska ancestors were buried along the Oregon Trail. Spotted Tail hunted buffalo at Bronco Lake, just west of my hometown. Nick Black Elk picked potatoes in Alliance, Nebraska, and Crazy Horse received his name-vision from Scotts Bluff, on the North Platte River just west of Horse Creek, where ten thousand mounted Plains Indians signed a treaty with the United States in 1851. In reclaiming my origins, F. O. Matthiessen's *American Renaissance* was certainly on my mind—recognition that the colonial severing with Europe and the rebirthing of a native literary culture had constellated in the 1850s—through Melville's sagas, Hawthorne's romances, Poe's ingenuity, Emerson's American scholar essays, and Thoreau's native soundings for this country's local genius. I also thought of the Greenwich and Harlem Renaissances of the 1920s, Marianne Moore editing *The Dial* and William Carlos Williams doctoring in Hell's Kitchen, Langston Hughes countering "I, too, sing America" and Malcolm X coming out of Omaha, Nebraska, my home state. I recalled Williams's *In the American Grain,* written in my parents' childhood, and Kazin's *On Native Ground,* published the year before my birth.

As I started teaching English and some American literature in 1969, Roger Buffalohead seeded a UCLA Native American program called High Potential, or "Hi Pot," scavenging for Indian students to enter the university on six months' remedial tutoring. I had grown up around Sioux Indians and been adopted into a Lakota family in northwest Nebraska, so I pitched in at UCLA, though our English Department was dominated by the Dryden Project. Why not give back? "I am as free as Nature first made man," John Dryden wrote in *The Conquest of Granada,* "Ere the base Laws of Servitude began / When wild in woods the nobel Savage ran," coining the oxymoron of noble savagery in 1672. Untenured in the early 1970s and a specialist in Victorian Studies, I was warned by older scholars that my native diversion was tantamount to career Russian roulette.

We recruited from Sherman Institute in San Bernardino, put out the word around California and the Southwest, found nineteen-year-olds at Arizona waterholes, and generally took any high school native graduate who showed aptitude or interest. Helping tutor English with Pat Locke and Art Zimaga, Sioux teachers from the Dakotas, I felt distantly related to home, no easy task in centerless Los Angeles. One of my Lakota students, Darrell No Dog, seemed a gifted artist, but caroused too much around the Alexandria Hotel, a flophouse near the Greyhound bus depot in ground zero Los Angeles. "LA ain't nothin' like South Dakota," Darrell said, dropped out, and went home. A Keams Canyon Navajo recruit named Danny Begay showed me his UCLA letter of acceptance stained with mutton grease. "Los Angeles is big enough," he said shyly, "to fill the Grand Canyon." At the end of the year, sixty-three of sixty-seven Indian students failed the minimum requirements to enter as UCLA freshmen.

In that spring of 1970, the United States invaded Cambodia, four Kent

State students were killed by National Guardsmen, and the campus rioted. A phalanx of three hundred black-leather motorcycle cops drove down Sunset Boulevard and swept the university. The faculty went on strike, while students asked for alternative courses. I was teaching an introduction to nineteenth- and twentieth-century British literature and honors freshman English, where a sixteen-year-old Cherokee, Allogan Slagle, showed promise of going on through college. In the middle of the strike, I met these classes, as scheduled, but added a seminar on American Indian literature, to meet off-campus in our beach apartment. I knew of only three Indian texts, John Neihardt's *Black Elk Speaks,* Scott Momaday's *House Made of Dawn,* Pulitzer winner the previous spring, and Vine Deloria's *Custer Died For Your Sins,* an early chapter roasting anthropologists in the 1968 *Playboy.* To these I added Margot Astrov's anthology of native oral literatures in translation, *The Winged Serpent,* Thomas Berger's *Little Big Man,* Clair Huffaker's *Nobody Loves a Drunken Indian,* Carlos Castaneda's *A Separate Reality,* Momaday's *The Way to Rainy Mountain,* and assorted mimeographs of poems, essays, and stories. The readings were a mixed bag, to be sure, but what did I know then? Muckrakers would soon allege fake, appropriation, and forgery over texts by "real" and "unreal" Indians, but this was a starting point in 1970. During that class, literally one seminar night on *House Made of Dawn,* my wife asked me to drive her to the UCLA hospital, where our daughter Rachel was born, in the middle of cultural revolution and a native renaissance.

I had students in those days who had occupied Alcatraz, Red Berets like Archie White, who came away from the campus riots with powder burns on his head. The spring of 1971, I scheduled an "Introduction to Native American Literature," and a hundred and twenty-seven students showed up. In the next few years, I spliced a course called Native American Voices between lectures on Victorian Fiction and Introduction to British Poetry. One of my Indian students, a soft-spoken young Papago, asked in class why I used the word *"Voices,"* and not *"Literature"* in the course title.

"Aren't Native Americans literate?" she challenged quietly.

"Well," I turned red-faced and hemmed, "oral literatures aren't printed, you know, they encompass more than set texts. We need to know everything from history to religion, art to archaeology, folklore to linguistics as contextual background. The word literature seems too limited to me." There was an embarrassed silence, and the class continued. Still, I thought about her objection, and thought to defend what I was doing as literature against the skeptics. What was literature, and what were its uses, through and beyond Pound's dictum of *language charged with meaning?*

I started thinking more about the contexts and contours of literacy, especially native texts. Grading essays that fall of 1973, freshly divorced and caring for my three-year-old daughter, I took a cabin break among the

Giant Forest sequoias and wrote an impromptu essay, responding to student midterms on native oral literatures. "Native American Tribal Poetics" was published in *The Southwest Review* the next year.

The Senior Americanist in my department chided me for suckering into Red Lit. Doctor Lemoine always smirked through smudged bifocals, as though he knew something you didn't.

"How could Indians speak a biblical King's English?" he pooh-poohed, blinking like the toad in *Paradise Lost,* blocking the hall in an orange-striped shirt and plaid bermudas. "Obviously some army private made up those fancy speeches." Obviously? . . . what about literary equivalents to native oratory?

"Wasn't the Bible written originally in Hebrew and Greek," I challenged him, "translated into Latin, again into English several times?"

"Yes, but those were scholars at work, not preliterate laymen." He was as pigheaded as I was.

"Jefferson put Logan's 1774 speech in *Notes on the State of Virginia,*" I kept arguing, "and compared it to Greek oratory. For godssakes, Logan's speech was in McGuffey's reader."

"Jefferson thought Indians were subhuman," he said and clamped his jaw hard. I never did know when to shut up in a stacked argument and could hear a loaded chamber spinning in the Russian revolver. My senior colleague gave me that knowing squint, stared at the acoustical ceiling tile, and we retreated into our respective cubicles.

Well, I continued arguing with myself, how could a cavalry recruit with a grade-school education make up something like Chief Joseph's surrender speech for the Nez Percé, near the Canadian border, winter 1876? "From where the sun now stands I will fight no more forever." Or Red Jacket's Iroquois quip to a missionary: "Brother! You say there is but one way to worship and serve the Great Spirit. If there is but one religion, why do you white people differ so much about it? Why do not all agree, as you can all read the book?" Come on, professor, weren't speakers in classic oral traditions of other tongues, say Homer or Diogenes, Buddha or Lao Tsu, capable of rhetorical elegance? What advantage does writing arrogate, or for that matter, does archive slumming dredge up? Maybe literacy has the opposite effect, I fumed to myself, dulling memory, squelching imagination, dumbing down the brain. Tribal leaders like Sitting Bull, after all, commanded attention and drew power through the spoken word. They led their people by lyric use of the native language. A man's word was sacred, yes, but could just as well be ironic. The Sioux Red Dog put the matter of removal succinctly in 1876, year of the Centennial and the Little Big Horn: "I think you had better put the Indians on wheels. Then you can run them about whenever you wish." Well, no matter, my obtuse colleague's resistance fueled my own. Maybe that's what the British meant by loyal opposition.

My UCLA chairman, the other Nebraska Bruin, advised me to "stop irking" the Old Guard, "if you know what's good for you," he added.

"I'm just trying to figure out my place here," I said with due respect, "to speak my mind."

"Do it on your own time," he put things directly, "after the tenure vote." It seemed I was caught up in something bigger than my own designs, on both sides of the Buckskin Curtain.

Why was I drawn to *native* America? To my White boy's reeducation back home, native tribalism seemed to do with extended kinship, a sense of family beyond blood. It came from the idea that we were all related across dividing lines, men and women, plants and animals, stones and trees, even the spirits and the dead. The ties crossed racial lines, as with the *hunka,* or brother-adoption ceremony, that Mark Monroe offered me in my hometown over thirty years ago. Being related, we took responsibility for each other, lifelong. "Grandfather, pity me," the Sun Dancers pierced their flesh and prayed, "I want to live." Ceremony here was as common as tipping your hat. Daily caring, even teasing or gossip, meant people connecting. In being related, we were rooted—as such we took care of others every day—tending the ground of our history, tilling the soil of our future, nurturing our daily seedings. An old-time "give-away," or *otuhan,* was the daily norm. Nothing was more important than family. I crossed the tracks to find and redefine my own sense of western culture next to my Lakota brother's history, a *native* American tradition, teaching literature no exception. "Remember, Ken, this here is your *tióte,* your home roots," Mark said when I returned to Alliance annually. "You have a big brother here, a home-place, a family." We learned from each other, neither becoming *the other,* but collaboratively respectful of turf and history.

The late 1970s and early 1980s were a decade of reeducation, building American Indian Studies at UCLA. I was trying to break out of the English Departmental confines of lit crit into a dozen related disciplines, the social sciences to the performing arts. Several directors of our budding Center came and went. We finally found an untenured Cherokee ethnomusicologist, Charlotte Heth, to run things, and the programs began to come together. Non-Indian colleagues in assorted disciplines worked cheek-to-jowl in those days—the historian Gary Nash, the archaeologist Clem Meighan, the lawyer Monroe Price, the ceremonial dance expert Alegra Fuller-Snyder, the anthropologist Johannes Wilbert, the psycho-biologist Doug Price-Williams, the musicologist James Porter, the art historian Cecelia Klein, the folklorist Bob Georges. Postdoctoral scholars came annually: Charles Ballard, Betty Parent, Susan Huff, Donald Fixico, Roxanne

Dunbar Ortiz, Walter Williams, Laura Coltelli, Donald Grinde, Troy Johnson, Clifford Trafzer, Susan Scarberry-Garcia. We added promising young colleagues, Pam Munro in linguistics, to Ken Morrison and Melissa Meyer in history, but where were the Indians? Native American faculty recruitment was dicey, since we had to work through established departments, setting research standards against native community needs and precious few human resources. A Choctaw ethnomusicologist did not make the cut in the Music Department. A Navajo health sciences expert went back to Arizona. A Cherokee librarian found work elsewhere. Symposium by symposium, Alfonso Ortiz to Wilcomb Washburn, the University of California, Davis, crew to Long Beach State Indian scholars, we networked and built up American Indian Studies. I saw my own role as an evolutionary subversive in the English Department, still an Anglophilic outpost of progress, where American Literature was regarded as a callow little brother to the Continental Great Tradition.

As Mark was building the American Indian Center back in my hometown (see *An Indian in White America* and *The Good Red Road*), at UCLA we built up our own Indian Studies library, started a scholarly journal in 1975, *The American Indian Culture and Research Journal*, and a Native American poetry series (nine titles to date). We sponsored research projects, counseled Indian students, and by 1982 offered the first graduate program in Native American Studies. Students like the Apache artist Lorenzo Baca and the Cherokee lawyer Leeann Herald were among the first graduates. Allogan Slagle went on to law school, teaching at UC Berkeley, then brokering tribal recognition and Indian law. My Yaqui-Mayan student Rebecca Pereyra Tsosie got a legal degree, too, and eventually settled into federal Indian law at Arizona State University. Margaret Archuleta became the Indian art curator at the Heard Museum in Phoenix. David Lee Smith took Reuben Snake's Nebraska place as Winnebago cultural historian, and Carolyn Marie Dunn went off to teach Indian Studies at Humboldt State University in northern California. A Pomo-Miwok, Greg Sarris, defensive tight end on the Bruin football team, took modern literature classes with me in the late seventies. Next door today, he's a UCLA Full Professor of Native American literature, a novelist, critic, and filmmaker of stature.

It wasn't "all my relatives" all the time. I was directing the graduate Indian program in 1985 when ethnic cleansing set in. The native staff, solid as a union cellblock, checked out en masse to take classes on suing their own Indian Studies Center and Cherokee director. They were led by a dissident associate faculty member from Montana, a disgruntled Yuki poet who resented my faculty direction, and a few graduate dog soldiers itching for another Little Big Horn. So, with disloyal opposition in the camp, Charlotte Heth and I went through several years of legal hassles, she resigned and went to the Smithsonian, and I pulled back.

A general malaise of White flight set in, as Indian Studies everywhere fell on hard times, shrinking nationally from fifty-five academic programs in 1985 to maybe a dozen in the country. Federal funds dried up, the National Endowment for the Arts and National Endowment for the Humanities wells went dry, the BIA stripped down to self-interest groups on the East Coast, and the State of California tilted against affirmative action. White boys were crying preferential bias across the country. By the mid-1990s, the University of California regents had voted against racial priorities, and the faculty was back to square one, when liberal colleagues paid Angela Davis out of their own pockets to teach philosophy. That was 1969, the year I showed up. Our nineties students were now primarily people of color, and UCLA counted some 120 Indian students. Sixty-two percent of the 1996 incoming freshmen were Asian-American, forty-two percent of our entire undergraduate population. From UCLA Watergate Republicans in the 1960s to rainbow coalitions in the 1990s, Whites had become a minority. Still, without affirmative action, Black, Hispanic, and Indian students might go the way of the carrier pigeon, if ex-Congressman Bob Dornan or Governor Pete Wilson had their say. In 1998 UCLA was ordered by public referendum and the board of regents to dismantle affirmative action admissions policies, the infamous ballot initiative, Proposition 209. Millennial California was a state of mixed persuasions.

During the 1990s, we rebuilt our center with strong faculty and staff, under the academic leadership of a Turtle Mountain Chippewa who had studied Russian and been the Harvard campus chess master. Duane Champagne may have been short on bedside manner, as were a number of harried earlier directors, but he ran a tight academic ship. Duane was assisted by Paul Kroskrity from linguistic anthropology, taking over the reins of the graduate program, and Carole Goldberg-Ambrose, associate dean of the law school. Hanay Geiogamah had since joined the faculty in theater arts. Paula Gunn Allen defected from Berkeley to bolster us in English, and Greg Sarris returned from Stanford to the fold. After leaving UCLA, the historian Melissa Meyer came back from the Midwest with her sociologist husband, Russell Thornton, another UC Berkeley crossover. Tara Brauner replaced Charlotte Heth and Ernie Siva in ethnomusicology, and Peter Nabokov teamed up with the World Arts and Cultures program. An Apache-Hispanic, Paul Apodaca, UCLA's 1996 graduate student of the year, was a potential colleague in folklore. There were casualties—our Navajo librarian, Vee Salabiye, dying the summer of 1996; affirmative action backlash; a few disaffected faculty, staff, or students (which goes with the turf). Despite setbacks, Indian studies was more or less on solid footing. We were one of the few remaining native programs in the country.

I relocated in Santa Fe to escape urban rot and academic sclerosis. Since 1990, I've been commuting on Southwest Airlines, loading up on peanuts and bonus tickets. So, this study may be my parting shot in the literary skeet shoot. *Dok-shá,* they say back home, "pay you back later."

NATIVE VOICES

Some tools of writing are the rhythm of language, the imagery & the thought conveyed. Out west, the frontier is on the edge of form. Not shape, but structure & organization of the writing. It is tribal, this hybrid & unfamiliar of the familiar. It's the part that comes from not belonging. Bawks. Words push into the new space. Tribal means belonging, but not belonging to civilization. This is the tension that results.

DIANE GLANCY, *Claiming Breath*

Sing with the Heart of a Bear reaches back a few thousand years, selects texts crucial to American writing this century, and respects the tribal and modern masters, in both the arts and social sciences—Dickinson, Sitting Bull, Boas, Pound, Sapir, Yeats, for starters, Milosz, Momaday, Kluckhohn, Hogan, Heaney, and Hughes, going on. Clearly my own predilections dictate the choices, neither English Departmental party line, nor countercultural cant. Some formalists will not be interested in mixed-blooded poetics that cross oral and literate texts. My literary plumb lines may not be everyone's, nor do I march with cultural missionaries, bearing a text to thump, who want *you* to discriminate from *their* biases. Hear me out. If not yours, these texts, contexts, and pretexts configure within my study.

Neither will this book satisfy isolationists with ivory horns to blow. *How* could I write about Sherman Alexie, an early press reviewer howled, when Ralph Salisbury, Carter Revard, and Peter Blue Cloud are out there, writing? So are two hundred other noteworthy Indian poets, twenty-eight represented here. Much publicized, Alexie continues a paradigm which I call a *Native American renaissance,* beginning with Momaday, Harjo, Hogan, and Welch. As well as editing the UCLA Native American Poetry Series, I have written about Simon Ortiz and Wendy Rose, Barney Bush and Paula Allen, William Oandasan and Gerald Vizenor, Judith Volborth and Louise Erdrich in other contexts elsewhere. This present verse discussion is more selective, biculturally patterned with analogues in canonical literary history. Covering a century of Native and American poetics, oral to written verse, the book cannot crowd every writer under one tent flap. Others will select otherwise, as they choose, and we may collectively, indeed collaboratively enter a new comparativist dialogue between ethnic and mainstream poetry. The point here is to open the corral. *Sing with the Heart of a Bear,* then, is a study of not just how we read American literary culture, but why our culture turns a decided native direction in the twentieth century. "American poetry at the end of this century," John Hollander prefaces *The Best American Poetry, 1998,* "seems elegantly to recognize the diversities of a native speech that has naturalized so many kinds of linguistic immigrant" tongues. A three-generational sequence arcs historically through this book, followed by gender discussions in overlapping eras of Mary TallMountain, Roberta Hill Whiteman, and Luci Tapahonso, then current luminaries Linda Hogan and Joy Harjo, paired with Linda Gregg, Jorie Graham, and Sharon Olds, finally Carolyn Forché. Other writers would fill and flesh out the discussions. I trust that new books will be written beyond this one.

CRITICAL TURF

I was discovering that like the postmodern universe, I too, am an eternally, multiply divided subject, waking these writing mornings at the top of a city high-rise in the midst of more concrete, steel, and plastic than one can readily imagine, from a sleep filled with dreams of home, echoes of my grandfather, chiding, calling.

PATRICIA PENN HILDEN, *When Nickels Were Indians*

Let me state, up front, what this book will *not* do. *Sing with the Heart of a Bear* does not pander to ethnic essentialism that would keep peoples and their cultures separated, mutually suspicious. Tribal nationalists can cast elsewhere—this is a book about cultural overlaps in Native and American poetry. Nor am I concerned, theoretically, with critical machines that were outmoded yesterday, broadsides au courant today, or prophecies fashionable tomorrow. John Wayne or Will Rogers, Wilma Mankiller or Tammy Faye Bakker: what does it all come down to, besides personal vendettas masked as culture wars? "Great hatred, little room," Yeats called Irish fanaticism, "weasels fighting in a hole." Essentialism too often masks self-interest. A 1998 *Aboriginal Voices* asks, "AIMster Gangsters from the past: Where are they now?" Minnie Two Shoes reports, "Over the years since the occupation, several members of AIM have gone on to become movie stars, book authors, recording artists, and tribal government officials." John Trudell (Dakota) has starred in movies and rock music, and Wes Studi (Cherokee) has appeared in a dozen films. Herb Powless (Oneida) is a Milwaukee businessman, and Dennis Banks (Chippewa) is a repatriation activist. Voice talent for the Disney cartoon, *Pocahontas*, Russell Means cameoed in *Natural Born Killers* and *A Song for Hiawatha*. Means sounded off with a ghost writer in *Where White Men Fear to Tread* as self-featuring *Last* of the Noble Savages, finding rehab God and Anglo grace in the movies, a script he abhorred at Wounded Knee '73. This is why I can't read Elizabeth Cook-Lynn, who titles her xenophobic Sioux polemic, *Why I Can't Read Wallace Stegner*.

Granted their cynicism, newly suburban, asphalt Indian writers—Wendy Rose, Gerald Vizenor, Ward Churchill, Adrian Louis, Sherman Alexie—resist the tribal pastoralism of the old ways, slanting away from the biospheric ethics of extended kinship. Their chant is not "all my relatives," as Plains Natives say, but *All My Sins Are Relatives,* as W. S. Penn entitles his life-story, a Los Angeles satirist claiming Sahaptin descent from Chief Joseph. His sister, Patricia Penn Hilden, self-featuring bluest-eyed-Indian professor of social history at UC Berkeley, daughter of an "ultra-white" DAR and an LA-assimilated Nez Percé father, calls her "urban, mixed-blood story" *When Nickels Were Indians:* "Indeed, for urban mixed-blood children, growing up among aliens, the only rest is with other mixed bloods. Only there is there no suspicion: *you* aren't Indian; *you* aren't white." Bifurcated irony is the mode here, disaffection the tenor, distemper the tone, a far cry from "beauty is all around me" in a Navajo Night Chant. Theirs is a questionable "house made of dawn, house made of evening light." Wendy Rose equivocally titles her new and selected poems *Going to War with All My Relations.* Like the children of other holocaustal survivors, these born-again warriors want not to be duped or deceived ever again; they will not swallow prelapsarian trust or the ceremonial pluralism of their ancestors. "I won't paint pretty pictures," says the Lakota artist Robert Penn in Omaha. "I'm nobody's dancing bear." Instead, these dog soldiers draw up the drawbridge, close the tent flap, and declare Indianness off-limits to all but the chosen. Intercultural harangue grinds their axe, acculturation remains their anathema, oddly so, since their own success as mixed-blood *writers* reconfigures tribal history by way of western literary tools.

Historically festering, these turf wars strike me as self-limiting. Is the charge of cultural appropriation, on other fronts, applicable to Ezra Pound, who revoiced Confucius and Homer in the Cantos? Should parochial history silence D. H. Lawrence, who took on Native American icons, eagles to his totemic red wolf in the *New Poems,* drumming and dancing with the Cochiti earth spirits of *Mornings in Mexico?* A scholar might puzzle what distinguishes cultural appropriation from research, respect, or reeducation. Is culture-stealing a one-way alley? Which side was co-opted and compromised when the Kwakiutl George Hunt teamed up with Franz Boas? When the Cherokee healer Swimmer worked with James Mooney? When the Omaha-Ponca ethnologist Francis La Flesche wrote about the Osage, or later collaborated with Alice Fletcher on the Omaha? We might question whether cultural "blood-sucking," as charged by a prickly press reader, remains true of all anthropologists, from the German Boas, to the English Douglas, to the American Geertz, who go outside their own ethnocentric backyards. Looking the other way, are Indian ethnologists Ella Deloria and William Jones through D'Arcy McNickle and Alfonso Ortiz suspect, too? A leave-us-alone policy, a compulsive separatism, would keep Indians forever apart, when two-thirds have left traditional lands for the cities, living fence-to-fence with non-Indians.

Who is empowered to speak for whom, and why? What about these blood-quantum sanctities, the privileges of "card-carrying Indians," as my

Sioux brother says, the DNA rights to tribal monopoly and cultural exclusion? This seems dangerously analogous to institutional racism in mainstream society. Should blood-privilege xenophobically restrict the flow of informed understanding around what is *American?* How few drops of blood, historical grief, and travel exotica equip or delimit us to tell a native story? Born-again, Buckskin Curtain watchdogs—no less than Don Imus, Rush Limbaugh, or Jesse Helms on the White-boy flap side—tell us to stay out and shut up. This muzzling goes against communal or pluralist traditions, indeed, tribal good will. We are never gag-ruled by the traditionalists or teachers of native cultures, but by dissidents longing for native empowerment—and I suspect their *own* appropriation of cultural identity, in the name of others *back home*, quasi-historically. The essentialist debate leads a late-century reader to ask: Who has privilege, cross-culturally, to what tribal story? Can we translate, compare, and appreciate cultures? Will *Native* ever connect with *American* literature?

Today, as Henry Louis Gates, Jr., sees it, margin *is* mainstream, while irate power blocs of mixed persuasions cry wolf, ranting *un*equal opportunity. Make no mistake, we stand at a crossroads of corrective racial apology, trying to reright cultural history. Our empathy is slipping, as in California, where I've taught for thirty years, struggling toward *affirmative* action to level the academic playing field. Popular referendums and court orders at this moment reverse an educational generation's work toward representative democracy and cultural diversity. To be replaced by what? The *rough beast* of blue-eyed, male prerogative again? The anarchy of shifting street politics, gangland turf, and self-aggrandizing tribal nationalism? Whether born in America or naturalized, blue-blooded or mixed, we all belong here as citizens of the country.

The Americas desperately need a fusional model of *mutual* interest, for once, where *your* mainstream and *my* margin, or vice versa, cross borders to share understanding, value, power, and grace. "Circle the wagons!" is a last desperate cry. Common manners would be to ask a stranger in, invite him to stay for a meal, and tell his story, though natives are rightly wary of unguarded openness. Walter Benjamin says this cultural courtesy is the origin of all narratives: homing farmer hosts traveling sailor, Emmaeus the swineherd welcomes Odysseus as stranger, the humbled warrior-king come home. And this is plain, old-fashioned manners, *hospitality*, wherever humans gather to claim themselves civilized and cultured and want to get along in peace with others. Our future turns on an extended kinship of mutual needs and aspirations, an intercultural native poetics, reaching across to each and all of us. The world will not survive without an enlightened reciprocity. "I tell my kids," Skip Gates says, "you can love Mozart, Picasso, even play ice hockey, and still be black as the ace of spades" (*The Boston Book Review*, May 1997). "Now you can feel free to like Mozart and

Coltrane. That is the ideal. Culture by choice. Not culture for a large political or ideological purpose."

BLESSED LISTENING

I know of no task so salutory to the poet who would, first of all,
put himself in touch with the resident genius of his own land.
MARY AUSTIN, *The Path on the Rainbow*

"Blessed / are those who listen," she writes, "when no one is left to speak."
And he: "To stay alive this way, it's hard. . . ."

Among hundreds, if not thousands of Native American poets writing, Linda Hogan and James Welch come forward among those surviving history. The Old West is still with us, albeit as popular art, no longer outright genocide. In the drive-in movie, Louise Erdrich hears John Wayne challenge Redskins to give up, "It is / not over, this fight, not as long as you resist." But resist they still do; it is not over yet, this reacculturation and relocation of peoples across the Americas. "I'm still here," my Pueblo colleague Paula Gunn Allen marvels daily, as she reawakens in a "movement toward recovery."

The pre-Columbian population was decimated ninety-seven percent by disease, starvation, slavery, and warfare, yet two million today live in the United States alone, another forty to sixty million repopulated in the Western Hemisphere. Historically alert, James Welch writes about the presence of the past in "In My Lifetime":

> His bones go back
> so scarred in time, the buttes are young to look
> for signs that say a man could love his fate,
> that winter in the blood is one sad thing.

The Native American present is a sometimes grief-stricken sense of loss, given the occlusion of animal life, land, air, water, and communal well-being. Yet Natives rise each morning, grieved and relieved to be alive, going on with James Welch:

> His sins—I don't explain. Desperate in my song,
> I run these woman hills, translate wind
> to mean a kind of life, the children of Speakthunder
> are never wrong and I am rhythm to strong medicine.

The Blackfeet once heard the voices of the gods in spring storms, opening their medicine bundles with the first thunder. To speak as children of thunder is, indeed, a sacred heritage, no less than Eliot's hearing a thunderous Sanskrit *Da* at the end of *The Waste Land.*

Over five hundred years of irreparable damage to the Americas have left native peoples denuded in the face of slaughter, witness to the devastation of their tribal ways, reduced to commercial icons. Charles Ballard looks back to a verdant paradise, as Orpheus called to an estranged love:

> We disbanded and were no more
> To choose finally is the Indian way
>
> But time was the trail went deep
> Into a green and vibrant land.

This tribal sense of loss, says Allen, leaves Indian people in "a state of perpetual grief . . ."; from there, "then you deal" with reality. "Why am I alive?" she asks, and "Where are we going?" In the acute aftermath of cultural shock, in the aching silences of genocidal delayed stress, the poets still bear witness. "You call me a drunk Indian, go ahead," Simon Ortiz stands up. And Anita Endrezze edges her defiance, "where I am silent as a bow unstrung / and my scars are not from loving wolves." Wildness was never suspect in the traditional ways, but honored as a test of courage, a quickened pulse. Natives would still be "at home" in the natural world, except that it is a "widowed" land, as Francis Jennings says, never a "virgin" one (*The Invasion of America*).

Why do so many Indians write poetry? Perhaps the tradition traces directly to the song-lines of ceremonial life, as in aboriginal Australia—landscapes of heritage and long history, the ritual and religion of the old ways recurrent, tribal beliefs in private voices made public. In Sioux country the stones speak. These earthen ancestral voices are still sacred and powerful, if muted (as in Ireland where four million natives, Yeats, Shaw, Synge, Wilde, Joyce, and Heaney among them, have recharged English literary history the past hundred years, in the face of cultural imperialism and colonial rule). The bedrock of American culture remains native grace. Joy Harjo looks up to old sky medicine:

> Like eagle that Sunday morning
> Over Salt River. Circled in blue sky
> In wind, swept our hearts clean
> With sacred wings.
> We see you, see ourselves and know
> That we must take the utmost care
> And kindness in all things.

Perhaps poetry, a form of visionary kinship, is the one means left to speak, when few are left to listen: "an ache or a need," Allen says, that rises out of silence. If poetry begins with Frost's lump in the throat, its tribal release will open the heart and clear the mind—and here the poets of Native America today are heard speaking of tribal shadings that must be imagined to be believed—"our voices the color of watching," as Lance Henson says.

The native lyric note is deep-struck, reverent, as with the Plains invocation to "pray for a vision." Poetry here is daily prayer, "sending a voice" homeward. What American poet-at-large today, in the secular slide and dispirit of modern verse, "prays" for visionary power homing among others? Jim Barnes asks of the other, "call him brother / semblance, prey." Spiritually graced, if troubled with uprooting, the native lines rise out of natural settings, guardian spirits, interdependent structures, and balancing organic energies. Along with William Carlos Williams, Mary Austin saw this native balance as "the old rhythm" coursing through all things, "the roll of thunder," for example, "or the run of wind in tall grass" *(The American Rhythm)*. "It leaves a track, a mold, by which our every mode of expression is shaped." N. Scott Momaday prays the reciprocity of earth and artist, as he crafts verse turquoise, a remembered gift of love:

> I will bring corn for planting
> and we will make fire
> Children will come to your breast
> You will heal my heart
> I speak your name many times
> The wild cane remembers your name.

Language is believed regenerative, even sacred, and makes things happen; a beloved's name heals, through the natural act of speaking, or in the silence after. By way of parallel placement and balanced perception, so too Austin called attention to "streams of rhythmic sights and sounds" in traditional reverence for physical settings, the indigenous cultural cadences—shifting winds, rushing streams, lapping lake waters, soughing pines, chattering aspen, whispering corn, or sighing shortgrass. Her passionate absorption in the land, natively inspired and perhaps dated (to a skeptic's slant), rallied modernists like Williams, Frost, Hemingway, and Fitzgerald, later Welty, Faulkner, Cather, and Jeffers, to consider their own native, local origins. Regional bounty filled the land everywhere. And shimmering angles of perception were patterned in slants of light, the horizon-shifting sun, or the ever shape-changing cycles of the moon.

Again, in his first published poem, "Earth and I Gave You Turquoise," Momaday finds solace in the patterns of native kinship:

> My young brother's house is filled
> I go there to sing
> We have not spoken of you
> but our songs are sad
> When Moon Woman goes to you
> I will follow her white way

Austin discovered poetic cadences in geological sweeps—valley sloughs, to prairie horizons, to mountain striations, to coastal fractures or unbroken sandy shores. If short on hauteur, she was long on climatological zeal, the healing physicality of the native landscape. The contemporary Kiowa poet honors these ongoing traditions, as he grieves personal loss:

> Tonight they dance near Chinle
>   by seven elms
> There your loom whispered beauty
>   They will eat mutton
> and drink coffee till morning
> You and I will not be there

Starting from a Pueblo vision of human and natural exchanges, Mary Austin went on to write her own life-story, *Earth Horizon*. "In the Rain Song of the Sia, Earth Horizon is the incalculable blue ring of sky meeting earth, which is the source of experience." The vision is tactile, physically inspiring, "rays of earth energy running together from the horizon to the middle place where the heart of man, the recipient of experience, is established, and there treasured." Horizon to radial center, this four-winds balance of energies places the human heart within natural forces, the spirit everywhere in the world. Hers is visionary hyperbole, granted, but fundamentally consistent with tribal ceremony. Native healers see design in spiderwebs, offering in anthills, grace in birdsong, not at odds with Blake's seeing eternity in a grain of sand or Whitman's reading his text in "leaves" of grass.

The renewed landscape of America flows artistically in all diversity and direction, moving rhythmically, collectively, even when seeming to be fractured. Observing the natural miracles of daily renewal, the Kiowa poet completes his vision of beloved reunion:

> I saw a crow by Red Rock
>   standing on one leg
> It was the black of your hair
>   The years are heavy
> I will ride the swiftest horse
> You will hear the drumming hooves

The ending strikes a romantic, even spiritual chord, as seen through our postmodern disillusions. Ceremonial aesthetics are out of fashion, sadly, in a fallen world; yet through native eyes, these song-lines arc toward a New World vision of the Garden, First Man and First Woman rejoined. Austin scratched for defenses of an American rhythm against the disbelievers. In the "stress recurrence" of physical bodies, she argued—breathing and heart-beating, tapping fingers or toes, rising or walking—came the muscular rhythms, the pulses of "the blood and the breath" that cadenced voice, "the breath, the *lub*-dub, *lub*-blub of the heart." William Carlos Williams spoke this way of the "variable foot" in natural American speech patterns, cadencing his triadic verse lines, consistent with tidal wave actions on the shore or wind traces in sand dunes. From Whitman and Lawrence, through Austin and Williams, down to Snyder, Bly, Creeley, and Ginsberg, the new American poem became a projective field of action, humanistically, as Charles Olson would see it, an "open form" in the natural world.

No less than Ezra Pound held that poetry derived from musical cadences, as music evolved from dance rhythms, and the farther they strayed, the less charged the poetic line. Franz Boas picked up the thought in his summary of Native American "Literature, Music, and Dance" in *Primitive Art,* the text that spellbound Sylvia Plath thirty years later: "that song is older than poetry and that poetry has gradually emancipated itself from music." Following suit, Austin pointed to "ripples of energy" in ceremonial song-lines: "rhythm pattern, sound sequence, incremental thought rhythm, rhythmic clusters, cadenced phrasing," narratives "rippling like the swallowing muscles of the snake." These natural patterns lay rhizomic strata through native settings. "Every important word is a fist well fingered with syllables," Austin held along with Sapir, an interjective poetics from the bear's heart.

So today's Indian poets inherit tools and attitudes from both sides of the Buckskin Curtain. Scott Momaday owes much to Yvor Winters' formal training at Stanford, as he honors his Kiowa singing and storytelling grandmother, Aho. James Welch learned blank verse from Richard Hugo and surrealism from Cesar Vallejo, as he translated Blackfeet traditions into twentieth-century poetry and prose. Hybrid empowered from the strengths of both sides, these multivoiced Indians are "caught between the two windows," Mike Kabotie sees in his "transistor Hopis" art, finally transcultural. So, too, with literature. "American poetry must inevitably take," Austin prophesied, "at some point of its history, the mold of Amerind verse, which is the mold of the American experience shaped by the American environment." And here flows the landscape of literature, as it resurfaces in Native American poetry today. Judith Volborth, a mixed-blood Blackfeet raised in New York City, self-educated in the public library, lets her imagination whisper:

> The-One-Who-Scatters-Leaves-
> Across-The-Snow
>
>   has departed.
>
> The only sound now
>
>   the flute-player
>   rising in my ear.

The images are not ornamental, but drawn from hushed wind or rustling brush—they invoke an occasion of quickened listening and attuned feeling. This alertness draws on deeper voices, the resonances of life lived beneath the skin's crust.

Native American poems hold dialogue with spirits in the land, not One-Self; a person prays "for" the Mother Earth and Father Sky, Paula Allen says, not "to" them. As with Moses humbled before the burning bush, or Blake catching ecstatic whispers of myths, or Dante moved to the bone by love, the language of these sacred textual moments is experience charged with meaning (to re-adapt Ezra Pound's modernist definition of literature, at all times, as "language charged with meaning"). Dreamer-of-the-Sun told Red Weasel, a Standing Rock Sioux, one hundred years ago, that he could pray with his mouth and be heard, "but if I *sing* the prayer it will be heard *sooner* by *Wakan Tanka*" (Densmore, *Teton Sioux Music*). No cultures ever stressed the need for spirit *and* form together, aesthetic *and* cultural fusion, more than Native Americans. "What you give, you get," Allen insists, the bear heart giving back.

The ranges of giving are stunning. From nila northSun's (*sic*) punk humor with its sassy talking back, to Scott Momaday's older symmetry, the terrain of invention and tradition covers pre-Columbian, oral-traditional times to postmodernist *lit crit:*

> *Earth* and *I* gave you *tur*quoise
> when *you walked sing*ing
> We *lived laugh*ing in *my house*
> and *told old sto*ries

The 7–5, 7–5 syllabic lines, no less than the traditional Chinese syllabics of Du Fu, gently sway between reversed trochaic and expected iambic rhythms, all the while spondaically insisting on counterbalance in conjunction. This rhythmic conjoining comes both through parallelism (the repeated "and") and gerund ("-ing," the object-in-motion of active endings). The binary function of the verbal noun is to keep people and things moving in ceremonial patterns. Earth *and* the earth-born, in Momaday's poetic, participate organically; nature and artist both receive and reveal what-is, an aesthetics of the real. There is grief here, sincere loss, but against individual grief play the timeless singing and laughing and storytelling, binding the people against their common loss.

Bouncing along with nila northSun in "moving camp too far," the rhythms are only more syncopated, compared with Momaday, more street-smart and hip:

> i can travel to pow wows
> in campers & winnebagos
> i can eat buffalo meat
> at the tourist burger stand

> i can dance to indian music
>   rock-n-roll hey-a-hey-
> i can
>   & unfortunately
>   i do

The newer Indian poets use, reinvent, and at times trash White culture and English, turning the language back on itself in ironic subversion.

Paula Allen experiments with polyphonic couplets, feeling delicately for a mediative frontier adjoining Whites and Indians:

> and i am not stone but shell,
> blue and fragile. dropped,
>
> i splatter. spill the light
> all over the stone
>
> nothing that can be mended.

Luci Tapahonso code-switches Navajo to English, trading on insistent differences, chuckling between cultures with her mother's brother, giving her polysyllabic native ear a bivalent range:

> Ah-h, that's the one that does it for me.
> Very good coffee.
>
> I sit down again and he tells me
>   some coffee has no kick but
>
> this one is the one.
> It does it good for me.

A simple pleasure, a quick look at Navajo life as it is lived.

In these poetries each voice is original, all share multicultural slippage and reconnection. Every voice rings true, within heterogeneous tribal contexts, far less party-line than *Poetry* magazine, for example, or City Lights Press. Channeling the unvoiced charge through a special voice, Allen offers, each "poem shapes space," as a coiled bowl or basket contains the literal significance of its material and space. The tare and texture of Red English comes up off the page, an interplay of image and rhythm, syllable and sequence. Barney Bush, cowboy-Indian poet, sings of "My Horse And a Jukebox":

> Powwow
> and I am in your
>   north country again
>   great beauty that holds

> the medicine to make
> people crazy

The ceremony of poetry is to bond and to heal, as with ancient tribal ritual, to purify and to inspire, to humble and to empower. The phrasing bows from an *other* world of silenced older texts, resurrections as real and pressing as daily prayer. Charged in laughter, immediate with love, the lines strike a reader less as verbal performance, more as cultural rite and human reality. Craft serves context ("Ask the fact for the form," Emerson added). The poets are not afraid to *get down:* John Trudell addresses "God" intertribally from the streets,

> I hope you don't mind
> but I would like to talk to you
> . . .
> I don't mean
>
> to be disrespectful
> but you know
> how it is
> My people have their own ways

Not free-floating, free-spaced art-for-art's sake, but verse muscled with the equivalent of tribal declaration, ritual poise, and personal tough love— these poems count deeply. Translative form and tradition recharge the lines:

> Becoming strong on this earth is a lesson
> in not floating, in becoming less transparent,
> in becoming an animal shape against the sky.

From Linda Hogan's natural graces in the right ways of nature—praying for the daily voice, fruitful cycles of crops, guardian animals, and healthy children—to Leslie Silko's talk-lines with deep needs to know the stories of her characters, to Simon Ortiz's lyric concisions among cut lines and incisive images, to James Welch's stunning honesty, come a persistent and real poetics of courage and candor. There is nothing silly or self-indulgent about beauty or form in the works. Everything earns its place, its traditional footing, even sacred clowning, *koshares* to *heyokas,* false-face fools to tricky ravens, coyotes to spiders, tribal gossip to the everyday lives of the people (recipes, lullabies, scandals, hunting and working songs, burial laments and birth lyrics). Subjects move from historical angers to spiritual intercessions by way of powers that "Move-what-moves." The presence of unseen life-forms fills the margins: shifting winds, seasonal through-lines, river currents, lake depths, buds' secrets, hibernative promises, the seasonal return of birds, the continuances of language, prayer, song, laughter, and dance.

Geary Hobson speaks with great good humor of escaped buffalo at the Albuquerque airport,

> —roam on, brothers. . . .

Ancestral powers move through personal lines, *are* the voices of the poets. "All my relatives," the Lakota call out, *Mitakuye oyasin*, relative to all.

A word on this collection: the terms of inclusion & exclusion are simply two people's tastes and time—forgive our limitations. Paula Allen made up a list of poems, as I did, and we worked out a collated collection. The choices are not so much representative, as selective, in sampling Indian poetry for uninitiated readers, first published in the 1992 *Jacaranda Review*. Margot Astrov must have faced a similar dilemma of what to include, then what she could say in *The Winged Serpent* in 1945, as A. Grove Day wondered just how far he could go a few years later in *The Sky Clears*. We need texts to work with, a body of poems, before we can begin to say anything helpful around them. In the menu of the moment recipes could change, palates shift, harvests vary. Nevertheless, these poems represent the talent out there, the conversations these days in Indian Country. The voices come from rhythms at work in contemporary native poetry, the unbroken spirits of surviving Native Americans—the diversity, energy, multiplicity, and complexity of our native Americas.

From nurturing compassion to bitter humor, the verse can be at once comic, ironic, and sad. "This late in the 20th century," Sherman Alexie begins the collection, "There are so many illusions I need to believe." And from a previous generation, Ray Young Bear speaks of leaving,

> i pressed my fingers
> against the window, leaving
> five clear answers of the day
> before it left, barking down the road.

"Yes," the elder Mary TallMountain consoles her last wolf from a hospital bed, "I know what they have done."

Poetic lines cross boundaries here, meet conflict head-on with what Paula Allen calls "right-on perception." She adds, "it's the way we are, regardless of where we are"—in country or city, on or off the rez, traditional or acculturative, younger or elder, breed or blood. Tribal peoples "write with and for the Indian world," in all kinds of voices. These Native Americans challenge and redefine and reassert their places in America, after five hundred years of assault and displacement. In their work we can recognize and renew freshly the *native* in American culture. Leslie Silko hears ancient bear voices singing:

Don't be afraid
    we love you
    we've been calling you
    all this time.

Go ahead
    turn around
    see the shape
    of your footprints
    in the sand.

SHERMAN ALEXIE *(Coeur d'Alene-Spokane)*

Seattle, 1987

This late in the 20th century
I cannot look at a lake
without wondering what's beneath it:

drowned horses   snapping turtles   cities of protected bones.

Yesterday, the sun rose
so quickly on cable television I thought it a new day   beginning
but it was just another camera trick.

How the heart changes
when this city fills with strange animals
the reservation never predicted

animals formed by the absence of song.

Downtown today, a street magician
so clumsy I fell in love
and threw a dollar bill into his top hat.

There are so many illusions I need to believe.

PAULA GUNN ALLEN (*Laguna Pueblo-Sioux-Lebanese*)

Something Fragile, Broken

1.
i had seen something
i had wanted

and sorrow is not to enter
into it:

a sparrow falling: a tiny
fragile egg, crushed

it was in the grass then
fallen, dead.

reached out, that hand,
palm open, such care

fallen anyway, all the way
to the ground

where it smashed.
the slate stones that ringed

the lily pond of my grandmother
held it, blue and broken.

sorrow was not to enter
into it. but it did.

and i am not stone but shell,
blue and fragile. dropped,

i splatter. spill the light
all over the stone

nothing that can be mended.

2.
sorrow was not to enter this

but it did. and i
was not to weep, or

think such things or
let you see that this,

which was not to be entered,
was born and broken before

entering. not in tears
exactly, not fallen in

that way, but still
and i knew what would not

be spoken. a circle that
would not be broken

shattered anyway, or died.
like ripples on the lake,

when the stone has sunk
deep beneath the surface,

die. sorrow has no part
in it. some things just

don't go on. some circles
come undone. some sparrows

fall. sometimes sorrow
in spite of resolution,

enters in.

CHARLES BALLARD *(Quapaw-Cherokee)*

Time Was the Trail Went Deep

Time was the trail went deep
From the granite ledge of the Verdigris
—On west to rivers flat
And a rolling sea of grass

We followed the Arkansas to New Town
Of the creeks and veered off
To low hills in the north
Where we camped in those final days

Having walked to never look back
Having talked to carry through
We disbanded and went no more
To choose finally is the Indian way

But time was the trail went deep
Into a green and vibrant land

JIM BARNES (Choctaw)

Tracking Rabbits: Night

The moon in your eyes is best.
Believe it:

light and shadows
stand distinct.

The thing to know
is how to blink

and keep tied to tracks
when the ground grows granite hard.

Take a parallel course: dead on. The tracks
are blue steel, and you are to catch the moon.

Beware long curves; never cut across.
A whistle will sometimes slow your prey.

When you are close you will have to
link up with his shadow,

pant with him,
stop with him,

snort at a crossing
he distrusts.

When he heads home
ride him into his steamy bed,

put your hot hands
on his dark hot head,

call him brother,
semblance, prey.

PETER BLUE CLOUD (Mohawk)

Coyote, Coyote, Please Tell Me

What is a shaman?

A shaman I don't know
anything about.
I'm a doctor, myself.
When I use medicine,
it's between me,
my patient,
and the Creation.

      Coyote, Coyote, Please tell me
What is power?

It is said that power
is the ability to start
your chainsaw
with one pull.

      Coyote, Coyote, Please tell me
What is magic?

Magic is the first taste
of ripe strawberries and
magic is a child dancing
in a summer's rain.

      Coyote, Coyote, Please tell me
Why is Creation?

Creation is because I
went to sleep last night
with a full stomach,
and when I woke up
this morning,
everything was here.

      Coyote, Coyote, Please tell me
Who you belong to?

According to the latest
survey, there are certain
persons who, in poetic
or scholarly guise,

have claimed me like
a conqueror's prize.

    Let me just say
once and for all,
just to be done:
    Coyote,
he belongs to none.

BARNEY BUSH *(Shawnee-Cayuga)*

My Horse And a Jukebox

Powwow
and I am in your
    north country again
    great beauty that holds
    the medicine to make
    people crazy
I look for you in the
    early morning cause
    I didn't 49 last night
    they say you will be
    coming—
In the dust around
    the arena or somewhere
    in woodsmoke
    I'll sort of be watching
    —we both know—
    about how nights turn cold
    the leaves fall too soon
    and the grey mystery
    of glancing at each other
over pool tables and
    jukeboxes
It was a good foreign
    feeling walking up the
    street carrying food
    orange maple leaves falling
    at our feet
and a carload of
    Oklahoma Indians
    pull up—want to know
    what we're doing
    a good feeling the
    cold lake country
    where I keep missing
    you
and hear only rumors
after you've gone———.

CAROLYN DUNN *(Creek-Seminole-Cherokee)*

Sleeping with the Enemy

I.
I say Nissei
You say
Africa
hey
Little boy with
skin so dark
eyes shaped almond
dark like shiny onyx
Mama Africa's upon us.
You wear your father's mask
face dark yet
fair
and call for the one thing
you never had.

From somewhere deep within
I thought I heard a song.
"Send me your 1000 paper cranes,"
cracked white bones
brittle against the
terraced tiles of
home.
Skin falling like
leaves
leaves turned to ash
in the flicker of an eye.
She sleeps with the enemy
eyes dark of the blackest night.
The sky turned to heaven
if there's anything left.
The world ends with the
tiniest whimper
1000 paper cranes
crumpled in between
snow capped
stones.
Underneath
we're all bones.

ANITA ENDREZZE *(Yaqui)*

Return of the Wolves

All through the valley, the people are whispering
the wolves are returning, returning
to the narrow edge of our fields, our dreams.
They are returning the cold to us.
They are wearing the crowns of ambush,
offering the rank and beautiful snow-shapes
of dead sheep, an old man too deep in his cups,
the trapper's gnawed hands, the hunter's tongue.
They are returning the whispers of our lovers,
whose promises are less enduring than the wolves.

Their teeth are carving the sky into delicate antlers,
carving dark totems full of moose dreams: meadows
where light grows with the marshgrass and water
is a dark wolf under the hoof.
Their teeth are carving our children's names
on every trail, carving night into a different bone—
one that seems to be part of my body's long memory.

Their fur is gathering shadows, gathering
the thick-teethed white-boned howl of their tribe,
gathering the broken-deer smell of wind
into their longhouse of pine and denned earth,
gathering me also, from my farmhouse
with its golden light and empty rooms, to the cedar
(that also howls its woody name to the cave of stars),
where I am silent as a bow unstrung
and my scars are not from loving wolves.

HARRY FONSECA (Maidu)

Coyote

I

Some say that Coyote first appeared on a raft
That Coyote created the world
That Coyote is very old the first one
That Coyote put the stars in the universe
That Coyote fucked up the planets
That Coyote is the giver and taker of life
That Coyote stole fire for the people
That Coyote can change the seasons.

II

Some say that Coyote dances in a feather cape trimmed with flicker quills
That Coyote plays a flute and is the best dancer around
That Coyote has more clamshell and magnesite beads than you can imagine
That Coyote can make redbud burst into bloom by staring at it
That Coyote wanted to be a falling leaf and tried it
That Coyote was looking for figs and followed a male
That Coyote is a poet
That Coyote is a fool

III

Some say that Coyote is on the streets and in the alleys
That Coyote lives in L.A. and San Francisco and eats out of garbage cans
That Coyote talks to his asshole and usually takes its advice
That Coyote howls at the moon because it never stays the same
That Coyote doesn't like change
That Coyote is change

IV

Some say Coyote wears a black leather jacket and hightop tennis shoes
That Coyote thinks Rose is a good singer
That Coyote eats frybread peanut butter and jelly
That Coyote will use you if you don't watch out
That Coyote will teach you if you let him
That Coyote is very young the new one
That Coyote is a survivor

Some say Coyote is a myth
Some say Coyote is real

I say Coyote is
I say Coyote
I say Coyote

NIA FRANCISCO (Navajo)

Roots of Blue Bells

Female spider
swept her legends into her palms
    then   gently blew on it
           like   powder
she blew   dampness
       of her breath
     felt in the southern wind

     Powdered roots
of blue bells   water cress leaves
       blossoms
and rosemary shrubs
only the she-bear knows the mixtures
for she   sunbaked them
high on the mountain top in Crystal

     She-spider
blew the powder
onto the deep   deep wounds
    and holocaust of USA
    and global pains
then
she sat
on life-giving mountains
    while she spun
webs   and webs
    of unspoken legends
into looms of Milky Way

She spun
the blackness of Universe
as clothing for the twins
     Night
who is the twin of day
     Day
who is the twin of night

MARY ANN GERARD (Blackfeet)

The Bear

I was at this powwow.
My baby was wrapped in a star quilt.
She was sucking on a pink plastic baby bottle,
sleeping through the drum.

I was in the prison
of being in a crowd, alone.

The fry bread was hard and dry,
but I tore a piece off
and saw you "straight dance" by.

You wore a grizzly bear's Spirit.
When you looked at me
strawberry vines grew and curled
around my ankles,
fragrant twisting tendrils
whipped the fringe of my orange shawl.
Then you went on by.

I turned around to see
if some other woman sat behind me,
but no one was there except Grandpa Buffalo,
sleeping like my own baby, Magpie.

I have never kissed a bear on the nose,
but later that night
grizzly bear fur warmed me to sleep
after we fed on strawberries
wilder than any bobcat spirit
could conjure up.

JOY HARJO (Creek)

Eagle Poem

To pray you open your whole self
To sky, to earth, to sun, to moon
To one whole voice that is you.
And know there is more
That you can't see, can't hear
Can't know except in moments
Steadily growing, and in languages
That aren't always sound but other
Circles of motion.
Like eagle that Sunday morning
Over Salt River. Circled in blue sky
In wind, swept our hearts clean
With sacred wings.
We see you, see ourselves and know
That we must take the utmost care
And kindness in all things.
Breathe in, knowing we are made of
All this, and breathe, knowing
We are truly blessed because we
Were born, and die soon, within a
True circle of motion,
Like eagle rounding out the morning
Inside us.
We pray that it will be done
In beauty.
In beauty.

LANCE HENSON *(Cheyenne)*

anniversary poem for the cheyennes who died
at sand creek

    when we have come is long way
    past cold grey fields
    past stone markers etched with the
    names they left us

    we will speak for the first time to the season
    to the ponds

    touching the dead grass

    our voices the colour of watching

GEARY HOBSON *(Cherokee-Quapaw-Chickasaw)*

BUFFALO POEM #1
(or)
ON HEARING THAT A SMALL HERD OF BUFFALO
HAS "BROKEN LOOSE" AND IS "RUNNING WILD"
AT THE ALBUQUERQUE AIRPORT—SEPTEMBER 26, 1975

—roam on, brothers . . .

LINDA HOGAN (Chickasaw)

Blessings

Blessed
are the injured animals
for they live in his cages.
But who will heal my father,
tape his old legs for him?

Here's the bird with the two broken wings
and her feathers are white as an angel
and she says goddamn stirring grains
—in the kitchen. When the birds fly out
he leaves the cages open
and she kisses his brow for such
good works.

　　Work he says
　　all your life
　　and at the end
　　you don't own even a piece of land.

Blessed are the rich
for they eat meat every night.
They have already inherited the earth.

For the rest of us, may we just live
long enough
and unwrinkle our brows,
may we keep our good looks
and some of our teeth
and our bowels regular.

Perhaps we can go live places
a rich man can't inhabit,
in the sunfish and jackrabbits,
in the cinnamon colored soil,
the land of red grass
and red people
in the valley
of the shadow of Elk
who aren't there.

　　He says the damned earth is so old
　　and wobbles so hard

98

you'd best hang on to everything.
Your neighbors steal what little you got.

Blessed
are the rich
for they don't have the same old
Everyday to put up with
like my father
who's gotten old
     Chickasaw
     chikkih asachi, which means
they left as a tribe not a very great while ago.
They are always leaving,
those people.

Blessed
are those who listen
when no one is left to speak.

MIKE KABOTIE (Hopi)

Transistor Windows

Sitting by kitchen window
gazing over Hopi village of
Shungopavi, named after a
spring where reeded-plants grow
  and
watching autumn skies light up
with orange as the September
sun sinks into the deep abyss of
the mighty Grand Canyon.

The blue of evening creeps
over mesas and apartment
dwellings of the Hopi as
children play and shout in
the cool of purple dusk.

To the east, Mishongnovi and
Walpi light up and twinkle
as Shungopavi quiets down
for evening supper.

Inside mother's house, once my nest,
beans boiled for supper and green
chili burned and smothered us with
choking smoke, as we all laughed
with tears in our eyes.

Relaxing, we turn to watch the world
through television windows; seeing
bloated black children starve in
Africa; Arabs and Jewish people
hunting each other on barren
deserts with devastating arsenals
  as
lovely young American maidens sell us
the stunned viewer on the secrets of
youth, as my aging mother and aunt
chuckle and crack Hopi jokes.

Outside, kachina cloud-priests have
gathered over the Hopi mesas, lighting

the skies with bright lightning and
crashing thunder that a deaf-mute German
caught so well in his sonatas.

Caught between the two windows, I pondered
the confusions and hunger of the modern
transistor Hopi.

ADRIAN LOUIS *(Northern Paiute)*

Because

Because I have a choker of trading post beads
and an ancient ribbon shirt
stored in some forgotten box
and because these city streets are cancerous
and I have caromed off too much concrete
today I bought you some violets.

In the flower shop
the pruned plants ache
disdaining man's best intentions.
We stroll in dusk's park where a toadstool sprouts,
ephemeral and phallic, I must be its sun
and the warmth I call love
can be only allusion
to the secreted why of common addition
because I have a choker of trading post beads
and an ancient ribbon shirt
stored in some remembered box.

N. SCOTT MOMADAY (Kiowa)

Earth and I Gave You Turquoise

Earth and I gave you turquoise
   when you walked singing
We lived laughing in my house
   and told old stories
You grew ill when the owl cried
We will meet on Black Mountain

I will bring corn for planting
   and we will make fire
Children will come to your breast
   You will heal my heart
I speak your name many times
The wild cane remembers you

My young brother's house is filled
   I go there to sing
We have not spoken of you
   but our songs are sad
When Moon Woman goes to you
I will follow her white way

Tonight they dance near Chinle
   by seven elms
There your loom whispered beauty
   They will eat mutton
and drink coffee till morning
You and I will not be there

I saw a crow by Red Rock
   standing on one leg
It was the black of your hair
   The years are heavy
I will ride the swiftest horse
You will hear the drumming hooves

moving camp too far

i can't speak of
   many moons
   moving camp on travois
i can't tell of
   the last great battle
   counting coup or
   taking scalps
i don't know what it
   was to hunt buffalo
   or do the ghost dance
but
i can see an eagle
   almost extinct
   on slurpee plastic cups
i can travel to pow wows
   in campers & winnebagos
i can eat buffalo meat
   at the tourist burger stand
i can dance to indian music
   rock-n-roll hey-a-hey-
i can
   & unfortunately
   i do

SIMON J. ORTIZ *(Acoma Pueblo)*

"And The Land Is Just As Dry"
line from a song by Peter LaFarge

The horizons are still mine.
The ragged peaks,
the cactus, the brush, the hard brittle plants,
these are mine and yours.
We must be humble with them.

The green fields,
a few, a very few,
Interstate Highway 10 to Tucson,
Sacaton, Bapchule,
my home is right there
off the road to Tucson,
before the junction.
On the map, it is yellow
and dry, very dry.
Breathe tough, swallow,
look for rain and rain.

Used to know Ira, he said,
his tongue slow, spit on his lips,
in Mesa used to chop cotton.
Coming into Phoenix from the north,
you pass by John Jacobs.
Who pays them $5 per day in sun,
enough for quart of wine on Friday.
Ira got his water alright.
Used to know him in Mesa in the sun.
My home is brown adobe
and tin roof and lots of children,
broken down cars, that pink Ford
up on those railroad ties.
Still paying for it
and it's been two years since
it ran, motor burned out,
had to pull it back from Phoenix.

Gila River, the Interstate sign says
at the cement bridge over bed
full of brush and sand and rusty cans.

Where's the water, the water
which you think about sometimes
in empty desperation?
It's in those green, very green fields
which are not mine.

You call me a drunk Indian, go ahead.

CARTER REVARD *(Osage)*

Driving in Oklahoma

On humming rubber along this white concrete
    lighthearted between the gravities
of source and destination like a man
    halfway to the moon
    in his bubble of tuneless whistlin
at seventy miles an hour from the windvents,
    over prairie swells rising
    and falling, over the quick offramp
that drops to its underpass and the truck
    thundering beneath as I cross
with the country music twanging out my windows,
    I'm grooving down the highway feeling
technology is freedom's other name when
    —a meadowlark
    comes sailing across my windshield
    with breast shining yellow
    and five notes pierce
    the windroar like a flash
    of nectar on mind
gone as the country music swells up and
    drops me wheeling down
    my notch of cement-bottomed sky
    between home and away
    and wanting
to move again through country that a bird
    has defined wholly with song
    and maybe next time see how
he flies so easy, when he sings.

WENDY ROSE *(Hopi-Miwok)*

The endangered roots of a person

I remember lying awake
in a Phoenix motel. Like that
I remember coming apart accidentally
like an isolated hunk of campfire soot
cornered by time into a cave.
I live even now
in an archaeological way.

> Becoming strong on this earth is a lesson
> in not floating, in becoming less transparent,
> in becoming an animal shape against the sky.

We were born
to lose our eyes in the Sun Dance
and send out lengths of fishline
for the clouds, reel them in
and smooth away all the droughts
of the world.

> Sometimes Medicine People shake their hands
> over you and it is this: to drop your bones
> into the sand, to view yourself
> bursting through the city
> like a brown flashflood.
> The healing of the roots
> is that thunderhead-reeling:
> they change and pale
> but they are not in danger now.

That same morning
I went for coffee down the street
and held it, blowing dreams
through the steam, watching silver words
bead up on my skin. The Hand-trembler said
I belong here. I fit in this world
as the red porcelain mug
merges in the heat with my hand.

> On some future dig
> they'll find me like this
> uncovered where I knelt
> piercing together the flesh
> that was scattered in the mesa wind
> at my twisted-twin birth.

CAROL LEE SANCHEZ *(Laguna Pueblo-Sioux-Lebanese)*

Conversations from the Nightmare

we have mounted
the burning ash
and counted jawbones
in the pits of

darkened dead
and dying all around

our striped bombs
a-bursting comfort
and ease
trip through
the red white and blue of

darkened dead
and dying all around.

melted leaves will
mix with bones
carrion fish will
travel far
to cover this dust
and ash of

darkened dead
and dying all around.

a concrete
high-rise tombstone
Old Glory and napalm
Phnom-Penh and

darkened dead
and dying all around.

MARY TALLMOUNTAIN *(Koyukon Athapaskan)*

The Last Wolf

the last wolf hurried toward me
through the ruined city
and I heard his baying echoes
down the steep smashed warrens
of Montgomery Street and past
the few ruby-crowned highrises
left standing
their lighted elevators useless

passing the flicking red and green
of traffic signals
baying his way eastward
in the mystery of his wild loping gait
closer the sounds in the deadly night
through clutter and rubble of quiet blocks

I heard his voice ascending the hill
and at last his low whine as he came
floor by empty floor to the room
where I sat
in my narrow bed looking west, waiting
I heard him snuffle at the door and as
I watched
he trotted across the floor

he laid his long gray muzzle
on the spare white spread
and his eyes burned yellow
his small dotted eyebrows quivered

Yes, I said.
I know what they have done.

Hills Brothers Coffee

My uncle is a small man
in Navajo we call him little father
   my mother's brother.

He doesn't know English but
   his name in the white way is Tom Jim.
   He lives about a mile or so
   down the road from our house.

One morning he sat in the kitchen
drinking coffee
   I just came over, he said,
   the store is where I'm going to.

He tells me about how my mother seems to be gone
everytime he comes over.
   Maybe she sees me coming
   then runs and jumps in her car
   and speeds away!
He says smiling.
We both laugh just to think of my mother
   jumping in her car and speeding.

I pour him more coffee and
   he spoons in sugar and cream until
   it looks almost like a chocolate shake
   then he sees the coffee can.
   Oh, that's the coffee with
   the man in the dress, like a church man.
   Ah-h, that's the one that does it for me.
   Very good coffee.

I sit down again and he tells me
   some coffee has no kick but
   this one is the one.
   It does it good for me.

I pour us both a cup and
   while we wait for my mother,
   his eyes crinkle with the smile
   and he says

yes, ah yes, this is the very one
(putting in more cream and sugar).

So I usually buy Hills Brothers coffee
once or sometimes twice a day
I drink a hot coffee and

it sure does it for me.

JUDITH VOLBORTH *(Blackfeet)*

Native Winter
(for Brenda)

It is dusk

the water-bugs
gathered the shadows
close to them at the
center of the lake.

The Crows

have ceased their
gossip and

The-One-Who-Scatters-Leaves-
Across-The-Snow

has departed.

The only sound now

the flute-player
rising in my ear.

In My Lifetime

This day the children of Speakthunder
run the wrong man, a saint unable
to love a weasel way, able to smile
and drink the wind that makes the others go.
Trees are ancient in his breath.
His bleeding feet tell a story of run
the sacred way, chase the antelope naked
till it drops, the odor of run
quiet in his blood. He watches cactus
jump against the moon. Moon is speaking
woman to the ancient fire. Always woman.

His sins were numerous, this wrong man.
Buttes were good to listen from. With thunder-
hands his father shaped the dust, circled
fire, tumbled up the wind to make a fool.
Now the fool is dead. His bones go back
so scarred in time, the buttes are young to look
for signs that say a man could love his fate,
that winter in the blood is one sad thing.

His sins—I don't explain. Desperate in my song,
I run these woman hills, translate wind
to mean a kind of life, the child of Speakthunder
are never wrong and I am rhythm to strong medicine.

ROBERTA HILL WHITEMAN (*Oneida*)

Patterns

If I could track you down to have you taste
the strawberry shaded by beggar's green,
the winter wheat, remote as sunlight
through low moving clouds, we'd face
the squash blossom, fixed in its quiet temple,
and breathe in rhythm to our own beginnings.

Instead I step without your echo
over the cucumbers' tapestry of tendril
and woolly stem. The corn, my blind children,
mingle with wind and I walk naked
into their midst to let them brush my hips
with searching fingers, their cuffs alive with rain.

When I ask if they are happy,
a few by the fence whisper "Yes." It comes
through the rows, yes again
and again yes. My feet take root
in rings of corn light; the green earth
shouts more green against the weighted sky,

and under poppies of ash, patterns emerge:
lilacs collecting dark beneath the sheen of elms,
cedar buds tinting air with memories of frost,
a tanager's cry deep inside the windbreak,
my life's moire of years. When my jailers,
these brief words, fumble with their bony keys,

I listen to the arguments of flies, to the long
drawn-out call of doves, for lessons in endurance.
Moths, twilight in their wings, dance above the oatleaf
and I know you stand above the same muted sea,
brooding over smoke that breaks
around hollyhock's uneven pinnacles.

For a moment, we are together,
where salt-stunted trees glory in the sun, where verbena
and jasmine light the wind with clean tomorrows.
I felt us there, felt myself and not-myself there.
We lived those promises ridiculed in solemn days.
We lived with a hunger only solitude can afford.

ʒ(•)ʒ

(Native) American Verses

If there are then complex Native/American poetries and postmodernist fusions, what are the diagonal poetics, *singing with a different heart?* Writers come of disparate minds, swayed by idiosyncratic visions and divergent drumbeats. The American rhythms, mountain to woodland, plain to sea, remain diverse and variable, tribe to tribe, margin to mainstream. And tribal peoples stand sovereign, "domestic dependent nations," within post-colonial economies and dominant technologies, not to mention native writers under the literary thumb of the Great Tradition, Euro-American critical academia, and the publishing industry. How does a verse dialogue *within* American cultures line up today?

> A day!
> The wings of the earth
> lift and fall
> to the groans, the cold, savage thumpings of a heart.

GALWAY KINNELL, "GOING HOME BY LAST LIGHT"

Galway Kinnell, Irish-American poet, was born in 1927, a boom-or-bust year at the peak of the modernist renaissance, in a Rhode Island place deriving its name, Pawtucket, from the Algonkian. Along with Sharon Olds, he teaches creative writing in the NYU graduate school on an island called *Manahatta,* once a Delaware Indian thoroughfare. A wandering Western Hemispheric native, Kinnell has made a courageous life of words in a land where such work is suspect. He has received distinguished awards, among them the fabled MacArthur "genius grant," a Pulitzer and an American Book Award for *Selected Poems* (1982), the Shelley Memorial Award from the Poetry Society of America in 1973, and the 1974 Award of Merit from the American Academy of Arts and Letters. Despite these honors, rumor has it, he is still followed to his readings by a packaged suit in the mail. In some sense, then, Galway Kinnell represents contemporary American poetry coming out of modernism, wrinkled suit and all.

Kinnell has translated major French writers—Bonnefoy, Hardy, Goll, Villon—and published a novel, *Black Light*. Since 1960, he has been principally known for his original, searching verse: *What a Kingdom It Was* (1960), *Flower Herding on Mount Monadnock* (1964), *Body Rags* (1968), *First Poems 1946–1954* (1971), *The Book of Nightmares* (1971), *The Avenue Bearing the Initial of Christ into the New World* (1974), *Mortal Acts, Mortal Words* (1980), *Selected Poems* (1982), *The Past* (1985), *When One Has Lived a Long Time Alone* (1990), and *Three Books* (1993).

A distant New Jersey godfather, William Carlos Williams, asked pointedly some years back, "Good Christ what is / a poet—if any / exists?" Iconoclastically American, the question takes us to the origins of culture. Among world ancients, the poet was a powerful sage, preserver of tradition, medium, healer, lawgiver, teacher, holy one: the Taoist prophet of mystic pragmatics, the Confucian collector of common wisdoms, as Pound proselytized, the Homeric singer of epic tales, the Gaelic advisor to the king. These pre-poets were what Shelley, among the first moderns two thousand years later, saw as "antennae of the race." They registered, reified, and refined the language of "a man speaking to men," Wordsworth felt, "the real language of men in a state of vivid sensation" (Preface to the *Lyrical Ballads*). By the nineteenth century's end, Baudelaire came to regard poetry, in an elegy over Poe's tomb, as a means to distill *"mots de la tribu."* Eliot pressed the ferment further, to "purify the dialect of the tribe," and Williams vowed, contrariwise, to keep genuine "the speech of Polish others" in verse, "the language of the tribe." Pound insisted on the dance music behind all this metaphor and murmuring. To sing the tribal tongue, in short, collates miscellaneous eponyms for poetry, ancient to modern, immanent in the music of our common dialect, as Sitting Bull's Lakota still speak of *singing with the different heart of a bear*.

Galway Kinnell is the only poet in my thirty UCLA years, besides a sidewalk Allen Ginsberg, to *sing* his poetry, indeed, to chant *from the heart,* as we say, a verse vision of America that culminated with reciting "The Bear" over two decades ago in Los Angeles. His was a performance without a written text, and Kinnell changed my sense of the poetic word, giving poetry and its audience a true voice, "carried alive into the heart by passion," as Wordsworth prefaced his ballads, "homage paid to the native and naked dignity of man." The poet became the bear, internalized the wild, bit down on wild excrement, crawled inside the kill, and asked gut-wrenching questions of the blood spilled in words. Such is a Western organic poetics and the oral tradition of the "word sender" where I come from—the Lakota "sending a voice" to the "Power-that-Moves-moves," or *Takuskanskan,* on the northern Great Plains. Words, chanted and enchanting, carry us into the Real world, Dickinson might say, the moving One within this one of many worlds, many surfaces and diversions. Such words call on power, in the Native American tradition—healing, wisdom, beauty, goodness, truth, passion—all the "old" values or *hozhó*, as the Navajo say, the reciprocal balance of all good things. And this word-sending comes in response to what we must live with, unpoetically, a sometimes terrible beauty, in an all-too-often fallen mortal world, which Yeats saw as "the desolation of reality."

Today, every poet seems to be the "last" romantic, twisted visionary, or first *scop*, that is, "railing bard," as the Druidic poets were called in ancient Ireland, Celtic precursors of W. B. Yeats, Seamus Heaney, and Galway Kinnell. We live at the other end of an Adamic dream—face down in Dante's descent, estranged, our hearts devoured by terrible angels of love. It is a particular "New World" dilemma, a postmodernist stance, if you will, a skeptic's riff. The "conquest of America," according to Tzvetan Todorov, "heralds and establishes our present identity," for, so contends this philosopher-historian, "We are all the direct descendants of Columbus." Or we are children of Orpheus, Rilke might say farther back in the West, Greek chanter of losses in song-lines that chart our loss-as-gain. The first "American" book published in New England, only recall, was George Sandys's 1627 Jamestown translation of Ovid's *Metamorphosis,* where in Book 10 Orpheus loses Eurydice and gains his true elegiac voice at the cost of life. His animistic metamorphosis seems a western paradigm, a blues given.

Kinnell's American "fall" into the abyss of the westering mind, lost in history, takes him by way of Yeats's "foul rag-and-bone shop of the heart" to nightmares of war, open wounds, visionary drunks, street drifters and deadbeats, broken-hearted sows, gutted porcupines, and disemboweled bears. He walks the dirtied *C* avenues of Christ today, hears the cries of homeless urban survivors, staggering sundown dreamers who parse and wonder the poetics of sacrificial blood. Yvan Goll, in Jewish exile, came to New York City to die and write his New World *cri du coeur, Lackwanna Elegy* in 1943, the middle of the Second "Great" War. Kinnell translated Goll's lament at the end of the 1960s: "America / The tongues of your rivers burn with thirst," the poet prophesied, "The arms of your sequoias ask pity of the storms." Bearing "asphalt" eyes and a "mercury" head, an "Indian woman" with a rattlesnake in her teeth will come to exorcise the "white ghost" of racial hate:

> America beware of your past
> Of the Katchinas filled with menace.

No less than Hart Crane's invocation of Pocahontas in *The Bridge,* Goll's warning is a spirit howl worth heeding, a critical gender inflection. Kinnell's lines bridge a necessary Euro-American translation into present native voices: prophecy, challenge, introduction to modern American poetry and native difference.

NOT LIKE YOU

About twenty years ago my Laguna Pueblo friend, now UCLA feminist colleague, Paula Gunn Allen, was trying to explain Indian-White cultural differences. I knew the social science paradigms, for example, the 1957 Spindler Report which detailed personality types and sociocultural patterns as pantribal "Indian" characteristics—restraint, generosity, individual autonomy, stoicism, courage, natural awe, in-joking, immediate concerns, spirituality, and supernatural dependence. Better than that, I knew examples and exceptions, growing up in northwest Nebraska among Sioux and pioneer-cowboy types (see *Men Down West*). Educating me in native differences, the Buckskin Curtain threw up a barrier to frontier dialogue. "We're not like you, Ken," my Lakota brother, Mark, told me, over and over, by word and living context, and thus the *need*, personal and professional, we both felt, for our adoptive kinship and adult work.

But Paula, whom I met in Flagstaff in 1977, was a Laguna-Sioux-Lebanese woman from New Mexico. Hardly the northern plains warrior type, she was still a fierce native feminist to be reckoned with, listened to, taken seriously, early on known for a legendary poem, "A Cannon Between My Knees." Short and solid, curly-haired and firm-jawed, slow-eyed and hot-wired, she was nobody's Penelope or Pocahontas, nobody's fool, nobody's pushover.

"You know, Kenneth," Paula would say, voice crackling, "no two Indians are alike, and God knows, no tribe much like, or likes, another." Long pause, drag on her black cigarette, careful thought: "—but there *are* broad cultural differences that draw tribal peoples *together against* mainstream White thinking, the Tom Sawyer and Donald Duck stuff. We have a common enemy, you guys." She winked and put out her cigarette. "So let's get down to particulars."

Talking culture is like predicting weather—an educated guess, often a wing-and-a-prayer promise, tentative, revisable, but worth hazarding, if for no other reason than having some idea of how to dress for the streets. Alfonso Ortiz, the Tewa anthropologist traveling from the Southwest deserts to California coasts, always started our telephone conversations puzzling weather reports, just to guess what we were getting into. How do we get into culture? Barre Toelken boils his adoptive Navajo family's ethos down to "sacred reciprocation." This daily give-and-take of natural world and spirituality involves an interaction, Toelken says, something like rodents gathering blue juniper berries, children re-collecting the eaten-out shells and making "juniper eye" necklaces ("ghost beads," Anglos say) to ward off nightmares or to keep someone from getting lost in the dark. The interconnection of plant, animal, spirit, and human is key here, all in processive balance, seasonal bounty, rooted beauty, grounded goodness— *hozhó,* the Diné say.

Where I come from, to repeat, the Sioux talk of four-winds-balance and the "Power"-that-"Moves"-what-"moves," *Takuskanskan,* a four-by-four Prime Moving that inter-connects sun, moon, earth, wind, and so on, through *Wakán Tanka,* the Great Mystery, or *Tunkáshila,* the Grandfather Spirit. Everything's related, connected by odd and even symmetries that balance out, as the old-timers say, two-legged, four-legged, winged, crawling, and rooted beings. "Behold a good nation," Nick Black Elk says, "walking in a sacred manner in a good land!" Equally important, as Barre Toelken's Navajo father queries the Empire State Building, then a B-52, "How many sheep will it hold?" That is, how does *your* cultural frame-of-reference compute in *my* worldview?

Paula drew lines on several bar napkins and wrote above each column, *Native American Oral Tradition* and *Euro-American Textuality.* Opposite *Matriarchy* she wrote *Patriarchy,* then added, "You do know, I'm sure, that ninety-two percent of the tribes were matrifocal. Women have a powerful place of origin in Native America, don't you forget it. When we want a piano moved, we don't ask men, Pueblo women just move it." First son in a Presbyterian family of three boys, I kept my mouth shut, though I knew some hearty pioneer women who ploughed fields and roped calves. Opposite *Oral Transmission* Paula scribbled *Established Canon.*

"Storytelling and singing were passed on word-of-mouth, Momaday reminds us, one generation from extinction. The voice, the ear, the breath and heartbeat, the body—these human functions physicalized living tribal languages. Think of speaking, listening, and remembering as critical to cultural survival. How's that stack up against New York publishing houses and the Great Tradition? Machine in the Garden, eh, printing press down to personal computers?" Again, I shut up and nodded, though I'd grown up in a village without radio or TV and been teaching the art of the spoken voice as good writing for many years. "There's got to be a participant audience to keep the story going," Paula said with a raised eyebrow, "a call-and-response culture to continue the song."

I remembered a line from D. H. Lawrence, observing how everyone got caught up in the Cochiti Corn Dances, "No spectacle, no spectator."

"Yeah," Paula said, "all chorus, no soloists, no distance from stage to pit, eh? Shakespeare would like that, don't you think?"

Then she wrote *Complementary* on the oral side, *Conflictual* on the textual side. "Indian stories background crisis, mostly, Western fiction foregrounds heroic resolution. Tribal people don't like to fight over who wins, you see."

Well, yes, I did see, though this native dialogic seemed in itself a bit adver-

sarial, after all. Her brain in high gear, Paula went on, "Storytelling rein-
forces communal advocacy, novels plot adversarial confrontation. The sto-
ryteller merges with his participant audience on one side; the artist stays
isolated from the reader on the other, across the text." Peering directly
into my face, she asked, "Do you get it?"

"Well, sort of," I hedged, "connection against cloister, the way pioneers
learned to stick together in wagon trains and sod houses. You're pitting
discussion against soliloquy," I took the bait, "dialogue and monologue."

"Bingo, Little Beaver, you're beginning to think like an academic In-
dian."

Paula took another napkin and scratched *Egalitarian* on the left, *Hier-
archical* on the right. Under those she jotted *pluralism* and *individualism,
positional* and *willful, kin* and *loner, copartnership* and *dominance, physical land-
scape* and *existential space*. "Gets pretty thick in here," she muttered to her-
self, and lit another cigarette. "You have to have an IQ above wet cement
to think like this," she added, "but we'll work on it."

I grinned weakly and bit my lip. The West's heroic individualism as a
rationalization for everything from conquistador and colonizer, to robber
baron and junk bondsman had crossed my mind more than once, none
too happily. This was my White-boy cultural history on the firing line, no
heroic contrast through native eyes. It seemed Christian to bite the bullet.

"The Indian world is basically metaphysical, with physical spirits in all
things, coyotes and spiders, corn mothers and raven chiefs," Paula said,
wrinkling her brow, "as opposed to a secular separation of church and
state, workers driven by a materialist economy, a fallen earthly existence
under heaven with angels *en pointe* . . . I learned that in Catholic girls
school," she chuckled. "But the business of America is business, no?" she
tossed in, "masculine power making money?" I couldn't argue, even if I
could think of exceptions, beginning with my mother's sense of decency
and my father's working-class honesty. How do we get from personal ex-
emption to cultural representation? I wondered to myself. How does cul-
tural history shape us, after all?

Paula stared at the smoke curling into dark corners, then wrote
Quest(ion)ing opposite *Author(ity)* and glossed them, *What's going on?* up
against *Who's in charge?*

"You see, Ken," she footnoted the phyla, "this is a question of the
anonymous, unmonopolized sacred in all things, rocks and runes to ra-
vens and rainbows. It's what the Sioux call strangely *wakan*, as distinct
from Yahweh saying I AM THAT I AM to Moses from the burning bush.
Pantheism versus monotheism, more or less. Momaday has this poem,
you know, 'Earth and I Gave You Turquoise,' like saying, '*we* came up
with this wedding bracelet *together*.' Contrast that with Coleridge's 'little-
god' who *makes up* a romantic poem by himself, all alone in Kubla Khan.

Get the difference, Kemo Sabe?" I was starting to, though it felt like sitting in pilgrim stocks. Something told me we couldn't simply dismiss white-bread Americans as godless heathens, the history of displacing Native America notwithstanding, and something else whispered the need for reckoning and making amends, but not without digging up the broken bones. I knew many non-Indians who would side, more or less, with my Pueblo friend's polemic. "A good anger is a good thing," John Fire said years ago, peeing down Teddy Roosevelt's nose at Mount Rushmore. The Black Hills have been sacred to the Lakota for centuries. Presidential monumentalism there is a Native insult.

Paula placed *Community* across from *License.* "You've heard the Lakota call *Mitak' oyasin,* as folks up there say, 'All My Relatives.' Think about that against Walt Whitman's Kosmic myself-at-the-center stuff, the unauthorized and natural given world up against the copyrighted *logos,* you know. It's the old egocentric final word of a patriarchal Power, compared with a bunch of women gossiping. The silent voice in a stone, the burning coal on Isaiah's tongue."

"A lot to bite off there," I said meekly, "a lot to chew."

"No doubt about it, my friend," she agreed, "but if we're ever to negotiate the distances between our cultures, we'll have to start with a candid sense of both sides, Emily Dickinson to Sitting Bull."

"Differences, eh?" I mused and picked up the line of reasoning. "Keith Basso says that the White Man generally is what the Indian *is not,* from an Apache point-of-view, both sides making each other meaningful, as stereotyped opposites."

"Yes," she chimed in, "to a modest or shy Apache, a curious White man is pushy."

"And a strong-willed, work-driven Anglo sees the Apache as fuzzy, even lazy."

"You got it, buddy, both sides misread the other. Things are understated for the reserved Indian, overstated for the go-get-'em American. *Both* projections are cultural inventions, set off by tourists, missionaries, anthros, bureaucrats, cowboys, and cavalry—and on the other side parade images of medicine men, warriors, squaws, dusky maidens, noble savages, and zany seers. That's historical show biz, you know, from Pocahontas and Hiawatha, to Tonto and Chief Dan George." She lit another cigarette. "It's endless, Ken, simply stringing out for five hundred years behind us, and who knows how long ahead of us?"

"Maybe we can do something about the misreadings," I offered, "as teachers, as writers."

"Maybe," she closed the distance, smiling, "but don't hold your breath. These myths hang on like chiggers."

ACROSS CULTURES

Over two decades ago, field research for *The Good Red Road* found me au-
diting an American poetry film series in Jamestown, North Dakota, where
I was thinking about American Indian oral poetry and American literacy.
To see and to hear poets on film, admittedly contrived, still brings an au-
dience closer to the flesh of voice, the speaking body, the local context.
The films catch the shadow of an oral tradition where poet-singers and
tellers move in cadence, in ceremonial tongue, in transport. The effect of
such poetry is to *move* us, to renew and to restore us collectively, to reaffirm
what-is, the way *we* do things, the right senses.

"The Amerind makes poetry because he believes it to be good for him,"
Mary Austin says in *The American Rhythm*. "He makes it because he believes
it a contribution to the well-being of his group. He makes it to put himself
in sympathy with the *wakonda,* the *orenda* or god-stuff which he conceives
to be to some degree in every created thing. Finally—and on almost every
occasion—he makes it to affect objects that are removed from him in the
dimension of *time and space."* Why does any American make poetry, we
might ask today, and to what effect? What are the connections and differ-
ences, the continuities and distances between American and Native Amer-
ican cultures, seen through their verses?

As impressions gather and parallels deepen, I recall D. H. Lawrence
warning that America would simultaneously destroy and glorify the Indian.

> The bulk of the white people who live in contact with the Indian today would
> like to see this Red brother exterminated; not only for the sake of grabbing
> his land, but because of the silent, invisible, but deadly hostility between the
> spirit of the two races. The minority of whites intellectualize the Red Man and
> laud him to the skies. But this minority of whites is mostly a high-brow minority
> with a big grouch against its own whiteness. (*Studies in Classic American Liter-
> ature*)

This chapter gives that intercultural choler a forum—the run of a dialogue
with "native" American poetries. America could listen to Native America
for a change, instead of excluding or missionizing or, most insidiously,
exotically *othering* the native among us. The mixed-blood Eskimo, Knud
Rasmussen, took a dogsled across the Arctic for three years in the 1920s
and was courteously received by an Inuit woman in her igloo, who impro-
vised a song for him:

> *The lands around my dwelling are*
> *now more beautiful from the day when*
> *it is given me to see*
> *faces I have never seen before*

The NET films on American poets come from the mid-sixties, when American and Native American song-lines began to cross over: Frank O'Hara, the knowing New Yorker; Hart Crane, the visionary suicide; Michael McClure, the magician; Gary Snyder, self-disciplined in a black Japanese student uniform; Brother Antonius, cursing his reprobate listeners; Phillip Whalen, walking alone at the San Francisco Legion of Honor; Richard Wilbur, lucid and articulate; Robert Lowell, the staring, intense New Englander; Luis Borges, blind and touching in Argentina; Lawrence Ferlinghetti, Beat hipster fearful of America's future along its clogged freeways; and Allen Ginsberg, trickster of great talent. All men of talent in the countercultural sixties (where are the women and poets of color?). All, in one way or another, American, even Borges, so savored by American intellectuals. Next to these American writers, sample some recent collections of American Indian literature and life-history that surfaced from 1960s ethnopoetics, from linguistic anthropology to freely adapted reworkings to contemporary verse: *The Winged Serpent,* edited by Margot Astrov; *The Sky Clears,* edited by A. Grove Day; *The Magic World,* edited by William Brandon; *Shaking the Pumpkin,* edited by Jerome Rothenberg; and *Carriers of the Dream Wheel,* edited by Duane Niatum (sixteen contemporary American Indian poets, updated in 1988).

The differences between American and Native American poets, American and American Indian seers, play off each other in cultural, historical, and traditional terms. No slur is intended toward individual talents—magicians, shamans, healers, seers, prophets, alchemists, all in older traditions of mediation between the given and the dreamed worlds. I am disturbed, nonetheless, by a tendency to ignore, to alienate, to other or to co-opt America's native poets; at the same time, we can be encouraged by the poet's centrality and tribal dignity in Native America. "I know that if you cut deeply into any Indian poem," Mary Austin forewords *The Path on the Rainbow,* "it yields that profound and palpitant humanism without which no literary art can endure."

Soliloquies. In cities people imagine the cosmos of their own questionings. Individuals hole up in defensive burrows and emerge to forage for a livelihood, merchandise, culture, entertainment. Allen Ginsberg cruises through "A Supermarket in California":

What thoughts I have of you tonight, Walt Whitman, for I walked down the sidestreets under the trees with a headache self-conscious looking at the full moon.

In my hungry fatigue, and shopping for images, I went into the neon fruit supermarket, dreaming of your enumerations!

What peaches and what penumbras! Whole families shopping at

night! Aisles full of husbands! Wives in the avocados, babies in the tomatoes!
—and you, García Lorca, what were you doing down by the watermelons?

The land, given its country sense of free space, still allows for communities, tribes, clans, for superstition and sorcery and feeling as a part of the natural landscape of magic—something larger than *one-* self. Animals, plants, stones, ancestors, gods, even nothing, as echoed in the Southwest deserts, or resonant on the Great Plains, or shadowed in the Northern woodlands. Native nothing. Emptying out. The Ojibwa sing,

> *as my eyes*
> *look over the prairie*
> *I feel the summer in the spring*

Poetry—not just communication, Frank O'Hara says, chanting away the city—music, better still, witchcraft! "Reading poetry makes your blood run a different way."

"A poet is prompted by . . . a muse or the Holy Ghost, not sound or sense." Prompted by, O'Hara says, moved, inspired, encircled by the poem, a spiritual nimbus.

Luis Borges waited until his sixties to marry, purblind now in the film, after his mother served as "my eyes," he says smiling, for thirty years his sight going, vision growing. The blind bard, visionary seer: Black Elk, Homer, Milton, Yeats, and Joyce late in life. The poet listens to see. In *The Way to Rainy Mountain,* N. Scott Momaday remembers his grandmother Aho, naked, blind, and praying in Kiowa at her bedside: "The last time I saw her she prayed standing by the side of her bed at night, naked to the waist, the light of a kerosene lamp moving upon her dark skin. Her long, black hair, always drawn and braided in the day, lay upon her shoulders and against her breasts like a shawl."

Borges's wife now sings, yes *sings* his poetry back to him, and his head nods and sways, keeping time with her melody, his lyric sound and sense. He surely fell in love with her rich contralto voice, her pitch and resonance and range, her liquid trilled *rs.* Fell in love with her sound and touch, her smell, but most of all her audible grace. Poetry, in love, and singing—poetry in the body's balanced motion, the dancing feet, up through the visceral organs, past the breath and heartbeat, rushing out through the throat and mouth, in dignity and passion, with care. A. Grove Day writes in *The Sky Clears:*

The Indians made poems for many reasons: to praise their gods and ask their help in life; to speak to the gods through dramatic performances at seasonal celebrations or initiations or other rites: to work magical cures or enlist supernatural aid in hunting, plant-growing, or horsebreeding; to hymn the praises of the gods or pray to them; to chronicle tribal history; to explain the origins of the world; to teach right conduct; to mourn the dead; to arouse warlike feelings; to compel love; to arouse laughter; to ridicule a rival or bewitch an enemy; to praise famous men; to communicate the poet's private experience; to mark the beauties of nature; to boast of one's personal greatness; to record a vision scene; to characterize the actors in a folk tale; to quiet children; to lighten the burdens of work; to brighten up tribal games; and, sometimes to express simply joy and a spirit of fun.

Frontier American poetry: irrepressibly the ego, Emerson's I / eye / aye (the ethics of private property, Protestant self-help). *Ego ergo sum.* The freed pioneer on his own, the daring explorer, the hungry conquistador, the "new" man inventing on the go, Columbus and Cortés, Custer and Cody. Walt Whitman boasts a *Song of* My*self:*

> Walt Whitman, a kosmos, of Manhattan the son,
> Turbulent, fleshy, sensual, eating, drinking and breeding.

American Indian poetry: the tribe, anonymously sung (familial ethics, extended communal use, all our relatives). No one corners the market on poetry or property. No signed first editions. Oral poetry alive in dream, vision, song, speech—the tribal body and tongue, collectively. The people and goods in common. Giveaways, feasts, potlatches, sharing wealth and poverty, the world together. Maria Chona recalls a cactus gathering camp in her Papago childhood:

> Everybody sang. We felt as if a beautiful thing was coming. Because the rain was coming and the dancing and the songs.
>
> *Where on Quijota Mountain a cloud stands*
> *There my heart stands with it.*
> *Where the mountain trembles with it.*
>
> That was what they sang. When I sing that song yet it makes me dance.

American poetry: the now, the new, the present action, pitched & hot—. Ginsberg crawls out of mid-American alley dives to

Howl!

American Indian poetry: the past manifesting the present, the old revealed timelessly new, regenerative traditions, even stasis and stillness as sources of cool energy.

Listen!

American poetry: vicariously facing death alone, somewhere in the future here and now. Fear as an exercise one step removed from necessity. The displacement of horror movies, pathologies, footnotes, midnight television, police reports, the news as bad news. T. S. Eliot warns in *The Waste Land:*

> I will show you fear in a handful of dust.

American Indian poetry: the lyrical brevity of life, the vulnerability of the tribe, the word, the sacred rituals, only to be lost or forgotten by a negligence of memory. Still the extrahuman cycles of change remain constant, and thus ritualized—moon, sun, stars, seasons, tides, generations. The Nahuatl sang when Cortés came:

> *we only came to sleep*
> *we only came to dream*
> *it is not true*
> *that we came to live on the earth*
>
> *we are changed into the grass of springtime*
> *our hearts will grow green again*
> *and they will open their petals*
> *but our body is like a rose tree*
> *   it puts forth flowers and then withers*

American poetry: the shining mind, technique and craft, formulaic complexity and idiomatic sophistication, showing the poet's unique vision and skill. Gary Snyder lists "What you should know to be a poet":

> the wild freedom of the dance, *extasy*
> silent solitary illumination, *entasy*
>
> real danger. gambles. and the edge of death.

American Indian poetry: the "heart's eye," as the Lakota say, *çanté istá*, the senses and sense profoundly simple. Not to be unsettled by sentiment, common beauty, shared power, and tribal riches. The Pawnee Hako cautions:

> *Remember, remember the sacredness of things*
> *running streams and dwellings*
> *the young within the nest*
> *a hearth for sacred fire*
> *the holy flame of fire*

American poetry: the freed human being, free even of his gods and past, to question his freedom along a vast frontier. Galway Kinnell ends "The Bear":

> wandering: wondering
> what, anyway,
> was that sticky infusion, that rank flavor of blood, that
>   poetry, by which I lived?

American Indian poetry: the traditionally free, self-designated "real peo-
ple," as over a hundred tribes directly or indirectly called themselves. And
they believe in the gods, spirits, spells, animals' intelligence, plants' knowl-
edge, stones' centers. And they, too, are free in their beliefs, not Puritani-
cally, but by tradition and necessity free of confusion and doubt. Free not
in the short range of this time and place, but in the larger sense of forty-
thousand-year-old traditions (the San Diego Museum of Man carbon-14
dates a skull, found on Santa Rosa Island off the southern California coast,
at forty-four thousand years). Forty-thousand years, or more.

"They have assumed the names and gestures of their enemies, but have
held on to their own, secret souls," Momaday writes of his ancestors in
House Made of Dawn, "and in this there is a resistance and an overcoming,
a long outwaiting." And they keep themselves, are kept, secret and sentient,
within their religious sense of the magic world. The Kiowa poet says in
"Carriers of the Dream Wheel":

> They are old men, or men
> Who are old in their voices,
> And they carry the wheel among the camps,
> Saying: Come, come,
> Let us tell the old stories,
> Let us sing the sacred songs.

American poetry: experimental, exploratory, pugnacious, daring, exhi-
bitionist, energized, alive. Charles Olson makes the declaration for "free"
verse, via William Carlos Williams:

PROJECTIVE   VERSE
(projectile   (percussive   (prospective
                            vs.
                   The NON-Projective

American Indian poetry: free of technical gyrations or party-line dogma,
still traditional as highly developed cultural history, the generational wis-
dom, the tested life forces. Play taken seriously. Rhyme and image as kin-
ship, not technique—the bridge of an arcing imagination. The Navajo pray:

> *In beauty*
> > *you shall be my representation*
>
> *In beauty*
> > *you shall be my song*
>
> *In beauty*
> > *you shall be my medicine*
>
> *In beauty*
> > *my holy medicine*

American poetry: the sharp wit, jokes at the expense of politicians, suburban ghettos, advertising, housewives, businessmen, machines, stupidity, excess, waste. Defensive humor, edged, barbed. The social bite, teeth in the smile. Charles Bukowski, beat-up poet of Los Angeles bars and byways, advises in "making it":

> make money but don't work too
> hard—make somebody else *pay* to
> make it—and
> don't smoke too much but drink enough to
> relax, and
> stay off the streets
> wipe your ass real good
> use a lot of toilet paper
> it's bad manners to let people know you shit or
> *could* smell like it
> if you weren't
> careful

American Indian poetry: primally funny. Jokes to integrate the tribes, laughter to free deepest fears. Open laughter. Ribald, scatological, wild, instructive, liberating humor. The Paiute recall the ribald old days, an off-color creation story reworked by Jerome Rothenberg:

> In the old time women's cunts had teeth in them.
> It was hard to be a man then
> Watching your squaw squat down to dinner
> Hearing the little rabbit bones crackle.
> Whenever fucking was invented it died with the inventor.
> If your woman said she felt like biting you didn't take it lightly.
> Maybe you just ran away to fight Numuzoho the Cannibal.
>
> Coyote was the one who fixed things,
> He fixed those toothy women!
> One night he took Numuzoho's lava pestle
> To bed with a mean woman
> And hammer hammer crunch crunch ayi ayi
> All night long:
> "Husband, I am glad," she said
> And all the rest is history.
> To honor him we wear our necklaces of fangs.

American poetry: on the page, black and white, printed, though exploring, even there, the dimensions of the human voice, the terrain of spaced sounds, the freedoms, as in Williams's variable foot and all the variations thereof. Again, the good doctor asks in "The Wind Increases":

> Good Christ what is
> a poet—if any
> > exists?
>
> a man
> whose words will
> > bite
> > > their way
> home—being actual
> having the form
> > of motion

American Indian poetry: song-poems chanted, drums beating and feet drawing life from mother earth with the pulse and heartbeat, the gourd and rattle and feather fan, even the eerie eagle bone whistle of the Plains. Singers sing from visions, their own inherited and shared lines in the tribe. Each sings his variant in the drumming-dancing-chanting-rattling-tribal circle. The pan-Plains Ghost Dance of the late nineteenth century prophesied cultural resurrection and a return of the old ways:

> *I circle around*
> *The boundaries of the earth,*
> *Wearing the long wing feathers,*
> *As I fly.*

American poetry: lonely artists in urban crowds, on freeways not very free, blue down alleys and sewers and bars and slums. Here, de-civilized in the bowels of middle-class America, the poets feel an underground measure of wild alienation. Ashfault. Seventy percent of the surface of central L.A. is pavement, driveway, and parking lot. Ezra Pound caught an image of ghostly return after the First World War:

> Haie! Haie!
> > These were the swift to harry;
> These the keen-scented:
> These were the souls of blood.
>
> Slow on the leash,
> > pallid the leash-men!

American Indian poetry: the reservation outside city limits, "a sovereign nation" of people united in the land, villages buried in the elements, earthen clay flesh, sumac skin, veins of pipestone and turquoise, animal skeletons, sacred stones, kin with creatures, the two-leggeds, four-leggeds, many-leggeds, no-leggeds, wings of the air, and all colors of all things. The Navajo chant of sunrise:

> *House made of dawn*
> *House made of evening light.*

House made of the dark cloud.
House made of male rain.
House made of dark mist.
House made of female rain.
House made of pollen.
House made of grasshoppers.

American poetry: secular, tough, independent, from the knowing gut, the smart viscera, down to our *hips in things,* as Olson says of Melville—tangible, stringy, carnal, concrete. Pound excoriated his times in "Hugh Selwyn Mauberley":

frankness as never before,
disillusions as never told in the old days,
hysterias, trench confessions,
laughter out of dead bellies.
V
There died a myriad,
And of the best, among them,
For an old bitch gone in the teeth,
For a botched civilization

American Indian poetry: sacred, visionary, on spiritual target (even scatologically and comically), utilitarian, the essentials necessary to live as one must, a warrior or a sacred clown or an ordinary person. Death a stone's throw from the tribal camp. Death the pitch of the mind beyond the heartbeat. The Lakota imagined:

A wolf
I considered myself,
But the owls are hooting
And the night
I fear.

American poetry: rich, abrasive, various, full of it, inventing. Lawrence Ferlinghetti caught the hiphop beat in "A Coney Island of the Mind":

the poet like an acrobat
    climbs on rime
        to a high wire of his own making
and balancing on eyebeams
        above a sea of faces
    paces his way
        to the other side of day

American Indian poetry: stripped to the essentials, the polished ancestral bones, the elements deep within sinew and flesh and blood and skin. The Lakota sang around Custer's time:

> *Soldiers*
> *You fled.*
> *Even the eagle dies.*

American poetry: the Model T Ford, the stock market in the printing business, libraries, ticker tape, farms, ranches, cities, railroad trains, soda shops, fire hydrants, baseball, basketball, golf, tennis, hockey, and football three nights a week on "tele"vision (the popcorn and hot dog of Kultur, Pound might say), Disneyland, Hollywood, McDonald's, Marilyn Monroe and Billy Graham and Lester Maddox and Rod McKuen and Howard Stern. Insatiable consumers. James Wright worried, "Lying in a Hammock at William Duffy's Farm in Pine Island, Minnesota":

> To my right,
> In a field of sunlight between two pines,
> The droppings of last year's horses
> Blaze up into golden stones.
> I lean back, as the evening darkens and comes on.
> A chicken hawk floats over, looking for home.
> I have wasted my life.

American Indian poetry: sun, moon, trees, bush, boulder, pebble, arrowhead, sacred blue lake, medicine pipe, holy land of the Black Hills *(Paha Sapa!)*, the buffalo *(Tatanka!)*, and the "sacred dog" *(sunka wakan)*, as the Sioux named the horse. The centaur, colors of the land in every time of day and night and season, indeed, *the colors of the night*. Medicinal herbs, handcraft in praise of hands that shape things with human care through nature, warning of a deadening technocracy, an old jeremiad, still unheeded. Kindness, touching the world sparingly, the tribe at large, always measured freedom in the tribal village extended. Momaday speaks of *Green* in "The Colors of the Night":

> A young girl awoke one night and looked out into
> the moonlit meadow. There appeared to be a tree;
> but it was only an appearance; there was a shape
> made of smoke; but it was only an appearance; there
> was a tree.

American poetry: maximal.

> I have had to learn the simplest things
> last. Which made for difficulties.

("MAXIMUS, TO HIMSELF," CHARLES OLSON)

American Indian poetry: minimal.

> *The water bug is drawing*
> *the shadows of the evening*
> *toward him on the water*

(QUECHUAN, ANONYMOUS)

American poetry: the fox, the crab, the vulture at the innards. Internal warfare, ulcers, the mind in torque. The cultural tension, finally, of having nothing in too much, too much having, nothing. Robert Creeley recounts in "I Know A Man":

> As I sd to my
> friend, because I am
> always talking,—John, I
>
> sd, which was not his
> name, the darkness sur-
> rounds us, what
>
> can we do against
> it, or else, shall we &
> why not, buy a goddamn big car,
>
> drive, he sd, for
> christ's sake, look
> out where yr going.

American Indian poetry: open anger of necessity, based on spiritual regard for living creatures and their emotional needs, freedoms, huntings. Honor and apology to the buffalo, the bear, the wolf, the deer, for animal life sustaining human life, which in turn will sustain plant and animal life, in the end, the continuing, integrating all. The ecosystem, natural, holy. Earth our household. The attitude is what counts, taking no more than one needs. The contemporary medicine man, John (Fire) Lame Deer, concludes:

> I believe that being a medicine man, more than anything else, is a state of mind, a way of looking at and understanding this earth, a sense of what it is all about.

American poetry: the loner artist, the renegade, the rebel, the underground invisible man, minority cultured. The exiled, dog-eared gadfly, unheard, unheeded in our century by H. L. Mencken's "boobsgeoisie." Poetry in hipster coffee houses. Poetry in the *little* magazines. Poetry in universities, criticized. Poetry in school, on the page—but not on the streets, or in the home at night, or at work, or driving to work, or in the elevators, or on commercials, or in the peoples' minds and hearts. Advertisements crowding public places. Poetry banished from the daily common living/loving lives of people. Poetry the province of the professor, the pointy-headed intellectual (the masses growl), the egghead and bookworm, sex maniac, commie pinko (Mao wrote poetry), queerball, long-haired freak. Knifing irony as a self-condemning way of life. Before jumping off a Minneapolis winter bridge to his death, waving to the crowd, John Berryman pleaded in "Henry's Confession":

> —*If* life is a handkerchief sandwich,
>
> in a modesty of death I join my father
> who dared so long agone leave me.
> A bullet on a concrete stoop
> close by a smothering southern sea
> spreadeagled on an island, by my knee.
> —You is from hunger, Mr. Bones.

Native American poetry: *Pahuska,* the "longhair" with dignity. Chief Joseph. Sequoya. Black Hawk. Touch-the-Clouds. Poetry sung all day into the night, as Italians sing Verdi working on roads, or in washhouses, markets, brothels. Poetry the province of the people. Poets as holy men. Warriors. Chiefs. Seers. Healers. Sitting Bull was a poet, a medicine man, a warrior, a visionary, a chief, and a martyr. Pontiac. White Antelope. Handsome Lake. Poetry integral with tribal life and daily naming, poetry the circle itself, spherically projective, the people's ambient spirits in their songs. Anita Endrezze writes in "Red Rock Ceremonies":

> With low thunder, with red bushes smooth
> as water stones, with the blue-arrowed rain,
> its dark feathers curving down
> and the white-tailed running deer—
> the desert sits, a maiden with obsidian eyes,
> brushing the star-tasseled dawn from her lap.
>
> It is the month of Green Corn;
> It is the dance, grandfather, of open blankets.
>
> I am singing to you
> I am making the words
> shake like bells.

American poetry: still hung up on Europe, though less so now, as poets mature, novelists invent, but still worry down under whether the country hasn't come of age ("literary scholarship of the United States hangs out its tongue with eagerness while it paws the scrap heap of Europe," Mary Austin grouses in *The American Rhythm*). Little traditional regard for the past beyond the prodigal son's split with the Old World Father—and because of that split, the poet renegade guilty all the way back, mythically and historically, through the Protestant and Roman Catholic, then Roman and Greek cultures, in search of origins, originality, family, parentage, history. W. S. Merwin laments in "Homeland":

> The sky goes on living it goes
> on living the sky
> with all the barbed wire of the west
> in its veins

and the sun goes down
driving a stake
through the black heart of Andrew Jackson

American Indian poetry: mature as Confucius, and dating before, as playful, as sacred, as right naming, metaphoric, and knowing of human behavior, the target of all poetry. Wisdom pungent as the smell of sage. The world as a projected metaphor in the imagination, which itself is a natural phenomenon, the self *within* the world, psychically concrete. Grounded mysticism: the world flowing through the medium of self, a current. Self as part of a world so infinite and marvelous that it is only imaginable. Magic. Imagination. Image. Mage. *Magikos,* ancient Greek for sorcerer, the first poet. The South American Uitoto in Columbia said of creation:

Nothing existed, not even a stick to support the vision: our Father attached the illusion to the thread of a dream and kept it by the aid of his breath. He sounded to reach the bottom of the appearance, but there was nothing. Nothing existed indeed.

American poetry: to be read once, then left for a newer poem, never redundant, for god's sake, never repetitive. Few refrains, fewer ballads (only to study the poem can one repeat it). Merwin worries in "Whenever I Go There":

And once more I remember that the beginning

Is broken

No wonder the addresses are torn

To which I make my way eating the silence of animals
Offering snow to the darkness

Today belongs to a few and tomorrow to no one

American Indian poetry: chanted daily, all day long, into the powwow ("making medicine") night. Each person sings a song carried personally, from a dream, throughout his life, like a name—Sweet Grass Woman—as the people mean beauty and necessity and naming to each other, in a daily renewal of trust, kinship, kind-ness. Like a name—Sweet Grass Woman. Like a name—Sweet Grass Woman. The Papago made up their world with peoples' names, Rothenberg says:

A shaman has a dream & names a child for what he dreams in it. Among such names are Circling Light, Rushing Light Beams, Daylight Comes, Wind Rainbow, Wind Leaves, Rainbow Shaman, Feather Leaves, A-Rainbow-as-a-Bow, Shining Beetle, Singing Dawn, Hawk-Flying-over-Water-Holes, Flowers Trembling, Chief-of-Jackrabbits, Water-Drops-on-Leaves, Short Wings, Leaf Blossoms, Foamy Water.

American poetry: private ceremony, personal vision, singular imagining. Primal poetic space in the secret labyrinths of the mind. Uncommon poetic contexts. Wallace Stevens looked at a blackbird thirteen ways:

> Icicles filled the long window
> With barbaric glass.
> The shadow of the blackbird
> Crossed it, to and fro.
> The mood
> Traced in the shadow
> An indecipherable cause.

American Indian poetry: ceremony, oral tradition, *the people,* an inherited place for communal poetry. Preverbal contexts for sacred silence and speech: gesture, dance, music as moving space, event, ritual to formalize a primal setting. Ceremony remains accessible to the voice in time of need or play. Song-chants in the foreground, middleground, and background of tribal life. James Welch still listens to Blackfeet ancestors in "Snow Country Weavers":

> Say this: say in my mind
>
> I saw your spiders weaving threads
> to bandage up the day. And more,
> those webs were filled with words
> that tumbled meaning into wind.

American poets long to be *Native* American. List the translators of tribal poetries in the past thirty years: Merwin, Levertov, Olson, Snyder, Berg, Wagoner, Norman, Tedlock, Duncan, Creeley, Kelly, Rothenberg. Even non-American poets long to go Native, since the Renaissance and a discovery of the *New* World and the Natural Man. Montaigne on the "cannibals." Rousseau on the "noble savage." Marx and Engels on the communal Iroquois. Kafka on the back of a disappearing Indian pony. Dylan Thomas, on his hands and knees, playing Indian in the Welsh gorse.

"Now I could be what I wanted," the medicine man John Lame Deer told a New York artist, Richard Erdoes, immigrated from Vienna, "a real Sioux, an *ikçe wiçasa,* a common, wild, natural human being." His Lakota grandfathers sang:

> *You cannot harm me*
> *you cannot harm*
> *one who has dreamed a dream like*
> *mine*

American poets all know and work with and celebrate, in their own difficult ways, the country's poetic voices. That's the poet's job—to do with

what he is and has, among the people. So America needs more poetry of
the tribe, Native American poetry, and can listen to ancient voices in this
land. Simon Ortiz remembers his childhood in Acoma, a New Mexico
Pueblo village, dating its people's history before Christ:

> I was talking about song as poetry, song as motion and emotion. Song as the
> way in which I can feel those rhythms and melodies and how those things
> give me energy. . . . poetry is the way in which we make the connection be-
> tween all things. Poetry is a way of reaching out to what is reaching for you.
> Poetry is that space in between what one may express and where it is received.
> Where there is another energy coming toward you—it's that space in between.

(II)

MODERN SHAMANS

FIVE

⁑(•)⁑

Mythic Mothers

Defining ethnopoetics in the *North Dakota Quarterly,* Sherman Paul notes that "revisionist work, so much the work of women, is not adventitious, and should remind us that in the search for the primitive, which to a considerable extent is a search for the feminine, women should not be left out of the account." Gender and ethnicity swing on reconnective poetic hinges, the silenced voices of others speaking from sealed hope chests and repressive patriarchies. The *native* in American verse may well be feminist-as-cultured-other, tribally singing out of carefully wrapped medicine bundles and clan genealogies.

DICKINSON'S *PRIVILEGE TO DIE*

My Barefoot-Rank is better.
EMILY DICKINSON
TO T. W. HIGGINSON, 1862

"If we turn to the best of Emily Dickinson's poems," Edward Sapir reviewed her newly published verse in *Poetry* magazine, May 1925, "we find the fruits of her healthy ignorances in a strange, unsought, and almost clairvoyant freshness." Sapir, a linguistic ethnographer and German student of Franz Boas, translated acres of Native American oral texts; with a keen ethnopoetic eye, he titled his review, mentioned earlier, "Emily Dickinson, a Primitive." The last word means "first" (Latin *primus)* and implies *primal* or *primary,* as discussed. So "Primitive" points to the original or natural—*native*—something we come from and need to return to, possibly. Richard Sewall, in turn, notes the literary range of Dickinson's "prehensile mind and burrlike memory," referencing the Bible to the Brontes. Devouring "the luscious passages" of Shakespeare after her 1864 eye surgery,

Dickinson wrote a friend, "I thought I should tear the leaves out as I turned them." Sewall adds, "She never learned to pray, she said, and she persisted in calling herself a pagan." The "consuming flame" of Dickinson's "primitive freshness" and "spiritual passion," Sapir concludes in 1925, leads toward "a fresh, primitive, and relentless school of poetry that is still on the way." The native bear-heart sings her differences.

Dickinson's verse was rhythmically *cut* and naturally scalloped. It more or less followed the Euro-American musical line that Ezra Pound tried to rescore in poetry. Pound championed the classical grace of Sappho, Homer, and Confucius, through the frontier concisions of T. S. Eliot, H. D., and e. e. cummings—spare, elemental, essential. "Above all to be precise," Pound translated Confucian Odes, "At the gulf's edge / Or on thin ice." As his colleague and college friend, Bill Williams, put it, "penetrant and simple—minus the scaffolding of the academic." These were modernist terms of American Literature in the mid-1920s: "clean and sharp," as was said of a Yeats poem, "like the blade of a knife," no less than Dickinson incising, "She dealt her pretty words like Blades—/ How glittering they shone—/ And every One unbared a Nerve / Or wantoned with a Bone—" (no. 469). Such essentialist terms coincided with the rediscovery of Native American oral traditions, freshly translated and first anthologized by George W. Cronyn in *The Path on the Rainbow,* as the Great War ended and various modernist and ethnic renaissances began. Dickinson spoke to all of them:

> To see the Summer Sky
> Is Poetry, though never in a Book it lie—
> True Poems flee—

How do we reconnect *native* and *American* literature? In "Poetry," Marianne Moore calls art "imaginary gardens with real toads in them," versed inventions of the real: in the modernist garden of verbal delight, grumps and groans and shrieks foul our artificially rhymed lives, from toad blemishes, to bats sleeping upside-down, to death by drowning. The garden goes fallow to a desert, then a wasteland. Over our century, ecstasy shades into terror, as Ted Hughes says of Dickinson and his suicidal wife, Sylvia Plath: it's what doesn't fit, what surprises us, what bothers or disturbs or terrifies our certainties—the lisp in our likes, the un/likes in our likenings, "feelings of strangeness and awkwardness," Wordsworth warned the *Lyrical Ballads* reader. "If I read a book [and] it makes my whole body so cold no fire ever can warm me," Dickinson told Thomas Wentworth Higginson in 1870, "I know *that* is poetry. If I feel physically as if the top of my head were taken off, I know *that* is poetry. These are the only way I know it. Is there any other way?" So the paradoxical dis-figurations in what we poetically figure throw reality back into art, bewilderingly, like curvatures of black-hole space. "After all, when a thought takes one's breath away," Higginson prefaced the first 1890 Dickinson edition, "a lesson on grammar seems an impertinence." Twentieth-century art, then, can be the poetry of misfits (misread "ignorant" or "primitive"), reconsidered truly back through western lyrical ballads, revealing the real. As Sapir said of Dickinson's *barefoot rank*, "a strange, unsought, and almost clairvoyant freshness."

Thus, Moore calls for the "raw" and the "genuine," if we are "interested in" *it*, the untranslatable poetic referent of reality. Emily Dickinson (1830–1886), a genuine and intimate voice, has the true inner ear for *it*, the poem idiosyncratically present, while her twin sister in eastern Massachusetts, Sylvia Plath (1932–1963), is a poet of eclipsed eye under the moon's hooded bone. "Dickinson and Plath are sisters in an Orphic cult," Norman Dubie feels, "that dismembered Orpheus with the serrated edges of sea shells" (*The Clouds of Magellan*). Between these lethal sisters stands Marianne Moore, a verse iconoclast tendering modernist reprises of old rhythmic forms.

Ted Hughes speaks of the "naked voltage" in Dickinson's poems—the wildly leaping energy in those errant dashes, interruptive commas, and plunging line breaks. Hughes clearly connects Dickinson with the "blueish voltage" of Plath, his wife a century later, whose "burningly luminous vision of a Paradise" is overseen by a lunar muse, "bald, white and wild," spotlighting death. Dickinson ritualized dying, and Plath made death an obsessive art; both gave their lives to the poet's calling. If Emily Dickinson was, in Sapir's words, an "American Primitive," an *original* (indeed, aboriginal, *from* the *origin*), then Sylvia Plath was a neoprimitive sibyl sibling. Recently pushing the politically correct margins, Hughes poeticizes the "aboriginal thickness" of his wife's lips and nose, "broad and Apache," in "a prototype face / That could have looked up at me through the smoke / Of a Navajo campfire" ("18 Rugby Street," in *Birthday Letters*). This shamanic sister seer wrenched poetry out of the ladies' parlor and pitched it into the witches' cauldron. No less than Stravinsky, Kandinsky, Gauguin, or Picasso, Plath a generation later was fascinated with the rediscovered arts of tribal cultures, particularly from Africa and the Americas. Hughes in *Winter Pollen*, for example, cites the "explosive transformation" of Paul Radin's African folklore on his wife's poetics, "the original primitive thing" in anthropological excavations of ancient oral texts, and in another essay he notes the alembic chemistry of C. M. Bowra's *Primitive Song* on both their writings. "Though the contents of primitive poetry vary greatly from those of modern," Bowra writes, "its manner of composition is something which we can understand and recognize as related to what our own poets have told of themselves." Plath and Hughes were no exceptions.

The Inuit Orpingalik told Knud Rasmussen in the 1920s, as quoted earlier in Bowra, "Songs are thoughts, sung out with the breath when people are moved by great forces and ordinary speech no longer suffices. . . . When the words we want to use shoot up of themselves—we get a new song." If Lorca's *Duende*, the in-house presence of artistic genius, is to be found anywhere in modern reading, Hughes argues, it will be "in the section on primitive literature." When "ordinary speech" fails, the Inuit says, and we small humans "feel still smaller," the shaman's songs thaw the ice and "shoot up of themselves." No less than for the premodernist, as Dickinson wrote, "my whole body so cold no fire can ever warm me." The poet queries: "Is there any other way?" Hughes feels that the hymn and the riddle, center and circumference of Dickinson's imagination, fired her verse into a voice for all times and peoples. Heart straight to heaven, whether primitive or modernist, chant and crux cross in genuine cultural literacy.

Both common and original, the early modernist muse of Amherst wrote from the bear's terrible heart. Dickinson canted lines of poetry from an idiomatic American voice, speaking among "Us," but to herself, a paradox of community and cloister. It is as though each of us, "She" and "Us," were characters in a cubicled canvas, each separately facing a special way, speaking in soliloquy, and all the voices were some Chorus heard by an imagined "God."

> The last Night that She lived
> It was a Common Night
> Except the Dying—this to Us
> Made Nature different

Does "Nature" differ, or do we defer (dis-liking) in the face of dying? The bear-hearted difference here registers an otherness not to be denied: its strangeness signifies a real alterity. And what is untranslatably strange— what is lost in translation, as Frost said—suggests a positive poetic slippage. Dis-like creatively disturbs the imagination into the significance of a reality deferred. No way around it, the poets insist, though we deny moment to moment—we all die.

Art, nevertheless, comes from living speech—the common diction of "a Common Night" (of dying) uncommonly registered, reified as verse. From Wordsworth's language of "man speaking to men" through Williams's "speech of Polish mothers" and Eliot's "dialect of the tribe," this is the Euro-American experiment in *freeing* verse. A democratic pluralism opens the wings of the poet's sanctum to the people's murmurings.

In Dickinson the "heard" is concretely "seen" on the page, more or less exactly as it is spoken, glitches and all, all in focus, no wasted motion. Selection, distillation, and precision of daily breaded speech render her poetry. It's an American invention in alchemizing verse from daily dialect, catching rare spittle on the common tongue, overhearing the everyday observation and giving it due. This means testing the democratic whole of many individuals all deferring, demurring, debating, cussing and discussing life in broad swatches—Emerson, Thoreau, and Whitman, down to Williams, Moore, and Bishop, as *Sing with the Heart of a Bear* will show, on through Native American men and women writers, Welch and Hogan to Gregg and Olds, Momaday and Harjo to Graham and Forché.

This common tongue requires privacy, even isolation, to be overheard and recorded purely. So Dickinson insisted more and more, as she aged, on the solitude of one's own reflections among the masses, in a world that pretends sociability. Is democracy a veneer for self-embrasure, she questioned, a collective curtain, perhaps, for a private spirit in public confessional? "The Soul selects her own Society—". Over a hundred years ago, Dickinson struck the first note in a leitmotiv that was to become modern *Existénce,* via Kierkegaard, Heidegger, Camus, and Sartre. Nietzsche tolled the opening chord, *"Gott ist tot,"* of nineteenth-century existentialism with a receding Deity, and Dickinson stopped going to services, though she never lost faith in devout questions. Science and industry were fast dissecting and straining collective life; nationalism was subsuming the One in the Many. The poets and thinkers protested with the aloneness (al-one-ness) of Emerson's individualism: registering both the release of freedom in the New World, and the terror.

What did it mean to lose all that institutional scaffolding and walk barefoot through a secular wilderness? Hughes thinks that Dickinson "is not sure she likes the looks of this soul-thing. Her ecstasy—'ecstasy' is one of her favoured words—is also terror, convincingly." What lurked outside primary consciousness, beyond public scrutiny, beneath the social facade? The contraries of self and not-self, of estranged Me and distant Other, troubled Dickinson's imagination to "Zero at the Bone." This below-freezing chill predicated death, her nonbeing, alone. Life would come full circle, she sensed, without benefit of divine rescue or interceding others, to end as it began, at the "Hour of Lead" in nothing.

"I stepped from Plank to Plank," Dickinson says in a two-stanza poem, toward the "precarious Gait" that "Some call Experience." Not to be hobbled, she begins the soul's Journey in a Western pilgrimage—from Eric the Red and Columbus, to Green Peace and Voyager today—meeting the unknown, the wilderness, the frontier of the Other. As in the Latin root *experiri,* or "risky crossing," this is a meeting of village and wilderness, poet and savage, citizen and other "at the forest's edge," with no certainties, few negotiations, dissolving treaties—. Yet the "inquiring mind" *dashing* about reflectively, Heather McHugh says in *Broken English,* frees the reader "into the meaning of the moving moment." Dickinson's poetic foot, a hesitant step, must be constantly modified, searching, uncertain in its progress toward . . . "radiance always an incipience."

The mystery of consciousness here opens a compelling space in time—

the ancient "way" to personal truth, to know in the going, the truth *of* the unknown. So temporality is physicalized, space-time is given a personal voice in what we might call chronotopes of reflectivity (mentioned at the outset, borrowing Bakhtin's sense of time fleshed through physical landscape, *chronotope* as the topology of time-made-flesh—a people's living heritage signified experientially and historically, Hindu Mount Everest or Buddha's bo tree, in heartland America, perhaps, Mount Rushmore or the Sun Dance cottonwood). Chronotopes of reflectivity, then, suggest that getting to know the American cultural unknowing in things personalizes a radically uncertain frontier wisdom, the chronotope (or time-space) of consciousness itself in motion. Dickinson's is the "power of *running* metaphor," Alfred Kazin says, "the linking of incommensurables" never before anticipated, "roaming this world as if it were interstellar space" *(God and the American Writer)*. The world is not so much object, then, as moving subject, Heraclitus might say. Better yet, the poet gives us voiced motions as "verses" *(versus,* the plough's turn to the next furrow, that is, poetic line)— hence, Dickinson's quatrains of passage. There's an art, in passing, to all this, "the poem as a ploughshare that turns time / Up and over," Seamus Heaney says in " 'Poet's Chair.' "

In Dickinson's running reflective chronotopes, we witness less a landscape reified in words or images, more a consciousness felt in passing— through the stirrings of a voice both set in motion (and hushed) by circumstances—by gravity, by reality, by loss, finally by death. Most of all, the poet's sacramental voice is humbled by its own honesty in recognizing the changing faces of things, against a reader's unanswerable human need for something to hang on to. The need is all, yet nothing satisfies, short of death as metaphor for completion, and even here, the world moves on. The poet's spirit seems more restive than restful.

With Dickinson there is forever the delicacy and difficulty of motion through a wilderness of space, a mutability and mutation archetypally American. Mortality is registered in uncertain, self-correcting metrics. No native hunter or planter ever touched the underbrush more searchingly. Her iambs stutter across commas, her trochees plunge and suspend— everywhere hymnal meter, in the Old World sense, meets the free measure of an unexplored topos. Here lies Dickinson's primitive modernism, parsing a landscape measure that just precedes formal measuring. "It was back to the foot pace on the new earth," Mary Austin says of New World metrics in poets like Whitman, Frost, or Sandburg *(The American Rhythm),* "ax stroke and paddle stroke. So it is that new rhythms are born of new motor impulses." The "*lub*-dub, *lub*-dub of the heavy-footed Nordics," Austin thinks, met a more precarious gait in wilderness forests. Among pioneers and frontiersmen there was less traversing of fields than touching down through the uncertain soil of native undergrowth.

And where did the iambic stride of the émigré Englishmen originate? Ted Hughes, poet laureate of England (who should know of these matters), starts a thousand years back across the Big Water with the "two-part, alliterative accentual line [that] served as a spinal column" of Anglo-Saxon verse ("Myths, Metres, Rhythms," in *Winter Pollen*). By Chaucer's time, Norman French was grafting a vowel tissue of iambic pentameter ("Whan that Aprill with his shoures soote / The droghte of March hath perced to the roote") over German and Scandinavian spondees, rooted in four-beat, medial caesura rhythm. After a few centuries, this rhyming musicality, in turn, was countered with irregular Latin iambics by Wyatt's muscular rhythms: a "hand-wrought, gnarled, burr-oak texture" of rough pentameters, Hughes feels, grafted from Petrarchan sonnets ("They fle from me that sometyme did me seke / With naked fote stalking in my chambre"), which broke ground for Shakespeare's blank verse speeches, on to Wordsworth's walking monologues ("I'd rather be / A Pagan suckled in a creed outworn"), through Hopkins's *sprung* rhythm in "The Windhover," first published in 1918, when Cronyn's *Path on the Rainbow* surfaced ("No wonder of it: shéer plód makes plough down sillion / Shine, and blue-bleak embers, ah my dear, / Fall, gall themselves, and gash gold-vermilion").

Here at end-century, Emily Dickinson, a priest's sister across the Atlantic, enters our Euro-American verse-line history with her four-and-three-beat hymnal meters, stretching, suspending, and breaking across uncertain terrain. "It is this leap of the running stream of poetic inspiration from level to level," Mary Austin says in *The American Rhythm*, "whose course cannot be determined by anything except the nature of the ground traversed, which I have called the landscape line." Austin contends that all traditional verse forms, wherever local in the world, come from *aboriginal* rhythms, "in the sense that they are developed from the soil native to the culture that perfected them." Whether Greek, Roman, Celtic, or English, all feed into the evolving metrics of American poetry, still further freed and remetered in a new landscape across the Atlantic, for forty millennia filled with two thousand native tongues. "The physical basis of poetry appears, then," Austin sweepingly summarizes, "as the orchestration of organic rhythms under the influence of associated motor and emotional impulses, recapitulated from generation to generation." Suspending skepticism for a moment, consider the argument via a native poetics, grounded in the biodiversity of organic nature the world over, from Bashō's tonal haiku syllabics, to Petrarch's fourteener hendecasyllabics, to Wyatt's iambics, to Whitman's anapestic leaves of grass, to Lawrence's free-verse-fired spondees, to Heaney's Anglo-Irish, northern "word-hoard":

> "Keep your eye clear
> as the bleb of the icicle,

> trust the feel of what nubbed treasure
> your hands have known.''

William Carlos Williams offered the "variable foot," a triadic phrase-cadence, as an original American syntax, hence the scalloped verse line in his modern epic poem, *Paterson*. All these experiments in form—syllabics, to metrics, to free verse, to howling vowels and crashing consonants, to scalloped triads—feed into a native poetics, original and recreative, *singing with the heart of a bear that is different.*

In direct line with Austin's *American Rhythm* and Bowra's *Primitive Song*, the book that turned his wife toward her own native poetics, Ted Hughes roots the native coherence of mythology, meter, and rhythmic cadence in local cultures, relatively indigenous: "Perhaps in primitive groups, or in small nations that are still little more than tribal assemblies of ancient, inter-related families, where the blood-link can still be felt, the conditions for it are more likely." Think of Yugoslavian burgs where Alfred Lord found evidence of Homeric oral-formulaic traditions still alive; or African heart-land peoples drumming story-songs village to village; or Tibetan hamlet healers curing soul-loss by walking traditional paths in the Himalayas; or Pueblos, for several millennia along the Rio Grande, dancing and chanting seasonal renewal at the spring equinox; or New England villages ringing with Protestant hymns. Hughes steps back:

> To see the full irony of this Battle of the Metrical Forms and this intertangled Battle of the Modes of Speech, in Britain, you have to be Welsh, Scots or Irish. You have to be one of those, that is, who failed, in successive defeats, to stop the Anglo-Saxon, the Scandinavian and finally the Norman invaders stealing the country from beneath them. Just as Chaucer's rhymed iambics displaced the Germanic alliterative sprung rhythm, so that long clangorous line had in turn displaced the verse forms of the indigenous Celtic peoples, who held in common one of the most evolved and sophisticated poetic traditions in world history.

Seamus Heaney calls this Anglo-Irish countervoice "the guttural muse," where consonants strike off internal vowels, and the cave of the mouth still rings with oar splash and sword clang (*Preoccupations*). Perhaps, among other considerations, it helps to be *native* American to see this battle of tribes and tongues on American soil, as seen later from TallMountain through Tapahonso.

Imagine a century ago the New World poet, Emily Dickinson, walking across an uneven terrain, an overgrown aboriginal game path through her father's woods, where the Euro-American way of meter, rhyme, and imagery is newly laid down in four- and three-beat hymnal lines which she is singing to herself (Martin Luther's "A *mighty fortress is* our *God* / A *bulwark never failing*; / Our *helper He*, a*mid* the *flood* / Of *mortal ills* pre*vailing*"). Here

the strangeness of nature, or of the ways-things-actually-are—the unex-
pected hummock and furrow along old game paths—all interrupt the poet's
anticipations of the foot, or rhyme scheme, or traditional metaphor, even
as her four-and-three-beat line quatrains, trimeter answering tetrameter,
show up in popular hymns, ballads, work songs, spirituals, and American
folk cultures current today (a slaver's hymn turned into Black spiritual,
"A*mazing grace,* how *sweet* the *sound,* / that *saved* a *wretch* like *me* / I *once* was
lost, but *now* am *found,* / was *blind* but *now* I *see*"). But in an original way, note
how the poet's actual verse lines push off from iambic singsong with drilled
spondees, caving run-ons, odd slant rhymes, all manner of torqued syntax:

> I *willed* my *Keep*sakes—*Signed* a*way*
> What *portion* of *me be*
> As*signable*—and *then* it *was*
> There *interposed* a *Fly*—
>
> With *Blue*—un*certain stum*bling *Buzz*—
> Be*tween* the *light*—and *me*—
> And *then* the *Win*dows *failed*—and *then*
> I *could* not *see* to *see*—

Dickinson's rhymes—*Keepsakes, me be, assignable, Blue, Between, me, see to see*—
repeat the long ee's insistently, to be tripped up by the voweling spondee
me be and the enjambed tangle in the assemblage *assignable*. And then the
fly buzzes, *interposes* itself between the slant *light* and the fatal seer—and its
uncertain noise, its *stumbling* insect *Buzz,* darkens the whole of reality. Time
stops: *and then* / *I could not see to see*—Her dash holds the dying eternally.
That is, time doubles and sticks to itself, like a broken disk of seeings, a
stopped clock seen stopped, and the poet can no longer *see to see* out the
Windows of consciousness. *Keep-me-be-tween-see* all are blotted out and swal-
lowed by the feasting, low-voweled *Buzz,* the winged worm called a fly. So
the difficulties of going (walking-talking-thinking) encounter traps where
the poet sticks (and dies) on stutters, on ticks, on errant commas and er-
ratic dashes—the buzzing flies of syntax. The mind's stumblings up against
infinity, the drops in footing on ground falling away, the broken frames of
light in shuttered rooms among the dying—all anticipate Sylvia Plath's dis-
junctive leaps toward immortality, the deadly art of defying norms by taking
life in one's teeth and spitting out all the illusory safe bets.

Through all this, Emily Dickinson writes with the deep courage of a mind
that entertains isolation, fragmentation, and momentary assemblage of
pure thought and feeling. Her poetry turns on a fine independence, even
eccentricity, as she recognizes "Much Madness is divinest Sense—" the
Odd may be our All, the loner our one and only. Hers is not a tribal com-
posure. She "demurs" against "the Majority," against the frosted chill of
oncoming death: "It made no Signal, nor demurred, / But dropped like

Adamant." The gravity of death, the weight of dying, is Adam's labor, Eve's curse. And she hesitates, or shyly objects, as the poems (de)mur/mur, remaining demure, sedate, reticent, coy. Her insight is special, not public or communal, except in the common finality of dying. Each death is its own ceremony. Her verse gathers funereal icons of thought, shards of image, New England cuneiform. Radically oral with the finest ear imaginable, Dickinson refuses to give in to the normative "Majority" of any conventional or noisy resolutions. "Like Us," she says of shared lives, "like Frost," she says of not-life in chilling similes that look forward to cummings's experimental courage to own up to death ("Buffalo Bill's defunct"), to Williams's three-step metrics ("The descent beckons"), to Plath's flat assertions of diamondlike, deadly will ("Edge" the week before her suicide). All this turns on a minimalist precision: "it's a small centimeter that makes art," Segovia, the master classical guitarist, said just before his death.

Humor, delight, play, and extravagance of image thicket Dickinson's work. She counters the dour posture of the white-bodiced spinster of Amherst: "my hair is bold, like the Chestnut bur—," as she wrote Higginson, as quoted, "and my eyes, like the Sherry in the Glass, that the Guest leaves." Dickinson was fully what Lawrence might have called "woman alive," though she never married (and why should she?), and she published but a dozen of her own poems (written for a select audience of one or two). Her metaphors free a reader through dazzling thought: "the Fields of Gazing Grain" when Death stops for her, or the corpse drops "like Adamant" into the grave, or "plashless" butterflies leap and swim "off Banks of Noon." Though delicately, even quietly rendered in deft iambic syllabics, her world is truly outrageous, genuinely different, idiosyncratically itself:

> Inebriate of Air—am I—
> And Debauchee of Dew—
> Reeling—thro endless summer days—
> From inns of Molten Blue—

As in the falling light and shadow and bruised ear of Theodore Roethke's work, we scut from terror, to tinkling phonemes, to bone-piercing truths: "Being, but an Ear, / And I, and Silence, some strange Race / Wrecked, solitary, here—".

She is definitely "here," in the iconoclastic consciousness of the poems. A slant musicality winds through the spoken words, off rhymes, near chimes, slurred cadences, jagged stanzas of thought. Dickinson rhymes "listens" with "Distance" in a poem that begins, unforgettably and colloquially, "There's a certain Slant of light." It's this contracted "Slant" that defines her world, indeed, underlines it, may even be said to reveal the real of her angled vision, where others would gloss it smooth or straight. Austin saw this as unpredictable "ripples of energy" in the new American rhythms of "the landscape line," all the more so in Dickinson—variant foot, oblique image, off rhyme, bent light. The contracted "there's" is unmistakably hers, and undeniably prosaic in anapestic American metrics ("There's a *cert-*"). Her everyday attempts at pattern and art are constantly interrupted by the "Slant" of truth unnoticed (and parenthetical synapses, in the pauses that follow, to correct our misjudgments). "None may teach it— Any—" she says of that "Slant." It leans toward an all-inclusive "nothing," remaining open to anything, and is most often revealed in apt negations of anticipation, refusals of what Williams called "easy lateral sliding," where we lose the target in a simpler distraction. Her oblique truth is registered in an errant hyphen ("I heard a Fly buzz—when I died—"); or in a stubborn comma that won't budge, even for a verb ("That oppresses, like the Heft / Of Cathedral Tunes—"); or in line breaks that plunge into infinity, only to dredge up more weighted metrics ("Or Butterflies, off Banks of Noon / Leap, plashless as they swim"); or in a parenthetical outrider of thought that can't be dislodged ("And then a Plank in Reason, broke, / And I dropped down, and down—/ And hit a World, at every plunge, / And Finished knowing—then—"); or in repetitions where we least expect, or changes where we expect repetition ("As We went out and in / Between Her final Room / And Rooms where Those to be alive / Tomorrow were, a Blame").

The poet believes, a century before James Wright wrote it down, that "fear is what quickens me." In poem no. 974, she says the Soul's intimation of immortality is "best disclosed by Danger / Or quick Calamity—"

> As Lightning on a Landscape
> Exhibits Sheets of Place—
> Not yet suspected—but for Flash—
> And Click—and Suddenness.

So the indirect perception of God's "Flash" is as though sheet lightning flared *behind* the clouds, illuminating the evanescent silhouette of a buried landscape. This sheet-lightning flash carries what Hughes calls "naked voltage" in her dash synapses. We see in snatches: slant light, distant chord, quick luminance, brief synapse. Alternately and momentarily blue-lighted, the truth is flashed, through darkness and occlusion, off layered "Sheets of Place." Seamus Heaney in his 1995 Nobel acceptance speech, perhaps also thinking of Hopkins's "terrible crystal," spoke of discovering "the crystalline inwardness of Emily Dickinson, all those forked lightnings and fissures of association." There is always another Voice (the Master?) behind the voices of the storm, another bolt behind the diffused charge that "sheets" our ghostly sense of place on earth.

As with slant rhymes that bind, or misplaced commas that plough up sense, scattered hyphens set off the truth, capitalized. Stuttered rhythms strike different (ear)drums. So does syntax twist and invert and reverse expectations to yield more deeply embedded truths: "His notice sudden is—" she says in the snake poem, the transitive-of-motion as a whispered kiss coming last. Or again in the deathwatch poem, "The last Night that She lived":

> As We went out and in
> Between Her final Room
> And rooms where Those to be alive
> Tomorrow were, a Blame
>
> That Others could exist
> While She must finish quite
> A Jealousy for Her arose
> So nearly infinite—

"We" and "Her" and "Those" and "Others" seem loosely grouped and estranged all at once, *others* all in what critics are fond of calling alterity these days. It seems as though some form of temporal gathering were casually coming and going around the dying, as people go "out" and "in" the rooms of time, busying futile daily arts before death. And "tomorrow" *was* there, she remembers, such that time dissociates into the past-future, a split sense of bracketing death all around us. We scramble about, as mortality scurrying through many rooms, shuffling here and there, our present nowhere, lost in the scuttle of out and in, the dying breaths.

Dickinson's capital letters cause us to pause and guess what is being said behind what's said—rooms behind rooms. Both the concrete and the abstract exist together in this language of verbally physical ghosts. The language doubles, with spirits behind each *Thing*, presence italicized, as it were. And the rhymes riddle, rather than reassure: "quite" ties into "infinite," the inconsequential with the never-ending, the colloquial or offhand filler with the final endlessness. Her composite puzzle of reality quizzes and dis/comforts, to say the least, disturbs us into finer awareness, less arrogance. The hymn and the riddle, as Hughes says, chant and crux, transfix us. What we harmoniously (de)claim is usually what eludes us.

Throughout the verse, poetic cadences are begun and interrupted by *things*-as-they-are. With death's attention,

> We noticed smallest things—
> Things overlooked before
> By this great light upon our Minds
> Italicized—as 'twere.

Mysteries edge out certainties. Summer slips off "as imperceptibly as Grief." In the autumnal beauty of America are both loss and anticipation: "A courteous, yet harrowing Grace, / As Guest, that would be gone." All is evanescence, a stranger and more nameless flight than Shelley's skylark or Keats's haunting nightingale. "There's no wing like meaning," as Stevens says, yet still stranger meanings ruffle like ghosts:

> And he unrolled his feathers
> And rowed him softer home—
>
> Than Oars divide the Ocean,
> Too silver for a seam—
> Or Butterflies, off Banks of Noon
> Leap, plashless as they swim.

The generic ghost of a "bird" leaps time and space, beyond Dickinson's abstract *Thing*. Hers is a transcendental vision of the transforming moment when flight is all, the metaphor dissolving the hardness of mortal reality, swooping us up into the "plashless" moment, the epiphany as reflective chronotope.

We have the neoprimitive truth of one woman's nature in premodernist America, the Amherst of "New" England, and more. This poet can be joyous: "Much Madness is divinest Sense—". Whimsical: "the little Tippler / Leaning against the—Sun—". Terrible: "—and then / I could not see to see—". Sapir concludes of this American Primitive, "She gained solitude, and held on to a despair that was linked to joy by their common ecstasy." Her art combines in patterns and disruptions—to reveal, or to suggest, or to pray, at least, for "differing" patterns of perception, Anglo-Saxon to *native* American. To our ears, straining for symmetry, her irregularities at times may fail to cohere, her reality escaping us. Thus, beyond the "landscape line" we imagine a Paradise, possibly a God, where the echoes of our prayers and stammers may be heard perhaps in clearer harmonies (Our Fathers or Mothers Who Art . . .). And we make our poems of her poetry, our new American rhythms.

Finally, in death, she may be "grasped of God," but in consciousness never by God. Like Wordsworth's Lucy, rolled in "earth's diurnal round" with senseless "rocks and stones and trees," we each and all become "of" the world in death. There is room for honest Christian doubt here, a true humility before the end and God's uncertain grace. She earns "The privilege to die" long before Plath. No wonder the Holocaust poet Paul Celan found translating her verse into German electrifying. And thus we must add Rilke's "terrible angels" in the *Duino Elegies—Jeder Engel ist schrecklich*—the harrowing spirits remain (un)revealed, sensed but never seen or heard, in the hushed murmurings of human consciousness. The closest Dickinson can come to hymnal God lies in "plashless" flights of winged things, in leaps of butterflies off "Banks of Noon," or in still "Slants" of winter afternoon light. And seasoned by fall, by Eve on the edge of the Garden leaving, Adam penitent, she reserves and sings the warrior poet's "privilege to die."

MOORE'S DETERMINATE IT: *IT'S CONSCIENTIOUS INCONSISTENCY*

Even more than Dickinson, whose poetic resurrection framed her own literary debut, Marianne Moore loved the organic nature of plants and animals. She was a biology major at Bryn Mawr and went on to teach at the Carlisle Indian School, 1911–1915, when the Sauk and Fox Olympian, Jim Thorpe, was a student there. No neoprimitivist, and not a world traveler like her friend Elizabeth Bishop, still Moore loved the natural world at-large, the natural way things worked best. Call her a poetic naturalist, an aesthetic realist. She was a bright and bold woman with high regard for wild things, for native sports (especially baseball, car racing, and tennis), for good art (in the best sense of those words), for the right way to do things. Dickinson would have admired Moore's old-fashioned good sense, Plath may have thought her oddly brilliant. Paul Celan translated her as well as Dickinson into German.

Vladimir Nabokov once noted "the passion of the scientist," reversely empowered, "the precision of the artist." In our native New World, contrary truths cross-furrow modernist ground. Just so Marianne Moore: small, red-haired, spark-eyed and spunky, yet decorous. She was an Irish-American poet who taught stenography at Carlisle Indian School, then moved into a fourth-floor Brooklyn apartment life-long with her mother. In "Efforts of Affection" Elizabeth Bishop sketches a remembered house of integrity:

> The atmosphere of 260 Cumberland Street was of course "old-fashioned," but even more, otherworldly—as if one were living in a diving bell from a different world, let down through the crass atmosphere of the twentieth century. Leaving the diving bell with one's nickel, during the walk to the subway and the forty-five-minute ride back to Manhattan, one was apt to have a slight case of mental or moral bends—so many things to be remembered; stories, phrases, the unaccustomed deference, the exquisitely prolonged etiquette— these were hard to reconcile with the New Lots Avenue express and the awful, jolting ride facing a row of indifferent faces. Yet I never left Cumberland Street without feeling happier: uplifted, even inspired, determined to be good, to work harder, not to worry about what other people thought, never to try to publish anything until I thought I'd done my best with it, no matter how many years it took—or never to publish at all.

Our unwed positivist was an inveterate Dodger fan, when baseball still ruled Brooklyn; she watched televised games with the janitor and his wife in their basement apartment and never missed a home game. Moore paid homage to the physical, exercising on a trapeze hung in her apartment doorway and playing a spirited game of tennis.

This poet frequented zoos and circuses sacramentally. To repair a bracelet, she once clipped a few hairs from a baby elephant's forehead with nail scissors while Elizabeth Bishop preoccupied the parents by way of stale brown bread at the zoo rope's other end. Marianne was as interested in the nature of machines as the workings of nature. Upon request, she came up with several hundred names for the Ford Edsel (imagine Eve naming four-wheelers in Eden): Mongoose Civique, Hurrican Hirundo, the Impeccable, the Resilient Bullet, the Ford Fabergé, Turbotorc, Thunder Crester, Pastelogram, Regina-Rex, Andante con Moto, Turcotingo, Utopian Turtletop. The Edsel was finally named after Henry's grandson.

A touch old-fashioned in a modish way, Moore wore her red hair formally coiled. She showed a fondness for broad and low, felt or straw hats and proper attire (she noticed such things of appearance). For two years Marianne Moore and Elizabeth Bishop called each other "Miss." Bishop draws a portrait of her friend of thirty-five years:

> Marianne's hair was always done up in a braid around the crown of her head, a style dating from around 1900, I think, and never changed. Her skin was fair, translucent, although faded when I knew her. Her face paled and flushed so quickly she reminded me of Rima in W. H. Hudson's *Green Mansions*. Her eyes were bright, not "bright" as we often say about eyes when we really mean alert: they were that too, but also shiny bright and, like those of a small animal, often looked at one sidewise—quickly, at the conclusion of a sentence that had turned out unusually well, just to see if it had taken effect. Her face was small and pointed, but not really triangular because it was a little lopsided, with a delicately pugnacious-looking jaw. When one day I told her she looked like Mickey Rooney, then a very young actor (and she did), she seemed quite pleased.

Marianne learned to tango, and she loved to ride in the front seat on the wildest roller coaster. As she said in *The Paris Review* of Williams's writing, "he is willing to be reckless; if you can't be that, what's the point of the whole thing?" To catalogue the traits of a woman who wrote naturalistically from open secrets and modest silences, "self-reliant like the cat—,"

—a persnickety wit
 —a microsyllabic ear
  —a precise, exacting eye
   —a self-effacing ego
    —a scrupulous regard for the things of others
—a microcosmic sense of the poem as the-world-of-living-things-in-miniature
       —a touch old-world, indeed, proprietous
     —a dash eccentric
   —a classic modern
 —an original American.

She was never condescending, never negative for the sake of it, though firm in what certain things were *not* (a positive negative)—truth was all. Along with her mother, Marianne showed an antique fondness for double and triple syntactic negatives, which reversed field to right wrongs in broader human contexts. "Distaste which takes no credit to itself is best," she said of unlikeables, "Snakes, Mongooses, Snake-Charmers and the Like." And further, of obscure verse: "we do not admire what / we cannot understand: the bat . . ."—but to such are we drawn (base/ball fans, elephants, wild horses, business documents). Moore first arranged to meet the younger Bishop, a student recommended by the Vassar librarian, at the doorway to the reading room of the New York Public Library. If she suspected not liking someone for the first time, the poet-editor arranged to meet them at the information booth (a quick exit) in Grand Central Station.

Ms. Moore was laureled with sixteen honorary degrees. In 1951–52 she won the Triple Crown in poetry, as Randall Jarrell quipped, the National Book Award, Bollingen, and Pulitzer Prizes. Moore redefined the verse line for herself: a bit Latinate, that is, quantitative or syllabic, even polysyllabic— and, again, certainly accentual (or not so certainly, as the case may be) so that "accentual-syllabic" verse becomes *her* way of writing an idiosyncratic democratic poetry that makes no apology for what it isn't (easy), or won't (conform, normalize), or persistently resists (gloss). She was as gifted and careful about her measures as Dickinson and Sitting Bull. Form has its place in the natural world (nature is never formless) to be enjoyed. It will delight one of clear eye, ear, & mind—"how pure a thing is joy," she wrote, her favorite word of praise being *gusto*. The mind is, indeed, "an enchanted" (if limited, alas) "thing"—about five pounds of grey matter that glistens imaginatively "like the glaze on a / katydid wing—". By nature and defi- nition, it minds things in our little emotive stores of senses. "Where there is personal liking we go," the poet assures us most naturally in "The Hero." We like what we are, by nature, mostly, even when we are dead wrong.

Our minds scour the grounds of being, skeptically sniff the air, chomp down on "reality," and, enchanted, shine

> like the dove-
> neck animated by
> sun; it is memory's eye;
> it's conscientious inconsistency.

Still, the poet adds,

> Unconfusion submits
> its confusion to proof; it's
> not a Herod's oath that cannot change.

An honestly resistant mind can right itself, gyroscopically, through double negative (change its wrong mind). It's not what won't be (Herod's slain infants) but *will* be (the Word made flesh will *not* not-be). *In*consistencies become consistent, curiously in the mind's own iconic justification, where knowledge is necessarily of the self, primarily *primitive*, that is, primary or naturally original. Such is Moore's comic, honest celebration of our individually obdurate, flaming minds embodied through evolutionary biology and animal kin ("don't laugh," she cautions of her "wood-weasel" emergent). We, thinking with "regnant certainty," dominate all . . . the world around, we think (as with Stevens's jar in Tennessee). In Moore's zoosphere, we remain wildly and exquisitely obtuse, delightfully unperturbed with the rest of the world's (the whole world's mostly) objections to our enchantments—our reversible fields of the mind's play with "reality." One's song is another's squawk, one's meter is another's muck.

Such parochial local color holds true for broad cultures, made of so many gyroscopic individuals composing a group. Mary Austin was Moore's organic contemporary and Western Sierra sister at the turn of the century, and in *Earth Horizon* she steps forward as an emancipated natural woman. Her native voice recalls itself sensuously and syllabically, with a twist of Frost's contrary tension, even a smatter of Dickinson's phonemics. "All these *things* came *back* with the *shat*tered *bril*liance of *light* through *stained glass*," she begins chapter six in rolling hexameter:

> I remember the orchard with great clumps of frail spring-beauties coming up through the sod; the smell of budding sassafras on the winds of March, and the sheets of blue violets about rotting tree-trunks in the woodlot.

With a breath of Bronte moor wind, her traversing prose pushes anapests against trochees, reverses pace with lyric spondees, compels iambs toward great gusty spaces. Moore would have admired her *gusto*.

> I remember the tree toads musically trilling, the katydids in the hickory tree by the pump, and a raw Yorkshire lad who had come to work for Father, not able to sleep because of them.

Austin's cadences move acoustically through natural rhythms, primal sights and smells, to visual sequences and characters in dramatic motion.

> I more than recall the hot honey-scent of red clover, and the heavy, low flying bumble-bees; long walks in winter over the snow with Father, and the discovery of green fronds of fern and leafy wild blackberry vines under the edge of February thaws.

The writer's physical imagination, rolling with Wordsworthian iambics, brings back a sensuously graced childhood for contemplation. Her reflective cadences are prose cousins to Moore's elaborately natural poetics, both writers feeling into the genuine speech and daily pattern, the commonplace intelligence, for a genuine narrative, native and artistic. "As they came forth normally," Austin wrote in *The American Rhythm*, "the prose rhythms of folk narrative are as distinct as their speech idioms. In all of them there is a basic rhythm of perceptivity, the mind of the story-teller working on his plot . . . rippling like the swallowing muscles of the snake." As Parry and Lord rediscovered, two thousand years after Homer sang Greek epics to a lyre's lilt, the way an artist patterns words to tell a story will sequence, and become, the storytelling itself, the word-sending. Mary Austin's "rhythm" is her American text.

Moore, the poet, writes a little tighter lines. She counts her phonemes, and they click into place, each consonant lettuce-fresh, each vowel a tiny lagoon for the tongue to swim. Her syntax feels like thin tissue (not muscular like Frost, sculpted like Pound, or scalloped like Williams). She thinks each word, probing its depths and testing its edges, turning sounds upside down to shake loose all the scuttling meanings; she then places the assemblage, always, right-side-up, as it should be, on the decorous line, more or less . . . though the lengths seem at times all awry. That is, until one counts their orderly coveys (bird-like they perch on branches of lines) and remarks how real to the symmetry of teeth, the rounded mouth and budded tongue, indeed, how "like" to human the visual and vocal designs of the lines. (Dickinson would clap in praise!) The phonemes swell and shrink in accord with organic logics, orderly as mathematics: "miracles of language and construction," Bishop remarks.

> Marianne was intensely interested in the techniques of things—how camellias are grown; how the quartz prisms work in crystal clocks; how the pangolin can close up his ear, nose, and eye apertures and walk on the outside edges of his hands "and save the claws for digging"; how to drive a car; how the best pitchers throw a baseball; how to make a figurehead for her nephew's sailboat. The exact way in which anything was done, or made, or functioned, was poetry to her.

"Contractility is a virtue," Moore wrote of snails, and of "the principle that is hid" in poems. Or of apple seeds in the poem "Nevertheless": "the fruit / within the fruit." This organic image, seed within seed, tactiley and naturally answers Stevens's "poem within a poem" *(Adagia)*. The mode is analogy—the metaphor, comic simile. A wood-weasel, for example, creeps by as "determination's totem," the embedded humor no less penetrant than Dickinson's wit or Darwin's marvel. The poems and their animals seem to live a life of their own, as the poet did, "inconceivably arcanic."

Well, perhaps they are a bit artificial (at times) but nobly so, well-made. Let's say honest, if archaic (who isn't, too soon?): "it is not for us to understand art," *that* cat says among monkeys "in articulate frenzy." No species too strange (apteryx to kiwi), no setting too silly ("Bird-Witted"), no subject too shimmering ("Like Gieseking playing Scarlatti"), no syllable too small (it, art, if, bat, eat, cr*i*tic, po*e*try). She spells out her own terms in "If I Were Sixteen Today":

1. Whatever you do, put all you have into it.

2. Go to the trouble of asking, "What good does it do?" rather than "Why Portuguese? I may never use it."

3. Don't look on art as effeminate, and museums as "the most tiring form of recreation."

4. I would, like Sir Winston Churchill, refuse to let a betrayal rob me of trust in my fellow man.

5. One should above all, learn to be silent, to listen; to make possible promptings from on high. Suppose you "don't believe in God." Talk to someone very wise, who believed in God, did not, and then found that he did. The cure for loneliness is solitude. Think about this saying by Martin Buber: "The free man believes in destiny and that it has need of him." Destiny, not fate.

And lastly, ponder Solomon's wish: when God appeared to him in a dream and asked, "What wouldst thou that I give unto thee?" Solomon did not say fame, power, riches, but an understanding mind, and the rest was added.

Her friend Bishop recalls Moore as "one of the world's greatest talkers." At the heart of New York modernism, this Bryn Mawr woman of the first decade knew Austin, Pound, Eliot, Stevens, Williams, and all "The Others" of the Greenwich Renaissance and after. She edited *The Dial* and published countless new writers, and assisted in the New York Public Library. Moore would not have missed notice of Mary Austin's celebrated play, *The Arrow Maker,* about an Indian shaman woman unsuccessfully in love, produced 1911 in New York's New Theatre, within months of Roger Fry's neoprimitive-modernist art exhibit in London, through which "human character changed," according to Virginia Woolf. "In the winter of 1910–11," Austin writes in *The American Rhythm,* "The Poetry Society took notice to the extent of inviting me to address them" on Native American verse as the "mold" of American poetry. Hers was an argument Moore or Williams would consider, one that Fry or Picasso would draw from African to postimpressionist art, or that Pound might raise in the *ABC of Reading,* down through *Confucius to Cummings:* "It ought not to be necessary to justify the relationship between Amerind and American verse, seeing how completely we have accepted the involvement of Hellenic and Pelasgian influences in the best of Greek literature. Nobody denies the intermingled strains of British, Celtic and mixed Nordic elements in the best of English," Austin adds.

Classic could be organic, then, at its best; modernist was neoprimitive, from Paris and London, to New York and Chicago with the 1912 advent of *Poetry* magazine. At the masthead, a New World Sappho of Irish-American heritage, Moore was freshly steeped in Dickinson's slant muse, amused even more so than her predecessor. Well, with a plain sense dose, yes, of Elizabeth Bishop tossed in. Her poetry "gives the impression of a passage through," William Carlos Williams wrote. "There is a distaste for lingering, as in Emily Dickinson. As in Emily Dickinson there is too a fastidious precision of thought where unrhymes fill the purpose better than rhymes.

There is a swiftness impaling beauty. . . ." Moore's modestly precise modernism anticipates the woman's verse of Denise Levertov, even Linda Gregg, Jorie Graham, or the arcanic stringencies of Adrienne Rich, Louise Glück, Mary Oliver, and Sharon Olds today. There was Gertrude Stein, after all. There were Amy Lowell, Hilda Doolittle, and Edna St. Vincent Millay. There have always been women doing as they do, Dickinson and Moore among the first Euro-Americans (back to Sappho, up through Anne Bradstreet) to be recognized as major modern poets, in a through-line today recognizing Luci Tapahonso, Linda Hogan, and Joy Harjo, among other Native American women poets.

Poetry? "I, too, dislike it[,]" Moore sniped, but not snidely. Often we *dislike* what we choose or must do: do daily and then carp. This domestic woman carried scribbled verse slips of paper in her mouth from ironing to washing dishes, as Dickinson filled her baking apron pockets with daily jottings. Moore was constantly pressing against the dead foliage of language, the cast-off rags of street sayings, the trash of newspapers, baseball scores, racing forms, Wall Street ticker tape—for precisely the right syllable to suit the *thing,* whatever at hand. It surprised her, as flushed spirits will, as animals can, as we surprise ourselves. Moore learned to drive a car at seventy years of age. Her world is our jack-in-the-box hall of mirrors— bestiary, mortuary, test tube, and vegetable garden, all in one. Steeple-jacks all, we climb above our Main Street to paint the gilded star of hope, a red-and-white DANGER sign on the sidewalk far below.

Poetry, too, is of this world, climb as we will and "damned" as we fall, Williams said, from beginning to end—but more often than not, it is our piecemeal grace, our mental salvation, our verbal body's bread and everyday sacrament. "Nevertheless," Moore wrote,

> Victory won't come
> to me unless I go
> to it

At least if "one" (an *other* minding) is so inclined, not reclined, s(he) is "interested *in*" it, po-*et*-ry, as Williams saw her work, an *art*-iculated porcelain garden. Toads in her syllabic compost turn into bumps-of-another-color; phonemes metamorphose as princes of thought, royalty of a natural kind. What a weird business, this art, what a quirky life!

Not if one *is* a poet, Dickinson would side with Moore: the "genuine," on one hand, is as the gentle, genteel, jaunty, and gentlewomanly, all cognate (human-*kind,* the genus), so-called *Homo sapiens,* suspected *Homo ludens.* The "genuine" is precisely and passionately, as Nabokov says, the genius of the scientist and artist alike, as is poetry, on the other hand, "raw," which moves naturally, both rare and everywhere about us in native poetics, parsing the bear's heart. Stringing a bow from Dickinson and Austin, through Moore to Plath, a woman's cadence sets a modern poetic through-line—an American rhythm of sights and sounds, scenes and sequences, series and scenarios. "It is human nature," Moore wrote in "A Grave" of a man facing the sea, "to stand in the middle of a thing." *In medias res,* Moore would say, a native democracy of poetry. On the postmodernist side of Sylvia Plath, perhaps we must taste our meat more tender, just a breath of blood, and skim our ears and skin our eyes, disrobed to rawness. Better, as Simone Weil argued in the 1920s, to *decreate* the cooked back to the steamy animal afoot, than simply to realize the "raw" wherever we find *it: re,* regarding *res,* the "things" at hand, and *-alize,* as in conceptualize it alive. Poetry stalks ideal game in real dreams—the "genuine" of Dickinson's w*it,* the "raw" of Plath's reality.

The genuine and the raw, then: the real and the naked, honest and unadorned. American women at either end, and in the middle of it, come forward as newly liberated, even neoprimitive modernists. Naturalists and poets lean toward a common agreement, at least, on what-is, whatever registers *true.* These seers, Sitting Bull and William James through Galway Kinnell and Sharon Olds, seem truly American, native, modern as in alive to the country's present (Leonardo was so, Pound would argue, as was Confucius, or Pythagoras, or Beethoven in their own cultures). "The exact way in which anything was done, or made, or functioned," Bishop concluded, "was poetry to her." It's the tic within the tick: an origin in the original, an immigrant Irishman's daughter rooted in Whitman's Brooklyn.

Elizabeth Bishop immortalizes the word-sending, ambient truth of her poet-friend in an "Invitation to Miss Marianne Moore":

> From Brooklyn, over the Brooklyn Bridge, on this fine morning,
>   please come flying. . . .
> Come with the pointed toe of each black shoe
> trailing a sapphire highlight,
> with a black capeful of butterfly wings and bon-mots,
> with heaven knows how many angels all riding
> on the broad black brim of your hat,
>   please come flying. . . .
>
> With dynasties of negative constructions
> darkening and dying around you,
> with grammar that suddenly turns and shines
> like flocks of sandpipers flying,
>   please come flying.
>
> Come like a light in the white mackerel sky,
> come like a daytime comet
> with a long unnebulous train of words,
> from Brooklyn, over the Brooklyn Bridge, on this fine morning,
>   please come flying.

PLATH: MS. *RAW*

. . . every genuinely shamanic séance ends as a spectacle *unequaled in the world
of daily experience. The fire tricks, the "miracle" of the rope-trick or mango-trick type,
the exhibition of magical feats, reveal another world—the fabulous world of the gods
and magicians, the world in which* everything seems possible, *where the dead
return to life and the living die only to live again, where one can disappear and
reappear instantaneously, where the "laws of nature" are abolished, and a certain
superhuman "freedom" is exemplified and made dazzlingly* present.

MIRCEA ELIADE, EPILOGUE TO Shamanism

*Behind these poems there is a fierce and uncompromising nature. There is also
a child desperately infatuated with the world. And there is a strange muse, bald,
white and wild, in her 'hood of bone,' floating over a landscape like that of the
Primitive Painters, a burningly luminous vision of a Paradise. A Paradise which
is at the same time eerily frightening, an unalterably spot-lit vision of death.*

TED HUGHES ON SYLVIA PLATH, Winter Pollen

If poems are in Moore's words "imaginary gardens with real toads," Plath's
reptiles turn darkly real. They fester and rot in Eve's Inferno of fallen vines,
a "radioactive" Eden, her husband writes in *Birthday Letters.* Cursed off-
spring, the poems spurt blood and belch black smoke and hiss their in-
human dissent: "a stink of fat and baby crap," the mother says of her
infants in "Lesbos." Self-condemned by her father's death when she was
eight, Plath was trapped in *existénce,* scornful of *nature,* cursed with con-
sciousness, disdainful of alterity (as Sartre said in *No Exit,* Kazin notes, hell
is "other people"). The reassertion of natural rights to a living art does
not always work out in America; from patriarchal curse to self-violence, our
frontier gamble with death is a real one. Not much chance for neoprimitive
rebirth here, more cul-de-sac existentialism, a fatally self-made poetics.

Plath's "raw" nature strips the skin from reality. "I am red meat," she
warns in "Death & Co." We see the projected wounds of hyper-thought—
bleeding from unwanted, obsessional sexual entry and insatiable, sucking
offspring. Intensity is everywhere, raging, internally sizzling; yet from with-
out, the poet is stone-faced in a skin mask. The mother muse hides out by
indifferent moonlight, "her blacks crackle and drag." Children, "all the
dead dears," must cover their cloven souls to survive, if only for a little
while, as Medusa shamanically casts spells to dispel the night's terror. She
hexes love, chants death's threat to a dramatic stall, holds off Dickinson's
imminent eternity, for just a second. Stage directions splicing acts of *The
Winter's Tale* come back to haunt this study's through-line, *"Exeunt omnes
pursued by a bear."*

The Master may be dead, but never forgotten. By way of a Ouija board,
"Prince Otto" spoke to his daughter from the dead, but he was under gag
rule from the Colossus, the title poem of her first collection. The "bald,

white tumuli of your eyes" remained occluded, and Otto Plath's daughter
could "never get you put together entirely":

> A blue sky out of the Oresteia
> Arches above us. O father, all by yourself
> You are pithy and historical as the Roman Forum.

According to a carbon typescript found by her husband, Plath's final and
finest excoriation, *Ariel*, was to be titled *Daddy* until the very last. So God
the Father is daughter-cursed among men. Daddy's vampire German Soul,
his "fat black heart," must be staked with word-sticks. A woman's father,
son, or lover (here Otto Plath, Nicholas the first-born boy, or Ted Hughes
her husband) violate the old Edenic tryst, though it's never quite clear why
(the telephone's "muck funnel" in muffled whispers secretly tells on Him).
This is an old misogynist tragedy, as Greek as Atreus and Medusa, with
American Gothic twists—Cassandra's melodrama, Electra's tension,
Helen's promiscuity, Clytemnestra's hysteria. This woman's anger burns
deadly white, beyond reason or grace. Hatred, an inverted voice of passion,
is her cause for living, momentarily.

In November 1959, as Hughes reconstructs his wife's journals, Plath
dreamed that she died and abortively tried to reassemble "a giant, shat-
tered, stone Colossus." This dismembered father image worked itself,
Hughes thinks, into a breakthrough poem called "The Stones." He reasons
that the turning point in Plath's life, the birth of "her real poetic voice"
and "rebirth of herself," came through the dream tradition of shamanic
"magical death," followed by demonic "dismemberment," then resurrec-
tion "with new insides, a new body." To what end? In the *Listener*, a year
after Plath's death, Hughes concluded of the shaman's practice: "His busi-
ness is usually to guide some soul to the underworld, or bring back a sick
man's lost soul, or deliver sacrifices to the dead, or ask the spirits the reason
for an epidemic, or the whereabouts of game or a man lost." An inter-
mediary daemon, the shaman bets lives against the odds, a marginal guide
through crisis. And so it was with Plath's abortive quest to reconstruct the
shattered Colossus of her dead father, Prince Otto "Full Fathom Five," to
whom, as a failed shaman, she could go only by way of suicide. A New
England wyrd far beyond Dickinson, her self-prophesied death is prefig-
ured in "Witch Burning," or in the infamous "Lady Lazarus":

> Dying
> Is an art, like everything else.
> I do it exceptionally well.
>
> I do it so it feels like hell.
> I do it so it feels real.
> I guess you could say I've a call.

It was brassily imitating Roethke by way of "The Stones," Hughes feels, that shattered the old Sylvia and momentarily raised "a new self out of the ruins of her mythical father." The next month, December 1959, Plath set sail from America with her English husband, got pregnant with her first-born, Frieda (named after Lawrence's wife), and placed her first collection of poems with Heinemann. Within three years, she bore two children, wrote her novel and best verse, and took her own life on the anniversary of the Heinemann contract for *Daddy*, published posthumously as *Ariel*. Out of this brittle crucible came Plath's most brilliantly disturbing work, bridged by "The Stones," whose last lines end *The Colossus:*

> Love is the bone and sinew of my curse.
> The vase, reconstructed, houses
> The elusive rose.
>
> Ten fingers shape a bowl for shadows.
> My mendings itch. There is nothing to do.
> I shall be good as new.

Hers is the Edenic myth as American homily or kitchen commonplace; the homemade cliché betrays, as it wounds and teases anew a suicidal Eve. *I shall be good as new.* According to Hughes, Plath is the dangerous shaman dying, again and again, conversing with the mute dead colossus and traversing hell in self-resurrecting, poetic spectacle. "It's the theatrical / Comeback in broad day / To the same place."

Plath was stranded in personal crisis and the magical vice of *making* art. W. B. Yeats, poet-hero of both Plath and Hughes, passed through the Celtic twilight calling on Irish myth to dream himself anew, legendary heroism to battle time, folkloric spirituality to revive Gaelic culture, and his own wild imagination to reconfigure English poetry as tribal chant. "This was pure shamanic thinking of the most primitive brand," Hughes describes Yeats's reborn gods of the Irish renaissance. "It was closer to the visions of the Sioux Shaman Black Elk than to anything in the political or even poetic traditions of Western Europe," Hughes thinks. "Primitive man knows nature," C. M. Bowra wrote in *Primitive Song*, the study that momentarily reshaped Plath's poetry, "because he lives with it and in it and by it. . . . he has a factual, realistic experience, which is more intimate and more expertly first hand than that of any zoologist or botanist."

Plath was fascinated with the lines Bowra drew from contemporary poetry to primitive song, lines that Dickinson, Austin, and Moore would have traced with interest, but Sylvia could not draw from the tribal catalyst. She abhorred cultural context. Plath buried her poetics in herself and aborted shamanic transformation, contrasted with another English-transplanted American a generation before, T. S. Eliot, who placed individual crisis in traditional history. Bowra contends that a tribal song-poet calls for desired ends from nature, reciprocal exchanges with animals, plants, and spirits, for survival and renewal itself: "Primitive man hardly ever sings of nature simply from delight in it for its own sake." Plath knew no nature or community outside her own writing, nor did she trust in life-sustaining ways, finally, her own *nature*. She lived for the tenuous, thesaurus-driven *makings* of lines that broke up psychically as she made them. We are back between the opening terms of this study, the made and bearing arts of poetry.

Bowra's division of secular and spiritual song-poetry cuts to the bone of Plath's verse-for-her-own-sake. "So, while nature is both his home and his hunting-ground," Bowra summarizes of the primitive singer, "it is also the seat of supernatural powers. . . . His unceasing traffic with nature only convinces him that there is much more in it than meets his eye, and though this in no way diminishes his watchful keenness, it forces him to look on nature with questioning wonder and uneasy awe." Here is the glitch in the shaman's trance: Plath's final glance backward, literally her last poem, is one of mixed dread and scorn, as the night blacks "crackle and drag." Bowra concludes in *Primitive Song:*

> Primitive man is surrounded by forces which he cannot control or understand, and he hopes that by finding the right words he may gain some hold on them. This applies equally to prospects for hunting and the weather, to birth and death, to puberty and marriage, to the growth of trees and plants, to the supply of animals and of water. Though he has a vast and precise knowledge of the natural world as he studies it in his search for food, he does not begin to understand how it works, and he turns to magic as a means to get what he wishes.

Chant magic could not charm the poet from her own darkness, nor could she find her dispossessed way back into any tribal community, but left cookies and milk for her infants as she lay her napkined head in an unlit oven.

As much as Plath draws on shamanic magic, she fails the journey home to grounded people, time, or place; her poetry exists for itself alone, a wellwrought curse, an existential cul-de-sac. Her verses carry American diction to extraordinary poetic limits, as a housewife's muttering turns into witch's liturgy. There are no given line lengths (one-beat to five-beat cadences). Erratic, brilliant rhymes come sparingly: "perfected" / "accomplishment" in "Edge," or "Each dead child coiled" tolling nascent dentals, or "serpent" / "empty," or with her black mare on Hampstead Heath before sunrise, "Stasis in darkness" and "The dew that flies / Suicidal, at one with the drive."

Plath has one of the finest ears in American poetry—not Dickinson's Inner Ear ("Being, but an Ear"), but the concise acoustic echo of a highly attuned "outer" ear, estranged from things, stunned by their impact, listening painfully. "Catgut stitches my fissures." She records a world in bruising certainty, with no spiritual or communal undertones. At the same time, this poet can throw it all in the fire—reject her aural genius, mock her art, self-combust with brilliant smack rhymes: "hell-dull, dull as the triple" in "Fever 103," or "Incapable / of licking clean," or "The indelible smell / Of a snuffed candle," or "low smokes roll," or "yellow sullen smokes," and finally, in rhythmic parody, "element" that "will not rise." An incessant oral imagination is at work here.

> What is it
> Survives, grieves
> So, over this battered, obstinate spit
> Of gravel?

Her hyperkinetic aural sensitivity fixates and rings changes on a single syllable, "the sluttish, rutted sea," much as Robert Schumann the composer was possessed of the note A that would not vacate his brain.

Plath's self-made poetic is an isolate consciousness stranded awake, where *existénce* eats itself alive, an insomniac's nightmare. The late verse sounds as though it were written posthumously, A. Alvarez says. Hers is the romantic temper gone occult, slanted away from Hughes's tracking of shamanic verse through the Great Tradition—Shakespeare's Lear in white heat, Keats afire in the longer Odes, Yeats in epic quest of Oisin, Eliot smoldering in *Ash Wednesday*. "Once you've been chosen by the spirits, and dreamed the dreams," Hughes concludes, "there is no other life for you, you must shamanize or die: this belief seems almost universal." Shamanize or die: for Plath there was no relief from thought, no lessening of life's tension, no whimsy enough, or humor, or play that lightened the bone-numbing load of reality. Her wicked wit seared things. Her focus was fierce, relentless. Dickinson's "Zero at the Bone" slid into the anorectic, even leukemic perfection of Plath's deadly art as "the Hour of Lead." The verdict: "Somebody's done for."

So Plath could not complete the uncertain journey that Dickinson began. Plath is as *un-American* as the 1960s, as radical as Anne Sexton and Allen Ginsberg, as maverick as Colonial revolutionaries two centuries before her in Boston. Her mind self-combusts, her poems decreate before us; imagery immolates itself, as feelings go up in sulfurous smoke. The white heat, the powdery ash add up to postincendiary poems. Dickinson's hesitant step, her delicate inner ear and "plashless" sense of elusive beauty, her icy courage to travel with Death, all burn out in Plath. A true revolutionary with a death wish, then, Plath will smash, burn, rage, and plunge on her black mare into the eye of the red sun like the "suicidal" dew—all sustained for the sake of a sensational artistic genius, what "art" is left in the wreckage of postmodernism. The artist's tricks undercut themselves, exposing the lie of language. All traditions, all human assumptions—poetry, family, society, God, the State, beauty, hope, salvation, love—are up for grabs. Dickinson's commas, dashes, reversed feet, iconoclastic "arts" are all stripped, charred, scraped to the bone. So a barren, lidless, shamanic moon hangs in the night sky as Plath's final icon, indifferent to suffering, no grace, no ornamentation worth saving. At a price, the artist dies before our very eyes. If Emily Dickinson's season is early fall, then Sylvia Plath's is dead winter, when she killed herself in February 1963, as cited, the anniversary of the contract for *Ariel,* three years before.

Certainly Plath saw herself a prisoner of her privacy, a vestal sacrifice to her art—not the "demurer" of chosen hesitations that italicize meanings, but the shamanic obsessional whose magic fails. For the tragic visionary in post–World War II Euro-America, there is no choice left in the matter. So recorded in her journals, Plath is woman-cursed monthly by the "wet, mussy spurt of blood." Her metaphors are overpowering, inexcusable, not to be forgotten: "There's a stake," Daddy, "in your fat black heart." The language itself, Germanic in origin (Otto Plath taught German for a living), is *his* trap: "a barb wire snare. / Ich, ich, ich, ich, / I could hardly speak." The thin toppling "I" in this "language obscene" spills from a wrenching child ego, devoured by bitter birth and premature death. Plath's protest is the curse of the life-condemned, who like Berryman or Celan spit in the face of the torturer-ghost (not man enough to stay alive for her to spurn face-to-face): "Daddy, daddy, you bastard, I'm through."

"Black milk of daybreak we drink it at sundown," Celan off-rhymes in "Death Fugue," *Schwarze Milch der Frühe wir trinken sie abends.* Rilke's "terrible angels" become avenging succubi. "We are as flies to wanton boys," Lear says in the wake of his daughters' patricidal rebellions, "they kill us for their sport." But here there's no buzzing, no blue when the poet dies— only the incendiary snap of an insect aflame and a hooded bone of moon staring down, "nothing to be sad about." "She is used to this sort of thing," Plath scraps sentiment in her last line, "Her blacks crackle and drag."

Where is this tragic vision—soured gender, toxic aesthetics—seeded in America? Is there any grounding in a native poetics at our century's end?

$\stackrel{\scriptstyle \equiv}{\scriptstyle \in}(\bullet)\stackrel{\scriptstyle \equiv}{\scriptstyle \ni}$

Adamic Savages

Westering Adam is not doing much better than Ms. Plath, *femme fatale* of our *fin de siècle*. Dickinson made dying an art, and a century later Plath turned the art of dying into fatal dare. Moore's "imaginary gardens" fester raw with holocaustal curses, crawling with fallen angels and lethal toads. Where is Old Man Bear in all this? Paul Celan wrote in *Lichtzwang* (1970), the year he threw himself into the River Seine, two years before John Berryman leaped to the frozen Mississippi:

> What you've heard, what you've seen, in
> Ward a thousand and one,
>
> day-and-nightly
> the Bear Polka:
>
> you're back in school,
>
> you will again be
> he.

"The Garden Master's gone," Berryman mourned the early death of his manic-depressive friend, Theodore Roethke. If the mother-poet as naturalist, Eve to Emily, dead-ends in Plath's rage toward an absent Daddy, where does the verse pioneer head in our new land?

BERRYMAN'S BLUES

Lord of happenings, & little things,
muster me westward fitter to my end—
which has got to be Your strange end for me—
and toughen me effective to the tribes en route.
JOHN BERRYMAN, "A USUAL PRAYER"

For American men, now over half a millennium, it's been *westward ho!* down west of west to what Plath's sibling-suicide, John Berryman, deems "Your strange end for me" in his posthumous *Delusions, etc.* Dickinson's *Master* or Plath's *Colossus* seems to have abdicated a heaven haunted by Berryman's *Lord of happenings, & little things.* His vagrant Be-ins carry a blur of casual sixties chaos. This late Berryman quatrain heaves against a normative iambic foot, trips up the made blank verse of Shakespeare & Co. "Lord" could lead into a quasi-serious prayer, with Dickinson's slant homage and biblical undercut in the capitalized possessive, "Your." Striking a minimalist swagger, the blessed ampersand "&" colloquializes little things with beat informality. The dactylic army talk of "muster me" (soldier of the revolution, civil war, cavalry, or fortune) and alliterative adverb "westward" head out toward dusk. Showdown, pardner: the sundown of Manifest Destiny and nadir of Eden, prefiguring Adam's last "strange end for me." And does "fitter" wildly suggest stronger (Gold's Gym trim), or madder (Hamlet's jabber), or normatively forced (Moral Majority fitting) toward the inevitable dying? The poet suffers a lifelong threat of suicide, in the wake of his own father's sorry end (the inherited patronymic of everyman, oddly enough, John Smith). A hyphen suspends it all ironically, an end that doesn't— . . . here in a poetry, of sorts.

And, puzzling an American rhythm, where does a reader find the opening foot in the third line—"Which" or "got"—as the monosyllabic splat of "got to be" rocks toward a spondaic thump, "Your strange end"? Berryman comes on as the fallen, postmodernist rhymer, a staggering swag, & stranger than Thou, by God (a strange god indeed) Who condemns his supplicant son to dying forlorn *(Forsaken me?)* by His last words. *Kyrie eleison:* mercy me, the lost Adamic soul in the West, estranged, asking, but not trusting salvation. It's all a bit too, giddy. Mother of God, where have you?— oh dolor, blue blood of Christ.

A prosaic riptide careens beneath the iambic hexameter of the tentative lyric, resistant to being counted or scanned: "and toughen me effective to the tribes en route." The clicking *t*s poeticize the clatter of trail talk, the chatter of the West. *Toughen me* "effective," Big Daddy, the frontier voice dares, thicken my skin: test me sore to my bones, make it & me work once more—circled wagons, marauding savages, westering.

This is the poet-man down west, word-trickster at-large, anticipating his sorry & melodramatic mortality, suspended lifelong (closure as pathos?). He wrestles with the rhythm of the American frontier (the streets, the military, the sixties, men on the run) up against the loosened rules of blank verse, bluesing the unknown. The rhymes hide in-line, tricking the form: *happenings/things, westward/my end, got to be/end for me, effective/en route.* The iambs are jammed slant with trochees—five beats become six or more— and alliteration replaces end rhyme, as rhythm primally takes back the poetics. The heaving lines reach way back across the Big Water and rock in asymmetric Anglo-Saxon rowing halves (3/2, 2/3, 3/2, 2/2/2), wilder than Pound's opening Homeric Canto ("And then went down to the ships")—slant literate, sly aesthetic, odd poetic.

Verse man tilts in crisis here, the way back east erased, Indian tribes & a "strange end" dead to the west. Twisted formal trails, the singing bear silent. Daddy's gone, Mommy's mute. A forced-march, trail-of-tears, prisoner-of-life, holocaustal trek westward without our "Lord of happenings" on the horizon. Life hunkers down to "little" bytes and lumped "things." Plain style, plains blues. It's a minuscule, inarticulate art, gunny sacked in slack American diction—oblique, ironic, fearful, all with "a certain slant" of off-beat ceremony.

Posthumously, Berryman ends with American *macho:* "toughen me effective." There comes a slightly odd appeal for armor & aesthetics, John Wayne mixed with Milton. "Tribes en route" recall savages in the path, haunting the forests, wilderness in the (un)certain mortal "end" of things, pioneers, land grabbers, gold rushers, bushwhackers, mountain men and desert rats, river pilots, politicians, and realtors running out of continental freedoms and exhaustible resources. The journey terrifies.

"Than longen folk to goon on pilgrimages," Berryman opens his last laments, *Delusions, etc.*, with Chaucer amid passages of madness. *"Lord, have mercy on my son: for he is lunatick, and sore vexed: for ofttimes he falleth into the fire, and oft into the water. "* America has been a land of maddened journeys for a long time, from the Bering Strait to the *Mayflower*, Eric the Red to Cortés, Ellis Island to fearful border passages across a Rio Grande wasteland. "April is the cruellest month," Eliot intoned a broken iambic, "breeding / Lilacs out of the dead land, mixing / Memory and desire, stirring / Dull roots with spring rain." Pilgrims seem to have lost a certain amount of faith in crossing the Big Water, or the infidel desert, since Chaucer's time. "I saw the best minds of my generation destroyed by madness," the first and last *Beat* rhymer howls. "—Kitticat, they can't fire me—," Henry drops his canceled last words in a waste basket, before jumping. Landing near the coal docks and rolling down the river slope, John Berryman was identified by his thick glasses and a blank check.

The Th/inky Death

> The marker slants, flowerless, day's almost done,
> I stand above my father's grave with rage
> often, often before
> I've made this awful pilgrimage to one
> who cannot visit me, who tore his page
> out:. . . .
>
> NO. 384 *The Dream Songs*

Just two months into the "Great" War, two days before Dylan Thomas in Wales, John Alleyn Smith was birthed cesarean in McAlester, Oklahoma, October 25, 1914, the same day Sylvia Plath would be born eighteen years later. Pound, Keats, and Sexton were all born the last Halloween week of October, full-blown Scorpios. At Berryman's birth, World War I started as a picnic, to be over by Christmas, and scudded to an end four years later, apocalyptically, for an entire generation of Euro-American men. Eliot's *Waste Land* was its elegy, Pound's *Cantos* its aftermath, Fitzgerald's *Great Gatsby* its epitaph, Hemingway's *In Our Time* its indictment. Berryman's life was bracketed by a "first" world war and an Asian "conflict" that broke America; a second global war and a Korean Communist massacre scuttered in between. The poet was at war with himself, let alone the world, all his life.

Little John's father, John Alleyn Smith, Sr., failed as an investment banker in two states, Oklahoma then Florida, where divorcing his wife and betrayed by his partner in 1926, he put a .32-caliber slug through his heart. "Father being the loneliest word in the one language," the son sang. His mother remarried her sixteen-year-senior landlord in two months, and eleven-year-old John, now a Berryman, began growing up to his tragic end. "Each jack be the custodian of his desires / from which he sprang & sullen then he slept / until a coda of blaming."

Poor eyesight kept John Berryman out of the Second "Great" War, a global slaughter we came to know through Hitler, Hirohito, Dachau, and Hiroshima. Delayed stress, endemic trauma, and holocaustal shock piled up the toxic flotsam of a "military-industrial," so tagged in the sixties, postmodernist complex—radioactivity, smog, racial violence, international terrorism, with recent epidemics of global warming, AIDS, teenage drug suicide, and millennial hysteria. In 1943 Berryman began writing "The Nervous Songs," to become *The Dream Songs* that won the Pulitzer in 1965, accompanied later by *His Toy, His Dream, His Rest,* which in turn won the National Book Award and Bollingen Prizes in 1969—the renowned Triple Crown of American poetry. Berryman was Mark Van Doren's protégé at Columbia, Robert Blackmur's colleague at Princeton, nobody's icon at Harvard. He was poet-friend to Delmore Schwartz, Robert Lowell, Randall Jarrell, Theodore Roethke, and Saul Bellow, the cursed generation of the Depression thirties, "Analysands All," the rhymer jabbered. In 1953, Berryman stood outside Dylan Thomas's hospital room as the Welsh bard died of "grievous insult to the brain," brought on by eighteen bourbon doubles in the White Horse Inn ("I think that's the record") and a medical misdiagnosis ("His bare stub feet stuck out"). Berryman's first of three wives, Eileen Simpson, wrote a biography of these Tidewater fugitives, *Poets in Their Youth,* a sobering anti-testimony to genius, booze, philandering, self-pity, and manic-depression. Lost son of a suicidal father, our modern poet is nobody's hero.

> I'd like to scrabble till I got right down
> away down under the grass
>
> and ax the casket open ha to see
> just how he's taking it, which he sought so hard
> we'll tear apart
> the mouldering grave clothes ha & then Henry
> will heft the ax once more, his final card,
> and fell it on the start.

"I have a living to fail," Henry boasts, brother to Roethke in the Lost Son syndrome. In crucifixing blasphemy and ritual self-splendor, the suicide dies solipsistically for his suicided father, who has forsaken *me*. Berryman's patriarchal ghosting (Hamlet with a chortle) comes on as poetic *dream*, the night's interior sweats and druidic whisperings, displacing a prosaic day in *songs*. These are not Black Elk's dream vision songs, not Two Shields "word-sending" a bear-hearted lyric to the north wind, but more the *heyoka*'s crazy inversions, the contrary warrior challenging death on a day he is wildly willing to die. These demonically enchanted tongues ring madly vatic in a wilderness of things—the poet-as-tortured-bearer of native culture, cursed cousin to Yeats, Sitting Bull, Langston Hughes, or Homer, pleading their visionary redemption. "What did I do to be so black-and-blue?" Satchmo sang not long ago in Carnegie Hall.

Occult, obsessive singer-poets are addressed in eulogy throughout *The Dream Songs:* the "majestic Shade" of W. B. Yeats, the "Garden Master" ghost of Theodore Roethke, Wallace Stevens, Robert Frost, Delmore Schwartz, Randall Jarrell, William Carlos Williams, Sylvia Plath, Ernest Hemingway. Half of these bards are self-condemned suicides, "taking cover," as Berryman said of his jump from a Minneapolis bridge to the frozen west bank of the Mississippi. As in Dante's Wood of (negated-name Wonderland) Suicides, their muse seems a terrible mystery, an orphan death the only "mother of beauty." Henry sifts his archaeology of loss, "Collating bones" in a death rattle of laughter and American cliché, boozy slur and street dialect, nonsense and babble, as Helen Vendler catalogues, "baby-talk, childish spite-talk, black talk, Indian talk, Scottish talk, lower-class talk, drunk-talk, archaism and anachronism, megalomaniacal self-aggrandizing images, hysteria and hallucination, spell-casting, superstition, paranoid suspiciousness, slang, and primitive syntactic structures of all sorts—sentence-fragments, incorrect grammar, babble, and so on" (*The Given and the Made*). There's lingual range here to match a continent's voices.

Mistah Bones comes on as our common American "pal," one of us lost, the persona of a terrified child-artist, left behind with his father's gun. Everyman John Smith, rechristened Berryman, grows up the schmuck, the average guy, the desperate and failing American anti-hero—low as rat, roach, or the dog's tail, a "goatish" satyr-poet, "Henry Pussycat." Not bear-heart, but coyote appetite fuels his hunger, and sex is his primal drive, the male province to conquer and collect. "All the girls, with their vivacious littles," he flutes, stud of the walk in man's mating *game*. This from the small, shy, myopic boy who threw himself on the train tracks after a bully beat him up, a collegiate swing dancer and tennis dandy who failed at high school football and ice hockey. He's almost the wise fool now, Lear's or-phaned jester within verse nonsense. Joking sets his truth-stage, if he must exit before the tragedy ends; the poem's the thing to catch the errant mind, reality in slippage.

This is age-old Trickster stuff, the sport who outwits the hero-king. He tests the rules playing with limits. Berryman regenerates by dying on stage, then crawling out of the pit, the New World, comeback kid. Henry wears many masks, changes multiple shapes, a beast-god from lowest to highest possibility (over probability) in a protean reality, open, unfixed, evolving. A comic loser, he survives defeat to bounce back for another go-around. The poet relaxes the tension in given forms, plays the margins, improvises solutions, or connives new ways of looking at impossible odds, archetypally making things up. In the old spring mythos that Northrop Frye equates with comic resurrection (*Anatomy of Criticism*), Trickster rejuvenates spirit by scandalously driving out fate's scapegoat, interactively draws together all the potential victims in festive bacchanal, and renews an old covenant of hope, albeit hopeless in the final brag over death, the autumnal reaper opposite spring's joker.

Here is the Lunatick son inversionally "trying to hit the head on the nail," his madness clarifying disorder in what Roethke called "the kingdom of bang and blab." The down-driven, the hidden, the reverse reality comes up through his lucid insanity. His puns, contradictions, riddles, and crazy metaphors torque all images anew, wrench hidden meaning out of the wrought phrase, squeeze fresh blood from drilled diction (modernist po-etics gone wild to seed). A wag of a rhymer, Henry clowns around bizarrely, the joke catching in his throat, singing a funny sobbing, all the stops pulled out in this minstrel masquerade. His dreams rise above pain's rainbow of analysis.

> These Songs are not meant to be understood, you understand.
> They are only meant to terrify & comfort.
> Lilac was found in his hand.

The Dream Songs descend from an old idea of poetry as "ode" or talk-song, indeed, Homeric lyric in war-ridden times. So, too, these dream-songs move from elegy and dirge, Milton's "Lycidas" and Tennyson's "In Me-moriam," through homily and prayer, Donne to Hopkins, to the confessional lyrics of Thomas, travel talk, political detritus, daily news, and the Black jazz-blues of Bessie Smith. The lines turn on the "music" of talk, the song in spoken outpourings. A racing nervous jabber at times, the speech is comically idiomatic American (Williams's cheeping birds, Thomas's barking dogs, Roethke's slithering snails). This lingual rhythm-and-roll lapses across the Big Water to Browning's soliloquies or interior monologues, that is, blank verse dramatic monologues, as verse-speech came to be known, but with a difference, fractured from Fra Lippo Lippi and J. Alfred Prufrock: the quirky, subdividing selves of dramatic interior dialogues. Under the Trickster muse, Berryman's self splits futilely to save itself from self-damnation. Our cursed priest of the bleeding psyche finds his origins in Hopkins's "dark" sonnets, the "terrible crystal" of self-consciousness, where Berryman says the soul "ached itself awake." Lorca's *duende* is in the home, a daemon in the hearth, a devil in the cellar—Freud's house of the psyche, afire and damned. Dionysian, visionary, bacchanalian, postromantic, these are the dithyrambics of a tormented Narcissus, splitting infinitely into ruptured, refracted shards of jabbering selves: *Henry*, a White man in blackface, a.k.a. *Mistah Bones*, along with his dark alter-ego end man, trailed by a baby-blubbering orphan, a maniacal womanizer, a tortured teacher, a crazed dreamer, a bookish harlequin, an imminent suicide. Sex, booze, madness, vision, laughter, loathing: the poetics of manic-depressive brilliance, the sizzling contraries, the odd extremities, the fatal edges of Mister Trixter's dissolved boundaries. His is the immoral minority: never-the-norm, anti-institutional, anti-Christian, heretical and blasphemous, a fallen Catholicism cut loose from ideology. The cursed poet finds delight in defying God and any worm crossing his path.

Beat and revolutionary, his is also backtalk American jive: curious, new, twisted, original, cantankerous, brash, immodest, selfish, compassionate, unstable, questing, regenerately violent. "You do. She do. I will be with you-all, / in a little little silence, Mr Bones." The poet, as Plato feared, is anti-state, anti-bourgeois, anti-academic, anti-moral-majority, while cutting up among them all. An iconoclast with a passion to knock down false idols, a compulsion to play against the limits, John Berryman is an anti-establishment American Original: White boy with a lip, a cross, a curse, an attitude, brandishing a ludic poetics.

The form of *The Dream Songs* is somewhat straight-forward, a pentameter ballad stanza, irregularly rhymed, borrowed from Yeats. Three such stanzas make a song-poem in 5/5/3 iambic measures, crazily quilted, but surely, steadily, maddeningly sequential through over a thousand such gyrations. As with Lowell's blank sonnets, Roethke's mad ballads, Pound's Vorticist cut and driven Cantos, slant rhymes rise up rhythmical to the coursings of the lines, a river true to its own depths, shallows, and bends. Harmonic echo, metric overtone, wry assonance, and surging alliteration all ride the lines in service of the musical phrase, as Pound had it, a poetry of classical background, intellectual instinct, and improvisational hip-hop presence. A new land, a new tongue, an old poetic tradition: Europe released, freed, street-smart, reborn, yet old as nominal Adam, honed as Homer, sly as Shakespeare. Berryman worked on a definitive edition of *King Lear* to his death.

The Dream Songs are doubly inventive, form *re*invented in the nature of poetic chaos theory. They are demotic and democratic in the broadest sense, demanding but not elitist (master of the maudlin), and having it all ways, yet not un-traditional. Dante, Wyatt, Donne, Blake, Wordsworth, Keats, and Yeats deeply inform the poet's sensibility, indeed, his craft, as a "man speaking to men," albeit in wild & crazy tongues, more so even than Whitman, cummings, Roethke, or Lowell. He out-beats Ginsberg, Kerouac, and Ferlinghetti. His verse is blurringly pluralist, from English Departments to local bars, sherry parties to beer brawls, innumerable trysts to three marriages (and three children), Shakespeare to Charlie Parker, intellectual soiree to father's suicide. His is the imagination of a very large continent, still uncivilized by European standards ("the pure products of America / go crazy," Williams declared in "To Elsie"), natively wild ("a dash of Indian blood"), geographically free ("sheer lust of adventure"), psychically unrepressed (the crack-brained "truth about us"), haunted by ancient griefs ("somehow it seems to destroy us"), undermined by modern tragedies ("no one to witness and adjust"). Yet the work is hilariously energized, at times madly lucid, delightedly crazed, terribly so—and always complexly charged, reversing dangerous fields of play, sobbing, shouting, guffawing, sneering to-get-it-Out. Berryman the savant, the sad hero, the wise fool, the cracked genius, the native trickster fallen away from Hemingway's heroics.

> Mercy! my father; do not pull the trigger
> or all my life I'll suffer from your anger
> killing what you began.

"Hell talkt my brain awake," Berryman recalls the curse of consciousness in "the thinky place," chased by "the thinky death," patronymic self-destruction. The mind devours its heartfelt, bereft "Song," raging against feeling all-that-is, self-loathing and dark gloating as "his lonely & his desperate work." In the logic of his illogic, the poet comes off as exiled prophet, crazed visionary, Tiresian tragedian with a slant grin. "—Mr Bones, we all brutes & fools," a blackface bro chortles for all the fallen children. His is the energy of a new world gone crazy: no ground, no stability, no staying, but an ungraced Western culture of speed, curse, and greed where "all nouns become verbs." It's Fenollosa at a crazy pitch, Pound in the Pisan tiger cage, convicted of treason, about to be shot, a dream nightmare with poetic vengeance. "I have a living to fail," Henry grieves: "Leaves on leaves on leaves of books I've turned / and I know

nothing, Henry said aloud, / with his ultimate breath." Laughter checks
the sob welling up, a humor of sadness "In a state of chortle sin."

This is wild confessional when it works, maudlin drivel when it doesn't.
The dreamed songs are mostly outpourings of an "unloved," hence failed,
lover, at base "the original crime: art, rime." His tricks begin with ungraced
idioms, American speech in its raw immediacy. "If all must hurt at once,
let yet more hurt now, / so I'll be ready, Dr God. Púsh on me. / Give it to
Henry harder." From hymnal to pop, ballad to hip schtick, the lines dance
with vitality and vulgarity snatched from the everyday, the lowly native
sources of poetic diction and rhythm. "—Try Dr God, clown a ball, / low
come to you in the blue sad darkies' moans / worsing than yours, too."
The muscled bone lines sinew a restless movement under the diction (Em-
ily Dickinson's "mad-dash punctuation without the words," Lowell says).
Pattern is always betrayed by creative disjunction, fracturing the expected,
revealing a new beauty in what doesn't cohere, or behave, or always make
sense. "—If life is a handkerchief sandwich, // in a modesty of death I
join my father / who dared so long agone leave me." Maybe this kind of
poetry conveys the shaman's song at heart—the strange ripple beneath the
familiar, the defacilitated mind, the turgid feeling ruptured by destiny and
obdurate things. The indecipherable maze beckons. All's a come-hither,
inversional. "My lass is braking. / My brass is aching."

Berryman ends blue-eyed American male as desperate Dionysian singer.
A father-suicide haunts his lyrics, his blues as elegy, cry, howl & groan from
a descendental patriarchy. The blood sins of the father curse a son's loins,
mother a runaway betrayer or bourgeois bore, young lovers "wylde for to
hold," and bewildered, many mistresses in distress. What have we come to?
Mister Trixter rocks betwixt and between modes and motives: Is Henry a
good "bad" guy? a beat songster gone sour? a lucky stiff fallen on hard
times? The American Adam eyes his end, unredeemed, Old Man Bear am-
bles off.

Everywhere a violent nonsense challenges norms: an elbowed poetic dic-
tion and wrenched metrics, kneecap "low" subjects and lower feelings,
swag and brag of blue-eyed machismo (a loner's cover for pathos?), alcohol,
affairs, insanity. Berryman's sins fall and dazzle as the deadly virtues of his
vices. "Henry" is king of comic despair (his wife's Jewish dentist, Henry
Glickman, in blackface?). The *poète maudit* laughs crazily at loss, sings the
lonely blues, suffers dispossession (the title of his first book, *The Dispossessed*
in 1948) and endless displacement, no less than exiled Indians, Blacks,
Jews, or Baudelaire in jail with syphilis. With the likes of James Wright or
James Welch, Ernest Hemingway or Sherman Alexie, he knows Western
dispossession, the grief of homelessness, the dislocated native. His is, finally,
a fractured genius, a posthumous *Delusions, etc.* The last joke leaks through
the tragic mask, a "springy" dancer's jump from a winter Mississippi

bridge, again a break in the formal verse pattern to lift the fatal load of verse. It's a wicked aesthetic, a mad way to go.

The American frontier lies here on the line itself, the ploughed versing ground, the turn of the till in the soil, ringing against the rocks. "I perfect my metres / until no mosquito can get through." Internal and slant and off and identical rhyme lurch across the fissures, scandalously lusting for connection, for coupletting and stitching, out of desperate loneliness. "All the girls, with their vivacious littles, / visited him in dream: he was interested in their tops & bottoms / & even in their middles." Assonance and consonance thicken the insides, callous the outsides of the poet's lowings. "—I saw nobody coming, so I went instead." Adam's mad, westering, wild-visionary Fall across a horizon of possibilities: how Whitey has fallen from bearing hard times.

ADAM AGAIN

How, then, postlapsarian, do we speak of American man as Adamic Savage? From Henry Nash Smith's *Virgin Land* through R. W. B. Lewis's *The American Adam*, including Leo Marx's *The Machine in the Garden* and Richard Slotkin's *Regeneration Through Violence*, scholars have tracked the Edenic Fall through the New World. Yet this was not a "virgin" land, Francis Jennings notes in *The Invasion of America*, so much as a "widowed" land, since Native Americans already occupied the hemisphere. American innocence seems more Edenic elegy, less a feature of the landscape. "There may be always a time of innocence," Wallace Stevens wrote in "The Auroras of Autumn," his last great poem, "There is never a place." Innocence is an emigrant act of the mind, recalling what might have been, mostly is not, and may never be. The Fall is grieved by everyone.

So there are two stories here, pre- and postlapsarian, mythic and historic, tensely superimposed at the autumnal heart of the American psyche: a springtime Adam, at ease, naming things in the Garden, and fall Savages, at large, killing things in the Woods. European-shadowed by myths of noble savagery, American men are compelled by both, end up playing out both. At some later point, summer's Eve enters the story, "an unbelievinge Creature, namely Pohahuntas [*sic*]" in the New World, saving John Smith in his own words and later marrying John Rolfe, and the miscegenated pair Fall, again, into a reality of time-and-place, as Powhatan's favorite daughter becomes a court-acculturated Lady Rebecca of the English Renaissance. "Be thou the mother of thousands of millions, and let thy seed possess the gate of those which hate them," Genesis prophesies of Rebecca. "Two nations are in thy womb."

In this country's mythology, sex and gender remain old, renewable schisms for the American Adam and Eve; the fascination and fear of race pose newly awakened guilts. Listen to the cry in poetic terms. "Less and Less Human, O Savage Spirit," Stevens titled his couplets on "the god in the house" of America: "It is the human that is the alien, / The human that has no cousin in the moon." Alien to the human, this lunar icon was Plath's calling, the doomed *other* her pale Eve: "It is Adam's side, / this earth I rise from, and I in agony." Hughes recalls his wife's poetic break-through, November 1959, "But now that she was resurrected as a self that she could think of as Eve (as she tried so hard to do in her radio play *Three Women*), a lover of life and of her children, she still had to deal with every-thing in her that remained otherwise, everything that had held her in the grave for three days, 'The Other.' " A lonely savage, indeed, then shadows the clearing, axed of trees, eradicated of women and Indians, unrhyming under a hooded moon. "She confronts her own moon-faced sarcophagus," Hughes says of his dead wife's posthumous *Ariel*, "her mirror clouding over, the moon in its most sinister aspect, and the yews—*blackness and silence.*"

"Savage" derives from *sylvan*, that is, natives born in the dark forests. For pilgrims and pioneers, the shadowy woods were an *other's* obstacle to agrarian progress, as were bears, wolves, and wild children of such dusky forests. The "naked" bottom of a pubescent Pocahontas cartwheeling "all the fort over" aroused first John Smith's "unbridled desire of carnal affec-tion: but for the good of this plantation, for the honour of our countrie, for the glory of God, for my owne salvation, and for the converting to the true knowledge of God and Jesus Christ an unbeleeving creature, namely Pokahuntas." John Rolfe took the abducted princess in 1613, married this teenage Algonkian (against Puritan taboos of miscegenation), and sailed her to England, where he raised Pocahontas to Lady Rebecca in the court of James I, not far from Shakespeare's Globe Theatre and the public Bear Gardens. Blanched of gamey brio (her Powhatan name meaning "playful, lively"), Princess Pocahontas bore a son and died four years later at Graves-end, 1617, trying to sail back to her homeland. Some four million Tide-water descendents claim lineage through Pocahontas's son, who moved back to his Virginia tobacco plantation almost four centuries ago.

Americans early on harbored two obsessions, de Tocqueville noted, cut-ting down trees and killing Indians, perhaps a single template in the fron-tier mind—all in the civilizing interests of "clearing" the land for settle-ment farming. Thus, the land of the free and home of the brave—originally a wooded native homeland for the bear and the "savage"—was felled by ax and cleared by musket, whereby Richard Slotkin reads the "bloody loam," à la William Carlos Williams, as an American paradigm, "regener-ation through violence." Today, the country would be reborn, native, sing-ing with a different heart.

The slaughter of paradisal mystery: it is the second triad of the Adamic myth, the sexual expulsion, sacrificial birth, and suffering labor that doubled up the Puritans. In the "virgin" new land of the early 1600s, praying-town profligates who did not kneel twice a day were shot, hanged, or burned at the stake. Thieves had their ears cut off, deserters were broken on the wrack, profaners lashed, blasphemer's tongues run through with bodkins. Men in America are particularly haunted by this Puritan history. Ezra Pound goes global in thunderous recoil, William Carlos Williams peers carefully into the local tribal detail, Wallace Stevens intones Adam back into the imagined Garden, and Theodore Roethke lies down in its tangled roots. These conversions have led toward a *native* American writers' renaissance, in the making since 1890.

RE/NEWING *THINGS:* EZRA POUND

In London before the Great War, Ezra Pound found a Polish-French sculptor, Henri Gaudier-Brzeska, forging his own tools "as independent as the savage," Pound said, under the railway arch in Putney. Pound liked to discover genius, and in this case he unearthed an original. At the Albert Hall one day, he and a friend were grubbing for "good amid much bad" new art, Ezra remembers, "and a young man came after us, like a well-made young wolf or some soft-moving, bright-eyed wild thing. I noted him carefully because he reminded me a little of my friend Carlos Williams." Pound stopped "before a figure with bunchy muscles done in clay painted green" and stuttered over the artist's name, "Brzsjk—" again, "Burrz-issksk," and again, "Burdidis—." He then "heard a voice speaking with the gentlest fury in the world: *Cela s'appelle tout simplement Jaersh-ka. C'est moi qui les ai sculptés."*

Had Gaudier, with Pound's Chinese poems in his pocket, not been killed at twenty-four in the second year of the "Great" war, he would have joined this century's greatest sculptors, a Vorticist master among artists like Epstein, Brancusi, and Modigliani. Gaudier left brilliant sketches of panthers, stags, and horses, and some thirty sculpted pieces in stone and metal—wild animals, nudes, dancers, wrestlers, and the torqued marble "hieratic head" of Ezra Pound, bristling with physicality. The young sculptor was a native genius, self-taught, self-inspired, self-sufficient, living for his "virile" art alone, "original, new, primordial," as Gaudier described his ideal modern architecture. He dismissed *beaux arts* and extolled the primitive, Africa to Assyria to Egypt to China, writing with pencil from the French war trenches of the "Paleolithic vortex, man intent upon animals" in the Dordogne caves. Gaudier was the modernist embodiment of Fry's neoprimitive Bloomsbury exhibit in 1910, through which "human nature changed," according to Virginia Woolf. With Pound, Gaudier held forth heatedly on "exogamy, or the habits of primitive tribes, or the training of African warriors, or Chinese ideographs," which the young sculptor could decipher on sight. As noted, this man "forged his tools" from old steel spindles in a mud-floor studio under a railway bridge; "he cut stone until its edge was like metal."

Modern art, for Pound, was anciently modeled from "energy cut into stone, making the stone expressive of its fit and particular manner." Thus Gaudier's incised stone and fired metal gave Pound tangible images for making verse new: the word edged with physicality, the verse rhythm muscled in space, the image cut in time, the idea concretely luminous in the mind, as discussed earlier. The image as vortex, Pound said, became "a radiant node or cluster" from which and through which ideas were "constantly rushing." Pound's renewed modernist text, sculpted into history with Gaudier's "swift moving apprehension," would read as a "ball of light in one's hands," the word as power illuminated by Mallarme's "flash of intellect." The language might come up off the page ideogrammatically, as in the ancient Chinese texts (via Ernest Fenollosa's studies), and with a primordial torque the world would once again regenerate through art.

Gaudier despised overly civilized art, Hellenic decorations, for example, the "curled nubilities and discreet slits" of "those *damn* Greeks," warmed over in modern museum pieces. His own "virile" sculpture, he wrote in *The Egoist,* March 16, 1914, was "continuing the tradition of the barbaric peoples of the earth (for whom we have sympathy and admiration)." So for Pound, admiring Egyptian stone carvings and early Chinese bronzes, "Make it new" became the modernist motto, an ideogrammatic gold inscription from an ancient Chinese bathtub, renewing the Western frontier of American verse. Adam the procreative wordsmith, Eve bearing the scripted body: modernism reborn globally.

In a canonical Western tradition, Pound was originally, boldly American, an intellectual born on the frontier of Hailey, Idaho, 1885. There's classical precedent for Ezra: to teach, to stir the mind, Marianne Moore saw in Pound's work, to afford enjoyment. "To inform, to move, and to delight," as Cicero says in *De Oratore: ut doceat, ut moveat, ut delectet.* St. Augustine later inflected the axiom as *docere, flectare, delectare* in *De Doctrine Christiane.* As a cultural journalist advising "the people," Pound reacted in strident counterattack to bad criticism:

> The supreme crime in a critic is dullness. The supreme evil committable by a critic is to turn men away from the bright and the living. The ignominious failure of ANY critic (however low) is to fail to find something to arouse the appetite of his audience, to read, to see, to experience.
>
> It is the critic's BUSINESS *adescare* to lure the reader. Caviar, vodka, any hodge-podge of oddities that arouses hunger or thirst is pardonable to the critic.
>
> He is not there to satiate. A desire on his part to point out his own superiority over Homer, Dante, Catullus and Velasquez, is simple proof that he

has missed his vocation. Any ass knows that Dante was not a better racing driver than Barney Oldfield, and that he knew less of gramophones than the late Mr Edison. ("Examples of Civilization" in *Guide to Kulchur*)

Kicked out of his first and only college teaching job, for harboring a lady friend overnight in his quarters, Pound was even harder on pedagogues:

> In no case let one's sons spend money on "education" offered by cowards who dare not answer specific questions about their own subjects. The modern and typical prof holds his job because of his slickness in *avoiding* the thesis, because he crawls under the buggy rug of a moth-eaten curriculum in sheer craven terror of known fact and active discovery. That is what the half-louse is PAID for. ("Watch the Beaneries" in *Guide to Kulchur*)

His given Christian name, *Ezra*, was Hebraic for "help." This prophetic namesake suggests darker Old Testament severities behind pale Galilean charity. The surname tells all, Pound: as a noun, a norm—the measure of weight, mass, or force—or in his own image of the sculpted ideogram, a monosyllabic stone *cut* into the weight of time. The verb "pound" explodes—to hit against, to thrust, to smash. All this energy surged through his Vorticist magazine, *Blast!* in 1917 of the "first" *World* War, Gaudier the sculptor and Rupert Brooke the writer dead in the French trenches, artifice shattered by political economics, Wyndham Lewis drafting a modernist upheaval at home. The traditional verse line buckled. "To break the pentameter," Pound wrote in 1945, Canto 81, "that was the first heave." And the trochee thrust up against the iamb, irrevocably for modernist verse, counterweighted measures of the new Pound line.

In a station of the Parisian Metro, Pound received a contrapuntal vision of Orphic descent, as discussed in the beginning:

> The apparition of these faces in the crowd;
> Petals on a wet, black bough.

With the image as "the poet's pigment," the trochee *Petals* bursts against the ghostly iambic image of "the crowd" at the verse's turn. The spondaic chiseling of dentals and labials, *wet, black bough,* thrusts the couplet onto the bole of the tree of life and death. Inspired technique, ancient art, steady focus—mystery crafted *"hokku-*like," Pound said—the shamanic poet-tree anticipated Yeats's "great rooted blossomer" to come a decade later. "In a poem of this sort," Pound wrote in the Gaudier monograph, "one is trying to record the precise instant when a thing outward and objective transforms itself, or darts into a thing inward and subjective." Still, the would-be master advised, "The churn, the loom, the spinning-wheel, the oars are bases for distinctive rhythm which can never degenerate into the monotony of mere iambs and trochees." The natural world of bodies-in-motion mulched Pound's aesthetic soil, "the ground sense necessary,"

Williams argued in a burial tract for the mind's airy forms. Even bearlike Wallace Stevens, six-feet, two-inch large red man reading, suspected worldly envy of the departed angels, weeping "to step barefoot into reality." The Forms of Reality?—variously natural. Around Pound's era, the pianist Wanda Landowska remembered first experiencing 2/4 time as a Polish farm child watching a cow milked; her harpsichord and her Scarlatti, her metronome and her Bach, were *in* her milking hands, no less than Mary Austin intuited *an American rhythm* in the pitch and roll of shortgrass prairie landscape.

Pound. The man *matters,* like him or not. He tells us so, as poetry *must* move us toward exacting passions—"so much depends," his doctor-friend said, "upon" the working craft. To do so, the poet sings in the old styles renewed, Homer, Confucius, Dante, Daniel, Villon, Chaucer, and Shakespeare, for starters. *Confucius to Cummings* (1964) was his titled canon of good works near his death. It is time for America to go international and historical, Ez says, time to grow up to "other" countries from which she comes. Verse = *moving* lines, "language charged to its utmost with meaning," Pound thumps the sounding board, riding on the intonations of voice, the pluralist possibilities of tongues (16! in eight hundred pages of Cantos or "songs"): from the Anglo-Saxon sea rhythms and yoked *kennings* ("trim-coifed Circe") with their muscular consonance ("that swart ship"); to the Italian aria assonance in open vowel "endings" at the illusive closures of Latinate nouns (*libretto, canzoni);* to the lyric, crisp whispers of French, the lover's language of tipped palate and sibilant light *("Le paradis n'est pas artificiel");* to the consonant grist, muscular thrust, and Germanic "cut" sculpted into words ("Swartest night stretched over wretched men there"); to Virgil, via Dante's Tuscan, and Latin syllabic "quantities" of verse rhythms, softly pedaling over modern twists and turns of phrase ("Lie quiet Divus" and *"Venerandam"*); to chiastic ("crossing," X or *chi* in Greek) Dionysian mysteries, a dialect of Greco-Roman twined cultures long lost ("Kimmerian lands") recorded 2,500 Homeric years ago—the beginnings of Western seeing, dithyrambic dancing, Apollonian pattern (*"Eidos"* = the knowing "eye" for things & sounds & sights, Pound etymologized: "Aphrodite" "orichalchi"). And back, back round to "Cathay," or China, and Confucian play with the useful truths of everyday things: functions of form, right beauty, the good goods ("They have all answered correctly," Kung said, "That is to say, each in his nature" [C13]). And more—

Which is to say that history and art do not come easily, normatively. They emerge hard, indeed, but beautiful, in fact, moral as hard-won truths, moving as Sitting Bull's warrior songs. And this matters most: the "unwobbling pivot," as the Chinese sages said, the center within, the due mean of each in his or her own "nature," as the ancients say, *wei wu wei* ("not" to go against nature). Pound brings a moral intensity to bear on the *fine* arts of the West, rarefying Williams's terms "in the American grain," a classic burst against slack thought. The poet has Washington's adamant spirit of fixed place in a new land (to the death a revolutionary) and Jefferson's pluralist idealism, coupled with Ben Franklin's curiosity (a bit French, too) of light-ning-charged *things*. An eighteenth-century revolutionary "enlightenment," one might say, rational to an ecstatic fault. The Eastern rule of thumb, counterbalancing: "Have no twisty thoughts." This does not rule out Frost's use of the "straight crookedness of a good walking stick," counterpoint in verse rhythms or rhymed thoughts, but demands the exact and exacting line: "Above all to be precise / At the gulf's edge / Or on thin ice."

Yes, arrested after the war for speaking his mind, as best he could—straight on, *á la Americáine*, from the center, where the heart loves best, Confucius in Pound's coat pocket in the landing-strip cage south of Pisa—and with this core to ride out the "fall" into reality, the Odyssean descent into the hell of twentieth-century economic politics, the next Adamic step down and forward from the receding frontier. To be delivered up by soldiers to St. Elizabeth's Asylum, rather than shot as a traitor—twelve years locked up with psychotics—let out by Frost's FBI intervention through Archibald MacLeish and Robert Kennedy.

Some things said in the Cantos had to be recanted ("'my worst mistake," Pound told Allen Ginsberg in 1967, "was the stupid suburban prejudice of antisemitism, all along, that spoiled everything—"). How could a man named Ezra be anti-Semitic? he challenged under psychiatric guard. Potentially this raises the personal wrong in our civic "rights," exposed oftentimes as a mistake, perhaps, an inexact caesura in the mind's synapse, a misplaced "foot" (in mouth): to wit, a radio speech to our boys from the political Other, an ex-patriotic position on the wrong side in the Allied / Axis Second "Great" War. Charles Douglas on paper banking sparked Pound's anticapitalist engine. His economic theory of usury was misapplied, possibly, culturally or historically misdirected (and misunderstood?) on racial terms that indicted the Rothschild banks of England, scapegoating ethnics in the mad 1920s, in short, a mad glitch in the brain's computer. "To confess wrong without losing rightness:" he asked to the end in Canto 116, 1965 or so, after Frost, Plath, Roethke, and Williams died in 1963, the year John Kennedy was assassinated. By then Pound had been dreaming up over a hundred Cantos for some sixty years.

User-friendly, this poet?—roughly at times, and only to those who will work with him. Imagine taking battle lessons from Sitting Bull. Readers willing to re/view the "a-b-c" progression of their own basic learning—the logic of their reading, the actual phonemes of speech and poetic articles of faith—will be better off, even perhaps pleased and a bit richer verbally, in the long run, certainly bolder. No short gains here, few windfalls, fewer quick-profit margins, no aesthetic junk bonds. Don't "fake it," Pound advised the young writer, and stay curious (*Paris Review* 1960). Original sin, usury; first hybris, false ease; prime heresy, false gods; undeserved gains, corruption; throwaway glitter, decadence; adjectival splendor, silly in its painted-on fustian. True beauty, or none at all, nature so crafted as to remain natural. Pound reacted wolfishly to nineteenth-century "emotional slither." Mostly, "have no twisty thoughts," he checked sloppy feeling with the mind's chiseled counsel, as Williams vowed to speak of the "idea" only *in* terms of "things," a real world of poetry everywhere, of real words, streetwise to court-sweet, of tangible thoughts and physical feelings and concrete things: *claritas,* back with Joyce to the Latin of medieval scholastics, clarity in idea, direct feeling along the parabolic lines of thinking, penetrant seeing of the "thing itself." So Joyce, granted a life annuity through Pound stumping his friends, stamped a "visa" on his young artist, the unsaintly displaced Stephen of kinchly thought: knife-blade vision, a dark voyage into the lighted world on a piece of paper. Modern seafarers, trans-lators, Odysseans, that is, heroic pilgrims on high-sea journeys. These are watery passages through medial verbal "things," stirred by old and new Masters, more traditional, perhaps, more classical or hierarchical than the average American, say Williams, would have them, the "new" American rolling up his sleeves as an answer to Greek and Latin. How much historical ground will we stand in the logography of literature? What *must* we learn? How listen or record "the word"? We must draw lines. "Not Ideas about the Thing but the Thing Itself," Stevens concluded his *Collected Poems* (winning his second National Book Award in 1954, the year of his death).

For Pound taught the modernists primally *how to* read: not so much in order to conclude, though we make judgments, weigh evidence, listen acutely, "read" our "passages" in passing, and pass back for a second astonished glance. And not to preclude any "Confucius to Cummings" in the classic anthology, but to witness and to recreate, as best we can, women and men, nature's creative genius (which may include, indeed, more of the "feminine" or so-called subjective than Pound could muster). This means feeling toward things, too—*in medias res*—a world chock-full of interpenetrant objects ("interpass, penetrate" [C81]) with ideas and emotions (not "CONTRA NATURUM," but art that *art* "of" nature, as in bearing the making: "The green casque has outdone your elegance" [C81]). That is, we respond to these musically chosen, intrinsically designed, inmotion particles of words ("things-in-themselves") from the *whole* of nature and human history, primitive to modernist, Confucius to cummings, natively poetic. We are *of* our history, surely, which hangs larger even than the Sum of our present parts, coming after our precedents, followed by our antecedents. In short, cultured ancestors and successors gather around and beyond us, as with the language itself, spoken or recorded: "those that returned," Stevens imagined the large red man reading, "to hear him read from the poem of life." Pound wrote ninety-one books; countless masters before wrote God-knows-how-many-more (. . . we're still at it . . .). His be-loved Cantos alone filled 800 pages. "Properly, we shd. read for power," he insisted in the essay, "Zweck or Aim" in *Guide to Kulchur.* "Man reading shd. be man intensely alive. The book shd. be a ball of light in one's hands."

To what end? "And then," the first Canto opens in 1916, the middle of the First "Great" War that took dear friends and cherished artists. "So that:" the opening chant "ends," as it opens to more than a hundred more Cantos for half a century more, from the bottom of Odysseus's descent into Hades, through "what thou lovest best." The hibernating Greek hero, the original draft resistor, as Joyce said, is told by the blind bisexual seer, Ti-resias, that only he will survive to come home, confronted by his beloved companion sailor, Elpenor, dead, and his true mother, Anticlea, dead too after these twenty years, both alive when last the king looked (time, the blink between, even for a bearlike king). Only you, listener, will survive. The only heroic thing to do, all-too-human, only modern as well: *go on.* "Make it new" again. Finally back to his wife, Penelope, who isn't dead, thank god, and his living son, Telemachus, who will take the place of his comrade, homeless, namelessly unburied, who will be-come a second son. *"A man of no fortune, and with a name to come,"* Elpenor gives his masculine epitaph to his captain. So Pound, who imagined and voiced and rescribbled it all, kept going on for fifty more years . . . so many names "to come" and *be*come. His son Omar bears on.

How can an American "begin" to end with a Canto at the bottom of Greek epic myth?—only to pause in the breach, consider, draw breath, and proceed. The eighty-sixth Canto, from the 1945 Pisan cage on the blistering beach near Tombolo, tells us, "Master thyself." Not far from Keats dying with Homer a few miles northward out to sea, Pound was lucky to have Con-fucius in his pocket when the Allies landed. "What thou lovest well is thy true heritage." *History* makes us the bearers of love of truth, the *en passant* of ancestral wisdom: "Master thyself, then others shall thee beare." Subject or object, "thee"? For Pound, different from Plath or Berryman, the per-sonal "other" is intersubjective, best seen as both doer *and* done: *shall thee beare,* to carry, to put up with, to engender, to gestate and to birth, to reveal or bare. *Sing from a bear's heart that is different.* And he ends, "Here error is all in the not done, / all in the diffidence that faltered . . ." (ellipsis his).

This wracked, arrogant, and brilliant man of almost ninety years, con-victed of treason, condemned by moderate men for his seditious opinions, committed for over a decade to an insane asylum where he played tennis, chess, wrote more books and held forth for friends, still writing those blasted / be-loved "songs,"—here he *falters* (ellips, slips?) writing beyond the invitation in the elliptical light through the passageway. Athena's light came into his tent, he swore, the muse visited the expatriate, a condemned prisoner in 1945 at the age of sixty. There's caesura in closure: it will be another thirty or so Cantos still, before he dies twenty years later at eighty-seven in jeweled Venice. He just couldn't keep quiet, this old man, or silence the inspired voices, no less than Dickinson or Sitting Bull.

As long as humans breathe, they may speak; as long as they move (and move us, even in anger or sadness) we sense they are thinking. Indeed, feeling. Literature is "news which STAYS news." And this is Pound's Euro-American, classically neoprimitive place among the poets: through blasted and crafted shards of traditional literary history, personalized from all man-kinds, he forces us to think, charms us to sing along (*cantare*, no less than Bowra's depiction of the primitive singer or Two Shields singing with a differing bear's heart), moves us to move with or against him (to dance dithyrambically, even as Dionysius). He charges our Edenic resettlement in a New World to take place through a global context. *Docere, flectare, delectare.* His is the whole human weight of why we write, and in trying harder (some pray) to write well.

"Pull down thy vanity," Pound thunders and hymns, "Learn of the green world what can be thy place / In scaled inventions or true artistry" (C81). This seems the call for a native poetics the globe over.

IT IS AN IDENTIFIABLE THING

. . . we have no words. Every word we get must be broken off from the European mass. Every word we get placed over again by some delicate hand. Piece by piece we must loosen what we want.
WILLIAM CARLOS WILLIAMS, *The Great American Novel* (1923)

> *so much depends*
> *upon*
>
> *a red wheel*
> *barrow*
>
> *glazed with rain*
> *water*
>
> *beside the white*
> *chickens.*

Apart from Pound's thunder abroad, so much depends on what back home, a red wheelbarrow? For a moment, peer through a knothole into Williams's smallest poem, his most well-known "local assertion," broken off and loos-ened, as microcosmic emblem of the local American lyric: scan a sixteen-word poem stripped of filigree, unadorned, even anti-formalized. From the 1913 Armory Show on, Williams, Pound, Hartley, Demuth, Moore, and all the Others were "streaming through" a break in the old conventions: "—the poetic line, the way the image was to lie on the page was our immediate concern."

Surely there's more here than meets the eye. The ear, perhaps, picks up a stuttering iambic step, say, of a man (paternally English) trundling something across the barnyard (chicken manure?). But where, in this uncharted farmland, does the foot fall? The metric stress is ambiguously pitched: "*so much*" might make light of how much, and "*so* much" bears a trochaic heave that could overload the slight line. Yet together, iamb tilting against trochee, improvisationally and indeterminately metric, the opening catches us in the pitch of needing to know, and unknowing. "There's a *certain Slant* of *Light,*" Dickinson demurred with an anapest, and Frost churned the slurred line with trochees, "*Some*thing there *is* that *does*n't *love* a *wall.*" This is measure freed to informal responsibilities of speech, poetry metrically loosened, American-*formed.*

Classically Western, this rolling sense of beginnings expresses the personal urgency, the rocking weight-in-motion, of not knowing where to put the "foot" as we shoulder the load in a new land. Thus, we must step (speak, think) carefully . . . *upon* the second line. This preposition is a single verse unit, and as such, it's the syntactic *wheel* of the machine, as it were—the rolling fulcrum of the line above it. By now we begin to *see* the game: a parodically imitative "wheel / barrow" couplet, rolling along, which leads into a second stanzaic movement, minimally precise, "a red wheel" (one syllable shorter than its corresponding tray of a line above). Barrow itself, nub of the poem, evolves from Old English *bearwe,* cognate with *bear.* This third line is composed of two spondees enjambed toward an inverted foot, a trochaic "*bar*row," which serves as the wheeling reverse pivot, indeed, of the second line (as with Pound's "*Pe*tals"). And still it's one continuous motion ("an unimpeded thrust," Williams wrote a friend in 1921, "right through a poem from the beginning to the end"). The poem trundles a wheel barrow along freshly, as barnyard metaphor of America (working man's humor), to a trochaic "*glazed,*" surreally highlighted by its own acoustics. Then, leaning iambically further, the line "with *rain*" tumbles toward a trochee, "*water,*" into the third microcosmic couplet. All this to be completed in four syllables, trailing yet a third preposition, "be*side,*" now normatively iambic, as a near rhyme within the line, "the *white,*" drops with delicate trochaic twist to "*chick*ens."

No title, without punctuation, minimal diction, tilting rhythm, and modestly internal rhyme *(depends/upon, wheel/barrow, beside/white/chickens):* it's not much of a poem, an English formalist might object. What makes it tick? What catches in the eye, cocks the ear? Three modest prepositions—*upon, with, beside*—place these barnyard minims in visual apposition, or a kind of contingent spatial rhyme, as in Alexander Calder's counter-gravity-balancing mobiles. Syllable to syllable the ear rolls (wheels) iamb upon trochee, the eye composes (glazes) red with white, as the mind centers (depends) on a barrow beside the chickens. It's elemental—a figure / ground design scanned in twenty-two slim syllables. And perhaps it adds up to no more than a small comic lesson in the necessity of things in themselves, ideas in action, here the basics of a rudimentary machine (rediscovering the New World wheel, the rolling fulcrum of Western-moving-man). Work-ethic poetics, workman's details, working-class humor. This artist gets the job done—scoops out the coop, fertilizes the turned ground, cleans the Augean stables as wry Hercules in minuscule. Williams's first book of poems ("bad Keats, nothing else—oh well, bad Whitman too") was printed at his own expense in 1909 and sold four copies at the local stationery. A retired printer stored the remaining hundred copies on a rafter under the eaves of his old chicken coop, where they were accidentally burned ten years later. On through the red wheel barrow, Williams "scribbled" another fifty years, whether anyone noticed or not.

"A poem is a small (or large) machine made of words," Dr. Williams introduced *The Wedge* in 1944. Here with the wheel barrow, we find a homely poem, a wheedling machine, without which no artisan on the farm could work, or work so well, to redefine poetry in American hands ("the artist figure of / the farmer—composing /—antagonist," Williams wrote early on in *Sour Grapes*, 1921, a year before "the great catastrophe" of Eliot's Anglophilic *Waste Land*). This, and its attendant good humor (who are we kidding?), offer no small tasks to the poet-as-nativist-farmer, low as these basics stoop to the ground. "Nothing can grow unless it taps into the soil," Dr. Williams says in his autobiography, originally titled *Root, Branch, & Flower*. Things must work from the beginnings: poems, farm tools, fertilizer, the farmer's eye and step, and, for that matter, ear. The artist renders Adam again barrowing the Garden, doing an honest day's work with words, a neoprimitive tenet refreshed.

Early on in "The Farmer," Williams sketches his anti-decorative, or "—antagonist," nature of art from the ground up. In the "blank fields" of a cold March, the page freely strewn with "browned weeds" of words, "the artist figure of / the farmer" paces the native soil. A rough figure of the artist looms (elsewhere pirouettes off-stage "in a soiled undershirt") cleaning up, pondering, mugging, practicing. Ejected from Eden, Adam-the-farmer plans a fallow reentry, as "the world rolls coldly away," *composing* a design for a "harvest already planted" in his mind. Distractions conspire against him, so he uses them in freer design of things, as in "The Bitter World of Spring":

> And, as usual,
> the fight as to the nature of poetry
> —Shall the philosophers capture it?—
> is on.

Before planting comes the plotting. Through, as well as against (archetypally American), the wet, blank space of spring, the poet, thinking, re-seeds his fields in the American grain, for he is no wanderer, but a pacing, planning husband of local nature. Randall Jarrell wrote, ". . . one exclaims in despair and delight: He is the America of poets," and adds, "so American that the adjective itself seems inadequate." Williams's freely patterned verse is a detailed tract of agrarian husbandry. The pro-creative antagonist demarks territory, plots things-in-space, composes from a barren text to harvest his labor in season, just as the poet-farmer paces and thinks and plans in order one day to give thanks for native abundance. No less than Dickinson's primal freshness, the poet ambles here as neoprimitive.

Why this elementary exercise with a farmer-poet or red wheel barrow, an agrarian step down from Stevens's "supreme fictions" published the same year, 1923? Scrutiny, for one thing, a sharper look at things. There's humility, for another, and perhaps a native sense of humor. "That is the poet's business," Williams ended his *Autobiography*. "Not to talk in vague categories but to write particularly, as a physician works, upon a patient, upon the thing before him, in the particular to discover the universal." Medicine and verse, Williams insists throughout his *Autobiography*, give a precise focus on immediate things: "Was I not interested in man? There the thing was, right in front of me. I could touch it, smell it. It was myself, naked, just as it was, without a lie telling itself to me in its own terms." Minimal art unclogs the ear and clears the eye, indeed, checks the mind from easy somersaults into making "sense" of things. Tight focus resists self-reflexive nonsense (Narcissus with a silly grin). The "thing itself" speaks itself, painted a cautionary red against pastel gloss.

In a lighter wheeling vein (doesn't poetry play and please?), why not compose an organic riddle, a living machine-in-motion, to pass the work-day, shift the load, ease the labor, dung out and tidy up the hutch of poetic tradition, redefining itself in the New World? With no schooled "rhythms of privilege," our "raw earth" non-English immigrants didn't come "to express themselves in pentamic hexameters," Mary Austin wrote in 1923, about the time Williams's Puerto Rican mother moved in with the family and the red wheel barrow poem showed up. Thirty years later, mother and son translated the Spanish novel of Quevedo, *El Perro y la Calentura*. "There was scope in the new America," Mary Austin held in *The American Rhythm*, "for play on the Homeric scale."

So *be* original and useful, the poet implies with a wink, if not instructively playful—or as Moore said smiling, genuine and raw—within the given verbal landscape. Williams admits through a flowering biblical weed, "The Pink Locust":

> I am not,
> I know,
> in the galaxy of poets
> a rose
> but *who,* among the rest,
> will deny me
> my place?

His singing was indeed different, his bear heart true. And why not make art (Dickinson might say) sufficiently puzzling to resist nonessential "readings"? Why not deny critical last words, if not Pound's Big Ideas ("often brilliant but an ass," his college chum Bill said), other than the job at hand—setting the scene, focusing the essentials, traversing the yard in four syllabic-accentual passes (junior couplets), worthy of Moore's candid scrutiny? Work with "the humility and caution of the scientist," the doctor noted his training. The landscaped line in the New World, Austin thought, was "shaped by its own inner necessity," and Williams searched for the "intrinsic" form of local speech. This verse cannot be measured conventionally, the poet insisted, but must be entered in*to* variably, for itself alone, the singular mind on a singular image (red wheel barrow), thinking and seeing cleanly (glazed with rain).

Williams grounds the lines humanly. He starts over, in effect, with fresh clarity, working humor, and good sense: poetry as humus, the native soil of the New World, the local talk or dialect of the folk. His is a new kind of objectivist verse (a word-world of "things" in themselves)—an Adamic experiment in anti-formalist artistry through an exercise in syllabics, plain diction, and gently barrowing rhythms. The red barrow poem acts out, too, the ways that the working world resists poetic dither: "to refine, to clarify, to intensify," the poet insisted, "that eternal moment in which we alone live." No one but Williams could say it this way. "Such must be the future: penetrant and simple—minus the scaffolding of the academic, which is a 'lie' in that it is inessential to the purpose as to design" (*Notes in a Diary Form* 1927). In October 1948, the good doctor wrote:

> We can't have a new (or old) poem built on a no-good or worn-out framework or underbody. . . . We've got to *begin* by stating that we speak (here) a distinct, separate language in a present (new era) and that it is NOT English. . . . It must be regrown from the ground up—from the skeleton out *before* the flesh, the muscles, the brain can be put upon it.

What in God's name *is* a poet, as the wind increases, if any inhabits the new land?

It is all in "The Poem," sounds that should be sung, as in native oral ceremonies, or Homeric epics, or Confucian folk melodies, but yet "Seldom a song." So we make what we can melodically of "isolate flecks" given off, trying to catch "the strange phosphorus of the life" of our people in historical recovery, "nameless under an old misappellation," finding "particulars, wasps, / a gentian." A stinging truth of our world, the bitter yellow-flower root of the gentian contains a gastrointestinal tonic that heals: "—something / immediate, open / scissors, a lady's / eyes—waking." Wait just a minute, a reader protests, if the gentian is a healing wasp of particular truth, what do the crossing blades of a cutting tool have to do with a lady's eyes—waking up? Simple, one is "open" and closes down to slice, often in a woman's hand; the other, closed, opens to cut into the desired attention—"centrifugal, centripetal." These are the interpenetrant dialogics of odd opposites, brought playfully and disturbingly together in a poem, out and in, open and closed, thought and object. "Say it: no ideas / but in things." The doctor-poet could open rocks like flowers, turn trees into waterfalls, interconnect wasps and gentians, cross blades and scissoring eyes, or see wheel barrows as . . . wheel barrows.

"What, then, is a romantic poet now-a-days?" Stevens asked in a cheeky preface to Williams's *Collected Poems, 1921–1931*. "He happens to be one who still dwells in an ivory tower, but who insists that life would be intolerable except for the fact that one has, from the top, such an exceptional view of the public dump and the advertising signs of Snider's Catsup, Ivory Soap and Chevrolet Cars; he is the hermit who dwells alone with the sun and moon, but insists on taking a rotten newspaper." The same could be said for Fitzgerald's "great" Gatsby after the "Great War" that killed Gaudier.

After a year in Paris, 1923, with Brancusi (afternoons in the studio), Joyce (dinners and white wine), Yeats (a reading for the chosen), Hemingway (a deadlock set of tennis), Gertrude Stein, H. D., and Sylvia Beach on his voyage to *pagany*, Williams went home where he belonged for good. When he left Paris, Mina Loy sketched the doctor-poet as a "wild Indian," maverick that he was, and Pound continued to lecture his college friend on parochial limitations. "Paganism, polytheism, culture fastening on culture to seek some common root: Greek, Chinese, Latin, even American!" Alfred Kazin notes of Pound's poetics in *An American Procession*. "His was the intoxication of returning to the roots of poetry, to an ancient world in Asia even more than to pagan Greece and Rome. Paganism: the living out of roles *in* nature, first by the gods and then by men. Paganism: an identification with the energy patterns in nature *[paideuma]*, not the modern habit of seeking to study nature by dominating it." And Williams insists in counter-measure:

> —to tell
> what subsequently I saw and what heard
>
> —to place myself (in
> my nature) beside nature

                       —to imitate
             nature (for to copy nature would be a
             shameful thing)
                   I lay myself down:

The global modernist sifts back and forward through the recovered "pa-
pyri" of history—Sapphic bits in mummy guts and crocodile stuffing, Fro-
benius scooping up a potsherd, the Altamira caves and Le Trois Frères
opened in 1917 in the French Pyrenees. Culture "begins when one HAS
'forgotten-what-book'," Pound says in his *Guide to Kulchur,* and history ad-
vances not back to, but toward "the primitive," that is, the essential,
whether for medicine man, epic singer, or modernist poet. If Pound is the
bearlike poet as warrior-teacher, Williams is doctor bear, the poet-as-realist-
healer with the cleansing north wind.
      Less windily proselytizing than Pound, but no less *pagan,* Williams held
out for the local detail, the daily dialect, the "ground sense necessary" to
stay put and create from the given. Words were his healing compost, speech
a tribal rhizome. "The study of medicine is an inverted sort of horticul-
ture," he said in *Kora in Hell.* Language as herbal medicine was no less
essential to the doctor-poet than to Sitting Bull or any *native* American
healer, still present, who tells the old stories to root the people tribally,
who sings the old bear-hearted songs to keep the culture vital. "As a writer,
I have been a physician, and as a physician a writer," Williams begins his
Autobiography, "and as both writer and physician I have served sixty-eight
years of a more or less uneventful existence, not more than half a mile from
where I happen to have been born." By the early 1950s, at the end of his
autobiography, Williams is lecturing to Reed College on tribal culture.
"The tribe, a term I borrow from the ethnologists, was the theme of much
that I had to say of the arts. Culture, that martyred word of the subjectivists,
came more and more to be my thought." He speaks in a vein unpacked by
Bowra throughout *Primitive Song.* The measure of culture—"its depth, its
thickness"—matter as much to a poet, Williams says, as to "the magician,
the sorcerer."
      The Edenic descent underlay it all: poetic terror of loss as an opening
into reality, the regenerate energy of breaking free, falling from the mass.
The pragmatics of mortal defeat, his poetics: exit from the old Garden
myths, enter the unknown new. "If you can bring nothing to this place /
but your carcass," his father's mother, Emily Dickinson Wellcome, says
from her grave, after grubbing life for a hundred years, "keep out."
      America to Williams was the pure bastardry, tawdry romance, and care-
less westering of runaways from another world, mixed with the native, the
genuine and *raw* of Moore's interest in poetry. As with the mothering do-
mestic, Elsie, fallen from one virgin renaissance across the water to a second

native rebirth—a regenerative violence teaches the "broken-brain" truth about our incomplete human condition. We strain for golden rebirth and suffer the waste of indifferent gods, no one interceding to save us, no one to drive the car for the other. The yacht-like beauty of form betrays Adam once again, one cheap romance to the next. In a miracle of recovery and loss-that-becomes-gain, the broken forms of our lives reveal the underlying terror and truth of a new world, falling from and yet through, the worldly beauty and waste of our native poetics.

≋(•)≋

SEVEN

Reimagining the Garden

The contemporary New World freshly recorded, petal to wheel barrow, eagle skirr to coyote shadow, stirs in yet another renewal—a resurrection from postlapsarian war and urban wasteland, as modernists stitch up broken Renaissance dreams, reimagining a native Eden, indigenously envisioned. Revision and reconstruction are never simply idyllic. From Pound to Williams, through Stevens and Roethke, a post-Columbian vision of fallen Adam and Eve, repatriated in the Garden, ghosts the literary landscape.

In the Days of Prismatic Color

> not in the days of Adam and Eve, but when Adam
> was alone; when there was no smoke and color was
> fine, not with the refinement
> of early civilization art, but because
> of its originality; with nothing to modify it but the
>
> mist that went up, obliqueness was a variation
> of the perpendicular, plain to see and
> to account for: it is no
> longer that
>
> MARIANNE MOORE

STEVENS'S EARTHY ANGELS

"Dear fat Stevens," Williams piqued his amicable rival, "thawing out so beautifully at forty!" (*Kora in Hell*). Stevens was four years older than Williams, five younger than Frost, and also educated at Harvard 1897–1900 in the arts. His first book of poems, *Harmonium* (1923), the same year as

Williams's *Kora in Hell,* was not published until he was forty-four, married, and rooted in the business world. Stevens lived as an intellectual of means, a Connecticut executive of Hartford Accident and Indemnity, who walked two miles to work each day, musing. Elsie, his lifelong wife, bore a daughter, Holly, entering the world the year of her father's first book. Years later, Holly Bright edited her father's posthumous letters, poems, plays, and essays, *The Palm at the End of the Mind.*

It was all there, in the beginning of the poet's world, and more being said, just before the end, when Stevens published his *Collected Poems* at the age of seventy-five. This gathering won both the 1955 Pulitzer and National Book Award for Poetry (a second time). His last poem in the collection, "Not Ideas about the Thing But the Thing Itself," still holds to nature's harmony, the horizon note of middle C. A sunrise birdsong in early March, a "chorister whose c preceded the choir," whether "scrawny" or not, could inspire an aging poet to yet a "new knowledge of reality," at the end of his life, as at the beginning. "Not as a god, but as a god might be," the ringed men chant their Sunday morning devotions to a rising sun, "Naked among them, like a savage source." Where is the native bear's song among these hearts of difference?

When Americans visit a zoo in Oklahoma, Kafka says, they look constantly over their shoulders. Placing this country's origin in *Native* America, Stevens begins his collected verse with a parable of the new land, "Earthy Anecdote," a frontier beast fable of horizon-note *Oklahoma* ("red-earth" from the Choctaw) territory. Here buffalo once stampeded by the thousands, before White men invaded Indian hunting grounds. Later huge herds of cattle were driven north from Texas, a trail soon crossed by tens of thousands of wagons heading west, and then came the great land rush of squatters (Sooners), grabbing homesteads before legal settlers could get there. Luis Borges catalogues the global folk bestiary of griffin, troll, or unicorn in *The Book of Imaginary Beings*—animals dreamed more real than any in a zoo—and so Stevens imagines the unfettered genius of the wilderness in a wild "cat" made up of "fire" (as in wildfire), birth-startling, leaping in the way of "bucks" (male-at-large ungulates, warriors, cowboys, sodbusters). The natural and surreal worlds merge, and the imagined wild sparks strangely geometric arts, a wilder algebra of images ("the pleasure of disturbance," Robert Pinsky says of poetic variation). As the phonemic clatter of the poem tumbles out, the herd *swerves* right and left in "swift, circular" lines (a herd geometry of stampeding masses among red dust swirls), while hidden syllabic rhythms order the wilderness symmetrically, perhaps pointlessly. Unfazed, the firecat bristles and leaps on, a fabula of prairie fires, dust devils, and primal dreams.

In the brief margin of the final stanza break, the new land ages, its people grub in, after a time the country settles down: "Later, the firecat closed his bright eyes / And slept." Even Edenic fire needs its time of sleeping coals, its rest. From firecat to Plato's ghost, leaping and loafing rhythms cadence most of Stevens's poems: again and again, the garden closes down, oafish Adam tamed by a young girl's whispers, "Heavenly labials in a world of gutturals." Past ten o'clock disillusionment, middle-class houses "haunted / By white night-gowns" drowse through the dark, no dreams of "baboons and periwinkles" lighting up an aging New World. Yet erratically, as the firecat swerves the bucks this way and that, "here and there" an old drunken sailor "asleep in his boots, / Catches tigers / In red weather." A wildfire, primitively native, original, the bear's heart singing, is nascent in all things, primally colored and dream vivid, indefatigable. By the time of Stevens's last poems, such as "An Ordinary Evening in New Haven," the loss of any spirit simply rekindles another. "The plainness of plain things is savagery," Stevens nods to the native given, recreating "the big X of the returning primitive."

One level of Stevens's most convincing poems, notwithstanding their wild dashes of pigment, keeps the tone simple and direct, the musings, say, of a man walking along daydreaming (Wordsworth striding the gravel cottage path, Dante walking cobbled Florence, Mandelstam pacing his plank-boarded study). As though falling asleep, the talk stays just this side of metaphor, the direction of the poem slightly tilted toward meaning, but offset. Ideas lie under the textual surface, images embedded in things. The reference to "bucks," for example, stretches to the four directions, a "firecat" bristles without provocation, a "blackbird" means thirteen or more things. Then a "snow man" stands empty of sentiment (hence densely full of suggestive negative space), and a barren jar in Tennessee can be just that, "grey and bare," still trying to order the wilderness, a mute sign of imposition. The reader's role is to puzzle and unpack the images ("one last look at the ducks"), to imagine the implications quizzically ("Rationalists would wear sombreros"), finally to hear the music within the sensual motion of the verses ("good, fat, guzzly fruit" in the Crispin's new land).

In a singing land, renamed the *Carol*-inas, the lilacs wither down as the butterflies flutter up, fugally. Already children critique the love in parental voices: "Timeless mother, / How is it that your aspic nipples / For once vent honey?" The buried rhythmic rhyme, "is it" and "aspic," aspirates something afoot. Aspic is an herbal lavender used for perfumes, oddly as well for asp or snakebite. It is also a rendered fat stock for serving choice meat dishes. Aspic seems a strange adjective for nipples, yet perhaps not to the "new-born" suckler—elixir (aesthetic), snake oil (antidote), fat stock (appetite). The perfumed "milk of human kindness," so Lady Macbeth would unsex her sentiments, may turn acrid at times, fallen from New World innocence. "Life is a bitter aspic," the poet concludes later in "Esthétique du Mal": "We are not / At the centre of a diamond." No "terrible crystal" lies at the heart of reality, as Hopkins feared, but the swallow of loss—a lounging woman finds no aesthetic grace on Sunday morning, a single word fails to save. Stevens's worldly poet fears the imagination disembodied:

> The greatest poverty is not to live
> In a physical world, to feel that one's desire
> Is too difficult to tell from despair. Perhaps,
> After death, the non-physical people, in paradise,
> Itself non-physical, may, by chance, observe
> The green corn gleaming and experience
> The minor of what we feel.

Yet in the beginning, for infants hearing nurturing voices and periodically later, a mother's milk may be sweet, temporally, as the children wonder, "For once vent honey?" A third aspirant, "For once," in the triple spondee, "o*nce* vent h*on*-," puzzles the human kindness here "vent." The odd verb implies windy (Latin *ventus*) discharge, the aesthetic risk in Stevens's work ("mere sound," the poet grills himself, "to stuff the ear"?). And the Mother (Earth), timelessly seasonal, coming and going in a Carolina Garden, answers musically: *"The pine-tree sweetens my body / The white iris beautifies me."* The stressed voweling, or caroling, within "p*i*ne-tr*ee*" and "b*o*d*y*" (ai-ee and ah-ee), then "wh*i*te *i*r*i*s" and "b*eau*t*ifi*es" (ai-ai-ih and oo-ih-ai) sweeten the reply in lovely song, worthy of a place named "the Carolinas." Stevens's voweling lyrics come from a trans-Atlantic, Norman-English tradition. Keats developed prosody on "the principle of Melody in Verse," his friend Benjamin Bailey wrote in 1818, turning on "open & close vowels . . . interchanged, like differing notes of music to prevent monotony." A century later, Pound swore of metrics, "we will never recover the art of *writing to be sung* until we begin to pay some attention to the sequence, or scale, of vowels in the line, and of the vowels terminating the group of lines in a series." Rounding off the Edenic couplet, our earthy mother's "body" still end-rhymes with "me."

A New World Eve, pregnant in a spring tree, pining, is still sweet with white flower, blossoming ("Petals on a wet, black bough," Pound saw in war-torn Europe, despite "an old bitch gone in the teeth"). The "great, rooted blossomer" of the Last Gaelic Romantic gets another chance out west: in and out of war, ravished and regenerate, Stevens holds out, the earth still renews herself by imaginative, impassioned music ("Their ancient, glittering eyes, are gay," Yeats chanted). Postmodern or Futurist, art still refreshes. "Natives of poverty, children of malheur," as Stevens rhymed in heroic couplet, "The gaiety of language is our seigneur" ("Esthétique du Mal"). Postromantic or pre-apocalyptic, the feminine beautifies our world, whether a "terrible beauty" born of sacrifice ("Death is the mother of beauty"), or the "green corn gleaming" after the withered flowers of evil. The drunken, old sailor in bed with his boots still dreams "tigers / In red weather," beyond disillusionment of ten o'clock, when the night-gowned women in white, untouched, have retired. And the "firecat," that wildfire catalyst to inspiration, lights "red earth" along the Oklahoma frontier, in the beginning a long time ago, still imaginable in the American West. The cat fires an untamable native heat, a new world energy of transformation, as Stevens holds to the alchemy of imagined art, the "supreme fiction" of Adamic belief—believing the native myth of the original land to be regeneratively real.

Following Roy Harvey Pearce's lead on the Adamic mode of American self-creation, Emerson through Whitman, Joseph Riddle concludes that Stevens "wills to establish himself once more in absolute innocence, at the origin, so that like Adam he might create his world and himself anew" (*The Clairvoyant Eye*). No matter how bad it gets, how many give up, or die, more émigré singers will come across the waters, after the fall and dream a new world from fallen ashes. Poetry's music charges us, awakens us to a world of natural renewals, as Nietzsche said, an *eternal recurrence.* "Going back to Connecticut is a return to an origin," Stevens wrote of his home state the year of his death. "There are no foreigners in Connecticut. Once you are here, you are—or you are on your way to become—a Yankee." Here stands the New England romantic at the heart of old world irony, Dickinson countering Frost and Plath. The palm sways at the end of the mind, the grackle cackles when the golden "bird's fire-fangled feathers dangle down."

Six-feet-two and two hundred pounds, Stevens conveyed a puzzling mix of bearlike physicality and dandy diffidence. In 1936 he won a bar fistfight with Hemingway. And yet his was, he deferred, an unremarkable personal life. When asked for a biographical note from the *Dial* in 1922, the poet declined: "I am a lawyer and live in Hartford. But such facts are neither gay nor instructive" *(Letters).* Stevens traveled for the company, collected fine art, drank good scotch, and wrote privately. This 1900 Harvard aesthete in the *fin de siècle* came from Pennsylvania Dutch stock. All his life he pursued the ideal within the real, the "absolute fictions" of men and women peopled with the "necessary angels" of the earth, "in an age angrily secular, romantically anti-romantic, and resignedly naturalistic," Riddle notes. He kept the old poetic dreams alive, from Adam, through Columbus, to Keats and Yeats. His poet was a new world discoverer, an original innocent, a dreamer of the real world. Finally, "Real and unreal are two in one," Stevens felt on an ordinary evening in New Haven. His "new" haven was a second refuge, or heaven on earth, for an aesthetic Adam to "seek," as mortally embodied spirit, "The poem of pure reality."

The modernist new world is part comic's dream, part cynic's nightmare—the esthétique or aesthetic of ill—and truly a joker's fall into reality. Stevens suspects,

> That there lies at the end of thought
> A foyer of the spirit in a landscape
> Of the mind, in which we sit
> And wear humanity's bleak crown;
>
> In which we read the critique of paradise
> And say it is the work
> Of a comedian, this critique;

In "The Comedian as the Letter C," Crispin the clown, "affectionate emigrant" and "odd Discoverer," sails from "Bordeaux to Yucatán" and northwest, a born-again, modernist Christopher Columbus. Crispin goes in search of "the veritable ding an sich," that is, the worldly word-made-flush, "a vocable thing." In the beginning, the salty poet records:

> Nota: man is the intelligence of his soil,
> The sovereign ghost. As such, the Socrates
> Of snails, musician of pears, principium
> And lex.

Crispin plunges into "a savage color" of "tidal skies," only to beach on an old shore, "the mint of dirt, / Green barbarism turning paradigm." On the coast of the New World, he colonizes Carolina from a "savagery of palms," bunkers down on land, and turns a fortune, "Exchequering" (all the *c* sounds possible, Stevens said, the consonant cash of the poem). Four curly daughters later, Crispin's New World turnip turns into the same Old World lump. "Glozing his life with after-shining flicks," he must settle for musing on "plain and common things," as all men have. Poetry finally comes from what is at hand, early and late, everyday; the *real* world is the poem. "The plum survives its poems."

Replaying the rediscovery of Eden-via-America, Stevens was, perhaps, the last Adam before postmodernism to be naming things again (the first American paradigm all over)—signing on a second time around, freed in imagining beings in the garden by what they might be called. The *Ding an sich,* however, the "thing in itself," fell to earth by name, one tongue to another (Old English cognate German to contemporary American English), cognitively lower in the descent of cultural hegemony ("language drift," linguists call it), through a millennial century of great wars and aesthetic chaos. The man on the dump (Baudelaire, Eliot, Fitzgerald) surveys his articled waste of creation, "The the" of his garden gone junk. He faces dung *an sich* and makes a dirge of it, by making up more earthy sounds from the ground up: not moon or nightingale, but "elephant-colorings of tires" and "the blatter of grackles." Adam's "The the" ends "The Man on the Dump" in wisely ignorant desire for the . . . real world, as yet unformed, unrealized, Columbus again. This "the" is a genuine article of unknowing which precedes, and leads to, the noun-things of the new world, "dogs and dung." In this case, the article "the" predicates leaning into things of being, a verbal torsion around "the," without assertive push, indeed, sans the connective and kinetic energy of any verb. Still, the well dressed, bearded man knows, "It can never be satisfied, the mind, never." In some odd sense, the mind seems an attendant article to reality, an indefinite article to be called "the . . .".

So, too, Stevens continually raises questions *of* the preposition's position before and after things in a globed world, placing noun-particles sequentially within each other's context. Ariel says of the planet on the table,

> Some affluence, if only half-perceived,
> In the poverty of their words,
> Of the planet of which they were a part.

Things and thinkers remain appositional, ideas syntactically intelligible only next to one another, objects contingent, sounds rhymed, rhythms scanned, stanzas repeating designs. So the word's *Things* work out of the world's designs-in-things, like rabbits from rabbit shadow hats. "Every poem is a poem within a poem: the poem of the idea within the poem of the words."

As Pearce says of "transempirical" reality within the real of Stevens's paradise, the "thing in itself" generates a process of decreating our fallen and fixed world, next discovering a fluid one, and finally recreating a living one-in-process, things-in-thoughts, by way of words. "It is a world of words to the end of it," Stevens says in "Description Without a Place," at least certain of uncertainty, "In which nothing solid is its solid self." The *Ding an sich* is thus the desire for naming the world, Adamically, and the fated acceptance of poetic kinetics—wanting fallen "things"—moving, without finality, or even substantiality, as an end in itself. Perhaps this is better said as "thing-ing in itself," or even better, via Fenollosa on verbal nouns in Chinese calligraphy, the natural genius "to *thing*" all things as creative forms of energy, more or less in motion.

Stevens thus straddles the "see-saws" of subject-object phenomenology (the conjugating swing of present-past epistemology: he sees thing-*ing*, knows he saw some-*thing*). Roy Harvey Pearce sees Adam's seesaw as a "dialectical compromise" between thinking and things, *denken und Dinge (The Continuity of American Poetry)*. Thus, Stevens delights in seeing himself seeing things—subjective interpenetration with objective things, loading the argument toward phenomenological thinking-as-things-in-interactive-process, indeed, or Valéry's "pure" art as the interplay between the mind's eye and the body's form. We know the dancer through her dancing, the seashore girl in her singing beside the sea's "mimic motion" (the embodied rhyming of ideas of order at Key West: she as Eve by the sea, Adam as son by the sun). Hers is the world "she sang and, singing, made," and his what he heard and saw. The maker is reborn in remaking her song. "She was the single artificer of the world / In which she sang." When the girl leaves and silence falls, the "glassy lights" of anchored fishing boats, "tilting"—now of the Adamic onlooker's making, after listening attentively— still blessedly order the night's descent, in words "dimly-starred" and fragrantly portaled, "of ourselves and of our origins, / In ghostlier demarcations, keener sounds."

All this, more or less grounded in the New World, is a process of Adam cogitating things through words, unendingly. While contemplating a half-glass of water as alembic of conditional thinking, "Fat Jocundus" finds

> In a village of the indigenes,
> One would have still to discover. Among the dogs and dung,
> One would continue to contend with one's ideas.

Stevens opts for the sylvan side of the Adamic story "in a village of the indigenes," the nascent bliss of new beginnings. "I am a native in this world," insists the man with the blue guitar, "And think in it as a native thinks." His is the natural wonder of a free imagination, trusting the visible world, "green's green apogee" in summer credences, gliding natively through the forest of words—albeit iambically and often in the shadows of modernist philosophical fears, what J. Hillis Miller charts as the disappearance of God and personal reconstructions of reality. (At the turn of the century, Stevens, as did Eliot, studied philosophy at Harvard, where Frost learned Latin and Greek). Early and late, Adam's dream holds out against dispirit, as the green plant finally "Glares, outside of the legend, with the barbarous green / Of the harsh reality of which it is part." Stevens distills postlapsarian grace from the "muddy centre" of being, in "Notes Toward a Supreme Fiction," and extracts thanks from "an unhappy people in a happy world." The true poet—Adam in process, Ariel about to be set free, Columbus setting sail—sees the "seeming" reality of things in an ever regenerate world.

> The first idea was not our own. Adam
> In Eden was the father of Descartes
> And Eve made air the mirror of herself,
>
> Of her sons and of her daughters. They found themselves
> In heaven as in a glass; a second earth;
> And in the earth itself they found a green—

Green through glass to grey Tennessee jar, the perceived world is its own word reward. As Crispin discovers on new land, "what is is what should be." Stevens affirms his acceptance of it all in "Of Modern Poetry,"

> The poem of the mind in the act of finding
> What will suffice.

ALL INDIANS

The perplexed claim that "We Are All Indians" appears in Stevens's notebook of titles, *From Pieces of Paper,* most for poems never written, or if so, lost to us, as George Lensing has documented from the Huntington manuscripts. Only in the strictest Edenic sense of an Adamic Uhr-father could all be distantly Indian, and Stevens ironically parses what Roethke elsewhere calls "the longing" to go native.

Three poems in *Harmonium,* Stevens's first book, map out the decreation of Adam's ego, the rediscovery of a non-self or native Other, and the elegiac recreation of a poet's fallen world; a fourth says about all that can be said generically about the poetic process. "Anecdote of the Jar" sets the artifice of self free in a new garden land, "The Snow Man" clears the weeds of sentiment, and "The Emperor of Ice-Cream" resurrects flesh from fatal dumbness. "Thirteen Ways of Looking at a Blackbird" turns the radical imagination loose in a world of decreative renewal.

First, a note of frontier context. "At fifteen years of age," William Carlos Williams records in *In the American Grain,* "Samuel Houston, born 1793, Scotch-Irish, ran away from his brothers of whom he was a charge and joined the Cherokee Indians of Western Tennessee." Three years later, Sam went back to school, got himself elected governor of Tennessee, and married Eliza Allen, who abandoned him after three months. So Governor Samuel Houston resigned, "left everything behind him and took the descent once more, to the ground." Sam rejoined the Cherokees, now relocated in Arkansas, "took an Indian woman for his wife," and lived eleven years with the tribe. Houston came back to civilization a third time, defeating Santa Anna at San Jacinto, and was elected governor of Texas, then United States senator. He married once more, was considered for the presidency and favored by Abraham Lincoln. "When in deep thought," the historian adds, Sam "whittled pine sticks."

Next to the one-page epitaph on Lincoln, "Descent" stands as *In the American Grain*'s shortest chapter, but with the good doctor's minimalist precision, a sketch with rich significance. His most prized poem in the variable foot, "The Descent," emerges from the Houston sketch, turning defeat into gain by discovering the "ground sense" to face mortal facts, and earning "a poetic knowledge, of that ground." Regenerative from the earth, men like Lincoln, Franklin, Washington, and Père Rasles "come up from under," making their way originally and courageously, natively, through "a strange New World." And Sam Houston marked his own trail over the Cumberland Gap into Tennessee wilderness.

In the American West, what does this mark mean? Before God created Eve, according to Genesis, He gave Adam the power of naming Creation, "and whatsoever Adam called every living creature, that *was* the name thereof." This primal gesture has been the subject of much speculation, from religion and philology, to feminism and ecology. What does it signify to stand on a hill, supposedly for the first time, and reorder "the slovenly wilderness" of God's creation? "And God said, Let us make man in our image, after our likeness: and let them have *dominion* over the fish of the sea, and over the fowl of the air, and over the cattle, and over all the earth, and over every creeping thing that creepeth upon the earth" (emphasis mine). Adam's dominion is an age-old arrogance, especially when Old World individuals invade New World tribes.

The opening "I" of Stevens's Tennessee tale, "Anecdote of the Jar," places his empty glass container on a "wild" hill in quatrains of perfect iambic tetrameter, four-by-four—except for the dactylic trip in the third line, "*slov*-en-ly *wild*-er-ness," adding an unruly syllable in the wrong place. The stumbling-step is trailed by a diminished "Surround that hill" and flat trimeter in the last quatrain, "The jar was gray and bare." No matter the roughage, the "round" jar *makes* the wilds "Surround" the hill, and a wilderness "sprawled around, no longer wild." Artificially tuned and unnatural, strange in the wilderness, "The jar was round upon the ground." So the "slovenly wilderness" is enslaved by rhymed likenesses (Slavs in Slovakia?), or at least the I / eye of the glass jar would like to think so. Not only round, surround (Sir?), around, and ground sound poetically forced, even nonsensically rhymed; dauntless, the glass artifice rises "tall and of a port in air." Is this bombastic jar, then, part of a nautical window in the air, sailing into space above ground, or perhaps a harbor to God's heaven in the sky, a chalice of divine interconnection? Like the Puritan "city of light" on a hill above savagery, this brittle palisade seems Pecksniffian self-mockery ("a high-toned old Christian" jar). Adamically parodic, "It took dominion everywhere," in a state already renamed from a Cherokee village, *Tanasi* (place names make Stevens continuously aware that we stand on previously named, indeed inhabited, *native* American ground). Lingual disorder frays imposed order. Listen closely: five words in the poem sprawl erratically across triple syllables, *Ten*-nes-*see, slov*-en-ly, *wild*-er-ness, do-*min*-ion, and *eve*-ry-*where*. An odd cross rhyme, Tennessee and wilderness, sandwiches the repetition of the word "hill," then the second quatrain gives up on rhyme, and the final stanza slips into mock couplets, "everywhere" / "gray and bare" and "bird or bush" / "Tennessee." What savagery is deformalizing the old iambic rhythms and closed rhyme schemes that tied everything down in place? Helen Vendler sees the jar's "awkward sublimity" as a palinode recanting Keats's "Ode on a Grecian Urn," that is, "a vow to stop imitating Keats and seek a native American language that will not take the wild out of the wilderness" *(Wallace Stevens)*. Is this Mason jar pastoral, then, beautiful, true, or natively anecdotal in a new land named after a Cherokee village?

It's an odd poem, indeed, with a metaphor that teases the relationship between seeing through a glass jar (darkly?) and the first-person eye / I / aye (Walt Whitman's exuberance?) as intrusive human consciousness. No small matter that Stevens published the poem originally in October 1919, *Poetry* magazine, as mentioned, with thirteen others under the general title "Pecksniffiana." Eliot's fastidious Prufrock was all the rage by this time, appearing with his "Love Song" five years prior in *Poetry*. The Victorian sanctimony of Dickens's unctuous hypocrite (forcing poor Mary Graham to marry him) is the peck-and-sniff English nuncle of this puritan eye. There's a self-reflexive roundness afoot, a glass rhyme circling back on itself. This rounding eye oddly rivals sun, moon, and earth itself. A little humility, some humor would help. In "Le Monocle de Mon Oncle," also in *Harmonium*, Stevens anticipates the artificial Edenic sin of a looking-glass jar in Tennessee:

> This luscious and impeccable fruit of life
> Falls, it appears, of its own weight to earth.
> When you were Eve, its acrid juice was sweet,
> Untasted, in its heavenly, orchard air.
> An apple serves as well as any skull
> To be the book in which to read a round,
> And is as excellent, in that it is composed
> Of what, like skulls, comes rotting back to ground.

Stevens loves the ah-oo diphthong of "round" and concocts near rhymes for almost every letter in the alphabet (astound, brown moon, clown, down, found, gown, hound, etc.). "I cannot bring a world quite round," sings the man with the blue guitar, "Although I patch it as I can." Not two-dimensionally "round," but spherical in space, a global being, the moon-like poem should embody "an inherent order active to be / Itself, a nature to its natives all / Beneficence," Stevens says late in *The Auroras of Autumn*, by way of a poem aptly titled, "A Primitive like an Orb."

The crack in the "round" jar is hubris, the formal liability of poetry riding too high, as his critics chided ("a grandee crow," Berryman elegized in "So Long? Stevens": "brilliant, he seethe; / better than us; less wide"). That gray glass jar is bare, pontificate of air, falsely domineering. "It did not give of bird or bush, / Like nothing else in Tennessee." Again, the artifice of "of," as in apart from, is not a part *of* the given world. A glass-house art seems unnaturally withholding, stands above creation "Like nothing else." And again, as in "tall and of a port in air," the problem comes down to an overreaching ego, a glassworks "I" about to topple in the wild. This artist manqué connects to, but rawly overreaches *other* ideas of order in God's green earth, blessedly, unselfconsciously native. Man the maker must learn to bear native origins:

> Oh! Blessed rage for order, pale Ramon,
> The maker's rage to order words of the sea,
> Words of the fragrant portals, dimly-starred,
> And of ourselves and of our origins,
> In ghostlier demarcations, keener sounds.

From airy "port" to "fragrant portals," it will take more than a glass eye or tinsel ear to sing naturally *of* natural order in the new world, more than rage to grace "petals on a wet, black bough." The poet seeks native being embodied, the bearing of his makings ("Beauty is momentary in the mind—," Peter Quince sings at the clavier, "The fitful tracing of a portal; / But in the flesh it is immortal"). To perceive anything is to redefine it, to name it one's own and impose consciousness on it. So just seeing things changes them (as ethnologists like Edmund Carpenter have shown of first contact between aboriginals and explorers). Yet we're all *interpenetrant*, Williams says, or biologists like A. Lorenz have argued of the "Butterfly Effect," Beijing to Moscow, where an insect's flight affects life halfway around the globe. "I am what is around me," the poet wrote in "Theory." How do we not-go against an Other's nature, then? How does the artist best enter nature, if he must?

Comic correlative to the red wheel barrow, the glass jar offers a study in perception and artistic imposition, teasing us into self-awareness, without sealing bias toward an art-of-nature. Arrogant or unassuming, what else do we have but consciousness, whether an executive poet in *Connecticut* (Mohegan "place of the long river") or a glass-eyed immigrant on an Indian hill in *Tanasi*? "As part of nature," Stevens wrote of the poet in Havana, "he is part of us. / His rarities are ours: may they be fit / And reconcile us to our selves." Williams would lie down and add his own nature, within nature, to natural things. "The poem is a nature created by the poet," Stevens noted in his daybook. Reading more than his share of modern philosophy, Stevens knows that seeing things changes the scene, naming alters any nature. He wonders how far a poet can go, how artificially the garden has been rhymed, from Plymouth Puritan and Connecticut Yankee, to Tennessee woodsman and Key West beachcomber.

Likeness can falsify as it connects, whether bad rhyme, poor pun, or cheap image. Tone undercuts or affirms, and no rhythm need be imposed on creation. The scene must be freshly seen, the metric foot felt, understood on its own terms and drawn out of the land through artistic cadence, if there is to be an American rhythm that works naturally in verse. Austin, Williams, Pound, Moore, even the immigrant Lawrence got down to the terrain natives walk, the minims of American speech, to write of their new land. "In the world of words," Stevens held his ground, "the imagination is one of the forces of nature." He must answer their call for a native poetics, if his writing is to be "a pheasant disappearing in the brush"— evanescent, resplendent of iris neck and scarlet cockles, speckled with a spray of tail feathers, Old World émigré (the wild pheasant was not native to the Americas). Even at its bleakest, verse should shine in the mind's eye: "A poem is a meteor." As a postscript in *Adagia*, Stevens adds renascently, "(Poet,) feed my lambs." What could the poet learn, not from largesse, but from a Euro-American loss of ego, bear-hearted sacrifice?

"The Snow Man" is one long sentence in five oddly rhymed tercets, crystallized as verse. Like Frost's image of ice melting on a stove, the poem reveals itself as it slides along, warmed dangerously by human touch. The lesson is clear: leave a snow man alone, and it exists for itself, unchanged; touch the snow, and the artifice goes away, as it goes along. An object measures differently in motion than at rest, variously cold and hot: watch it disappear. Instead of the expected iambic opening ("I *placed* a *jar*"), the poem begins impersonally, with a tentative trochee, almost spondaic, "*One must have* a *mind* of *win*ter." Right away, reverse field, the poem catches us in metric crux ("the trochee's heave," Pound said). A leveling cold serves to brace entry and numb stresses into anapests, even spondaic trochees: "and the *boughs* / Of the *pine-trees crust*ed with *snow*." The lines keep rocking with phonemic upheavals, "*juni*pers *shagged* with *ice*," and "*distant glit*ter / Of the *Jan*uary *sun*." A falling dactyl bridges the stanza break, "*glit*ter / Of the," down to the iambic spondee, "*same bare place*" that leans across the gap "For the *list*ener," who finally "beholds / Nothing that is not there and the nothing that is." The last dazed line, twelve syllables shagged tetramically like rime ice, or hoarfrost, arrives as the poem's "terrible crystal" of negation and rediscovery: an initial trochee, "*Noth*ing," an anapestic spondee, "that is *not there*," an anapest falling trochaically, "and the *noth*ing," to a final affirmative iamb, "that *is*." Form is intrinsic rhythmic function: the interruptive patterns of spoken American syntax shoulder against the iambic meter, with errant anapests and trochees stringing out the talk-song, Frost might say, against the more regular metric strictures. A verse line should spring from the resilient strength of natural form, Frost argued for keeping the metric net up, "The straight crookedness of a good walking stick." And what comes of these thick poetics?

"The Snow Man" is an ice-sketched landscape, like Frost's "Desert Places," but its lyrically graced, barren chill leads to more than personal despair. Only the snow man knows himself, the poem knows of itself. Anthropomorphic sentiment, creating a human effigy of snow, must be balanced with the objective knowledge that "misery" plays a false part in this scene. Learn of winter from winter, Bashō would say. Pine, juniper, spruce, and leaves rough or "shagged" with snow (that is, "bearded") are just what they are to "a mind of winter." The trees are, after all, *ever*greens, Vendler notes, and January the "new" year. Imposing summer's loss on the image, a human sense of misery, or worse, the listener feeling "nothing himself," could melt the snow man in elegiac sentiment. Here is where the Other, outside our perceiving self, must be respected as a projection that both is, and is not: ourselves perceiving, Adam on time's seesaw, and a native *it* as *nothing that is. Is* is *was,* time's fall dictates, just *as* we perceive it. Thus the primitive, or primal *Id,* literally "it," is never here, but over there—the not-me or Other as a dark Narcissus flitting in the lost, forbidden shadows of consciousness, the singing bear's heart in shadowy silence. In postmodernist alterity, the other brother, Baudelaire's *hypocrite lecteur,* mirrors the dream ghost of my libido, the me-I-fear, or *not-me* me at the heart of my perceived being.

So the snow man is our wintry opposite, here, out there. This anti-man translates culturally as the natural or primitive self artifacted, the wild or savage native, disowned, driven down under the veneer of civilization. This distorting sublimation is an autumnal tug on the modern mind, fall eulogist to spring lyricist, especially in Adamic America, where "the poverty of dirt" haunts a "World without Peculiarity." It is only one step further from abject to reject, Plath's total disillusion. A truly native poetics, in Stevens's terms, calls this Dionysian Other forth to challenge Apollo's radiant order: "disillusion as the last illusion, / Reality as a thing seen by the mind," while the aging poet walks New Haven on an ordinary evening, "Everything as unreal as real can be, // In the inexquisite eye." The native aesthetician addresses the Academy of Fine Ideas,

> The winter wind blew in an empty place—
> There was that difference between the and an,
> The difference between himself and no man,
> No man that heard a wind in an empty place.
> It was time to be himself again. . . .

Winter has its rightful barren place, cold its purpose, especially to the "native" man bare with snow. Just so, "The Hour of Lead" is Dickinson's respite "after great pain," scrimmed by an alchemical "Slant of light, / Winter Afternoons": "As Freezing persons, recollect the Snow—/ First— Chill—then Stupor—then the letting go—." Stevens goes a philosophical step further than release. When we recognize loss, or error, or nothing that we thought was there (like imagining a ghost at the window) we come to recognize, in a sequence of loss-and-recovery, the positive absence of the empty space ("negative space," Hans Hofmann says, where the canvas has no marks, inviting and soon defining what marks may come). This abstinence recognizes a Zen-like world not overly filled, a "nothing" that frees natives in a new land. The power of art is often what is left unsaid, excess taken away, understatement, implication, or most powerful of all, white space or silence around what is said, aptly, that is, poetry. In "No Possum, No Sop, No Tatters," the visionary poet starves until "Snow sparkles like eyesight falling to earth," and January comes down to

> The savagest hollow of winter-sound.
>
> It is here, in this bad, that we reach
> The last purity of the knowledge of good.

From "snow man" to "emperor of ice-cream," Stevens's senses of mortality and poetics are sweetened seasonally. Yet something is up in the off-beat gusto of Stevens's favorite poem, its "essential gaudiness" festing an elegiac ice cream party at a bawd's wake. The "Call" begins with trochaic imperative for the cigar-roller, swarthy man of the streets, to whip up ice cream "In kitchen cups." The curious Latinate phrase, "con*cupi*scent *curds*," rises and falls with an added anapestic syllable, opening "cup" in an elongated phonemic "-*koop*-". This odd adjective, syllabically curdy, means "eagerly desirous," that is, lusty, bawdy, with a tinge of nonsensical gaiety. The modifier sweetly parodies Puritan sexual prudery ("lustful" curds of ice cream!). No less than John Calvin equated sex with original sin, "all defiled and crammed with concupiscence," Alfred Kazin notes in *God and the American Writer;* "or, to sum it up briefly," Calvin writes, "the whole man is in himself nothing but concupiscence" (*Institutes of the Christian Religion,* Book 11, Chapter 1). So be it in Adam's own words, the poem proclaims, let the body be celebrant of its own high and low, fantail to bunion, in Stevens's words "concupiscence" to "destitution" (*Letters:* to Leonard C. van Geyzel, May 16, 1945).

"Let the wenches dawdle in such dress," the elegist calls for a lusty renewal of the stale, "As they are used to wear"—suggesting both everyday lounging wear, chemises or less, and "wear" they are *used* in, paid to be in and out of, connoting hired "wenches." Yet Julia Kristeva's *jouissance* flavors all this, the feminine prerogative, letting pubescent boys bring recycled flowers in old newspapers. The poem elegiacally fetes a tawdry scene, muscular and mysterious, still joyous in its romping rhythm and rhyme: "Let be be finale of seem. / The only emperor is the emperor of ice-cream." The trimeter refrain's assonance plays musically with and against its cognitive density. The iambic spondee, "Let *be be*," is anapestically reversed in the end result, how things appear, "fin*ale* of *seem*," as the line rides on four long ee's, creating a sort of giddy realism to face the last rite or final word. "Let be be the finale of seem," Stevens wrote to Henry Church, "is let being become the conclusion or denouement of appearing to be: in short, ice cream is an absolute good" (*Letters*, June 1, 1939). Recreant repetition is the key: what is is (what seems is all there is), fallen or renewed, *finale* and all. The be-ing of seem-ing is our end, so let *seem* finally *be*.

This little nonsense ditty takes a serious turn at the stanza break. Someone and somethings are missing. The woman's dresser, where she "used to wear" lingerie, lacks "three glass knobs" (three-in-a-jar trinity?), and her bedding may be too short to cover both head and feet. Her prone body, mocking how the wench lived, lies flat in the indignity of death. "If her horny feet protrude," those limb ends tell us "how cold she is, and dumb." So a wench is dead, stretched out cold at the ice cream party. The dresser deal "knobs" transpose to "horny" bunions, glass to skin calluses. No empty jar lies here, rounding the wild, but a woman's body in its cool opaque skin, thickened from walking the earth. Her "horny feet" index a prosaic, if bewitching reality, bunioned and "dumb" as the "slovenly wilderness": feet are the earthen root, nonetheless, the vulgate "base" of a poetic meter iambically shamanic. She embroidered "fantails" on her bedsheet, her tail-end art. Those curlicues may cover her face, if they cannot mask her feet, which grounded her in reality, finally in death. So, for a fourth and final call, "Let the lamp" of nature "affix its beam," the sun its sundown flame, as the seeing eye celebrates an inner light in mortal darkness, a comeback optics of imagining sunrise reborn at sunset. As elsewhere, the well dressed man with a beard finds,

> After the final no there comes a yes
> And on that yes the future world depends.
> No was the night. Yes is this present sun.

Dreaming *jouissance* is critical. The imagination, Stevens said in his *Letters*, is "like light, it adds nothing, except itself." The "supreme fiction," lighting us to the end, is to *be*-lieve in our world, "my green, my fluent mundo," as one lives and faces death in others (no less than Emily Dickinson a-wake or Sitting Bull the sash-wearer). Poetry is to imagine well what must be. "The final belief is to believe in a fiction," Stevens wrote in *Adagia*, "which you know to be a fiction, there being nothing else. The exquisite truth is to know that it is a fiction and that you believe in it willingly" (reflective chronotope turned precept).

With rhyming comic finality (come/dumb/beam/cream), the refrain rides on a boisterous iambic pentameter, "The *only emp*eror *is* the *emp*eror of *ice-cream*." The fourteen syllables curdle in a spondee (as with the twelve-syllable, shaggy last line of "The Snow Man"). There's a youthful break in the pace, a jump-rope skip completing the Falstaffian form. From bunioned foot to embroidered fantail, earthly base to fanciful end, this elegy resists loss by making art of what seems to be, seeing what is, delightfully. It is an act of the imagination at a wake, the final test, to return to childhood joy in "cream" made of "ice" (Carolina "aspic nipples" sweetened). A concupiscent summer is whipped up from winter's absence, the snow man's "nothing" curdled by sweet belief.

Out walking his home town, Stevens realizes in the evening, as Williams showed in *Spring and All,* "So lewd spring comes from winter's chastity." Subject to object, feeling to fact, Stevens concludes after seventy years, "We keep coming back and coming back / To the real: . . . to the object // At the exactest point at which it is itself." Old World to New, mortality haunts the Columbian Adam, leaving the fallen garden to discover expulsion in the moment of *re*discovery:

> The rock is the gray particular of man's life,
> The stone from which he rises, up—and—ho,
> The step to the bleaker depths of his descents . . .

This poet would fly by the totem of night. In his *Letters* Stevens said of the blackbird sequence, "This group of poems is not meant to be a collection of epigrams or of ideas, but of sensations." In what senses? Among the Russian formalists, a theorist named Viktor Zhirmunski published a study of rhyme in 1923 when Stevens's first book, *Harmonium,* appeared beside Williams's *Kora in Hell,* Donald Wesling recounts in *The Chances of Rhyme,* specifically focusing on off-rhyme and what his Russian colleagues called "making it strange." The device of inexact rhyme calls self-reflexive attention to a literary text and language-as-medium, Zhirmunski said, through a sequencing effect: defamiliarizing a reader entering the text, defacilitating the interpreter with verbal intricacy, and retarding the critic's progress digressively. The effect is to slow down time, heighten awareness, and open radical interpretive possibilities, where assumption blocks intuition, or arrogance shuts down understanding. Similarly, in *Shakespeare's Meanings* Sigurd Burkhardt writes of Shakespeare driving a verbal wedge between sound and meaning, in order to free his language from expectation and cliché. As with off-rhyme, so with slant images—beyond critical paraphrase, slightly gnomic—they throw the poem into what Yeats called "radical innocence," positions of witness and testament, less interpretation, the bear's heart all the more singing *différence.* A poem must be, Auden noted, more than anyone can say about it. Just so with the blackbird sequence, a poem of optics and phonics, among other things, shattering reality into irregular facets of a mysterious jewel that reflects spectral colors, iridescent light from a black diamond. At least thirteen ways into this, each angle of refraction redefines the blackbird, as each moment shifts the image.

To begin, the trochaic title is strangely reverse of blank verse (the only pentameter in the poem): "*Thir*teen *Ways* of *Look*ing *at* a *Black*bird." The trochee's insistently reverse rocking, beginning with that superstitious surd,

*thir*teen, an indivisible number with no stable root, sets up an inverse po-
etics, or radical set of "Ways"—that is, passages or mental journeys—of
"looking at" (not so much seeing) a bird the color, all colors, of the night.
This is trickster stuff, as Ted Hughes darkly develops in *Crow*, the off-comic
possibilities of god as Harlequin who tosses disappearing dice with reality.
The poem shows us seeing a "black" bird as surd pronoun, *it*, treading
syllabic night terrain, searching for winged focus on a disappearing, then
reappearing radical. Call it the *blackbird factor*, the unpredictable quark of
reality, the poem's decentering center. Disruptively patterned, this wild
shadow is its own original being, in motion.

Oddly enough, the first tercet is a still scene, the minimalist quiet of
Oriental landscape painting brushed with haiku delicacy. "A*mong twen*ty
*snow*y *moun*tains," the line opens, rising and falling reversely, "The *on*ly
*mov*ing *thing* / *Was* the *eye* of the *black*bird." Can this be iambic meter, when
six of the seven two-syllabled words are trochaic, and the second line en-
jambs a trochee spondaically, *"thing / Was"*? What are the metrics? Twenty-
one syllables in three lines, 8/6/7, focus on "the eye" of a blackbird among
"twenty" whitened mountains. The reader's eye and ear move back over
the syllables, searching for clues to movement in the landscape, and fix,
sideways, on the blackbird slanting at an angle. So the equation seems to
be twenty mountains, plus one black eye (a perceptual pun?), in twenty-
one micro-syllabics, or $n + 1$, as the blackbird factor to begin. We can always
count on one radical in any given set, moving among counted numericals.
Still more, while one blackbird eye moves visibly, the other remains hidden,
we imagine (the back side of things), suggesting forces behind or beneath
the surface visual image. *(Not) see it new* would be Stevens's take on "Make
it new," Pound's modernist formula from the Chinese. That which is be-
yond us remains irreducibly the Other, to be noted, respected, acknowl-
edged, if not altogether seen. Like the other side of the globe, or the dark
side of the moon, or the libido's reservoir in the id, we must also *imagine
it new*, as this Other eye is always turned away, but always there. For Stevens,
it must be imagined because it is, even if we can't quantify or touch it, as
with an electron, a black hole, the square root of three, or a perfect human
union. Shamanic riddles, the quizzical chill or slant truth of Dickinson's
work, say, always lie hidden behind the mask, beneath the surface of or-
dinary things. There's mystery in the old mundo, marvelous in the mun-
dane, as ordinary things harbor extraordinary potential. This won't be an
easy poem to track.

Through the rhyming acoustics of three, tree, and there, the second
tercet toys with lingual, hence metaphoric triangulation: "I was of three
minds, / Like a tree / In which there are three blackbirds." Perhaps the
optic reference is two eyes focusing on one tree, $a + b = c$, or in a folkloric
vein, mortality witnessing the tree of life-and-death, the indivisible trinity

completed on the cross (three is the first surd with no square root). Also note that it takes two eyes, focusing diagonally, to create one three-dimensional, in-depth image. Perceptual reality is complex, to say the least, and at its simplest, most mysterious (Leonardo spoke of "the vanishing point" in his three-dimension rendering of the Annunciation, Gabriel, Mary, and a distantly dissolving river). The meter of the third line is uncertain, "In *which* there are *three black*birds," perhaps, and the formal arc of the poem less and less calculable. Still, a unified diversity hovers *there*, one consciousness "of *three* minds," like blackbirds *three*-in-one-*tree*. The poetics tilt dangerously off-center, just shy of nursery rhyme magic. Subtract an *h*, or add one and shift the *r:* the slightest change changes everything, three-tree-there, yet the whole remains one cross-stitched homologue, an optic riddle and odd-sense rhyme.

The next couplet implies that the mind *mimes* the world it sees in motion, as a blackbird whirls in autumn winds. Nature shows itself a "pantomime" or dumb show without words, its essential action preceding language. The fourth section, all four lines starting with *a*, or alpha, hints that no anaphoral coupling, Adam to Eve, man to wo-man in the beginning, is complete without a decentering third radical, the blackbird factor. Union comes from disunion, as even turns on odd. The dark stranger—Pluto to Orpheus and Eurydice—thickens the plot radically, realistically. The unknown other to a given rhyme or couplet keeps the poem going (Pinsky's "pleasure of disturbance"). So far, the text is playing with parts-in-motion of a whole, jockeying for kinetic position to view the blackbird's collective facets.

The fifth stanza questions which tonal cadence most makes way for beauty, in-*flec*-tion or in-nu-*en*-do, "The blackbird whistling / Or just after." Is it accent, or afterthought, that suspends sense—the word spoken, or the reflective silence that follows? The plot is in the pause. Just so, shadow to caesura, the longer sixth section shows the triple remove of the blackbird's shadow, crossing icicles of "barbaric glass" outside a "long window." Here "bar*baric*" (from the Greek, *ethnoi* for foreigners who stutter *bar-bar* like sheep) modifies the scintillant dactyl, "*ic*icles," and we sense how many optic removes the eye, a fluid sphere refracting light in a black pupil, must *see through* to catch a fleeting glimpse, a dark image of a darker flying object. *Icicle,* literally Old English "ice of snow," traces back through Frost's melting verse on a stove to the snow man's wintry Otherness, the "nothing that is" out there. The blackbird's shadow darts back and forth outside civilization's glassed house (again the empty jar's echo). The radicals of remove prove multiple, metrically tracing "in the *shad*ow / An inde*ci*pherable *cause,*" as Plath says pointillistically of the retreating horseman in "Words," those "inde*fa*tigable *hoof*taps." *Window, shadow, to and fro, mood,* and *shadow*

REIMAGINING THE GARDEN   *213*

come together as the first true rhymes of the poem: an echoing sense that
we've reached an inner corridor, a winged truth.

In high rhyme now, the poet addresses those "*thin men* of *Had*dam" to
ask why they follow Yeats to Byzantium after imagined "golden birds,"
when the real blackbird walks at the feet of their women, looking up. Not
fantails, but fleshy feet give the physical downbeat of art ("let be be"), the
"under"-standings that Poldy Bloom glimpses following a woman's skirt up
the stairs, or admires on library chairs under reading women. High diction
and formal metrics amount to little, lacking the ground sense and sensual
counterstress of the blackbird's fetching antics, deconstructing all art that
climbs too high. And so the bird flies off the page, over the horizon, "the
edge / Of one of many circles," from viewer's eye to global curve; and just
so quickly, it reappears in an Edenic green light, drawing bawdy cries of
ecstasy. Recall the first poetic speech as interjection (Ah! or Ha!), here
from "the bawds of euphony," those academic wenches of high art. Even
critics can be moved from fustian to ecstasy by springing resurgence ("the
green corn gleaming").

The eleventh set trips metrically uneven, the poet riding "over Con-
necticut / In a glass coach," again reminiscent of the artifice of the Ten-
nessee jar. Through the rattling glass of a formal poetic (train) coach, a
mistaking "fear pierced him"—the shadow of his carriage, that high-riding
"equipage" of art, seems the steely shadow of the blackbird, a decreative
omen sparking creative fear. And so, penultimately conclusive, the Hera-
clitean river flows ever onward, never to be stepped in twice the same, the
blackbird still flying—and it is about to snow, that in-between "evening all
afternoon," when slant light haunts the study, and the end anticipates a
new beginning: "The blackbird sat / In the cedar-limbs." Cedar is the
dream wood the world over, Lebanon to the Dakotas, the tree of see-ing
visions, and in it still sits the bird of all-colored night, shadow of shadows.
In a world of radical unrest, he will momentarily close as the fixed radical,
reality's shifting point-of-reference, just as the poem opened with one black
eye among twenty snowy mountains. Poetry comes from a voice about to
sing, Valéry said, and Stevens's verse rises out of blackbirds soon to fly.

Stevens is entering and modernly reinventing an old avian tradition.
"The wing is the corporeal element which is most akin to the divine," Plato
insists. Man cannot fly, so he marvels winged things and dreams of angels.
"Of the nature of the soul," Plato says in the *Phaedrus*, "let me speak briefly
and in a figure. And let the figure be composite—a pair of winged horses
and a charioteer." The "imperfect soul," Plato thinks, loses her wings,
drooping in flight, and "at last settles on the solid ground—there, finding
a home, she receives an earthly frame." So mortals fall into reality, as
in Stevens's end words of the *Collected Poems*, the gold-feathered "bird's

fire-fangled feathers dangle down" from the mind's last palm (tree or hand?). Back to the fallen New World, Roethke elegized "The Dying Man," dedicated to W. B. Yeats, the "last" Romantic: "he dares to live / Who stops being a bird, yet beats his wings / Against the immense immeasurable emptiness of things." From Dedalus escaping the minotaur's cave on wax wings, to Christ as griffin, part-eagle-and-lion, to Shelley's skylark and Keats's nightingale, to Hopkins's windhover and Dickinson's generic "bird" with a worm, *plashing* like a butterfly off "Banks of Noon," to Williams's dead father as a fallen sparrow and Ted Hughes's enigmatic crow, poets dream of flight, angelic transcendence, melodic transfiguration, and the fated fall. Idiosyncratically, Stevens's bird is black, an omen of the night, and unpredictable, a chaos theory clown. Its iridescent darkness signals the given, the other to ordering human light, and as such an antidote to fixed opinion. Still at the end of things, palms down, "The bird's fire-fangled feathers dangle down." Because readers of reality cannot know the blackbird, only look at it in flight and see it seeing, we see ourselves looking at a native totem of the radical imagination, listening to Yankee shamanic song. The world over this is the shaman's riddle: when Orpingalik's Inuits feel "thawed up" in an ice-floe and fear to use words, small people feeling still smaller, he tells Knud Rasmussen, "the words we need will come of themselves," indeed, words "shoot up of themselves—we get a new song." We come away singing the wisdom of unknowing, if lucky, the conditional human perception of our tricky place in nature's mystery play. Though humans cannot fly, we can imagine Others who do and find significance in our difference. As Stevens noted in *Adagia,* "There is no wing like meaning."

An aphoristic or riddling magic lurks in the corners of Stevens's poems. He trades on the shaman's tricks, the mind's quirks, male variance and female wile, as readers look twice and critics change their minds. The texts sway like Japanese koans, the rhythm of one hand clapping, the squawk of the crow's split tongue, the silence of tamarack or maple unfallen in the New England forest. This poet dreams before the Fall, an Adamic savage with original wonder. He feels the child's acceptance of a world without Dickinson's slippage, or Frost's after-bite, or Plath's crackling blacks. In their shadows, Stevens concludes "A Primitive Like an Orb":

> That's it. The lover writes, the believer hears,
> The poet mumbles and the painter sees,
> Each one, his fated eccentricity,
> As a part, but part, but tenacious particle,
> Of the skeleton of the ether, the total
> Of letters, prophecies, perceptions, clods
> Of color, the giant of nothingness, each one
> And the giant ever changing, living in change.

Always the discrete, incomplete part begs a large whole, an imagined *harmonium*. The concrete particle clings tenaciously to itself within a worldly context of not-self. The nothing beyond itself defines *it* as a part of reality, or an interrelating definition within the dynamic whole: "any stick of the mass / Of which we are too distantly a part," the poet celebrates in "Less and Less Human, O Savage Spirit."

Stevens wrote gracile verse with underwater grace, the dancing porpoises and seals at Key West where he wintered, say, drifting seaweed and swaying kelp. With a heliotropic (sun-shade) imagination, he wrote as a man meditating daylight at leisure, reflecting night aesthetically: "a response to the daily necessity of getting the world right," the poet defended such reflective pastime, or time out of daily time. Stevens took the philosophic nature of time, light, and reality seriously, meditatively coming "to regard poetry as a form of retreat" from the unreal real, he wrote Harriet Monroe in 1922 *(Opus Posthumous)*. But this pause from the workday, as well, spawned a special "nature created by the poet," he added in *Adagia* ("at ease," Italian *ad agio)*. Neither lucrative work nor labored craft, Stevens's verse traces a "pure poetry" of mind meeting matter, and vice versa. His art is the craft of craft in personal off-hours, where work is never work, but serious play, the pure joy of creative thought. "Poetry is the gaiety (joy) of language" *(Adagia)*. It is an angelic "jovial hullabaloo" early on, a "miraculous multiplex" by the poet's late life, but always, and more than for any poet of his time, writing for Stevens is sensual, ideational harmony (and pleasure) of words musically in motion: "the green corn gleaming."

Such aesthetic thought may be philosophical insurance to an American businessman. It was not the monetary hedge against hustling lines in the streets (before law school Stevens scraped by as a New York journalist), nor was it the material carapace of worldly possessions stocked against spiritual poverty (for a man of wealth). His were aesthetics set in motion by the mind's self-delighting interplay with August things and April ideas as yet unsavored: "A text of intelligent men / At the centre of the unintelligible." Then again, for Stevens poetry served as assurance of another kind, if anti-insurance in some sense, since what isn't possessable and doesn't pay *does pay off* in its release from American materialism, burgher stupor, male arrogance, or the opiates of wealth.

Poetry earned Stevens an enlightened gaiety and gained him a measure of modernist immortality. Art to him was spiritual insurance, a psychic anti-bank account. A commuter riding over Connecticut in a glass coach, his own shadow, mistaken for the trickster's dark innuendo, startled the poet strangely awake: "The river is moving. / The blackbird must be flying." That's the way things worked for Stevens: ice cream, snow men, drunken sailors, clattering bucks, wincing widows, or passing blackbirds necessitated angels of reality, "decreative" (indeed procreative) pauses, leaping

Oklahoma firecats, red weather, and echoing reflections. His angel was always surrounded by *paysans*, as the poet searched continuously for the *native* in America, the Euro-American fusion of old and new poetics. In the Great Bear's shadow, his savage "nothingness," if a mute god in the house "less and less human," was coolly "vermilioned." Helen Vendler argues: "To create the new we must first de-create the old, and the reality of de-creation (as Stevens called it, borrowing the word from Simone Weil) is as strong as the reality of creation. It is for this reason that Penelope's web becomes for Stevens the very image of human desire: woven afresh every day, it is unraveled again every evening" *(Wallace Stevens)*. Or less politely, the poet shushed his winged soul's wincing in "Puella Parvula":

> Keep quiet in the heart, O wild bitch. O mind
> Gone wild, be what he tells you to be: *Puella.*
> Write *pax* across the window pane.

Stevens's goal was the ideal in the real, fact and imagination one. As he jotted in "Notes Toward a Supreme Fiction," perhaps his finest long poem:

> To find the real,
> To be stripped of every fiction except one,
>
> The fiction of an absolute—Angel,
> Be silent in your luminous cloud and hear
> The luminous melody of proper sound.

His was a "blessed," if all too bestial "rage" for human order, a harmonious *is*.

So Wallace Stevens seems a Renaissance man, Raleigh in Roanoke regenerate through verse, further enlightened by the philosophy of an eighteenth-century age of reason, finally tempered for three centuries in Puritan New England and reborn a modernist. That is, Stevens stands as a "pure" intellectual pilgrim resisting Christian asceticism (the "high-toned old" hymns of wincing widows) and spiritual repression (the spinster "nave" of institutions). His neoprimitive rhythm catches Adam singing to himself, reentering the imaginary Garden, with "raw" and "genuine" angels silent in the hyacinth. If Stevens had moments of autumnal sighing, a post-Romantic yearning for Keats; if at times he even gave in to a wintry mind of postmodernist despair, he still believed in the "orb" of the "primitive" and sang "this gorging good" in "huge, high harmony" with the green voice of Edenic summer, glorious, warm, and mellow, through the mind's blue shadows. Stevens was, after all, a lyricist, an artist of true voice, a word-sender. He played the blue guitarist above the spinster "catarrh" of a virgin soul, alone as Eve or Emily Dickinson in the garden, but joyous as Whitman or Navajo Changing Woman, singing a new world.

No less than Two Shields chanting "a wind from the north comes for

me," the Adamic Savage fingers his forest of phonemes, and Stevens's re-
flexive "Large Red Man" reads aloud from his kitchen "poem of life"—a
clutter of pots, pans, and tulips—while the "ghosts" of the departed creep
back to listen: "They were those that would have wept to step barefoot into
reality."

A CANTICLE FOR THEODORE ROETHKE

The Garden Master's gone.
JOHN BERRYMAN

Born 1908 in Saginaw, Michigan, at thirty-three Theodore Roethke pub-
lished his first book, *Open House,* and went on to win the Triple Crown in
poetry (as did Marianne Moore and John Berryman), a Pulitzer, Bollingen,
and two National Book Awards, plus Guggenheim, Fulbright, and Ford
Foundation support. Though Roethke joked that his canonical Harvard
elder would "play the flitter-flad" and "plink the skitter-bum" of verse,
the younger gardener inherited Wallace Stevens's "anguish of concrete-
ness!"

> Roar 'em, whore 'em, cockalorum,
> The Muses, they must all adore him,
> Wallace Stevens—are we *for* him?
> Brother, he's our father!

An inch taller than Stevens at six-foot-three and bearishly bearded, Ted
Roethke was more savage, less sylvan, all too much a lost son of this world.
"And things throw light on things," he chanted the back-draft of small
beings, "And all the stones have wings." He would have understood Sitting
Bull's meadowlark songs and lamentational *Tunkáshila,* or "grandfather"
stones. Stanley Kunitz found "news of the root, of the minimal, of the
primordial" in his friend's verse: "The life in his poems emerges out of
stones and swamps, tries on leaves and wings, struggles towards the divine"
(*A Kind of Order, A Kind of Folly*). Roethke's verse made music of all the live,
dumb things, a pantheistic elegy over falling into the New World.

Roethke sang from Garden grief, lost, banished by the Father, mother-
less. His Adam descended from Darwin's swamp, east of Eden: "This frog's
had another fall." Rather than Eve's "aspic nipples" venting honey,
Roethke was slapped awake by "the lash of primordial milk!" and thumbed
a son's raging expulsion. Michigan's wildest poet wrote in evolutionary
verse, formal to free, verging on shamanic Mother Goose, heard in both
German and English daily as a child:

> By snails, by leaps of frog, I came here, spirit.
> Tell me, body without skin, does a fish sweat?

> I can't crawl back through those veins,
> I ache for another choice. ("Unfold! Unfold!")

His verse was all outdoors, in the spirit of endangered beasts and a botched civilization begging native redemption. "Who cares about the dance of dead underwear," he satirized the modernist wasteland dirge, "or the sad waltz of paper bags?" Roethke called for "the great rage of a rocking heart," as did his Welsh counterpart in pastoral ecstasy, Dylan Thomas. "I sing the green, and things to come," the American declared in "O, Thou Opening, O." He could blurt with impunity, "The lark's my heart!" or "The rat's my phase," and write of going Indian in "The Longing,"

On the Bullhead, in the Dakotas, where the eagles eat well,
In the country of few lakes, in the tall buffalo grass at the base of the clay buttes,
In the summer heat, I can smell the dead buffalo,
The stench of their damp fur drying in the sun,
The buffalo chips drying.

> Old men should be explorers?
> I'll be an Indian.
> Ogalala?
> Iroquois.

As Sitting Bull sang two generations before, "So I have been a warrior / and now it is all over, so / I know to bear against hard times." Roethke's hard-time wilderness was of words, primarily, an obsessive acoustics of mad rhyme and rhythmic rattle on the edge of *heyoka* gibberish. He battered the senses of speech until sense broke through. "Have mercy, gristle:" the poet counseled himself along a long alley, "It's my last waltz with an old itch."

In tribute to Lawrence, "Give Way, Ye Gates," Roethke howled of Adam as crucified Christ in the Garden, Eve seduced to be Mary, man's primal lot the Expulsion, our lives wastelanded:

> Believe me, knot of gristle, I bleed like a tree;
> I dream of nothing but boards;
> I could love a duck.

> Such music in a skin!
> A bird sings in the bush of your bones.
> Tufty, the water's loose.
> Bring me a finger. This dirt's lonesome for grass.
> Are the rats dancing? The cats are.

His mad synapses gambled with sense and hexing passion. In "Her Becoming," the poet called on "the wild disordered language of the natural heart," through the influence of craft, "to bring the language back to bare, hard, even terrible statement."

No less than Berryman, Roethke's art was a bursting struggle with the muse. He recounts "that particular hell of the poet" when he could not write, a midlife crisis at forty-four, teaching pentameter at the University of Washington, and feeling like a fraud. Suddenly the room was charged with Yeats's presence and "The Dance" came in thirty minutes, a formal poem of an ambling poet-bear "remembering to be gay." The troubled bear-heart sways back to iambic life cadence. "Yes, I was dancing-mad," the poet concludes, "and how / That came to be the bears and Yeats would know." Looking back, Roethke confesses, "I felt, I *knew,* I had hit it. I walked around, and I wept; and I knelt down—I always do after I've written what I know is a good piece." A writer feeling the muse, or sacred mentor, come personally to inspire creation is not uncommon, whether pathological or spiritual—Dante led by Virgil through the Inferno, Machiavelli among his Ancients writing *The Prince,* Herbert inspired with God's Word, Blake feeling Milton's ghost enter his left foot, Yeats awakened in southern California by Irish spirits to *A Vision,* or in our own day, Pound typing Pisan Cantos by Athena's light in his prisoner-of-war tent, Merrill communing with Auden through his Ouija Board, Hughes catching the Thought-Fox on paper, or Heaney disinterring the Bog Queen in *North.* No less than Sitting Bull's birdsong, Roethke's logic swings on the native hinge: "If the dead can come to our aid in a quest for identity, so can the living—and I mean *all* living things, including the sub-human. This is not so much a naive as a primitive attitude: animistic, maybe" *(On the Poet and His Craft).*

Since God "is in all things," the poet reasons from St. Thomas, He can be called through snail, clod, birdsong, or Eucharist. Rilke gazed at his tiger for eight hours to write a lyric. Roethke gathers around him a lifetime of creatures abandoned from the Garden, cicada to towhee, clam to banana, geranium to quince. He would be Adam to all the oddly living in a field of light, siskin to kingfisher, cyclamen to oriole:

> My heart lifted up with the great grasses;
> The weeds believed me, and the nesting birds.
> There were clouds making a rout of shapes crossing a windbreak of cedars,
> And a bee shaking drops from a rain-soaked honeysuckle.
> The worms were delighted as wrens.

This garden poet regards the word as vatic root: sprung from underground, dark beneath us, tangible, mysterious, tuberous. Where did it come from? Be-fore us (fore-being)? At the other end, the word blazes as riotous blossom, "chrysanthemum" (golden flower), "smilax" (bindweed, or climbing asparagus), "nasturtium" (nose-twist). Even more than Stevens, *Things* compel him, physically touching, granite to slime, icicle to hot coals. Roethke, as in roots—tangled, tenacious, thrilling with life—his grandfather had been Bismarck's chief forester in nineteenth-century Germany. His father and uncle glass-housed twenty-five acres of the Saginaw Valley in northern Michigan to grow New World green things, as their boy nursed in the mulch:

> Hunting along the river,
> Down among the rubbish, the bug-riddled foliage,
> By the muddy pond-edge, by the bog-holes,
> By the shrunken lake, hunting, in the heat of summer.

He knew the "native" in American, the untamed in the dark wood, the primitive in the Indian, for he was of their world, as his Old World fathers tended virgin timber (the last pure Michigan stand in the First World War) and replanted forests felled by careless pioneers.

The brilliant lyric, with its grenading half-line, is there early in *The Lost Son*. "*Where were* the *green-house*s *going*," the boy in "Big Wind" asks with double spondaic trochees, alliterative gerunds dropping right and left, "Lunging into the lashing / Wind driving water / So far down the river / All the faucets stopped?—". The diction is downwind American, unadorned, as fact exceeds the word. A dwarfed adjective in the title fails to measure up to the wind's gusting bigness. So the first metric step, "Where were," is blown off balance, and the skidding gerunds lash back and forth, "going" wind-wild. There's no letup from start to finish, no full stop in the poem, rather a boy's breathless witness of "the old rose-house," fragilely glassed against the elements, as "she rode it out," an epic battle full of heroic equestrian simile ("She hove into the teeth of it"), chiasmus ("Ploughing with her stiff prow"), kenning ("Bucking into the wind-waves"), Anglo-Saxon alliteration ("Where the worst wind was"), and Old English rowing rhythms from Pound's Odyssean Canto ("*Flinging long strings* of *wet* a*cross* the *roof-top,* / *Fi*nally *vee*ring, *wea*ring themselves *out, merely* / *Whi*stling *thin*ly *un*der the *wind-vents*"). The blown gerund is the poem's pivot; the noun-become-verb, or object-in-motion, keys the child's excited imagination, his belief in the myth of the stormed ship as America's night-sea journey to renewal. His is a hothouse drama of civilization, the Adamic Garden under glass, seen more heroically than from Stevens's empty jar or glass coach. An innocent and vulgar practicality wins out here, a true American grit, as the drained manure-machine drives steam to the far end of the hothouse, and animal feces save the roses. An old frontier story comes round: the rough men with a boy-witness save *her*, the rose-house of mother culture. The excited living being of roses takes every bit of ingenuity, strength, and courage that a vernacular hero can muster to salvage from the night storm wilds.

Old, dark, working harpies haunt Roethke's early poetry. "Frau Bauman, Frau Schmidt, and Frau Schwartze" are revered as greenhouse earth goddesses, real women reified in myth who godmother Edenic flowers:

They teased out the seed that the cold kept asleep,—
All the coils, loops, and whorls.
They trellised the sun;

The tenacity of these midwifing muses hovers over the boy's first night sense of loss:

Now, when I'm alone and cold in my bed,
They still hover over me,
These ancient leathery crones,
With their bandannas stiffened with sweat,
And their thorn-bitten wrists,
And their snuff-laden breath blowing
lightly over me in my first sleep.

The hard Frauen life is lightly born, their feminine legacy elegized in the boy's coarse loving lines, no less than Dylan Thomas with his agrarian aunt in "After the Funeral." Young Roethke knew a calloused father, too, an unsettled mother, in the dancing trimeter of "My Papa's Waltz," from which the boy could never recover:

The whiskey on your breath
Could make a small boy dizzy;
But I held on like death:
Such waltzing was not easy.

Four trochees spring against the waltzing monosyllables of the iambic quatrain—*whiskey, dizzy, waltzing, easy*—and the slightly giddy rhymes, straining for reassurance, leave the sense of something celebrated, yet not quite right. An American mixture of violence and gaiety, a touch inebriate, tinges a moment when "mother's countenance / Could not unfrown itself." Something's wrong, and can't be righted with form or bonhomie. The third stanza records the small signs of brutality and love that trouble the poem:

The hand that held my wrist
Was battered on one knuckle;
At every step I missed
My right ear scraped a buckle.

Still absolutely iambic, the narrative is bruised from pain behind the father's belt, and a "battered" knuckle on the child's wrist imprints the young poet's ear, wounded by the hard-rhyming "buckle" of a man's labor. And then the rhythm breaks, troubling time, form, and memory: "*You beat time on* my *head / With a palm caked hard* by *dirt.*" The boy addresses his dad directly in a whisper of anapestic spondees, a love-banged stutter-step hard to scan. Time is battered, knuckled into the boy's brain by his gaily obtuse, work-beaten father. We are left puzzling a drunken dad waltzing his son off to bed. Is this Adam's curse, to sweat and swear on the earth for bread, to come home drunk to a disapproving wife and bewildered son, "Still clinging to your shirt," who will record the genesis of his own broken time, wounded ear, and grief-joy of growing up inebriate to sleep? In America, the poet staggers under Adam's heritage.

"The Waking" is his Edenic *darkness visible*, as William Styron titled his own writer's anguish, the fodder and compost for a fallen son of Stevens. Keats notes in a letter, "The Imagination may be compared to Adam's dream—he awoke and found it truth." Postlapsarian and postmodernist for Roethke, waking is torturous and sleep dangerous in a poet's battered candor. "Now I lay me down to sleep," Protestant children are first taught, "I pray the Lord my soul to keep. / If I should die before I wake, / I pray the Lord my soul to take." Roethke measures out his prayer primordially, "I wake to sleep, and take my waking slow." His is a sleep-walker's slow waking, either to sleeping mortal dreams, or to dreaming awake, and uncertainty is the minor key. "Was it a vision, or a waking dream, / Fled is that music," Keats ends his nightingale ode: "—Do I wake or sleep?" The poet tilts on edge, feeling his way forward for words, his fate in the given mortality he is born to: "I feel my fate in what I cannot fear." And he follows an old theme, *Homo viator*, a myth peculiarly American, the pilgrim-as-child. The boy-poet is not a hero, but a seeker, a young pioneer without a map, Columbus to Huck Finn. "I learn by going where I have to go."

The villanelle turns on just two rhymes in nineteen lines, absolutely regular iambic pentameter, but for a trochaic tremor in three initial phrases, *"God bless the Ground!"* and *"Light takes the Tree;"* and *"Great Nature has"*— mortal leanings (burial, crucifixion, death) where the leaves shudder on the old Garden Tree. "The lowly worm climbs up a winding stair," and when nature does "another thing" to "you and me," we'll not be there. So "lively" takes hands with "lovely," and the creative irresolution of the poem steps to a close, steadied by the meter's tremor beneath the ongoing iambic foot, simply rhymed: "I wake to sleep, and take my waking slow. / I learn by going where I have to go."

The child's innocent wisdom comes just before the end: "What falls away is always. And is near." Again the vowels control the open-mouthed tone with soft interjection (ah-*ah* uh-*a* ih-*ah*-a *ae* ih-*ih*). Listen to the vowels for a line's inner music, Keats, Pound, and Auden told generations of poets. The internal rhyme, sliding from "away" to "always," locks in the natural motif of loss quickening the soul: "And is near." We carry our wants most closely to the heart and think by feeling them. In the present-past of time, we have not what we have, but have had, then desire, as in the double sense of wanting, a creative need born of "What falls away." This innocent courage of the fallen, inseparable from fear, wakes the poet to dream his way as the way goes, steadied by unknowing, to "see feelingly," as blind Gloucester in *King Lear*. Carolyn Forché will borrow this courageous epigraph from Machado's tomb, *Caminante, no hay camino / Se hace camino al andar*, that is, "Sojourner, there is no path, / You make the path by going" *(The Country Between Us)*. And still this is a child's prayer, an invocation of innocence and courage, to learn the age-old truths "by going where I have to go." As in the poet's elegy for a fallen student, no relative, no beloved, but an intimate stranger, the words reach beyond poetic invention—

> Over this damp grave I speak the words of my love:
> I, with no rights in this matter,
> Neither father nor lover.

Roethke was Adam exiled, a tempest "thing of darkness" more Caliban than Ariel, at home with the lowest plants and animals, weeds and worms, minnows and toads: "All things innocent, hapless, forsaken," he wrote of the meadow mouse. With Blake's animistic empathy, he confessed, "I'm sure I've been a toad, one time or another. / With bats, weasels, worms— I rejoice in the kinship." In the "anima of animals," as Stevens said, Roethke prayed "Pure as a worm on a leaf" among a "diocese of mice." He shepherded a fallen botany and bestiary of rat and goat, slug and oyster, crab and saxifrage, stickleback and parsnip, shrike and cockroach. He wrote through a dark time, when "the eye begins to see": "I live between the heron and the wren, / Beasts of the hill and serpents of the den." The poet worshipped in the New World, a native, at the axed roots of virginal trees cleared for pastures.

And the trees dwarfed him (as they staggered Columbus). The German language thicketed him in childhood, the dark light *(schwarze Licht)*, the consonant scree and cavernous vowels *(Öd und leer das Meer*, Eliot in *The Waste Land* murmured with Wagner's dying Tristan). His father's native tongue looked back to a time of German folktales and Gammer Gurton's nursery rhymes, before St. Francis's Latin, or Dante's Tuscan, or Chaucer's Norman suffused Old English. In good Saxon style, the young Roethke went in endless pursuit of wild verb endings for his verbal nouns, his unstable gerunds—and it all came down around him early on. He heard the cries in Williams's "bloody loam" ("that sucking and sobbing" underground, Eurydice's grief, Orpheus's heartbeat). He felt the tug of the slug, watched God's snail *glister* forward, heard the tulips bloom, and ate potatoes raw in their monkish hoods. "Who stunned the dirt into noise?" the poet cried. The corn stood savage in his father's garden, the new world riotous. "The roses kept breathing in the dark." It was, as for Dylan Thomas in Wales at the time, a force with a green fuse that would not stop shifting, or growing, or exploding. And then it was, suddenly, late fall harvest. "It was beginning winter, / An in-between time." The endless seasons cascaded from the limbs of living trees, and wherever leaves fell, more leaves appeared, as with men, and he could not stop it. He cried from the abyss:

> Be with me, Whitman, maker of catalogues;
> For the world invades me again,
> And once more the tongues begin babbling.
> And the terrible hunger for objects quails me.

So he sang the losses, articulated his blues, priested the language, as Two Shields sang with the heart of a bear for the cleansing north wind. Roethke made the dark his own daughter, the elegy his hymn, the dirge his father's delirium. He dug to the taproot and let the earth enclose him. A compost flood of death mothered this lost son.

The poet was not without elegiac compensation for his losses, triggering a decentering vitality. Roethke's childhood imagination leaped out and ran wild in hopscotching images:

> Toads brooding wells.
> All the leaves stuck out their tongues;
> I shook the softening chalk of my bones,
> Saying,
> Snail, snail, glister me forward,
> Bird, soft-sigh me home,
> Worm, be with me.
> This is my hard time.

Erotic strangeness invades these one-liners; off-rhyming "tongues" and "bones" with "home," "Worm," and "time," the lyric of the stunning half-line attentively italicizes what a child can't understand, a hexing cauldron of fears. With shamanic uncertainty and poetic inscrutability, the lines are unredactable, disturbingly *wakan*, as the Lakota say. Speaking in tongues, the phonemes vowel together, the non sequitur metaphors startle without settling. Everywhere, softly desperate, the spondaic rhythms insist on dumb kinship with underground beasts and the sighing birds. These last words, the poem as hushed confessional to a barely sensate nature, madden to silence, the voice of a man nearly voiceless, a manic stagger beyond Sitting Bull bearing "hard times," the Adamic son scrambling for a hole in his "hard time." This bear-heart sings truly different. The reader looks at odd words, riddling ideas, whispered sibilance, reverse rhythms, and slant rhymes for what they strangely are and suggest, without knowing. "I could love a duck." A Halloweeny incoherence cautions reading assumptions from or into things, a creative nightmare loosens the reader from adult imperative. The rat-poet as lost child has the courage to ask, by way of Job, "Hath the rain a father?" Rubbed in the dust of "father and mother," he circles death and returns to "big roses, the big bloody clinkers" of his young Michigan greenhouse. At the still center of the turning world, a child listening, the light returns to calm: "It will come again. / Be still. / Wait."

Post-native and tribeless, Roethke's lament is that of the lost connection to nature, the suppressed knowledge of totemic animals, the descent from the given world of creatures and guardian spirits (thus the homeless or *unheimlich* terror of modern existence). These dark riches, loamed in loss, disturb a postmodernist reader into strange and marvelous insight, disruptive of false order. The power of the uncanny releases the poet into gut consciousness, the old instinct of animal alertness, returning to preternatural knowing before Adam invented "nature" in a word. "We think by feeling," the poet wakes to know. We read our feelings through a positively awakened fear that feels into, around, beneath, and behind the masks of things invoked, but not truly named.

So for Roethke, Adamic necromancer of the fallen pastoral, the logics snapped. The more he let go, the purer he sang, the more he let go: "jogging back over the logging road." He learned to trust the child's night, adult slippage, the shifts of language, nature's outrage, his own fear. "Has the worm a shadow?" Metaphor branched him beyond—his one-way bridge to the next failed synapse, the shape of fire.

> Mother me out of here. What more will the bones allow?
> Will the sea give the wind suck? A toad folds into a stone.
> These flowers are all fangs. Comfort me, fury.
> Wake me, witch, we'll do the dance of rotten sticks.

It was enough to keep going, to leave the latest loss behind, strike out and in more deftly, American pioneer, all the time hitting motherlode paydirt, but never stopping to unrift the logical ore veins. Leave the getting-out and getting-on to those following. "What does what it should do needs nothing more," he wrote cryptically in "The Manifestation." Roethke fed on the verbal vision, words fleshed with indecisions, dripping of things. "In the first of the moon, / All's a scattering, / A shining." A rose on the seashore took the poet back to his "true place" in the country of song. "I think of American sounds in this silence," he wrote, as Sitting Bull listened to meadowlarks and magpies for lyric counsel:

> On the banks of the Tombstone, the wind-harps having their say,
> The thrush singing alone, that easy bird,
> The killdeer whistling away from me,
> The mimetic chortling of the catbird
> Down in the corner of the garden, among the raggedy lilacs,
> The bobolink skirring from a broken fencepost,
> The bluebird, lover of holes in old wood, lilting its light song,
> And that thin cry, like a needle piercing the ear, the insistent cicada,

And the ticking of snow around oil drums in the Dakotas,
The thin whine of telephone wires in the wind of a Michigan winter,
The shriek of nails as old shingles are ripped from the top of a roof,
The bulldozer backing away, the hiss of the sandblaster,
And the deep chorus of horns coming up from the streets in early morning.
I return to the twittering of swallows above water. . . .
I think of the rock singing, and light making its own silence.

Beyond the urban din, Roethke's world of verse was so real as to be irreducible, a trap for critical paraphrase, a rapture. "My meat eats me." He moved forward by "a perpetual slipping-back" and believed cyclically, as Hughes later found in *Wodwo*, "that to go forward as a spiritual man it is necessary first to go back." A throwback in America's heartland, then, a neoclassical primitive, his was the song of a man who could taste his own blood from first breath, whose death sang in his veins and danced stones, an exiled Narcissus, dark Orpheus. The Great Bear whispered in his ear, "(I measure time by how a body sways)." Dionysius replaced Christ at the other end of Yeats's cosmic seesaw, Apollo swallowed by the sea, castrated by Aphrodite. His brain burned through the would-nots, the "stinks and sighs" of our American middle class, "In the kingdom of bang and blab." The Puritan forbidden swelled his primitive fruit, Eve heaved in his air. "I want the old rage," he challenged, "the lash of primordial milk." Satan soured his drink, Babel composed his blessing. This song-poet rewrote the rules of sense and made us feel interjectively what we knew in the beginning with all native singers: "We think by feeling. What else is there to know?" He knew this—

Who rise from flesh to spirit know the fall;
The word outleaps the world, and light is all.

§(•)§

EIGHT

Seer, Shaman, Clown

How do Stevens's Oklahoma firecat or Roethke's elegiac Iroquois transpose to Momaday's great Kiowa bear or Welch's Blackfeet Montana blues? Somewhere along the way, probably by the mid-sixties, the modernist icon slants toward shamanic totem, indeed, tribal ceremony evolves into all-nations powwow. The Beats go wild, native is in. Just so, song-poems slide toward performance riff, and postmodern deconstructionist proves trickster-for-hire. The bear's heart twists with ironic literate difference.

> *The American Indian is the vengeful ghost lurking in the back of the troubled American mind. . . . That ghost will claim the next generation as its own. When this has happened, citizens of the USA will at last begin to be Americans, truly at home on the continent, in love with their land. The chorus of a Cheyenne Indian Ghost dance song —* "hi-niswa' vita'ki'ni" — *"We shall live again."*
>
> GARY SNYDER, "Passage to More Than India"

Jaime de Angulo, a Parisian Basque born in 1888, came to Wyoming as a cowboy at sixteen; by twenty-four, he had earned a medical degree from Johns Hopkins. The "Buckaroo Doctor" moved to a Monterey cattle ranch in 1920, befriended Robinson Jeffers and Henry Miller, and mastered seventeen California Indian tongues. He did field work for linguists at UC Berkeley, Boas, Kroeber, Radin, Lowie through Sapir, and translated for Carl Jung. Ezra Pound lauded him "the American Ovid" for his beast fables from Native America. Williams called him "one of the most outstanding writers" he'd ever met. Marianne Moore corresponded with de Angulo, Kenneth Rexroth became his friend, and Jack Kerouac wrote him into *Desolation Angels*. Following a tragic accident and second divorce in 1940, de Angulo lived as a hermit in Big Sur, writing *Indians in Overalls*. His correspondent-mentor was Ezra Pound in Washington, D.C., committed to a mental hospital, convicted of treason. De Angulo's secretary was the poet Robert Duncan, who typed manuscripts at home and recalls "two brilliant old cranks, the one living in a cage, the other dying of cancer, contemplating the irony, and the absurdity, and the humor in their respective fates."

De Angulo wrote of his intractable friends, the California Pit River Indians, "I never saw such a goddamn lot of improbable people." In turn, the Pit Rivers called Whites tramps or "wanderers" *(enellaaduwi)*, rootless after the Gold Rush, "smart, but they don't know anything." During the 1920s modernist period flourishing back East, de Angulo was taken in by these native Californians, a decade after the last Yana Indian, Ishi, stumbled into an Oroville slaughteryard. De Angulo and his Indian friends slept in ditches, traveled where they liked, and lived off the land, mostly on rabbits. Though a "damn fool white man," as his medicine friend Sukmit teased, de Angulo made a pretty good "Indian white man," Old Mary conceded.

Is, kaakaadzi, the Pit Rivers greeted their adopted White man, "Person, you are living." De Angulo lived his linguistics down into the ditches and drunken brawls, less catalogues of grammar in the accepted style, than the diction and syntax of everyday Indian talk and life. "Decent anthropologists don't associate with drunkards who go rolling in ditches with shamans," he groused of academics not wanting to sponsor his fieldwork. De Angulo mastered the bi-tonal, singsong Pit River speech patterns, gambled in the hand-game marked bones with tribes to the north, joined to "sing together" waking the spirits of *damaagomes,* and soaked up the native rhythms of movement—dancing, even dreaming and breathing their songs, stories, creation myths, coyote tales, impromptu speeches, and personal quarrels. From these he wrote the picaresque fable, *Indian Tales,* in the tribal voices of animal guardians.

"What do you know about electricity?! Electricity doesn't work that way," de Angulo would shout at Sukmit.

"Hell, what do you know about *damaagomes?*" Sukmit charged. "You are nothing but a white man, a goddamn tramp."

"No, I am not a white man!" the Basque doctor insisted.

"Yes, you are a white man," the medicine man held firm, "you are a white man forever!!"

"You two always quarreling like two old men," Old Mary chided from the campfire. "You Indian, you white man, ha-ha-ha! You both crazy!!"

De Angulo recalls: "So I sent them back on the train. Funny-looking pair they made at the station, bewildered, he with his long hair and his black sombrero, his long arms and his hump; she clutching a bundle; and her gray hair under a bright silk handkerchief we had just bought for her.

"I spoke a word to the conductor for them. He smiled broadly: 'Sure I'll take care of them. I know Indians. I was raised in Oklahoma.' As the train pulled out, Old Mary gave me the Pit River goodby: *'Is tus' i taakaakzee,* Man, live well! *Ittu toolol hakaadzi-gudzuma,* We also will live.' "

INDIAN WHITE MEN

I was standing beside old Tom Bird, and he was crying. He felt my eyes and turned, the bloody lance upright in his hand, paying no heed to the tears running down the sides of his big nose and into his mustache.

"Damn you, boy," he said. "Damn you for not ever getting to know anything worth knowing. Damn me, too. We had a world, once."

JOHN GRAVES, "THE LAST RUNNING"

The 1967 San Francisco *Be-In,* "A Gathering of the Tribes," was a modern bohemian Thanksgiving, replete with buckskins, feathers, body paint, designer drugs, chanting and dancing. The countercultural gathering was advertised by a photo-poster of a Plains Indian on horseback approaching a powwow, the carbine in his left arm replaced by a guitar (a hippie spin on Edward Curtis air-brushing an alarm clock or skillet from a teepee). "Him big bureaucracy running our fillingstations," Allen Ginsberg parodied *America* in street jive, "That no good. Ugh. Him make Indians learn read. Him need big black niggers. Hah. Her make us all work sixteen hours a day. Help." How did beat poetry and pop music unsaddle frontier warfare and the work ethic, and today's Indian shoot to a countercultural icon?

"Know then, that the more savage, that is, the more alive and freedom-loving a people is," Johann Herder promoted the oral literatures of ancient peoples, "the more savage, that, alive, free, sensuous, lyrically active, its songs must be, if it has songs." Late-eighteenth-century Europe birthed the American Revolution along with Rousseau's noble savage, as the West reincarnated a native Adam, in Hebrew "red earth." The Indian was born again, neoromantically, and New World disciples flocked to the wilderness, some as convicts and killers, some pilgrims, some just trailing along. "You laugh at my enthusiasm for savages," Herder added, "as Voltaire laughed at Rousseau for wanting to walk on all fours." Tribal songs, or "arrows of a savage Apollo," the philosopher assured his friend, one day would "pierce hearts and carry souls and thoughts with them." By the American 1920s, a native renaissance was in the making among other cultural re-birthings, to flower collaboratively across the Buckskin Curtain by the 1960s.

"So that when I say that I am not, have never been, nor offered myself, as an authority on things Amerindian," Mary Austin doubled back to (un)cover her tracks in *The American Rhythm,* "I do not wish to have it understood that I may not, at times, have succeeded in being an Indian." Given White bigotry, middle-class urbanization, and native resistance to encroachment, hers is candid equivocation with a history. Is this double or triple negative, then—or not "at times" Indian—a White woman going native? Waffling interculturally, Mary Austin wants to be indigenous, but is not and cannot be—though she puzzles *"not* at times, [to] have succeeded in being an Indian." The bifurcated Indian White (Wo)man would have acculturation both ways—neither exclusively Red, nor White, but cross-culturally mediating "the forest's edge." If indeed hybridly naive, Austin spoke across divided minds, split tongues, doubling hearts, warring Americans. A tall order, resisted on both sides, Austin's bridging raises the intercultural history of Indians and Whites still "treating" three centuries later, bucking great separatist suspicion on both sides. Cultural fusions and hybrid aesthetics come at cost of sovereignty for both, and neither fancies being half of the other. Why collaborate, why blend worldviews, why cross?

Going Indian, for all its naive loose ends, has a long colonial tradition that favors native cultures. Ben Franklin marveled that so few captured pilgrims returned to the fold, when all the captive natives, if they could escape stockades, went back to the blanket. John Eliot, "the Apostle of the Indians," jumped the palisade to minister with indigenous peoples, and Hawthorne gave him infamous stature in *The Scarlet Letter*. Daniel Boone and Sam Houston lived among tribes, as Williams chronicled, "native savages." Thoreau tracked the New England moose with Indian guides, Muir hiked native trails through the California Sierras, and Neihardt found Nick Black Elk awaiting him in South Dakota by spring 1931. Cynics sneer at these nature lovers who go native; the deeper issue may be why crossovers seek alternatives to migrant America—what benefit on both sides?—and finally how natives cross back and forth to access the goods, including literacy, of Euro-American cultures. Isolation is no twentieth-century solution, since everything from medicine to motor vehicles, television to the Internet, ties us together already.

The early modernist William Blake identified with American natives in *The Marriage of Heaven & Hell:*

> I also asked Isaiah what made him go naked and barefoot three years? he answered, the same that made our friend Diogenes the Grecian.
> I then asked Ezekiel. why he eat dung, & lay so long on his right & left side? he answerd. the desire of raising other men into a perception of the infinite this the North American tribes practise.

"Stupid fucking white man," the Apsaroke Nobody (played by Gary Farmer) says as he digs a bullet out of William Blake's heart (played by Johnny Depp) in the Wild West *film noir, Dead Man* (1996) written, directed, and produced by Jim Jarmusch.

Ancient Greeks to American Indians, biblical prophets to ecstatic poets and modern filmmakers, a mythopoeic native stalks the West, even if native cultures are not exactly welcoming. "What I am really handling, you see, is the Myth of America," Hart Crane wrote Otto H. Kahn in 1927, explaining why Part II of his masterpiece, *The Bridge*, was called "Powhatan's Daughter," focusing on Pocahontas as "the mythological nature-symbol chosen to represent the physical body of the continent, or the soil. . . . showing the continuous and living evidence of the past in the inmost vital substance of the present." Poets live by myths, and the native in America is our prime creation story. Eve to Pocahontas to Mother Earth ecology, how is "the Myth of America," apart from clichéd culture-mongering, rooted in a gendered, chthonic nativism? Four years earlier, Williams exclaimed plangently in *In the American Grain:* "The land! don't you feel it? Doesn't it make you want to lift dead Indians tenderly from their graves, to steal from them—as if it must be clinging to their corpses—some authenticity?" Here lies the crux of ethnocentric debate across the Buckskin Curtain. Struggling to appropriate authenticity, how much do Indian Whites sentimentalize, steal, or shamanize from Native America, and conversely, how much do they give up or back? What do native cultures stand to gain crossing over? Is there any defense for going native, or American, or fusing both? "I think, if we're lucky," Carter Revard, the Osage scholar-poet, says, "we'll have writers come along who know the mythical dimensions and are very, very honest, fiercely, unflinchingly, almost meanly vivid about the tough parts of Indian life and will not neglect either dimension. Which really means I'd like to see American Indian writing be a standard for this country" *(Survival This Way)*. If not the standard, native writing is setting benchmarks toward native empowerment and mainstream collaboration, from the poetry of Momaday and Hogan, to the fiction of Erdrich and Welch, to the filmmaking of Sarris and Alexie.

In this century alone, Williams, Lawrence, Austin, Crane, Vachel Lindsay, Lew Sarett, Marsden Hartley, Harriet Monroe (directing *Poetry*), John Neihardt, Jaime de Angulo, Charles Olson, Robert Creeley, Gary Snyder, W. S. Merwin, David Waggoner, Howard Norman, Brian Swann, and Jerome Rothenberg have been among the outside tribes of poets parting the Buckskin Curtain, with some authenticity, but why? Some artists distrust immigrant estrangement in the New World and seek "deeper footing in their native soil," as Austin prefaced the Cronyn anthology. From Puritan repression to bourgeois work ethic, the fear of touch, sensual play, and the earth itself has historically stiffened the American psyche. This immigrant armor has kept citizens uptight, particularly White men, and distant from others. In Yucatán in 1950, Charles Olson wrote Robert Creeley of Mayan contact on buses and in marketplaces: "their flesh is most gentle, is granted, touch is in no sense anything but the natural law of flesh, there is none of that pull-away which, in the States, causes a man for all the years of his life the deepest sort of questioning of the rights of himself to the wild reachings of his own organism" *(Human Universe)*. The native Indian, natural in America, seemed to Olson "a curious wandering animal like me." *Like,* but not the same: going Indian is still no answer to White émigré anxiety. The intercultural crux, not to be "like" others, as Williams said of poetic analogy, is to discover and invent *as others* have found their own native paths. Not "like the Greeks," the good doctor argued in *Paterson,* but "to invent as the Greeks invented, for to copy Nature would be a shameful thing." Olson added a tract on open field poetics, "Projective Verse," that Williams included in his *Autobiography:* "But if he stays inside himself, if he is contained within his nature as he is participant in the larger force, he will be able to listen, and his hearing through himself will give him secrets objects share."

Secrets objects share: the phrase reaches down into the loam of America, into myths of stone, root, stream, beast, and human, sharing a native land. Watching Navajo sand-painters encircle themselves with beauty, Jackson Pollock left the borders of his canvas and waded into tribal art. Behind organic petitions this century stand Rilke's letters to a young poet, Franz Kappus, which became seminar reading for the 1960s: "He can remember that all beauty in animals and plants is a quiet enduring form of love and longing, and he can see animals, as he sees plants, patiently and willingly uniting and increasing and growing. . . . And those who come together in the night and are entwined in rocking delight do an earnest work and gather sweetnesses, gather depth and strength for the song of some coming poet. . . ." From Thoreau, through Whitman and Crane, to Olson, Duncan, Bly, and Snyder, every other nativist poet has "wanted to be a Red Indian, basically," as Seamus Heaney remembers Bay Area sixties counterculture (*Ploughshares*). The children of Williams were running wild, Beats on the West Coast going natural—Snyder, Merwin, Olson, Kinnell, Ferlinghetti, Creeley, Dorn, McClure, Spicer, Whalen, Duncan, Wakoski, Waggoner, Rexroth. "The only poetic tradition is the Voice out of the burning bush," Allen Ginsberg proclaimed at the decade's beginning. At its end, Jerome Rothenberg and the anthropologist Dennis Tedlock had coined the term "ethnopoetics," that is, poetics of the Other (Gk. *ethnoi*), and started the journal *Alcheringa* (named for the tribal dreaming stone in aboriginal Australia), featuring primitive translations and contemporary American poetry. Rothenberg gathered global tribal poetries, *Technicians of the Sacred,* in 1969 (the year of Momaday's Pulitzer) and *Shaking the Pumpkin* in 1972, traditional Native American oral poetries "re-expressed," as Austin said, textually. A horde of native anthologies followed.

By 1983, Brian Swann was casting the net for essays on traditional native literatures, *Smoothing the Ground,* later with Arnold Krupat *Recovering the Word,* and then a Smithsonian series, *On the Translation of Native American Literatures*—crossing linguistics, literature, social sciences, performing arts, folklore, religion, and philosophy. The two East Coast editors collected *Everything Matters: Autobiographical Essays by Native American Writers* in 1998.

As a self-reflexive, theory-wielding academic, Krupat went on to question the legitimizing credentials of "Indian autobiography" *(For Those Who Come After)* and to deconstruct Native American literary canons *(The Voice in the Margin)*. More recently, he has postcolonialized the field in a mélange of academically personalizing essays, *The Turn to the Native,* culminating in "A Nice Jewish Boy among the Indians." That same banner year, 1983, Jerome and Diane Rothenberg collected three centuries of Euro-American essays on the ethnopoetics of tribal and contemporary poetries, *Symposium of the Whole,* its title lifted from Robert Duncan, answering Plato's censored Republic: "all the old excluded orders must be included. The female, the proletariat, the foreign; the animal and vegetative; the unconscious and the unknown; the criminal and failure—all that has been outcast and vagabond must return to be admitted in the creation of what we consider we are."

Placed next to Donald Allen and Warren Tallman's *The Poetics of the New American Poetry* (1973), a considerable body of work now represented American Indian and nativist poets, crossing mutual issues: the native ethics of the ecosystem, wilderness as natural freedom, the resident genius of plants and animals, the primacy of dreams and visions, the artistic need for tradition and ritual and community, tribal responsibility and tolerance of others. Most recently, William Clements in *Native American Verbal Art* (1997) considers the complex stretch of anthropological linguistics from such pioneers as Matthews and Densmore, Underhill and Parsons, through Dell Hymes and William Bright today. Besides the ethnic textual mapping of Franz Boas and Edward Sapir, among others—down through Dennis Tedlock on reinterpreting Zuni and Mayan sacred stories, Donald Bahr recording and transcribing Arizona Yuman songs, and Anthony Mattina on Canadian Red English, for example—scholars are beginning to discuss the evolution of ceremonial song performance, where the sacred walks through tribal song-stories, into translated ethnographic texts as tribal poetry. Paul Zolbrod ponders the crossings of oral culture and poetic lineation in *Reading the Voice: Native American Oral Poetry on the Written Page* (1995). "What are the measured qualities of the singing voice?" he asks us to ask of Native American translations, as formal questions become comparative cultural issues. Through an evolutionary process of historical conversion, the Manifest Destiny of competitive ambition and monotheistic creation have been challenged by communal respect, tribal interdependence, and interspecies collaboration. Slowly, the West has been changing its battle hymn from rugged individualism to a polytonal collaborative chorus.

Across the postwar Atlantic, Seamus Heaney and Ted Hughes emerge as nonmetropolitan poets, respectively distinct, connected by nativist Celtic traditions, the Indians of the British Isles. From Lawrence emigrating to New Mexico and finding Whitman's nativist muse among the Pueblos, to Heaney teaching in 1970 at UC Berkeley and more recently ensconced at

Harvard, to Hughes marrying Plath and breaking wilderness trail as British poet laureate for late-twentieth-century English-American verse, the Anglo-American literary channel has become less cross-Atlantic, more interactive and continuous (not to mention the regional literary underpinnings of New *England* and every "English" Department in the country turning an ear to American Studies). Native has come to signify national treasure.

Tracing back through Yeats to Wordsworth's north country, poets like Heaney or Hughes did not have to grow up around the court or the academy to be artistically gifted. Heaney out of the troubled north of Ireland represented the Gaelic agrarian native, Hughes from the northern wilds of England tracked the Yorkshire heath hunter. Both gave voice to the country poetics of working peoples, the poetry of "common things," as Frost said, "seen by the uncommon people." The uncommon modernist vision goes back to the newly married W. B. Yeats in 1918—the end of the Great War and advent of Cronyn's *Path on the Rainbow*—passing through San Bernardino, California orange groves in a railway sleeper car, when the spirits woke the couple with gnomic "metaphors for your poetry," eventually written out as *A Vision*. The muses visit native poets, the *duende* inhabits the artist's house, the spirits appear with visions, when the attitude is honoring and proper respects are paid (contrasted with wasteland ghosts haunting trashed cultures). Ancestors rise up, spirits talk from the land. "I have always listened for poems," Heaney says in *Preoccupations*, "they come sometimes like bodies come out of a bog, almost complete, seeming to have been laid down a long time ago, surfacing with a touch of mystery." Lakota visionaries long spoke this way of ancestral stones, *Tunkáshila,* the "grandfather" voices, and sang from the land with hearts of bears.

An Irish Catholic provincial, Heaney came from thatched farm and den folk, ploughed field and rough pitchfork. The primitive footings of primary beginnings were his bedrock: "that order of poetry," he said in his Nobel acceptance speech, "where we can at last grow up to that which we stored up as we grew." As a child, he hid in the throat of an old willow, or perched in a beech tree fork above "the liver-thick mud" of Mossbawn, a five-century-old family farm. In the Belfast Public Library, he first read Hughes on butchering a pig and knew suddenly that country life could field poetry: "the living speech of the landscape I was born into. If you like, I began as a poet when my roots were crossed with my reading." Those roots went down through the Irish "bog as the memory of the landscape," the boy-poet knew: "The bog was a wide low apron of swamp on the west bank of the River Bann, where hoards of flints and fishbones have been found, reminding me that the Bann valley is one of the oldest inhabited areas in the country." History grounded the native poet, the land charged him, just as meadowlarks and stones empowered Sitting Bull. Teaching in Berkeley by 1970, Heaney was challenged by the myths of the American West, the primacy of the Red Indian icon, and answered with a poem about his bog-land ancestry:

> We have no prairies
> To slice a big sun at evening—
> Everywhere the eye concedes to
> Encroaching horizon,
>
> Is wooed into the cyclops' eye
> Of a tarn. Our unfenced country
> Is bog that keeps crusting
> Between the sights of the sun.
> . . . .
>
> Our pioneers keep striking
> Inwards and downwards,
>
> Every layer they strip
> Seems camped on before.
> The bogholes might be Atlantic seepage
> The wet centre is bottomless.

In the Western iambic gait of native verse, Homer to Yeats, Heaney muscled his lines with a singer's amblings and a seer's sense of mystery: "poetry as divination, poetry as revelation of the self to the self, as restoration of the culture to itself; poems as elements of continuity, with the aura and authenticity of archaeological finds, where the buried shard has an importance that is not diminished by the importance of the buried city; poetry as a dig, a dig for finds that end up being plants" *(Preoccupations)*. Augury, insight, acculturation, tradition, discovery, excavation, seeding—natives harvest the poetry of an agrarian pioneer, rooted in history, no less than Williams, or Roethke, or any tribal American writer stirring in the sixties.

North in Bronte country, Ted Hughes grew up moorish wild, at the age of eleven writing "fantastic happenings and gory adventures" set in the American "Wild West," west of the Great Divide. He thought at an early age of poems as animals. "They have their own life, like animals, by which I mean that they seem quite separate from any person, even from their author, and nothing can be added to them or taken way without maiming and perhaps even killing them. And they have a certain wisdom. . . . Maybe my concern has been to capture not animals particularly and not poems, but simply things which have a vivid life of their own, outside mine. However all that may be, my interest in animals began when I began." To capture the other, to touch without altering: no less than Hemingway catch-and-release fishing the Big Two-Hearted River, or Lawrence glimpsing the red wolf of New Mexico. At home in northern England, Hughes caught the flash-stink of "The Thought Fox," his first successful poem:

> Across clearings, an eye,
> A widening deepening greenness,
> Brilliantly, concentratedly,
> Coming about its own business
>
> Till, with a sudden sharp hot stink of fox
> It enters the dark hole of the head.
> The window is starless still; the clock ticks,
> The page is printed.

Stalking poems as wild animals, Hughes went on in his first collection, *The Hawk in the Rain,* dedicated to Sylvia Plath, to write of macaw and vampire, hag and horse, hawk and jaguar:

> The eye satisfied to be blind in fire,
> By the bang of blood in the brain deaf the ear—
> He spins from the bars, but there's no cage to him
>
> More than to the visionary his cell:
> His stride is wildernesses of freedom:
> The world rolls under the long thrust of his heel.
> Over the cage floor the horizons come.

This primitivist bestiary was a sensation in 1957, followed by the medieval Caliban figure, "half-man half-animal spirit of the forests," *Wodwo,* a decade later (bastard issue of Beowulf), and then the dark trickster, *Crow,* inspired by northern Plains Indian myths:

> Black is the earth-globe, one inch under,
> An egg of blackness
> Where sun and moon alternate their weathers
>
> To hatch a crow, a black rainbow
> Bent in emptiness
>   over emptiness
> But flying

Hughes insisted on the prehistoric origin and primitive ancestry of *Homo sapiens.* "It is only there that the ancient instincts and feelings in which most of our body lives can feel at home and on their own ground." Reviewing C. M. Bowra's *Primitive Song* for *The Listener* in 1962, Hughes began, "We imagine primitives to possess some of the qualities of ideal poetry—full of zest, clairvoyantly sensitive, realistic, whole, natural, and passionate; and so we might well look at their songs hopefully." Not cynically and without bigotry, cliché, or "blood-sucking" appropriation, but respectfully, "hopefully"—the poet comes to "the forest's edge" to collaborate and to enrich the common vision by means of an interjective poetics, as Momaday learned at that time studying with Winters. Initially in *Primitive Song,* "blood kinships with our civilized poetry" captivated Hughes, and two years later he reviewed Mircea Eliade's *Shamanism* in the same journal: "every poetic language begins by being a secret language," Eliade wrote in his epilogue, "that is, the creation of a personal universe, of a completely closed world. The purest poetic act seems to re-create language from an inner experience that, like the ecstasy or the religious inspiration of 'primitives,' reveals the essence of things." Sylvia Plath and Ted Hughes pored over these thoughts, no less than Michael Dorris and Louise Erdrich, mixed-blood conjugal writers a generation later, answered neoprimitive longings with their own natively collaborative stories and song poems.

Receptions were mixed. Gary Snyder was writing "Shaman's Songs" as early as *Myths and Texts* in 1960, inciting Leslie Silko's tub-thumping "An Old Time Indian Attack" and Geary Hobson's "The Rise of the White Shaman as a New Version of Cultural Imperialism" (*Yardbird Reader*, 1976). "The Shaman-poet is simply the man whose mind reaches easily out into all manners of shapes and other lives, and gives song to dreams," Snyder claimed of "Poetry and the Primitive" in *Earth House Hold*. His nativist essays and verse, *Turtle Island*, won a Pulitzer in 1974, contested by some Indian activists charging appropriation. Michael Castro defended the Zen native in *Interpreting the Indian*, the one study of contemporary and Native American poetry this century: "Snyder's poems look closely at trout, deer, quail, dolphins, manzanita, mushrooms, and berries and, like Williams's poems on flowers, trees, and animals, Snyder's reflect an acute awareness of living nature, a sense of an intelligence to be found there, and a respectful, observant, participatory relationship with it akin to the Native American's." Akin, but not the same kind—related, but not blood relative—the nativist poet turns shamanic, to root his visions in native America, and to get out of his own culture's lockstep mind and skin.

"A reading is a kind of communion," Snyder said in a 1964 interview with Gene Fowler. "I think the poet articulates the semi-known for the tribe. This is close to the ancient function of the shaman. It's not a dead function." A decade later in *The Old Ways* (1977), Snyder was setting the shaman squarely in the poet's tribal camp: "The philosopher, poet, and yogin all three have standing not too far behind them the shaman; with his or her pelt and antlers, or various other guises; songs going back to the Pleistocene and before. The shaman speaks for wild animals, the spirits of plants, the spirits of mountains, of watersheds. He or she sings for them. They sing through him. . . . In the shaman's world, wilderness and the unconscious become analogous: he who knows and is at ease in one, will be at home in the other." If Picasso could be inspired by African masks, or Gauguin by Polynesian women, or Kandinsky by the American West, or Kafka by an Indian pony, the American poet could be moved, natively, by shamanic song.

There are some ground rules and cautions. The shaman is a step re-
moved from tribal priest, a shadow behind pillars of ceremony. Of necessity,
tribally speaking, a shaman uses ritual ecstasy or magical terror at a dan-
gerous perimeter to consciously *reorder* the supplicant's sense of reality.
Religion, medicine, art, necromancy, and philosophy coalesce across the
boundaries of ordinary practices. Always in process or on a journey, a sha-
man works on the liminal fringes of tribal givens and knowns, usually os-
cillating "at the forest's edge" between clearing and wilderness—without
certainty, dicing with danger, vulnerable to mishap. The shaman gambles
with overwhelming mysteries and perceptual odds, the life of the spirit
(imagination and psyche) in the balance. A shaman is a seer, on one side,
rolling bones with blind fate, a sacred clown on the other, if surviving the
losses. American poets, in a sense, can be seen to enter this tradition as a
tenet of the frontier: Plath was swallowed up in shamanic darkness, Stevens
sang the trickster's blackbird factor, and Roethke spun burled visionary
images across a heartland landscape.

By midcentury, New World Indian writers were on the horizon with mod-
ernist tools. The young Scott Momaday met Faulkner at a Virginia military
academy in the early fifties, as mentioned, and decided to become a writer.
Only a decade later, Yvor Winters was proclaiming him one of the five most
important American poets, along with Emily Dickinson, in *Forms of Discovery*.
The Kiowa writer finished a dissertation on Frederick Tuckerman, pro-
jected a critical study of Dickinson, and went on to UC Santa Barbara in
1963 as an assistant professor. Six years later at UC Berkeley, while Seamus
Heaney visited the faculty, Momaday won a Pulitzer for the novel, *House
Made of Dawn*. Meanwhile in the late sixties and seventies, Simon Ortiz and
Joy Harjo were training at the prestigious Iowa Writers Workshop to be-
come nationally recognized poets. James Welch and Roberta Hill studied
the native art of blank verse with Richard Hugo at the University of Mon-
tana. Paula Gunn Allen, now a leading UCLA ethnic feminist, did her doc-
torate in American Studies with Robert Creeley at the University of New
Mexico. Leslie Silko corresponded with James Wright in Europe *(The
Strength and Delicacy of Lace)*, and the North Dakota poet Louise Erdrich,
fresh from Johns Hopkins, met her future husband, Michael Dorris, run-
ning the Native American Studies Program at Dartmouth, still an "Indian"
college to Indians. Both became million-dollar best-sellers in the 1980s,
collaborating over on-and-off-reservation romantic sagas. By the nineties,
Greg Sarris was tossing *-emic* (insider scoop) tribal essays in the faces of
MLA literary critics, *Keeping Slug Woman Alive;* chronicling native California
dreamer-healers in *Mabel McKay: Weaving the Dream;* auctioning a short-story
collection to the big eastern commercial presses, *Grand Avenue;* and with
Robert Redford writing and coproducing an HBO movie from his fiction.

Fall 1998 Sarris published a three-generation saga of California mixed-bloods, *Watermelon Nights,* and signed a movie contract with John Travolta to write the Carlisle Indian School story. Sherman Alexie, Spokane–Coeur d'Alene *enfant terrible,* was popping up in the counter-culture journals, *Caliban* and *Hangin' Loose,* tossing off half a dozen chapbooks of riff verse, and storming prose fiction with a collection of short sketches, *The Lone Ranger and Tonto Fistfight in Heaven;* a first novel, *Reservation Blues;* a second novel on its heels, *Indian Killer;* and an all-Indian studio film with Cheyenne-Arapaho director Chris Eyre, *Smoke Signals,* in five short years. Alexie's native crew is producing a second film from *Indian Killer.* Crossing the Buckskin Curtain, these writers were not playing Indian, looking backward, or insisting on essentialist separatism, but diversely and collaboratively voicing the concerns of natives today, both for their own peoples and toward non-Indian viewers.

Native poetry can be tiered in generational folds from the 1960s through the 1990s. Three overlapping male writers cross shamanic roles of "philosopher, poet, and yogin" this century, as Snyder has noted: N. Scott Momaday, Oklahoma seer of old traditions and tribal elders, trained formally at Stanford by 1963; James Welch, native surrealist and dark magician, poet-turned-novelist in Montana after his first verse collection in 1971; Sherman Alexie, stand-up trickster and postmodernist Washington Indi'n, hip celeb by the age of thirty in the early nineties. "If the shaman in touch with higher spirits is the prophet of Native America," Lewis Hyde writes in *Trickster Makes This World,* "then trickster, his laughing shadow, is a prophet with a difference." The difference between trickster and shaman could be parodic realism, between shaman and priest, percentage of conviction. A priest carries the command of tradition, a shaman negotiates tribal margin and mainstream, a trickster parodies the priest's aspirations and the shaman's bivalence. Momaday enters contemporary American poetry about where Stevens got stuck between objects and thought, negotiating a collaborative native poetics ("Earth and I Gave You Turquoise") out of the modernist interplay between crafted and natural things. Welch bears up between the anguish and self-defeat that broke Berryman down; this Blackfeet keeps going with winter in his blood, where Plath got mad and quit. Fox-tailed essentialist, Alexie mugs and rails where Roethke fell on his knees. If *Nobody Loves a Drunken Indian* was the title of a 1950s pop fiction made into *Flap,* a movie starring Anthony Quinn, "Everybody Loves a Literary Indian" could be the lead review in a 1990s *Publishers Weekly.* Indian White Men and Native American writers have come a long way down the literary trail, from William Carlos Williams and Jaime de Angulo to N. Scott Momaday and Sherman Alexie.

OLD SONGS MADE NEW: MOMADAY

Eve my mother, no.
I am come from another.
She lies in the peneplanes
Of the Medicine Wheel and
In the red sediment of the Llano,
Older by planets than Eve.

N. SCOTT MOMADAY

Navarre Scott Momaday was "born between" the "great World Wars," as he himself says, in Lawton, Oklahoma, 1934, to a mixed-blood Cherokee writer-teacher, Natachee Scott, and a full-blood Kiowa painter, Al Momaday (the grandfather's name, Mammedaty, means "Walking Above"). He seems a man with background, firm ground beneath him, as self-recorded in *The Names* and elsewhere—native history behind, earth heritage all around. With his father a gifted artist and storyteller, his mother a writer and educator, there is something a bit archaic, natively formal, in the shape and sound of Momaday's verse—a dignity of voice, anciently learned, bearing the weight of ancestral history. "It is lyrical and reverent," the artist told Charles Woodard, "and it bears close relationship to Indian oral tradition. That is my deepest voice. It proceeds out of an ancient voice. It is anchored in that ancient tradition" (*Ancestral Voices*).

After growing-up years in Midwest and Southwest Indian Country (Oklahoma, Arizona, and New Mexico BIA schools where his parents taught), Momaday went east for mainstream education, no less than Charles Eastman attended Boston Medical School for his medical degree in 1890. There is native precedent: During the 1760s, Samson Occom, the Mohegon minister and Methodist founder of Brothertown, raised British money to fund Dartmouth College for Indians with sermons on the execution of Moses Paul. Algonkian students such as Caleb Cheeshateaumauk and Joel Hiacoomes studied English, Hebrew, Greek, and Latin at the Harvard College for Indians, founded in Cambridge in 1656, as detailed in Helen Jaskoski's *Early Native American Writing*. In the last century, the Sauk and Fox ethnologist William James attended Harvard with Wallace Stevens and was tutored by Franz Boas at Columbia; the Cherokee writer John Oskison graduated from Stanford and attended Harvard with Stevens and James in 1898–1899; the Flathead historian D'Arcy McNickle studied at Oxford in the modernist 1920s; and Alfonso Ortiz, Guggenheim and MacArthur scholar, earned his doctorate in anthropology at the University of Chicago in 1967, then taught at Princeton, before returning to New Mexico. Mainstream education did not cripple, but enhanced these native scholars' resources.

"We don't want to *freeze* the Indian in time," Momaday told the 1970

First Convocation of American Indian Scholars in San Francisco, "to cut him off at a certain point in his development. We don't want to end up with a 19th century man in the 20th century." In his final high school year at Augustus Military Academy, Fort Defiance, Virginia, young Scott was on the fencing team and honored in public speaking, a Kiowa of culture, to be sure, on both sides of the Buckskin Curtain. "[The Indian] has to venture out, I think, beyond his traditional world," Momaday said in 1970, "because there is another very real world. And there are more worlds coming, in rapid succession. But it is possible for him to make that adventure without sacrificing his being and identity." After a B.A. in political science, minoring in speech and English at the University of New Mexico, Momaday spent a year at the University of Virginia law school, 1956–57. There he met William Faulkner and decided that he wanted to write like the legendary southerner. Two years later, Momaday was married and awarded the Stegner poetry fellowship at Stanford.

These personal details bespeak a modern finesse, post-Oklahoma and otherwise, in this young artist's development off the reservation. His Kiowa heritage found an intercultural voice. By 1959, young Momaday met Yvor Winters at home near Stanford and began his most important literary mentorship. "Write little, do it well," advised the master in *Forms of Discovery,* where he enshrined his Kiowa charge among the five leading poets of American literary history. Momaday still speaks of the Stanford lion as a second father. The Oklahoma author's imagination seems always on an elliptical course home to native, if not mythic, origins. Fifteen years, a Pulitzer, a Fulbright, Academy of American Poets Prize, *Premio Letterario Internazionale Mondello* (Italy's highest literary award), and eight honorary doctorates later (his work translated into Russian, Polish, German, Italian, Norwegian, and Japanese), Momaday told his literary biographer, Matthias Schubnell, about the 1974 Fulbright to Moscow: "One of the things about Russia that I could not have anticipated was the amount of time I would spend in my mind in the Southwest" (Tucson interview, December 1981). "I saw Grendel's shadow on the wall of Canyon de Chelly," he muses in *The Names,* "and once, having led the sun around Hokinini Mesa, I saw Copperfield at Oljeto Trading post."

In the Presence of the Sun: Stories and Poems, 1961–1991, dedicated to the poet's four daughters, gathers twenty years of drawings, beside some thirty years of verse, free to formal. In addition, Momaday has "written a good many other things," the preface notes, essays to plays to fiction, chief among them the Pulitzer novel, *House Made of Dawn.* "Our first choice is N. Scott Momaday's *House Made of Dawn,*" the 1969 Pulitzer committee announced, "because of its, in the words of one of the members of the jury, 'eloquence and intensity of feeling, its freshness of vision and subject, its immediacy of theme,' and because an award to its author might be considered as a recognition of 'the arrival on the American literary scene of a matured, sophisticated literary artist from the original Americans.' "

The novel tells the story of a postwar Indian man, Abel, raised by his grandfather on the Jemez Pueblo in New Mexico. Abel is orphaned before the war in which he fights overseas, then convicted of murdering an albino Indian in a postwar, drunken spell, and relocated in the dark heart of Los Angeles 1952, a native struggling to come back to the Southwest. The narrative is paradigmatic of a pan-Indian quest to return home in the New World, now for well over four hundred years. Abel, the agrarian, slays the equestrian Cain, a mutant figure of bewitched White corruption, and comes back ritually to run with the early spring sun at his grandfather's death. The lines scan in pentameter: "*He* could *see* the *can*yon and the *moun*tains and the *sky*. / He could *see* the *rain* and the *riv*er and the *fields* be*yond*. / *He* could *see* the *dark hills* at *dawn*. / He was *run*ning, and *un*der his *breath* he be*gan* to *sing*. / There was *no sound*, and he *had no voice*; he had *only* the *words* of a *song*. / *And* he *went run*ning *on* the *rise* of the *song*. / *House* made of *pol*len, *house* made of *dawn*. *Qtse*daba." A deeply settling blank verse cadences the prose in iambic pentameter with voweled off-rhymes at line-ends ("beyond / dawn / sing / song / song / pollen / dawn") and rooted within lines ("canyon / mountains / rain / went running on / under / began to sing / no sound / only / And he went running on"). This is a poetic prose, to be sure, a native pace that knows its ground and foot. No American novel this century catches the Indian, Spanish, and Anglo rhythms of the Southwest better than Momaday's *House Made of Dawn,* and many have imitated the model that set off a Native American renaissance (Silko, Allen, Welch, Glancy, Campbell, Hogan, Erdrich, among others).

Momaday came of age in northern New Mexico near Santa Fe, where Mary Austin, Mabel Dodge Luhan, Georgia O'Keeffe, Willa Cather, and Alice Corbin Henderson lived by the 1920s. After recovering from tuberculosis through a Santa Fe sanitarium in 1918, Yvor Winters had taught grade school near there, in the coal-mining town of Madrid, in 1922. Winters came from graduate school at the University of Chicago, where he had joined the Poetry Club and collaborated with Harriet Monroe, the editorial dynamo behind *Poetry* magazine's 1917 and 1920 nativist reworkings by Sandburg, Bynner, Skinner, Lindsay, Sarett, Lowell, and Austin. In Santa Fe, Winters also met Alice Corbin Henderson, the poet who lauded *Poetry*'s aboriginal verse in "A Note on Primitive Poetry." Corbin Henderson wrote her own nativist versions of *Indian Songs,* laureled Stephen Crane as "an Indian poet," and strongly reviewed Cronyn's *Path on the Rainbow,* all in *Poetry* magazine, 1917 through 1919. Borrowing her books and advice, the young Winters wrote his own one-line verse, natively inspired, "The Magpie's Shadow," marveling Densmore's Chippewa translations as "among the most endlessly fascinating poems of my experience" *(Uncollected Essays and Reviews).* In the same essay, "The Indian in English," Winters compares

Jeremiah Curtin's Wintu *Songs of Spirits* with Blake and places the ethno-poetry of Densmore, Matthews, Russell, and Curtin "with no embarrass-ment beside the best Greek and Chinese versions of H. D. or Ezra Pound." Mary Austin had made her case.

Thirty years later, the modernist curtain was drawn open for young Momaday. By 1951, the Stanford doctoral student A. Grove Day published a full ethnopoetic study of American Indian translations in *The Sky Clears: Poetry of the American,* dedicated to "Yvor Winters—Singer of Power." Thus a nativist red-line ties Dickinson, Tuckerman, Austin, and ethnopoetic translation at the turn of the century, through modernism in the 1920s (Pound, Williams, Stevens, Moore, and company), to Winters's native rhythms in academia (the 1930s through the 1950s), to a native American renaissance beginning with Momaday's 1969 Pulitzer debut. A tangled through-line, the track nonetheless crosses and recrosses Native and Amer-ican literacies, both directions. "I look at the people whose writing I admire most—," Momaday told Larry Evers in *Sun Tracks* (1976), "people like Herman Melville and Emily Dickinson and Isak Dinesen, who is one of my favorite writers; and it seems to me that their attitude toward language is virtually the attitude which informs the oral tradition. It is the storyteller's attitude. Too few writers have developed that understanding of literature, but it's possible that the things which separate oral tradition and written tradition are more apparent than real, and that they can be virtually one and the same thing." Neither oral nor literate voice tips the scales, neither native nor immigrant falls beneath; "the storyteller's attitude" lyrically fuses cultures. Completing the native circle in the 1990s, Momaday has come home between the Sangre de Cristo and Jemez Mountains again to Santa Fe, still teaching at the University of Arizona. In 1997 he was nomi-nated for a Nobel Prize.

The Way to Rainy Mountain refracts the Kiowa tales of "old woman" in *The Journey of Tai-me,* a rare book "archetype," Momaday says, where the handmade pages are textured as parchment of an old woman's skin, her voice warm and thin as Oklahoma wind on a summer evening. Each small tale arcs from the upper right-hand page across a sepia canvas. *The Way to Rainy Mountain* adds several more dimensions to Kiowa oral tradition: the tribal muse speaks through Momaday's paternal grandmother, Aho, born in the dawn of the Kiowa migration south; ethnographic history comes by way of non-Indian documents by Mooney, Parsons, and Mayhall; the elegiac journey is recorded in Momaday's own voice, retracing the tribal pilgrim-age, Montana to Oklahoma in the 1960s; the father's visual witness—re-cording his own mother's stories for his son—appears in Al Momaday's drawings of horse, spider, buffalo, skull, cricket, water and storm spirits, the falling stars, and figures of the landscape. *The Way to Rainy Mountain* is a deft and delicate collage of Plains Indian history, gracefully written, per-sonally told in fine prose poetry, again near perfect blank verse with voweled off-rhymes at the ends of cadences. *"There, where* it *ought* to *be,* at the *end* of a *long* / and *legendary way,* was my *grandmoth*er's *grave.* / *Here* and *there* on the *dark stones* were an*cest*ral *names.* / *Look*ing back *once,* I *saw* the *moun*tain and *came a*way."

The Names, a family memoir, carries the Momaday story into the characters of his boyhood, and *The Ancient Child,* a recent novel, fictionalizes the author's life through a mixed-blood California painter, Set (Kiowa for bear), who returns to Oklahoma and his Indian heritage, reclaiming his grandmother's medicine bundle and native role as an artist. Momaday has been drawing and painting watercolors through the nineties, writing plays (*The Indolent Boys* premiered on the Syracuse Stage in New York, 1994) and carrying on philosophical kitchen table dialogues as theater pieces between Uhr-Set, the Kiowa Bear-Man, and Yahweh (Los Angeles 1998). This man *sings with the heart of a bear,* indeed, the dream traditions of word-senders long before him, still extant. Since his Stanford doctoral thesis on Frederick Tuckerman in 1963, Momaday has planned a study of Dickinson's poetics and, more recently, a play about George Catlin, the mid-nineteenth-century painter who traveled among Plains Indians, sketching and recording initial Euro-American observations. In the Santa Fe *Viva* weekly Sunday column, August 6, 1972, "A Love Affair with Emily Dickinson," Momaday wrote that the New England godmother taught him "the mystery and miracle of language," and in the process, "the art of intellectual survival."

Despite professional interests in prose fiction, memoir, drama, and ink-and-water-color, "I'm basically a poet," Momaday said to Bettye Givens (*MELUS* 1985), and a "cross-cultural" one at that, he told Louis Owens (1986). "Is it fair to say that your theory of literature and the imagination," Matthias Schubnell asked in 1981, "is rooted both in the oral tradition and in modern literary concepts?" "Absolutely," Momaday answered without pause *(Conversations).* The "magic of words," he explained to Joseph Bruchac a year later, survives in the poets and singers of the world: "The Anglo-Saxon who uttered spells over his fields so that the seeds would come out of the ground on the sheer strength of his voice knew a good deal about language" *(Survival This Way).*

Momaday's poetics, as related to Mary Austin's intuitions of an American rhythm, lie embedded in "Earth and I Gave You Turquoise," his first published poem in the 1958 *New Mexico Quarterly,* written on a college weekend break "at one of the second grader's desks of the Jemez day school." To recapitulate from chapter two, "in the presence of the sun" the artist collaborates *with* "the remembered earth," the original earth maker, drawing native characters and stories out of the landscape, everyday lives among plants and animals. Momaday's sense of design comes through syllabic speech rhythms, placing people in their daily living among common images. The poem's story is told by way of native images, common voicing of nature's craft. Natural object is best metaphor, Pound said, so this poem turns on the given healing power of turquoise (said by natives to heal aged eyesight), in the ritual presence of a lover's death: an owl's cry near Black Mountain, planting corn and wild cane, children and fire, a brother's grieving house and Moon Woman reflected on the water, dancing by the Chinle seven elms, Navajo loom and mutton and coffee, a Red Rock crow standing on one leg, black hair and drumming hooves. As with many of Momaday's early poems, tutored by Winters, the 7/5/7 syllabic count distantly echoes a poet such as Du Fu, Chinese master many centuries back, and American modernists such as Marianne Moore. From Emily Dickinson in New England, to Mary Austin, Harriet Monroe, Alice Henderson, and Willa Cather in New York, Chicago, and Santa Fe, to D. H. Lawrence in Taos and Georgia O'Keeffe in Abiquiu by the late 1920s, nativist configurations lattice this writer's life, Northeast to Southwest. "I was at Harvard yesterday," young Momaday, on a Guggenheim to study Dickinson's manuscript variants, wrote Winters, November 1, 1966, "and I had a long and careful look at Emily Dickinson's herbarium; it is a remarkable thing. There was an introduction to astronomy in her father's library. . . ." Momaday seems to wed Stevens's imagination with Moore's eye, to fuse Dickinson's ear with Williams's exacting mind—native musical phrasing, painterly precision, acoustic fine tuning, all flared in a tribal landscape and literary history, Navajo, Spanish, and Pueblo voices texturing American English.

The preface to *In the Presence of the Sun* refers to the open secret of language, naming ceremonies and talking mysteries, neolithic to modern art. Just so, his father's Plains Indian eidetic tradition comes from "rock paintings to hide paintings to ledger book drawings to modern art." A "man made of words," Momaday regards poetry to be "old and elemental expression, as venerable as song and prayer." If a reader looks closely, the preface ends, "it is possible to catch a glimpse of me in my original being." The visual artist glimpses himself from the side, a cloudy gravure close-up in the self-sketch framing the preface, again a second time closing the book.

The collection opens with a poem from Momaday's first year at Stanford, "The Bear," the author's totemic guardian and acknowledged relative of Faulkner's Old Ben in *The Bear*, also his final authorial by-line in the book of poems: "He is a bear." As in Sitting Bull's lyrics—healer in digging herbal roots, warrior for his strong heart, wise advisor with his intelligence—Old Man Bear crosses many tribes as a guardian spirit, worthy of great respect and power. The Kiowa arrowmaker Pohd-lokh named young Scott "Rock-Tree Boy" for the laccolith called Bear-lodge or *Mato Tipi* by the Lakota, otherwise known as Devil's Tower in northeastern Wyoming. "This past weekend I went into the Black Hills, to Devil's Tower (what a sad, inappropriate name for that unique, holy—but older than Christianity holy—place)," Momaday wrote Schubnell, August 25, 1982. "I discovered,

I think, where the children were playing, where the girls were running, and the bear after them," referring to the Kiowa creation myth that opens *The Way to Rainy Mountain* and recurs to pattern *The Ancient Child.* "There are no bears at the monument now, I am told. But, you know, . . . I am quite sure that a grizzly, an old thick animal, resides there somewhere in the Bear Lodge Mountains. He keeps an eye on Tsoai, surely. That is his trust. There is no Tsoai without the bear." The poet keeps a roughly carved wooden bear on his writing desk, Joseph Bruchac reports, and sees his guardian brother as "human-like, adventurous, powerful, curious, extremely confident," as he told Bettye Givens: "I have this bear power, I turn into a bear every so often. I feel myself becoming a bear, and that's a struggle that I have to face now and then." Today, the artist is still tracking that legendary namesake, "Uhr-Set" sitting down to powwow with Yahweh at a kitchen table in millennial dialogues (*In the Bear's House*).

Again in 5/7/5/7 syllabic precision, "The Bear" shifts from human to animal-spirit, entering the poet's body of verse—back thirty years to his beginning lines, all the way back some thirty thousand years to Kiowa tribal origins, cognate in New World evolution with bear, coyote, turtle, and cricket. The wounded bear's tracks and marks are scarred in time and place. These geological and biological scars leave mortal wounds on the mother earth, as at Devil's Tower. The guardian "old man" is caught by startling absence in Momaday's last lines (the shamanic trick Hyde calls "erasing angel"), the buzzard flight coterminous with a bear's exit in 5/7 syllabics:

> Then he is gone, whole,
> without urgency, from sight,
> as buzzards control,
> imperceptibly, their flight.

This glimpsed going off leads into the blank verse of "Buteo Regalis," catching in flight the sharply detailed hawk's vision (western ferruginous rough-legged hawk, the poet told Gaetano Prampolini), a bird's eye over the wilds—

> Aligned, the span bends to begin the dive
> And falls, alternately white and russet,
> Angle and curve, gathering momentum.

—which falls into the third poem, "Comparatives," from mountain to sea, eagle to fish here caught between, "fissure of bone / forever," the fossil of an inland sea. This time there is no breaking vision in the end, but a glimpse, again, a Williams's watercolor sense of broken shard:

> It is most like
> wind on waves—

mere commotion,
mute and mean,
perceptible—
that is all.

The collection moves through "Earth and I Gave You Turquoise," on to the free verse of "Simile," the deer's fleeting image an objective correlative or quietly appropriate image for estrangement:

What did we say to each other
that now we are as the deer
who walk in single file
with heads high
with ears forward
with eyes watchful
with hooves always placed on firm ground
in whose limbs there is latent flight

It seems an etched insight, the spirants "what" and "with" and "whose" pacing an anaphoral litany of retreat.

Four Plainview poems (the first a sonnet) open with heroic couplets, sibling to Winters's Magpie borrowed from Curtin's Wintu translations: "There in the hollow of the hills I see, / Eleven magpies stand away from me." Again, the verse closes softly, fading out. The image disclosed, disappears: "They are illusion—wind and rain revolve—/ And they recede in darkness, and dissolve." From this modernist impermanence in the mode of Stevens, the gathering moves to a ballad variation, reminiscent of Frank Mitchell's translated Navajo horse songs:

I saw an old Indian
At Saddle Mountain
He drank and dreamed of drinking
And a blue-black horse

A prairie-fire tone poem, then a riff on an old western folk song, à la Langston Hughes, round out the opening sequence: *"Johnnycake and venison and sassafras tea."*

Clearly, Momaday experiments with the mythos and metric syllabics of Native American verse rhythms crossing into modernist forms. He was directly influenced by Thoreau, Tuckerman, Dickinson, Muir, Lawrence, Austin, Dineson, Faulkner, and Stevens, among other modern writers of the native and natural world. "You are an Indian in a white man's world and are doubly isolated," Yvor Winters wrote his advisee, April 21, 1965, "but the fact gives you a remarkable point of view." At Stanford, Winters taught Momaday mainstream tenets of verbal concision, image precision, musical phrasing, and symbolist indirection, tools compatible with a native storyteller's elliptical plain style, winter-count eidetics, Sun Dance drum-beat, or the haunting power of Native American chanting. His grand-mother's storytelling and great-grandmother's singing set a lyric pulse keening in the young writer's heartbeat, and a conscious craft matured as he grew and traveled. Dickinson showed Momaday "economy and preci-sion," he told Charles Woodard, to "present a great idea in a very few words," as Pound had taught Winters in modernist credos. With a true sense of Pound's Oriental ideogram, this Kiowa poet then weds generic rhythms, Oklahoma and New Mexico, to twentieth-century formal accul-turations, beyond the wasteland.

Stevens would turn a firecat eye, a booted sailor's ear, a Tennessee jar's neck, to catch the syllabics of these native tigers in red weather, bear to eagle, geese to horse, crow to buffalo, deer to coyote. "As important as books are," Momaday wrote on the Argentine blind poet, Jorge Luis Bor-ges, "—as important as writing is, there is yet another, a fourth dimension of language which is just as important, and which, indeed, is older and more nearly universal than writing: the oral tradition, that is, the telling of stories, the recitation of epic poems, the singing of songs, the making of prayers, the chanting of magic and mystery, the exertion of the human voice upon the unknown—in short, the spoken word" (*The Man Made of Words*).

"I believe that a man is his name. The name and the existence are indivisible," Momaday told Schubnell. A man does not give, but is *given* and *bears* a name, earned according to tribal custom, and he is *made of* the word. "The Delight Song of Tsoai-talee" records the author's own cele-brative name-song, eco-tribal and anaphoral, in the manner of Old Testa-ment cadences, or Amhairghin's legendary "rhapsody on landing in Ire-land" over three millennia ago. One of three druids with the invading Milesians, Amhairghin allegedly sang:

> I am the wind which breathes upon the sea,
> I am the wave of the ocean,
> I am the murmur of the billows,
> I am the ox of the seven combats,

Douglas Hyde translated this epic boast at the turn of the century, and Lady Gregory retranslated it (the origin still disputed), no less than Washington Matthews rendered Navajo chants and David McAllester retranslated "The War God's Horse Song." *Tsoai* means rock-tree, Momaday tells us in *The Names,* for the volcanic laccolith near Sundance, the Lakota Bear-lodge, denigrated Devil's Tower by Whites. *Talee* means boy. So young Scott was tribally named "Rock-Tree Boy" by the arrow-maker grandfather, Pohd-lohk, for an ursine geological mystery that Kiowa ancestors encountered in their eighteenth-century journey southeast across Wyoming. The Kiowas hold to a story about seven sisters, chased into a magical tree by their brother-turned-into-a-bear, who scored the bark, and the sisters then climbed on into the sky as the Big Dipper or Ursa Major, to this day "kinsmen in the sky." And to this day, the bear-brother roams the earth, shadowing all of Momaday's writing in fear and delight:

> I am a feather on the bright sky
> I am the blue horse that runs in the plain
> I am the fish that rolls, shining, in the water

These images are small eidetic explosions in the brain, like firing stars. "I am a wild boar in valour," Amhairghin boasted, "I am a salmon in the water," and Momaday continues:

> I am the shadow that follows a child
> I am the evening light, the lustre of meadows

The name-song unravels a story about the sky in its relation to the earth:

> I am an eagle playing with the wind
> I am a cluster of bright beads
> I am the farthest star
> I am the coldest dawn

A quiet caesura centers the cadence, a snowman's chill, then with cold scintillant distance come peace and renewal:

> I am the roaring of the rain
> I am the glitter on the crust of the snow
> I am the long track of the moon in a lake
> I am a flame of four colors

Again, to see is to believe and to feel the power of song—singing from the bear's different heart—the creative inspiration of the maker, who is made by his singing, in the manner of Wallace Stevens and the seaside girl, here a Kiowa Amhairghin high on an intermountain native plain:

> I am a deer standing away in the dusk
> I am a field of sumac and the pomme blanche
> I am an angle of geese in the winter sky
> I am the hunger of a young wolf
> I am the whole dream of these things

The singer chants himself alive, standing "in good relation" to earth, gods, beauty, and "the daughter of Tsen-tainte." The communal principle of beauty and balance, of joy and delight, of youth and seasoned wisdom strings the song-poem's tribal bow, "all my relatives," as Plains singers call out. Anthropologists call this "sacred reciprocity," the give-and-take of people, creation, and spirits—the social aesthetics of tribal poetics. *Re* and *pro* are the roots of re-ci-pro-cal gift exchange, Lewis Hyde reminds us, "going to and fro between people" *(The Gift)*. Gift relating is a tribal maxim. "You see, I am alive, I am alive," the Kiowa poet concludes.

From here the book turns to a visual image, a watercolor of Rock-Tree Boy's namesake, the beginnings of Kiowa tribal consciousness. Always with Momaday, we are part way into myth and sacred landscape, visual and aural media, the remembered earth and its speaking-image past. So with "Head-waters," the opening poem in *The Way to Rainy Mountain*, comes a tribal emergence myth—moving through a hollow mother log, "wild and welling at the source." It is Aho's story, a grandmother's creation myth, and no small matter that *a-hó* (the accent reversed) means "thanks" in Kiowa dialect. *Thanks*, also, to a western and native sense of combined form in this tightly rhymed, slant-knit construction. With reversed trochaic entry ("*Noon* in the *inter*moun*tain plain:*") and spondaic arrests ("*scant tell*ing" "a *log hol*low" "*Stand brim*ming" "*What moves?*"), the tetrameter of this octave rides on exacting metrics. The rhythmic horizon line comes in eight-step syllabic verse, easing into iambics:

> A *log, hol*low and *wea*ther-*stained,*
> An *in*sect *at* the *mouth*, and *moss*—
> Yet *wa*ters *rise* a*gainst* the *roots,*
> *Stand brim*ming *to* the *stalks. What moves?*
> What *moves* on *this* ar*cha*ic *force*
> Was *wild* and *well*ing *at* the *source.* [emphasis mine]

There is a kind of Darwinian Indian poetics, as later in Linda Hogan's writing, a hesitant precision, even comma arrest ("the mouth, and moss—") worthy of both his grandmother Aho and her contemporary, Emily Dickinson.

The page turns to the closing elegy in *Rainy Mountain*, standing before Aho's grave in "Rainy Mountain Cemetery." Sealing the rhymes with vow-eling long *o*s and high *ee*s, this elegiac petroglyph rides on a sculpted mu-sicality, following Pound's terms, the mind chiseling the heart's grief. The poem interlocks in rhymed iambic pentameter, ritually slowed with spon-dees and tangible abstractions, wavering between the conception of death and the concreteness of stone:

> Most is your name the name of this dark stone.
> Deranged in death, the mind to be inheres
> Forever in the nominal unknown,
> The wake of nothing audible he hears
> Who listens here and now to hear your name.

But Aho cannot speak, or the name be spoken, as in many tribal ways of quieting the dead:

And silence is the long approach of noon
Upon the shadow that your name defines—

The remembrance ends in a variation on Pound's arresting spondees ("*Pet-als on a wet, black bough*"), iamb to spondee to dactyl, back to iamb: "And *death* this *cold, black dens*ity of *stone.*" *Aho* can only be shadowed in stone, a concrete space taken away, an earth elegy sculpted by the grieving grandson. He knows the dignity of the event, as with Dickinson among the dying, and rediscovers the presence of his grandmother's ongoing Kiowa spirit, in his own rebirth and age-old acceptance of a mystery that cannot be named or explained. "I know to bear against hard times," Sitting Bull sang his death song.

Those who follow the ancestors, as in the ancient migrations, move on and carry the dream wheel of tribal stories and ritual songs. The "Wheel of Dreams," primal, circular, mobile, unending, carries on in living voices, chanting and dancing in a tribal round, spinning the names of ground and sky back to a native "red-earth" Adam. The poet's role is not so much to name, as to remember and repeat the ancient "aboriginal" namings, that is, names "from" the "origins" of all things. Old to young, dead to living, these voices circle and recycle in an arced continuum:

> They are old men, or men
> Who are old in their voices,
> And they carry the wheel among the camps,
> Saying: Come, come,
> Let us tell the old stories,
> Let us sing the sacred songs.

Age makes language sacred—what is remembered binds us across time. Not "make it new," so much as "remake it *natively,*" Pound could have rephrased modernism by the century's end—to live again with each generation, passing in and passing on, continuing the dream. The end of Black Elk's Great Vision, translated and *recreated* by John Neihardt in high English style, comes to mind as the paradigm: "But I was not the last; for when I looked behind me there were ghosts of people like a trailing fog as far as I could see—grandfathers of grandfathers and grandmothers of grandmothers without number. And over these a great Voice—the Voice that was the South—lived, and I could feel it silent.

"And as we went the voice behind me said: 'Behold a good nation walking in a sacred manner in a good land!' "

And yet, in this modernist century, and three preceding it, Native Americans have been decimated by everything from germ warfare, to cultural genocide, to outright military invasion, conquest, and retention camps called reservations. Removal, poverty, insult, and neglect scar their present history. To repeat, their numbers in the territorial U.S. shrank from a pre-Columbian four or six million, to a quarter-million around 1900. Natives have rebounded to some two million at present. As no others here, Indians know impermanence, loss, and reemergence. They keep going on.

In "Anywhere Is a Street into the Night," Momaday sidles up to the iced windows of Stevens's blackbird shadows:

> Desire will come of waiting
> Here at this window—I bring
> An old urgency to bear
> Upon me, and anywhere
> Is a street into the night,
> Deliverance and delight—

As with the fine-line drawings of the book—agitating the margins of tangible things, tentatively approaching and slanting away—the mind brushes and busies the outlines of things, hesitant of their obduracy:

> And evenly it will pass
> Like this image on the glass.

Dactylic plunges ("*Here* at this" "*old urgency*" "U*pon* me, and" "De*liverance*" "And *evenly*") challenge the chary iambic advance of the line. All things will pass, indeed, just as a man's own image fades in panes of vision, a visionary impermanence where he cannot step twice into the same river. In Black Elk's day, the Lakota came to a recognition that the unnamable Creator is no single or static being, rather a kinetics of earth and sky, continuously moving, "the Spirit-that-Moves-moves."

The opening section of *In the Presence of the Sun* comes to fine close with a poem (this text's epigraph) dedicated to Georgia O'Keeffe, born a year before Eliot and two after Pound. She was Momaday's elder artist-friend in northern New Mexico, where the young Indian poet experienced his own coming of age, and again resides today. There is a free-verse ease, a native dignity and constructed reversal in the lines, beginning with the swinging rhythms of the title. "*Forms* of the *Earth*" could be a form of Platonic organics, Sequoia to Seattle, from Athens to Ab-i-quiu. Momaday and O'Keeffe first met in the painter's Abiquiu home, 1972; the young poet returned there to talk, over late lunches of goat cheese and wine, as the elder woman's eyesight faded. "When I first saw her," Momaday told Schubnell, "I marveled because her hands were huge and very bony and gnarled and rough—beautiful, but not feminine." Lacking blossoms and buildings that she saw and painted with her husband, Alfred Stieglitz, in New York City of the 1920s, O'Keeffe said that she took up bones and stones in New Mexico to paint as flowering desert forms (Santa Fe now houses these paintings in the Georgia O'Keeffe Museum). "All around there were beautiful objects," Momaday remembers her home, "Clean and precise in their beauty, like bone." So the poet brings "a small, brown stone," and the purblind painter (no less than blind Aho knitting, then praying at her bedside) describes it with a fingertip of the mind's eye:

> At once, accordingly you knew,
> As you knew the forms of the earth at Abiquiu:
> That time involves them and they bear away,
> Beautiful, various, remote,
> In failing light, and the coming of cold.

This is the elegiac beauty of the ends of things, spiritual beginnings in a southwest landscape—God's naturally architected garden of sweeping bajadas, sandstone escarpments, volcanic swells and granite scree, river-bed caliche, basalt petroglyphs millennia old—and everywhere the red earth, flushed with ochre and strawflower yellows, muddied with the porous crunch of adobe, the cobalt blue sky overhead, spackled at night with ten thousand thousand stars pinpricking cactus, chamisa, thistle, sagebrush, piñon, juniper, and scrub brush, and higher up on the mountain slopes rise the chattering aspen, ancestral cottonwood, old oak, spruce, and tall pines. A native poetics, indeed, for painter or poet, for any artist rooted in the landscape and spirit of local American place.

> These figures moving in my rhyme,
> Who are they? Death and Death's dog, Time.

Back to folktale and ballad, "The Strange and True Story of My Life with Billy the Kid" takes up the comic elegy of romance in the West. Truly American, frontier callow (an Indian boy identifying with the young White outlaw), the section is whimsical with boy-heroics, yet folklorically true as a smoking six-gun to the American frontier. Momaday recalls in *The Names* that Indians play cowboys and desperadoes out West, and in moments of empathic self-identification, the down-trodden identify with the loser. Billy Bonney was born Henry McCarty in New York City, 1859, and died twenty-one years later in New Mexico by gunshot, legend has it, having killed one man for each of his years. These oddly romantic prose pieces of history and rocking-horse lullaby ("Ride, Billy, Billy") charm like Mexican *corridos*, the ballad legends of Pancho Villa, say, or Gregorio Cortés. Momaday's charms canter along like the dreamy folklore of the West, all adolescent longing, callow and long-necked, refusing wasteland disillusion.

"Riding Is an Exercise of the Mind," the collection opens, the narrator riding his pony, Pecos, into a Jemez landscape to face off hostile Indians, flanked by his ghostly partner, Billy the Kid (who also appears in *The Ancient Child*). The "Two Figures" that open the section, Death and his dog, Time, reappear at the end, as adolescent fancy closes down the charm of legend and western storytelling in popular myths: a cow*boy* musing, bullets and bullshit, whores and widows, horses and snakes, bravado and betrayal. Over all hangs the early mortality of a young nation in a new land, discovering its desires and limitations, resisting native maturity.

The third section, "A Gathering of Shields," itself a separate collection, hand printed by a Santa Fe art dealer in limited edition, returns to Kiowa culture. Always protective medicine, a shield is both crest and defense, a decorative announcement of self and protective mask: "It charms you, frightens you, disarms you, renders you helpless." Four by four, these sixteen shields tell their own stories and remain "meditations that make a round of life," traditionally, like axial tepee poles or circular quadrants on a turtle shell. "These stories ought to be told in the early morning or late afternoon," the author advises, "when the sun is close to the horizon, and always in the presence of the sun." From the winter of 1833, when the stars fell, as recorded in the earliest tribal winter counts on buffalo skins, to the shield that was brought down from Rock-Tree in Wyoming, dogs and horses, soldiers and warriors, bears, spiders, and captive boys with names like Christian, Elijah, and Mas o Menos, tell the story of Kiowa migrations, from Yellowstone to Smoky Hill River, walking, the equestrian centaurs, wandering to incarceration. The old man, Give Him Back, tells his wife, "My old eyes were hungry for it," catching the 1833 falling stars attentively in his shield, an emblemized moment of "wonder and fearful delight."

The book ends with elegiac charms, occasional tombstone epigraphs. The impetus seems to be words as come-hithers, say, semiprecious syllabic stones on a brown-wrist bracelet: "She died a beauty of repute, / Her other virtues in dispute." One of these charms, preceding a formulaic "Prayer" of thanksgiving for Aho, stands in tribute to the most ancient of Native American origins, "Mogollon Morning." The poem goes on, from Aho's graveside in Rainy Mountain Cemetery, to the author's own contemplation of death:

> The sun
> From the sere south
> Splays the ocotillo.
> Cold withdraws. Still I stand among
> Black winds.

The softly sibilant alliterations, from the archaic but still viable "sere," to the more spiny cactus, "*ocotillo*" (microcosmic trochees), layer the verse attentively. The line breaks are uncharacteristically interruptive, a rhythmic slowing from Dickinson to Plath, Roethke to James Wright, that stills the poem:

> The long,
> Long bands of rock,
> Old as wonder, stand back.

I listen for my death song there
In rock.

The native poet prays to the earth gods, to ancestral bones, to cactus and rock, sun and wind, shadow and tortoise, to *keep him,* spondaically, going. In *Life,* July 1971, Momaday wrote: "The native vision, this gift of seeing truly, with wonder and delight, into the natural world, is informed by a certain attitude of reverence and self-respect. It is a matter of extra-sensory as well as sensory perception, I believe. In addition to the eye, it involves the intelligence, the instinct, and the imagination." Even "At Risk," as Momaday ends the book, he would still be charming his reader, purling the rhythms of the land, chanting stones and spirits among natural ancestral memories:

> And there was I, among ancient animals,
> In the formality of the dance,
> Remembering my face in the mirror of masks.

BLACKFEET SURREALIST: WELCH

As Robert Graves pointed out in The White Goddess, *the convergence of many ancient religions and shamanistic lines produces the western lore of the Muse.*
                                        GARY SNYDER, *The Old Ways*

Our twentieth-century Muse has grown a bit witchy. Much of modern American poetry leans toward darker tenets of shamanic surrealism, from Merwin's drunk in the furnace and carrier of ladders; to Kinnell's body rags and book of nightmares; to Ted Hughes's crow, Wodwo, and hawk in the rain; to James Wright's blossoming pear tree ("the dark / Blood in my body drags me / Down with my brother"). Wright cries after dusk, near the South Dakota border:

> Dead riches, dead hands, the moon
> Darkens,
> And I am lost in the beautiful white ruins
> Of America

Modern verse is a litany of the lost, the dispossessed, the down-out-and-forgotten, the undesirable and detestable. Unloved and lonely souls sing their blues off-key, but still they sing with a beating heart that is different: "I speak of flat defeat / In a flat voice," Wright says. *Outside* Fargo, North Dakota, behind a railroad boxcar or under a viaduct, whether in the moon shadow of Sioux warrior or flanked by stabbing Chippewa men, the poet laments his nativist "black Ohioan swan," reduced to oily scales in a polluted wasteland river:

Here, carry his splintered bones
Slowly, slowly
Back into the
Tar and chemical strangled tomb,
The strange water, the
Ohio river, that is no tomb to
Rise from the dead
From.

But rise they do, these poets, on the blackened wings of history, dreaming with Norman Dubie of Black Elk checking Virgil in chess. "I watched Black Elk speak to the flies on a drying buffalo skin. He addressed them as cousins. I have so much to learn" (*The Clouds of Magellan*).

I spent this night, the only white
in the Napi Tavern where the woman tending bar
told me she's your aunt. A scene of raw despair. Indians
sleeping on the filthy floor. Men with brains scrambled in wine.
A man who sobbed all night, who tried in strangled desperation
to articulate the reason. And the bitterest woman I've seen
since the Depression.

RICHARD HUGO, "LETTER TO WELCH FROM BROWNING"

James Welch was born of Blackfeet and Gros Ventre lineage in Browning, Montana, 1940, the first year of the Second World War. The young Indian studied at the University of Minnesota when Berryman taught there. He earned a college degree from the University of Montana, where he went on to an MFA in poetry under Richard Hugo, and has since taught part-time at Cornell and the University of Washington. Hugo had left Yale for wilderness recovery near his Washington birthplace and settled into fishing, drinking, swiving, and teaching poetry in Missoula. Maudlin boy of the fallen West, this nationally recognized White poet, no less than Winters with Momaday, midwifed Jim Welch, a.k.a. "Chief Boiling Whiskey," into the birth canals of American letters. Hugo "opened up a world of writing to me," Welch remembers coming of age under Hugo's tutelage, a "first real" and finally "main influence." Poetry "wasn't something you had to be a genius to do, or wear a black cape," but come to naturally, "an ordinary person with a certain amount of imagination, a certain ability with language" (*Four Winds*). The native in poetics came surreally to this young Blackfeet, and Hugo added some pointers on craft, notably the heartbeat blank verse line back through Yeats to Shakespeare.

Since his 1971 debut as a poet, *Riding the Earthboy 40*, Welch has shifted to fiction, as with so many other native writers, from Silko and Erdrich, to Hogan and Alexie. *Winter in the Blood* (1974) began as a Montana landscape poem; *The Death of Jim Loney* (1979) followed with the tragic antiheroism of a mixed-blood, self-martyed drunk; *Fools Crow* (1986 *Los Angeles Times* Book Prize) dropped back into frontier Blackfeet history and myth; and *Indian Lawyer* (1990) brought Native American affairs down to the present, a kinsman like Ben Nighthorse Campbell from Colorado, running for Congress. In 1994, Welch revisited the Little Big Horn with the documentary filmmaker, Paul Stekler, and co-authored *Killing Custer*. The PBS documentary of that rewitnessing, "Last Stand at Little Big Horn," won James Welch an Emmy.

This native writer resists illusions: begin with the earth and bone of reality, the blood definition of gritty landscape and given history, and go on from here. As writers from William Carlos Williams to Ray Carver swear necessary, he works against the grain from a rooted "ground sense" to scour the present of "sentimental crap" soaked up in junction bars, cheap motels, and roadside eateries. "Only an Indian knows who he is," Welch argues in "The Only Good Indian" (*South Dakota Review* 1971), "—an individual who just happens to be an Indian—and if he has grown up on a reservation he will naturally write about what he knows. And hopefully he will have the toughness and fairness to present his material in a way that is not manufactured by conventional stance. . . . What I mean is—whites have to adopt a stance; Indians already have one." That stance is shaped realistically in winter-locked towns like Moose Jaw, drunk tanks of Heart Butte, and dry fishing holes near Havre and Harlem, Montana. Welch etches into the page the elemental, truncated existence of modern Indians, toxic, bored, desperate on the rez:

> there isn't much to do
> nights
> Heart Butte
> in the dead of spring.

"Up there in Montana," the writer says, no less than O'Keeffe in the Southwest, "there are bones all over the place and the wind blows all the time. All of the towns that I write about, all of the country, is real." So real that it hurts: for centuries the Blackfeet were born into an exacting climate, a winter in the blood, no less than Stevens's anti-totemic snow man. *Nothing* is where they begin, far northwest, "a quick 30 below" zero, Christmas Eve on the Great American Desert, bordering Canada. In Harlem, Montana, the poet turns to "disgusted, busted whites" and "raven-haired stiffs":

> I have plans to burn my drum, move out
> and civilize this hair. See my nose? I smash it
> straight for you. These teeth? I scrub my teeth
> away with stones. I know you help me now I matter.
> And I—I come to you, head down, bleeding from my smile,
> happy for the snow clean hands of you, my friends.

"Fifty years ago," George Grinnell wrote in 1892, "the name Blackfeet was one of terrible meaning to the white traveler who passed across that desolate buffalo-trodden waste which lay to the north of the Yellowstone River and east of the Rocky Mountains." During "the winter of starvation" in 1883–84, more than a quarter of the remaining Blackfeet starved to death, as the government systematically destroyed the buffalo and brought the last hostile tribe onto a frozen reservation. They were supposed to farm potatoes, eat beef, wear stiff boots and trousers, and sing Christian hymns. "Onward, Christian soldiers, Marching as to war." They are still resistant today.

"Magic Fox" opens *Riding the Earthboy 40*. To work a quarter-section of Montana farmland for potatoes, say, one crop in five years on the average, is an exercise in "riding" the unsteady earth, indeed. Welch's father farmed the forty acres of an allotment abandoned by the Earthboy clan, ghosted by buffalo-hunting nomads, toxified by poor soil, severe weather, broken promises, chronic poverty, and chemicals, from cheap booze to pesticides and poisonous waste. So the earth tilts, tipsy, loosely metaphoric. The young poet's dreams swing from fantasy to cold reality. Images hit the ground, likenesses drop to things-as-they-are:

> They shook the green leaves down,
> those men that rattled
> in their sleep. Truth became
> a nightmare to their fox.

Reality is a foxy game. Day turns to nightmarish magic; love swirls among falling leaves, a nervous dance of memory and desire; the poetic line breaks dangerously on oddly unstable images. The traditional death chant—to meet the rattling darkness—snores leaves off the Sun Dance tree of life and death:

> He turned their horses into fish,
> or was it horses strung
> like fish, or fish like fish
> hung naked in the wind?

Coyote's wily cousin, the Euro-American fox, is neither sharp-eyed nor quick-clawed enough to untangle a mare's nest of fish, horses, or stars (possibly just spoiled fish), redundant images of a bad catch, bagged ponies, or falling stars. In fact, the stars fell on Blackfeet ancestors, and are still falling. Smallpox, like red-skin stars, killed two thirds of twenty thousand Blackfeet in 1837, four years after the Leonid meteor showers recorded far south by Momaday's Oklahoma ancestors (*The Way to Rainy Mountain*). There were successive plagues in 1845, 1857, and 1869. By the 1880s, Blackfeet horses were shot by cavalry or led away like so many fish on a barbwire stringer, as the remaining three million buffalo were slaughtered by government-paid marksmen, and the reservations staked out. The Sun Dance tree was pulled down, replaced by cross and flag pole.

The poet-shaman a century later is haunted by a fallen past that skews his present. A blonde seductress teases him into nightmare with boozy dreams. He wakes to dangerous sleep, delirious with the toxins of failed medicine, the dark firewater instability of magic and metaphor out of balance. In the second poem, "Verifying the Dead," a "woman blue as night" steps from a medicine bundle and chants a slant rhyming world "like this far off." A blue earth mother, sister to the blonde witch, sings of the old ways gone, echoed in a cold wind off a hard place. Owl Woman's song ghosts the century's end:

> In the great night my heart will go out;
> Toward me the darkness comes rattling.
> In the great night my heart will go out.

A new kind of shamanic realism informs this poet's voice, definitely on edge, tilting away from perpendicular. As with Plath, his poetics take life-and-death chances with reality. A Blackfeet medicine man was known as "a heavy singer for the sick," Grinnell notes, and an "all-face" shaman could be ostracized or killed for failure to heal the people. "The shamanic 'miracles' not only confirm and reinforce the patterns of the traditional religion," Mircea Eliade adds a positive note, cached by Plath and Hughes, to the poetics of shamanic uncertainty on a good day, "they also stimulate and feed the imagination, demolish the barriers between dream and present reality, open windows upon worlds inhabited by the gods, the dead, and the spirits." Just so, realistically twisted, the poet's voice bites through winter-count histories with a shaman's tongue, mysterious, ritualistic, unflinching. He chants "finicky secrets," hawked through the long winter night in strangely troubling phrases, wheeling on paradox, tilting through slant parable.

"I like to warp reality a little bit," Welch admits. Images spin out of ordinary associations, visions-turned-nightmares shadow the dark side of day-to-day Indian life.

> Meaning gone, we dance for pennies now,
> our feet jangling dust that hides the bones
> of sainted Indians. Look away and we are gone.
> Look back. Tracks are there, a little faint,
> our song strong enough for headstrong hunters
> who look ahead to one more kill.

No less than Berryman or Hugo, Welch writes poetry of startling half-lines and broken images. Common syntax and diction tense against metered line lengths, enjambed or broken at midpoint. Fragments of shattered metaphors impact in commonplace rhythms, logic falters along staggered lines of thought, lines bang to abrupt full stops. Ideas implode verse lines in smack rhymes: "*—instead* he *spoke* / of a role so *black* the *uncle* died / out of *luck* in a westend *shack.*" With postcard sarcasm his iambic rhythms look for "mountains to bang against."

> Sky is all the rage in country steeped
> in lore, the troubled Indians wise within
> their graves.

"Everywhere, rhythm raged," the poet says in "The Versatile Historian": the iambic downthrust of Sun Dance drumbeat, the agony of a piercing chest-to-post tether, the sere of the sun, bang of the earth, and sudden vision, the sacrificial breaking down and breaking through. The old gods come back in heartbeat, breath, and pulse, as Welch writes from the elliptical concision of a surreal Indian vision—spare, explosive, essential—a hard beauty crying for a vision of redemption and renewal: "quick paces and a space of mind," the rhymer says of "Birth on Range 18."

Myths of the West begin with cowboys and Indians, and historically these fuse into one, down west in Montana. So, too, men in riding boots move differently from Hartford executives in dress shoes, or Yankee farmers in galoshes—Wallace Stevens walking to work, or Robert Frost out mending walls. Montana cowboys, especially broad-shouldered, thin-hipped Indians, stride, mosey, or lope across a hardpan landscape, torso upright, heel forward, knee bent, hip shifting with the canter—and thus the heel-stressed counterpoint—a dominant male pace out west, a horizon beat for riding fence. So the inbred rhythms, including speech patterns, are irregularly stressed iambics, with spondees pitching a rise-and-fall pace, meeting a landscape weedy and ditched with surprises. And so among Indian cowboys, "Surviving" opens with a spondaically driven storm, out of season, pounding the open range:

> The *day-long cold hard rain drove*
> like *sun* through *all* the *ce*dar *sky*
> we *had* that *late fall.* [emphasis mine]

Meter gets no more driven or sprung. The fabled oral tradition is here a confessional telling, men lamenting around a fire, making up lies, storying their sins.

> We *hud*dled
> *close* as *cows* be*fore* the *bel*lied *stove.*
> *Told* stories. *Blackbird cleared* his *mind,*
> *thought* of *things* he'd *left* be*hind, spoke:*

More get-down gritty than Stevens's thirteen ways of looking at things, Blackbird's story tells of sexual abuse, the rape of the virginal earth, native desecrations, while dreaming of "ways to make the land":

> "That *thin girl,* old *cook's kid, stripped na*ked
> for a *coke* or *two* and *cooked* her *special stew*
> *round back* of the *mess tent Sun*days."
> *Spar*rows *skit*tered *through* the *black brush.*

With impacting spondees, three to a line, the cowboy rhythms belly up to a dubious trickster's rail—abuses of the feminine, of the land, of the self by Indians themselves in a surreal new, grainy reality, the postmodernist "dirty realism" to tell the truth, for better or worse. And who is the listener, the frame narrator, sparrow to blackbird, speaking with deep-chill candor, "Zero at the bone," but today's acculturated Adamic Indian?

> That *night* the *moon slipped* a *notch, hung*
> *black* for *just* a *sec*ond, *just long enough*
> for *wet black things* to *sneak away* our *cache*
> of *meat.* To *stay a*live this *way,* it's *hard. . . .*

These loping rhythms, rammed home with the triple spondee, *"wet black things"* (lifted from Pound's night-vision "wet, black bough"), carry the heart across a stubblefield of painful dismay and pain and gritty confessional—through which shine the single-winged angels of truth, not to mention bear-heart beauty. "To stay alive this way, it's hard. . . ." These Indians struggle "to bear against hard times," no less than Sitting Bull a century ago.

By now, it seems clear what James Welch is stereotypically not: a new-age, born-again scout who runs conferences on wellness or conducts vision quests for a small fee. This poet writes dense, unsettling texts on delirium tremens, failed visions, and lost dreams. He's not an off-reservation urban Indian who likes to give public readings, but a shy, even reclusive writer, private like Emily Dickinson. He's not a bow-and-arrow hunter, feeding his tribe wild game, but an artist of the real, warning his people about fat addictions and quick toxic fixes. Welch knows the double-edged knife of anger, the suckhole of self-doubt, and the necessary courage of a "now-day Indi'n," in the face of historical betrayals, a national culture of opiates and greed, a paradise going downhill fast. He's no fool to essentialist self-deception, the human propensity to take it easy, to cut corners, to con oneself into a stupor of conceits about *other* people's wrongdoings. Nor is Welch an eco-poet with feel-good fairy tales about Grandfather Eagle or Grandmother Spider. His deer and bear are shot by hunters with scoped .30–30 rifles, who target practice on rabbits, rats, and coyotes. His father's pastures are leased by White ranchers with government-protected interests. His mother's game is stalked by weekend sportsmen, tagged and taxed by state wildlife officials, whose revenue builds more asphalt roads into Indian wilderness areas.

> If we raced a century over hills
> that ended years before, people couldn't
> say our run was simply poverty or promise
> for a better end. We ended sometime
> back in recollections of glory, myths
> that meant the hunters meant a lot
> to starving wives and bad painters.

James Welch is not a buckskin warrior in headdress, but a blue-jeaned, fiftyish man in horn-rimmed glasses with a definite writer's squint. He's not an AIMster gone Hollywood, a chief on the take, but a member of the Montana State Parole Board, a lifetime writer and sometime teacher, a husband. He's not a "holy man" or medicine person who can cure cancer, but a poet-novelist with a sharp eye for scams, a quick tongue in print, a heart that's been broken more than once by self-delusion, and a flint-rough mind to keep things as straight as possible, given the limitations all around.

> Let glory go the way of all sad things.
> Children need a myth that tells them be alive,
> forget the hair that made you Blood, the blood
> the buffalo left, once for meat, before
> other hunters gifted land with lead for hides.

Welch is not an axe-to-grind Indian, but a mature writer with a sense of honor, justice, and especially truth, even when it offends. This poet sings from the wounded heart of the bear. He's not an old-time oral tradition-alist, or a high modernist, but his own man with his own stories and voices and struggles to speak "straight ahead," as Dr. Williams said—neither trick-ster nor visionary, necro-romantic nor apocalyptic, eco-naturalist nor urban cynic—but a modern-day, mixed-blood Montana Blackfeet / Gros Ventre with things on his mind, back and forth, across the Buckskin Curtain.

> Comfortable we drink and string together stories
> of white buffalo, medicine men who promised
> and delivered horrible cures for hunger,
> lovely tales of war and white men massacres.

America's federal holidays, Thanksgiving, Christmas, and Easter, are not exactly traditional holy days for Sun-dancing Plains Indians. An ancient religious concept of *humilitas,* the power of sacrifice, underlies Native American traditions of questing for words, dreams, and images to live by. "Pity me, I want to live," the Sun Dancers, tethered to a tree of life, pray in flesh-piercing ceremonies akin to Christ's agony. Vision seekers cry to spirits, "Listen." The ritual loss of self leads to spiritual gain, as paradoxically, winter warms the blood, hunger sharpens the eye, and the lonely mountain top leads back to the people. Given these conditional reversals that humble true hunters, driven by necessity to survive, tribal peoples developed an old humility before elemental truths. In "Thanksgiving at Snake Butte," riders crest a holy mountain to find rock-scored petroglyphs:

> the smooth stones of our ancestors, the fish,
> the lizard, snake and bent-kneed
>
> bowman—etched by something crude,
> by a wandering race, driven by their names
> for time: its winds, its rain, its snow
> and the cold moon tugging at the crude figures
> in this, the season of their loss.

The old ones lived their lost names, hunted for their lives, imaged the needs of seasonal losses, and turned to the animals in themselves, hunter as hunted, less as more under a "snow-fat sky." Thanksgiving, then, cuts two ways: the positive ritual loss in the old seasonal ways, designed to meet necessity with strength through abstinence, and a more recent history of cultural loss after the first Algonkians, dialectal ancestors to Blackfeet speakers, gave Pilgrim thanks in 1621. "No one spoke of our good side, / those times we fed the hulking idiot," recalls the renegade who wants words, "mapped these plains with sticks / and flint."

So, too, Christmas comes to Moccasin Flat in a winter blizzard: "*warriors face down* in *wine sleep.* / *Winds cheat* to *pull heat* from *smoke.*" The spondaic rhymes are desperately buried beneath verse cadences. Charlie Blackbird, twenty unpassable miles from God and booze, long surviving "wet black things," stabs at his fire with crude flint. Out of luck and liquor, drunks suck radiator anti-freeze, tribal chiefs eat snow, and elk run wild in the high country. A twist-tobacco crone named Medicine Woman spits at her TV to predict the end-of-the-day news. She translates the Christian myth as a creation story, children begging explanation from her stale breath:

> Something about honor and passion,
> warriors back with meat and song,
> a peculiar evening star, quick vision of birth.
> Blackbird feeds his fire. Outside, a quick 30 below.

The Savior's birth and sacrifice mean something very old, very present to Sun Dance winos facedown in their own need, Indians awaiting commodity staples, children swallowing mother myths to keep them going, and lone men, freezing on Christmas Eve, named after blackbirds.

Stevens's snow man could spirit this tribe. Ghost Dancers across the

Great Plains joined hands in the late 1880s, danced in circles, and chanted Christ's native resurrection with the buffalo, until they fell down with visions, or at Wounded Knee, December 29, 1890, were butchered by cannon and bayonet:

> The whirlwind! The whirlwind!
> The new earth comes into being
>   swiftly as snow.
> The new earth comes into being
>   quietly as snow.

In "Dreaming Winter," the fallen Sun Dancer knows with Berryman's Henry and vaudeville clowns making handkerchief sandwiches, that "only hunger" drives him wild: "wobble me back to a tiger's dream," beside Stevens's drunken sailor spying "tigers in red weather." Where is that Tennessee jar now? "I could deny them in my first hard springtime," the poet leans on his reader, "but choose amazed to ride you down with hunger." So wake to sleep with Roethke's troubled quest, ironically belied by the Three Kings and Saint Peter's heavenly keys, of going where men have to go:

> Have mercy on me, Lord. Really. If I should die
> before I wake, take me to that place I just heard
> banging in my ears. Don't ask me. Let me join
> the other kings, the ones who trade their knives
> for a sack of keys. Let me open any door,
> stand winter still and drown in a common dream.

It's clear that Welch has read fallen modernist peers, Eliot to Plath and Berryman, and reciprocates tricks and visions. In "Legends Like This," he sees Easter as "three dark poets / dying in the sight of God." Why has America forsaken the Indian, Wright or Roethke might ask, never bothered to learn his true name? One renegade, resurrected on the northern plains, dreams with hostiles at Wounded Knee in 1973 to burn His church and hide out "for a long, long time."

"Earthboy calls me from my dream:" the title poem ends, "Dirt is where the dreams must end." This fragment opens the novel, *Winter in the Blood*, and etches a surreal credo—an end-stopping, anti-sentimental realism—as the cleansing ground sense of renewal. If hope is to have a modest chance, may it be in plain-style romance. Blackfeet creation myth speaks of Old Man, *Na'pi* the sun, wedded to Old Woman, *Kipi'taki* the moon, in a dialogic tragicomedy. Their marriage involves a contrary dialogue in making-things-up, creating humans as they are, as opposed to how a fool might like them (twenty-fingered, vertical-mouthed, pubic-navel immortals, Old Man wishes with first-choice, male priority, and he is rightfully put down by a more pragmatic Old Woman with her last-word, realistic finality). They gamble on mortality—a buffalo chip to float on the water, he says, a stone to sink, she says—and humans must die. So these two give birth to a daughter, who dies. "We have to change this," Moon-Mother pines; "we can't," Sun-Father sighs, "we fixed it."

Behind Earthboy's forty-acre fall, riding his quarter section of dirt, lingers a pastoral memory of the Judeo-Christian Old Man as Adam, or "red earth," and the cursed ground of Eden, dust to dust: "Earthboy: so simple his name / should ring a bell for sinners," the title poem opens. Earthboy has fallen down "dirty" as a creator-clown, cursing sky and land, Adamically surreal in expulsion:

> The dirt is dead. Gone to seed
> his rows become marker to a grave
> vast as anything but dirt.
> Bones should never tell a story
> to a bad beginner.

"Mistah Bones," as Berryman calls his death-clown, is the surreal archangel with a flaming sword east of Eden, under the "hooded bone" of Plath's Old Woman moon in her final poem, "Edge." Adam's son, Na'pi's descendant, refuses disillusionment and rejects false sentiment, reading the bones as resistant signs:

> I ride
> romantic to those words,
>
> those foolish claims that he
> was better than dirt, or rain
> that bleached his cabin
> white as bone. Scattered in the wind
> Earthboy calls me from my dream:
> Dirt is where the dreams must end.

Contemporary "blood to bison" and "desperate in my song," James Welch speaks with the voice of thunder "In My Lifetime." Na'pi created Adam as a fool in his own image, while Thunder gave the Blackfeet a medicine bundle to be opened with His first words in spring, along with voices to pray for rain on the Great American Desert:

> With thunder-
> hands his father shaped the dust, circled
> fire, tumbled up the wind to make a fool.
> Now the fool is dead. His bones go back
> so scarred in time, the buttes are young to look
> for signs that say a man could love his fate,
> that winter in the blood is one sad thing.

The poet drinks the wind of the sacred run after wild game, chants the thundered earth rhythms, drums the sky for rain, and translates breath into off-rhyme life.

> His songs—I don't explain. Desperate in my song,
> I run these woman hills, translate wind
> to mean a kind of life, the children of Speakthunder
> are never wrong and I am rhythm to strong medicine.

Welch bootlegs the running meters of thunder speaking, more heartbeat-stressed than Eliot's "DA" in a modernist wasteland, from ancient rites of passage into crafted metrics. The text is a native poet's vision quest, updated.

The myth of Icarus, Greek immigrant, appears as a sign out of context to a drunken Indian who envisions "his future falling" in "Two for the Festival." The inebriate poet comes stumbling on "awkward rhymes," as Grandpa went "stumble-bum down the Sunday street," cradling a blind toad and fingering "thirteen lumpy stones." The "all-face" toad in the old days was associated with a medicine man, whose coiled hair likened him to the horned toad; his sacred "buffalo stones" for hunting are now reduced to the surd thirteen, in coven with Stevens's blackbirds. All this medicine power—totems, beasts, myths, and chants—cannot prevent the fall of Icarus or the pitch of the Indian. Fox hugs his stones in fear. One more drink for the road, and the acculturated drunk lurches home, "dreaming winter" of stones, bones, and neolithic knives. "Bears are in the cabbage again," Lester Lame Bull hallucinates. "Elephants are whispering in backyards." The inebriate vision is surreally fixed, comically sad and stale, an old trickster trap, still lethal.

The last section of *Riding the Earthboy 40*, "The Day the Children Took Over," tempers the hand-to-hand spondees of the opening section, "Knives." It pulls back from the "renegade" bitters of the second part, and moves beyond the splintered image of the poet weaving styptic spider webs, old medicine for wounds, "to bandage up the day" in "Snow Country Weavers." With winter coursing in their blood, native kids redefine a season of cold beauty "in their own image" as a creative time of counterplay, while a cultural blizzard locks mothers, lovers, statesmen, and priests in the arms of White losses. So Old Man's mask shows up in the final poem, "Never Give a Bum an Even Break," borrowed from W. C. Fields. Welch's spring bundle of Earthboy riding chants opens in the "fall" of Indian time and closes drumming up a "comic rain" in spring.

Still hostile, but comically, the poet leaves whitebread mirrors and crouches with a fellow bum to blow up the acculturative bridge. Old scores must be settled—broken treaties, lands stolen by "a slouching dwarf with rainwater eyes," chronic poverty and despair, toxic commodities, co-opting acculturation, termination threats—and Indians look to their own alternatives. The "all-face" shamanic clown resurrects as contemporary shaman, warrior, and vision quester in a white freezing desert, chanting his bitters, laments, and contraries through poetic "masks / glittering in a comic rain."

FUTURIST HIP INDIAN: ALEXIE

Alexie is not writing the intellectualized masturbation that passes for so much of today's poetry. He is a singer, a shaman, a healer, a virtual Freddy Fender saying, "Hey baby, que paso? I thought I was your only *vato."*
ADRIAN C. LOUIS, FOREWORD TO *Old Shirts & New Skins*

But I haven't met an Indian writer out there who isn't arrogant—or a writer in general who isn't arrogant. . . . I don't pretend I'm not.
SHERMAN ALEXIE, *Indian Artist,* SPRING 1998

With Sherman Alexie, readers can throw formal questions out the smoke-hole (as in resistance to other modern verse innovators, Whitman, Williams, Sexton, or the Beats). Parodic antiformalism may account for some of Alexie's mass maverick appeal. This Indian gadfly jumps through all the hoops, sonnet, to villanelle, to heroic couplet, all tongue-in-cheeky. "I'm sorry, but I've met thousands of Indians," he told *Indian Artist* magazine, Spring 1998, "and I have yet to know of anyone who has stood on a mountain waiting for a sign." A reader enters the land of MTV and renascent AIM: a cartoon Pocahontas meets Beavis and Butt-head at the forest's edge, Sitting Bull takes on Arnold Schwarzenegger at Wounded Knee '73. The Last Real Indian has a few last words.

A stand-up comedian, the Indian improvisator *is* the performing text, obviating too close a textual reading: youngish man, six-foot-two or so, born in 1966 at the height of hippie nativism, from Wellpinit, Washington, now living in Seattle and taking the fin de siècle literary world by storm (an Indian Oscar Wilde?). After a century of benign neglect, Indian literature has hit an inflationary spiral with six-figure book deals and million-dollar movies. New York publishers have been humping this sassy, talk-back satirist as the last essentialist hold-out, a commercially successful Crazy Horse of mass marketing. The "most prodigious" Native American writer to date, Alexie told a Chicago *Sun* reporter asking about his brassy novel, *Indian Killer,* October 1996, to which the reporter queried, "Indian du jour?" Our young hero replied, "If so, it's been a very long day. How about Indian du decade?" Millennial Indian *extraordinaire?* The reporter raised the controversy over *Granta* naming Alexie one of the twenty "Best Young American Novelists" for *Reservation Blues* (not a novel), and Sherman snapped: "To say I was on the list because I'm an Indian is ridiculous: I'm one of the most critically respected writers in the country. So the *Granta* critics . . . essentially, fuck 'em" (October 31, 1996, *New City's Literary Supplement*). Starting with Native American writers, Alexie's competition includes no less than Allen, Erdrich, Harjo, Hogan, Momaday, Ortiz, Silko, TallMountain, Tapahonso, Welch, and Whiteman, among others (not to mention non-Indians like Toni Morrison, Norman Mailer, Cormac McCarthy, or Rita Dove). If "most critically respected" in a specific fictional genre of *Indian Killer* (thriller violence with racial undertones), his closest rivals are Tony Hillerman, Gerald Vizenor, Mickey Spillane, and Stephen King, an acknowledged model, John Steinbeck and the Brady Bunch tossed in. "He's young," says my elder brother back home, "he'll ripen, given time."

A breed Spokane and Coeur d'Alene, not just anybody, but thirteen-sixteenths *blood,* according to his poetry: "I write about the kind of Indian I am: kind of mixed up, kind of odd, not traditional. I'm a rez kid who's gone urban" *(Indian Artist).* What kind of an Indian is this?—a photogenic black mane of hair, dark-framed bifocal glasses, high-school class president, bookworm nose broken six times by bullies (he reminisces), English lit college degree from Eastern Washington State (after passing out as a pre-med student in his anatomy class, twice). His work is wizened with poetic anger, ribald love, and whipsaw humor. The crazy-heart bear is dancing comically, riding a wobbly unicycle, tossing overripe tomatoes at his audience. "This late in the 20th century," the poet says in *Red Blues,* "we still make the unknown ours by destroying it." His firecat imagination plays tricks on the reader, for our supposed good, for its own native delight and survival. "You almost / believe every Indian is an Indian," the poet swears to Marlon Brando.

Sherman: not so much a rhymer in the old sense, as a circus juggler who can eat apples, he says, while juggling. A college graduate who played basketball sixteen hours a day to keep from boozing with his cronies: Seymour chugging beer as a poet writes poetry (up to the last one that kills you) and Lester dead drunk in the convenience store dumpster. Alexie's sister and brother-in-law, passed out in a trailer, died by fire when a window curtain blew against a hot plate.

The boy mimed everyone in his family and still won't stop talking. "I was a divisive presence on the reservation when I was seven," he told an *LA Times* reporter, December 17, 1996. "I was a weird, eccentric, very arrogant little boy. The writing doesn't change anybody's opinion of me." Promoting his new movie, *Smoke Signals* (coproduced with Cheyenne-Arapaho director Chris Eyre), the writer describes himself today as "mouthy, opinionated and arrogant," a court jester's cross of Caliban, Groucho Marx, and Lear's Fool, but underneath, "I'm a sweetheart" (*Denver Post,* October 20, 1997). He's the best native example yet of Lewis Hyde's wiley hinge-maker, Trickster, the infant Prince of Thieves, Hermes stealing into Olympus to claim legitimacy: "Wandering aimlessly, stupider than the animals, he is at once the bungling host and the agile parasite; he has no way of his own but he is the Great Imitator who adopts the many ways of those around him. Unconstrained by instinct, he is the author of endlessly creative and novel deceptions, from hidden hooks to tracks that are impossible to read."

Artistic grist and ironic survival are inseparable in this verse, tracing a short lifetime of basketball (a team captain "ball hog" in high school), beer, TV, rez cars falling apart, pony dreams, fetal alcohol syndrome (FAS) babies, and fancy-dancing drunks. "You call it genocide; I call it economics," Custer snorts. A warm-up for fiction and the movies, poetics are wrapped up in the politics of native poverty, torqued metrics, and ethnic protest: dime store Indi'n princesses and back-alley vision questers, 7–11 heroes and Vietnam vets, Marlon Brando and Crazy Horse. No insurance CEO or village doctor, Alexie has the near fatal, comic bravado of surviving an everyday rez, where every day is a blow to the stomach and a blaze of understanding. Being Indian means you're hanging on for dear life, hanging in there with catastrophic humor, kicking back at sunset, staggering through the '49 to dawn, laughing your ass off and on again (the short fiction says), and accepting that bottom line of your neighbor's butt next to you, misplaced, displaced, re-relocated into the present Red reality, so real that it hurts. So unreal in its hurtful beauty, so surreal that it makes you blink and smile to see another dawn. *"How do you explain the survival of all of us who were never meant to survive?"* It's a long walk from Sitting Bull bearing "hard times" to Charlie Blackbird "surviving." Alexie takes to Internet chat rooms for essential defenses of native sovereignty and intercultural access to America's power structures, particularly publishing and the movies.

So, from Momaday's visionary form, through Welch's shamanic rhythm, here's a surreal trickster savage in two-dimensional poetic cartoon. Rather than close reading or parsing the lines, his work elicits charged reaction, critical gut response, positive or negative argument. Reading Alexie's work triggers a recoil from the shock of Indian reality, like looking into the Sun Dance sun, going blind, and slowly regaining sight, stars and blackspots and sunbursts floating across the field of perception, so you know it's *your* perception, anyway, at last, of reality: *"whiskey salmon absence,"* the poem "Citizen Kane" ends. Firewater, relocation, vanishing American. The images, concretely charged as Pound's Vorticist objects, are loaded in disconnections: the poison where food swarms, desperate homing, the absence that starves Indians to death. "Rosebud" is not a child's movie sled but a desperately poor Sioux reservation in the Dakotas.

"But, I mean, I really love movies. I always have," Alexie said in "Making Smoke" (*Aboriginal Voices* May–June 1998). "I love movies more than I love books, and believe me, I love books more than I love every human being, except the dozen or so people in my life who love movies and books just as much as I do." His favorite films are *Midnight Cowboy, The Graduate,* and *Aliens.* The writer goes on, "I mean, screenplays are more like poetry than like fiction. Screenplays rely on imagery to carry the narrative, rather than the other way around. And screenplays have form. Like sonnets, actually. Just as there's [*sic*] expectations of form, meter, and rhyme in a sonnet, there are the same kinds of expectations for screenplays." There are two dimensions in Alexie's work, screenplay to verse, often no more than two characters in the short fiction, *The Lone Ranger and Tonto Fistfight in Heaven.* His work is mostly minimalist drama, back to the first Greek plays, *alazon* to *eiron,* dreamer to realist, fool to cynic. Toss in commedia dell'arte, Punch and Judy, Laurel and Hardy, Amos and Andy, Lewis and Martin, Red Ryder and Little Beaver. The embedded third dimension of this post-holocaustal comedy is cultural landscape, for lack of a better term, devastated native homestead. So a third character might be salvage-surrealist, Old Man absent and implied, as with Welch's winter-in-the-blood Na'pi. The third-dimensional axis then is Indi'n humor, a vanishing point of survival in the canvas of a hidden spirit world, including Trickster mimics, all around and behind us. Alexie takes Welch's foxy shaman a skitter-step forward to tease Mary Austin: "Sweetheart, history / doesn't always look like horses."

Poetry comes on not so much a text as a comic ruse, a razored one-liner, a reader's riff to wake up America. The world is Indian as a coyote magician who makes every ordinary day a trick of survival, a vanishing act, a raw joke. A reader's breath catches in the throat and comes out laughing strange, still . . . a breath it is, of life. It gets you going, brothers and sisters, a buzzing, rattling, weeping, yipping imagination. Cry so hard you begin to laugh: run so fast you lap your shadow: dream so hard you can't sleep: think so hard you startle awake like a child. "Maia gave birth to a wily boy," the Homeric hymn begins, "flattering and cunning, a robber and cattle thief, a bringer of dreams, awake all night, waiting by the gates of the city— Hermes, who was soon to earn himself quite a reputation among the gods, who do not die." Crossing Ginsberg with Creeley, Hughes's Crow with Berryman's Mistah Bones, Alexie brews a homeboy devil's own humor. The voice makes junkyard poetry out of broke-down reality, vision out of delirium tremens, prayer out of laughter. "When my father first smiled," the poet recalls, "it scared the shit out of me."

Look back at "Seattle, 1987" (appendix to chapter three), an early Alexie poem, first published in *The Jacaranda Review* and tracked to *Old Shirts & New Skins.* It sets up in triads, with one-line answering interstices, but the rhymes are lame (century / lake / it) and the rhythms scattered, three to seven beats. The poet sounds mysteries "beneath" a lake at the century's end: "drowned horses snapping turtles cities of protected bones." The gaps between the old horse-culture icons (*sunka wakan*, the Lakota called horses, "holy" or "super dog"), toothy denizens, and tribal runes space the poem across the page, as a "camera trick" jump-starts the sun on cable TV. "How the heart changes," the poet laments urban strangers, made without totemic "song." No dance, no song, Pound said, no poem. No tradition carries, no metaphor steadies, no structure holds, no tribal village binds. Instead, a clumsy magician gets a dollar bill in his top hat: the poet falls in love with street trickster failure and confesses, à la James Wright's "wasted" life, "There are so many illusions I need to believe." The tone is flat, failed romantic, a touch sardonic, beat. This young Indian is holding out for vision, needing to believe, tricked by MTV and sidewalk magic, laughing up his sleeve. His is more performance than poem, more attitude than art, more schtick than aesthetic. Definitely talented, deeply impassioned, hyphenated American-Indian, but to what end?

Indi'n vaudeville, then, stand-up comedy on the edge of despair. A late-twentieth-century, quasi-visionary clown tells the truth that hurts and heals in one-liners cheesy as the Marx Brothers, trenchant as Lenny Bruce, tricky as Charlie Hill's BIA Halloween "Trick or Treaty." The stand-up poet marvels in dismay, "Imagine Coyote accepts / the Oscar for lifetime achievement." There's an old trickster-teacher role here in a young Indian's hands—jokes draw the line, cut to the quick, sling the bull, open the talk. "White Men Can't Drum," Alexie announced in *Esquire Magazine*, October 1992, roasting the new-age men's movement, all the Wannabe fuss and fustian.

"How do you explain the survival of all of us who were never meant to survive?" asks the verse straight man.

"There is nothing we cannot survive," the poet swears.

Surviving war is the premise. In *The Summer of Black Widows* (1996), Alexie's sixth poetry collection in as many years (composing by computer), "Father and Farther" (also performed on the rock cassette, *Reservation Blues*) recalls a drunken basketball coach and a losing team. "Listen," his father slurs, "I was a paratrooper in the war."

"Which war?" the boy-poet asks.

"All of them," he said. Quincentennial facts: Native Americans as a composite are the only in-country ethnic group that the U.S. has declared war against, 1860–1890. Some existing 560 reservations, 315 in the lower forty-eight states, are natively seen from inside as occupied POW camps. Think of it as the delayed stress of contemporary Indian America: the post-traumatic shock of surviving Columbus to Cotton Mather, Buffalo Bill Cody to Andy Jackson, Chivington to Custer. "Goddamn," the general says, again and again, "saber is a beautiful word," in ironic cut against Auden's penchant for "scissors." World War I Indian volunteers, as cited, gained Native Americans dual citizenship in 1924. Code Talkers in World War II made natives national heroes. Korea, Vietnam, and Desert Storm's chemical poisoning brought tribal veterans into millennial terror.

In 1993, the UCLA American Indian Studies Center published *Old Shirts & New Skins* as no. 9 in the Native American Poetry Series. Old shirts, not stuffed new suits: new 'skins, Redskins reborn, sloughing "old" skins. There are always two sides to things, bicultural ironies to new-age lies, & the "blessed ampersand," hip shorthand to a coded new tongue, the with-it Indi'n poet. There's no text "set" here as such, but more a radical riff, something spilled over, a virus, a toxin released, a metastasizing anger. It's a "reservation of my mind," the poet says. The opening epithet equates, "Anger x Imagination = poetry," in the amplitude & invention of the angry young Indian. One shot short of death, Seymour says, drink as you write free verse, no matter if "our failures are spectacular." Maverick Trixter talks back, makes a different kind of poetry for people with differences: "it was not written for the white literary establishment," Adrian Louis says in the foreword to *Old Skins & New Shirts*.

A double buckskin language frays the edges of bicultural America, questions the multiple meanings of reservation, red, risk, Cody & Crazy Horse, Marlon Brando & John Wayne, Christ & Custer, who *died for your sins*. The critic is left with notes to bumper-sticker poetics, insult & antagonism, the fractious come-hither. Poetry as disruptive tease, a sideshow of historical truth & poetic hyperbole. Or, to borrow from the social sciences, "privileged license": tribal teasing tests boundaries, deepens resilience, insures survival, bets on renewal. Not without the warrior history of Old English insults, *flytyngs*, hurled across a river a thousand years ago in "The Battle of Maldon." LA South Central Blacks doin' the dozens, *Yer granmother wears combat boots!* The Last Poets in Harlem chant, *Niggers like to fuck each other.* . . . El Paso Hispanics drive *slow 'n low riders*. Inventories of abuses, imagined & otherwise: hunger of imagination, poverty of memory, toxicity of history, all in the face of cultural genocide and racial misrepresentation and outright extermination, to challenge musty stereotypes of vanishing, savage, stoic, silent, shamanic, stuperous Indians. Poetry is never bread enough & doesn't pay the bills, "damned from beginning to end," Williams says. Who could quibble aesthetics in this setting?

money is free if you're poor enough

Are there any connections with canonical American poetry? Start with Langston Hughes's essentialist pride in the Harlem Renaissance, "I, too, sing America," not just Walt Whitman fingering leaves of grass, or Carl Sandburg shouldering Chicago. Allen Ginsberg howled his native place in the 1950s: the marginalized, dispossessed, discriminated, hipster, homosexual, Jewish, offbeat antihero. It's an old revolutionary American motif, the lost found, the last first, the underdog bites back. Sylvia Plath's rage and exhibitionist daring to die for us as Lady Lazarus: "Out of the ash / I rise with my red hair / And I eat men like air." Ted Roethke's lost-son, lyric blues: "Thrum-thrum, who can be equal to ease? / I've seen my father's face before / Deep in the belly of a thing to be." John Berryman's brilliant mad comic pain: *"These songs were not meant to be understood, you understand, / They were meant to terrify & comfort. / Lilac was found in his hand."*

A kind of Indian antipoetry breaks form at the millennial end. Alexie pushes against formalist assumptions of what poetry ought to be, knocks down aesthetic barriers set up in xenophobic academic corridors, and rebounds as cultural performance. He can play technique with mock sonnet, breezy villanelle, unheroic couplet, tinkling tercet, quaky quatrain in any-beat lines. The rhymer trades on surreal images and throwaway metaphors in a drunken villanelle: *Trail of Tears . . . trail of beers.* The rush of his poems is an energy released, stampeding horses, raging fires, stomping shoes: the poet as fast & loose sharpster in accretive repetition. Alexie likes catalogues, anaphoral first-word repetitions, the accumulative power of oral traditions. There is something freeing about all this—free to imagine, to improvise, to make things up, to wonder, to rage on. Sharpening wits on quick wit, his poetry runs free of restrictive ideas about Indians, poems, ponies, movies, shoes, dreams, dumpsters, reservations, angers, losses. His lines break free of precious *art* . . . but free for what, that matters? Do we care? the hard questions come tumbling. Do we remember, or listen closely, or think carefully, or wonder fully, or regard deeply enough?

Readers certainly learn about New Rez Indi'ns who shoot hoop, stroke pool, fancy dance, drink beer, snag girls, hustle, hitch, rap, joke, cry, rhyme, dream, write everything down. These Computer *Rad* 'Skins write verse that does not stay contained in formal repose: does not pull away, or shimmer in the night sky, or intimidate the common reader, but comes on full as a poetry that begs visceral response. Often cartoonish, a gag, a point-of-view gimmick, more "like" *Virtual Indian.* "There is no possible way to sell your soul" for poetry, Alexie said in LA (December 17, 1996), "because nobody's offering. The devil doesn't care about poetry. No one wants to make a movie out of a poem." This trickster has made one movie, as mentioned, and cast another from *Indian Killer.*

Call it a reactive aesthetics, kinetic pop art, protest poetics to involve and challenge late-century readers—cajoled, battered, insulted, entertained, humored, angered to respond. A poetry that gets us up off our easy chairs. Tribal jive, that is, streetsmart, populist, ethnocentric, edged, opinionated, disturbed, fired up as reservation graffiti, à la John Trudell's Venice, California, rock lyrics, a Cherokee-breed Elvis as "Baby Boom Che." Alexie joins the brash, frontier braggadocio of westering America, already out west a long time, ironically, a tradition in itself, shared with Whitman, Lawrence, Stein, Mailer, Kesey, Kerouac, Ginsberg, Vonnegut, Bellow, Heinemann,

Mamet. Huckster, con man, carny barker, stand-up comedian, Will Rogers to Jonathan Winters, Cheech & Chong to Charlie Hill. The impudence of the anti-poetic Red Rapster, daring us not to call this poetry. "I'm not a rapper," Russell Means crows of his punk album, *Electric Warrior*, "I'm a Rapaho!"

"You'll almost / believe every Indian is an Indian," Alexie carries on. *Frybread . . . Snakes . . . Forgiveness*

III

TRIBAL SIBYLS

§(•)≩

NINE

Blood Sisters

As tribal men were moving from reserved warriors and ceremonial "word-senders" to postwar healers and tribal leaders (then further parting the Buckskin Curtain as prize-winning writers, professors, Nobel nominees, and moviemakers today), where were native women? The second half of our century has witnessed the acceleration of freedoms in Affirmative Action, much debated of late. The emancipation of women, receiving the vote just three years before American Indians in 1924, compounds ethnic liberation with gender revolution. Among all peoples of color, First Americans (as Canadians refer to Natives) come forward to speak their minds and image their dreams. Women stand in the front lines. Their "reservations" and aspirations signal a double liberation, uniquely original, of both ethnicity and gender.

> Later generations could look back and perceive that there had existed, in the beginning, a possibility of assimilation, acculturation, integration — as symbolized by Pocahontas and the English captain [John Smith] — a possible alternative to dispossession and genocide.
>
> FRANCES MOSSIKER, *Pocahontas*

In the 1890s, as the frontier closed on reserved Indians, Mary Austin married and moved to Inyo, California, along the eastern Sierra slopes of the Mojave Desert. Here she suffered a passionless marriage, bore a sickly child, and struggled to rebirth her *native* self at the century's end. "As for the other things that came to me by way of my Indian acquaintances," Austin records in *Earth Horizon*, "they are the gifts of a special grace which has been mine from the beginning, the persistence in me, perhaps, of an uncorrupted strain of ancestral primitivism, a single isolated gene of that far-off and slightly mythical Indian ancestor. . . ." If this sounds all too mystically *wannabe*, recall that the reservation system had just bottomed from the Indian Wars, 1860–1890, and the Wounded Knee Massacre was soaking into the Dakota landscape. Across the Western Sierra foothills, Ishi was living alone in a cave. "In the common esteem, not only are the only good aboriginals dead ones," Austin knew firsthand in the redneck California foothills, "but all aboriginals are either sacred or contemptible according to the length of time they have been dead" (*The American Rhythm*).

This young woman bucked frontier Indian-bashing, gold-rush violence, and artistic skepticism. Against racial and cultural xenophobia rampant in her day, no less than Jaime de Angulo or Washington Matthews, Austin cast her lot with a militarily conquered, culturally maligned, and materially destitute people stigmatized as "vanishing." She knew better: Austin nativized her life toward the "deep heart's core" of intercultural America, as Yeats wrote of his own acculturated Ireland in 1890, by way of tribal history and culture. American rhythms brought our writers home to the land, and early rerootings flowered into our century. "Once in his life," Momaday would weigh in two generations later, "a man ought to concentrate his mind upon the remembered earth, I believe":

> He ought to give himself up to a particular landscape in his experience, to look at it from as many angles as he can, to wonder about it, to dwell upon it. He ought to imagine that he touches it with his hands at every season and listens to the sounds that are made upon it. He ought to imagine the creatures there and all the faintest motions of the wind. He ought to recollect the glare of noon and all the colors of the dawn and dusk. (*The Way to Rainy Mountain*)

From Southwest horizon note to Momaday's lyrics today, Austin hears *the remembered earth*, a writer's natural presence rooted in American landscape. Whether prescient, or just precocious and fed up with frontier Anglophilic obtuseness, she turned to more ancient American myths in the matrifocal bedrock—to heal personal heartaches and to nativize her cultural bearings.

Bedridden and breast-dry in the late nineteenth century, a young mother Mary converted to tribal America, another White pilgrim gone over the palisade. Her daughter's Paiute wet-nurse opened the taproot of "ancestral primitivism," self-described in the third person of *Earth Horizon:*

> That winter, when she lay sick in bed day after day with no help but the uncertain visits of Indian women, she grew gradually aware, by the way the child throve, that the *mahala* [Indian woman] was nursing it along with her own beady-eyed, brown dumpling. Mary roused herself sufficiently to have the Doctor see the Paiute woman to make sure that they ran no danger, and for the rest, since the mahala was shy about her service, accepted it gratefully in silence. Two or three years later, because Mary's child was not talking as early as it should, that mahala came all the way to Lone Pine to bring her dried meadowlarks' tongues, which make the speech nimble and quick.

It was in experiences such as this that Mary began genuinely to know Indians. There was a small campody up George's Creek, brown wickiups in the chaparral like wasps' nests. Mary would see the women moving across the mesa on pleasant days, digging wild hyacinth roots, seed-gathering, and, as her strength permitted, would often join them, absorbing women's lore, plants good to be eaten or for medicine, learning to make snares of long, strong hair for the quail, how with one hand to flip trout, heavy with spawn, out from under the soddy banks of summer runnels, how and when to gather willows and cedar roots for basket-making. It was in this fashion that she began to learn that to get at the meaning of work you must make all its motions, both of body and mind.

Renativized, Mary Austin gathered up her life, eventually divorced her non-directional husband, and found, through conversations with native healers and William James (Henry's brother) in a San Francisco hospital, "that the true Middle of my search was in myself." She heard tribal elders summon "a wind out of your own past," keening toward a native pantheism.

Just so in the East, Doctor Bill Williams, respecting the tribalized Boone and Houston as acculturated warrior-husbands, honored a *native savagery* across immigrant and rooted cultures: "he saw and only he saw the prototype of it all, the native savage," Williams wrote of Daniel Boone *(In the American Grain)*. Mary Austin, in turn, felt "the ancestral motions of consciousness on its way to wider consciousness," a fusion of the new medical psychology and older aboriginal ways. "What I got out of William James and the Medicine-Man was a continuing experience of wholeness, a power to expand the least premonitory shiver along the edge of primitive apprehension" *(Earth Horizon)*. Her quest in the New World, as with all émigré estrangement, was to relocate her own in-depth being naturally, to come home in America. In end-of-the-century terms, Austin got down to the "ground sense necessary" of Native America and spiritually raised herself up again. It was her personal renaissance as recreative midwife between tribal and self-help Western ways.

"Neither wife nor widow," this emancipated, turn-of-the-century woman went back to champion American nativism for East Coast modernists, from *Poetry* magazine and the *Nation* to *Bookman* and *The Dial*, writing some thirty books and giving hundreds of lectures. After twelve years of storming New York literary circles, Mary Austin was feted at the National Arts Club, January 8, 1922, a dinner attended by the publishing elite, including Hamlin Garland, Carl Van Doren, and Witter Bynner, D. H. Lawrence's Southwest friend and president of the Poetry Society of America. She spoke on "American Literature as an Expression of the American Experience," and from these remarks later developed *The American Rhythm*.

Austin campaigned across the country for teaching "Amerind" poetry in the public schools. Staying during the 1920s in Los Gallos, Mabel Dodge

Luhan's house, Austin collaborated with her younger protégé, Ansel Adams, about Tewa matriarchy in *Taos Pueblo* (1930). In the "freeflung mountains, untrimmed forests," Austin felt "the joy of the wide, unrutted earth." She sought out the pulses of an American rhythm, crossing the country as a young woman—physically to walk, stride, canter, gallop, and ride, whether on feet, horseback, overland stage, or eighteen-mule borax team across landscaped "ripples of energy." Here, no less than Williams's variable foot, Austin conceived of "the landscape line" in poetics, "the nature of the ground traversed." She felt this horizon note bodily in native rhythms and rendered it physically in heartbeat metrics. Back East, her doctor compatriot held his New Jersey ground among the modernists:

> I am not,
>   I know,
>   in the galaxy of poets
>   a rose
>   but *who,* among the rest,
>   will deny me
>   my place?

Williams sensed a native poetics that coursed in aural cadence, clustered syntax, and organic sequence, moving locally through a given landscape and language. The good doctor's Others were listening to Austin. "No, we are not Indians but we are men of their world," Williams wrote in the American grain of the early twenties. "The blood means nothing; the spirit, the ghost of the land moves in the blood, moves the blood." From here spiritually, Williams tracked back to Kentucky's Daniel Boone, "the foremost pioneer and frontiersman of his day," and the Americanization of Adam in an "orchidean" New World. "To Boone the Indian was his greatest master. Not for himself surely to be an Indian, though they eagerly sought to adopt him into their tribes, but the reverse: to be *himself* in a new world, Indianlike." To learn from those gone before and take his place among them, grounded in the New World: "the native savage" was the new Adamic American.

Eve was his equal. Austin's public role as a tribal feminist early in the century, her insistence on the "native note" in American verse—resonant with her eco-textual sense of landscape and regional culture ("its skyey influences, its floods, forests, morning colors")—position her as godmother to a Native American poetics. She was close friends with Jack London and Sinclair Lewis, Elsie Clews Parsons and Frances Densmore, Mabel Dodge Luhan, Willa Cather, and John Collier, commissioner of Indian Affairs. In company with native women writers such as Gertrude Bonin (*Zitkala-Sa*), Ella Deloria, and Mourning Dove, Austin helped to midwife the organic surge in American literary studies—beyond Cooper's romances

and Longfellow's polyglot Hiawatha, extending Thoreau's unfinished mag-
num opus on Northeast native cultures and Lawrence's rediscovery of
Southwest Indians. In the spirit of Williams back East, doctoring the native
genius of America, out west Mary Austin would take literature from the
nervous hands of an Anglophilic academy and give it back to the American
people in their own dialects of local knowledge. Over the course of the
century, Winters, Hugo, Ginsberg, Snyder, Creeley, Rothenberg, Norman,
and Swann followed collaborative suit with "recreative" tribal poetics.

"We all of us come out of school with our heads canted over one shoul-
der," Austin wrote in *The American Rhythm,* at some lost "trail" patrifocally
cast by "shadow-pictures." Williams worked all his life to step freely west-
ward into America, away from a Puritan British patriarchy. Frost underlined
the point in verse recited at John Kennedy's 1961 inauguration: "The land
was ours before we were the land's." In the face of dissident skepticism on
both sides of the Buckskin Curtain, redneck racism to tribal essentialists,
Austin turned to a native poetics out of respect and need, loosening the
reins of blue-eyed canonical liturgy, from across the Big Water to "talking
leaves" at home. "We walk around and we wonder," the poet Roberta Hill
Whiteman said to Joseph Bruchac, "where do these thoughts come from?"
She remembered Lance Henson telling her, "They come from your feet.
When you're walking on the earth they come up through your feet." White-
man continued, "Up, up, up into your head. And women, you know, in
Oneida culture, in the traditional culture, have this close connection be-
tween their feet and the earth. This idea of being close to the earth. When
you dance, you know, you're close to the earth. You don't jump around,
you massage the earth. And I like to think of that connection, that the earth
is telling us things" *(Survival This Way).*

Austin lived among Native Americans, traveled the continent stirring
up interest in their deep-rooted cultures, and translated their songs and
stories into contemporary forms ("the many thousand-year-old culture of
the race that we displaced"). She knew firsthand the matriarchal power
of native women. This woman, thrall to none, advocated the native spirit
of our common America, the rhythms in our new land, mothered since
time immemorial by matrilocal tribal cultures, fathered by the big sky. In
so doing, Mary Austin and other ethnographic feminist advocates of her
time—Alice Corbin Henderson, Elsie Clews Parsons, Ruth Benedict, Al-
ice Fletcher, Natalie Curtis, Gertrude Kurath, Ruth Bunzel, Frances Dens-
more, Ella Deloria, Dorothy Dematracapoulou—made way for a genera-
tion of American Indian writers by the century's end, especially the
women, doubly empowered through feminine and ethnic ground swells,
so clearly in resurgence today. Listen closely. With the power of mother
bear hearts singing, these voices carry millennia of matrifocal native views
into the next century.

ATHAPASKAN ÉMIGRÉ: TALLMOUNTAIN

Mary Randle TallMountain was born "a hugger mugger meld" of Atha-paskan / Russian-Irish lineage in the last year of the Great War, one hun-dred miles south of the Arctic Circle and two hundred west of Fairbanks, Alaska. On a clear day the five-year-old child could see Siberia from Nulato. Mary TallMountain could have been an adoptive half-sister to Mary Austin's infant Ruth, suckling from a Paiute wet-nurse, while the women gathered sedge roots in the eastern Sierras. TallMountain remembers "pure, won-derful snow" by Mukluk Creek and the Yukon River going by "incessantly": "I see myself a tot beside the mystical Yukon River—she who centered my mindset early, who colored the lives of all my Indian forebears, that river remote, stately, mischievous, illogical, and rowdy, whose beauty coils unforgettable in the seedbed of my mind." Her unmarried Anglo father absent, her Koyukon mother contracting fatal tuberculosis, Mary was "adopted out" at the age of six, psychically torn from her native family. Fifty years passed before she could return. At that half-century remove in the 1970s, the cabins were still moss-covered, reindeer antlers tied to the eaves, a boardwalk leading through the village.

In the early seventies, Paula Gunn Allen found the renamed Mary Ran-dle working as a secretary in San Francisco, drying out from a grievous half-life of alcoholism. Mary took a paragraph about her Athapaskan brother's retreating footsteps to Allen, then a professor of Native American Studies at San Francisco State. The teacher went out for doughnuts and came back crying. "What are you going to do about it?" Mary asked this Laguna woman. "I'll tutor you," the Indian literary professor replied.

A mixed-blood, writerly adoption clicked into place. For one and a half years, Mary wrote sixteen hours a day on a Selectric typewriter that became her "altar." Each Tuesday she brought Paula work for feedback, word-by-word retrieving a gifted childhood through elder rewakening. "Over the years I've known her," Paula Allen introduces *The Light on the Tent Wall: A Bridging* (Native American Series no. 8, UCLA 1990), "Mary has been close to death several times."

> She's always in the hospital, or just coming home. She's always breaking some-thing, or repairing something. Her heart is always breaking. Her eyes are huge now, magnified into great almonds as her sight fades from looking into the misted distances for so long. She goes on and on. Like her poems, like her people, like her city, like her faith, like her earth, she continues, facing and besting unconscionable odds. She's always dying, and always keeping on.
>
> Who is this woman, this survivor, this half-breed, this poet, this friend? If you know the land of her origins and the cadences of the People, if you recall the rhythm of Roman liturgy, the solemnity of the Mass, if you read this

collection with care, hearing the eerie, powerful silences that surround the words, you will know who she is, what extinction is, and what survival engenders.

With pointillist country diction and rattling tree-branch rhythms, Mary's voice could sweeten the pit of winter. She writes in river rhythms and the steady shushing stride of snow-walkers, easy-boned natives, storytellers naturally cadenced in Frost's "talk-song" meters. Hers is not the quicksilver insight, but a narrative lyric, prosaically coming on, no jammed or enjambed line breaks. TallMountain's word gathering stands free-winded, like her mother's tuberculosis platform, built by a sister outside their Alaskan cabin window, "where she could breathe fresh air."

After seventy-six years of passionate living, Mary died September 2, 1994, in Petaluma, California. She survived much grief and passion, many insights and illnesses, little money or recognition in her own time. The TallMountain Circle, sponsored by the Tenderloin Reflection and Education Center in San Francisco, keeps this singular woman's spirit alive, through her writings and the works of those following her. In addition to a complete bibliography of her writings, they have reissued *A Quick Brush of Wings* (1991), *Listen to the Night: Poems for the Animal Spirits of Mother Earth* (1995), *haiku & other poetic forms* (1996, edited by Kitty Costello, Mary TallMountain's literary executor), *Goddesses We Ain't!: Tenderloin Women Writers* (1992), and *Celebrating Mary TallMountain: A Memorial Tribute* (1995).

Mary counterpoints loss with come-on lyrical lilts. This self-taught writer senses where her native cadences course, when the currents run deep, where the accents trip off the consonants and the good bones lie heavy with meat.

> By the fires that night
> we feasted
> The Old Ones clucked,
> sucking and smacking,
> sopping the juices with sourdough bread.
> The grease would warm us
> when hungry winter howled.
>
> Grease was beautiful—
> oozing, dripping and running down our
> chins,
> brown hands shining with grease.
> We talk of it
> when we see each other
> far from home.
>
> Remember the marrow
> sweet in the bones?

The controlling motif is a long homecoming, "Koyukons Heading Home."
Never more than two years in any one job or dwelling, for over three-
quarters of a century TallMountain carried a native trust that would not
quit or submit, a Franciscan grit, a catholic *ab*original faith. Mary believed
in a tent filled with women. A steady image, a beacon for over half a century,
shone through suburban California and the San Francisco Tenderloin,
both inside and outside—a light through her mother's abdomen, an image
of her native silhouette as *a light on the tent wall.*

> in
> the Eddy Street ghetto—
> Union Square—
> the mission barrios—
> any place where the Third World gather

Even the hop pickers' field canvas in the California thirties Depression
translucently kept her coming home with the poor, the dispossessed, the
hungry, and the hopeful, all the land over. As with Austin's self-narration,
Mary TallMountain fictionalizes herself:

> She shut her eyes tightly, remembering the way supper fires guttered and
> gleamed on those summer nights outside the open tents where the hop pick-
> ers stayed, the murmuring voices of Indian women preparing food at small
> rusted stoves, the warped pipes curling smoke away into the blue-black sky;
> and the women's shadows stirring with a kind of grandness on the tent walls.
> From a gambling tent Pa had pointed out to her, she heard laughter and the
> slap of cards.

This tentflap image kept on going for half a century, kept TallMountain
going through all her struggles to hold her Koyukon head high in winter-
white America, still "white as last winter's ptarmigans."

> He don't talk right, don't
> Know when to sit down, get up.
> He make too much talk talk.
> *Gisakk* come, he go.

In the broken eloquence of native voices, under the weight of an oppres-
sor's tongue, her adoptive White culture comes, and goes, as native women
see and say it, through labor-intensive transition and the acculturative
limbo of translation. Mary's male siblings are missing, including Brother
Wolverine, the intractable trickster blood-brother, whose captive fur
warmed an orphan child, distant and alone, in an all-white winter:

> *snaa',*
> I miss you
> when the children shout

> down by the slough and
> when I see leaves of *k'eey*
> dance in the white wind

She dreams of lynx-trimmed mukluks on her lost brother, Bernie, *"Soogha* eldest brother I never knew," and imagines her cross-blooded parents as "My Wild Birds Flying."

TallMountain relearned her adoptive and native languages, with a Koyukon glossary of forty-nine terms in *The Light on the Tent Wall*—the dual-tongued systems of accommodation, love, and loss, on either side. As an elder in her seventies, the poet looked back:

> serene I sip
> chamomile tea from
> English bone china
> yet by strange legerdemain
> of mind I feel
> drumbeats somewhere
> passing

What did she truly remember, from being six in Nulato, or dream more than half a century later, or creatively make up, in free verse and short story? TallMountain dedicated "Continuum III," a series of linked poems, to her verse mentor, Paula Gunn Allen; two raggedy, ecstatic, Sapphic feminists connect as grandmother poets:

> Last night you read poems
> about trumpet vines and tamarack
> in Laguna Pueblo—
> a purple dawn twenty years ago.
> I know.
> There's a place in my mind
> filled with sea wind,
> deep in Oregon dogwood, lupine,
> freckled with wild strawberries.

Mary's rhymes gently reassure, her lines chart the distances come, the distance to go, for herself and love of a "Marked Man," all men somehow branded to be taken or go away:

> It's far, there to here,
> Counted by insolent freeways,
> Marching mountains,
> Alkali pale under a miner's moon,
> Beautiful and terrible.
> Indians must go everywhere.

Her people, wherever they are, or may go with "last night's rotgut / whiskey throats," call out in the easy, singsong meters of wandering Athapaskan

tribes: "WAIT! I'M GOIN' WITH YOU / LEAVIN' THE GALLUP BLUES."
Just as surely as the sun rises, or winter turns to spring, "I *think* you'll *come
again* / to*night, Hoho*kam *In*dian *man*," TallMountain sings the soft true
rhymes of reverse balladry, in 3/4 measured couplet, no less than Emily
Dickinson's hymnal verse.

Mary enjoyed herself among people, clearly, after seventy years a new-
found focus and status as native elder with words for the younger. With
Athapaskan features she gave grandmotherly readings—plucked eyebrows,
coquettish lashes, and short-cut, grey-flecked hair. The poet wore plastic-
rimmed glasses, framing wide-open brown eyes, and dark, single-bead ear-
rings. She drawled her vowels, almost cowboy-fashion, the leftover dialect
of long night talks through spirits and smoke.

Mary would characteristically giggle and cover her mouth through bursts
of wellspring laughter. There was a hilarity deep down inside, province of
the wolf and wolverine, the fanged trickster warriors who saw her through
terrible losses—a childhood untimely ripped from the Yukon, her mother's
tragedy from tuberculosis, her brothers' deaths from the same (she never
saw a second brother in another village). Her father disappeared for sixty
years until she found him in Phoenix. Renamed Lois on the "Outside,"
along the West Coast in Atascadero, Mary-Lois grew up estranged from
herself. She was torn apart again by the financial ruin and death of her
adoptive physician father, raising chickens unsuccessfully when she was a
teenager in the Depression. Her adoptive mother committed suicide not
long after. Lois Randle drifted into joblessness and hardscrabble times and
finally tried legal secretarial work to stabilize her life. She fought battles
with depression and broken hearts and alcoholism, two bouts with cancer,
a quadruple heart bypass in her seventies . . . from which she awoke laugh-
ing, the doctors told her. "In her way TallMountain is Coyote," Allen
writes, "and like that quintessential old survivor, she knows that if you're
going to face death, and if you're going to engage the sacred, you'd better
have your sense of humor intact."

That cackling wolverine won't shut up, the wolf can't die. Mary had too
much to tell her cat, Emily Dickinson, about "good" grease and other things,
about humor and survival, about "positivity" in the face of devastation,
about having a good heart in a tough world. She knew accepting, caring, for-
giving, and putting up with all of us in a wilderness of losses, a traffic-rushing
darkness of metal and eight-to-five dungeon of concrete. Mary learned the
simplest and most difficult of wisdoms, how to take each breath with joy, with
care, with appreciation, a twinkle in her olive-brown eyes and an irrepressible
hoot in her throat. "Goood grease!" She consoled the last wolf in her city,

Yes, I said.
I know what they have done.

"Going Home" in confessional conveys the tender prose immediacy of an alcoholic's prayer. "I started on the road of the silent, secret drinker," she admits, stopping at the Brown Dog Bar in San Francisco for a "morning stinger," when she realized, stunned, that the light was darker, the traffic heading west, and it was evening, the "day had gone" another direction. So then, she "quit drinking, cold turkey. It took a long, sweating time, but it worked." And the advent of Paula Allen, "a wonderful friend and tutor," and "word-smithing," in place of drinking: renewal, rebuilding, finally reconciliation with her eighty-four-year-old, estranged White father, a sometime musician and writer, sharing his last two years in Phoenix. Mary said she learned "much from him about how to forgive, to sharpen my perceptions." She heard her mother's last words, through her lost father: "Tell my girl I love her. I wanted her to have the best life she could have, that is why I adopted her out."

Still, there were leftover angers, dismissing a redneck "Through a Wineglass Darkly":

> Go back to Wahoo, Nebraska
> With your yellowheaded woman
> In her white angora sweater
> And her twenty-five dollar hairdo

And always, back home with her mother's sister in far-flung Alaska, "There Is No Word for Goodbye":

> She looked at me close.
>> We just say, *Tlaa*. That means,
>> See you.
>> We never leave each other.
>> When does your mouth
>> say goodbye to your heart?

TallMountain's siblings were canine, the last wolf her brother, an ivory malamute her friend, a coyote lamenting her totem. The suburban hound in her, "a bridging" between village and wilderness, heard the old calls, "Calling our brother home."

> oh sister
> how those Nulato sled dogs howl
> at sunset it
> haunted me a lifetime

Alfred Robinson eulogizes Mary: "There are not many who face the prospect of apocalypse with such courage, wit, and great good humor. . . . Her work, like seasoned oak, is full of heat and fire, simplicity and compassion, maiden-comely and elder-wise." The poet chose her "epigraph" from T. S. Eliot's "Little Gidding":

And all shall be well and
All manner of thing shall be well
When the tongues of flame are in-folded
Into the crowned knot of fire
And the fire and the rose are one.

Eliot and TallMountain—an American expatriate in England, taken in, an Alaskan native in California, going home—both found lasting expression and a sense of peace, writing their own Western poetics. The posthumous poem, "Or Green Tree Lizards," catches the ongoing presence of this native poet:

I want a room she says
where I can watch the sea
through thin silk curtains blowing
I need a place to think
of Tibetan wind pictures
or green tree lizards and
sometimes pray

there's still so much of me
to learn

CHILDREN AND EXILES: CROW DOG AND WHITEMAN

It is the women above all—there never have been women, save pioneer Katies; not one in flower save some moonflower Poe may have seen, or an unripe child. Poets? Where? They are the test. But a true woman in flower, never. Emily Dickinson, starving of passion in her father's garden, is the very nearest we have ever been—starving.

Never a woman: never a poet.

WILLIAM CARLOS WILLIAMS, *In the American Grain*

*Black-eyed susan
rich orange
round the purple core*

*the white daisy
is not
enough*

*Crowds are white
as farmers
who live poorly*

*But you
are rich
in savagery*

Arab
Indian
dark woman
WILLIAM CARLOS WILLIAMS, *Spring and All*

Honoring maverick independence as native originality "in the American grain," Williams needles Neopuritans closeting creativity: "To live against the stream, Emily Dickinson, about the only woman one can respect for her clarity, lived in her father's back yard." Walled against wilderness, the Puritans mistook "pure" White blood, empty of native sense and worldly mystery, for God's abstinent grace in a savage land. Hybrid "cross," as Natty Bumppo mutters in Cooper's Leatherstocking Tales, was miscegenational anathema for the English colonists, from John Smith on down. In a chapter on the mixed-blood sachem, Jacataqua—the doctor-poet's only female American portrait among twenty sketches—Williams laments a Puritan whitewash of women and native Others: "these want meat," the eighteen-year-old, Abnaki-French Amazon challenges Aaron Burr. "You hunt with me? I win." A native warrior-woman fully empowered, Jacataqua serves as Williams's indigenous matriarch of color.

In the American Grain also cross-examines the high modernist pedestal of the 1920s. Slaves had been free fifty years before women got the vote following the Great War, and both were still held back by institutional history. Postwar urban conformity was the nominal emancipation legacy in a democratic revolution. Facing extinction and cultural genocide by the 1880s, so, too, Indians were reserved with wild animals in the shadows of native forests. A woman like Emily Dickinson, contained in her second-story, circular bedroom, remained daughter-thrall to a legal patriarchy, no vote, no marketplace privilege, no place in canonical poetry. "God was penurious with me," Dickinson wrote in a letter, "which makes me shrewd with Him." Her mentor editor, T. W. Higginson, called her meters "spasmodic." Still less than White men, women were manumitted outside the American mainstreams of power, not much better than savage or slave. Dickinson's closeted verse served as silent prodigal sister to bardic Whitman, closer to Sitting Bull than Longfellow, more the metrics of a bear heart singing than bluebird lyrics.

Williams hectors the fear of direct contact, repressing our native senses, sexual and otherwise, that purses American lips and stiffens the patriarchal soul. "Our breed knows no better than the coarse fibre of football, the despair we have for touching, the cheek, the breast—drives us to scream in beaten frenzy at the great spectacle of violence—or to applaud coldness and skill." Thus, inversely unrestrained, came the bloody campaign west and regeneration through brute force, to be lamented bloodlessly in the femininity of a "starving" poet. Williams's America hungers for the female sachem's vigor, "primitive and direct," the cross-gendered articulation of women and men openly challenging each other, "speaking straight ahead." Denying our common human touch in a new world, the good doctor feels, all Americans, native and immigrant, fall homeland dispossessed: "Lost, in this (and its environments) as in a forest, I do believe the average American to be an Indian, but an Indian robbed of his world—." Meanwhile, a British poet, born in the coal-wasted groves of Arthur's Sherwood Forest, imagined a liberated woman of the future, Ursula Brangwen in *The Rainbow*. By the 1920s, D. H. Lawrence had emigrated with his emancipated German wife, Frieda, drafted the free verse of *Birds, Beasts, and Flowers* under Southwest evergreens, and gone over to native Americana in the Taos mountains—near Mary Austin's adopted Santa Fe, north of O'Keeffe's beloved Abiquiu, not far from N. Scott Momaday's eventual home in Jemez Springs, New Mexico.

The man who "came through" Victorian repression turned God into a wild swan, seduced by a boldly sensual Leda:

> Come not with kisses
> not with caresses
> of hands and lips and murmurings;
> come with a hiss of wings
> and sea-touch tip of a beak
> and treading of wet, webbed, wave-working feet
> into the marsh-soft belly.

This was a poet who knew a woman's carnal desire, the mortal longing for godly touch, an artist's true risk of mystery. "What is the knocking at the door in the night? / It is somebody wants to do us harm. / No, no, it is the three strange angels. / Admit them, admit them." He canonized the "sucked blood" of the mosquito's "devilry," the sexual "fissure" of the cracked pomegranate, the fig's "womb-fibrilled" succulence, the turkeycock's Red Indian "fire." Lawrence heard the Christ-like tortoise "crucified into sex." He saw the "soft-bellied" phallicism of the exiled regal snake, smelled the orgasmic stink of the he-goat, sensed the blood-mountainous elephant, smiled at the "belly-plumbed" kangaroo. Mabel Dodge Luhan's *Lorenzo* adopted the "sickle-masked" eagle in New Mexico and his own totemic spirit, the dawn-bearded red wolf, homeless in America. Always the blood roar called Lawrence out of his mother's Middlesex house to witness life in the making, a libidinous scene sexually arresting, poetically afire:

> Then the great bull lies up against his bride
> in the blue deep bed of the sea,
> as mountain pressing on mountain, in the zest of life:
> and out of the inward roaring of the inner red ocean of whale-blood

the long tip reaches strong, intense, like the maelstrom-tip, and comes to rest in the clasp and the soft, wild clutch of a she-whale's fathomless body.

A blood rainbow arcs between heaven and earth, male and female, Zeus and Leda,

> the burning archangels under the sea keep passing, back and forth,
> keep passing, archangels of bliss
> from him to her, from her to him, great Cherubim
> that wait on whales in mid-ocean. . . .

Lawrence recalls ancestors in forgotten heat, prehistoric timber afire with life, an archaeological vulcan bedrock in a language "rare and orchid-like," lost to civilization, singing through the bear's wild heart. He sees the "long-nosed, sensitive-footed, subtly-smiling" primitive genetics of moderns rooted in Tuscan cypress:

> There is only one evil, to deny life
> As Rome denied Etruria
> And mechanical America Montezuma still.

WARRIOR WOMAN

While men rage and lament the marketing of America, Indian women go underground to reemerge revolutionary witnesses, as documented by Richard Erdoes in one of his four "as-told-through" Sioux biographies, *Lakota Woman* (1990). It is a more in-your-face, silently authored telling than Greg Sarris weaving Mabel McKay's life together, or John Neihardt translating Black Elk's great vision. These life-stories are not poetry per se, but they contextualize literary texts personally and indicate the cultural, indeed political, contexts behind Native American women's verse—profiles, stories, and historical events necessary to the native poetics of contemporary Indian America. The people, within and behind the texts, remain central to contemporary Indian culture, where text has not erased self, nor aesthetics slipped into deconstruction. The hermetically sealed purity of a line to one culture may be lifeless abstraction to another, just as performance poetry, ceremonial liturgy, or creation myths and tribal bestiaries can offend staunch defenders of parlor taste and measured verse in print. Not so long ago, Momaday's prose and Cronyn's *Path on the Rainbow* were shelved under anthropology in UCLA's bookstore. Ethnic literature still gets a separate aisle, an alcove of color a long way from mainstream writing. Whether categorized in the social sciences, the performing arts, or folklore and oral literature, life-histories are small reminders of the intertextual nature of Native American studies and tribal cultures.

Mary Crow Dog is a Rosebud Brulé *iyeska,* or Lakota mixed-blood with a White father, who took her 1973 stand with militants defending Wounded Knee. She washed dishes and sewed sleeping bags from rags. Her friend Annie Mae Aquash, a Micmac later assassinated, cooked and kept spirits high with talk and laughter. Other women held bunkers and "manned" guns. They held out for seventy-one days in winter along Wounded Knee Creek, where three hundred Minneconjou Sioux were butchered in 1890 by Custer's reformed Seventh Cavalry. A Roman Catholic chapel with a basement of AIM militants looked down on America's Auschwitz. Below the knoll where half the slaughtered women, children, and old men were dumped in a mass grave, Crow Dog bore a child during battle, named after Pedro Bissonette, later also killed. "In that ravine, at *Cankpe Opi*," Crow Dog remembers, "we gathered up the broken pieces of the sacred hoop and put them together again."

Crow Dog began as no Indian princess. Like TallMountain's father, her White dad turned away from "all that baby shit" to a bottle in Omaha. Her mother found work a hundred miles away from her own children, Crow Dog says, then remarried a wino who let the kids start drinking at ten. On the South Dakota prairie, near He Dog in a homemade shack with no electricity, heating, or plumbing, Grandma Brave Bird and Grandpa Noble Moore "raised us on rabbits, deer meat, ground squirrels, even porcupines." Then Mary was abducted to Catholic boarding school at St. Francis, a practice Indians have long seen as kidnapping, no less than John Rolfe sailing his child bride, Pocahontas, to England.

This young girl stole vestry wine and could drink a quart of hard liquor at twelve. She was raped at fourteen. This student rebelled against the nuns' strictness and was kicked out of St. Francis for publishing an underground newspaper, *Red Panther*, as well as decking an abusive sister. She joined the American Indian Movement for dissident power and pan-tribal unity to talk back: "My aimlessness ended when I encountered AIM." This young Red revolutionary married a medicine man, Leonard Crow Dog, after "the Knee." His people, the Crow Dog clan or *tiospaye*, were self-exiled Lakota renegades, even among their own people. Leonard spent two years in a federal penitentiary, he claims, for healing the wounded and conducting spiritual ceremonies at Wounded Knee. The family homestead was burned down by arsonists, friends died mysteriously of exposure or in strange car wrecks. While the FBI and state troopers harassed the Crow Dog extended family, Mary gave birth to three more children and made Indian coffee that would "float a silver dollar." She figured out how to deal with stubborn Sioux men, "the worst gossips in the world," including Leonard, whom she eventually divorced: "our men were magnificent and mean at the same time. You had to admire them. They had to fight their own men's lib battles." Mary began to speak out against the violence among her own Indian people, the substance abuse and wife beatings, the FAS births. In turn, she learned to accept, to forgive, and to help her brothers. "Facing death or jail they had been supermen, but facing life many of them were weak." Remarried in her late thirties, Mary Crow Dog carries on, committed to her people. "A nation is not lost," she repeats, "as long as the hearts of its women are not on the ground."

NIGHTSMELL IN OUR EARS

I resent you once told me how I'd never know
what being Indian was like. All poets do. Including
the blacks. It is knowing whatever bond we find we find
in strange tongues.
RICHARD HUGO, "LETTER TO HILL FROM ST. IGNATIUS"

Born in 1947, as her father was studying music and mathematics at the University of Wisconsin on the GI Bill, Roberta J. Hill is a Wisconsin Oneida mother of three children, Jacob, Heather, and Melissa. In 1980 Bobbi married her second husband, Arapaho artist Ernest Whiteman, and divorced in 1997. Hill completed a B.A. at the University of Wisconsin and an M.F.A. at the University of Montana in 1973. In younger years, she worked for Poets-in-the-Schools Programs in Minnesota, Arizona, Wyoming, South Dakota (Rosebud Sioux Reservation), Oklahoma, Montana, and Wisconsin. She has taught American Literature at the University of Wisconsin, Eau Claire, and completed a doctorate in American studies at the University of Minnesota. Professor Hill now teaches English and American Indian studies at the University of Wisconsin, Madison. Under her married name, Roberta Whiteman, Holy Cow! Press published a first book of poems, *Star Quilt* (1984), illustrated by Ernest Whiteman, and recently *Philadelphia Flowers* (1997). She has received an NEA Fellowship and the Lila Wallace–Reader's Digest Award and traveled China with the 1988 Sino-American Writers group. Roberta Hill is, simply put, a poet who thinks. "I work as hard (consciously, unconsciously) as I can to hear the music of the voice that speaks through me," the poet says in *The Third Woman*. "I sense that I am trying to regain an image of wholeness. Before that can occur, I feel one must be aware of what is left."

The Iroquois word Oneida comes from *oneyote a ka* or "people of the erected stone" in upstate New York. Transplanted from native Oneida lands to the Midwest, this poet-mother has learned coyote's peacemaking patience, ironically composite and comically renewing. In *Star Quilt* she writes iambic verse with a vision courageously oblique, a line off-center, an identity fluidly stable in commitments to her children, husband, and life-work:

> Look west long enough, the moon will grow
> inside you. Coyote hears her song; he'll teach you now.

> . . . . In your fear, watch the road, breathe
> deeply. Indians know how to wait.

These blank verse "Lines for Marking Time" don't come easily. Her logic skitters, her lines search, her images disassociate. There is lightning in her star quiltings, thunder in Oneida northeast stone origins. Hill trusts the maternal spirit of her mother, who died when Bobbi was nine, and her father's music. Charles Hill taught mathematics and played trumpet, guitar, banjo, and violin. "Dad would sing the laughing song on that other shore," even re-relocated as a *Wisconsin* Oneida, a life wracked with work, cigarettes, alcohol, and hurt. *"I 'uni kwi athi? hiatho*—father's name," the poet adds in the glossary to *Star Quilt*. "He never told us what it meant." When Hill's father died, "I threw myself away," the poet says, and moved to Montana.

Roberta Hill fingers the pained edges of words with blues candor and chanted courage. Long anapestic lines thread things together with buried midway rhymes. Blackbird hears a woman whisper, "Stranger, lover, the lost days are over," and the poet catches herself in bursting pentameter: "I stand drunk in this glitter, under the sky's grey shelter." Through a Halloween of domestic necromancy, this housewife's couplets carry on with "the grace that remains": she hears "fat sing up bread," the "clock echoes in dishtowels." Her matronly modernism is no less challenging than Sexton or Plath, no less medicinal than the songs of Owl Woman or Sitting Bull. "Rare and real, I dance while vegetables sing in pairs." So this coyotess takes her "Leap in the Dark": *"Truth waits in the creek, cutting the winter brown hills. / It sings with needles of ice, sings because of its scars."* The scar carries her song, as in the Homeric wound and bow, old tribal values in the face of modern ennui and feminist rage: sacrifice saves the people, sets the artist free, releases poetry.

Grown lean on government commodities and tribal omens, the poet's ear is seasoned lyrically by need, White hurt, and tribal hunger:

> We stand on the edge of wounds, hugging canned meat,
> waiting for owls to come grind
> nightsmell in our ears.

The old totemic coyote, recreant and regenerate, howls just off the margins, illuminating her way home in "The Recognition":

> Crazed, I can't get close enough
> to this tumble wild and tangled miracle.
> Night is the first skin around me.

Hill's brilliant and desperate American tutor at the University of Montana, Richard Hugo, taught her to trust the strange tongues, the startled insights, coyote's yellow eyes and yips toward bonding losses. "More than land's between us," Hill paid tribute in "Blue Mountain" to the middle-aged Anglo poet, who asked their common losses be sung as collaborative gain. "Chant to me in your poems / of our loss and let the poem itself be our gain," Hugo counseled in *31 Poems and 13 Dreams.* "You're gaining / the hurt world worth having. Friend, let me be Indian." As with James Welch, her Montana peer, Hill learned by Hugo's example the patterned natural rhythms of blank verse, the essentially iambic foot of Euro-American metrical lines, the lyric irony of a postmodernist temper, all the while listening to the bear's spine as her native tuning fork. She plays off Western form natively, originally.

The Dakota painter Oscar Howe also served as Roberta Hill's teacher later in South Dakota, no stranger to surreal and cubist visions. For half a century, he taught and painted a wildly beautiful world where inner vision-ary structures and modern tonal surfaces shared a canvas interplay of planes and forms. Hill wrote "Woman Seed Player," penultimate in *Star Quilt,* about Howe's painting by the same name: "you said no one had ever gone full circle, / from passion through pattern and back again / toward pebbles moist with moonlight." From all these mentors, lost mother and alcoholic father, children and husbands, Anglo poet and Dakota painter, sea fire and grey stone blood, Hill asks the contrary's humor to heal her wounds: "Oh crazy itch that grabs us beyond loss // and lets us forgive, so that we can answer birds and deer, / lightning and rain, shadow and hurricane." Re-ality—what things are—finally blesses her surreal lines. This poet-mother-bear of the Turtle Clan concludes for her firstborn, Jacob, "Son, we've little time and much learn." The lessons are traditional, the wisdoms daily generational, the faith natural.

> After every turn of innocence and loss,
> in the awful stillnesses to come,
> when we give what's true and deep,
> from the original in ourselves,
> love, the final healer, makes certain
> that we grow.

Winter will be remembered "as a cleansing, / like a note held high and long / above a vast terrain."

Roberta Hill attended the University of Wisconsin to be a scientist or a doctor, like her father's Mohawk mother, Dr. Lillie Rosa Minoka-Hill (the poet is presently writing her grandmother's biography). Roberta graduated with specialization in literature and psychology, introduced to contempo-rary poetry by Peter Cooley. The poems in *Star Quilt* were written mostly in the 1970s, at the University of Montana with Hugo and Welch, then teach-ing all over the Midwest and settling on the Rosebud Reservation in South

Dakota and birthing two kids, as Mary Crow Dog was bearing her own children nearby on the prairie. In "Beginning the Year at Rosebud, S.D.," Hill recalls:

> Raw bones bend from an amber flood of gravel,
> used clothing, whiskey. . . .
>   My empty hands ache
> from stains and cigarette smoke. I am a renegade,
> name frozen at birth, entrails layered with scorpions.

"Seven miles from Porcupine," down the road in Pine Ridge, Wounded Knee '73, "tanks chill the prairie."

On the plains, Indian women make quilts with configuring stars for their children and grandchildren. The mother blanket connects "the generations to one another and to the earth," the notes say. Vision questers may take this quilt on the mountaintop. So the book opens with a poem about weaving, one of the oldest of women's work, sibling craft to Mabel McKay's California Pomo culture: basketry, textiles, quill work, beading, gossiping, singing, birthing lives in patterns. Learned from pioneers, quilting is one of the newest of native arts for Indian women, no less than "tear" shirts in Oklahoma, the reuse of rags, renewal from cast-off scraps. So the star blanket signifies ancestral passing on, star vision to sky gods, recycling the spirits.

> Star quilt, sewn from dawn light by fingers
> of flint, take away those touches
> meant for noisier skins,

The poem's form, terza rima, goes back to Dante, but the rhymes are modernist, oddly interlocking in somewhat irregular patterns, loosely tied, but still shaped: "patches" jumps a stanza to find "marshes"; "pine" locks into "legend" and lies dormant until "geraniums," "velveteen," "fingers," and "skins"; and "Chinook" (warm *snow-eater*, an Inuit northwest wind) finds "locks," "heart," "touches," and "dust" across six tercets. A touch old-fashioned, these poetics are charred with modernism and five centuries of Indian-White dissension. The images skitter just ahead of the poem's logic, the narrative decenters, on-and-off target. The poem's pentameter drifts sideways, signifies pattern slyly, turns and scuts under a metaphoric fallout, not far from Dickinson's sheet-lightninged places, a star shower of thoughts, forms, and feelings. Despite modernist imbalance, the last lines of "Star Quilt" reroot Indian love in the mother earth, a marriage no less bitter than any other after a time of losses:

> anoint us with grass and twilight air,
> so we may embrace, two bitter roots
> pushing back into the dust.

The poet weaves lines, weds lives together, as in the old traditions of Grand-mother Spider creating life-patterns, binding up the days with styptic webs.

As the poems tumbleweed along, the reader settles into an associative logic of scattered rhythmic images, not exactly following it all, certainly not tracing a straight line, a plot curve that coheres from opening iamb to closing spondee. It's more a constellating of fragmented lines, rope-stitched meters, buried rhymes, and broken-lined images that scatter and spray over a prairie landscape of hard-won love.

> Small long cloud slung over a low mountain.
> Dreams gather in these mists. I've lived
> as a misshapen thing, bound by water and geese
> in flight. Lights flicker up hard against bald stone.

Indecipherable images are witness to a crazy-quilt personal story of a heart that sings with *different* tones, among gutted native histories.

The poems are slant-rhymed and canted in loping meters, as with Welch, only more so, sideways thrust, densely impacted and filled with associative imagery. A blank verse horizon line stays some balance. Hill chants in drilled spondees of "The Old Woman in a Shoo":

> Hungry for a creek
> with its churning full tilt tumble
> down a rock-gutted wash,
> she gathered the remnants of tears
> in those puddles oil slicks had changed
> into one dull hue.

The poet's child would stay wild, her creatures free of rational tethers, her imagination unfenced. She claims a youngster's questions can be answered metaphorically with "delightful idleness" and untamed intensity, as in "Variations for Two Voices":

> What do we do?
> We hide. We bargain.
> We answer each question
> with a difficult anger,
> map the future for heartache
> and rattle old bones.

This is a mother speaking in tongues, by uncoded images, not to be un-derstood, but reckoned with, if read in trust. She is an othered *native* Amer-ican, resisting the logic-chop co-option of difference. Hers is the swaying spirit of Roethke, in the kingdom of bedlam and babble, coupled with Hugo's pizazz, only more furtive, more feminine. As with Plath or Sexton, there's witchery afoot:

> We unstuck a walking stick walking
> down a wall and shoved it in a jar
> where it hung, a crooked finger.

"Waist deep in dying" at midlife, Hill's lines wryly anticipate Adrienne Rich or Sharon Olds, in domestic frenzy of kitchen cries and vacuum sobs. She skips across a hopscotch of imagining, but not so flatly raw, or spiritually braised, or roughly bruised as mainstream sisters. Roberta Hill trades more in cluttered metaphor and heart's ache, refusing to clean poetic house. Her lines come more from faith than fury, in an old hope of survival, a willingness to learn from the native land, helter-skelter, but to dream a world of words aplenty, even if the pale rider does not return. Ringing in the margins are Plath's "indefatigable hooftaps":

> Tomorrow. The right cadence,
> the right words are wedged
> in the hoof of the horse
> that took you
> beyond the clatter of dishes
> and toys, beyond the market
> bartering rifles,
> beyond broken glass
> or the need for shoes.

This mother's children are still there, evidence of her own fertility and care. The natural world blossoms, bears fruit, and graces her with mysterious bounty. There are men who *can* love steadily. Hill finally takes her stand on the side of the living, up against the odds, saying to her son Jacob:

> We're caught in some old story.
> I'm the woman winter loved
> and you, the son of winter, ask
> where did he go and why.
> This poem gets cut to just one sentence:
> You grow old enough and I get wise.

Keep your other ways, this mother tells her children, and dream of rebirth, "of an absolute silence birds had fled." The schools will assault your native sense of time and self, she warns Heather entering kindergarten:

> Too willing to be wrong, she knows our clock
> doesn't tock the same as theirs, and I'm afraid
>
> she'll learn the true length of forlorn,
> the quotient of the quick
> who claim that snowflakes never speak,
> that myths are simply lies.

But patterns emerge, if we "breathe in rhythm to our own beginnings" with the "corn, my blind children." The imagination will harvest shadows where fingers never reach:

> lilacs collecting dark beneath the sheen of elms,
> cedar buds tinting air with memories of frost,
> a tanager's cry deep inside the wind break,
> my life's moiré of years.

The Iroquois carry the longhouse of five fires in the spine of their being, the poet believes, moving on, always. As "wind finding wind in North Dakota" with her second husband, people learn to wait gracefully, to love longer, to live with mystery and irresolution, whether poetry or mortality:

> Charmed by illusion,
> by nature consistently cruel and kind,
> born to confusion,
> perhaps we shouldn't plan to arrive at the end
> of love, but should move inside its mystery. . . .

Modern poetry is intimate talk, Auden said, overheard. With implied distance and indirect affinity, second-person addresses scatter throughout a collection dedicated to many different people, teacher or daughter, neighbor or son, friend or lover or husband: *you* her intoxicated, working-class father, *you* the bereaved friend, *you* the friend's husband who rode away, *you* the one-time beloved, occasional lover, dead child, or drunken hustler, *you* her husband and children, finally—*you* turns into us, the world-as-other-reader becomes ours together. Hill even addresses a "mute hunger" to "Teach me / your crisscross answer / to the cackling of gulls."

Emily Dickinson comes out of her father's garden to track feral song-lines—always a woman, forever a poet. If *Star Quilt* requires thick unraveling of a mare's nest of images, of impacted rhythms, and of tangled feelings—rage, to inebriation, to ecstasy and grace—the way leads toward rebirth, a renaissance still in the making. "You hunt with me? I win," Jacataqua challenges Burr. There are reborn feminine voices, native rhythms afoot in the land. "One finds in this work," Carolyn Forché writes in the foreword, "a map of the journey each of us must complete, wittingly or not, as children and exiles of the Americas." Native mothers, their lovers, husbands, and children *re*form new families and "dream of rebirth" from "this slow hunger, / this midnight swollen four hundred years."

> Some will anoint the graves with pollen
> Some of us may wake unashamed.
> Some will rise that clear morning like the swallows.

The latest poetry, *Philadelphia Flowers* (1997), speaks even more person-
ally to her children growing up and away, absent parents, renegade rela-
tives, lost lovers, remaining husband, separation, and many friends. The
lines are full of lessons. Aunt Jo, her father's sister in "Your Fierce Resis-
tance," showed "how I could cut through the crap of my circumstance /
with thought and a fine bladed anger." A natively edged temper works
through good medicine, an accepting maturity, a tribal forgiving. With a
soft surreal nod toward T. C. Cannon's canvases, the poet speaks to "Van
Gogh in the Olive Grove," or she asks "Reparations" from a deer she hit
"driving full tilt" around a forest curve: "This bundle contains a healing
sound—/ a blast of wind to waken trees." The poet tracks her anger of
dispossession to personal grace, the thoughtless brutality of the pioneer
"wagon people" in winter 1873, to "Unbinding Anger" in middle-age. "I
walk this good road between rock / and sky," she writes early about wagon
train invasions of the West, down to love's renewal by calling back her
wayward children:

> Somewhere a girl prizes an aimless path,
> running barefoot on the grass
>
> of crisp blue mornings. Somewhere a boy
> carries a leafy branch
> above him down the road, waving
> its elation. I want them back.
>
> They will not come alone,
> but bring the old woman I'll become,
> the one driven to dance lifelong
> with the bones of wishes.

Philadelphia Flowers unfolds with a blousey natural sense of native lives
lived. The lines are less impacted, the images less dense, the lyric notes
crisper than earlier work, even if the wounds of Indian history lie deep in
this woman's "bones," as an anthropologist tells her. The bitter rootedness
and native rage, answered by redemptive riff, the sorrow and exorcist song,
followed by natural grace—all unearth a paleontology of dispossession and
ragged-edge survival and lyric courage to go on loving. The poems grow
on a reader with the effect of a loose-leaf personal album, a tribal binder
of family, friends, and tribal ground. This is the poet's world, her people,
her thoughts and feelings, from Oneida to China, dismissing the Bering
Strait migration "theory" as just that ("diminishes indigenous peoples'
sovereignty"), to staking a native claim for equity at Independence Hall.

> I was tracking my Mohawk grandmother
> through time. She left a trace
> of her belief somewhere near Locust and Thirteenth.

A homeless Philadelphia woman thrusts flowers into the poet's hand near Indian Campsite: "At least, I'm not begging," hence Hill's "bouquets of poems / to anyone who'll take them." Wild loss flowers in lines on the injustice of the Founding Fathers, the unhallowed ground of genocidal racism, the lies of brotherly history and sorrows of relocated native peoples. The poet turns directly to the reader:

> I tell you they're planning to leave our reservations
> bare of life. They plan to dump their toxic
> wastes on our grandchildren. No one wants to say
>
> how hard they've worked a hundred years.
> What of you, learning how this continent's
> getting angry? Do you consider what's in store for you?

The poems are not tidied up, or compressed into modernist icons, but unedited in their honesty, open to all through their singing defiance, in the manner of Williams or Hugo. Roberta Hill is taking her stand at midlife as a native woman, a mother letting go of her children, remembering all things native and human.

This Oneida poet thinks locally and globally, trusts a Beijing friend is rising on "the other side" as she goes to sleep. Across the Americas all the way to China, Du Fu to Empress Hsaio-Jui, literary travel seasons Hill's "nomad" grievance globally with "common heartbeats":

> The moon on the rim of my world
> skims westward over ripples of cirrus haze.
> It is the orange sail of a junk
> I follow, traveling in indigo twilight.
>
> Do you know in order to sleep
> I read Tibetan poetry? Chinese History?

In the wolf-dung fires lit by a Mandarin sentry, Roberta Hill finally knows that all "barbarians" will one day gather to cross the Great Walls and Buckskin Curtains of history:

> Dark as roots, your eyes uncover mine and make
> me hesitate, waiting for some splendor
>
> to rise within this moment
> where we yet may call a greeting
> instead of bleeding for each other.

WOMEN WEAVING STORIES: MCKAY

We sat for hours—talking, laughing, and sharing family memories and stories. The conversation switched easily between Diné and English and, at times, a rhythmic blending of the two.

LUCI TAPAHONSO, *Blue Horses Rush In*

Of some six hundred American Indian "autobiographies" published, more than four out of five are told, not written by native informants. Thus the native "self" is more accurately an Indian transcribed and edited by a non-Indian scribe, silently redacting the text, erasing the contexts of interview and setting. In this collaborative no man's zone, the texts normalize ethnic differences and co-opt alterity. Indian bi-/autobiography lies at a multicultural frontier of texts, Greg Sarris contends in *Keeping Slug Woman Alive*, as intertribal dialogue between speaking and inscribing cultures. Sarris urges translators to foreground individual circumstances, contextual field data, interpersonal dynamics, and subjective reflections in their life stories of Native Americans.

All of Sarris's learning, personal to academic, comes home in writing about his Pomo granny in *Mabel McKay: Weaving the Dream* (1994), an "as-told-through" collaborative biography. The genre was popularized when John Neihardt teamed up with Nick Black Elk, though this Pomo woman is no Sioux visionary. Mabel McKay, 1907–1979, was one of eight women chosen to be honored in the 1991 National Women's History Month poster. She was an adopted sister of Essie Parrish, who consulted with the Kroebers, collaborated with Robert Oswalt on the pioneering ethnographic study, *Kashaya Texts*, and worked on twenty-four ethnographic films as California's primary native informant. In the late 1960s, Essie Parrish welcomed Robert Kennedy into the Pomo Roundhouse, gave him a Kashaya basket three weeks before his death, and prophesied that he would "see no more moons."

Six generations back, when Greg Sarris's great-great-grandfather, Tom Smith, was conjuring among Northern California Indians, a medicine man named Richard Taylor dreamed and prophesied an invasion, "A world of white people and strangers. New world that was no world." Mabel Boone was born midway into the confusion of native exile—a shocking new world with roads going everywhere, the dreamer warned, even "to the moon." Mabel was a young girl when Ishi, last of the Yanas, staggered into the Oroville slaughteryard. The indigenous California Indian population had been decimated by over ninety-seven percent in half a century. Yet California was, and still is, among the most densely populated corridors of Native America, some 242,164 people in the 1990 census. Yokuts, Wappo, Yuki, Konkow, or Costanoan tuck away in cultural pockets of buried history, undergrounded tradition, indigenous as Sequoia redwoods.

Thus, many California Indians live displaced as strangers among themselves, mixed-bloods questioning both sides of their lineage. In Greg Sarris's case, they may be hybrid orphans, wandering and wondering who they are, where they fit in, when they can come home. On the down side, infighting, bickering, gossiping, and hexing suspicions fever tribal lives, on and off the reservation. "Poisons" spread everywhere, endemic with the internalized oppression of chronic unemployment, poor education, ill health, malnutrition, substance abuse, cultural loss, homelessness, and historical dispossession. Most everybody suspects everybody else of something.

"Why me?" Sarris asks. Why should he, nobody among Indians, illegitimate breed among Whites, be asked to tell Mabel's story? The healing design is built into her narrative as a life-story explanation, but it takes time. "Our old people were our books," Mabel would say. "They were living books, they spoke to us." The first definition of Indian life is collective, for better or worse, tribal, compassionate, and traditional. Those in need need to be taken in. Mabel Boone was given up by her mother and raised by her grandmother. She did not bear her own children. McKay healed strangers with her Dream songs, wove basketry all her life, and died the last of the Cache Creek Pomo. Her story is one of adopting herself and her people into families across cultural boundaries, "took-ins" mothered by childless women. Hers are the homeless coming home. And it is the stories that bring people home, make them belong, keep them coming back, to continue telling more stories.

"Now you listen to me. This is what I'm saying, what Essie was talking to you about. This has rules. It's your life," Mabel tells the young doctoral candidate Sarris about her microcosmic basket of talking "rules," the size of a pencil eraser, passed on to him. It's complicated, she warns, so listen closely. As a writer, Sarris will be *telling her tell her story* and in the narrative *hearing his own.* How does this work? Listening to the world speak, listeners become the stories they retell, native and otherwise; their stories interweave with all the others, struggling to belong. "Watch," the spirits say, "how it turns out." And to university students like Sarris, spending a "long time studying" knowledge, Mabel says on a personal note, speaking obliquely to her apprentice: "You have to know me. How what I say, it turns out. And that's a long time. That's knowing me." Such is the formula for *Weaving the Dream,* buried in the mother loam of feminist wit: the patiently woven, unwinding narrative of everyday detail and embedded spiritual Dream, going down to the bear-hearted stream and digging for native roots to coil and weave basket-stories, binding up and healing the people, going on.

McKay's twentieth-century biography is a working life of real, off-reservation Indians. Her people gather sedge and dream spirits, can apples and weave baskets, wash lettuce, scrub brothels, and dance the Charleston for fifty cents in a traveling carnival. Her life has a range that would baffle any purist. Mabel Boone McKay is remembered in the Sebastopol cannery, her baskets are preserved in the Smithsonian. She makes a living as a dish scrubber, house cleaner, elderly caretaker, clothes washer, cattle herder, vision storyteller, Bole Maru dancer, university lecturer, basket weaver, and sucking doctor. McKay attending to daily detail, to the story unfolding, to the Dream turning out—turns her attention to the world realizing itself, all of us in the story. An adopted Pomo sister from a neighboring Miwok tribe, ethnocentrism means little to her. It's all alive, all unfolding, all inclusive, "white people and strangers," native to immigrant, despite the poisons. With her young narrator, we keep coming back to hear ourselves woven into the fabric of community, through the delicate textures of the tiny feathered basketry. We listen to the old ones talk—to include us all in a story woven against loneliness, estrangement, and the isolating despair of age. In fear of dying alone, sadly so, people fail living together, and their despair poisons modern life. On the other hand, if people listen, the spirits of the old ways bring them back tribally. We are one among many, the ancient Dream reassures, never only alone, ever going on collectively in time.

So, too, for the storyteller, no stranger to modern displacement. "Greg, you're part of the gang," Essie Parrish's daughter, Violet, tells him offhandedly in pink curlers, standing in the open door of her house trailer and smoking a cigarette, "get in here and quit acting like a stranger." A generation before, Violet's mother took in Mabel as a doctor woman, across Pomo-Wintun tribal boundaries. "You don't have a people," Essie Parrish said. "You will be the last of your people. But you will have a people. You know who I am, and I know who you are. You'll be part of me, my people." With that the plot is set. "Watch how it turns out," the spirits told Mabel as a child hearing voices that troubled her. The Indian way—watch how, listen hard, learn from those who have gone before—in order to know oneself among others, including the spirits living in things, baskets, rattles, bones, shells, sedge roots, deer, hawk, salmon, and raven. The tribal self is never alone, never without stories or history, always seeking a place to come home.

From spirit poisoning to arthritis, homelessness to cultural genocide, the world can be a fearful place for medicine women too, as with Essie Parrish and Mabel McKay, adopted sisters, digging for healing roots. "They sat down with their handpicks and garden trowels and began working. They worked a long time, digging and cutting, piling wet soggy roots on newspapers and gunny sacks." When the two doctor-women break for plastic thermos cups of coffee, Essie says that an engineered dam will soon flood all this. The nonnative world will encroach in the centuries-old marsh of willow, sedge, and redbud gathered for sacred basketry.

A reader feels heart-breaking loss here, true grief for disregarded peoples, but no apocalypse, as Sarris tells an ongoing story that will not give up: "sitting there in that afternoon spring sun, Mabel felt something timeless, endless, something familiar and forever about digging roots by the water with another woman." Not the tragedy of Ishi, last of the Yana, nor the grief of Pocahontas, abducted Algonkian princess buried at Gravesend—but a Native America that keeps on going on, binding itself up with talk, gossiping to pull the people in line, weaving small baskets of sedge and bird feathers to keep the fraying lines tight, the spirits listening. McKay's K-Mart plastic shopping bag is filled with ceremonial objects when she travels. Her heart stays strong with compassion for lost children, her mind sharp with native humor, her soul clear as the sedge root stream that sustains her. A deft native wit keeps her resilient and resourceful, from joking about lunch at the Woodland "Happy Steak" with the Pope, John Paul II, who requested a meeting with her, to calamine lotion as a cure for poison oak, or dying her hair to stay young.

Testy, oblique, rooted, McKay's Indian humor grounds Sarris in his narrative. She is simple and direct, if elliptically coy. Not fancy, but effective, never hung up in words—Mabel trusts the Dream behind the intertribal talk, the heartblood within a breed hand, the pulse of the people. "When we're dancing," McKay would say, "we're praying." This woman is guided by the spirit behind conflicting things, the essential through-lines among people, across generations. Her baskets, stories, and dreams weave the estranged Sarris into tribal patterns that bring him home, storytelling, the old way in a new medium.

Roots and baskets, dreams and stories, the buried past and the unfolding future join across differences, conflicts, dispossessions. McKay's presence makes readers aware of the reality of Native America here among us. Not exotic shamans or visionary medicine men set apart, not tragic warriors or hapless princesses back there, but human beings, young boys to elder women, alive today. They question their own past and hope for a promising future; they struggle between cultures and choose hybrid survivals, celebrating who they are in our commonly confused world of native possibility and careless loss. Finally, we are "all related," the orphan narrator discovers at his Stanford graduation party, doctorate in hand, life story still being spoken. With the fusional storyteller adopted into the tribe, we all have "Lots of family, Jews. Catholics. Filipinos. Mexicans. Indians." *Mitak' oyasin,* the Sioux say back home, all my relatives. We must all take one another in, to keep surviving.

Watch in the end how the homecoming works. "While trying to help her," Sarris discovers as McKay's mixed-blood amanuensis, "while trying to trace her story, I traced my own." His profligate father was a Miwok-Filipino roustabout from up north and USC football player, Emilio "Meatloaf" Hilario, who boxed professionally and drank himself to death. His abandoned mother, dying in childbirth, was Bunny Hartman, a Jewish-German and Irish debutante from Laguna Beach. Orphaned at birth, Greg Sarris grew up an illegitimate street kid in Santa Rosa foster homes, hanging out with Indians and Hispanics. The intercultural designs, Native Americans to "white people and strangers," are endlessly interwoven across the years, from *Grand Avenue* through *Watermelon Nights*. "Her story, the story, our story," the narrator finds himself inscribed in his own accounting of McKay, her own weaving. Why is anyone included, asked to stay and listen? Sarris puzzles his connection with Mabel. Why should he be invited finally to come in and add a story to all the others? "Because you kept coming back," the old woman, straight and plain, settles on the book's last words.

NAVAJO HOME CODES: TAPAHONSO

About the age of Greg Sarris and Navajo mother of two daughters, Luci Tapahonso was born in 1951 at Shiprock, New Mexico, in the middle of eleven siblings. She has published five volumes of poetry: *One More Shiprock Night* (1981), *Seasonal Woman* (1982, illustrated by the Navajo painter R. C. Gorman and introduced by John Nichols), *A Breeze Swept Through* (1987, with Klee-like drawings by the Flathead artist Juane Quick-to-See Smith), *Sáanii Dahataal: The Women Are Singing* (1993, cover by the Navajo painter Emmi Whitehorse), and *Blue Horses Rush In* (1997). During the 1980s, Tapahonso taught as an assistant professor of literature at the University of New Mexico, Albuquerque. While Associate Professor at the University of Kansas, she lived in Lawrence with her Cherokee second husband. She enjoys two granddaughters and a grandson through her daughters, Misty Dawn and Lori Tazbah Ortiz. She now teaches at the University of Arizona.

Tapahonso's poetry meshes naturally shifting voices with cultural perspectives, a bifocal kind of code switching. Her verse calls on cultural aesthetics to cadence formal poetics: how to live and why in *hozhó,* the Navajo say, the good life. *"Hozhó* expresses the intellectual concept of order," Gary Witherspoon explains, "the emotional state of happiness, the moral notion of good, the biological condition of health and well-being, and the aesthetic dimensions of balance, harmony, and beauty" *(Language and Art in the Navajo Universe).* All this in a single word, *hozhó,* though the artist uses words less for themselves than for what they carry and convey.

The *Diné* have been traveling a long time, Athapaskans from western Canada seven centuries ago, and their speech has traveled, carried much, and changed, too, not the least in a century of English acculturation. "We call him *Shúúh* because he is always ready to hear a story," Tapahonso says in *The Women Are Singing.* "After we eat, we like to sit around the table and talk for hours and hours. That's how we found out he knows how to talk that old Navajo—the kind we hardly hear anymore. That language is ancient and some words we know the feeling of, but not exactly what they mean." So, between old and new Navajo, code switching to English and back, people know *the feeling* of words, sometimes, but not exactly *what they mean.* It becomes a matter of intuiting sense behind sound, feeling things *in my bones,* as her grandmother knows that their mother has died, before her brother speaks it. Tapahonso's mother-in-law says of baking bread, "I just know by my hands, / just a little like this is right, see?" All this reading between the words, looking inside a text, listening beneath the sounds is bound up in endless talking and boundless silence. Luci's mother, hoeing a field, tells her that "the mother is always ready with food, stories, and songs for the little ones." Just so, Juane Quick-to-See Smith, Flathead artist, illustrates the book with a childlike bounce—a deft use of color and form, ludic squiggles for women and horses, figures-in-motion, as in Miró or Kandinsky or Anasazi petroglyphs across the southwest, lines that meander significantly.

Poetry is a model for parenting, Tapahonso believes of her extended family, passing on values to the next generation, continuously. In living well and invoking blessings for others, the Navajo show younger ones *how to be* by being their best selves in a "house" made of dawn and evening light.

> Yippee!
> Lori said when we sat down to eat.
> She knows where she comes from.

So children come foremost in people's minds, modeled on the elders caring for them. The mother's model is kind, trusting, accepting, even in the face of betrayal or death. After her husband's brother dies, a sensual marriage continues to honor the couple's "own tender lives." There's a complete absence of aggression here, a sweet gentleness and faith in *hozhó.* For the poet, this balance registers in a contained voice—careful, discrete, microsyllabically concise. Humility and openness seem the tentative cultural aesthetics of what Richard Preston in *Cree Narrative* calls the "conditional" model of a tribal world, where the Diné originate in western Canada, dependent on everything around for survival, plants, animals, spirits, and all others. Thus, the poems effect a lower-case softening of Tapahonso's voice, not unlike Pound correcting himself in the late Cantos: "What thou lov'st well shall not be reft from thee."

> Learn of the green world what can be thy place
> In scaled invention or true artistry,
> Pull down thy vanity

As in the good the world over, *"Master thyself, then others shall thee beare."*

Luci Tapahonso's English has a slightly broken, pointillist quality, syllable-by-syllable, where breath "talks" as a second language is learned. With the title poem, commemorating her two daughters' births, we see in *A Breeze Swept Through* that dawn breeze, first breath, Grandpa's song, the mother's opening poem, and all winds around incorporate what the Navajo call the soul, the "in-standing wind," that breathes life through all creation. A Diné origin myth holds, as recorded by John Bierhorst in *In the Trail of the Wind:*

"It was the wind that gave them life. It is the wind that comes out of our mouths now that gives us life. When this ceases to flow we die. In the skin at the tips of our fingers we see the trail of the wind; it shows us where the wind blew when our ancestors were created." "Remember the Things They Told Us," the poet advises her children:

> When you were born and took your first breath, different colors
> and different kinds of wind entered through your fingertips
> and the whorl on top of your head. Within us, as we breathe,
> are the light breezes that cool a summer afternoon,
> within us the tumbling winds that precede rain,
> within us sheets of hard-thundering rain,
> within us dust-filled layers of wind that sweep in from the mountains,
> within us gentle night flutters that lull us to sleep.
> To see this, blow on your hand now.
> Each sound we make evokes the power of these winds
> and we are, at once, gentle and powerful.

Language is the expression of knowledge, just as speech is the outer form of thought, and wind is the external breath of the "in-standing wind" soul. In *"Dit'óódí,"* the poet hears her husband's voice nine hundred miles over the telephone:

> I hear words from your mouth,
> wet and warm with breath.
>
> It is said that the wind enters each newborn,
> a whoosh of breath inside, and the baby gasps.
> It is wet with wind. It is holy. It is sacred.
> ....
> Tell me words of healing,
> words of holiness.

Navajo philosophy is daily poetic here.

Language does not intrude between speaker and listener, but minimally opens a cedar hogan door to Navajo lives, ceremonially tied together. As a child, Luci sat wrapped in Diné blankets, looking at the stars, listening. She writes in *Blue Horses Rush In:* "Such summer evenings were filled with quiet voices, dogs barking far away, the fire crackling, and often we could hear the faint drums and songs of a ceremony somewhere in the distance." To "talk beautifully" without pretense is a Diné sign of culture and wealth, and the "combination of song, prayer, and poetry is a natural form of expression."

Tapahonso recalls going back from Kansas to her bilingual Shiprock upbringing in *The Women Are Singing:* "The songs the Yeibicheii sang, that the radio played, and that my mother hummed as she cooked are a part of our memories, of our names, and of our laughter. The stories I heard that weekend were not very different from the stories I heard as a child. They involved my family's memories, something that happened last week, and maybe news of high school friends. Sometimes they were told entirely in Navajo and other times in a mixture of Navajo and English."

Code-switching linguistics aerate the meeting grounds of cultures. Between languages, "words" are clearly what things *are called.* A Navajo personal computer is "talking metal," and a battery is the "car's heart." These are not to be reduced to clichéd artifacts (frontier "talking wire" or "firewater") but to be regarded as they are, functional cross-listings, fusional dialects, code-switching crossings of Indian-mainstream traffic between cultures. Red and White are all in this country together, despite what we call things: we are similar human beings, with separate inflections and dictions. We have differing sounds finally for the same things. Two sisters laugh about a husband's affair with "Ruthie" in a la-di-da poem about infidelity, comeuppance, and forgiveness, *"Yáadí Lá":*

> she fed the kids fried potatoes and spam and they watched TV.
> later her sister came over, she said,   he's gone, huh?
> *ma'ii' alt'aa dishíí*   honey, i won't do it again   *'aach' ééh*
> *noo dah diil whod.*   (old coyote was probably saying
>   in vain: honey, i won't do it again.)
> they just laughed and drank diet pepsi at the kitchen table.

The lines are sprinkled with an insider's Navajo, the poet's own first tongue of family privacies and Southwest regional commitments. The voice switches back and forth, poetically truncated, in a bicultural brand of Red English ("Joe Babe," Diné say, for acculturated boarding school girls "who teased their hair, wore lots of mascara, and wore white go-go boots when that was the style"). The poem thus works in a pan-tribal spoken dialect. "It does it good for me," Tapahonso's uncle says of good coffee, the Indian drink of preference. The effect is one of finely modulated, feminist Indian humor. "I have grown strong in your laughter," Tapahonso tells her daughter Lori, explaining that an infant's first laugh brings the extended kin together for a ceremony of feasting, passing the child around, tasting rock salt, and breaking bread as signs of lasting health and Diné belonging.

A light trickster's wit salts the verse, then, a woman's oblique, nurturing sense of comic survival. Children embody the future, a home sense to swing from, a generational past with elders, land, tribal history, and communal culture, including recipes for preparing food, the most stable of all literacies, anthropologists say. Most consistently, Tapahonso's poetry resonates to the tuning flute of her own Navajo voice, filtering through a naturally visual imagination—careful, everyday, inventive selections from the common languages of both cultures in her life:

he came home the next evening and handed her his paycheck
signed. the kids brought in his sacks of clothes and sat
back down to watch the flintstones. he sat at the table
and said   i deserve everything you do to me.
   you're just too good for me.
. . . .
he sat awhile not saying anything then went out to get
some wood.   she called her sister up saying:
   ma'ii nádzá!   want to go to town tomorrow?
   ayóo shibééso holó, hey!   (coyote's back
   and I have money to blow now!)

This narrative verse rides on an unassuming feminist focus, as well as a verse-line sense of visual balance and respect for margins. The "good" symmetry of *hozhó* is horizontally patterned by way of Williams's free-verse indentations. The spatial arrangement of words on the page, ordering the breath, is not so much an issue of metric lines, as the fluid symmetry of speech, syntax, and visual space. A loping poetic cadence meters the everyday phrasings of tribal life, as lyricized through a woman's special point-of-view (mother, lover, girlfriend, wife, among others, flirt, witness, confessor, and storyteller).

Tapahonso's daughters step in and out of the poems; her subjects remain consistently a sense of family, home, and extended kin—that is, who, and among whom, and where a person belongs. She writes of earthen births, native children, beloved siblings, uncles and aunts, parents and grandparents, lovers and husbands, rivals, cowboys, coyotes, sheep, dogs, and horses. Hers is a *gynocratic* grace, Paula Allen would say, a woman-empowered strength, coming from matrilineal tribal tradition. Tapahonso's grandmother broke wild broncos, according to one poem, and her former mother-in-law bakes incomparable bread. The poet speaks often of tribal food—husked corn, deep-fat frybread, mutton stew and tortillas, green chiles and sopapillas, blue corn mush, Spam, Diet Pepsi, Hills Brothers Coffee. Luci serves a hot brewed cup to her mother's brother, Tom Jim, as they talk things over in lines translated word-for-word from Navajo:

   I sit down again and he tells me
     some coffee has no kick but
   this one is the one.
   It does it good for me.

The Southwest animates her verse landscape—arroyos, buttes, mesas, washes, bajadas, mesquite, chamisa, sagebrush, cholla, greasewood, piñons, desert chaparral, cottonwoods, willows, and tamarack brush, peaks and intermountain plains, and the alluring Chuksa and Lukachukai Mountains: "there is nothing quite like this to see." In local names, naturally, lie details that inform and focus people's lives, that "stalk" us tribally, the Apache say, and keep us in line: Shiprock, Ganado, Keams Canyon, Red Rock, the Rio Grande and the San Juan River. Powwows, rodeos, raisin-eyed cowboys, dance competitions, "willie nelson and a can of beer," mirror sunglasses, blue jeans, pollen blessings for school daughters, sudden deaths, desert highways into the sky, Chinle and Albuquerque and Dulce and Gallup locate her poems among real events in Indian places today. The voice is quick, and quick to shift with a woman's sharp wit in nurture and teasing, gossip and prayer, hurt and care, discipline and midnight writing, sharp invective and dawn pollen blessings: "the good spirits in the gentle-bird morning." Hers is the humor of a people who delight in going on adventures, assured of traditional home—a Navajo people who love and forgive and care for their own over vast journeys, wrenching acculturations, and odd accommodations that prove positive in the long view. Tapahonso writes of "REALLY HOT CHILI!!" on feast days with her first husband's Acoma people:

> Myself, I don't eat it straight.
> It's better mixed with beans or the kids' stew,
> which is plain without chili.
> They tease me about it but it's okay.
>
> I'm Navajo: fry bread and mutton are my specialty.
> Like my brother said I get along on sheep thrills.
>
> Some Pueblos just don't understand.

This poet is happy to be alive, to be Navajo, to be woman. She will not be embarrassed by elemental delights in a good laugh, unquestioned love for children, her husband's workday return, or her grandfather's quiet song at a dawn birth. In the matrilocal art of baking bread, she finds setting for a poem about her mother-in-law, the poem as being-and-belonging—not conflict, but accepted texture, culture-as-art. She knows the feminist freedom of her matriarchy, even tracing back through the Yellow Woman stories to extramarital affairs. "Early Saturday, the appaloosa runs free near Moenkope," she sings in "She Says." Luci Tapahonso is disarmingly upfront about the goodnesses all around her, above the historical losses. "I drink a hot coffee and / it sure does it for me." It is this sophisticated innocence, this lyric naturalism, that makes the poems singularly enjoyable, especially Navajo, and specially womanist.

She ends her fourth book with "that going home business." The Diné have been going on a long time, wandering and migrating, circling the Southwest like native gypsies. Wherever they go, their spirits go with them. And so when Tapahonso leaves Shiprock to see Paris in 1987, her grandmother says, "Remember who you are. You're from Oak Springs, and all your relatives are thinking about you and praying that you will come back safely. Do well on your trip, my little one." This granddaughter comes to know, by absence and distance, where she's from, who she is, why she's going and coming back home. "I never missed Indians until I went abroad," Tapahonso marvels, sprinkling a corn pollen blessing from the top of the Eiffel Tower. She goes away to come back, learns to lose in order to have a good sense of place, listens (stops talking) to speak, and talks (stops worrying) to sing. In line with Frost at the Yankee far end of the country, the poem is her talk-story-song about Navajo life in the Southwest, Dinetáh. Not her story, but a people's, as Black Elk told John Neihardt, carries the collective voices of past and present. "This writing, then, is not 'mine,' " the poet says, "but a collection of many voices that range from centuries ago and continue into the future." From tiered calico skirts and bright velveteen shirts, Canyon de Chelly to Bosque Redondo, Yeibicheii songs to Navajo radio, traffic deaths to "jokes about cowboys, computer warriors, and stuff," Luci Tapahonso talk-sings her way lyrically home. "For many people in my situation, residing away from my homeland, writing is the means for returning, rejuvenation, and for restoring our spirits to the state of *hozhó*, or beauty, which is the basis of Navajo philosophy. It is a small part of the 'real thing,' and it is utilitarian, but as Navajo culture changes, we adapt accordingly."

Yá'át'ééh!

TEN

Millennial Women

From Pocahontas to Sacajawea, Pound to Plath, where do we all fit in? TallMountain to Welch and Tapahonso, how do notions of native ethnicity, gender divisions, and the natural world come together? Momaday to Alexie and the postmodernists, what is still wild, what do we mean by *American Primitive?* Approaching the millennium, we speak of a native poetics, yet wild still seems to be *other* than we *think* we are, a principle of contraries, without and within. Since civilization has "despatialized" the wilderness, bulldozing desert, forest, jungle, and mountain, Hayden White argues that the "Wild Man" no longer exists *out there,* contained by *other* forces, but many think that "the Wild Man is lurking within every man." So our wild Other, irrational or subconscious, inner or repressed, serves as antiself, the not-me within: unbounded, mutable, formless, unstable, dynamic. We associate primitive, or primordial, or primal with the natural self here, versus the artificial or civilized self, and come up with a manmade split forking at a millennial crossroad: to be artificially wild, pretending to be natural (as in *virtual reality,* New World reborn to New Age naive)—or to be vitally wild, naturally formed (postformalist to nativist), the "raw" and the "genuine" of Marianne Moore's interest *in* poetry. We are back to a tension between "making" or "bearing" art, where this study began. On all sides of all curtains, can we listen, through grief, anger, alterity, and reciprocity, to stages of cultural reconciliation? Ideally, to be civilized is to enhance the nature in us, without sacrificing art, emotion, or wildness around us (not-to-go against nature's ways, the Confucian says). If wilderness is a natural core, a first principle, a natural locus and logo, could *the wild* offer a given pattern for human interaction, even a native poetics? What if the bear and human hearts sang together of their reciprocal differences?

We dream a natural world restored and a human kinship at peace. If

313

only we did not clear-cut the trees, separate the clearing from the forest. Unfortunately, we continue to fell forests, plow clearings, reserve Indians and animals, and remake nature; we place jars in Tennessee, making things up. Given this imposition, could we not listen to the contrary in Williams, adding our nature less arrogantly to nature? Following Linda Hogan's eco-poetics, can humans be wild things, positively, even honestly differing others? Perhaps the *wild* can be that in us that *is us*—a natural self that remains preconscious and healthy, even oppositional or dangerous, while the choosing mind makes the most of what it knows, and trusts the rest, and decides what's right from what is felt and known, follows what moves us in positive directions. We have words for this: inspiration, instinct, sense, élan vital, even recent "chaos theory," which posits design behind all naturally apparent disorder.

Between cultures, granted, lie reasons for tragic resentment and smoldering rage, and we all must listen. The rules here, especially in art: don't rule out alterity; don't confuse wildness with license; keep the rules revisable; trust the mind as natural (naturally the extension of the body, determined within sense, by the deconstructive or oppositional *other*). If Confucians advise *not*-to-go against nature, most of our folly comes from unnatural acts, that is, not following the natural course of things from the native beginnings. We tend to reject what we misread as other. "Have no twisty thoughts," Pound translated the Chinese master, stick to the "unwobbling pivot." Our operable idea of the Good could be a *reciprocal alterity*, where the Other-becomes-Us: the [not] not-me, that is, comes back as our negated negative Other. With interactive cultural principles, we can take our place among others, without fearing difference or silencing opposition. We could move through the world with radically *other*-othering force. We might choose our own being and tolerate antibeing, honor past mysteries, present differences, and future changes. We would not go *back* to nature, going Indian, but be nature, ourselves, natively born to this land, as poets ask.

> *Let that be the poetry we search for: worn as if by acid through the duty of our hands, steeped in sweat and in smoke, smelling of lilies and urine, spattered by the professions that we live by, inside or beyond the law.*
>
> PABLO NERUDA, "TOWARDS AN IMPURE POETRY,"
> *Caballo verde para la poesía*, 1935

In 1929 among the California Wintu, Harry Marsh sang this jilted lover's song, tongue-in-cheek, said to be the most popular tribal song of its day, translated and published by Dorothy Demetracopoulou in *Anthropos* (1935), an international journal of ethnology and linguistics published in Vienna:

> Down in the west lying down
> Down in the west lying down
> A beautiful bear I found
> Tearing up clover in fistsful.

Also in 1929, Witter Bynner, translator of Confucius and other Chinese masters, published a collection of North and South American nativist poems, *Indian Earth,* dedicated to his traveling friend, D. H. Lawrence:

> Your gods are here, deeper than any spade;
> And when you lie on the earth under the sun,
> They whisper up to you ancestral spells
> From your own roots, to rot these foreign hearts.

A different bear song is being sung on either flapside of the Buckskin Curtain, one humorously lyrical, the other cross-culturally derisive, inside and outside tribal boundaries. On which side do Americans stand, or do we straddle both, historically at odds with others, trying to cross over?

The canon is permeable, especially by a Native American renaissance of the last three decades. After publishing three dozen books in fifty years, the first about the time Harry Marsh sang "Down in the west lying down," Robert Penn Warren wrote the long narrative poem in 1983, *Chief Joseph of the Nez Perce, Who Called Themselves the Nimipu, "The Real People,"* and was named the first Poet Laureate of the United States. *Chief Joseph* begins with Thomas Jefferson addressing native leaders in Philadelphia: "Made by the same Great Spirit, and living in the same land with our brothers, the red men, we consider ourselves as the same family; we wish to live with them as one people, and to cherish their interests as our own." Whether or not historically accurate of Jefferson's sentiment toward Others, these gestures of reconciliation "as one people" strike a needed chord between American native and newcomer, across the killing fields. Penn Warren's historical poem comes to dramatic pitch in the winter of 1877, when Joseph and his straggling Nez Percé, driven from their beloved Wallowa Valley in northeastern Oregon, surrender to Bear Coat Miles within forty miles of the Canadian border. This passage concludes Joseph's surrender, restored to the army scribe's firsthand translation:

Tell General Howard I know his heart. What he told me before I have in my heart. I am tired of fighting. Our chiefs are killed. Looking Glass is dead. Toohoolhoolzote is dead. The old men are killed. It is the young men who say yes or no. He [Joseph's brother] who led the young men is dead. It is cold and we have no blankets. The little children are freezing to death. My people, some of them, have run away to the hills, and have no blankets, no food; no one knows where they are—perhaps freezing to death. I want time to look for my children and see how many of them I can find. Maybe I shall

find them among the dead. Hear me, my chiefs. I am tired; my heart is sick
and sad. From where the sun now stands, I will fight no more forever.

The lines are heart-wrenching in English, no less than the originals, as with
Sitting Bull's speeches and song-poems fully translated: no more killing, we
want to live. "I know to bear against hard times." The essential diction,
spare images, and direct candor carry the reversing tension ("I will fight
no more forever") of Owl Woman's Papago elegy: "In the great night my
heart will go out. / Toward me the darkness comes rattling. / In the great
night my heart will go out." Issues of interethnic courage and accurate
translation fork at the crossroads, bicultural torque and empathic under-
standing, both ways. Penn Warren ends his epic in 1981, turning to a friend
meeting him at the Great Falls, Montana, airport, muttering cursed con-
trition:

> "It's getting night, and a hell of a way
> To go." We went,
> And did not talk much on the way.

We are left asking: Why does America still have "a hell of a way" to go, two
hundred years since Lewis and Clark with Sacajawea were guests of the Nez
Percé? Why should the country's first poet laureate be inaugurated in the
wake of Chief Joseph's surrender speech, "From where the sun now stands,
I will fight no more forever"? How much more ethnic cleansing must Amer-
icans endure, and where do women disrupt the battle?

A year later in 1984, Mary Oliver won the Pulitzer Prize for Poetry with
American Primitive, dedicated to James Wright. Among other Ohio verses of
lightning, pine woods, bobcat, blue heron, skunk cabbage, blackberries,
and bluefish stands the poem "Tecumseh," whose Shawnee name means
Shooting Star. Mary Oliver elegizes the warrior who lost Ohio (land of "beau-
tiful waters" to White pioneers. "Sometimes," she says, "I would like to
paint my body red and go out into / the glittering snow / to die." Do we
contemplate or reject this empathy as callow? Coming to terms with Native
American history, do we dismiss feminist-poetic wannabes as mindless ac-
culturists, or do we stay on to "listen / when no one is left to speak," as
Linda Hogan asks? Mary Oliver eulogizes Tecumseh:

> After the bloody and final fighting, at Thames,
> it was over, except
> his body could not be found.
> It was never found,
> and you can do whatever you want with that, say
>
> his people came in the black leaves of the night
> and hauled him to a secret grave, or that
> he turned into a little boy again, and leaped
> into a birch canoe and went

rowing home down the rivers. Anyway,
this much I'm sure of: if we ever meet him, we'll know it,
he will still be
so angry.

From male American poet laureate to female Pulitzer, a year apart, 1983–1984, what reconciliation beyond rage do we find in American literature today? Ethnic political correction has peaked; riding the crest of a domestic feminist revolution, the *other sex* is here to be heard and seen. In poetry, women seem to have an edge, publishing and running programs and writing criticism, from Helen Vendler at Harvard, to Jorie Graham at the Iowa Writers' Workshop, to the East Coast, long-haired daughters of Stanley Kunitz, Louise Glück, Lucie Brock-Broido, Sophie Cabot-Black, Marie Howe, and others. Women of color come doubly empowered: the Chippewa cause célèbre, Louise Erdrich, making millions on her fiction and publishing two volumes of poetry in the meantime; Sandra Cisneros, Sherrie Moraga, and Gloria Anzaldua as Chicana border revolutionaries; Maxine Hong Kingston, Amy Tan, and Cathy Song as Pacific Rim asteroids; Rita Dove, our first Black poet laureate, and Toni Morrison, our first Black woman Nobel novelist. The alterities of American culture are foregrounded literary issues, talked about and taught across the nation, nationally hassled by Harold Bloom, internationally hallowed by Hélène Cixous. Margin has definitely become mainstream, observes the Harvard Black scholar Henry Louis Gates, Jr. The Other has found a voice to speak with and back.

> *[Ted] Hughes's sensibility is pagan in the original sense: he is a haunter of the pagus, a heath-dweller, a heathen; he moves by instinct in the thickets beyond the urbs; he is neither urban nor urbane. His poetry is as redolent of the lair as it is of the library.*
>
> SEAMUS HEANEY, *Preoccupations*

Revolutionary Western men are still battling heroic odds through millennial crisis. In the dialectic of a native poetics (or depending on your taste, perhaps, a negative aesthetics) the poet laureate of England offers a decreative text, *Crow* (1970), inspired in part by African and Native American trickster figures. "My first subjects were Zulus and the Wild West," Ted Hughes told Ekbert Faas. After Plath's suicide, the poetry to bring Hughes back was antisong, the true singing of a tone-deaf, perhaps to us, beast-god-bird, who makes noise for itself alone, undecorated, unloved, unwanted, but undeniable. "You see, I throw out the eagles and choose the Crow. The idea was originally just to write his songs, the songs that a Crow would sing. In other words, songs with no music whatsoever, in a super-simple and a super-ugly language which would in a way shed everything except just what he wanted to say."

The purpose of this anti- or de-formalist energy returns poetry to the primordial wild, the incorrigible animal-in-us that candidly saves us, despite ourselves. This Trickster libido or scavenger survivor crawls out of a disaster and feasts on the carnage. Calvin Bedient calls its energy, after Schopenhauer and Nietzsche, "the will not to die." Necessary evil, then, Crow is our anti-totem: "the tooth is the clue to existence," Hughes says. Thus, in the natural world to "crow" is a poetry of acculturation to disaster, a reawakening noise beyond shock or silence. "They are like fat thrown on the fire," Hughes says of his antipoems: "ugly to both eye and ear, they yet spit and sizzle, are frantically there. They are fully as discordant and provoking as a crow's call—." This deconstructive voice also questions social certainty, the institutional hammerlock of empire, state, church, and economy, revolution to devolution. Crow takes us back to our younger disruptive selves.

Hughes was an early reader of Thomas, Lawrence, Hopkins, and Donne: "Blake I connect inwardly to Beethoven, and if I could dig to the bottom of my strata maybe their names and works would be the deepest traces. Yeats spellbound me for about six years. I got to him not so much through his verse as through his other interests, folklore, and magic in particular." Add to these Chaucer and Shakespeare, "the poet I read more than all other literature put together." Indeed, Robert Greene first satirized the Bard as a black acting bird in *A Groatsworth of Wit:* ". . . an upstart crow, beautiful with our feathers, that with his tiger's heart wrapped in a player's hide supposes he is well able to bombast out a blank verse as the rest of you; and being an absolute Johannes Factotum, is in his own conceit the only Shake-scene in a county." In his Ecco Press collection, *The Essential Shakespeare* (1991), Hughes speaks of the high-low, split tongue that gave Shakespeare access to multiple languages and cultures: Roman colonized Celt for four hundred years, and their combined detritus was overrun by Anglo-Saxon German, in turn invaded by Norse, the whole cultural collage flooded by Norman French in 1066. The resulting stew pot four centuries ago in "Shakespeare's hybridization and crossbreeding" of tongues, one might hazard, parallels Native America today. Hughes summarizes: "At each stage, the inner sense of a double nation—where a native, autochthonous breed of indigenes, speaking an old language, with old local emotional allegiances, was ruled over and oppressed by people of a foreign stock, speaking a distinctly different language, with allegiances to the continent—rearranged itself and deepened. Shakespeare's enforced intermarriage of the racial strains within his poetic style was in this sense a political and social act without precedent." The principle of the bard's diction, most basically, is patterned contrast. "*What* a *piece* of *work* is *man!*" Hamlet muses in rocking Anglo-Saxon monosyllables. "And *yet,* to *me, what is* this quin*tessence* of *dust?*" the prince ends, anapestically crossing Latin with Germanic roots.

Any poet in English this century, Hughes contends, digs into the abyss of life-energies, trying "to locate the force which Shakespeare called Venus in his first poems and Sycorax in his last," the all-powerful, bewitching mother of Caliban, beating heart to pulsing vagina. "Above—the face, shaped like a perfect heart," the poet reads a fragment of an ancient tablet in *Crow.* "Below—the heart's torn face." As Prospero concludes *The Tempest,* "This thing of darkness I / acknowledge mine." Out of the dark, Hughes connects modern poetry with violent release:

> Behind Blake's poem is the upsurge that produced the French Revolution, the explosion against the oppressive crust of the monarchies. Behind Yeats's poem is the upsurge that is still producing our modern chaos—the explosion against civilization itself, the oppressive deadness of civilization, the spiritless materialism of it, the stupidity of it. Both poets reach the same way for control—but the symbol itself is unqualified, it is an irruption, from the deeper resources, of enraged energy—energy that for some reason or other has become enraged.

This rage can only be answered and healed, Hughes feels, through the "old method" of poetic ritual and tribal ceremony, the balancing four-winds of deeply rooted, natively rhythmic stories and songs:

> When the wise men know how to create rituals and dogma, the energy can be contained. When the old rituals and dogma have lost credit and disintegrated, and no new ones have been formed, the energy cannot be contained, and so its effect is destructive—and that is the position with us. . . . What is the alternative? To accept the energy, and find methods of turning it to good, of keeping it under control—rituals, the machinery of religion. The old method is the only one.

"Primitive shamanism," Hughes restates his wife's shared interests, stands as the oldest of poetic methods. The modern artist must turn back to tribal medicine:

> . . . becoming and performing as a witch-doctor, a medicine man, among primitive peoples. The individual is summoned by certain dreams. The same dreams all over the world. A spirit summons him . . . usually an animal or a woman. If he refuses, he dies. . . . Once fully-fledged he can enter trance at will and go to the spirit world . . . he goes to get something badly needed, a cure, an answer, some sort of divine intervention in the community's affairs.

We have come to a millennial Delphi. "How can a poet become a medicine man," the British laureate ponders, "and fly to the source and come back and heal or pronounce oracles?" The Great Bear's othering heart, deeply rooted in native vision, is a singing start.

Poetry "is nothing if not that," Hughes swears, "the record of just how the forces of the Universe try to redress some balance disturbed by human error." In native poetics, a reader might conjecture, the artist's method, seer's madness, and poet's necromancy reassert the primacy of the word's *effect* over preformalist rules of composition. Yet is the word determined by blood or culture, if one must choose, nature or nurture? *What is poetry?* postmoderns ask: *That which moves us . . . to . . . ?* Though the range is vast, a native poetics crosses between Western antipodes, balancing tensions: symmetry to disruption, metrics to free speech, rhyme to blank verse, high diction to low talk, order to rebellion, Apollo to Dionysius, *hozhó* to *Taku-skanskan,* specifically, the Navajo harmonious good to the uncontainable Lakota Power-that-Moves-what-moves. The combinations and permutations are creatively endless.

Nevertheless, how do we consider the negative *effect* of modern verse? Crow's lineage begins primally:

> Screaming for Blood
> Grubs, crusts
> Anything
>
> Trembling featherless elbows in the nest's filth

In the postviolence of a civil war, Native American massacres, and two world wars, the West comes up against reverse dactylic truths (*"Scream*-ing for, *An*-y-thing, *Trem*-bling *feath*-er-less *el*-bows in"). Here blisters our *dis*-like of historical reality, by way of Hughes's Crow: we know little, we feed on dead things, we scavenge after war, we live on others' misfortunes, we destroy "other" differences, we laugh in the face of fear, we lose (control) more than we gain, we hunger, we lust, we die. It is a litany of modern rage, a confessional of all we fear. "Crow's First Lesson" is God trying to teach him to say *Love:*

> And Crow retched again, before God could stop him.
> And woman's vulva dropped over man's neck and tightened.
> The two struggled together on the grass.
> God struggled to part them, cursed, wept—
>
> Crow flew guiltily off.

These are poems of gender wars, blood carnage, and affirmed disillusion, the energy released in accepting the dark gods. All that is—that we don't like—still *is.* To confront the *dis*-like is to step into reality as-it-is, not as we would "like" it, or would sentimentalize or prettify it.

Crow is the comic black carrion eater who lives necrophilically on dead meat and castoff garbage. He crawls out of the "foul rag-and-bone shop of the heart," Yeats says of circus animal-man, generated in the "frog-spawn of a blind man's ditch." The black bird croaks everything we don't want to hear: the squawk of gawkish hunger, the belch of ego, the dark nothing at the pupil's center. He is sibling to the Aztec antigod of the sun's "feathered serpent" in Nahuatl myth—the god of night, Tezcatlipoca, omniscient and omnipresent, "like the darkness, like the mind," say the ancient texts. "Crow's Theology" realizes "two Gods—"

> One of them much bigger than the other
> Loving his enemies
> And having all the weapons.

So Crow is a god who decreates our reality: a god of energy released in failure, design revealed in broken order, pattern revealed in faulty plan. He's the energy of things going wrong, misbehaving, disrupting, and frustrating that shows up in distortion, exaggeration, grotesquerie, cruelty, and violence. Here the *un*-natural and, to us, unknown redefine what we think to be nature's way. Our dark angel in the blood, Crow humbles and makes us candid.

In a slightly less dark light, perhaps, Crow is the comic curse of the real, since failure characterizes civilization as much as its success: the unwanted, all-powerful truths in a mistaken world around us, a war of existence, hunger, and ego on a personal level, that lead to death and destruction in a public arena. Crow flies "the black flag of himself" over the Crucifixion:

> When God, disgusted with man,
> Turned towards heaven,
> And man, disgusted with God,
> Turned towards Eve,
> Things looked like falling apart.
>
> But Crow   Crow
> Crow nailed them together,
> Nailing heaven and earth together—
>
> So man cried, but with God's voice.
> And God bled, but with man's blood

But finally, Crow is failure and the survival of failure—a *native* American legacy, no less—lessons in how to lose and keep losing, without losing it all. Crow's incorrigible sense of going wrong keeps coming back for more. Like a ragged *heyoka* or off-color *koshare*, the holy fool keeps crowing with a dark humor, a raucous laughter outlasting loss. His grimace of resistance is called *risus sardonicus* in the medical world, the refusal to bow to the torturer, the victim's grimacing spit in the executioner's face. Crow steals owl's song:

> He sang
> How everything had nothing more to lose
>
> Then sat still with fear
>
> Seeing the clawtrack of star
> Hearing the wingbeat of rock
>
> And his own singing

Crow is a recreant spirit, regenerate in a scandalous, morbid, self-destructive modernism under the nuclear death threat, global entropy, ethnic cleansing, and toxic poisoning. He executes the executioner and takes everything back, doing away with the Serpent for Adam and Eve in "A Horrible Religious Error":

> They whispered "Your will is our peace."
>
> But Crow only peered.
> > Then took a step or two forward,
> Grabbed this creature by the slackskin nape,
>
> Beat the hell out of it, and ate it.

So there is no morality without Crow's inversional truths, Trickster's dirty humor and dark comedy as realistic grounding. His is the shock, the betrayal, the loss of knowing, and a new "terrible beauty," as Yeats said in the early 1920s, after the First World War and Irish Civil War. This "rough beast" reveals something of what we don't know, the slouching sphinx in the unknown. And that dark trickster power has long been associated with radical feminine sexuality.

SPLIT TONGUES: GREGG AND GRAHAM

The muses are often feminine in the West, attended by *wyrd* sisters, witches, and alleged hysterics (from Greek *hyster* for "womb"). All this century, women have been redefining that dark matrix. Monica Sjöö and Barbara Mor begin with biology, the fact that female chromosomes determine life from the start, and go on to argue that mother precedes father in a child's consciousness. Women gathering in villages invented speech, asserts *The Great Cosmic Mother,* and culture originated from matrifocal families. Old mother tongues call postmodern feminists back to Greco-Roman blood, the rites of Diana and Virbius at the Lake of Nemi near Rome, for example, where Frazer opens *The Golden Bough.* Goddess of the hunt, hearth, chastity, and moon, Diana protected women; for her renewal each spring, Virbius killed the old king at Nemi near Rome, a totemic key to blood sacrifice in Judeo-Christian history. So there was a time of goddesses in Western thinking, at least as feminists reimagine the stories, a time when *woman-born* of the Dark Mother meant incredible power.

   Today, a woman's voice is "crying in the wilderness," Sandra Gilbert introduces an English translation of *The Newly Born Woman* by European feminists, Hélène Cixous and Catherine Clément, "the voice of a woman, newborn and yet archaic, a voice of milk and blood, a voice silenced but savage." An Algerian Jewess in Paris, Cixous underscores Medusa's revolutionary laughter, the equation of madness, woman, childhood, and savagism. Clément sees the sorceress reinscribing paganism reproductively on her body. Gender, then, and attitudinal taboos divide biological conscious-ness. "Is Female to Male as Nature Is to Culture?" Sherry Ortner strikes the dissonant of a Western dialectic. The debate rages between nature and culture (Frazer), descent and consent (Sollors), mother and father (Freud), passivity and activity (Kristeva), heart and head (Jung), speaking and writing (Bakhtin), matter and form (Aristotle), night and day (Plato). Why the divisions? Women write fusionally, Cixous challenges, in bloody milk from the *wild* edge of culture, and *woman* is the *dark continent* to which all must return.

With hesitant care, Linda Gregg did just this, returning to Greece beside her master craftsman, Jack Gilbert, to seek the woman-spirit she could not name. There she glimpsed Aphrodite's elbow pushing up through the dirt in sunlight, the daughter born of her father's testicles in the frothy sea, goddess of passion, beauty, and desire. "But we must remember that it is still country on the other side of the border," Gregg cautioned early in *19 New American Poets of the Golden Gate,* "and there are things there which we do not have good names for." For lack of a translatable name, Gregg sought *Alma* in the Old World, "knowing" from the Arabic, "dancing-singing girl" from the Egyptian, "foster" from the Latin, "compassion" from the Greek for *alms.* In the Grecian dirt, the girl-poet found "Tokens of What She Is," lost coinages of real, unknowable things:

> She giving, knowing we are tokens of what She is.
> What comes to flower and bears. Lovers, poets, fools
> like singers for that world which will not come to me.
> The lack which I am. Which gives me speech.
> My voice as clues to Her absent grace.

Unfulfilled desire teaches the poet humility, acceptance, grace, and a certain beauty of wanting as healing, resonant with the Lakota "wind from the north [that] comes for" Two Shields. What she cannot have gives her "speech," poetry as the *desire to have,* a clue to the fallen goddess. In the old verities of Vermeer, the body is bathed and sometimes riddled with the light of lingual desire: "These words tell a story of my infinite caring, of a quaking there." Objects speak, mutely, as signs of a past passed, but ho-lographically remembered through loss. "These marks on paper tell of places within, / scratchings of the mind, spirit, and the other." After love-making, doors open spiritually, light shifts, baptismal water waits Orphi-cally, pears reawaken the senses:

> The door opens by itself after, showing the light
> has changed in the window of that other room
> where a glass of water stands waiting on a table,
> pears on a plate like gifts from centuries before.

The lines feel like Dickinson a century aged, pilgrim on a Greek island, without interjective wit or disruptive pulse. As with Mary TallMountain, Joy Harjo, and countless other poets from Sylvia Plath through Charles Wright, the slant-light muse of Amherst "was the first poet I really read," Gregg says. "She taught me there is a difficult, hard-to-understand, hard-to-translate, hard-to-write-about-or-explain place" (*19 New American Poets*). This Golden Gate daughter opens her heart to a power greater than the stony father, spreading her knees to menstrual flow and love loss, knowing the fertility of the torn womb, the spirit child that does not birth, but sings in the owl spaces of the night. Gregg submits to a god of ravished loss, gives over to loneliness and longing, going without, the ancient virtue of the soul's privacy:

> I sleep as a shard weary from earthquakes moving earth
> an inch at a time tilting each thing. The sea
> wearing away the land. Everything stronger than me.
> On the shard a reclining naked woman kissed by a god.

The glancing touch, retracted, grazes the truth of objects. Minimalist distance governs her graces toward small *things,* girl, flower, weed, or word, seen clearly and truly, *oleander, shard, widow, barley.*

"We Manage Most When We Manage Small," Gregg opens *Too Bright to See:* "We love a little, as the mice / huddle, as the goat leans against my hand." Focusing far to near, her poems turn on imagined absences, voices, silences, shadows, and longings—what she has had, and still wants, not having. "Different not Less," she argues for alterity: "We look into the night, or death, our loss, / what is not given. We see another world alive / and our wholeness finishing." The poet never gets the whole picture, only the suggestive piece, and we must read archaeologically through the broken particle, the ordinary fragment, to an imagined reality beyond.

In March 1890, the year Mary Austin started her breaking-through breakdown into *native* America, Heinrich Schliemann sailed to Hysilic, a Troy outside the walls of Troy, and struck a shovel into the foundations of that ancient Homeric city, inspiring Joyce, among others, to rewrite *Ulysses.* Schliemann died at Christmas in Naples, four days before Sitting Bull was assassinated in 1890, and was buried in Athens. A century after, Gregg follows his ethnopoetic lead, searching for classical precedents to her own *native* feminine muses in history's wake. *Muse, mother,* and *mystery,* Ruskin says in *The Stones of Venice,* are all cognate with *mouth,* probably rooted anciently in the animal moan *mu.* Gregg returns to the archaeological site of the primal muse, seeking the goddess-mother's visionary voice, tokens of She and Her, on the isle of Lesbos. There Sappho, a hundred years after Homer, trained young women in cultural arts. Mostly lost for over two and a half thousand years, pieces of her poetry were resurrected south of Cairo during Schliemann's time, as archaeologists found torn verse-strips of car-tonage stuffed in buried mummy and alligator bellies: an opening ledger of images, a middle column of actions, an end-strip of rhymes, set down here in Paul Roche's translated fragments.

> I See it Still and Feel it: The
> ... passion, yes
> ... utterly
> ... I can.
> ... shall be to me
> ... a face
> ... shining back at me
> ... beautiful
> ... indelibly

And on Lesbos, Linda Gregg found "fragments of stone, / one with the breasts of a woman on it and the name Elythia / as Greek letters cut into the marble." Like Ariadne's unrequited web leading Theseus from the labyrinth, Gregg's art is the archaeology of the midden, sifting the modernist ashheap of history, the corpse of the past, where we kneel, pray, eat dung, and come back from death to life. The feminine is revealed to her in shards, as the gods reveal their spirits mysteriously, before the mouth can stutter homage.

Hopkins wrote of a factory girl who lived on sacraments alone, and Gregg takes sanctity one step further with desire: true song is longing, as Rilke repeated with the Orphic wind, the soul's bread is wanting. "There Is No Language in This Country," she says of the borders "between things":

> Poetry
> does not live here, unless poetry truly is
> on the side of things that have no language.
> Like the earth, or people who live below the line
> of existence. Poetry is the voice of what has no voice
> to tell the difference between sand and dirt, rocks
> and heat, life and death, love and this other thing.

As with Cassandra behind Agamemnon, a war captive speaking in tongues, no less than La Malinche with Cortés, "this other thing" harbors a lone-liness after love's betrayal which is no thing, but bares a woman, kneeling in the dirt, to the paradox of desire for no-thing, distant, forlorn, untouchable. So the poet opens to *other* than what she thinks poetry is—the rest of the world, the unspoken words left out, to be said and sung as never before, in lyric loss and heart's desire.

Gregg honors a poet such as Lorca in "The Other Country," murdered to start a civil war, who gave us back the natural, unadorned speech of "good" people like Semele. Her name means *earth*, ravaged by Zeus to beget Dionysius, the human-god saving Ariadne from suicide when she was abandoned by Theseus. Or recall good women like Leda, mother of two sets of twins, paired love and war, or consider the Virgin Mary. We know what this life-poetry means, Gregg assures us, even if it means too much, or too little, to mean anything exactly to us. This is the goodness of not always exacting meaning, the common virtue of trusting, as Linda Hogan prays in Oklahoma. Sisters trust the slide of seasons, the blur of trees, the tumble of stones, the shyness of animals, the holograms of old religions, sodalities, and spiritualities. This is how we get back, more or less, to what got our ancestors through the heartaches, the griefs, the inconsolable losses of the past. This unspeakable language consoles us where the mind breaks and the heart cannot be.

Hers is a poetics of limits, of small things islanded or sequestered under a woman's still care. Less is more, indeed, in the eco-minimalism of Gregg's quietist imagination. The poet fingers the tenuous minims of restraint, peers through elemental scrims that block her from idyll or eternity, water, air, fire, earth. What she cannot have (constant love), what is lost or left behind (country childhood) leads the girl-woman to what she cannot understand, but trusts nevertheless. "There are things that they did," Gregg says of two horses in a paddock, "that I do not know." The not-knowing serves as a source of calling to, of imagining through denial. This restraint redefines the language of what-is as "tokens" of what we might have been, or be: broken particles plead the whole, potsherds speak of vanished cultures, middens and ashheaps testify to lives once lived. These cast-off shards of what was invoke the gods of want, the ghosts of an Other time or being.

A vanishing Eurydician grace speaks to a woman's fears of aging, a "tan and gray" dissolving, as in "The Color of Many Deer Running." As in Hill and Plath, the leaping loss of ghostly phonemes clatters rhythmically away: "Not one deer, but when many of them run away." With the spirit's abstinent faith, private witness of the "glistening" soul, her trees sing feminine, no less than when "Coleridge Saw the Harp as Invented Beyond Nature's Reason":

> Is it true women are the most supple form
> of agreement with the real?
> Do they make harps of themselves,
> singing with their earned bodies?
> Machines of sentiment the universe
> blows through, that winter comes to
> as it does to stone? These song-for-song,
> self-for-love, beaten as all exiles are.
> These that the Earth quickly cares nothing for.

These are the personal politics and poetics of estrangement, Carolyn Forché without a physical country between us. In Gregg's microcosmos, each woman is an islanded refuge to herself, ravished and abandoned into speech, lost as the lyric, tribeless. We cannot see *things*, only peer through them with desire— within words-as-things, spirits ring through interior shadows, the echoes in objects calling through. No heroic Athena, wise and all-powerful. No avenging Hecuba or menacing Medusa. No patient Penelope, innocent Nausicaa, or bewitching Calypso, but Sapphically broken and abandoned and bereft women of our commonly classical past, piecing their lives back together, alone, learning to love themselves, loving what they've lost.

How do modern women then "make" poems from despair? The second youngest, by one year, in the *Harvard Book of Contemporary American Poetry* is Jorie Graham. Helen Vendler musters her own "great tradition" of some three dozen postmodernist American masters, among them Stevens, Bishop, and Berryman, down to Merrill, Merwin, Plath, and Glück (besides Hughes, Hayden, and Dove, few Harvard rhymers of color). Everyone has favorites, but these poets constellate a contemporary star chart, of sorts, looking eastward.

Jorie Graham was born in Rome in 1951 and grew up in Italy. She was schooled at the Rome Lycée Francais, educated in philosophy at the Sorbonne, studied cinema at New York University with Martin Scorcese and worked in television. She took courses at Columbia University and completed an M.F.A. at the University of Iowa. In *Hybrids of Plants and of Ghosts* (1980), she ponders "The Nature of Evidence":

> how I would like to catch the world
> at pure idea—although, as with my profile, I,
> turning to it, find
> only myself again,
>
> and, no, it's not enough to understand
> it's there because it's gone.

For such dis- and reappearing evidence of our world, Graham has received many awards, including a Guggenheim, the Whiting Fellowship for emerging excellence, a MacArthur "genius grant," the Peter I. B. Lavan Younger Poet Award from the Academy of American Poets, and the Morton Dauwen Zabel Award from the American Academy and Institute of Arts and Letters. She now directs the prestigious Iowa Writers' Workshop where she got her graduate degree and has accepted a post at Harvard.

I first encountered Graham's writing fifteen years ago in Stephen Berg's *Singular Voices*, an anthology of single poems and self-commentary. On the evidence of one poem, I began a search for more. Her lines here—"spoken" into a tape recorder on a three-hour walk through Arcata, California, where she was then teaching in the late seventies—brought two paintings by Gustav Klimt into what Lakotas traditionally call *çanté istá*, or the "heart's eye." What

Jorie Graham said about "speaking" the poem while *walking among people and places,* à la Dante, Wordsworth, or Yeats, seems extraordinary still:

> I know I have a poem if I am moved in the first draft. By moved I mean choking in spots. . . . Somehow the outer world, with its incredibly unquestionable thereness, makes me justify my words in its midst as I move through it. It is harder to speak something untrue, dishonest, phony, or merely invented for the purposes of a poem, in the face of trees and power lines and other people's faces and evidence of joblessness and the damage done by the most recent rains. And then, too, I experience my work in the midst of their work, and must be honest not to feel ashamed.

Many masters come to mind: Dante with his vision of Beatrice feeding the poet's heart to Love, Roethke weeping on his knees and giving thanks for Yeats's specter with a dancing bear's sway, Williams assisting newborns of New Jersey Polish mothers, James Wright immortalizing the anonymously dispossessed in Ohio. This is an older tradition than Harvard, one of *humilitas* and mysteriously singing voices, of strange transports back to Grecian muses and daemons. In "Self-Portrait" Graham looks into things:

> Eye-level with the world
> something difficult is disappearing from our lives, something critical
> like emphasis
> or the blue
>
> deep-grooved river currents now reduced to pattern
> in the ice

The natural patterns, the deeper rhythms—made by wind and water, solar and lunar cycles, land and animal rhythms—are sliding away in these Eurocentric days. We respond to such Orphic voices with a tremor of recognition, a chill, a quickening or "fearful care," Graham says, as in the presence of Rilke's *terrible angels*. She writes "For John Keats":

> We live a harsh fecundity, it seems
> to me, the symbol tripping much
> too freely
> over everything
> it signifies.

Down west of west, this fecund weight comes through Louise Glück's Cassandra-like presence, or Carolyn Forché's tensing distances, or Roberta Hill Whiteman's star quilt dreams, or Sylvia Plath's unforgiving empty mirror. Eurydician visions trace back through a certain slant of wintry light, women elegizing the losses of supple love and natural grace.

The earliest colonists and later émigrés, immigrant pioneers all, go back to a European Mutterland, and so does Graham look back, philosophically and formally, to Old World origins and authenticities. Euro-American in her upbringing, three mother tongues splinter this poet's verse: her child-hood Italian among visual Renaissance masterpieces—Masaccio's stark ejection from Eden, Fra Angelico's weeping genius in painting frescoes of the crucifixion, Leonardo's magical vanishing points, Botticelli's joyous re-births. In "Masaccio's Expulsion," Graham writes:

> But this too
> is a garden
>
> I'd say, with its architecture
> of grief,
> its dark and light
> in the folds
> of clothing, and oranges
> for sale
>
> among the shadows
> of oranges

New World or Old, a Judeo-Christian Eden still haunts the metaphysical poet as a lost natural home, Lilith and Eve always her fallen sisters.

Secondly, there is the poet's schooled French, especially the Parisian sense of form, Rimbaud, Mallarmé, then Éluard—their cold, passionate artistry, their crafted beauty of mind, so admired by Stevens. Graham writes of Luca Signorelli carving into his son's corpse to reabsorb the body:

> then with beauty and care
> and technique
> and judgment, cut into
> shadow, cut
> into bone and sinew and every
> pocket
>
> in which the cold light
> pooled.

This pooling light in the body's shadowed cavity fills emptiness with the artist's mind. The imagination pools as remorseful flood in the corpse of the world: the poet as surgeon, as child-victim, as sacrificing parent, as explorer of the beloved's forbidden recesses.

Finally, Graham's early poetry, *Hybrids of Plants and of Ghosts* and *Erosion*, conveys a brand of English one could only call American—probing, origi-nal, sometimes plain, searchingly moral:

> And somewhere in between
> these geese forever entering and
> these spiders turning back
>
> this astonishing delay, the everyday, takes place.

If the ordinary life astounds us when it is disrupted or turned back, the delay—the poetic disturbance—trips our interruptive fall into salvation. Musing on "The Age of Reason," Graham asks,

> Isn't the
> honesty
> of things where they
> resist,
> where only the wind
> can bend them

Underneath any visionary catch in the voice or glitter in the eye, Jorie Graham's early poems course richly pragmatic, wondrously tough and detailed. "It is hard to speak junk, or write lies down," she says in *Singular Voices,* when walking among "the very real work of daily choosing and suffering." Her poems penetrate and record the perishable details of everyday things, here among Euro-American classics: Plato and passing geese, ambergris and St. Francis, Cézanne and the cross-stitch, the artichoke and Mark Rothko. "And I a name among them," she ends an early poem, "I Was Taught Three," on her native tongues. Graham recalls in "Syntax,"

> Spring we hunted bullfrogs.
> We caught the ones that sang.

From *The End of Beauty* (1987), through three more weighty volumes, *Region of Unlikeness* (1991), *Materialism* (1993), and *The Errancy* (1997), for a decade now, Graham's poetics have gone into philosophical orbit, eschatological "self-portraiture," as she freely titles her poems. The native in her poetics, it seems, has been muted by more global grandeur. A verse lesson: what is natural to some may seem unnatural to others. *Tempus loquendi, tempus taciendi.* A time to speak, the Romans said, a time to be quiet.

PRIMAL MOM: OLDS

> *It hangs deep in his robes, a delicate*
> *clapper at the center of a bell.*
> *It moves when he moves, a ghostly fish in a*
> *halo of silver seaweed, the hair*
> *swaying in the dark and the heat—and at night*
> *while his eyes sleep, it stands up*
> *in praise of God.*
>
> SHARON OLDS, "THE POPE'S PENIS"

An inverse to Linda Gregg's Greek pilgrimage, or Jorie Graham's Euro-American aesthetics gone west to Iowa, is Sharon Olds's California spunk, gone east to teach poetry at NYU with Galway Kinnell. Almost thirty years after going through Stanford in my class, Sherrie Olds came back to California to read at UCLA, April 1991: prim black linen suit, groomed salt-and-pepper hair, earnest wit, tailored Manhattan image. *Satan Says* had won the inaugural 1980 San Francisco Poetry Center Award. Her second book, *The Dead and the Living*, received both the Lamont Poetry Selection and National Book Critics Circle Award for 1983. *The Gold Cell* came out in 1987, and since then, *The Father* (1992) and *The Wellspring* (1996). Along with the Walt Whitman Citation for Merit, she was appointed New York State Poet, 1998 through 2000. With faux horror Sharon fears her own conception, looking back to her parents in May 1937, their fated graduation and marriage:

> they are kids, they are dumb, all they know is they are
> innocent, they would never hurt anybody.

"Do what you are going to do," she cries, deciding to be born against the odds, "and I will tell about it." My goodness, she does tell on her parents, and all of us by end-century.

Sharon Olds reads in bold simplicity, without gloss, no shop talk, no personal asides—the raw, direct lines on the page, the canvas raggedly unadorned, Moore's "genuine" interest in "it," more or less. She speaks with an ironic naiveté, a tremendous trust in the oddball ordering beauty of what-her-art-is: the poem as bald artifact, the poet as slant storyteller. Her innocence hangs as an underbite that drags on, after the flat lyric voice stops speaking its talk-lines.

> I want to go up to them and say Stop,
> don't do it—she's the wrong woman,
> he's the wrong man, you are going to do things
> you cannot imagine you would ever do,
> you are going to do bad things to children
> you are going to suffer in ways you never heard of,
> you are going to want to die.

Olds's candor is terrifyingly simplistic—a childlike assertion that wags as loose underclothing on a frayed clothesline. Her aesthetics hang throwaway—the everyday glimpse of a deeper life, the Williamsesque pirouette of the heart, in spite of it all. And the little performance tip of the head, the pert orchestrations, fall like a school teacher's assenting nods and warning shakes—to make sense of absurdity, to relieve the pressure of cruelty, to let us know it's just . . . a poem. This is, after all, a little daily quip, only a woman's life. The audience doesn't know where to clap or laugh, how to respond to the quaint humor that so disturbs, cloaked and soaked as it is, apparently, in such personally rich terror and fey confessional. Hers are the American fruits of childhood masochism, we are told, and parental sadism, all narrated with postmodernist rue and roughage.

A sinister innocence colors Sharon Olds's work. She draws on the pubescent voice of a young, postholocaustal America, refusing to grow up, something like *Alice in Wonderland* crossed with *Heart of Darkness*. The poet goes in witness of a world wickedly askew, twisted in "natural" ways with naive grotesquerie. Her voice is that of the idiomatic commonplace, liltingly in the presence of "the horror." With puberty staring wide-eyed at evil, her wicked similes use *like* tongue-in-cheek for the unspeakable. Marianne Moore's poetic *it* swells through the personal pronoun into a phallic phoneme, a poem titled "It." Risking what Williams called "the bastardry of the simile" for the all-inclusive sexual generalization, *it* slides consciously off its referent into wonder and terror:

> Sometimes we fit together like the creamy
> speckled three-section body of the banana, that
> joke fruit, as sex was a joke when we were kids,
> and sometimes it is like a jagged blue comb of glass across my skin,
> and sometimes you have me bent over as thick paper can be
> folded, on the rug in the center of the room
> far from the soft bed, my knuckles
> pressed against the grit in the grain of the rug's
> braiding where they
> laid the rags tight and sewed them together,
> my ass in the air like a lily with a wound on it

The twisted similes of sex always prove slant, not a comfortable or set metaphor, but a bastard likeness for what is unspeakably *like* what it isn't: her bare ass exposed "like a lily with a wound on it." This woman is stunned beyond words, silenced by the hyper-lingual power of *it:*

> and I feel you going down into me as
> if my own tongue is your cock sticking
> out of my mouth like a stamen, the making and
> breaking of the world at the same moment,
> and sometimes it is sweet as the children we had
> thought were dead being brought to the shore in the
> narrow boats, boatload after boatload.
> Always I am stunned to remember it,
> as if I have been to Saturn or the bottom of a trench in the sea floor, I
> sit on my bed the next day with my mouth open and think of it.

In bemused arousal, a sexy nightmare of America, the poet's thin-skinned callowness opens a bathroom door on candid bliss and sensual terror, the native Eve as pubescent Lolita or bewitched celluloid Carrie. Olds sees through her vaginal "slit" to another world of golden threads, in "A Woman in Heat Wiping Herself," another reality within and beyond her, somewhere else, where her children come *from:* she sees through a "body

that is far beyond our powers, that we could / never invent." Think of
Andrew Wyeth, the girl crawling in the wild grasses, or Grant Wood's
"American Gothic" pitchfork farmer and wife, mixed up with Gustav
Klimt's decadent glitter and scrimmed vaginal drains. Imagine a contem-
porary Pocahontas, just graduated from Bluebirds, off to YWCA camp to-
morrow, standing naked before a cracked mirror, with a doorway shadow
behind her. Think of Plath's outrage low-spoken by Dorothy in the Wizard
of Oz: unsettling mixtures, shifts in attention, surprises, kinks, quirks.
There's always a worm under the apple's polished red skin.

Puritan idealism comes up against a wild New World in the late twentieth
century. Olds's poetic grist is generated from a savage purism, as Yeats said,
"a radical innocence." Hers is a combination of repression and obsession,
a fear of the untamed and a fixation on the good-with-bad. "We need to
know how bad we are," she corrects an interviewer about the family values
blather of politicians and the religious right, "and how good we are, what
we are really like, how destructive we are, and that all this often shows up
in families." Olds questions convention: the morality of majority terrorism,
mob psychic rule in America—the tension of nature and nurture, the given
and the chosen, country and city—what is "there" and what the civilized
sort out and select. Philip Larkin put it more baldly in *High Windows,* "They
fuck you up, your mum and dad. / They may not mean to, but they do."

The history of women speaking out, from Anne Bradstreet (rewritten by
John Berryman in *Mistress Anne Bradstreet*) and Dorothy Bradford (rewritten
by Sophie Cabot-Black in *The Misunderstanding of Nature*), to Gertrude
Stein's dry wit and Erica Jong's "zipless fuck," gives Olds feminist lineage
back through the underbelly of the American renaissance, the dark mus-
ings of Poe, Hawthorne, and Melville, say, on women. "When I grew up
there were so few poems about women from a woman's point of view,"
Olds told a *Hungry Mind Review* interviewer, "so few poems about children
from a child's point of view" (Fall 1996). Beyond vamp, her poems puck-
ishly take off from how a suburban mother talks to children: simplify the
diction, squish the complexity, coo the hurt away, insist on honor and
goodness in the face of bad things, lullaby the devil to a "comfort zone"
of reality.

What brings us to this point of wild feminist enunciation in late century,
from Columbus spacing out the natives, especially the bare-breasted
women, at the foot of unimaginable forests? from Cortés challenging the
Aztec god-king Moctezuma, through his captured concubine, La Malinche,
and destroying the "orchidean" culture of Tenochtitlán? from Cotton
Mather praising God for five hundred heathen Algonkian souls sent to hell
in smallpox blankets, preceded by Pocahontas dying at Gravesend in 1617?
What brings us from the "bloody loam" of our post-Edenic past, down to
the sinister innocence of this parodically twisted sister, Sherrie Olds? An

infant dumped in a garbage can, "The Abandoned Newborn," offers a paradigm of the new world lost and found again in a wilderness, the baby named for the rescue medics, the story covered on the six o'clock news. The poet is left "standing here in dumb American praise for your life."

"What do I really see as American? . . ." Olds muses in her interview. "I see being born in war time, where the war wasn't, and where our neighbors who were Japanese were sent to camps. Being born in 1942, in San Francisco. That's American. Racism." This callow wonder registers the postwar shock of our twentieth century global Holocaust, that is, "the rainbow of pain" after Hiroshima, Julia Kristeva says, or the defoliating greenhouse effect; the delayed stress of Third World killing fields and soldiers come home psychically bleeding; the nuclear family under attack, our social shake-up, from Freud to Foucault to feminism; the implosion of institutions collapsing since the turn of the century, religion, state, nationalism, unmasked ideologies from capitalism to communism; the trash piles of advertising and crass materialism (junk bonds, forced buyouts, our national debt, taxpayer revolts, reversed racism and racial hatred like hemorrhaging arteries). Knee-jerk trashing of affirmative action, political correctness as ethnic revenge: you name it, we spoil it, the American Dream debunked, debased, desecrated.

So where does the poet turn? Back to the beginnings, to the first light of consciousness, where biology opens to psychology: primitive pubescence, the native child within, suburban *enfant savage*. The cops save a suicide from jumping, the longest day of the year in New York City—

> then they all lit cigarettes, and the
> red, glowing ends burned like the
> tiny campfires we lit at night
> back at the beginning of the world.

With adult nostalgia and childhood stamina, Sharon Olds goes wild, turns neoprimitive manqué, with the courage of the desperate, the hope of the damned, the cunning of the cornered. And we come upon the gilded given, the "gold" rat-hole of our present reality, the "cell" of our descent from animal nature. Is this gold cell a procreative biology, the physical world we live renewed in, or an enclosing penology, trapping us sexually in the body, in art, in the "word" cell? Everyday excremental riches stain our lives, from "the gold hole they say is in the top of the head," to golden urine during a water crisis, to saffron snot in elementary school, to teenage sex in the stained brass odor of a second-hand Chevy, to an amber hole in her father's bourbon-and-cigar-stained mouth, to the sepia shit of her constipated mother, to the "gold ball" of the mushroom cloud at the end of the world. Mirroring this gold-cell chaos theory, there is a ghastly beauty in our planned (scientifically and politically) apocalypse. How could things have gotten so hugely, so absurdly wrong? Is man, women ask, basely murderous, stupid, mad, or grotesquely naive? Are women victimized, shrewish, or passively complicitous? Could a mother's concern make a difference? We have come to live with cartooned horror, black wit, absurdist innocence in the face of Armageddon; through the power of comic hyperbole we become accustomed to dealing with an outrageous "reality." Have we so come to love our flowers of evil, glittering brightly from the counting rooms of Midas to Baudelaire's Parisian sewers, that the gold cells galvanize us?

The poet speaks with the Voice of America to the Free World, a near cliché or commonplace. Our roughcut, workaday, oddly real lives—commuting, punching the time clock, lunching, napping, knocking off, kicking back, channel surfing, snoozing, pigging out some more—come back in kitchen kitsch, pop candor, fey art, all stuffed into the poetic line. We hear the unpoetic grit of Our Country, given back whole, with art and devilish spin. The silly grin of reality slides over hunger and lust, human need and drive. Olds's scene is an ordinary day seen through representative eyes, a mom with a daughter and son in the suburbs, recollecting the nightmare of her own childhood with a defeated mother and an alcoholic father, who tied her to a chair as punishment for not eating dinner. This is realism taken seriously, and then some, pushed to absurdist fantasy. Call it kitsch verité, the *middle* class in Polaroid snapshot: mom and pop, gerbil and mouse, menstruation and teenage fellatio, suicide and rape, mugger and mailman, son and daughter, as though left over from a teen-angel croon, "this boy, this girl." It's *my* special claim, says our Poet-for-a-Day, on *"this"* virtually generic America.

Olds sees common things from odd corners of refraction, where fantasy takes off from the given: her father, sodden with cigars and bourbon, as Saturn eating his son; her mother as a distraught child throwing the brute out, then weeping in her daughter's bed; their nasty divorce when Sherrie was thirteen. Hers is the incestuous psychic grief of postmodernist America, women who hate their men, for good reason, possibly, their children aghast. A daughter's wagging-blade tongue cuts through pain talking back, watching the old man snore his life away, then die (she documents the going in a book-full of poems, *The Father*). This poet-child is gifted with unblinking uncertainty and innocent courage, to see and tell all this—a certain purgative confessional, a suburban poetics of witness that duck Plath's suicidal grief or Forché's politics. If a father's love is a mixed blessing, what does a mother do about loving her own son? She gathers Gabriel's "sunburn peals like / insect wings, where I peeled his back the night before camp," self-reflecting:

> I am doing something I learned early to do, I am
> paying attention to small beauties,

whatever I have—as if it were our duty to
find things to love, to bind ourselves to this world.

But is it art? Don't be silly; the imagination is capable of anything, the poet
suspects, the fantasy of fact, the terror of naiveté, the ranges of trust and
distrust, in one big bubble of fear. Art is the given, plus what you make of
it, within the forms or beyond them. Every poet for herself. "The loneliness
of consciousness," she concludes her interview. "I believe that we're very
far apart from each other and that there's no way to know very much about
each other at all."

This may be a poetry never heard before: a cartoon requiem, comically
parodic, of the fallen, the unredeemed, the ordinary, the unforgivable, the
petty, the boring. It dares *not* to be poetic. It's what we do, daily, put up
with, survive, and go on doing horribly or charitably to others, when chil-
dren become parents in America: cigarettes and breakfast cereal, frozen
orange juice and cottage cheese, subways and suburbia, laundry chutes for
hanging children by their heels and dental fillings to terrorize them even
more, California water shortage and New York summer camp, parental
fears and hyperbolic childhood innocence. Eden is middle class adrift. Lar-
kin goes on footnoting mum and dad, "This Be The Verse" in drear olde
Englande, the Mother Countrye:

> They fill you with the faults they had
> And add some extra, just for you.
>
> But they were fucked up in their turn
> By fools in old-style hats and coats,
> Who half the time were soppy-stern
> And half at one another's throats.
>
> Man hands on misery to man.
> It deepens like a coastal shelf.
> Get out as early as you can,
> And don't have any kids yourself.

Born-agains ignore the warning. In Olds's breakaway New World, poetry
comes on as graffiti, offbeat, off-color, off-putting street hieroglyphics. Her
lines are coarse and curious as public bathroom scribblings, not designed
to last as icons, but to string out as daily actions noted, then passed on.
"First Sex" breaks down all the barriers, transcends what the adult liars hid
of a lifelong contract with the life force. It's more than a girl can imagine:

> under my
> hand he gathered and shook and the actual
> flood like milk came out of his body, I
> saw it glow on his belly, all they had
> said and more, I rubbed it into my
> hands like lotion, I signed on for the duration.

This is "The American Way," as another poem has it, in our minds to be *Fucked Senseless*—our primal obsession, passively lethal, with the advertised wild in us and out there, essentially ignored as we are being violated. The "Singles problem" gets sorted out in "The Solution," creating a gym where people stand in lines answering one another's needs. Nobody stands in the *I Want to Fuck Senseless* line, just a pile of guns, but the *I Want to Be Fucked Senseless* line gets so long, they add portable toilets and a minister for births, deaths, and marriages. Finally the line snakes out the door into the fields and "across the nation in a huge wide belt like the Milky Way, and since they had to name it they named it, they called it the American Way." A pornographic joke balloons into the off-color image for today's virtual America, as the real pushes over into a Simpsons cartoon of itself, finally a sleazy metaphor beyond sex, beyond rage or censor, for our postmodernist abdication of freedom. Ours is an innocent vulnerability to exploitation, coupled with a wily propensity to take advantage of others (The Long Walk to Desert Storm) and survive the fucking around—an odd mix of cynicism and faith, resistance and belief in a fallen country, not unrelated to Ted Hughes's wild antics of Crow, only more nicely masked.

How is it to grow up blue-eyed American, all-in-the-family? the poems ask us to ask. They work in the art of shadowed casual allusion, the unraveling line: "Oh, by the way, Harry just lost his . . . ," a neighbor muffles the fatal news across our fence. What makes this suburban cartoon more poetic, a cynic snarls, than "Beavis and Butt-head"? Daring not to be Poetry, it challenges our assumptions about everything, family paradigms to the pope's penis. Its parodic realism gets right to it, tries to get it right, admits wrong, and turns the screw one turn, beyond mastery, to pedestrian mystery. The surprise catches us with insight, when we're least expecting it. Olds's exposé of lies grips us with the truth of our lives, mirrored: "Backwards and upside down in the twilight that / woman on all fours," she sees herself as a sensual "Iroquois scout" stalking her husband naked in the conjugal bedroom mirror. The craft of this ill-constructed set-up gets us contemplating our own artless unpoetic hook, getting us reading poetry again, after we've given up on William Shakespeare or Wallace Stevens or ethnic alterity. Olds counters the preciousness of poetry with a raspberry epiphany on the American Way. She opens the closed high modernist text, cracks the inviolable icon, mugs the smug artist, tweaks the condescending critic, guffaws at the arrogant academic. Anyone can read this stuff—but then what? The exposé of *any* one being some *one* special in the New World *is* the American Way, originally, and native poetry comes round democratically. Can we be entertained by humor at our own expense and come away refreshed, enlightened, charmed?

Native and American poetries seem to cross in Sharon Olds and Sherman Alexie, at least substantively cross cultures. Not only is Indian history a wretched instance of democratic colonialism in action, but the supposed Free World holds all of us, present and future, hostage under chemical and nuclear "gold cell" fallout. Old skins, new shirts, natives all, we're all in this together, "all my relatives." What's a blue-eyed mother or dark-skinned son to do, but bear witness and protest and scratch some dark humorous cell as antidote to the horror? The resistance may be satiric or parodic, a coarse raspberry or knowing smirk through the teeth or tongue-in-cheek, but poetic protest it is: Wake up, America, free our families and tribes from holocaustal nightmare and millennial terror.

Pound's "news" stays new as sound byte. A reader doesn't so much remember the lines as the gags and scenes: the suicide on the building ledge, the inebriate father sleeping, the distraught son with his dead gerbil, the pederast on New York City streets, the daughter going off to camp with her cello. We reread these poems asking, Is this really my world, are you kidding? And it is, more or less, true. What has this urban gas to do with Native American verse? Hogan's unadorned candor, Harjo's brassy riffs, Welch's surreal twists lend a native suspicion that Ms. Trixter has snaked into the cutting room of "I Love Lucy." Two Shields would turn from bearheart chant to coyote *heyoka* in this ceremony of contrary humors, the backwards-thinking parody of high art that grounds tribal vision in human reality. As with Sherman Alexie's stand-up monologues, such horseplay boils down to poetry as a performance of the real that we *get*, for a change— we get the "news" here, despite Williams's disclaimer. There is some of Plath's exhibitionist feminism, with less bitterness, though in order to protect our children, we want to know, as the mother does, "evil / in the human heart." There is much of James Wright's plain talk, without the devastating loss, even faced with the mushroom cloud, as we hold an infant in our arms watching TV. There is a dose of John Berryman's courage, with no self-destructive urges, even though domestic violence lounges on the couch, in the daughter's bed, down in the basement with the little pet animals dying. And there are occasional glimpses of Carolyn Forché's lyric innocence in postwar shock, without the political kickers, as suburbia is exposed for what it is, not so bad as most poets think—not Victoria in a tin trailer or Joseph carving soap bullets, but Gabriel saving water religiously, Liddy eating blood oranges after being lost: "oh my Lord how I / know these two," Olds closes *The Gold Cell* in "Looking at Them Asleep." Her children are not *like Hitler,* this mother insists, but decent and good. Back from camp and eating chocolate pudding in the kitchen, Liddy cries out, "*Oh, it's good, Mom, / it's good.*" We know chocolate tastes as good as Dr. Williams's plums taken from his wife's refrigerator. We don't worry where the sugar comes from, or who picked the fruit, we just eat it, like hungry children.

These poems deal less with guilt, more with a young mother's sweet determination to live in the native real world, to accept it, to make jokes about it, to go on going on, among children, pederasts, suicides, commuters, husbands, adulterers, rapists, popes, and all. Her self-portrait appears in "Why My Mother Made Me": "a big woman, stained, sour, sharp, / but with that milk at the center of my nature." She concludes this generative, self-reflexive text with a birthing metaphor of her father, holding his children by their heels down a laundry chute to fix the busted doorbell:

> so although it's a story with some cruelty in it,
> finally it's a story of love
> and release, the way the father pulls you out of nothing
> and stands there foolishly grinning.

What kind of a poetry do we have here, then? Not a construct, or a shaped artifact, but a riff, an improv, a sitcom art. Not a Po-em, made from nature, but a loose assemblage of words, spoken mostly, rambling anapests in American speech patterns that tumble into meaning as real culture. Prepositions and adjectives freely clutter the lines, as they do when we talk and make up stories in our own words, in order to get across what we're trying to say. "At thirty, when I started writing what felt more like my own poems, I felt: the end of the line is approaching and I'm supposed to stop there and rhyme, and I won't." The line lengths are funny, purposefully interruptive, not in the lightning way of Emily Dickinson, but more like a tongue-tied suburban housewife, rattling on about a car wreck, or a lost dog, or the burnt roast. Think of Jane Eyre as a bourgeois housewife, Emily Dickinson as a telephone operator, Huck Finn as a teenager in suburban California. *Bring it down,* Pound and Williams say, hip-to-life, as we, *the people,* know life in America. *Get down,* the young say today, with a wicked undercut, a Gothic *grunge* bent. "You'll almost / believe every Indian is an Indian," Alexie swears. There is simply no authority dictating the poem, no high art or ultimate truth, more something disruptive, random, and real to muse on, twisting in the traffic winds. Our true lives can be taken back from clichés, in newborn witness of the undressed daily truth. Behind all this chaos and casual realism lies an intent, it seems, to snare the reader in a woman's unadorned, unpoetic, unprepossessing musings *on "life,"* whatever we mean by that. She stares wondrously at the fornicating wife, staring back at herself naked in the mirror:

> I cannot get over her
> moving toward him upside down in the mirror like a
> fly on the ceiling, her head hanging down and her
> tongue long and black as an anteater's
> going toward his body, she was so clearly an

animal, she was an Iroquois scout creeping
naked and noiseless, and when I looked at her
she looked at me so directly, her eyes so
dark, her stare said to me I
belong here, this is mine, I am living out my
true life on this earth

ELEVEN

¾(•)¾

Mixed Rebirth

Native American women *sing with different hearts,* as the Lakota say. If Linda Gregg's potsherd minim is no longer a syllabic Western lever, as with the red wheel barrow or Carolina lilac, but a receding flyspeck on our cultural horizon, have we come to the blackbird of poetry's millennial end? If Jorie Graham has blotted poetry's physics with meta-vision, has the native ground eroded irreparably? If Sharon Olds has dusted Eve's obverse in parodic guffaw, where do native women and men take their stand among postmodernist poets?

> we have been guided from scattered wombs
> all the way here choosing choosing
> which foot to put down
> we are like wells moving
> over the prairie
> a blindness a hollow a cold source
> will any be happy to see us
> in the new home

"THE TRAIL INTO KANSAS," W. S. MERWIN

"Show me your original face before you were born," says a Buddhist koan. W. S. Merwin was born 1927 in New York City and grew up in New Jersey and Pennsylvania, the son of a Presbyterian minister. Truly American, he is a poet moving forward, each text a beginning and ending, compassed by the hard, fragile beauties of anticipation, discovery, loss, and continued seeking. Even the boys catching lice, Merwin quotes Heraclitus, deceived the wisest man in Greece. Homer could not answer their riddle: "What we have caught and what we have killed / we have left behind, but what has escaped us / we bring with us." In the American West, *culture* shadows the lice.

Merwin speaks in a quietly *cut* language, Pound would say, on the edges of appearing and disappearing at a century's ending. His verse recalls, from Auden on, modern poetry as an act of translation (reworking Robert Lowie's Crow ethnography, among others), rising out of the nameless original being, from nothing toward revelation. Stevens's snowman seems the modernist totem. We find ourselves moving through spaces barren of solace, unfamiliar, yet distantly echoing our lives. The world empty of human is open to us, our very breath an opening, our lungs free, as the Zen spaces in the net, or the plains medicine pipe stem. This poet tracks the places that life passes through, terrifying, difficult, chartless freedoms in the New World, footprints, echoes, shadows, the gaps where the wind blows, names themselves. Native American dispossession comes to be a metaphor of Americans everywhere, the homeless, endless tribe seeking itself: the intensity of setting out, the letting go of everything, the opening into a new terrain. "A phenomenology of darkness, then, of loss, absence and removal," Richard Howard summarizes Merwin's poetics in *Alone with America.* "And a prosody of pauses, of halts and silences which will let the language thicken to unwonted suspensions, enjambments which reveal, chiefly, *weight* to the ear hasty for conclusions, as they show *disparity* to the eye seeking recurrence."

A modernist poetry of departures, physical erasures, infrared transparencies: How do we tread these shadowy templates and quietist ironies? "Careful as men crossing a winter stream," Lao Tsu advised. To be certain in uncertainty, to feel the chill shadow of thought's flame, to set out unknowing on an unmarked path through others' lands begins the American journey, registered so reflectively in Dickinson or conditionally in tribal interrelationships. Hearing the voice catch in accepting mortal challenge, knowing that love is wanting what we cannot—all this is to enter the lowercase silk screens of W. S. Merwin's three dozen or so books to date. Despite all the prizes, a tentative poetics, to be surely unsure. So, too, is it to be postwar American, from the Revolution on—to honor the conditional candor of humanity up against the known end, to ask for courage, reflection, humility, and commitment—all in the searching, caring voice of the poet, poised to enter and echo the void. Enlightenment, Dōgen said, is like the moon on the water: the water does not get broken, the moon does not get wet.

Just four years older than Merwin, Denise Levertov came from Welsh and Russian-Jewish heritage in London, where her father, too, was a clergyman, though Anglican rather than Presbyterian. Levertov married Mitchell Goodman and migrated to the United States in 1948. Nineteen years later, *The Sorrow Dance* elegized her suicidal sister, Olga, and spoke against the Vietnam War in 1967. Borrowing Wordsworth's title from a poem about "two well-dressed Women" and "*wildish* destiny" on a solitary trek, "Stepping Westward" layers the measures toward feminist liberation:

> What is green in me
> darkens, muscadine.
>
> If a woman is inconstant,
> good, I am faithful to
>
> ebb and flow, I fall
> in season and now
>
> is a time of ripening.

The two- and three-beat couplets advance steadily across and down the page, tracking the contraries of a woman's cyclic rhythms, uncontradicting herself by containing "multitudes," as Whitman said in *Leaves of Grass*. An immigrant feminist, Levertov's range is consistently broadening, deepening.

> There is no savor
> more sweet, more salt
>
> than to be glad to be
> what, woman,
>
> and who, myself,
> I am, a shadow
>
> that grows longer as the sun
> moves, drawn out
>
> on a thread of wonder.

Step by dimeter step the couplets click into place, the diction willow crisp, the rhythm narrow hoofed.

> If I bear burdens
>
> they begin to be remembered
> as gifts, goods, a basket
>
> of bread that hurts
> my shoulders but closes me
>
> in fragrance. I can
> eat as I go.

Denise Levertov is a woman moving forward, on the road no less than Kerouac, but less driven, more consciously in tune with her needs and in touch with her heart. By midcentury, this country's feminism came to be seen as the gendered ethnicity of the Other, women something of a matriarchal class-race in themselves, seeking parity, if not full liberation. Back to the turn of the century, the revolution was ignited within social structures, beginning with mothers working during wars, here and abroad. Today in our own times, women go to work as writers, among other traditionally closed-shop professions, and challenge male dominance. "A feminine text cannot not be more than subversive," the Algerian-French feminist, Hélène Cixous, writes in *La jeune née (The Newly Born Woman):* "In ceaseless displacement. She must write herself because, when the time comes for her liberation, it is the invention of a *new, insurgent* writing that will allow her to put the breaks and indispensable changes into effect in her history."

Laureled by Williams as the poet of the future, Levertov has patiently championed women's rights, while soliciting the muse's visitation. She advocates poetic form as a natural *revelation* of intrinsic content in "Some Notes on Organic Form," originally published in *Poetry* (September 1965): "A partial definition, then, of organic poetry might be that it is a method of apperception, i.e., of recognizing what we perceive, and is based on an intuition of an order, a form beyond forms, in which forms partake, and of which man's creative works are analogies, resemblances, natural allegories. Such poetry is exploratory." No native poet would disagree. *Intrinsic* design or organic form shapes all native art, Mabel McKay to Linda Hogan, from basketry, to pottery, to weaving, to cooking, to hunting and planting, to language and ceremony. The native poet listens down inside, then draws revelations through the "deep heart's core" to the surface of language. Levertov translates a Toltec poem, "The true artist / maintains dialogue with his heart" *(The Poet in the World).* As in Merwin's verse freed of form and pretension, she discovers words to bring the world to light, a native sense of language and natural design that opens the canon to American Indian writings.

LISTEN AND SPEAK: HOGAN

> *If I spoke*
> *all the birds would gather*
> *in one breath*
> *in the ridge of my throat*

Linda Hogan's *If* turns on hesitation to speak, a careful, indeed feathered crossing from introspection into breath. "What we really are searching for is a language that heals this relationship," she writes in *Dwellings* of the fractured natural order, "one that takes the side of the amazing and fragile life on our life-giving earth. A language that knows the corn, and the one that corn knows, a language that takes hold of the mystery of what's around us and offers it back to us, full of awe and wonder." Linda Gregg goes back to archaeological runes in Greece to find postcoital traces of "Her," while Linda Hogan traces her native kinship in the New World to mixed bloods, fallen animals, slaughtered whales and exterminated wolves, skinned bears and sacrificed caribou and scavenger crows. The grace of her poetry waits for light to rise again, writing natural dawn back through an eclipse of sun and moon. In reemerging Native American consciousness today, this light, both personal and pan-tribal, illuminates, fires, even burns the poet's voice to speak of collective native concerns—a renewed dwelling of tribal families freed one day from suffering, violence, ignorance, and poverty, all too pervasive among the dispossessed peoples of Native America.

A mixed-blood Chickasaw from Oklahoma, Linda Hogan has adopted daughters who are full-blood Oglala Lakota, Tanya Thunder Horse and Sandra Dawn Protector: "sleeping with open mouths / full of moonlight." Hogan's *Eclipse* (1983), UCLA Native American Series no. 6, is dedicated to "gentle women" and her own children, looking to reconciliations for the survival of family, community, and the natural world. Sutured in the scars of history, her personal visions of Indian continuance are inseparable from contemporary feminist politics, but less strident, more encouraging than accusatory. This woman's voice spans tribes and traditional lands, racial and sexual schisms, native and mainstream fissures. Hogan adapts natural expressions of "the people" into the more specialized tongues of contemporary poetry. She overlays Darwin with Joseph Campbell, quotes Loren Eisely next to Luther Standing Bear, and among other American poets seeks a language of reparation and quickened listening that would bring natural science back into a continuously layered narrative with human myth. "Perhaps there are events and things that work as a doorway into the mythical world," she muses in *Dwellings,* "the world of first people, all the way back to the creation of the universe and the small quickenings of earth, the first stirrings of human beings at the beginning of time." Carrying on in Levertov's hopeful steps westward, Hogan seems a spiritual zoologist, whose scientific empathy bridges ecology and *Takuskanskan,* native humanism and earth caretaking. "Inside people who grow out of any land there is an understanding of it, a remembering all the way back to origins, to when the gods first shaped humans out of clay, back to when animals could speak with people, to when the sky and water were without form and all was shaped by such words as *Let there be.*"

> There is a voice crying in the wilderness, Catherine Clément and Hélène Cixous say—the voice of a body dancing, laughing, shrieking, crying. Whose is it? It is, they say, the voice of a woman, newborn and yet archaic, a voice of milk and blood, a voice silenced but savage.
>
> SANDRA M. GILBERT, INTRODUCTION TO *The Newly Born Woman*

Indian women today, Paula Gunn Allen observes, write from "a sense of familiarity with what is strange, a willingness to face, to articulate what is beyond belief, to make it seem frightening and natural at the same time"

(*Book Forum* 1981). These Indian women would return home, in peace, to raise their children in a promising future informed by the native past, taking their stands against misuses of the motherland and her peoples. Hogan, Harjo, and other native women take up the warrior-chant of bearing hard times where Sitting Bull, extradited from Canada to prisoner-of-war homelands, left Dakota Territory singing his bear-heart in 1890. If homelessness in some painful sense sums up our common modern condition, going home is even more acute for Indians. Their tribal sense of children and community, traditional regard for ancestral land, deep care for extended kin, plants, and animals, remembered cultural history, and ceremonial belief in the spirit of place have been challenged, dismissed, warred over, uprooted, relocated, and re-relocated in the twentieth century. The Winnebagos were "removed" five times in the nineteenth century. The largest state population today, 252,420 Indians in Oklahoma, represents some sixty tribes *off*-reservation from *other* states in the Union. "Red-earth" Oklahoma Territory was a dumping ground for tribes removed from eastern homelands, the Delawares and Five Civilized Tribes not the least among them. Among Hogan's models from Darwin to Dickinson, Elizabeth Bishop asks in "Questions of Travel":

> —A pity not to have heard
> the other, less primitive music of the fat brown bird
> who sings above the broken gasoline pump
> in a bamboo church of jesuit baroque:
> ....
> "Continent, city, country, society:
> *the choice is never wide and never free.*
> *And here, or there . . . No. Should we*
> *have stayed at home, wherever that may be?"*

Home is knowing who you are by where your people have roots, an ancestral sense of time and place—specific to relatives, animals, plants, earth, sky, the dead, and the gods. "Although I was born in Denver, Oklahoma is my tribal homeland, after the Trail of Tears," Linda Hogan wrote me in 1981, "and the place where most of my family remains: grandparents born and died in Indian Territory and very clear that it was the territory and not the state. It is the place of my blood and heart. The strongest energies of my growing up years are from Oklahoma soil, creatures, and people, from listening at night through the sound of frogs and insects, to the stories and lives of Chickasaw family and friends. Now, however, I am firmly rooted in the mountain lands of Colorado, the Red Rocks area. Transplant has taken. I have sent down a long tap root and want to stay here and probably die here. I've become familiar with the edible plants, with the seasons, the migrations of owls and geese, the deer herd, the position of stars and planets, when things grow, when the hills thaw and fall with rockslides, what goes on with the lives of the people."

Hogan's quest to come home gives voice to a distinctly modern and expressly native consciousness, after the long westering exodus of American and American Indian history. In *Calling Myself Home* (1978), she asks "Blessing" along the backroads of America, listening in the shadows of cultural eclipse:

> Chickasaw
> *chikkih asachi,*
> they left as a tribe not a very great while ago.
> They are always leaving, those people.
>
> Blessed
> are those who listen
> when no one is left to speak.

Blessing voices still rise out of her father's Oklahoma bottom lands—magpies and mosquitoes, spiders and salamanders, crawdads and catfish. In the older sense of a language of the earth, speech is never lost on those who listen. "How can we listen or see," she writes of bat sonar in *Dwellings*, "to find our way by feel to the heart of every yes or no? How do we learn to trust ourselves enough to hear the chanting of earth? To know what's alive or absent around us, and penetrate the void behind our eyes, the old, slow pulse of things, until a wild flying wakes up in us, a new mercy climbs out and takes wing in the sky?" This poet listens, beneath the brain's ceaseless scanning, to the pulse that Mary Austin called an American rhythm: "Sometimes I hear it talking. The light of the sunflower was one language, but there are others more audible. Once, in the redwood forest, I heard a beat, something like a drum or heart coming from the ground and trees and wind. That underground current stirred a kind of knowing inside me, a kinship and longing, a dream barely remembered that disappeared back to the body."

Eclipse honors the four winds, father sky, and mother earth in six gatherings. The lines ride gently honed in plain song, "a breath apart. / What soft edges." Hogan crafts phrases of common speech and weaves the lines in natural idioms, cadenced "so soft the snow lifts. / Stories of loss." The verses carry muted voices before sleep, quieting the world, awaiting the peace of home. Her poems carefully articulate common things once known, not yet understood and necessary to survival, as in the section, "Who Will Speak?"

> Nothing that belongs to us
> except this searching for words
> to say again what has been said
> and not heard.

The search for a poetic voice begins with a woman listening, then speaking through the hush of lyrically estranged, sometimes ghosted tongues. She turns to "Small Animals at Night" as though they were her adopted children:

> But hear them.
> They sing in their own heads
> in the shivering blue bones of an ear
> the voices here in grace
> in the hollows of this body.

The deer, the insects, and the birds lend images of quiet waiting, silent companionship, and winged light to an earthbound woman. With them she grieves the desecration of the land, history's forewarnings of destruction, through the translucent thin skin of humanity: "loving every small thing / every step we take on earth."

The poems show the physical world enveloped in burning light, emanating from the sun in eclipse, animating and illuminating fragile tissues through "lucent skin." As in Olds but less armored, the poet also knows the nuclear light's terrible power to annihilate all peoples. The solution is still human, still motherly, as in "The Women Speaking":

> Let us be gentle
> with the fiery creature furnaces
> smelling of hay and rum,
> gentle with the veils of skin
> that bind us
> to the world.
> Let us hold fierce
> the soft lives of our children,
> the light is inside them
> and they are burning
> in small beds of straw,
> beds of scorched white sheets,
> newspaper beds with words
> wrapped against skin
> the light burns through.

The last section of *Eclipse,* "Morning's Dance," portrays women weaving up the days through "a splintered warp of light" and "dancing home" through common dark. In this interplay of day and night, of matter and energy, of dark stabiles and light mobiles, Linda Hogan senses resurrection:

> Carbon
> red ochre
> we rise

> burning
> out of soil.

Since the early 1980s, Linda Hogan's work has gone even deeper and emerged more prolific—from the early poetry in *Calling Myself Home* and *Red Clay*, through *Eclipse* and *Savings*, then broader recognition in *Seeing through the Sun* (American Book Award from the Before Columbus Foundation) and *The Book of Medicines* (finalist in National Book Critics Circle Award), and more recently, two novels, *Mean Spirit* (Pulitzer finalist in 1991) and *Solar Storms* (1995), then a collection of essays, *Dwellings* (1996). In 1998 she published a third novel, *Power*. With Deena Metzger and Brenda Peterson, Hogan has edited a gathering of literary and scientific essays, *Intimate Nature: The Bond Between Women and Animals* (1998). She is collaborating on a study of interspecies connections to be called *Between Species*. Linda Hogan has received distinguishing support from the Guggenheim Foundation, Newberry Library, Yaddo Colony, National Endowment for the Arts, Five Civilized Tribes Playwriting Award, and a Lannan Fellowship. The poet has settled into teaching at the University of Colorado, where she received an M.F.A. years before.

Hogan is a fusional poet. Her Irish-American grandmother was an immigrant Nebraska pioneer, her Chickasaw grandfather an Oklahoma horseman. She gathers the *native* of her mixed American bloodlines into a singular voice with a gentle humor and graceful imagery.

> In my left pocket a Chickasaw hand
> rests on the bone of the pelvis.
> In my right pocket
> a white hand.

Pockets empty, as most poets, she's out of love, money, and patience with historical greed, but not without her own redemptive laughter:

> Girl, I say,
> it is dangerous to be a woman of two countries.
> You've got your hands in the dark
> of two empty pockets.

The hyphenated American sets the norm, however, in this bi-coastal country of natives and immigrants. The old adage of walking in another's moccasins, or shoes, may lift a woman, single-parenting two adopted daughters, out of her own dismals:

> Relax, there are other things to think about.
> Shoes for instance.
> Now those are the true masks of the soul
> The left shoe
> and the right one with its white foot.

Behind her good humor and honed common sense lie terrors, genuine metaphors of fear and wild imagining. Sylvia Plath and Sand Creek threaten this poet's sunrise, historically clouded, a blackbird's shadow over wily coyote.

> My hair burns down my shoulders.
> I walk. I will not think we are blood sacrifices.
> No, I will not watch the ring-necked pheasant
> running into the field of skeletal corn.

A plain-style metaphysician of verse, no less than Wallace Stevens or Jorie Graham, and head up with Levertov, Hogan keeps stepping westward in "November," a poem dedicated to Meridel LeSueur, listening for the native voice when no one is left to speak:

> I will walk into the sun.
> Her red mesas are burning
> in the distance.
> I will enter them. I will walk into that stone,
>
> walk into the sun
> away from night rising up the other side of earth.
> There are sounds in the cornfield,
> *Shh. Shh.*

Native verse in Hogan's hands is picked clean. Like the understated model she studied, Elizabeth Bishop, or the clear lines of Williams and Gregg, Hogan tries hard to make her poems not sound like poetry. No end rhymes, no blank verse or syllabic metrics, no stanzaic forms, no big metaphors or grand ideas—but a line stripped to essential thought. It hangs there bone-clean, often bent-kneed, bare and beautifully lean, with the light of awakened consciousness all around it.

> We have stories
> as old as the great seas
> breaking through the chest
> flying out the mouth,
> noisy tongues that once were silenced,
> all the oceans we contain
> coming to light.

With milk-and-blood-stained scripts, newly born women are reinscribing "the traces of paganism that triumphant Christianity repressed," Hélène Cixous writes: "woman is in a primitive state; she is the incarnation of origin." Before Greek tokens, *The Book of Medicines* opens with a history of biological evolution, interspecies exchange, the beginnings of language and art, all in red motifs: passion, birth, blood, greed, lust, anger, fire, fruit, dawn, sacrifice, redskin, stop. The most ancient Western artifact yet found is a 300,000-year-old marked bison rib from caves in southern France, where tribes painted running red bison on walls "after their kind," the poet adds. Primitive hunters imaged animals with their own blood, as they were honoring the hunted animal within. An inner totemic guardian teaches kinship for *Homo erectus,* even compassion for other beings. That alterity, out of respect for differences (Welch's *winter* in the blood), defines our first being, down inside, native American or tribal Eurasian: "Love, like creation / is some other order of things." Later, ancient Greeks painted crossroad markers red, plains Lakota painted grandfather *Tunkáshila* stones red, and the Cherokees elected "red" war chiefs. In time of sacrifice whose blood flows, the poet asks, and for what reason, hunter or soldier, mother or artist, lover or enemy? "This life in the fire, I love it, / I want it, / this life," the poem on Red ends in plain assertion, and opens to a section called "Hunger," whose flowing through-lines are water, milk, tears, se-men, and sweat (complementing red with white fluids, as in her mixed bloodlines, blood with milk in Cixous's prophecy).

The monosyllabic splat of the first poem, "Fat," slaps down a phonemic ring that hurtles like a stone thrown through the collection: Fat, Bear, Skin, Salt, Map, Drought, Milk, Tear, Glass, Drum, Two, Gate. For a century, sperm oil rendered from mountainous whale fat lighted New England through a smoky slaughter and set off one of many species holocausts. That blood-ocean also loosed unappeasable hunger on the land, bison to bear, carnage to native rape. Estranged whalers at sea lusted for women and dreamed dolphins to be mermaids, so they sexually abused the swimming mammals.

> They were like women,
> they said,
> and had their way
> with them,
> wanting to be inside,
> to drink
> and be held in
> the thin, clear milk of the gods.

This misbegotten atrocity, an old misreading of desire, twists out of hunger or lust into male violence, abusing the living, and we call it "love." The conjunction of simple diction, wretched arrogance, and stunning lyricism lifts this passage above any verse plane that tries too hard. The last line is Ledaen mother's milk, the nurturing feminine at the mammal's living heart, where displaced male killers batter reentry. And its mothering power is the compassion of adoptions, of caretaking the world, of holding those most vulnerable close and taking them inside us; here the maternal guard-ian is guarded by her own attempts at tenderness and understanding (compared with Sylvia Plath's tragic reabsorption of her offspring in the last poem, "Edge").

This poet sings softly with the ghost-heart of a bear. An old man rubs her back with bear fat, and she dreams the starving of horses, eating tree bark and each other's tails. Equestrian becomes Indian victim, warrior woman a BIA dependent mother on welfare:

> I slept a hole into my own hunger
> that once ate lard and bread
> from a skillet seasoned with salt.

Three bony dogs lead men into a cave, to grow fat on bear grease and wood-ash, and the dogs dream back to when they were wolves (the evolutionary descent of domestic dogs). The poet fears her own canine dreams of wilderness, before the time of taming and senseless killing, as she fears love, after the clumsy attempt to make wild things love us. "And now it is all over, so / I know to bear against hard times," Sitting Bull sang of his warrior past and present survival.

These poems turn on a startling simplicity, their directness arresting confusion or complication. Like the bison or the whale, Hogan says, "The bear is a dark continent," only more human, "that walks upright / like a man." Old Man Bear "lives across the thawing river," marks the poet's door with winter claws, and cries when a man shoots it. Bishop-ended and Lakota-hearted, the poem breaks into a final plane of clarity:

> Madness is its own country,
> desperate and ruined.
> It is a collector of lives.
> It's a man
> afraid of what he's done
> and what he lives by. Safe,
> we are safe
> from the bear
> and we have each other,
> we have each other
> to fear.

Not the wild, or the natural, or the original other, but each *other* / *to fear*— our self turned back on *it* self like the halibut's eye curving into horizon. The isolate human, a self broken off from animal being by monetary slaughter, fears the "terrible other" in itself, a fear of the other's fear, a mixed-blood confusion between red and white lineage. Caught between incompatibles, the hybrid poet proves animal-human. Is fear natural, and are we born so? She looks into the mountain lion's "yellow-eyed shadow of a darker fear" and glimpses a desperate shyness in all of us, turning away from the other's "other." Do animals instinctually fear the other, and do

we share their wild estrangement? If nature is composed of fearful differ-
ences, recognizing our radical and mutual alterity could join and save us.

And so we journey to a "clan of crossings," beginning with whales near
Tierra del Fuego, singing across the twenty-foot ocean drop that divides
the Western Hemispheric seas, then to a fetal whale with human face and
fingers, then to a child with vanishing gill slits (an embryonic sonogram in
the first trimester shows vestigial tail, flippers, and lateral eye sockets trac-
ing animal-human evolution). The poet says that she "spoke across ele-
ments" to the amphibious children, swimming like horses across the river:
"Dark was that water, / darker still the horses, / and then they were gone."
Our animal-human passages, evolutionary changes, mutations and meta-
morphoses make us sea creatures on land, wild things grounded. In the
Darwinian Indian world, amphibian breeds are caught between worlds,
mixed-bloods or Metis, mesteños or mustangs, coyotes or mutts. Hogan
voices a hybrid lament, back through creation stories and beast fables, of
shape-changing growth, adaptations, acculturations, the cross-blood al-
chemy of the natural world, "where moose becomes wolf and crow":

> Betrayal is crow's way of saying grace
> to the wolf
> so it can eat
> what is left
> when blood is on the ground,
> until what remains of moose
> is crow
> walking out
> the sacred temple of ribs

A shamanic crow calls through stripped ribs, lost bone fragments, no-things
left but hunger, longing, isolation, and need. Aching from hunger, the call
does not call back, starving from natural laws of necessity. This tooth-and-
claw necessity is "why war is only another skin," the next poem knows,
"and why men are just the pulled back curve of the bow." It is the hunters'
misfortune to be hungry; their arching need, their desire, strings a tension
to kill, for the deer's "hide / of light" to become, finally, human skin. The
hunter becomes the hunted, the wound becomes the bow of its own inter-
nal healing.

Which leads to the hollow virtue *Te* of "Bamboo," the first Chinese
writing on shells, next bones, then bamboo slats, and a "Map" of the
world's words, ice sister to water, salt brother to loss:

> But they called it
> ice, wolf, forest of sticks,
> as if words would make it something
> they could hold in gloved hands,

> open, plot a way
> and follow.

It is apparent, by now, that Hogan's poems track essential minims of a neolithic beginning and hold these primal elements up for inspection and comparison in the neoprimitive clutter of postmodernity. The poet knows natural magic and tribal ceremony through scientific observation: that every snowflake centers in a grain of dust, that ice carves away our land, that wolves circle into themselves. Blood instinct tells her, on the other hand, that words are preconscious and primordial, that things no longer answer by their true names, "and beneath us the other order already moves" like the bloodstream itself. Just so, Native American names live beneath half the states in the Union, Willa Cather's Nebraska as Omaha "flat water," James Wright's Ohio as Shawnee "beautiful water," Wallace Stevens's Connecticut as Mohawk "long water." The fluid mystery of water within being, vaporous or frozen in its seasonal changes, still channels native origins and changes.

We are walking reservoirs (water invented humans, an old saying goes, to move about on land); words are layered transparencies to our origins. The human need for fluid speech breaks the tongue loose, begging song, even when it betrays the call to truth. These origins cannot be named, but flow beneath a monosyllabic speech: "so we tell him our stories," the poem "Drought" says of thunder weeping rain, "in honest tongues." The virtue and mystery of this book lie in its plain speech, its prayer for help, slanting into strange reconsiderations of most basic being and need. Honesty before beauty bears the need of true art, where animals sing the human *through* themselves.

So a pre-Adamic Eve or Lilith stands in the Garden "Naming the Animals": "wolf, bear, other," as if s(he) made them up with imposed labels. Some animals are relegated to crawl, swim, and root like pigs in a wilderness, "where all things know the names for themselves," unspoken or stolen by no (wo)man. Yet names open us, if awkwardly, as speech rounds our mouths, to being in the true world:

> From somewhere I can't speak or tell,
> my stolen powers
> hold out their hands
> and sing me through.

Words are passages through the world—not ends in themselves, but messengers from the others, beneath, before, and beyond us—finally made of a ghost world of guardian "others." We are "made of words," as Momaday claims, no less than spirits and mysteries.

And so, a guardian "animal walks beside me," the poet says, what the Algonkian Cree call a *mistebeo,* arm's length to the left, a protector down on all fours, from "the house of pelvic truth" in "The Ritual Life of Animals." The basic drives—hunger, sexual thrust, shelter—come in ritual sacrifice, lowering ourselves to be the sacrificed, the violated, the excreted. "Love has pitched his Mansion / in the place of excrement," Yeats chants with Crazy Jane. Down on her knees, Hogan concludes the section "Hunger" with the smell of her white mother's breast, nipple to her nipple, white milk and red blood fusing in the beginning and ending of all journeys. We are regenerately back to the title poem "Hunger," wanting to be inside loving, to drink and be held in the "thin, clear milk of the gods." The poet finds herself gathered by her dead mother in "the thin blue tail of the galaxy," the Milky or Spirit Way, *gone south,* Plains Indians say, to the other world of nurturing heavens, beyond the northern lights.

"The Book of Medicines," the second section, answers "Hunger" with the elements snow, rain, ice, and cloud. Playing on the homonym "tear," for Chickasaw dresses torn from scraps along the Trail of Tears, Hogan recalls her descent from both pioneer and native Indian grandmothers:

> They walk inside me. This blood
> is a map of the road between us.
> I am why they survived.
> The world behind them did not close.
> The world before them is still open.
> All around me are my ancestors,
> my unborn children.
> I am the tear between them
> and both sides live.

White intruder and red captive, the poet is the weeping rip that separates, through tears, and is sewn together again. She is the human who desecrates, and the animal who suffers; together she dreams of returning by way of a "circle of revelations," through the mirrored hole of herself to

> ... the place wind blows through
> when winter enters the room,
> the wounded place
> Raven walked out from

Born white, grown black in the wilderness reflection of grey water, Raven, too, would go back,

> the way glass wants to go back
> to being sand
> and ice wants to return
> to being water on earth
> as it is in heaven.

The poet's voice is lived "in the cracks between thawing ice" and reaches "all the infinite way down / to where breaking and darkness / are simple powers." Hogan's prayer touches contemporary global history: she knows that the destruction of Hiroshima was by no means a simple or natural force, still trumpeter vine seeds, buried in clay bricks, sprout from the carnage (see *The Crazy Iris*). So, too, barley still sprouts from Irish ditches, Seamus Heaney reminds us, where IRA resisters fell with seed rations in their pockets. Chickasaw and Cherokee women caressed leaves when they left Georgia and carried living roots to Oklahoma on forced removal. "The peaches were green when we left Alabama," the Creek Itshas Harjo said, "and the wild onions plentiful here when we arrived." The stories of these losses lift descendants from historically embedded rage, bringing them back from tragedy by taking them through it.

Skin is our oldest connection, a transparent dream to the other that both separates and joins humans by touch. Just so, the blue skin drum of a mother's womb, the heartbeat itself, stretches to the heated water drum:

> and is the oldest place
> the deepest world
> the skin of water
> that knows the drum before a hand meets it.

Healing comes in giving in to the elements, accepting what is and has been done, believing in the oldest truths of things:

> Earth tells her,
> return all lies to their broken source,
> trust in the strange science of healing.
> Believe the medicine of your own hand.

Primally and primevally, water and blood find their common nexus flowing down to their fulfillment, letting go, running their course and then lying still.

> It is true our lives will betray us in the end
> but life knows where it is going,
> so does water,
> so does blood,
> and the full and endless dance of space.

The poem "Two" reminds us of loving that "Water falls through our hands as we fall through it." We are permeable reality, primarily fluid, conditional, evolving, and adaptive to countless forms of life. Water, the great mother of the sea, gives us life within, flowing red as blood; just so, the faith healing of Hogan's mother, Nebraska pioneer daughter, sees the poet through her hopelessness. "Nothing sings in our bodies / like breath in a flute." Our skin is a shaman's water drum, our voice an open flute, our skeleton a taut bow, and "this living is such a journey / inside a breaking

open world," the poet marvels in "Great Measures." Ours is a world break-
ing into blossom, as James Wright saw beyond the dead swan's shadow.

With "the weight of living / tugging us down and earth wanting us
back," Hogan steps into light, growing inch by inch with the children "like
trees in a graveyard." The poet chants mother, daughter, sister: "It is ocean
/ calling the river, / Water." And ends with "The Origins of Corn" as a
sensual dance between man and woman, bringing forth a miracle, another
life, to be called by the same Hopi word, "child" and "corn." Domesticat-
ing Mother Corn from wild grass 12,000 years ago, the Pueblos and Mayans
say, "We are corn." Back home, the Algonkian gift of green corn in 1620
saved English pilgrims from starvation, commemorated in our most Amer-
ican of feast days, Thanksgiving, a treating "at the forest's edge" that joined
both halves of Hogan's genetic lineage in conditional peace and bounty.
This inclusive dream, beyond the nightmare tears, encloses *The Book of
Medicines*.

What makes this woman's work Indian? A mixed-blood writer, conscious
of Indian-Anglo schisms, Hogan tries to put herself together as a modern
native American, Chickasaw relocatee to Nebraska pioneer, singing the
heart home. Mixed-American, she worries about our spiritual dispossess-
ions, and Chickasaw descendant, she reads the landscape for signs of dam-
age and living renewal, listens to its rhythms and feels for its wounds, talks
with and about plants and especially animals in her poems. Combining
spiritual intuition with environmental activism, the poet listens empathi-
cally, while the machines deaden our hearing. She asks blessing, grace, and
courage from her totemic (brother "clansman") guardians, bear, wolf,
raven, whale, coyote, blackbird. No less than any spiritual scientist—care-
taker of the natural world, and the natural part of ourselves—she listens
and observes the Other, even rapacious "far-hearted" men, as aboriginal
Bushmen say, for empathic understanding and interspecies exchanges. Her
human attentions, beginning with adopted daughters, reach out to *all* her
relatives as kinsmen, an extended tribal family drawing the Buckskin Curtain
open. Stories, places, events, revelations—from animal magic, to historical
markings, to strange happenings—tie her people tribally together, from
the old days (Coyote Old Man to Darwin), to frontier collisions of *both* her
peoples (Trail of Tears to Wounded Knee), to present acculturations (Eliz-
abeth Bishop, Ralph Nader, and Russell Means). Hogan is particularly con-
cerned, as a woman, about the threats of male violence to the biosphere,
whale oil to oil wells, mass slaughter of bison, wolf, and bear to chemical
pollution and radioactive waste. Hers is a full and critical agenda. She
mourns the raping of land and animals ("they had their way with them"),
mindless killing (from sport hunting wild "game," to overseas dirty wars),
and men abusing even themselves (love-grief, loneliness, rage, neglect).

What makes this poetry? Neither rhyme nor meter, metaphor nor

structure, but her *concision,* Pound would see, shapes the economy and
depth of thinking lyrically. In a phrase, Hogan's *searching simplicity* informs
and shapes the poetry. She holds the verse reins lightly in an old-time
buckboard ride through our native country, giving herself time and relaxed
attention to take in the landscape and the life. "Muse," Denise Levertov
reminds us, means "to stand with open mouth," childlike and yet elder-
wise, in attentive concerns for our scattered present and collective future,
across the distances. In "The Weight" Linda Gregg speaks of two horses
in the same paddock who sleep standing, throats curved against each
other's rump:

> There are things they did that I do not know.
> The privacy of them had a river in it.
> Had our universe in it. And the way
> its border looks back at us with its light.
> This was finally their freedom.
> The freedom an oak tree knows.
> That is built at night by stars.

Is Hogan's free verse prosaic, formalists might worry, her prose too lyric?
Only if a reader sits on form and disregards Jorie Graham's distinction
between the *run run* of story and the lyric disruption of song. Hogan's lines
startle a reader, no less than Bishop or Dickinson or Welch, into quickened
living. What Lowell called the *blazing out* in Roethke is here the burning
in, the imploding spark of Pound's "luminous detail." Use the natural
object as image, Pound advised, and Hogan listens—a starving dog remem-
bers it was wolf, a deer turns into a raven eating carrion, a dentist uses Chief
Joseph's skull for an ashtray. A Mimbres *kill hole* in the clayware of Native
America swallows Ishi, the last of 4,000 Yana.

The healing comes, Hogan concludes, when the animal-in-human is
regarded as a guardian spirit of this natural world, unnaturally threat-
ened by violence, greed, and ignorance. Healing quickens by regarding
the organic contexts of texts, the ceremonial regards of ancestors, ob-
served daily. Poems-as-stories, the everyday sacraments and sayings, fluidly
keep humans going on going on. Each breath is hourly measure of our
daily poetics, stepping rhythmically into life, patterning a return to famil-
iar truths through honest words. And native poetry is that by which we
live in "red" affinity, under snow, rain, ice, and cloud. "And far from
kingdoms, from caesars, from brawls, from the cravings of penis and
sword," Cixous, Algerian-Jew and blood-sister to all native women, con-
cludes of newly born womanists, "from the unnamable 'goods' of this
world, far from show and self-love, in harmony with each other, in ac-
cord, they live still."

SAX DANCE STICK: HARJO

I propose a different structure; it's not original but what I've learned from being around tribal peoples, and in my own wanderings. The shape is a spiral in which all beings resonate. The bear is one version of human and vice versa. The human is not above the bear, nor is Adam naming the bear. Male and female are equal, useful forces—there's no illusion of domination. We move together. Transformation is really about understanding the shape and condition of another with compassion, not about overtaking.

JOY HARJO, *Religion & Literature,* 1994 (IN *Spiral of Memory*)

Joy Harjo grew up wanting to be a painter, in the family tradition of her Creek grandmother and aunt. After writing acid rock lyrics at the Santa Fe Institute of American Indian Arts, she discovered poetry her senior year, 1973, at the University of New Mexico (recently a full professor there), the AIM year of Wounded Knee, then got an M.F.A. in 1978 at the Iowa Writers' Workshop. Reading Emily Dickinson early on, Harjo "fell in love with poetry—the soundscape of poems," as she told a *Bloomsbury Review* interviewer. Initially she was influenced by Leslie Silko (who gave Harjo her first electric typewriter twenty-five years ago at UNM) and Simon Ortiz (father of her daughter, Rainy Dawn). Galway Kinnell and James Wright gave her writing models, as did Richard Hugo and Adrienne Rich. On the radio John Coltrane and Jim Pepper, Bessie Smith and Count Basie belted out the music behind her get-down language. Half a dozen books later, Joy Harjo is still on the road, trekking the lower Forty-Eight in her red pickup and Europe annually, chanting free verse lyrics and prose poems, playing saxophone riffs with "Poetic Justice," her native rock band. Harjo's most recent collection, *The Woman Who Fell from the Sky* (W. W. Norton 1994), comes with a tape cassette of performance poetry and saxophone music. This native woman has received the William Carlos Williams Award from the Poetry Society of America, the Delmore Schwartz Award, The American Book Award, NEA and Witter Bynner fellowships, and the 1990 American Indian Distinguished Achievement Award. She has just coedited an anthology of North and South American native women's writing, *Reinventing the Enemy's Language,* published a children's book, *The Goodluck Cat,* and will soon release her memoir, *A Love Supreme* (a John Coltrane line).

Joy Harjo was born in Tulsa, Oklahoma, in 1951 to a Cherokee-Irish-French teenage mother and a Creek father with lineage back through Menawha, the warrior who resisted relocation from Alabama to Oklahoma in the Muscogee Redstick War against Andrew Jackson. Joy's mother divorced "that crazy Creek from Oklahoma," and the eight-year-old, no less than Sylvia losing Otto Plath at eight, remembers her Creek father as "tall, wild, and stubborn," eventually dying of asbestos poisoning, or "white lung," alone in a trailer, outside Oyster Creek, Texas, when he was fifty-four (interview, *MELUS* 1989). Her mother "waitressed or cooked in truckstops or cafeterias" and wrote "heartbreak" song lyrics at the kitchen table on a battered Underwood typewriter (interview, *Hayden's Ferry Review* 1990). Harjo went through rebellious, even suicidal periods of rejecting both sides of her mixed-blood, but grew up to decide that "all people are originally tribal," as she told Joe Bruchac: "We're all in this together." Her adult life is syncretic, multi-blooded, fully sensual, cross-cultural: "I'm not separate from myself either, and neither are Indian people separate from the rest of the world." She admits that her poems are "different," but try to be inventively "androgynous," strong and full of grace, bear-hearted, horse-footed, deer-quickened, eagle-visioned.

Without a Creek reservation, Joy was raised working-class suburban on Tulsa's north side, hearing the influences of "many musics": country-western radio songs, especially her mother's fondness for Patsy Cline; jukebox music and crooning around the house; Baptist preachers like her grandfather Henry Harjo; Creek stomp dance songs; Black jazz by way of her Alabama heritage; Motown at Indian school; "and always the heartbreaking blues." The "art of poetry," Harjo says in *Kalliope* (1991), "is not separate from the art of music." Her voice is clearly the fusional product of America, writ large, singing from the epicene heart of the bear.

Music and literature have a long interconnective history, as repeated through the ages. The Greek word *mousike* combined dance, melody, poetry, and elementary education, as mentioned earlier. Rhythm and lyric, dance and scansion, music and narrative have always gone together, from Confucius with his stringed instrument gathering Chinese folk music, to blind Homer with his lyre singing Greek epic tales, to Wyatt, Yeats, and Pound set to musical lines, to Ginsberg with his harmonium verse or Bob Dylan with his harmonica blues. Think of Langston Hughes with Black jazz backup, Louis Armstrong with his trumpet, Lew Serett with his Indian drum songs in the 1920s, Bessie Smith and Billie Holiday with hip-grinding lyrics, Jack Kerouac with Steve Allen improvising jazz on the piano, Leonard Cohen, Neil Young, Laurie Anderson, Black rappers (especially "The Last Poets" of Harlem), or Bruce Springsteen today. Listen to Bill Miller's Mohawk "Reservation Road" or the Dakota AIM leader-turned-rock-lyricist, John Trudell, with his Venice, California, "Grafitti Band" (*sic*), started by Jesse Ed Davis, the Kiowa backup guitarist for Eric Clapton. Play "Witchi Tia To," a tape of the Creek-Kaw saxophonist Jim Pepper blowing Manhattan jazz riffs with stomp dance rhythms, then listen to Joy Harjo reworking the rhythms with "Poetic Justice." All these literate musicians have a native context. From lullaby, to hunting and planting song, to love charm, to rowing chorus, to death lament, to vision cry, to ceremonial feast, to gambling counterpoint, to burial dirge, to renewal chant, to prayer—Native

American verses have been sung to drum, rattle, flute, or rhythmic foot for millennia.

Published by Thunder's Mouth Press in 1983, the same year as Hogan's *Eclipse, She Had Some Horses* is free-verse Indian riff, a combination of performance poetry and ceremonial improvisation, to the guardian spirit hoofbeat of wild female energies. If Plath in her last days heard the "indefatigable hooftaps" of a retreating rider, Harjo counters heartbreak deadend clatter with a galloping howl, a counterlove of contrary feminist voices reversing the field. She trades on the thunder and energy of horses in motion, icons of transformation, in chanted rhythms that accumulate power. Her long, pulsing lines drop unexpectedly into lyric resonance—the voice as an alto sax counterpoint, *wa-waah*, bending the *thrum-thrum* of a storytelling drive, here in the anaphoral chant of "Remember":

> Remember the sky that you were born under,
> know each of the star's stories.
> Remember the moon, know who she is. I met her
> in a bar once in Iowa City. . . .
> Remember the wind. Remember her voice. She knows the
> origin of this universe. I heard her singing Kiowa war
> dance songs at the corner of Fourth and Central once.

It's a Beat beat, cool, off-center, a hip *jouissance* in sixties countermeasure. And still there's hurt in her gently enduring, lyric humor—cut, incisive, penetrant—coming out of bars, booze, midnight highways and Kansas City moons, lovers always leaving, returning. Home is usually a horizon away, until she learns to carry it within her. This poet is not a nester, a domestic, or a suburban "nice" lady, though she's raised Phil Dayn and Rainy Dawn, two of her own children, alone. Horse-sister and crow-cousin, Harjo seems a woman in search of her own voice of power, her own radical style. She sways to her own demons and dreams, in short, an original she-bear and coyotess of native ways.

Harjo has created the persona, Noni Daylight, who shows up in "Heartbeat" as a fictional alter ego. Hers is the razor edge of desperate womanism, sneaking out the back door of her son's room in their apartment "for the hunt," driving Albuquerque all night, alone, with a pistol in her lap—tracking danger, heartbeat pounding, with "a fierce anger / that will free her." How Noni will get free is not yet clear (she has slipped into Barney Bush's writing), but her native determination is: to ease the "trembling ache" of a forbidden memory of woman-love in poems with women and children and other women, few men, coming down through Adrienne Rich, Audre Lorde, Paula Gunn Allen, Alice Walker, June Jordan, Meridel LeSueur, Tillie Olson, Gertrude Stein, and Gloria Steinem—old myths of women sufficient unto themselves, Amazonian archers with an incendiary

snap of fierce lyricism, hip-to-hip with Jack Kerouac. A smoky-throated du-
ende sidles up in "Nautilus":

> This is how I cut myself open
> —with a half pint of whiskey, then
>   there's enough dream to fall through
>
>   to pure bone and shell
>   where ocean has carved out
>
> warm sea animals,
>   and has driven the night
>   dark and in me
>
>   like a labyrinth of knives.

Her heart cleaves open cleanly in danger, fear, and courage. Back to Sap-
pho, this self-wounding performance with death as stage manager may be
the act Plath mastered too well. Native peoples have had enough of sense-
less death. Harjo's many horses constantly save her in powwow chants, old
tongues, new riffs, all mixed with bar talk, jukebox blues, come-ons, con-
fessionals, hip bravado, and a quiet determination to get through one more
dark night, alone, or with the one she's with. In "She Remembers the
Future," Noni Daylight asks whether to dream her poet "afraid,"

> "Or should you ride colored horses
> into the cutting edge of the sky
> to know
>
> that we're alive
> we are alive."

A history of one-horse affairs breaks her heart wide open to the oldest
love-story around, you and not-me, Orpheus and Eurydice in "What I
Should Have Said." With Leonard Cohen lyrics ("cold as a new razor
blade"), the goddess Diana comes on another kind in "Moonlight," a
woman protectress in the arms of a distant mother sky. Remember sisters
moon and wind, the poems chant, strangers met on street corners, or in
all-night bars, in reverse anthropomorphic, one-night-stand kinships. With
Willie Nelson ballads and whiskey blues in snappy juke lines, Albuquerque-
booted, Harjo thrusts a shoulder forward and boasts in "Alive,"

> I am free to be sung to;
> I am free to sing. This woman
> can cross any line.

The arts fuse, no less than artists cross cultures and forms. Lawrence
claimed the running rose flame for experimental verse, free of formal re-
straints. One leap wilder by century's end, wild-ass IAIA native canvases

hang above Joy Harjo's lines: Van Gogh crows in a wheat field behind T. C. Cannon's seated grandfather, Jean LaMarr's Buckskin princess before barbed wire and a jet fighter in the sky, Harry Fonseca's swish Coyote in "Swan Lake" and "Four Seasons," and R. C. Gorman's Navajo-Mexican woman under a serape.

Joy Harjo does not know Muskogee, but living in the Southwest, she studied Navajo in college and learned to speak it fairly well. She would take special note of David P. McAllester translating Frank Mitchell's "Enemy Slayer's Horse Song" in 1957 at Chinle, Arizona, with opening reference to Changing Woman, principal Navajo deity *(Coming to Light):*

> Now White Shell Woman, *na,* her child, since that is who I am, *na,*
> —with their voices, for me they are calling,
> —with their voices, for me they are calling, *ya'e, nege yana.*

In red feminist riff, more radically than Matthews, Cronyn, Momaday, or Swann reexpress the Navajo chants, Harjo reinvokes the Blessingway for traditional good luck with travel, livestock, and wealth in her title poem, "She Had Some Horses":

> She had horses with long, pointed breasts.
> She had horses with full, brown thighs.
> She had horses who laughed too much.
> She had horses who threw rocks at glass houses.
> She had horses who licked razor blades.
>
> She had some horses.

"Horsey" male and female combined, this intersexual icon for strength and sensitivity is itself a fusional breed in the New World, first released by Cortés's mounted conquistadors. The horse evolved toward the mustang or mixed-blood *musteño* traded and stolen north into Canada, spreading across the plains as a "centaur," Momaday says of Kiowa migrations by the eighteenth century, bred into Appaloosa by the Nez Percé, and coming to the Lakota as a transfiguration of "dog holy," *sunka wakan* or Super Dog. At fourteen on Scotts Bluff above the North Platte River, the legendary Crazy Horse or *Sunka Witko,* boy-named Curly, envisioned a horse so wildly strange that it seemed *witko,* not so much "crazy," as supernatural or otherworldly. The winter counts of a ledger historian like Amos Bad Heart Bull immortalized the flying hooves of Lakota ponies. General "Bearcoat" Miles said that the world had never seen finer equestrians.

Thus growing up in Indian Territory plains, Joy Harjo inherits a native iconography of passion and strength, of mobility and fecundity, of wild sensuality and thundering power—the energy, mass, motion, and nobility of Lakota *Takuskanskan,* the Creative Forces of "What-moves-moves" embodied in the four-legged centaur. "She *had* some *hors*es," the drum voice chants, all kinds in all times, and will have more. Like Linda Hogan's Oklahoma Chickasaw grandfather, her father's Creek great-grandfather, Menawha, was renowned for his horse sense, a famous equestrian thief. So the horse is Harjo's androgynous icon and imaginative catalyst, free to leap and gallop and graze where native instinct takes her, no less than Stevens ringed with blackbirds, Momaday inspired by eagle and bear, Sitting Bull mentored by meadowlarks, Roethke solaced by snail, or Dickinson spirited by singing birds, flies, and butterflies.

Harjo's more traditional voice, softened with ceremonial regard, comes through the collaborative prose poetry in *Secrets from the Center of the World*. She teams up with Stephen Strom, an astronomer at the University of Massachusetts, and responds verbally to his four-by-four-inch, pastel-washed photographs of the Southwest desert (analogues to Momaday's four-by-four ceremonial shields). The passages are tone poems, pure and simple, with clear lyric beauty, activated through a small aperture by "a fine depth of field." Consistent with "tribal vision," Harjo says, "it all flows together" in a Southwest kind of microcosmic *hozhó*. "All landscapes have a history, much the same as people exist within cultures, even tribes. There are distinct voices, languages that belong to particular areas. There are voices inside rocks, shallow washes, shifting skies; they are not silent." As mentioned and consistent among many tribes, the Lakota call these rock-voices *Tunkáshila*, both "grandfathers" and "stones," speaking anciently. The motions in such landscapes are "subtle, unseen, like breathing," Harjo says, and "if you allow your own inner workings to stop long enough," these sounds and motions move "into the place inside you that mirrors a similar landscape; you too can see it, feel it, hear it, know it." The formula is as old as prayer: envision, sense, resonate, and narrate a story, a sigh, a song. So the poet speaks through an aperture of sacred landscape, finding the land within the *scape,* the poem within the sound. This inner-outer cadence of self, in relationship to a given tribal landscape, generates an American rhythm of our common country. "From the mud hills of Nazlini to Moencopi rise, on the other side of Tuba City," Harjo writes of postmodernist Blessingways, "the earth Strom photographs speaks powerful stories. They are of its own origins as the keeper of bones; of survival; of the travels and changes of the people moving on it, inside it; of skies. And the stories change with light, with what is spoken, with what is lived."

"My house is the red earth," *Secrets* opens, focusing on a minuscule hogan washed in reds at "the center of the world." An imagined "fool crow," picking fat scraps near the corral, has nothing to lament of grief and survival, but simply "perches on the blue bowl of the sky, and laughs." Here caws Wallace Stevens in Navajo country, Van Gogh on the southwest desert, rescued from extinction by black trickster birds who rave truth.

"And understand how three crows at the edge of the highway, laughing, become three crows at the edge of the world, laughing." Evolutionary Indians like Harjo, Momaday, and Hogan know geological acclimation full well: "Moencopi Rise stuns me into perfect relationship, as I feed a skinny black dog the rest of my crackers, drink coffee, contemplate the frozen memory of stones. Nearby are the footprints of dinosaurs, climbing toward the next century." Seeing this world truly, that is, beneath the surface, shapes a landscape of the imagination. "It's true the landscape forms the mind. If I stand here long enough I'll learn how to sing. None of that country & western heartbreak stuff, or operatic duels, but something cool as the blues, or close to the sound of a Navajo woman singing early in the morning." A bilingual space-time or *chronotope* overlaps cultures, Dickinson's weighted slant of light as flesh-in-season, crossed with Luci Tapahonso's women singing: "To describe anything in winter whether it occurs in the past or the future requires a denser language, one thick with the promise of new lambs, heavy with the weight of corn milk." And the single-line lyric, resonant within Strom's square-box photo, hangs by minimalist symmetry. "In winter it is easier to see what my death might look like over there, disappearing into the misty, spotted rocks."

These sepia images invoke beauty, but even with the "patience of stones" word-pictures cannot express the world fully. "This land is a poem of ochre and burnt sand I could never write, unless paper were the sacrament of sky, and ink the broken line of wild horses staggering the horizon several miles away." Any given language, especially writing, goes only so far, Harjo says in *Tamaqua* (1992): "I'm always aware of the spectrum of other languages and modes of expression, including, for instance, cloud language, cricket singing talk, and the melodic whir of hummingbirds." She sensually concludes the poem, "Bleed Through":

> There are no words, only sounds
> that lead us into the darkest nights,
> where stars burn into ice
> where the dead arise again
> to walk in shoes of fire.

You must get up close, touch the center of things, with eye, hand, voice, and the imagination of all these in petroglyphic earth-stories. "My cheek is flat against memory described by stone and lichen. The center of the world is within reach. It is as familiar as your name, as strange as monsters in your sleep." The power of this landscape brings us back to ourselves, homing, with faith in the good beauty, Navajo *hozhó*. "I am witness to flexible eternity, the evolving past, and I know we will live forever, as dust or breath in the face of stars, in the shifting pattern of winds."

Harjo writes thin books, about the width of grassblade or knife. *In*

Mad Love and War comes on with mod girl love, the illicit sister stuff that crosses NOW, AIM, and an alternative All-Nations Drum pounding out, *We're here, we're queer, get used to it!* The collection riffles with an off-beat, zip-suit, razored energy; if you forget to laugh, to dance, to snort or to howl, the gaggle falls flat. A go-go stripper changes into a deer-like Sappho in a sleazy, all-night dive: "bar of broken survivors, the club of shotgun, knife wound, of poison by culture." The Indian woman dances naked on a table with blanket-ass courage, the beautiful goings-on of native transformation. "We were Indian ruins. She was the end of beauty." The oral traditional riff of this narrative song brings down-and-out natives back for one more vision. An undressed beauty transforms into a deer on a bartop among drunks, drawn back by evolutionary visions to an older world of unashamed freedoms. Her long-legged, raggedy-ass rhythms get down in lyric beauty, curling anapests and dactyls steel-string-bent:

> We are *all* in the *bel*ly of a *danc*ing god
> *swim*ming the *heav*ens, in this *whirl*ing *cir*cle.

Hot feminist licks sizzle Harjo's lines, in the book's dedication acknowledging "Leslie [Silko]'s" sense of story, "Audre [Lorde]'s" erotic courage, and editor/writer/ally "Brenda [Peterson]'s mad love," as in the Dylanesque "A Hard Rain":

> Until I awaken again to swollen clouds
> and your dark hand on my thigh
> the only hot sun I want to feel.

Catch the womanesque references of "Bleed Through":

> Her anger is yours and when her teeth bite through
> a string of glass
> you awaken, and it is not another dream
> but your arms around a woman
> who was once a dagger between your legs.

Sense the sexual imperative in "City of Fire":

> I will dream you a wolf
> and suckle you newborn.
> I will dream you a hawk
> and circle this city in your
> racing heart.
> I will dream you the wind,
> taste salt air on my lips until
> I take you apart raw.
> Come here.

Feel the vaginal heat in "Heartshed":

> I walk into another room inside
>   your skin house.
> I open your legs with my tongue.
> The war is not over but inside you
>   the night is hot
> and my fingers walk their way up your spine.
> Your spirit rattles in your bones and yes
> let's dance this all again
>   another beginning.

The maturing occurs here, the compassionate letting go—lovers, ex-husbands and fathers, children, angers, words themselves—in a smoldering dance of the living to live fully, to *bleed through* to the feminine power of blood. "I understand lovemaking is praising God with your body," Harjo told an interviewer in *Religion & Literature* (1994; in *Spiral of Meaning*, 1996). These are poems of women in their monthly letting go, in orgasm, in birthing, and in tending the living and the dead.

"The Real Revolution is Love," Harjo says in idiomatic dreams and prophesies, as savage Cassandra of a broke-down, getting-back-up native America, born of women. "I do what I want, and take my revolutions to bed with me, alone." Ours is *not* a foreign country, she insists, but the land of reborn, newly acculturated dreams, "the root of my own furious love." No less than Berryman or Alexie, this poet gets down *mad*, to the ground sense necessary of knowing herself *native*, however she was born or chooses to live. "Let me hear you / by any means: by horn, by fever, by night, even by some poem // attempting flight home," she says in "Bird." The war is on, still, by way of words, in wild leaps of faith. "To survive is sometimes a leap into madness." Any sign is salvation to a Creek hitchhiker going home: "Does the license plate say Oklahoma?"

Some Adrian Louis sass and Jim Pepper blues corn salt the prose poems—junkie angel music—by way of Bessie Smith and Billie Holiday, John Coltrane and Aretha Franklin, Richard Hugo and Barney Bush. Surreal-italicked images carry the poet back to the southwest desert, where "Spirits play crack-the-whip in the abyss" of "Day of the Dead," twisting into yet another lyric realism. "I have built a fire in the cave of my body, and hope the devil wind gives it a chance." She does not give up: "I will drink whiskey and slow-dance with slim boys, rock with glitter angels, before going home alone. Tomorrow I will feed the dead. Then I must find you." Her sister-in-redemption, Rebecca Tsosie, once a UCLA undergraduate, now a law professor at Arizona State, knows only too well "The Woman Hanging from the Thirteenth Floor Window":

This woman could be any number of women, or even ourselves. Her poem speaks to those of us who have felt the dull throb of pain at 4 A.M. when the cold glare of neon signs holds no comfort against the lonely grey drizzle of early city mornings. City nights are as hard and unyielding as the oily asphalt of city streets. Companionship in after-hours clubs is limited to pimps in purple-feathered hats and diamond-stuffed rings, to Black or Mexican proprietors that keep pistols in their belts and whiskey in their hands, and to other Indians who are as lost and lonely as you are.

This is the forbidden, break-your-heart, drop-dead romance of lost America, even if "(everyone is ultimately a relative)" in a Muskogee world. Tsosie continues:

I think of a young Hopi girl in Oakland. She is not more than sixteen and she is dancing with a Black man dressed in a flashy white suit. They are dancing to a passionate "Brown Sugar" that thunders from the jukebox and drowns out the city-sounds—the screaming sirens and the low moan of the trucks rolling on out of town. She is dancing sedately, her face a quiet mask, and the Arizona mesas and low thunder clouds appear for a moment in the smoky haze, and then are gone, gone far, far away so that not even a memory remains.

Harjo holds out for desire as the transforming vision of love: "Say all of this is true and more // than there are blackbirds / in a heaven of blackbirds." Her vision of an eagle has circled America on bus lines, in subways, along train tracks, as "American Poetry in the Streets," here in prayer verses from "Eagle Poem":

> Breathe in, knowing we are made of
> All this, and breathe, knowing
> We are truly blessed because we
> Were born, and die soon within a
> True circle of motion,
> Like eagle rounding out the morning
> Inside us.
> We pray that it will be done
> In beauty.
> In beauty.

A visionary kindness of all kinds of living patterns language, circles fire, wings being—the oldest, most natural kindnesses among extended kin. Rebecca Tsosie signs the coda:

Sometimes you feel that you can never go home again. Sometimes you feel that you have forgotten how to speak, that your eyes are hollow, burning sockets that are unable to cry. Pain releases itself in low, animal cries, in the chatter of teeth at the terrible cold of a city night, and in the desire to escape somewhere, anywhere, even out of a 13th story window.

At the root of the pain is fear—fear of the cold, anonymous city, fear of going back to the poverty of the reservation, fear of racists and rapists and of what the school will "teach" the children, fear of what vision the next drink will bring, and fear of what will happen if there *is* no drink ("Changing Women," UCLA undergraduate honors manuscript).

Harjo's most recent, and most visibly marketed book, *The Woman Who Fell from the Sky,* twists its title from an Iroquois creation myth, also a spin on a sci-fi, underground film, *The Man Who Fell to Earth.* Marge Piercy, Scott Momaday, Meridel LeSueur, Linda Hogan, Adrienne Rich, Sandra Cisneros endorse the book with blurbs, Indians and women of color, doubly othered, marching to a marginal beat that has become mainstream: "these poems make clear," Hogan says, "what is unspeakable in us and not yet come to words." Dedicated to her two *grand*daughters and "my other children," all eight of them, Harjo's book begins with a "prayer" of "reconciliation" arcing into the next century, climbing out of nightmares into miracles, never giving up, as with blood sisters like Tapahonso and Whiteman. The writer drops the pretense of line lengths, essentially, catching a prose riff that takes its own intrinsic time going along, from DNA, family clan talk, and Bell's theorem, back to Muskogee great-grandparents, in acts of strange cruelty (she says via the bumper sticker) and rare kindness: *"We cannot be separated in the loop of mystery between blackbirds and the memory of blackbirds."*

Clearly, from the title poem on, this poet wants to say something *different,* in an experimental form different from the norm, accessible, narratable, yet with a spin: "new psychic splits of space," in a "new literary tradition," apart from English conventions, "a combination of oral and written, a new movement," she says in *Kalliope* (1991). From here, all are relatives. "Ultimately, all people are tribal." A common diagonal crosses our lives, straight to gay, child to saint, lost to found peoples. "When you were born in this country," Harjo continues her interview, à la Austin, "you were born into the mythic structure of native peoples, the history that has gone on, is still ongoing" (in *Spiral of Meaning*). And elsewhere in *Tamaqua:* "You have to recognize that a few hundred years ago, aboriginal peoples were one hundred percent of the population of this continent. Now, we're one-half of one percent of the total population!" (in *Spiral of Meaning*). So a falling Dairy Queen mother-goddess named Lila is caught in the arms of Johnny "Saint Coincidence," panhandling outside Safeway, and the plot wobbles between chic despair and new age native regeneration.

Harjo composes on the go, backpack notebook to laptop computer in an Apache-owned restaurant. The intentional "truth teller of the culture" wants to "make a terrible music with our wise and ragged bones," from dead friends, to taxi drivers, to ex-husbands and lovers, in rescued fragments of memoir, digressive stories, echoing atrocities. Harjo records the

wild drama of her maternal Cherokee-Irish-French grandparents, who bore
six sons and one daughter, her mother:

> *When he returned nine months later she was near full term with*
> *a baby who wasn't his. He beat her until she went into labor and gave*
> *birth to the murdered child.*
>
> *Shortly after the killing my grandparents attempted double suicide. They*
> *stood on the tracks while a train bore down on them as all the children*
> *watched in horror. At the last possible second my grandfather pushed*
> *my grandmother off to safety and leaped behind her.*

No lines are ever free, and none come easy. Female Bretón down west,
hers is a Field of Miracles, Lucca to Albuquerque, with the leaning Tower
of Pisa, Bosque Redondo of The Long March, and Anasazi petroglyphs of
hump-backed Kokopelli and prehistoric animals. "The world begins at a
kitchen table," Harjo's final poem begins, "Perhaps the World Ends
Here."

> It is here that children are given instructions on what it means to be
> human. We make men at it, we make women.
>
> At this table we gossip, recall enemies and the ghosts of lovers.
>
> Our dreams drink coffee with us as they put their arms around our
> children. They laugh with us at our poor falling-down selves and as
> we put ourselves back together once again at the table.
>
> This table has been a house in the rain, an umbrella in the sun.
> . . . .
> Perhaps the world will end at the kitchen table, while we are laugh-
> ing and crying, eating of the last sweet bite.

TWELVE

A Terrible Innocence: Forché

The blood-dimmed tide is loosed, and everywhere
The ceremony of innocence is drowned;
W. B. YEATS, "A PRAYER FOR MY DAUGHTER"

Native women trade stories and gossip around a kitchen table at the world's ending. Are these elegiac voices *about* to sing, as Valéry anticipates poetry, or soon to fall silent? The news is mixed. From regional home to international family, men's wars to women's rebirthings, what options are left in the West? "All changed, changed utterly:" Yeats cried of his native Ireland, "A terrible beauty is born."

After Auschwitz, Theodor Adorno said, all documentation is barbarous, and yet perfidiously, native relocation camps, politicized racism, and cultural genocide remain. Our century has been a massive killing field of shattered hearts and silenced songs. Can any still *sing with the heart of a bear?* Among thousands of life-forms, native bears have been exterminated in most parts of the New World, no less than threatened American bison and Indians, relocated to national reserves as endangered species. Natural life-forms and Native Americans have survived five hundred years of a sustained holocaust, some ninety-seven percent attrition of sixty million natives. Cultural diaspora still fractures their lifestyles, warfare declared on their populations even today in parts of Latin America. The Lakota Pine Ridge Nation in South Dakota, where Crazy Horse, Sitting Bull, and Red Cloud sang with hearts of bears, reserves the poorest county in the United States, the highest rates of teen suicide, school drop-out, and unemployment. Diabetes, alcoholism, and traffic wrecks ravage the people. And still they hold on, holding out for their own language, traditional means of livelihood, tribal integrity, political sovereignty, ceremonial literacy. Perhaps at a flash point, Native Americans can teach the West something about cultural courage and spiritual reconstruction—the bear's survival chant as medicine, strength, and teaching—before we all go down dispossessed in history.

Today, the Polish refugee and distinguished Nobel writer, Czeslaw

Milosz, sifts Euro-American literary evidence of historical dislocation, indeed, cultural catastrophe, for keys to the next millennium. "How did it happen," Milosz asks in *The Witness of Poetry*, "that to be a poet of the twentieth century means to receive training in every kind of pessimism, sarcasm, bitterness, doubt?" This century's modernists deny any "Ode to Joy" above Western ennui, and postmodernists suffer worse disillusion. In the Holocaustal wake of his own Polish romantic history, Milosz finds extermination camp *barbed wire* to stand as the "perfect expression" of our collective historical nightmare. "Hell is both man-made," Joseph Brodsky adds of imprisoned writers, "and manned by man" ("Writer in Prison"). The legend of Viktor Jara during Pinochet's 1973 military coup of Chile, the day Neruda died, is a case in point. Dissident artists were rounded up by armed squads and huddled by the thousands in a soccer stadium. The people's musician, a Chilean Woody Guthrie, Viktor Jara began to play his guitar and lead the political prisoners in resistance singing. Ordered to stop, Jara kept playing, so a soldier mutilated his hand, the people say, and he *kept singing*. These native stories and bearheart songs in our time hurl across the Western Hemisphere.

Again the West hears Caliban railing against Renaissance speech, cursing, threatening, grumbling into mute tempest on an isolated island: "You taught me language, and my profit on't / Is, I know how to curse. The red plague rid you / For learning me your language" (*The Tempest* 1.2.365–67).

> always the silence remains kneeling.
>
> Every word is a doorway
> to a meeting, one often canceled,
> and that's when a word is true: when it insists on the meeting.
>
> YANNIS RITSOS, "THE MEANING OF SIMPLICITY"

"What can poetry be in the twentieth century?" Milosz pleads in "Ruins and Poetry." For the Polish refugee "there is a search for the line beyond which only a zone of silence exists . . . ." The ruins of poetry scatter in today's decentered, deconstructed, now historically reconstructed *text*—the printed door into darkness, smudged phonemes on a thin rectangle of *nothing*. This lost passage barely tracks across split minds and broken hearts, back to a native poetics, a reconciling of Native and Euro-American cultures. "In the dark times, will there also be singing?" Bertolt Brecht asked. "Yes, there will be singing. About the dark times." If retranslated accurately and reaffirmed interculturally, a native Western script could offer passage beyond illusory light, past failed speech, above fallen idols.

The bearheart song turns back on itself where this study began. A hundred years ago, the Gold Rush had already overrun California with speculation, violence, and greed that has not ceased to this day, Sutter's Mill to suburban mall. Mary Austin felt a mystery in the Sierra Nevada arroyos, "a lurking, evasive Something, wistful, cruel, ardent; something that rustled and ran" from despoiling boosterism, "the miracle-mongering of over-grown vegetation and inflated prices." Austin elegized the "low round hills on which the wild oats had dried moon-white and standing," and no less than Sitting Bull or Emily Dickinson, she dreamed of natural wonders: "Beauty-in-the-wild, yearning to be made human." From her midwestern childhood in "a perpetually widowed house," to a troubled young marriage in Southern California, Mary Austin was plagued with "the black spell" of wanting to know answers to a homeless sense of displacement, "cast away on a waterless strip in a dry year" *(Earth Horizon)*.

> She would lie in her bunk with fixed, wide-open eyes, hearing the cu- owls on the roof, the nearly noiseless tread of coyotes going by in the dark, the strange ventriloquist noises they kept up with their cousins miles away beyond Rose Station, hearing the slow shuffling tread of the starved cattle, momentarily stopped by the faint smell of the settlers' water-barrels, but too feeble to turn out of their own tracks to come at them.

In 1890 Mary Austin witnessed the depressive Fall, again, her own "complete collapse" the year of the Wounded Knee Massacre, the closing of the frontier, the assassination of Sitting Bull. "And meantime, the place of the mystery was eaten up, it was made into building lots, cannery sites; it receded before the preemptions of rock crushers and city dumps."

Austin's conversion to Native America came through this 1890s crisis of westering civilization. Yes, she was a bit daffy about her Indian soul and an intuited American rhythm—but no less courageous than natives seeking bicultural choices, both Native *and* American, through the narrow turns of the century, beginning with Mabel McKay adopted by the Pomo and Mary TallMountain working in San Francisco, Luther Standing Bear writing his memoirs in Los Angeles or Charles Eastman becoming a Lakota physician in Boston. The mixing already in motion, the hybrid middle could not be excluded. Mary Austin took on native positions, no less than mixed-blood natives becoming American in our time, Archie Phinney to Ella Deloria, N. Scott Momaday to Joy Harjo. In the land of little rain, "She began to learn how Indians live off a land upon which more sophisticated races would starve, and how the land itself instructed them." The spirit of place, embodied in a native people's cultural rhythms and historied instincts, would help to heal her émigré sense of homelessness, Old World and New become one world. Daily rituals and dialectal tongues, ancestral religions and tribal paradigms fused her American context and translative text, from the turn of the last century on.

And for those coming after, beyond disillusion in our own time, a native poetics still lies under our passage west. "I watched Black Elk speak to the flies on a drying buffalo skin," Norman Dubie dreams in *The Clouds of Magellan*. "He addressed them as cousins. I have so much to learn." New translations, revised approaches toward cultural diversity, correct mistranslations and misappropriations. "The writing of poetry *is* redemptive," Dubie says of Black Elk's flaming rainbow vision of the sky tepee, an analogue to Momaday's house made of dawn, a Navajo borrowing. What still twists beneath our stubborn toughness, where do human tenderness, beauty, or grace lie? Think back to Linda Hogan's elegy for a lost native America, "Blessed / are those who listen / when no one is left to speak." Who speaks for us? Writers can start by revising a poetics of witness where history, politics, art, and personal concerns coalesce, beyond holocaustal rage or millennial despair, hearing the bearheart sing again. It cannot be, and never was, simple or easy.

The Nobel German essayist, Elias Canetti, addressed an international Munich gathering in January 1976 on "The Writer's Profession." No one can write today, he said, without seriously doubting the "right" to be a writer. We come to words, and to our worlds, out of great suspicion and deepest need, the daily crises of loving; still, our "responsibility for life" must be "nourished by compassion," as through the global work of PEN or Amnesty International, for example. Back to *Gilgamesh* (and before), Canetti finds in the "early incomparable creations" of tribal poetries, "an inexhaustible spiritual legacy." As invaders everywhere, Westerners do not merit the host, yet the poet's tribal "resurrection" may initiate a "metamorphosis" toward grace. America's rebirth, through its own native poetics, could draw us all together, across our original differences, as Canetti concludes in *The Conscience of Words*:

> One shall seek nothingness only to find a way out of it and one shall mark the road for everyone. Whether in grief or in despair, one shall endure in order to learn how to save others from it, but not out of scorn for the happiness that the creatures deserve, even though they deface one another and tear one another to pieces.

A Western visionary, Elias Canetti speaks for natives in the Americas, as well as for all the world. Such a path leads to what Czeslaw Milosz terms the *Witness of Poetry*.

ADAM O'ER-REACHING

For me, Malintzin is at the heart of the very issues that Chicanas are struggling with today—race, class, gender, sexuality, and voice. Because she is so well known, she is associated with all Indian women and with all of us as mestizas. She represents the indigenous feminine aspect of this continent—the continent it-

*self as Mother Earth, which continues to be invaded, violated, exploited, tortured,
and killed.* . . .

INÉS HERNÁNDEZ-ÁVILA IN JOY HARJO AND GLORIA BIRD,
Reinventing the Enemy's Language

Many tongues rail and cry at the heart of our dispossessions since the dis-
covery of Native America. Misperceptions and mistranslations mar the first
exchanges between Old and New Worlds, Tzvetan Todorov observes in *The
Conquest of America.* As his journals record, Columbus on a ship without
women or children could not see the people for the exotic trees, animals,
and birds, never seen by Europeans. In 1493 he gave an Adamic new name
to the first of his "discovered" islands, San Salvador, or Saint Savior. So,
too, in 1519 Cortés renamed Vera Cruz under the shadow of the "true
cross" and Spanish crown. He made speeches to Montezuma through a
shipwrecked Portuguese sailor, Gerónimo de Aguilar. The conquistador's
"other" Latin tongue had learned Mayan speech as a captive and came
aboard the Spanish ship in Cuba. This Portuguese castaway heard Quiché
translated from Nahuatl, by way of the Spaniard's concubine, La Malinche,
or Doña Marina. The Aztec princess was born Ce Malinalli, the Chief of
Paynala's daughter, called Malintzin among her people, a figure still scape-
goated in Mexico as whoring betrayer, a *malinchista*. Why this misogynist
scapegoating where gender shadows ethnic abuse?

An Aztec minor royal child, Ce Malinalli had been sold to the Mayans
as diplomatic fealty. The Chief of Tabasco subsequently presented her at
seventeen as war booty to Hernán Cortés. On her insurrectional return
with the Conquistador, she spoke Nahuatl to Moctezuma, through royal
interlocutors. Four tongues, then, stuttered with mixed motives among
New World collaborators: Cortés, the soldier of fortune (Spanish); Aguilar,
the castaway sailor (Portuguese); La Malinche, the enslaved courtesan
(Quiché); Montezuma, collapsing emperor, fronted by royal emissaries
(Nahuatl). The Aztec king addressed the Spanish soldier of fortune by the
slur of his mistress, La Malinche, vulgarly translated as the Fucked.

The enslaved princess Doña Marina later bore Cortés an illegitimate son,
Martín, before he married her off to Juan Jaramillo, a young captain in
Honduras. Today, La Malinche is synonymous with La Chingada, derivative
of Aztec words for foul residue, garden seed, and alcohol. Octavio Paz
explains the connotations of breaking, ripping open, and voiding in *The
Labyrinth of Solitude:* "The Chingada is the Mother forcibly opened, violated
or deceived. The hijo de la Chingada is the offspring of violation, abduction
or deceit." La Chingada appears a complex Latin American term, then, a
verb of male aggression, now associated with the violated Mother, forcefully
penetrated and vanquished by the Father. Permutations on this term
lace Hispanic dialects across Latin America: *Se chingó*, something breaks;

chingones, political bosses; *gran chingón,* the macho male; *Vete a la chingada,*
go to hell, literally, "nothingness." La Chingada's "children" bear the
illicit fruits of the Black Legend, as Paz explains Latin resistance to racial
fusion from the Conquest, fueling the chingón embers of arbitrary and
illegitimate power. So in Mexican folklore, the violent male humiliates the
abject female, Paz argues, and La Malinche, "the Mexican Eve," is still
regarded as whoring betrayer, the native concubine of a Spaniard who
conquered the Aztec empire.

Doubling as the vanquished and resurrected sun god, Quetzalcoatl, Cor-
tés commanded in the name of Christ and a Spanish queen, while on the
other side teetered a declining Aztec king in an imploding empire. Moc-
tezuma abdicated his reign under Tezcatlipoca, god of highwaymen, war-
riors, and murderers ("omnipotent and omnipresent," the Aztecs said,
"like the darkness, like the mind"). And so the night-god-king of Tenoch-
titlán, orchidean island in the central valley of Aztec Mexico, surrendered
several hundred thousand devout warriors to the few hundred mercenaries
of a pale knight on horseback, Hernán Cortés, bearded, pious, rapacious,
gold-thirsty, impersonating the returning sun god. "The Spaniards are
troubled with a disease of the heart," Cortés said, "for which gold is the
specific remedy." Fray Pedro de Gante baptized fourteen thousand Indians
each day with his spittle, for lack of holy water in the New World. This odd
cleansing came some two decades before Pope Paul III declared Indians
"truly men" in the 1537 papal bull Sublimis Deus.

"We are all the direct descendants of Columbus," Tzvetan Todorov ar-
gues historically. Misreadings five hundred years ago still script collisions
and catastrophes in the New World, disastrous foreign policy, embargo,
counter-insurgency, military tyranny—"God for gold" in 1519, ideology
for arms today, as recently as the Contragate scandal. Up and down the
Americas, "the other" as native Indios remains alienably other, impover-
ished, rebellious, furtive, an outcast among his own people. Disappearing
Indians are still reserved as exotic and exploitable, and the feminist mestizo
divides conquistador and king: "it is in fact the conquest of America that
heralds and establishes our present identity," the Parisian semiologist sees.
A questionable history is certainly with us, in such respects, across the Amer-
icas and elsewhere.

> Piskata, hold your tongue, she says.
> I am trying to tell you something.
>
> CAROLYN FORCHÉ, "ENDURANCE"

Special-interest readers may not agree with my choices in writers for a
representative Native/American poetics, or my cultural boundaries, for
that matter, more permeable than palisaded. Carolyn Forché is "the giant

mosquito of cultural appropriation," an essentialist press reader carped; and a "pathetic" Mary Austin, in this reviewer's opinion, passed her "sad" life as "careless cultural appropriator." Why these peevish dismissals? More importantly, why do other Americans get interested in Native American cultures? Tolerant, for the moment, of Austin's crossover pathos or Forché's empathic co-options, we might ask why Americans, from "White Indians" like Boone and Houston, through writers like Swiss-immigrant Mari Sandoz and Black American Alice Walker, should want in varying degrees to trace and to adopt in some way a native heritage. Why should women from Austin to Forché, in particular white women poets, question mainstream American values and go searching for gender options, intercultural paradigms, literary fusions of margin and mainstream? And, at the same time, why should not native peoples, the majority living off reservations, interconnect and strategize pan-tribally, as the National Congress of American Indians, later the American Indian Movement, began doing half a century ago? The collective idea parallels one of our united states, in truth, nations, whose common goal is peace, prosperity, and unbiased opportunity. Why, for that matter, would writers of color—Rita Dove or Amy Tan, Louise Erdrich or Sandra Cisneros—seek mainstream publishing to honor their work? These questions poke at the opacity of the Buckskin Curtain, bracket the success of Gerald Vizenor, Leslie Silko, Greg Sarris, or Sherman Alexie. Should cultural separatism be the battle cry of born-again Indians, many from urban dislocations, throttle pan-tribal talk across the hating fields? This dialogue started in the seventies, was strangled in the eighties, and seems in danger of being silenced in the fin de siècle nineties, once again.

Carolyn Forché adds political empathy to cultural othering these days, and therein lie seeds of resentment. The poet tugs at our own complicity in a poetics of witness. She wants the reader-of-witness to feel, even to do something constructive like write a congressman, in the face of global suffering and greed. Unpopular in the United States, the witnessing poet informs a cultural model in other countries—Neruda, Lorca, Akhmatova, Hikmet, Celan, Breytenbach, Milosz, and Havel, to name a few. Still some critics, especially men in power and right of center, don't take to poets of witness. In *Sulfur 6,* for example, a skeptical Eliot Weinberger accuses Forché of "revolutionary tourism" and fetishized grief. What's all this othering, empathy with suffering, and political proselytizing? critics like Robert Hughes complain of a *Culture of Complaint.* When "the white American male starts bawling for victim status too," Hughes concludes, "maudlin narcissism" intersects a spiraling descent into "cultural triviality." In these "worst of all times for literary criticism," Harold Bloom mans *The Western Canon,* "the rabblement of lemmings" will hurl standards off politically correct cliffs. The Ivy League don thunders, "We are the final inheritors of Western tradition." Ethnic complaints boil down to heated cultural interface—empathy with a cause—as a contemporary imperative. Where do we draw and cross the line between taste and intolerance? Either we connect, collaborate, and translate across historical gaps, or we hole up, hate, and harass each other across chasms of gender, race, dialect, and religious difference. Our lives are on the line.

For a woman fusing intimate poetry and impassioned politics, Carolyn Forché is relatively young. Born in 1950 in the Michigan heartland, she grew up Roman Catholic around Detroit and went through a sixties "greaser" phase, her own label, in Vietnam-conflicted America. Educated locally, then internationally, Forché sees our country from within and without, speaking idiomatically from blue-collar Detroit, natively from the West, multilingually from intercontinental travel. Her Euro-American lineage collates Slavic-Irish ancestry in working-class Michigan, a college education and M.F.A. in the Midwest, and several Southwest years with Taos Pueblo Indians. On a Guggenheim writer's fellowship, Forché received an alternative education 1977–1980 in El Salvador, and eventually established global lines to Mallorca, Kiev, Prague, Latin America, Lebanon, and South Africa, traveling with her Time-Life photographer husband, Harry Mattison.

Where is this woman's native ground? First, the local tongue: "My mother was a poet when she was young," Forché told interviewers, August 1984 in Berkeley,

> and continued to write during my early childhood; she wrote fairy tales for us. So the act of writing—reading and writing—were something acknowledged as legitimate activities in our household. I was from a working-class family. My father worked ten and twelve hours a day, six and seven days a week, as a tool-and-die maker in Detroit. My memories of my father are of his leaving for work before light with a thermos bottle and a lunchbag, and coming home after dark with the empty thermos bottle.

Hers is working America, the émigré paradigm, where "free" verse has much to do with Gaelic fairy tales, mixed-blood families, and a laborer's empty thermos. Her work gives cause for thought. At a UCLA reading in September 1982, Forché described poetry as "a way of living inside my own mind," then added somewhat sadly, as she recalled her Irish mother and Slovak grandmother reading verse aloud, "I do wish that we loved poetry more in this country." Compatriot poets from elsewhere, Milosz, Yeats, or Neruda, carry Forché's cultural past forward, her personal sense of immigrant American history, still sifting the ruins of modern warfare. Pain challenges assumed zones of comfort. Among relocatees in this country between us, including Native Americans today, at a George Sand Bookstore reading in Los Angeles that same month Forché spoke of her poetry as "someplace where you can feel the grief of the world" (Los Angeles 1982), a grief that can bond or banish us from one another. The choices are critical. "There are two human worlds," she writes of South Africa, "and the bridges between them are burning." *The Angel of History,* the poet says in notes to her most recent book, replaces first-person lyric with an open, collective wound, "polyphonic, broken, haunted, and in ruins, with no possibility of restoration." Her current verse-in-progress lets the language "tear" itself open, she explained with a Lannan Foundation audience in Santa Fe, May 1998, to reveal what it is saying beyond what it says. She worries what will happen to human beings and the earth, a luminous global web, as we walk into the harsh light of the twenty-first century.

Forché grew up the eldest of seven children, nicknamed *Piskata,* or Slovakian "chatterbox," by a paternal grandma. Anna Bassarová Sidlovsky spoke "a funny English," Forché recalls. "This not Slovakia," Anna snapped. "This country a piece of shit." So the poet's genealogical muse, another kind of Beatrice altogether, stood as this "bossy, strong" paternal grandmother from Slovakia, whose given name means "grace," as Carolyn's name derives from "song." Anna challenged the family's relocation from foreign places far away to Michigan,

> . . . peeling her hands
> with a paring knife, saying *in your country*
> *you have nothing.*

The granddaughter's lifelong quest to ground herself in America, no less than Mary Austin or Linda Hogan, begins with Anna Sidlovsky's dedicatory poem, "Endurance," in *Gathering the Tribes.* How can Americans build, or rebuild out of cultural ground zero, the lines ask, our country from a bloody-loamed "nothing"? How can we survive the historical gap, the human dislocation from parent lands? Can we live with and beyond a native sense of dispossession? "We are so made," the poet fears in "Hive," a recent manuscript text about a bee colony, "that nothing contents us." The double hinge of that word, "nothing," falters between fated negation or positive absence, wiping clean or erasing all signs of life from a fouled slate, in order to start over.

Colonial exile tempers imperial arrogance, a woman's courage checks male drive. "One finds in this work a map of the journey each of us must complete, wittingly or not, as children and exiles of the Americas," Forché forewords Roberta Hill Whiteman's *Star Quilt,* as cited earlier. Despite the postwar losses, women strain to love and to forgive and to believe again. This is a terrible innocence, if you will, bracketed by Yeats's sense of Irish civil chaos and millennial apocalypse "slouching" toward Armageddon. In a native country between us, an Oneida survivor of indigenous genocide writes her "Leap in the Dark" mustering "the grace that remains":

> "Truth waits in the creek, cutting the winter brown hills,
> It sings with needles of ice, sings because of its scar."

The wounded bear's heart sings truly through its pain. A decade later, Forché reiterates: "For non-native Americans, America is a nation of exiles in search of a homeland, and now that this need for homeland has become interiorized, and is experienced as interior exile, the homeland sought has become figurative" (*American Poetry Review* 1988). Imagining reality no less than Stevens, we each look for the way back home, "inner émigré," as Seamus Heaney sees himself uprooted from northern "troubles" to southern Ireland, moving into a new millennium of stockpiled arsenals and prayers for peace.

The Michigan poet searches for home as a road-wizened feminist, for family and land sense, for tribe and history and native tongue. She forges her own politics, on moral and personal terms. "I'm interested in a deep morality," Forché told an interviewer for *The Jacaranda Review,* UCLA 1987, "one of compassion rather than of judgment." She insists that "Poetry is a necessity, not a commodity, a necessity" (*APR* 1988). Forché's cue may have come from Neruda, who remembers 1939 Spanish exiles in France, when he writes, "I Went Out to Look for the Fallen" *(Memoirs):* "Can poetry serve our fellow men?" the Chilean diplomat pressed himself. "Can it find a place in man's struggles?" History answered him. "As the first bullets ripped into the guitars of Spain, when blood instead of music gushed out of them, my poetry stopped dead like a ghost in the streets of human anguish and a rush of roots and blood surged up through it. From then on, my road meets everyman's road." A returning diplomatic poet, Neruda sailed exiled Chileans home and retired to Isla Negra to write, committing himself in leftist resistance to fascism. He died two years after receiving the Nobel Prize for Poetry, the day of Pinochet's 1973 takeover. Spain 1939 was the Chilean poet's turning point, no less than Forché's 1979 witness in El Salvador.

Forché's first book, *Gathering the Tribes,* won the 1976 Yale Series of Younger Poets Award. These early tribal verses dig down through skin and cellophane and asphalt to a native taproot in America: breaking through middle-class conventions, sexual barriers, taboos of thought, racial curtains, and a conflict of tongues into a chaotically pluralist, American cultural history. The poet gathers a legacy of emigrants, homesteaders, pioneering women, Indians, soldiers, priests, and steel workers with a maternal sensitivity "stubborn" as potatoes, elegiac as her given name. Carolyn mourns the loss of her fierce muse, Anna, who broke American soil in "Burning the Tomato Worms":

> Between apples and first snow
> In horse-breath weather

Birds shape the wind
Dogs chained to the ground
Leave their dung
Where the ditches have burned
And I wish she were alive
But she is big under the ground, dead

In the wake of Anna's resistance to foreign soil, Forché lives with determination to face her grandmother's charge of *"nothing"* in America. No metered poetics, no *poetic* style, but a fierce resolve to speak truly, from what concerns her with others in a new land. "The essence of any good lyric," Brodsky notes of writers in prison, "is compression and velocity." Neruda adds of *working* poetry, "Using language like clothes or the skin on your body, with its sleeves, its patches, its transpirations, and its blood and sweat stains, that's what shows a writer's mettle. This is style."

In the nativist matrifocal tradition of Whiteman or Harjo, Forché rejects the patriarchal daughter's legacy: a cloistered Emily Dickinson, a proprietous Marianne Moore, a suicidal Sylvia Plath. There is no Daddy, either to idealize or to castigate, no place to hide in the global village, no "refuge of otherness," the poet swears, only courage to speak out and the periodic grace of retreat. Americans are "born to an island of greed / and grace," an elder woman charges compassionately, in a country "where you have this sense / of yourself as apart from others" ("Return"). Yet, "I am not one of these," Forché defends her stance against daughters islanded in their father's gardens. Not only the solace, but the challenge of verse, historically charged, sends Forché back into the world, a lyric witness to history.

Reentry raises hard questions, since the radical dissonance of the sixties. Can the dissenter part and return, travel abroad and come back, given ethnic strains and global estrangements today? Canonical police reject ethnic contexts and gender campaigns. Tribal reconstructionists dismiss *wanabes* as New Age culture-mongers, and traditionalists fear mainstream erosion from the classics. Wanderers go home bearing terrible news, innocents abroad suspected as cultural terrorists at home. Immigrants continue to flood our shores. What does Michigan have to do with El Salvador, America with Slovakia, or Cortés with the contras? We recoil from our own complicitous entrapments in the politics of experience, retreat into our American myths of innocence. This "nothing" we inherit seems either an ironic negative or a positive caution. If a warning heeded, what language emerges from the privacy of informed witness, what does political history have to do with poetry? Forché puts her verse on the line: Can poetic witness do anything humanly for humanity, with grace beyond greed?

A post-Catholic, postlapsarian poet, Forché seeks a vision of home within the New World's desacralized landscape.

My grandmother, Anna, had often spoken of this kind of dislocation. She talked of coming to this country, of things that occurred in Europe before she came, of her father who was turned away at Ellis Island because of a sore on his leg. She never saw him again. When I was nineteen, I married—But it's difficult for me to talk about this. I've always harbored a dark sense that the world is at risk. (*APR* 1988)

So the poet's search for something of value inversely springs from a reassertive "nothing." She would begin by grounding "the country between us" in reconnective intimacies beyond material greed, loss, or conquest. No less than Williams or any Native American tribal ethic, hers is a "ground sense necessary" to begin again, to revise imperial myths, to free "the people" from a negative history of greed and guilt. No less than Hogan or Tapahonso, she would quiet the ghosts, bury the dead, and go on through the world. "In every generation of Slovak women," she translates her grandmother's charge in "Endurance," the Anna poem, "there had been one who wanders, restless-hearted, by ship or in an old car, and that measure of strange blood was passed this time to me" *(Singular Voices).* Her pilgrimage has taken the poet through Spain, Czechoslovakia, Central America, Taos Pueblo, the Middle East, Africa, and all over the United States. "So what has marked my adult life," Forché concedes, "is solitariness and search" (1984 Berkeley interview).

Politics and poetry don't mix well in the United States, at least *Poetry* magazine doesn't favor accusatory or radical postures invading patron parlors, let alone academic hallways. Despite Whitman, Pound, and the Beats, canonical Anglo-American verse has little been a voice of political resistance since the colonial revolution (ethnic poets, for the most part, remain outside these conduits of power, even as Helen Vendler squeezes a black trio—Langston Hughes, Robert Hayden, and Rita Dove—into her Anglo-American Harvard anthology of contemporary U.S. poetry, where neither Forché nor any other culturally politicized poet of color appears). Perhaps New World émigrés of Manifest Destiny, so young and still settling, see fit to stick with market *values* and *real* estate ethics, now *virtual* reality, preferring to indulge neither marginal dissent nor flimflam aesthetics. Yet a national disgrace, our marketplace *free* enterprise politics devalue the arts. In the early nineties, Robert Hughes calculates, the American taxpayer gave sixty-eight cents annually to support the arts, while Germans contributed twenty-seven dollars and the French thirty-two dollars a year. In truth, we do not put much stock in poetry, nor do we read much. By contrast, one in four Nicaraguans considers him or herself a poet, and most every Native American writer begins with poetry. Per capita, Czechs buy twenty times more poetry books than Americans, Italians recite Dante's canzoni by heart, and Andrei Vozneshensky fills a Russian soccer stadium for a poetry reading. Add feminine second-class status (non-voting until the 1920s) to the business-world inequity of women in America (seventy cents on a man's dollar still today), and a radical young feminist like Carolyn Forché might look elsewhere understandably for verse models.

The threat of isolation, the silenced tongue, generate a woman's need to go beyond our borders, to learn new languages and cultures, even ancient sources of her own speech. By the time of Forché's first slim book, the poet had attuned her ear to Russian, Spanish, Serbo-Croation, French, and Tewa tongues, "listening beyond grammar for the secret texts," Stanley Kunitz forewords *Gathering the Tribes*. And in calling for tribal community and common ground, Forché has radically canonized her position as a pilgrim of witness. The final arbiter is her own deepest honesty, the plain truth deeply plumbed. An old Slovak homily comes back clearly in her earliest poems, searching for Anna, her grace: "Eat Bread and Salt and Speak the Truth."

NATIVIZED POLITICS

By the time Forché was thirty, *The Country Between Us* had won the 1981 Academy of American Poets Lamont Prize for the best second book of poems in America. The Slovak daughter is drawn back in dislocations to Michigan, still haunted by Anna's admonition of *"nothing"* in this country, grieving and dedicated to the suffering of El Salvador, the Vietnam of the 1980s. History arcs back on her, as she parses truth in the wake of "that which is lost" in the final poem, "Ourselves or Nothing," writing of the globally dispossessed and condemned. "I decided to write narratives of witness and confrontation, to disallow obscurity and conventions which might prettify that which I wished to document" (*APR* 1981). How does this work?

Her cursed prose poem, "The Colonel," stalks readers with dead, severed ears. "One evening," she relates in terrible witness, "I dined with a military officer who toasted America, private enterprise, Las Vegas, and the 'fatherland' until his wife excused herself and in a drape of cigar smoke the events of 'The Colonel' took place. Almost a *poéme trouvé,* I had only to pare down the memory and render it whole, unlined and as precise as recollection would have it" (*APR* 1981). Such an unspeakable moment, selected from personal history, is a witnessing check poem. "Simply to keep watch over life," the political historian Terrence Des Pres wrote, as Forché records his search for the lost home in "Ourselves or Nothing."

The word "colonel," from the Latin for "little column," designates a midrank, upright officer (vertically at attention) in the field. It is suspiciously close, by way of the ear, to "colonial," which derives otherwise from the Latin for "farmer." Forché's little column of words, "The Colonel," carries the news as a kind of freelance prose poem from a Latin American colonial home—straight from the mouth of a military bureaucrat with a gun on the "cushion" beside him (the privilege of terrorism). Suburban order is the flag of the generic Colonel's family: "his wife" clearing the table, "his son" going out for the night, "his daughter" filing her nails. The "pet dogs" complete this domestic coven, all-in-the-family conventional, proper and expected, but for the gun on the pillow.

"WHAT YOU HAVE HEARD is true," the rectangular block of an alleged poem, among six other lineated texts about El Salvador, opens with hushed confirmation. Beginning with full capitals, the first four words could pass for a legal brief or diplomatic report manqué (Forché was serving as cultural diplomat on a Guggenheim, *The Country Between Us* her report to the people). This report is different. It does not look like or sound like a poem, at first, more a newspaper column—flatly descriptive, factual, reportorial. All this changes. The whispers of unspeakable rumor, the conspiratorial fears of oppression, the underground gossip of the streets leak through her reportorial column like small gusts of breath. A factual, mid-level diction breaks with maximal stress the need to tell all, in plain style disbelief and passionately embedded inscription. Hers is an anti-art that is an art of timed witness and indirect revelation. In journalistic wraps of the daily news, justified between margins, the lines carry a tone of clinical horror, echoes of controlled terror: all in the name of decency and diplomatic taste, Pentecostal "rack of lamb, good wine," and hemispheric trade. "His wife carried a tray of coffee and sugar."

The Colonel's violence is institutionalized with broken bottles cemented into the walls (to "scoop" a man's "kneecaps," the voice edges toward bloodshed, or "cut his hands to lace," nervously questioning terrorist art). More colloquially, the Colonel's windows are grated "like those in liquor stores." Martial law rules this neighborhood. A "gold bell" calls "the maid," and "The maid" (in repetitious servility) brings green mangoes, salt, bread—all uniform, all in order, all "his" orders, a man-*made*, emotionless, down-home horror under middle-class cushion. A TV cop-show in English imports American greed and violence, the commercial in Spanish capitalizes the local margin. What will happen? the reader wonders. How will this piece work out?

Metric line breaks are embedded in the syntax, curiously disguised not to look *like* poetry. The lines internally break into hymnal or ballad measure (five times in tetrameter, "His *wife* took *everything away*"), blank verse (sixteen times in pentameter, "The *moon* swung *bare* on its *black cord over* the *house*"), and Homeric meter (seven times in hexameter, "There were *daily papers*, *pet dogs*, a *pistol* on the *cushion beside* him"), only three lines in strictly "free" verse, three to seven beats. Sibilant hissing rhymes interlace the metric sentence endings ("house, English, house, lace, stores, Spanish, terrace, this, faces, themselves, voice"). Within the closing lines, the monosyllables "sack, ears, halves, hands, glass, rights, ears, last, ears, scrap, ears" and "pressed" siphon their vowels into a cluster of atrocities carried home as "groceries." Forché is much more of a poet, or anti-poet, than she lets on here. Her hidden rhymes and rhythms (both words from Greek *rhythmus*, as mentioned, meaning "flow") conceal the art of conspiratorial witness, the designs of a hushed poetics. "Tell all the Truth but tell it slant—" Dickinson cautioned, "Success in Circuit lies" (no. 1129). The off-poetic disguise is essential. How can she be an aesthete in witness of the horror? How can Forché appear to be ordering her lines, to be measuring her steps, to be decorating her images, in the face of the Colonel's controlled madness, his butchering orders? This paterfamilias finds it difficult "to govern" these days, to order his household, to keep the margins justified, to muzzle the press, to silence the cries of the disappeared. "Hello," the parrot parrots on the terrace, and the Colonel tells it to "shut up." The poet's cowitness, "my friend" (separate from household pawns), says "with his eyes: say nothing." Timing is all here, the slowly detailed opening, the building of tension with the pistol, glass, and grating, then more swiftly, the pressure of breaking open consciousness through undercurrent and sustained release of detail—all in the steadily mounting expectation of a narrative worthy of Chekhov. The poet goes subversive. "She dealt her pretty words like Blades—" Dickinson wrote, "How glittering they shone—/ And every One unbared a Nerve / Or wantoned with a Bone—" (no. 479).

So the Colonel brings out his grocery sack of ears, as casually as any collector might produce his stamps or chloroformed butterflies. "He *spilled many human ears on the table. They were like / dried peach halves. There is no other way to say* this." This cannot be said right, the subversive poet knows, no way except by way of a horribly failed speech, a terribly wrong image—"like dried peach halves"—the unspeakably excoriated simile. Language cannot bear this violence. The word "ear" disappears uncannily in the word "disappear." The *disappeared* bodies go earless, this wretched simile our evidence that they heard, but did not heed the Colonel's orders. Poetry is hopeless. Metaphor strains, words fail, the imagination shuns the truth, "—An Omen in the Bone / Of Death's tremendous nearness" (Dickinson, no. 532).

Yet one ear "came alive" in the Colonel's water glass. It's his awful party trick, his bad parody—little titular *column* of a military god-man with life-and-death whims. He orders *desaparecidos*, proved by souvenir ears. "*Some thing for your poetry, no? he said.*" That little Latin-Anglo hinge, "no?" is the dialectal trip wire of the whole poem. Such a small word to *reverse field* on the expectations of poetry, to trigger an obverse order. The negating disclaimer turns back in moaning o's, "*Something for your poetry, no?*" This is not so much poetry as anticolonial protest, not so much aesthetics as conspiratorial witness, or art beyond art. The failure of language goes deeper into human failures. Such is a poetry that breaks poetic illusion with the need to speak of the unspeakable, at whatever cost. "*As* for the *rights* of *any*one, / *tell* your *people they* can *go fuck* them*selves.*"

Foul words fit here. The Colonel comes clean in infamy, the truth no longer slant, but out in bad talk, self-condemned. A fallen, postmodernist diction, lower than any poet has gone before, is orally apt. The unspeakable is disgustingly cursed by his own words. Forché writes in postlyric, questionable witness of "the horror" with us, Conrad's Marlow in the New World, female, south of the border, bringing the news back home. "YOU, I, his, her, my friend, your people, they"—the disparate host of personal pronouns in "The Colonel" points to a complicity of crimes at *our* door. The poet's careful detailing of this petty CEO thug with a gun leads to our implicative connection, "the horror" at home today, not far south. "Blessed / are those who listen," Linda Hogan says, "when no one is left to speak."   ·

Some of the ears on the floor still beg mercy from a "scrap" of the Colonel's voice. This news comes from the bottom of the text, the prone axis that intercepts the Colonel's upright column and *justified* margins. Horizontal to his vertical order then, *some* of the ears lie "pressed to the ground"—trampled, still listening underground in resistance, keen to hear, to know, to witness, and to rise up against the Colonel's orders. Latin America is an Hispanicized Native America, fusional Old and New Worlds, "children and exiles of the Americas," Forché writes of Whiteman's Oneida *Star Quilt.* The nativized ghosts of atrocity speak through intense silence, the quiet of the *desaparecidos,* the horror weighing the poem's shadows. "There is no other way to say this," the poet says, but this much must be said.

"In every war someone puts a cigarette in the corpse's mouth," the poet makes note, as hard truth haunts her. "I dug maggots from a child's open wound with a teaspoon" (*APR* 1981). What is too horrible to say reduces her to simile, sacked ears "like dried peach halves," a device that admits its own failure to name things directly. In so failing, the simile breaks a frustrated silence beyond itself. Forché remembers horror with stunned clarity, a poet's post-traumatic stress: "The bodies of friends have turned up disemboweled and decapitated, their teeth punched into broken points, their faces sliced off with machetes. On the final trip to the airport we swerved to avoid a corpse, a man spread-eagled, his stomach hacked open, his entrails stretched from one side of the road to the other. We drove over them like a garden hose." A writer's trope tilts away in pain. "The imagination is not enough," Forché writes of an African Anna, mothering sixteen adopted children, the "smallest one tied to her back by a rag" (*The Angel of History*). Witnesses must see beyond the darkness. The failures of metaphor to rise above the real, the knots of talk, the breaks in syntax, the slippages in language . . . teach something about the need to go beyond what we think we can say, know, or do, our hands not tied by art, but freed in responsibility.

The *disappeared* spirits listen mutely in Salvador today, and Forché urges us to heed their brutalized cries. "There is nothing one man will not do to another," she reports of one-meter human cages, *La Oscura,* in "The Visitor." This is a truth some know, others fear to imagine, most want not to hear in our land of opulent opportunity (as privilege goes) above the poverty line. "To write out of such extremity is to incise, with language, that same wound, to open it again, and, with utterance, to inscribe the consciousness. This inscription restructures the consciousness of the poet" (*APR* 1988).

Forché's seven Salvadoran poems are dedicated to the memory of Monsignor Oscar Romero, a saint in the poet's eyes, assassinated in 1980 while giving mass in a hospital for incurables (in 1989 the Paulists released *Romero,* a major film about the Monsignor). And when *they* buried her friend, José Rudolfo Viera, murdered a few months later with two Americans in the Sheraton Hotel coffee shop by the *Mano Blanca* or "white gloves" death squad, Forché elegized his loss in couplets as the "one" always forgotten, the space between the double lines.

> I could take my heart, he said, and give it to a *campesino*
> and he would cut it up and give it back . . .

Life is muscled by Yeats's "deep heart's core," as Two Shields sings with the heart of a bear, yet postcolonial militancy rips the compassion from human touch.

> The heart is the toughest part of the body.
> Tenderness is in the hands.

Finally, the heart's witness lies in our hands, whose labor, craft, and love, "smelling of lilies and urine," Neruda says, distinguish humans from animals. The barbarous cruelties of men at war with themselves still mutilate the bear's heart:

> A boy soldier in the bone-hot sun works his knife
> to peel the face from a dead man
>
> and hang it from the branch of a tree
> flowering with such faces.

The traditional *shame tree* of Latin American cultures, a bounty tree here defaced, silences protest as a terrorist cross, a terrible death-in-life tree, a mute Sun Dance tree. Who will speak, as Hogan asks, when no ears are left, no eyes to witness? If men continue desecrating the tree of life, can the mother earth ever bear fruit?

The poet accepts the stigmata of those Salvadoran years in the late 1970s, posing as a woman doctor's assistant, her conscience crystallizing: "a young writer, politically unaffiliated, ideologically vague," she characterizes herself, "I was to be blessed with the rarity of a moral and political education—what at times would seem an unbearable immersion, what eventually would become a focused obsession" (*APR* 1981). Forché told Claribel Alegría's nephew, Leonel Gomez Vides, that she knew nothing about Central American military dictatorship, and he said, "Good, you know that you know nothing. Now, this is a good beginning" *(The Writer in Our World)*.

The writer had to bring this obsessional focus home—to her family and friends and lovers, to Anna and Victoria and Joey (her first sweetheart, an acolyte priest), and to readers in her poems, at the risk of misunderstandings ancient in the Americas:

> Now this feel of knife for fish,
> of bullet for something racing through
> the darkness, your voice
> slung on the wires that lapse
> scalloping the cold length
> of the country between us.
> It is another voice that calls me
> after all this time.
> It has nothing to say to you, Joseph.

What she can *not* tell her adolescent lover now matters. We listen beyond the words, read between the lines. We finger the empty spaces, filter the echoes of voices along the wires: the "disappeared" whisper *nothing* through shadow and silence. In Eastern Europe the poet writes "For the Stranger," a lover met on a train, "We have, each of us, nothing. / We will give it to each other" (the first poem written for *The Country Between Us*). Postwar lovers then give nothing to one another—a release from self-possession, from things, from finality. The heart insists, but for death and courage, that we give nothing, keep nothing, end up nothing, and go after "nothing" between—freely committed to seek ourselves . . . restless, relocating, questioning in a Western tradition now five centuries coming home.

How does a poet sing or shape lines from such loss and distance? During the September 1982 reading at the George Sand Bookstore, Forché spoke of her poetry as "those beautiful moments of reverie when I was able to put something down from the life." These reflective eddies pool before an illumining terror or beauty, they arrest and keep the mind going. And still, Whitman, Dickinson, Williams, Moore, and Bishop have gone before, as American poets in this scripted oral tradition, a poetry of the people's voices. Theirs is an aesthetics of engagement, what Clifford Geertz sifts as cultural evidence toward "an ethnography of modern thought" *(Local Knowledge)*. The social historian would "attempt to navigate the plural / unific, product / process paradox" that splits social science into bifurcated modes, "by regarding the community as the shop in which thoughts are constructed and deconstructed, history the terrain they seize and surrender." This community-specific or "local" knowledge, Geertz reasons, could "attend therefore to such muscular matters as the representation of authority, the marking of boundaries, the rhetoric of persuasion, the expression of commitment, and the registering of dissent." These ongoing, often contrary landscapes of American things and thoughts, physical and common, register in native poetries. "We are all natives now," Geertz observes, as Harjo noted in the beginnings. Parsing a self-reflexive, cultural hermeneutics—a poetics of witness—we "can bring the war back home," the social scientist argues, and perhaps come to a truce, then a new beginning.

But we are not unalike—"The Island"

What is compelling to this poet's audience is not just the public reading, or even the poetry alone, but the projected experience *in* the words. This poetic language is catalyst to a memory, charged with moral imagining, to overcome human estrangements, the gaps of time and space. "We must educate our sensibilities first," Forché says in the Berkeley interview. "And then write with the fullness of our being. . . ." Her double negatives cancel our canceled options; she would negotiate the fissures of history and circumstance, the voided nothing, antinomies tensing between what Yeats called choice and chance. Forché talks the body to attention and trusts in things, as she plumbs their recesses and questions absence. She uses form less for itself than to connect the reader with experience. This woman incants her witness in terrible innocence, the mind of a child searching for causes in hard times, intersected with tendoned irony and tender courage. Because "one" is always forgotten, the poet elegizes the unmentioned brother: "When Viera was buried we knew it had come to an end, / his coffin rocking into the ground like a boat or a cradle." The verse flows in an open design, iambically rocking, as craft covers itself. Poetic shape lies in the clarity and commitment of the experience, resistant to an imposed form, free to what it is, an elegy. Here dignity, grief, and grace come together in natural balance. More than artifacts or constructs, the poems then present "narratives of witness and confrontation," tensing with shape, like a blade struck in a block of wood.

Forché records reality viscerally. "WHAT YOU HAVE HEARD is true," the poet confirms the daily rumor and terror of a police state. Back home, the hushed news and local pitfalls stain her origins with a teenage friend, Victoria Champagne ("As Children Together"):

> Holding each other's
> coat sleeves we slid down
> the roads in our tight
> black dresses, past
> crystal swamps and the death
> face of each dark house,
> over the golden ice
> of tobacco spit, the blue
> quiet of ponds, with town
> glowing behind the blind
> white hills and a scant
> snow ticking in the stars.

The perspective narrows to a seductive art of simple beginnings. The heart's land pans away, an Orphic glance backward, not unlike Baudelaire's alchemy of Parisian sewers ("the golden ice of tobacco spit") glittering in *Les Fleurs du Mal,* but with a callow Midwest twist. Forché must not forget that Victoria and she sought "a way to get out" of blue-collar mid-America. Workers of all skins—her father, mother, siblings, and schoolmates—remain trapped in late-twentieth-century racism, the rages of urban poverty.

Salvador may be a fearful paradigm of "disappeared" voices, the mutism of all the dispossessed and disillusioned; since the auto industry layoffs, Forché adds, "sections of Detroit remind me, physically, of Beirut" (*APR* 1988). Always there is a life to be lived, for better or worse, but before or beyond words for most. Victoria, her last name now unknown, is rumored to be living outside Detroit in a trailer with her Vietnam-veteran husband. Victoria's *mobile* home is a rootless locus of delayed stress, and Forché calls to her of lost American sisterhood. "If you read this poem, write to me," she asks her childhood friend in a conspiratorial whisper over the years. "I have been to Paris since we parted."

How do we read this odd mixture of political irony, girlish daydream, and commonplace impulse to escape and reconnect? In conspiratorial intimacy, Forché weds the free-verse, lyric narrator that Sharon Olds can parody as an "Iroquois scout" sexually stalking her mirrored bed partner, with that terribly wounded survivor whom Linda Hogan seeks natively to harbor, comfort, and heal after centuries of homeland war. Can critics tolerate the unsettled tone, or readers sustain the unanswered appeal across feminist fissures, ideological killing fields, and gilded aesthetics? A cynic may be tempted to misread these private young codes, to discount personal fantasy in the face of political complexity. Terrence Diggory wondered if "sexual union" were not a fatigued "answer to political conflict" in Forché's poetry (*Salmagundi* 1983), and Kathy Pollit complained in *The Nation* of "the misty 'poetic' language of the isolated, private self." A sympathetic reader pares meaning from means, parts tissue from tendon within each

line—heartfelt sorrow from fey sigh, Maoist Paris from Symboliste salon—
to release a tenderness delicately strung, finely torqued.

> all things human take time,
> time which the damned never have, time for life
> to repair at least the worst of its wounds.

As in "Ourselves or Nothing," humans need time to reflect on experience,
particularly trauma, as the living die of time. We act out of entrapment
within ourselves, webbed in language. We dream apart from do, bearing
"silence at the pole of the appalled and the disappeared," Bedient says.
Today people millennially strain to imagine a choice beyond ambiguity and
indecision, a way to decide the lyric collective fate. Desires must lead to
actions. "In dreams," Yeats chants, "begin responsibilities." Williams
checks the postromantic sentiment, "Somehow / it seems to destroy us, /
No one / to witness / and adjust, no one to drive the car."

With careful and fixed attention the poet lives precariously at a certain
pitch. As epic softens to lyric, the lines catch poetry where it tremors and
still keeps life moving, the voice riding naturally on song's motion. Yeats
spoke of Homer's voice in *The Odyssey*, that epic homecoming from war,
"the swift and natural observation of a man as he is shaped by life" *(Dis-
coveries)*. Can a native poetry so move from personal to public witness today?
There is no other way for Forché: "politics" must begin personally, as does
"time" or "history." Verse, then, moves with the natural movement of a
life; a native poetic works out a personal vision in the currents of communal
language and collective history. And this poet is a woman shaped by the
terrible experience of lost innocence, deeply felt, personally honed, hold-
ing *nothing* back. "As for the rights of anyone," slurs her drunken colonel,
"tell your people they can go fuck themselves."

AGAINST DISREMEMBERING

The truth is a cursed wound cratering our war-torn century. Neo-catholic
in her compassion, Forché seems a woman obsessed with suffering, as doc-
umented most recently in *The Angel of History*, a book-length poem on the
trauma of modern poetic memory, also gathered in her new anthology of
globally repressed voices, *Against Forgetting: Twentieth-Century Poetry of Wit-
ness*. This poet speaks intimately of time and place raised to moral reflec-
tion, what Calvin Bedient calls "a penitent poetics" *(Salmagundi,* Summer
1996). Hers is less the heroic moment of classical epic than a strategic
courage in the contemporary world, where heroics are grounded, even
shattered, in daily survival. Personal choice lies at issue, form in question.
Back to Whitman and Lawrence, the poet searches for natural freedoms of
diction, imagery, thought, and the shape of the line. She goes to great

trouble to make art serve the human—it must be aesthetically honest, rather than decorating things. *The Angel of History* questions the first-person lyric of her earlier free verse with a number of interruptive witnesses, "attempting to rupture that voice, and to critique it from within in order to expose its artifice" (*APR* 1988).

From Beruit, to South Africa, to Salvador, to fascist-collaborative Paris, to Prague, the "angel of history" is caught, Walter Benjamin says in the epigraph, by a storm blowing in from Paradise. The angel's wings will not close, and he is thrust backwards into the future. *"The silence of God is God,"* murmurs Elie Wiesel, and God's name is reduced to *"a boneless string of vowels,"* Forché cites C. W. King on the Gnostics. The poet's inmate in a Paris mental ward, Ste. Monique in the Hôtel-Dieu, is a Polish-Jewish refugee named Ellie: "I say this God is insane." Delayed stress, the aftershock of war, can no longer be held off. The consequences of violence, to women and children, fall disastrous: "A woman broken into many women." Ellie fuses into Forché's paternal grandmother, Slovakian Anna, "coal-eyed in a field of bone chips."

> You loved the shabbiness of the world: countries invaded, cities bombed, houses
>   whose roofs have fallen in,
>   women who have lost their men, orphans, amputees, the war wounded.
> What you did not love any longer was a world that had lost its soul.

True torment flattens the lyric. Jewish children secreted, April to April during war, then trained to Auschwitz, singing, score an even more horrible waste land than Eliot, Fitzgerald, or Hemingway set down in the twenties after the First "Great" War. Night terrors haunt the poet, vultures from El Salvador body dumps invade her room. The *nuit blanche,* or "white night" insomnia, keeps her awake all hours, as Bedient notes, "a hand cupped over its speaking soul." This is a woman's post-traumatic terror: Linda Gregg in hell, the horror of becoming the other, Her, when she is hopelessly deranged by war:

> It was years before my face would become hers, yours, and hers, the other's, facing
>   each other through days, pain, the prisoner's visiting window.

These lines register the inverse terror of the Beijing Effect, a global tremor from Tiananmen Square, for example, when violence is felt all over the world as deafening pain. "These ruins are to the future what the past is to us," the poet thinks: we are the future, bearing the past, unbearably, the angel of history blown (apart) yet forward, his back turned to what lies ahead. The Recording Angel goes mute, amnesiac, Mnemosyne dismembered. *"Always say I was never there,"* Elias Canetti begs.

It is the end of the world, Cassandras scream: God is coming, history recorded in graffiti and bullet holes. Someone smears "Fuck" in dogshit on the atelier walls. Postmodernists live with a history of lies, evasions, and cover-ups, when an SS soldier can gloss the Chelmo death ovens, "To make charcoal. For laundry irons."

> And so we revolt against silence with a bit of speaking.
> The page is a charred field where the dead would have written
> *We went on.* And it was like living through something again one could not live
>   through again.

Art can never be art the same again, as Forché discovers a poetics in ruins:

> Surely all art is the result of one's having been in danger, of having gone through
>   an
>   experience all the way to the end.

Poetry approaches prose in running tare: leeched diction, colorless imagery, opaque density, shoeless metrics, end-stopped lines. No art without nature first, and then a *dangerous* art: no likeness until the artist knows unlike, hallucination, derangement. Forché comes close to an essentialist poetics of suffering, the desperate experiential necessity to speak and rise out of a text's context.

Her exiled grandmother's past is post-Holocaustal, a history of grief carried on, born again in women, where Prague was stomped in recent history, first by the Germans, then by the Russians. Anna's was "a ruined city," historically now, "a corpse in the armoire." Women piss standing up, a naked broken doll is trundled back and forth in a boy's bicycle basket. Is this, then, "a war without end," three thousand years from Troy to Tiananmen Square, where men's souls are *disappeared,* and women bear damaged progeny? Is "memory a reliquary in a wall of silence"? Write "nothing except what can be said," the poet vows, no unspeakably artistic lies, no grandiose aesthetics. Bear no likenesses over our heads, simply "bootprints in clay," drained fields.

"When my son was born I became mortal," the long poem opens, and ends with Holocaust children in ovens, then begins again with an ornamental garden in Hiroshima, *Shukkei-en,* and the giving back of likeness earned:

> By way of a vanished bridge we cross this river
> as a cloud of lifted snow would ascend a mountain.
>
> She has always been afraid to come here.

Nonerasable fragments of other's voices, in fleshed memory, in print, mark this terrible poem with misprisions, the sucked-in art of respeaking history. "Bear the unbearable," a radio broadcast tells Anna's war peers. Her granddaughter Carolyn hears a voice end "The Testimony of Light":

The way back is lost, the one obsession.
The worst is over.
The worst is yet to come.

A poet must go on, at unbearable cost, hearing Peter Schwenger wonder in *Letter Bomb. Nuclear Holocaust and the Exploding Word:*

> For if Hiroshima in the morning, after the bomb has fallen,
> is like a dream, one must ask whose dream it is.

ARMED NATIVE ART

"There is no savor / more sweet, more salt," Levertov continues to step westward, "than to be glad to be / what, woman, // and who, myself, / I am, a shadow. . . ." Politicized feminism lies at the heart of Forché's poetry, in what Bedient sees as our "print-besmeared and bomb-shrill century," from the admonitions of grandmother Anna, to the godmotherings of Teles Goodmorning in Taos, from her own mother Louise raising seven children and graduating from college beside her eldest daughter, to the *bruja* spells of Rosita Romero around the Pueblo in *Gathering the Tribes.* "They, the feminine ones," Hélène Cixous warns, "are coming back from far away, from forever, from 'outside,' from the heaths where witches stay alive; from underneath, from the near side of 'culture,' *from their childhoods.* . . . We, coming early to culture, repressed and choked by it, our beautiful mouths stopped up with gags, pollen, and short breaths; we the labyrinths, we the ladders, we the trampled spaces; the stolen and the flights—we are 'black' *and* we are beautiful." Dickinson's progeny, a woman's obliquely resistant, *slant* point of view governs native witness. With Forché, being woman reaches to the Sapphic orgasm of "Lalaloch" on a deserted Washington beach, to lessons in Spanish exile from Claribel Alegría in Deya, to Victoria's *québecoise* lyrics in Montreal, to chill affairs with strange men behind the Iron Curtain, to marriage and children into the next century.

A woman's care tonalizes the final humanist call in *The Country Between Us,* an ode of love in the broadest personal and political senses. Morally impassioned, these feminine carings move toward all the beloved and lost, as in her last ode, dedicated to Terrence Des Pres writing on the Holocaust in *The Survivor.* In his posthumous *Praises and Dispraises: Poetry and Politics, the Twentieth Century,* Des Pres speaks of Antigone as our sister, the Theban woman who died by her father-in-law-to-be's decree, trying to bury her revolutionary brother. Des Pres lists the revolutionary poets of modern politics—Milosz and Herbert; Akhmatova, Mandelstam, Tsvetayeva, and Pasternak; Neruda and Vallejo; Popa and Holub; Seferis and Ritsos; Hikmet—

> These poets come from places burdened by political torment but blessed with zealous care for poetry; and now they have gained an important hearing

among us despite the uncertain dignity of translation. If we should wonder why their voices are valued so highly, it's that they are acquainted with the night, the nightmare spectacle of politics especially. The sense of familiarity got from their poems resides in an undervoice, an emerging consciousness in common that we, too, are beginning to share.

Our lives are held hostage by military world order, Des Pres fears, an economy that defoliates the sister earth: "in a series of dislocations that drove Auerbach to the Bosphorus—that pushed Walter Benjamin to suicide at the Spanish border and Paul Celan to the bridge in Paris—politics intrude to mock the happy notion that we can be in the world but not of it." In this telling moment, the poet either speaks out, or stands mute. By way of her friend's example, Forché finds courage in "Anna Akhmatova's 'Requiem' / and its final *I can* when the faceless woman / before her asked *can you describe this?*" Plath fell at this precipice and Dickinson fell silent, Hogan began to listen and Harjo to sing, all blood sisters with the singing, bear-hearted warrior.

Feminist politics have become global issues, male and female challenges of "the other" in private violence (abuses of passion), parental failures (the unraveling family), and institutional penalties (disparate salaries and menial skills mired in gender). Why raise these differences? It was not fish, Clyde Kluckhohn notes, who discovered water. "In a world of rocket ships and international organizations," the social scientist wrote in a postwar modern world, *Mirror for Man*, "what can the study of the obscure and primitive offer to the solution of today's problems?" Kluckhohn opens with Boas as an epigraph: a social and artistic science of *the other* "may show us, if we are ready to listen to its teachings, what to do and what to avoid." It was right there, by 1928 around Austin, Pound, Moore, Williams, Stevens, and Pound—*Anthropology and Modern Life* by Franz Boas. "Studying primitives," Kluckhohn continues the Boasian dialogue of alterity in 1949, "enables us to see ourselves better." We human beings seem to translate reality *plurally* only when we see ourselves as others seeing us, in order to act or not to act misguidedly. So Joyce spoke through a wandering Jewish-Protestant Dubliner-alias-Ulysses, and Bakhtin wrote on dialogics toward the end of his life. *They* become interpenetrantly *us,* the *other* among us, not-other, primitive to modern, as Julia Kristeva brings us back to the stranger within ourselves. "But we are not unalike," the poet learns in a double twist of the tongue, translating Claribel Alegría, the Spanish exiled Salvadoran. "When we look at someone, we are / seeing someone else."

In Forché's poetry, these dialogics surface in intimate contraries; differences sever lives, as they strangely connect them. People gain one another in loss, in violation of dialogue, in witness of "nothing" left over. Where humans cannot speak, where the untranslated voices of the disappeared haunt the living, language stirs within itself, another tongue is loosened.

"Carolina," the exiled poet checks Forché's chattering, "do you know how long it takes / any one voice to reach another?" At best, poet and reader engage in narratives of exchange, witness, wanting, and calling to others; at worst, we misread and malign the other with a spur of impatience. Not all reviewers were as admiring as the Yale and Lamont judges, or the Guggenheim Foundation who gave Forché the time to write in El Salvador. Eliot Weinberger keeps sniping at a "game of revolutionary tourism" in Forché's work (*Sulfur 6* 1983). Yet *The Country Between Us* has been one of the largest sold *and read* collections of contemporary American verse.

Can the "other" then, male or female, dark or light, wealthy or poor, remain with local integrity and respect the *other?* Native Americans, for one complex of peoples, fear appropriation and co-option of sovereignty, rightly, the acculturative erasure of difference. Can the other be different and still be, as Genesis would have it, "one of us," an-other human? Julia Kristeva appeals to our recognition, psychologically and politically, of "a stranger within" so that "uncanny strangeness is no longer an artistic or pathological product but a psychic law allowing us to confront the unknown and work it out in the process of *Kulturarbeit,* the task of civilization" *(Strangers to Ourselves)*. "The foreigner is within us," she concludes. "If I am a foreigner," to repeat, "there are no foreigners."

As with the natural world, we can learn to bear, or even to like, the *dis*likes of modern distances within and "between us." Poetry can stir people to change the criminal conditions of poverty, to respond to violations of human rights locally, even globally through telecommunications. In the hushed "valley of its saying," Auden lamented Yeats's death, "poetry makes nothing happen," yet there are *other* points of view to "teach the free man how to praise." *I can,* Akhmatova said, and did write the requiem of what women saw outside a Russian prison. Native Americans have risen from holocaustal ashes to "reinvent the enemy's language," as Joy Harjo and Gloria Bird anthologize native feminist writings. In Forché's verse, a personal nothing inversely becomes a public *no-thing* that speaks through tensed silence, canceled syntax, a mutual sense of loss. Intimately to internationally, these politics stretch between us each day and speak to the countries we cohabit, the tongues we stumble across. Forché recalls a comrade in "Reunion," a poem dedicated to Billie Holiday:

> I can remember it now as I see you
> again, how much tenderness we could
> wedge between a stairwell
> and a police lock, or as it was
> as it still is, in the voice
> of a woman singing of a man
> who could make her do anything.

Something more than nothing, a woman must ask, is this "anything" worth the blues cost? Why does her man make her do anything? The young poet remembers with Victoria "when one of the men who had / gathered around you took my mouth / to his own there was nothing / other than the dance hall music / rising to the arms of iced trees." Or more archly, she hisses in *Gathering the Tribes* with Sapphic brass: "In the night I come to you and it seems a shame / to waste my deepest shudders on a wall of a man" ("Taking Off My Clothes").

So beyond the "deep heart's core" of Yeats, Penn Warren, Roethke, or Berryman in the last-romantic agonies of Anglo male fatigue, Forché honors the "toughest part of the body," the quartered heart, whose violence or "tenderness" must be expressed in the hands, no less than Sitting Bull took his stand "with the heart of a bear." The poet invokes the crafting hand, the loving touch, the tool-making and art-shaping extensions of the heart and mind that distinguish humankind, for better or worse. Hand-made arts speak of "a mutually shared physical life," Octavio Paz says in *In Praise of Hands*. "A glass jug, a wicker basket, a coarse muslin huipil, a wooden serving dish: beautiful objects, not despite their usefulness but because of it." With such regard for daily beauty, Pablo Neruda writes local odes to the elemental things of everyday life: socks, artichokes, stones, tomatoes, lovers in *Odas Elementales*. And Zbigniew Herbert in Poland bids us look lovingly at a loyal stool, or carefully at a pebble with its "calm and very clear eye." These seem the heroics of earth and hearth, not conquest, the arts of peace at home, paid at human cost and tempered in forbearance, literally, thought onward to consequences. Neruda calls this witness a native guerrilla warfare, "poetry's war against war."

How else should the Irish-Slavic daughter of a working mother and a tool-and-die maker write? Blooded to a proletarian tradition of hand-crafted, useful arts, Forché pays homage to Hispanic-Indian ideals of passion, political resistance, and individual courage. Salvador and Slovakia come together in the cultural *news* brought home to the Americas. In "Ourselves or Nothing," the poet describes her models of witness:

> They turned to face the worst
> straight-on, without sentiment or hope,
> simply to keep watch over life.

This observer knows local truth with fierce compassion. Politics and art, hardly incompatible to most of the world, yet somehow estranged in the States, can record personal history, and people will read it. Time includes us, our lives to be lived, yet goes beyond us to the next generation. These are not ideologies or conceptual glosses, deracinated from immediate contexts, but poetic realities, quick and exact, in texts that move us through particulars into history and future life.

As "native" Americans, indeed as blooded indigenes, Spanish-speaking native poets rise epically behind Forché: her exiled Salvadoran mentor, Claribel Alegría, Cesar Vallejo from Peru, Octavio Paz from Mexico, Gabriela Mistral from Chile, and above all, Pablo Neruda. "It is useful, at certain hours of the day or night," Neruda said of an "impure" poetic search, "to look closely at objects at rest: wheels that have crossed long, dusty distances, bearing their huge vegetal and mineral burdens, bags of coal from the coal bins, barrels, baskets and handles in a carpenter's tool chest. From them flow the contacts between man and the earth, like a lesson for all tortured lyric poets." What ties the poet to these and other great writers of Hispanic America—Rulfo and Galeano from Mexico, Llossa and Vallejo from Peru, Cortázar and Juarroz from Argentina, Márquez from Colombia—is the *mestizo* complex of native and émigré, the tribal tongues of *Los Indios* blooded to Spanish, Portuguese, and many others, by way of "Golden Age" landfalls.

Hybridity—cultural fusion—bears the history of Latin American peoples, in truth, Hispanicized Native Americans. A century before William Bradford wrote the history of Plymouth Colony, the first "Hispanic" historian of the New World, Garcilaso de la Vega, was born Peruvian in the mid-sixteenth century and known as *El Inca,* by way of his mother. History is grounded in truth. Given a poetry of human rights and impure reversals, Forché would not be deluded by pure art or shining ideologies, but would lie down with the bastard *things* that Williams saw fleshing ideas. "A poetry impure as a suit, a body, with soup-stains, and shameful attitudes," Neruda goes on, "with wrinkles, observations, dreams, vigils, prophecies, declarations of love and of hatred, beasts, convulsions, idylls, political beliefs, denials, doubts, affirmations, taxes."

Such a poet lives, struggles, loves, and writes for "the people," as Native Americans have long named themselves. No less than her tribal sisters, Hogan, Harjo, Tapahonso, Whiteman, or TallMountain, Forché resists the abuses of indigenous human rights. The native mother-poet witnesses and speaks against unjustifiable wrongs, in the face of overwhelming odds and daily indecisions. Cataclysm comes between us, more than any time in human history. The threat of ending could reunite us. "Ourselves or nothing" whets a dialectic blade imposed by this century's closure, indeed by the threat of apocalypse more real than millennial hysteria. Julia Kristeva writes of "Hiroshima, mon amour" that our "private pain absorbs political horror," as we hold the other's "deathly halo" in our arms. Death's "permanent wound" immanently opens contact within, all too explicitly without. If the barbed wire of death camps is our terrible icon, Milosz notes of modern nihilism, Canetti would open the tribal door through a dark eros of anxiety. Beyond our holocaustal "rainbow of pain," Kristeva concludes,

"We are survivors, the living dead, corpses on suspended sentence, harboring our personal Hiroshima in the hollow of our private world."

This is our terrible innocence moving native poets "simply to keep watch over life," not only locally, but at home in our common global village. Carolyn Forché seems a poet whose art comes naturally, swiftly from commitments to the living, from loyalties to the dead and prayers to honest gods. She is a bear-hearted poet who places her voice, values, art, and life on the line.

> everywhere and always
> go after that which is lost.
> There is a cyclone fence between
> ourselves and the slaughter and behind it
> we hover in a calm protected world like
> netted fish, exactly like netted fish.
> It is either the beginning or the end
> of the world, and the choice is ourselves
> or nothing.

Afterword: *The Bear's Tail*

. . . poetry can make an order as true to the impact of external reality and as sensitive to the inner laws of the poet's being as the ripples that rippled in and rippled out across the water in that scullery bucket fifty years ago. An order where we can at last grow up to that which we stored up as we grew.

SEAMUS HEANEY, *Crediting Poetry*, 1995 NOBEL LECTURE

Have we found "som murthe or som doctryne," since Chaucer was stinted by his Host, in all this "drasty rymyng"? At the forest's edge of our own times, *Sing with the Heart of a Bear* has traced an American rhythm from individual voice, to local tone, to regional ground, Scott Momaday to Georgia O'Keeffe: "At once, accordingly you knew, / As you knew the forms of the earth at Abiquiu." We are all interconnected, all related. Intrinsic aesthetic, particular dialect, and comparative dialectic move out into a global community, interculturally *treating* for mutual acknowledgment, the "country" between us.

As argued, the American rhythm this century begins with Dickinson's iambic hymnal measure, counterpointed, and Whitman's free verse "barbaric yawp" hewn into the modernist iambic line, Stevens to Roethke, strung down to the formalist airs of Jorie Graham and Hogan's interspecies insistence. A century ago, the linguistic anthropologists were laying postwar riprap for Cronyn's rainbow "path," a tribal coalition across the New World, so that Navajo *Talking God* and Lakota "word sender" were transcribed into print by 1918.

Native and American begin to cross by midcentury, and Williams's "variable foot" finally links up with TallMountain's lyric plain style. Pound's taut lines and cut images sculpt a measure of Momaday's tensile symmetry. Moore's syllabics cadence Tapahonso's pointillist, code-switching, Navajo-English rhythms. Later century fusions tie a literary epoch of evolutionary forms together. Lawrence's freed lines break out in the free-form blank verse of Olds, and Hughes's fierce torque can be felt in the high-tension, hardly-free verse of Forché. Revolutionary native poetics recycle in each generation. The wild-line sixties again fire up in the Ginsberg-Kerouac riffs of Harjo and Alexie. Neoprimitive becomes postmodern, tribal at last national. It's all mixed up, all mixed together, oral to formalist, regional to transcontinental. A comparative aesthetics comes up, over and over, with newly original, *native* American poetics. The one certainty is that Native and American are fusing.

As social scientists tell us, the "hybrid vigor" of global fusions comprises a country's strengths, poetic and otherwise. "The record of history likewise indicates," Clyde Kluckhohn reminds us, "that mongrel peoples are more creative than the more inbred groups. Almost all of the civilizations that humanity agrees were most significant (Egypt, Mesopotamia, Greece, India, China) arose where divergent peoples met. Not only was there cross-fertilization from varying ways of life, but there was also interchange of genes between contrasting physical strains" (*Mirror for Man*). Given the geometric combinations and permutations of our émigré-native, gene-pool intermix, Americans need not fear a turbid "melting pot" in the near future. This country's aesthetics remain *genuine* and *raw*, as Moore says of our interest *in* poetry, for a long time to come, cummings's blue-eyed boys to Williams's black-eyed susans. "We must never forget that four-fifths of the population of the earth consists of colored peoples," Kluckhohn looks at the big picture. "It does not mean pretending that differences do not exist. It does mean recognizing differences without fearing, hating, or despising them. It means not exaggerating differences at the expense of similarities. It means understanding the true causes of the differences. It means valuing these differences as adding to the richness and variety of the world."

The context of any text, debated in an American grain these days, warily circles *new* criticism of the well-wrought urn, itself once a revolutionary corrective to biographical history. Half a century back, context was thought to silence text and texture, elements now seen as cultural index preceding and shaping literacy. Given the multiple ABC of textual particulars—syllable, syntax, structure, style, sign, and sense—how do we translate across languages and cultures, coming full circle, without losing or making up whole new texts? Can we resist literary products of our own predilections? *Traduttore, traditore,* the Italian proverb warns, the "translator betrays," though Frost was cryptically fond of saying, as noted, that poetry is that lost in translation. We would be all the poorer for not trying to bridge cultures, and without rooted history or comparative aesthetics. The translative problems run legion, as everyone knows, just crossing from Romance to Germanic-based languages (Hamlet's "this quintessence of dust"), from musical phrasings of open-voweled phonemes to muscular patterns with consonantal cuts and spondaic end-stops (Welch's "wet, black things to steal away our cache / of meat"). Pattern and variation in rhythm alone, the expected (formal) and the spoken (natural) foot, may be intricately and variably interlineated with tone, pitch, weight, mass, and voice inflection, from the classical Spanish hendecasyllabic line, to Augustan heroic couplets. "The apparition of these faces in the crowd; / Petals on a wet, black bough." Add to phonemic inflection, syntax. "If words referred only to things," Kluckhohn says in *Mirror for Man*, "translation would be relatively simple. But they refer also to relations between things and the subjective as well as the objective aspects of these relationships. In different tongues relationships are variously conceived."

So poetics are not just syllabic constructs, but sequential sounds, personally registered: "words refer not only to events," Kluckhohn continues, "but to the attitudes of the speakers toward those events." Forché writes from empathic grief turned political fervor, Olds from wry tailspin, Hogan from mothering compassion, Tapahonso from Navajo wit and *hozhó*. These are deeply personal, dramatically public matters, revolutionary for unsilenced voices, especially among women and peoples of color. "When 'The Repressed' of their culture and their society come back," Cixous warns Parisians by way of radical Algerian-Jewish feminism, "it is an explosive return, which is *absolutely* shattering, staggering, overturning, with a force never let loose before." For the rest of us, circling the debates of power, Terrence Des Pres fears a dearly expended, deafening ache: "The press of the real is problematic for all of us but especially for poets because their art requires attention to humanity's sad still music that now, amid the awful nonstop roar of things, is hard to make out." Lyrically editing the crowd's "bang and babble," a writer configures the *shape* of the line, syllabic to accentual foot, poised couplet to ragged prose riff. Alexie's Spokane sass, Stevens's Hartford harmony, Pound's Venetian gaze cast their verse in distinctive tones, measures, and shades of voice, all crafted in diversity.

> *White men like to dig in the ground for their food. My people prefer to hunt the buffalo as their fathers did. White men like to stay in one place. My people want to move their tepees here and there to the different hunting grounds. The life of white men is slavery. They are prisoners in towns or farms. The life my people want is a life of freedom. I have seen nothing that a white man has, houses or railways or clothing or food, that is as good as the right to move in the open country, and live in our own fashion.*
> SITTING BULL, FORT RANDALL, 1883

What are our imagined cultural myths, revised these days, as Eden revisited, by way of Native and American creation stories? In some southern sense, La Malinche has come back as Cixous's hysteric-heroic-goddess, resurrected, to retranslate and to update the *conquest* of the Americas. More northerly, Sitting Bull has reemerged with Henry James's literary tools, a quick wit, a sharp eye, a fine ear, an accurate pen, Momaday through Alexie. James Joyce took Ulysses as his classical ethnic hero in the British Isles. Americans might look to Sitting Bull, *Tatanka Iyotanke*, an indigenous model for inspiration and true heart: the *poetic* man of action, generous and brave, trusted and eloquent. If this land is ever threatened or, God forbid, invaded, *Tatanka Iyotanke* stands as a model of native resistance, heroic courage, then firm, realistic negotiation. He knew when to fight, staked to his native ground with strength and honor, and when to cease conflict—when to defend and when to dialogue, when to speak and when to keep silent. Sitting Bull voiced all this, hunting, leading, husbanding, parenting, dreaming, warring against invasion, mediating peace, in words that commanded respect and vision.

To recapitulate, Sitting Bull was an interspecies *wicasa wakán* or visionary, beginning when a yellowhammer warned the boy of a threatening bear. The Lakota warrior sang bird cadences all his life, ceremonially and otherwise, especially meadowlark triads and cascading fourths, in a fine second tenor voice. The "Sioux" lark warned him of his death, December 15, 1890. Powerfully quick on his feet when younger, Sitting Bull would stake himself to the battleground as a red sash wearer in the Strong Heart *akicita*. The war chief dreamed of many upside-down, earless Bluecoats falling into his village, just before the Little Big Horn of 1876—and his people won that battle decisively when Custer did not listen. Sitting Bull led some twenty thousand Sioux in campaigns against white encroachment, from the 1850s through 1876; the unbeaten warrior negotiated settlements from then until his assassination in 1890. "I would rather die an Indian than live a white man," Sitting Bull said to his end. Still, he was adaptively civil and legendary in generosity, especially to strangers, adopting a nephew, One Bull, as his own son, beside a captive enemy Assiniboine boy, *Hohe* or Stays Back. Choosing to live as a Hunkpapa when given the choice to return to his people, *Hohe* was known later as Kills Plenty, then as Little Assiniboine, finally as Jumping Bull, the name of Sitting Bull's father. Sitting Bull was a compassionate leader who released the white captive Fanny Kelly, when others wanted to kill her or keep her as a hostage. The warrior-chief also adopted Frank Grouard, half-white and half-Polynesian captive mail carrier, as his brother and translator, his eyes and ears into the *Wasiçun* world. Grouard was renamed Standing Bear, then The Grabber, for the courage of a fighting bear.

Tatanka Iyotanke was a strong leader, a respected father and husband, a charismatic speaker, a holy man, a politician, and a gifted singer—"a man medicine seemed to surround," Robert Higheagle said in his Hunkpapa camp. Sitting Bull was loyal to his peoples' rights to the death. "Long Lance" Major James M. Walsh, Canadian Mounted Policeman, described the Hunkpapa warrior on September 11, 1880:

> He is the shrewdest and most intelligent Indian living. He has the ambition of Napoleon, and is brave to a fault. He is respected as well as feared by every

Indian on the plains. In war he has no equal. In council he is superior to all. *Every word said by him carries weight, is quoted and passed from camp to camp.* (emphasis mine)

Long Lance Walsh served as Sitting Bull's Canadian warden and interpreter, during Lakota exile 1877–1881. Wry and unbowed, *Tatanka Iyotanke* kept his dignity through government assaults on his homeland, broken treaties, the slaughter of the buffalo, and betrayal of promises to leave his people free in Great Sioux Territory "as long as the grass shall grow and the rivers shall run." Finally, Sitting Bull made the white easterner, Catherine Weldon, welcome in his cabin as "Woman-Walking-Ahead"; the year of his assassination, he even offered to marry her.

Sitting Bull was an inspired storyteller and a brilliant orator, truly a man of powerful language, as the Sioux said, a *word sender*. He left a pictographic autobiography of forty sketches and learned to autograph his name, free for ladies, one to five dollars for men. He gave signatures "with true reportorial grace," a reporter said. Traveling with Buffalo Bill Cody's Wild West, Sitting Bull adopted Annie Oakley, *Little Sure Shot,* as his daughter. "The one old man chief of all the camps combined," Wooden Leg put it. No poet has ever commanded a more attentive or responsive audience.

> *So I have been a warrior,*
> *and now it is all over, so*
> *I know to bear against hard times.*

With a spirit of place and people indivisible, from Aztec to Sioux, Wintu to Delaware, Native America is here to be heard, consulted, read, and respected. Men like Sitting Bull, James Welch, Sherman Alexie, or Scott Momaday are native poets, distinct within an American tradition of poetry, and real men for it. Native American women, Mary TallMountain to Joy Harjo, Mabel McKay to Roberta Hill Whiteman, voice their tribal integrities and differences, too, from mainstream feminists: *othering* involves not only mothering their own or nurturing took-ins, as Luci Tapahonso, Louise Erdrich, Joy Harjo, or Linda Hogan have done with child-raising, but as they say on the rez, "helping out" across the board. These mothers care for and adopt children, yes, but they also stand beside their fathers, husbands, sons, lovers, ex-lovers, or otherwise, forgiving their warriors' falls and faults, Mary Crow Dog says, as casualties of imposed historical calamities. They are strong women. History is their tomahawk to whet, institutional war their grievance, savagist racism their enemy. Tribal peoples may be anti-mainstream or even anti-white, but seldom male-bashing or female-trashing, even if sexual preference turns to their own gender. Nor does someone like Mary Crow Dog complain of being "a prisoner of biology," as Simone de Beauvoir would exempt women from pro forma childbearing. Kith and kin are the centers of Native America, clan and family the core;

whether one is gay or straight, on- or off-rez, children, elders, and extended family compose the tribal future, immediately present. *The people* are surviving evidence of a native holocaust and renaissance, to be celebrated.

In the specifics of gender wars, women of all color writing poetry voice a reorienting grace, a call for courage, sacrifice, atonement, justice, and equality in our New World. La Chingada returns as our interlingual translator, Old World native to New World interlocutor and lover. *Hijos de la chingada,* then, are not mestizo misfits, but hybrid fusions of power and intelligence, when cultures cross borders. In truth, Moctezuma's progeny continue to populate western Spain, since a conquistador took one of the monarch's daughters back home as his wife. So, too, Pocahontas lives on today, as "Lady Rebecca" Rolfe's descendants on the eastern seaboard. Sacajawea's story continues as Frenchman's wife-and-guide to Lewis and Clark. Tekakwitha, Iroquois maiden, reminds America of sainted sacrifice, next to her Roman Catholic rival for canonization, Father Junípero Serra, the slaver-priest. The New World native pogrom is known *by sacrificial blood-giving,* never forgotten. Mixed-blood leaders, men and women, have gone down in American history with heroic legacy: Squanto, Wampanoag translator, commandeered to England and back with the first colonists; Samoset, an Abenaki who greeted the Pilgrims at Plymouth in English learned from traders; Sam Houston, married into Tennessee tribal societies; Quanah Parker, mixed-blood Comanche chief; Crazy Horse, called Curly as a boy, with his brown hair and grey eyes, martyr among Sioux peoples; Pancho Villa, Mexican-Indian revolutionary; Essie Parrish, Miwok-Pomo Dream Dancer and healer; role models like Charles Eastman, Jim Thorpe, Mabel McKay, Will Rogers, Reuben Snake, Wilma Mankiller, Vine Deloria, Jr., Ada Deer, or entertainers like Buffy Sainte-Marie, Will Samson, Dan George, Graham Greene, Wes Studi, and John Trudell. From northern Metis or "mixed-bloods," to southern "runaway" Seminoles, from Mohawk high-steel workers and Penobscot loggers, to Montana Blackfeet cowboys, Pueblo weavers, and Salish fishermen in the West, Indians are among us, today, as American as anyone can claim, and writing.

If we could listen closely to American rhythms long in this land, update and rewrite the Edenic myth, by way of native creation stories, it might go something like this: *long ago, they say, only yesterday,* first-man Adam climbed from the animate dust of "red earth," surely, though the Maker comes from and in many forms, many names: Feathered Serpent, to Dawn-Light-Colored-One, to Talking God or Singing Spirit, to Old Man and Old Woman, to Turtle and Rabbit, or Spider and Snake, or simply the Light and Darkness. Or maybe it was all there, all along, no beginning, no ending, the *Power-that-Moves-moves.*

Imagine that Eve would not break from Adam's rib, as Dickinson grafted in her father's garden, but live right there among the original ninety-two

percent of matrifocal societies, four to six million strong in the pre-
Columbian United States land mass, certainly with Hogan's Chickasaw an-
cestors and Harjo's Creek forefathers of the "Five Civilized Tribes" in the
Southeast. They trace back forty, to sixty or more thousands of years of
migrations, Mongoloid to Caucasoid trekkers across the Bering Strait. More
mythologically, if you like, the first beings were emerging from a sacred
umbilical snake-hole, *Shipapuni,* in the Grand Canyon, or stepping off an
Iroquois Turtle Island raft, or born Blackfeet daughter of Sun and Moon,
or spawned Diné Coyote, or blessed Kiowa granddaughter of Grandfather
Snake and Grandmother Spider.

A native Adam does not privilege himself naming and numbering savage
creation, as Stevens feared the glass jar in Tennessee, but finds himself an
early evolving creature among others, interrelating things, as Welch's
Blackfeet people tell of the creation. *Na'pi,* or Old Man Sun, went first by
male prerogative, making things up obtusely, and his wife, *Kipi'taki,* or Old
Woman Moon, got the second, that is, last realistic word: ten, not twenty
fingers; horizontal, not vertical facial features; pubes hidden, not at the
navel. Tossing a stone, not a buffalo chip on the water, resulted in people
dying forever, not going away and coming back in four days, as Old Man
wished. Their child died, and Old Woman wanted to change the order of
things, but Old Man sighed, "We can't, we fixed it." And so with names,
with all things, trying to fix them accurately, dialogically, knowing that mor-
tality sweeps the whole creation away to other forms, to the spirits.

As Austin dissented, and Williams held out against his patriarchal peers,
neither does Adam hold *dominion* over all beings, but remains more as
Tapahonso's Navajo think, the firstborn Coyote of Old Man and Old
Woman, down the line in comically serious succession, finding his way
southwest from the north, picking up bits and pieces of things along the
journey. Nor does Adam hold sway over Eve, as Moore and Bishop resisted
among the Manhattan modernists, but owes his lineage and medicine bun-
dle, the pipe in particular, as Mary Crow Dog's Lakota say of White Buffalo
Calf Woman, to the mother earth beings, bison and eagle, wolf and bear,
horse and deer. Clan mothers, from Iroquois in the Northeast, to Pueblo
in the Southwest, to Civilized Tribes in the Southeast, to Klamath fishing
clans in the Northwest, keep these mother-rights firm in Native American
succession.

Original Sin, the forbidden apple of knowledge, does not turn on sexual
or intellectual transgression, as Pound suffered his own overreaching bril-
liance and incorrigible ego, but seems better illustrated in the Blackfeet
story of the Dung Suitor, as Roberta Hill, studying for her M.F.A. in Mon-
tana, might dream it. The chaste princess, whose excrement was so pure
as to be white, was too good for any village man, until a handsome dark
stranger showed up in winter and won her heart with his fine bearing and

dress. In spring, he said that he had to go, and as she tried to hold him, he slipped away. She followed, calling after him. Chinook winds warmed the earth, and the princess came to a moccasin of dung, then a legging of dung, then a buckskin shirt of dung, and finally to her lover, Dung Man, melting through his fine clothing. Chastened, she went back to the village and found a good husband.

The Expulsion from the Garden, the catastrophic Fall, would be told quite differently from Roethke's glass-house trauma in deforested Upper Michigan. Farther north, TallMountain's Koyukon relatives speak of *Takánakapsâluk* and her father out fishing off the Northwest Coast: the daughter fell overboard, and when she tried to crawl back into his boat, the father cut off her fingers. *Takánakapsâluk* sank to the bottom of the sea, where she became keeper of the sea animals, seal, walrus, porpoise, whale, and lived in a cave guarded by a snarling, three-headed dog, gnawing on a bone. Today, shamans in trances drop to the bottom of the sea to ask her forgiveness: circling the soul-stealing father and calming the dog, they approach *Takánakapsâluk* from behind and comb her matted hair, since she has no fingers. They turn her toward the light and beg propitiation for man's cruelty. The shaman shoots up the ancestral tube to his people, "I have something to say." The people confess their blood sins, "Let us hear, let us hear." If *Takánakapsâluk*, "Mother of the Sea," hears them, the game will be plentiful and the hunting successful. "Words will rise," the shaman says. If not, winter will be long and hard for the Koyukon.

Adam would not be cursed to sweat and labor for his bread, as Graham and Olds stigmatize western macho. Old Man might game for a living, like Coyote bargaining immortality, losing, but coming back for more. Or he might trick the dumb ducks in a shut-eye dance, or toss his eyeballs up in a tree to amuse and, unfortunately, to feed the crow, or generally misbehave all over the place, acting out how things go wrong and what not to do, losing and popping up somewhere else. Hinge-minded Trickster shows the wit to sharpen our wits, as Lewis Hyde says, the imagination to imagine a world. Mind waking up to mind, he would be playing the game we all must play, hopefully better, but always with Coyote's negative culpability, keeping us grounded, alert, and of good humor.

And Eve would not be cursed, giving birth in sorrow, as Gregg and Forché grieve, but more joyous-sad like Grandmother Spider in a sacred-secular beginning, who raises the twins of the Sun and Moon. So Momaday's Kiowa matriarchs tell it, happy to be taking care of the boys, keening such a handful. "The holiness of such a thing can be imparted to the human spirit, I believe," Momaday writes of his great-grandmother, "for I remember that it shone in the sightless eyes of Keahdineakeah. Once I was taken to see her at the old house on the other side of Rainy Mountain Creek. The room was dark, and her old age filled it like a substance. She was white-haired and blind, and, in that strange reversion that comes upon the very old, her skin was as soft as the skin of a baby. I remember the sound of her glad weeping and the water-like touch of her hand.''

Finally, justice, grace, and redemption would not come by millennial Second Coming—the terrible sword and four horsemen of the apocalypse, heaven and hell divided by the Angel of Eternity—but more as Alexie's Nez Percé cousins tell their own Orpheus and Eurydice elegy, the loss and seasonal recovery of the beloved earth. Jarold Ramsey frames this indigenous archetype by way of Archie Phinney's 1929 translations, his mother's Shahaptian native rhythms of winter and summer, the retreating and coming back of hope, going without and getting back to reality: "Darkness fell, and now Coyote listened for the voices, and he looked all around. He looked here and there, but nothing appeared. Coyote sat there in the middle of the prairie.''

These stories would be told, and others, by many different peoples, in different places and times, all across the country, Native American and those simply native, or recently immigrant, still coming. The languages would be diverse in the beginnings, but cross regional dialects and personal inflections, margin *in* mainstream—the male drives and female forgivings, the feminist cries and masculinist prayers, the countless tongues of others from far away coming closer.

The American rhythms of this land contour a native poetics, an openly fusional aesthetics. A complex and creative literacy is evolving in our interethnic new land. Seamus Heaney, the Nobel Oxford-Harvard poet-professor, crosses oceans with native rights to conclude his '' 'Poet's Chair' '' in *The Spirit Level:*

> My father's ploughing one, two, three, four sides
> Of the lea ground where I sit all-seeing
> At centre field, my back to the thorn tree
> They never cut. The horses are all hoof
> And burnished flank, I am all foreknowledge.
> Of the poem as a ploughshare that turns time
> Up and over. Of the chair in leaf
> The fairy thorn is entering for the future.
> Of being here for good in every sense.

SELECTED BIBLIOGRAPHY

Alexie, Sherman. "Beyond Talking Indian Chiefs." *New York Times* (October 23, 1994): 44.

———. *The Business of Fancydancing.* New York: Hanging Loose, 1992.

———. *First Indian on the Moon.* New York: Hanging Loose, 1993.

———. *Indian Killer.* New York: Atlantic Monthly, 1996.

———. *The Lone Ranger and Tonto Fistfight in Heaven.* New York: Atlantic Monthly, 1993.

———. "Making Smoke." *Aboriginal Voices* 5 (May/June 1998): 42–43.

———. *Old Shirts and New Skins.* Native American Series, no. 9. Los Angeles: UCLA American Indian Studies Center, 1993.

———. *Reservation Blues.* New York: Atlantic Monthly, 1995.

———. "Sherman Alexie." Interview by Charlene Teters. *Indian Artist* (Spring 1998): 30–35.

———. *The Summer of Black Widows.* New York: Hanging Loose, 1996.

———. "Well Spokane." Interview by Annabelle Villanueva. *LIT: NewCity's Literary Supplement* (October 31, 1996): L10–L11.

———. "White Men Can't Drum." *New York Times Magazine,* October 4, 1992, 30.

Allen, Donald, and Warren Tallman. *The Poetics of the New American Poetry.* New York: Grove, 1973.

Allen, Paula Gunn. " 'The Grace That Remains'—American Indian Women's Literature." *Book Forum: "American Indians Today—Thought—Literature—Art"* 5 (1981): 376–82.

Allen, Paula Gunn, and Kenneth Lincoln, eds. Native American Supplement to *The Jacaranda Review* 6 (Winter/Summer 1992): 53–111.

Angulo, Jaime de. *Indian Tales.* New York: Hill and Wang, 1953.

———. *Indians in Overalls.* San Francisco: Turtle Island Foundation, 1973.

———. *A Jaime de Angulo Reader.* Edited by Bob Callahan. Berkeley: Turtle Island Foundation, 1979.

Armstrong, Jeannette C. "Land Speaking." In *Speaking for the Generations. Native Writers on Writing*, edited by Simon J. Ortiz. Tucson: University of Arizona Press, 1998.

Astrov, Margot, ed. *The Winged Serpent*. 1946. Reprint, *American Indian Prose and Poetry*. New York: Capricorn, 1962.

Austin, Mary. *The American Rhythm: Studies and Reëxpressions of Amerindian Songs*. New York: Houghton Mifflin, 1923, 1930. Reprint, New York: Cooper Square, 1970.

———. *Earth Horizon*. Boston: Houghton Mifflin, 1932.

Bandelier, Adolph F. *The Delight Makers*. 1890. Reprint with an introduction by Stefan Jovanovich. New York: Harcourt Brace Jovanovich, 1971.

Basso, Keith H. *Portraits of "The Whiteman": Linguistic Play and Cultural Symbols Among the Western Apache*. Cambridge: Cambridge University Press, 1979.

———. *Wisdom Sits in Places: Landscape and Language Among the Western Apache*. Albuquerque: University of New Mexico Press, 1996.

Bataille, Gretchen M., and Kathleen Mullen Sands. *American Indian Women: Telling Their Lives*. Lincoln: University of Nebraska Press, 1984.

Baudrillard, Jean. *America*. London: Verso Press, 1988.

Beauvoir, Simone de. *The Second Sex*. Translated by H. M. Parshley. New York: Alfred A. Knopf, 1952.

Bedient, Calvin. "Poetry and Silence at the End of the Century." Review of *The Angel of History*, by Carolyn Forché. *Salmagundi* 111 (Summer 1996): 195–207.

———. "The Solo Mysterioso Blues. An Interview with Harryette Mullen." *Callaloo* 19 (1996): 651–669.

Berg, Stephen. *Singular Voices: American Poetry Today*. New York: Avon, 1985.

Bender, John, and David E. Wellbery, eds. *Chronotypes: The Construction of Time*. Stanford, Calif.: Stanford University Press, 1991.

Benjamin, Walter. *Illuminations*. 1955. Second edition translated by Harry Zohn. Edited by Hannah Arendt. London: William Collins Sons, 1973.

Berkhofer, Robert F. *The White Man's Indian: Images of the American Indians from Columbus to the Present*. New York: Random House, 1978.

Bernheimer, Richard. *Wild Men in the Middle Ages: A Study in Art, Sentiment, and Demonology*. Cambridge, Mass.: Harvard University Press, 1952.

Berryman, John. *Delusions, Etc.* New York: Farrar, Straus and Giroux, 1972.

———. *John Berryman: Collected Poems, 1937–1971*. Edited by Charles Thornbury. New York: Noonday/Farrar, Straus and Giroux, 1989.

Bierhorst, John. *In the Trail of the Wind: American Indian Poems and Ritual Orations*. New York: Farrar, Straus and Giroux, 1971.

Bishop, Elizabeth. "Efforts of Affection: A Memoir of Marianne Moore." In *Elizabeth Bishop: The Collected Prose*. New York: Farrar, Straus and Giroux, 1984.

Bloom, Harold. *The Western Canon: The Books and School of the Ages*. New York: Harcourt Brace, 1994.

Boas, Franz. *Primitive Art*. Oslo: H. Aschehoug, 1927. Cambridge: Harvard University Press, 1928.

Borges, Jorge Luis. *The Book of Imaginary Beings*. Translated by Jorge Luis Borges and Norman Thomas di Giovanni. New York: Penguin, 1974.

Bowra, C. M. *Primitive Song*. New York: World Publishing, 1962.

Brandon, William. *The Magic World: American Indian Songs and Poems*. New York: William Morrow, 1971.

Brinton, Daniel G. *Essays of an Americanist*. Philadelphia: Porter and Coates, 1890.

Brodsky, Joseph. "The Writer in Prison." *New York Times Book Review* (October 13, 1996): 24–25.

Brooks, Van Wyck. *The Confident Years: 1885–1915*. New York: E. P. Dutton, 1952.

Brown, Calvin S. *Music and Literature: A Comparison of the Arts*. Athens: University of Georgia Press, 1948.

———. *Tones Into Words: Musical Compositions as Subjects of Poetry*. Athens: University of Georgia Press, 1953.

Brown, Donald E. *Human Universals*. New York: McGraw-Hill, 1991.

Bruchac, Joseph. *Survival This Way: Interviews with American Indian Poets*. Sun Tracks Series, vol. 15. Tucson: University of Arizona Press, 1987.

Buechel, Eugene, S.J. *A Dictionary of the Teton Dakota Sioux Language*. Edited by Paula Manhart, S.J. Pine Ridge, S.D.: Red Cloud Indian School, 1970.

Bynner, Witter. *Indian Earth*. New York: Knopf, 1929.

Canetti, Elias. *The Conscience of Words*. Translated by Joachim Neugroshel. New York: Seabury Press, 1979.

Carr, Helen. *Inventing the American Primitive: Politics, Gender and the Representation of Native American Literary Traditions, 1789–1936*. New York: New York University Press, 1996.

Castro, Michael. *Interpreting the Indian: Twentieth-Century Poets and the Native American*. Albuquerque: University of New Mexico Press, 1983.

Celan, Paul. *Paul Celan: Poems*. Translated by Michael Hamburger. New York: Persea Books, 1980.

Cheyfitz, Eric. *The Poetics of Imperialism: Translations and Colonialization from 'The Tempest' to 'Tarzan.'* New York: Oxford University Press, 1991.

Cixous, Hélène, and Clément, Catherine. *The Newly Born Woman*. Translated by Betsy Wing. Theory and History of Literature, vol. 24. Minneapolis: University of Minnesota Press, 1986.

Clements, William M. *Native American Verbal Art*. Tucson: University of Arizona Press, 1997.

Coke, A. A. Hedge. "Seeds." In *Speaking for the Generations: Native Writers on Writing*. Edited by Simon J. Ortiz. Tucson: University of Arizona Press, 1998.

Coltelli, Laura. *Winged Words: American Indian Writers Speak*. Lincoln: University of Nebraska Press, 1990.

Cook-Lynn, Elizabeth. *Why I Can't Read Wallace Stegner and Other Essays: A Tribal Voice*. Madison: University of Wisconsin Press, 1996.

Cronyn, George W. *The Path on the Rainbow*. 1918. Reprint. *American Indian Poetry*. New York: Ballantine, 1991.

Crow Dog, Mary, with Richard Erdoes. *Lakota Woman*. New York: Grove Weidenfeld, 1990.

Curtis, Natalie Burlin. *The Indians' Book*. New York: Harper, 1907.

Day, A. Grove. *The Sky Clears: Poetry of the American Indians*. New York: Macmillan, 1951. Reprint, Lincoln: University of Nebraska Press, 1964.

Deacon, Terrence W. *The Symbolic Species: The Co-Evolution of Language and the Brain*. New York: Norton, 1997.

Dead Man. 1996. Written, directed, and produced by Jim Jarmusch. Los Angeles: 12-Gauge Production/Miramax. Motion picture.

Delany, Paul. *The Neo-Pagans. Rupert Brooke and the Ordeal of Youth.* New York: Free Press, 1987.

Deloria, Philip J. *Playing Indian.* New Haven: Yale University Press, 1998.

Demetracapoulou, Dorothy. "Wintu Songs." *Anthropos* (Vienna) 30 (1935): 483–494.

Des Pres, Terrence. *Praises and Dispraises: Poetry and Politics, the Twentieth Century.* New York: Viking, 1988.

———. *The Survivor: An Anatomy of Life in the Death Camps.* New York: Oxford, 1976.

Dickinson, Emily. *The Complete Poems of Emily Dickinson.* Edited by Thomas H. Johnson. Boston: Little, Brown, & Co. 1951. Reprint, Cambridge: Harvard University Press, 1955.

———. *The Complete Poems of Emily Dickinson.* Edited by Martha Dickinson Bianchi. New York: Little, Brown & Co., 1924.

———. *The Life and Letters of Emily Dickinson.* Edited by Martha Dickinson Bianchi and Alfred Leete Hampson. New York: Houghton Mifflin, 1924.

———. *New Poems of Emily Dickinson.* Edited by William H. Shurr. Chapel Hill: University of North Carolina Press, 1993.

———. *Poems of Emily Dickinson.* First Series. Edited by Mabel Loomis Todd and T. W. Higginson. Boston: Roberts Brothers, 1890.

———. *Selected Poems and Letters of Emily Dickinson.* Edited by Robert N. Linscott. New York: Anchor/Doubleday, 1959.

Dodge, Robert K., and Joseph B. McCullough, eds. *Voices from Wah'Kon-Tah: Contemporary Poetry of Native Americans.* New York: International Publishers, 1974.

Dow, Philip, ed. *19 New American Poets of the Golden Gate.* New York: Harcourt Brace Jovanovich, 1984.

Dubie, Norman. *The Clouds of Magellan.* Santa Fe: Recursos, 1991.

Dunsmore, Roger. *Earth's Mind: Essays in Native Literature.* Albuquerque: University of New Mexico Press, 1997.

Eastman, Charles A. (Ohiyesa). *Indian Heroes and Great Chieftains.* Boston: Little, Brown and Co., 1918.

Eliade, Mircea. *Shamanism: Archaic Techniques of Ecstasy.* Translated by Williard R. Trask. Princeton: Princeton University Press, 1964.

Eliot, T. S. *The Use of Poetry and the Use of Criticism.* Harvard Lectures 1932–1933.

———. "War-Paint and Feathers." *Atheneum,* no. 4668 (October 17, 1919): 1036.

Erdoes, Richard, and John (Fire) Lame Deer. *Lame Deer Seeker of Visions: The Life of a Sioux Medicine Man.* New York: Simon and Schuster, 1972.

Erdrich, Louise. *Baptism of Desire.* New York: Harper & Row, 1989.

———. *Jacklight.* New York: Holt, Rinehart and Winston, 1984.

Farr, Judith. *Emily Dickinson: A Collection of Critical Essays.* New Century Views. Upper Saddle River, N.J.: Prentice-Hall, 1996.

Fenollosa, Ernest. *The Chinese Written Character as a Medium for Poetry.* Edited by Ezra Pound. San Francisco: City Lights, 1936.

Finnigan, Ruth. *Oral Poetry.* Cambridge: Cambridge University Press, 1977.

Fisher, Dexter, ed. *The Third Woman: Minority Women Writers of the United States.* Boston: Houghton Mifflin, 1980.

Forché, Carolyn, ed. *Against Forgetting: Twentieth-Century Poetry of Witness.* New York: Norton, 1993.

————. *The Angel of History*. New York: Harper Collins, 1994.

————. "Carolyn Forché." Interview by David Montenegro. *American Poetry Review* 17 (November/December 1988): 35–40.

————. *The Country Between Us*. New York: Harper & Row, 1981.

————. "El Salvador: An Aide Memoire." *American Poetry Review* 10 (July/August 1981): 3–7.

————. *El Salvador: Work of Thirty Photographers*. New York and London: Writers and Readers Publishing Cooperative, 1983.

————. *Gathering the Tribes*. Foreword by Stanley Kunitz. New Haven: Yale University Press, 1976.

————. "An Interview with Carolyn Forché." By Constance Coiner and Stathi Gourgouris. *Jacaranda Review* 3 (Winter 1988): 47–68.

————. "An Interview with Carolyn Forché." By Kim Addonizio and John High. *Five Fingers Review* 3 (1985): 116–131.

————. "A Lesson in Commitment." In *The Writer in our World: A Symposium Sponsored by Triquarterly Magazine*. Edited by Reginald Gibbons. Evanston, Ill.: Northwestern University Press, Winter 1986.

Frost, Robert. *The Complete Poems of Robert Frost*. New York: Rinehart and Winston, 1949.

Fry, Roger. *Vision and Design*. New York: Brentano's, 1920.

Gates, Henry Louis, Jr. "Applying the Corrective: Henry Louis Gates, Jr." Interview by Harvey Blume. *Boston Book Review* 4, May 1997, 4–6.

Geertz, Clifford. *After the Fact: Two Countries, Four Decades, One Anthropologist*. Cambridge: Harvard University Press, 1995.

————. *Local Knowledge: Further Essays in Interpretive Anthropology*. New York: Basic Books, 1983.

Gibbons, Reginald, ed. *The Writer in Our World. A TriQuarterly Symposium*. Boston and New York: Atlantic Monthly Press, 1986.

Glancy, Diane. *Claiming Breath*. Lincoln: University of Nebraska Press, 1992.

Goll, Yvan. *Lackwanna Elegy*. Translated by Galway Kinnell. Fremont, Mich.: Sumac, 1970.

Graham, Jorie. *The End of Beauty*. Hopewell, N.J.: Ecco, 1987.

————. *Erosion*. Princeton, N.J.: Princeton University Press, 1983.

————. *The Errancy*. Hopewell, N.J.: Ecco, 1997.

————. *Hybrids of Plants and of Ghosts*. Princeton, N.J.: Princeton University Press, 1980.

————. *Region of Unlikeness*. Hopewell, N.J.: Ecco, 1991.

Graves, John. "The Last Running." In *The Portable Western Reader*, William Kittredge, ed. New York: Penguin, 1997. First published in *Atlantic Monthly*, 1959.

Gregg, Linda. *Alma*. New York: Random House, 1985.

————. *The Sacraments of Desire*. St. Paul: Graywolf, 1991.

————. *Too Bright to See*. St. Paul: Graywolf, 1981.

Grinnell, George Bird. *Blackfeet Lodge Tales: The Story of a Prairie People*. New York: Scribner, 1892.

Haffenden, John. *The Life of John Berryman*. Boston: Routledge & Kegan Paul, 1982.

Hallowell, Irving A. "Bear Ceremonialism in the Northern Hemisphere." *American Anthropologist* 28 (1926): 1–175.

Harjo, Joy. *In Mad Love and War*. Wesleyan: Wesleyan University Press, 1990.
———. "The Language of Tribes." Interview by Ray González. *Bloomsbury Review* 17 (November/December 1997): 18–20.
———. *Secrets from the Center of the World*. In collaboration with Stephen Strom. Sun Tracks Series, vol. 17. Tucson: University of Arizona Press, 1989.
———. *She Had Some Horses*. New York: Thunder's Mouth Press, 1983.
———. *The Spiral of Memory: Interviews*. Edited by Laura Coltelli. Ann Arbor: University of Michigan Press, 1996.
———. *The Woman Who Fell from the Sky*. New York: Norton, 1994.
Harjo, Joy, with Gloria Bird. *Reinventing the Enemy's Language: Contemporary Native American Women's Writings of North America*. New York: Norton, 1997.
Heaney, Seamus. *Crediting Poetry: The Nobel Lecture*. New York: Farrar, Straus and Giroux, 1996.
———. Interview by James Randall. *Ploughshares* 5, no. 3 (1979): 7–22.
———. *Poems 1965–1975*. New York: Farrar, Straus and Giroux, 1980.
———. *Preoccupations: Selected Prose 1968–1978*. New York: Farrar, Straus and Giroux, 1980.
Hilden, Patricia Penn. *The Spirit Level*. New York: Farrar, Straus and Giroux, 1996.
———. *When Nickels Were Indians: An Urban, Mixed-Blood Story*. Smithsonian Series of Studies in Native American Literature. Washington, D.C.: Smithsonian Institution Press, 1995.
Hill, Roberta J. *See* Whiteman, Roberta J. Hill.
Hoffman, Daniel. "Emily Dickinson Reconsidered." *Hudson Review* 50 (1997): 206–226.
Hogan, Linda. *The Book of Medicines*. Minneapolis: Coffee House, 1993.
———. *Calling Myself Home*. Greenfield, N.Y.: Greenfield Review, 1978.
———. *Dwellings: A Spiritual History of the Living World*. New York: Norton, 1995.
———. *Eclipse*. Native American Series, no. 6. Los Angeles: UCLA American Indian Studies Center, 1984.
———. *Mean Spirit*. New York: Atheneum, 1991.
———. "Of Panthers & People." Interview by John A. Murray. *Bloomsbury Review* 18 (July/August 1998): 5, 8–9.
———. *Red Clay: Poems and Stories*. Greenfield, N.Y.: Greenfield Review, 1991.
———. *Savings*. Minneapolis: Coffee House, 1988.
———. *Seeing Through the Sun*. Amherst: University of Massachusetts Press, 1985.
———. *Solar Storms*. New York: Simon & Schuster, 1995.
Hogan, Linda, Deena Metzger, and Brenda Peterson, eds. *Intimate Nature: The Bond Between Women and Animals*. New York: Fawcett/Ballantine, 1998.
Hollander, John. Introduction to *The Best American Poetry 1998*, edited by David Lehman. New York: Scribner, 1998.
Holquist, Michael. *Dialogism: Bakhtin and His World*. London and New York: Routledge, 1990.
Howard, Richard. *Alone with America*. New York: Atheneum, 1980.
Hughes, Robert. *Culture of Complaint: The Fraying of America*. New York: Oxford University Press, 1993.
Hughes, Ted. *Birthday Letters*. New York: Farrar Straus Giroux, 1998.
———. *Crow*. New York: Harper & Row, 1970.

————. *The Essential Shakespeare*. The Essential Poets, vol. 17. New York: Ecco, 1991.

————. *The Hawk in the Rain*. London: Faber and Faber, 1957.

————. *Ted Hughes: The Unaccommodated Universe*. Edited by Ekbert Faas. Santa Barbara: Black Sparrow Press, 1980.

————. *Winter Pollen: Occasional Prose*. Edited by William Scammell. New York: Picador, 1994.

————. *Wodwo*. London: Faber and Faber, 1967.

Hugo, Richard. *31 Letters and 13 Dreams*. New York: Norton, 1977.

Hyde, Lewis. *The Gift: Imagination and the Erotic Life of Property*. New York: Vintage/Random House, 1983.

————. *Trickster Makes This World: Mischief, Myth, and Art*. New York: Farrar, Straus and Giroux, 1998.

Hymes, Dell. *"In Vain I Tried to Tell You": Essays in Native American Ethnopoetics*. Philadelphia: University of Pennsylvania Press, 1981.

Jaskoski, Helen, ed. *Early Native American Writing: New Critical Essays*. Cambridge: Cambridge University Press, 1996.

Jennings, Francis. *The Invasion of America: Indians, Colonialism, and the Cant of Conquest*. Chapel Hill: University of North Carolina Press, 1975.

Kazin, Alfred. *An American Procession: Major American Writers, 1830–1930*. Cambridge, Mass.: Harvard University Press, 1984.

————. *God and the American Writer*. New York: Knopf, 1997.

————. *A Lifetime Burning in Every Moment: From the Journals of Alfred Kazin*. New York: HarperCollins, 1996.

————. *On Native Grounds: An Interpretation of Modern American Prose Literature*. New York: Harcourt, Brace, 1942.

————. *Writing Was Everything*. Cambridge, Mass.: Harvard University Press, 1995.

Kinnell, Galway. *The Avenue Bearing the Initial of Christ into the New World*. Boston: Houghton Mifflin, 1964.

————. *Black Light*. Boston: Houghton Mifflin, 1965. Reissue, San Francisco: North Point, 1980.

————. *Body Rags*. Boston: Houghton Mifflin, 1968.

————. *The Book of Nightmares*. Boston: Houghton Mifflin, 1971.

————. *First Poems 1946–1954*. Boston: Houghton Mifflin, 1974.

————. *Flower Herding on Mount Monadnock*. Boston: Houghton Mifflin, 1964.

————. *Mortal Acts, Mortal Words*. Boston: Houghton Mifflin, 1980.

————. *The Past*. Boston: Houghton Mifflin, 1985.

————. *Selected Poems*. Boston: Houghton Mifflin, 1982.

————. *What a Kingdom It Was*. Boston: Houghton Mifflin, 1960.

————. *When One Has Lived a Long Time Alone*. New York: Houghton Mifflin, 1994.

Kluckhohn, Clyde. *Mirror for Man: The Relationship of Anthropology to Modern Life*. New York: McGraw-Hill, 1949.

Kramer, Lawrence. *Music and Poetry: The Nineteenth Century and After*. Berkeley and Los Angeles: University of California Press, 1984.

Kristeva, Julia. *Strangers to Ourselves*. Translated by Leon S. Roudiez. New York: Columbia University Press, 1991.

Krupat, Arnold. *The Turn to the Native: Studies in Criticism and Culture*. Lincoln: University of Nebraska Press, 1996.

Krupat, Arnold and Brian Swann, eds. *Everything Matters: Autobiographical Essays by Native American Writers.* New York: Random House, 1998.

Kunitz, Stanley. *Interviews and Encounters with Stanley Kunitz.* Edited by Stanley Moss. Riverdale-on-Hudson, N.Y.: The Sheep Meadow Press, 1993.

———. *A Kind of Order, A Kind of Folly: Essays and Conversations.* Boston: Little, Brown, 1975.

Lame Deer, John (Fire), and Richard Erdoes. *Lame Deer Seeker of Visions: The Life of a Sioux Medicine Man.* New York: Simon and Schuster, 1972.

Larkin, Philip. *High Windows.* New York: Noonday, 1974.

Laughlin, James. *Remembering William Carlos Williams.* New York: New Directions, 1995.

Lawrence, D. H. *The Complete Poems of D. H. Lawrence.* Edited by Vivian de Sola Pinto and R. Warren Roberts. New York: Viking, 1964.

———. *Mornings in Mexico.* 1927. Reprint, New York: Knopf, 1934; London: Heinemann, 1956.

———. *The Plumed Serpent.* New York: Martin Stecker, 1926.

———. *Selected Letters.* New York: Penguin, 1978.

———. *Studies in Classic American Literature.* New York: Seltzer, 1923.

Levertov, Denise. *The Poet in the World.* New York: New Directions, 1973.

———. *The Sorrow Dance.* New York: New Directions, 1966.

———. *Tesserae: Memories & Suppositions.* New York: New Directions, 1995.

Lewis, R. W. B. *The American Adam: Innocence, Tragedy, and Tradition in the Nineteenth Century.* Chicago: University of Chicago Press, 1955.

Lincoln, Kenneth. *The Good Red Road: Passages into Native America.* With Al Logan Slagle. San Francisco: Harper & Row, 1987. Reprint, with a new epilogue, Lincoln: University of Nebraska Press, Bison Books, 1997.

———. *Indi'n Humor: Bicultural Play in Native America.* New York: Oxford University Press, 1993.

———. *Native American Renaissance.* Berkeley and Los Angeles: University of California Press, 1983.

———. "Yo, Ken! Alfonso here. . . ." *American Indian Culture and Research Journal* 22 (1998): 171–181. Also published in *Native Peoples Magazine,* Spring 1998, 34–40.

Lourie, Dick, ed. *Come to Power: Eleven Contemporary American Indian Poets.* Trumansberg, N.Y.: Crossing Press, 1974.

Lowell, Robert. *Collected Prose.* Edited by Robert Giroux. New York: Farrar, Straus and Giroux, 1987.

Marx, Leo. *The Machine in the Garden: Technology and the Pastoral Ideal in America.* Oxford: Oxford University Press, 1964.

Matthiessen, F. O. *American Renaissance: Art and Expression in the Age of Emerson and Whitman.* New York: Oxford University Press, 1941.

McHugh, Heather. *Broken English: Poetry and Partiality.* Hanover, N.H.: Wesleyan University Press, 1993.

McNickle, D'Arcy. *Native American Tribalism: Indian Survivals and Renewals.* New York: Oxford University Press, 1973. Reprint, 1979.

Means, Russell. *Where White Men Fear to Tread: The Autobiography of Russell Means.* With Marvin J. Wolf. New York: St. Martin's Griffin, 1995.

Merwin, W. S. *The Carrier of Ladders.* New York: Atheneum, 1970.

Milosz, Czeslaw. *The Witness of Poetry.* Cambridge: Harvard University Press, 1983.

Momaday, N. Scott. *The Ancient Child.* New York: Doubleday, 1989.

――――. *Conversations with N. Scott Momaday.* Edited by Matthias Schubnell. Jackson: University Press of Mississippi, 1997.

――――. *House Made of Dawn.* New York: Harper & Row, 1968.

――――. *In the Bear's House.* New York: St. Martin's, 1999.

――――. *In the Presence of the Sun: Stories and Poems, 1961–1991.* New York: St. Martin's Press, 1992.

――――. "A Love Affair with Emily Dickinson." *Viva,* August 6, 1972.

――――. *The Man Made of Words: Essays, Stories, Passages.* New York: St. Martin's, 1997.

――――. *The Names.* New York: Harper & Row, 1976.

――――. *The Way to Rainy Mountain.* Albuquerque: University of New Mexico Press, 1969. Paperback reprint, 1976.

Monroe, Mark. *An Indian in White America.* Edited by Carolyn Reyer, with an afterword by Kenneth Lincoln. Philadelphia: Temple University Press, 1994.

Moore, Marianne. *A Marianne Moore Reader.* New York: Macmillan/Viking, 1965.

――――. *Complete Poems.* New York: Macmillan/Viking, 1967.

Nabokov, Peter, ed. *Native American Testimony: An Anthology of Indian and White Relations, First Encounter to Dispossession.* New York: Thomas Y. Crowell, 1978. Reprint. New York: Harper & Row, 1979.

Neihardt, John G., trans. *Black Elk Speaks: Being the Life Story of a Holy Man of the Oglala Sioux.* 1932. Reprint. New York: Pocket Books, 1972.

Neruda, Pablo. *Memoirs.* Translated by Hardie St. Martin. New York: Farrar, Straus and Giroux, 1977.

――――. *Selected Odes of Pablo Neruda.* Translated by Margaret Sayers Peden. Berkeley and Los Angeles: University of California Press, 1990.

――――. "Towards an Impure Poetry." In *Caballo verde para la poesía* (Madrid), no. 1 (October 1935): 1–3.

Newsletter of The Institute for the Preservation of Original Languages of the Americas, Native Language Network (Fall 1997): 1, 6.

Niatum, Duane. *Carriers of the Dream Wheel: Contemporary Native American Poetry.* San Francisco: Harper & Row, 1975.

――――. *Harper's Anthology of 20th Century Native American Poetry.* San Francisco: Harper & Row, 1988.

Olds, Sharon. *The Dead and the Living.* New York: Knopf, 1987.

――――. *The Father.* New York: Knopf, 1992.

――――. *The Gold Cell.* New York: Knopf, 1987.

――――. "Rooms of Passion and Loss: An Interview with Sharon Olds." By Patricia Kirkpatrick. *Hungry Mind Review* 39 (Fall 1996): 26–27, 44–49.

――――. *Satan Says.* Pittsburgh: University of Pittsburgh Press, 1980.

――――. *The Wellspring.* New York: Knopf, 1996.

Oliver, Mary. *American Primitive.* Boston: Little, Brown, 1983.

Olson, Charles. *Selected Writings.* Edited by Robert Creeley. New York: New Directions, 1966.

Ortiz, Simon J. *Speaking for the Generations: Native Writers on Writing.* Tucson: University of Arizona Press, 1997.

Paul, Sherman. "Ethnopoetics: An 'Other' Tradition." *North Dakota Quarterly* 53 (Spring 1985): 37–44.

Paz, Octavio. *In Praise of Hands: Contemporary Crafts of the World.* Greenwich, Conn.: New York Graphic Society, 1974.

———. *The Labyrinth of Solitude and Other Writings.* Translated by Lysander Kemp. New York: Grove, 1985.

Pearce, Roy Harvey. *The Continuity of American Poetry.* Middletown, Conn.: Wesleyan University Press, 1961. Revised edition, Princeton, N.J.: Princeton University Press, 1987.

———. *Savagism and Civilization: A Study of the Indian and the American Mind.* Berkeley and Los Angeles: University of California Press, 1988. Revised edition of *The Savages of America* (Baltimore: Johns Hopkins, 1953).

Penn, W. S. *All My Sins Are Relatives.* Lincoln: University of Nebraska Press, 1995.

Peyer, Bernd C. *The Singing Spirit: Early Short Stories by North American Indians.* Tucson: University of Arizona Press, 1989.

Pinker, Steven. *The Language Instinct: How the Mind Creates Language.* New York: William Morrow, 1994.

Pinsky, Robert. "An Interview with the Poet Laureate." By Tom Sleigh. *American Poet* (Winter 1997–98): 26–33.

Plath, Sylvia. *The Collected Poems.* Edited by Ted Hughes. New York: Harper & Row, 1981.

———. *The Journals of Sylvia Plath.* Edited by Ted Hughes and Frances McCullough. New York: Dial, 1982.

Pound, Ezra. *ABC of Reading.* New York: New Directions, 1960.

———. *Gaudier-Brzeska: A Memoir.* New York: New Directions, 1970.

———. *Guide to Kulchur.* New York: New Directions, 1970.

Pound, Ezra, and Marvella Spann, eds. *Confucius to Cummings: An Anthology of Poetry.* New York: New Directions, 1964.

Preston, Richard. *Cree Narrative: Expressing the Personal Meaning of Events.* National Museum of Man Mercury Series. Canadian Ethnology Service Paper, no. 30. Ottawa: National Museum of Canada, 1975.

Ramsey, Jarold. *Reading the Fire: Essays in the Traditional Indian Literatures of the Far West.* Lincoln: University of Nebraska Press, 1983.

Riddle, Joseph. *The Clairvoyant Eye.* Baton Rouge: Louisiana State University Press, 1965.

Rockwell, David. *Giving Voice to Bear: North American Indian Myths, Rituals, and Images of the Bear.* Niwot, Colo.: Roberts Rinehart, 1991.

Roethke, Theodore. *The Collected Poems of Theodore Roethke.* New York: Doubleday, 1966.

———. *On the Poet and His Craft: Selected Prose of Theodore Roethke.* Edited by Ralph J. Mills, Jr. Seattle: University of Washington Press, 1965.

———. *Selected Letters of Theodore Roethke.* Edited by Ralph J. Mills, Jr. Seattle: University of Washington Press, 1968.

Rothenberg, Jerome, ed. *Shaking the Pumpkin: Traditional Poetry of the Indian North Americas.* Garden City, N.Y.: Doubleday, 1972.

Rothenberg, Jerome and Diane. *Symposium of the Whole: A Range of Discourse*

Toward an Ethnopoetics. Berkeley and Los Angeles: University of California Press, 1983.

Sapir, Edward. "Emily Dickinson, A Primitive." *Poetry* 26 (May 1925): 97–105.

Sappho. *The Love Songs of Sappho*. Translated by Paul Roche. New York: Penguin, 1966.

Sarris, Greg. *Grand Avenue: A Novel in Stories*. New York: Hyperion, 1994.

———. *Keeping Slug Woman Alive: A Holistic Approach to American Indian Texts*. Berkeley and Los Angeles: University of California Press, 1993.

———, ed. *The Sound of Rattles and Clappers: A Collection of New California Indian Writing*. Tucson: University of Arizona Press, 1994.

———. *Watermelon Nights*. New York: Hyperion, 1998.

———. *Weaving the Dream: Mabel McKay*. Berkeley and Los Angeles: University of California Press, 1994.

Scully, Tames, ed. *Modern Poetics*. New York: McGraw-Hill, 1965.

Shepard, Paul, and Barry Sanders, with an afterword by Gary Snyder. *The Sacred Paw: The Bear in Nature, Myth, and Literature*. New York: Viking, 1985.

Sjöö, Monica, and Barbara Mor. *The Great Cosmic Mother: Rediscovering the Religion of the Earth*. San Francisco: Harper & Row, 1987.

Slotkin, Richard. *The Fatal Environment: The Myth of the Frontier in the Age of Industrialization 1800–1890*. New York: Atheneum, 1985.

———. *Gunfighter Nation: The Myth of the Frontier in Twentieth-Century America*. Norman: University of Oklahoma Press, 1991.

———. *Regeneration Through Violence: The Mythology of the American Frontier, 1600–1860*. Middletown, Conn.: Wesleyan University Press, 1973.

Smith, Henry Nash. *Virgin Land: The American Frontier as Symbol and Myth*. Cambridge: Harvard University Press, 1970.

Snyder, Gary. *Earth House Hold: Technical Notes and Queries to Fellow Dharma Revolutionaries*. New York: New Directions, 1969.

———. *The Old Ways: Six Essays*. San Francisco: City Lights, 1977.

———. *The Practice of the Wild*. San Francisco: North Point, 1990.

———. *Turtle Island*. New York: New Directions, 1974.

Sollors, Werner. *Beyond Ethnicity*. New York: Oxford University Press, 1986.

———. *The Invention of Ethnicity*. New York: Oxford University Press, 1989.

Spindler, George D. and Louise S. "American Indian Personality Types and Their Sociocultural Roots." *Annals of the American Academy of Political and Social Science* 311 (May 1957): 147–157.

Stedman, Raymond William. *Shadows of the Indian: Stereotypes in American Culture*. Norman: University of Oklahoma Press, 1982.

Stevens, Wallace. *The Auroras of Autumn*. New York: Knopf, 1950.

———. *Collected Poems*. New York: Knopf, 1954. Reprint, New York: Vintage/Random House, 1990.

———. *Harmonium*. New York: Knopf, 1923.

———. *Letters of Wallace Stevens*. Edited by Holly Stevens. New York: Knopf, 1966.

———. *The Necessary Angel: Essays on Reality and the Imagination*. New York: Knopf, 1951.

———. *Opus Posthumous*. Edited by Elsie Stevens and Holly Stevens. New York:

Knopf, 1957. Reprint, Milton J. Bates, ed. New York: Vintage/Random House, 1990.

———. *The Palm at the End of the Mind: Selected Poems and a Play.* Edited by Holly Stevens. New York: Knopf, 1971.

Styron, William. *Darkness Visible: A Memoir of Madness.* New York: Random House, 1990.

Swann, Brian, ed. *Coming to Light: Contemporary Translations of the Native Literatures of North America.* New York: Vintage, 1994.

———, ed. *On the Translation of Native American Literatures.* Washington, D.C.: Smithsonian Institution, 1992.

———, ed. *Smoothing the Ground: Essays on Native American Oral Literature.* Berkeley and Los Angeles: University of California Press, 1983.

———, ed. *Song of the Sky: Versions of Native American Songs & Poems.* Foreword by Paula Gunn Allen. New York: Four Zoas, 1985.

———, ed. *Wearing the Morning Star: Native American Song-Poems.* New York: Random House, 1996.

Swann, Brian, and Arnold Krupat, eds. *Recovering the Word: Essays on Native American Literature.* Berkeley and Los Angeles: University of California Press, 1987.

TallMountain, Mary. *Celebrating Mary TallMountain.* Compiled by Yvonne Yarber. San Francisco: TallMountain Circle, 1994.

———. *Continuum.* Marvin, S.D.: Blue Cloud Quarterly, 1988.

———. *Good Grease.* New York: Strawberry Press, 1978.

———. *The Light on the Tent Wall, A Bridging.* Native American Series no. 8. Los Angeles: UCLA American Indian Studies Center, 1990.

———. *Listen to the Night: Poems for the Animal Spirits of Mother Earth.* San Francisco: Freedom Voices, 1995.

———. *Nine Poems.* San Francisco: Friars Press, 1977.

———. *Quick Brush of Wings.* San Francisco: Freedom Voices/Red Star, Black Rose, 1991.

———. *There Is No Word for Goodbye: Poems by Mary TallMountain.* Marvin, S.D.: Blue Cloud, 1982. Reprint, Oakland: Red Star, Black Rose, 1990.

Tapahonso, Luci. *Blue Horses Rush In: Poems and Stories.* Tucson: University of Arizona Press, 1997.

———. *A Breeze Swept Through.* Albuquerque: West End, 1987.

———. *One More Shiprock Night.* San Antonio: Tejas Art, 1981.

———. *Sáanii Dahataal / The Women Are Singing.* Tucson: University of Arizona Press, 1993.

———. *Seasonal Woman.* Santa Fe: Tooth of Time Books, 1982.

Thomas, Dylan. *Portrait of the Artist as a Young Dog.* New York: New Directions, 1940.

———. *Selected Letters of Dylan Thomas.* Edited by Constantine Fitzgibbon. New York: New Directions, 1966.

Todorov, Tzvetan. *The Conquest of America: The Question of the Other.* Translated by Richard Howard. New York: Harper & Row, 1984.

Toelken, Barre. "Poetic Retranslation and the 'Pretty Languages' of Yellowman."

In *Traditional Literatures of the American Indian,* edited by Karl Kroeber. Lincoln: University of Nebraska Press, 1981.

———. "Seeing with a Native Eye: How Many Sheep Will It Hold?" In *Seeing with a Native Eye. Essays on Native American Religion,* edited by Walter Holden Capps. New York: Harper & Row, 1976.

Torgovnick, Marianna. *Gone Primitive: Savage Intellects, Modern Lives.* Chicago: University of Chicago Press, 1990.

———. *Primitive Passions: Men, Women, and the Quest for Ecstasy.* New York: Alfred A. Knopf, 1997.

Tsosie, Rebecca Pereyra. "Changing Woman: American 'Native' Poets." Manuscript. UCLA, 1985.

Turner, Frederick. *Spirit of Place: The Making of an American Literary Landscape.* San Francisco: Sierra Club Books, 1989.

Two Shoes, Minnie. "AIMster Gangsters from the past: Where are they now?" *Aboriginal Voices* 5 (May/June 1998): 28–29.

———. "How activism shaped the life of Wes Studi." *Aboriginal Voices* 5 (May/June 1998): 28–29, 30–31.

Ulibarri, Sabine R. *Mi Abuela Fumada Puros / My Grandpa Smoked Cigars.* Berkeley: Quinto Sol, 1977.

Underhill, Ruth M. *The Autobiography of a Papago Woman.* Memoirs 46. Menaska,Wis: American Anthropological Association, 1936.

———. *Singing for Power: The Song Magic of the Papago Indians of Southern Arizona.* Berkeley and Los Angeles: University of California Press, 1938.

Utley, Robert M. *The Lance and the Shield: The Life and Times of Sitting Bull.* New York: Ballantine, 1993.

Valéry, Paul. *The Art of Poetry.* Introduction by T. S. Eliot. Bollingen Series vol. 45, no. 7. Princeton, N.J.: Princeton University Press, 1958.

———. *Selected Writings.* New York: New Directions, 1980.

Vendler, Helen. *The Breaking of Style: Hopkins, Heaney, Graham.* Cambridge: Harvard University Press, 1995.

———. *The Given and the Made: Strategies of Poetic Definition.* Cambridge: Harvard University Press, 1995.

———. *The Harvard Book of Contemporary American Poetry.* Cambridge: Harvard University Press, 1985.

———. *The Music of What Happens. Poems, Poets, Critics.* Cambridge: Harvard University Press, 1980.

———. *Part of Nature, Part of Us. Modern American Poets.* Cambridge: Harvard University Press, 1980.

———. *Wallace Stevens: Words Chosen Out of Desire.* Cambridge: Harvard University Press, 1986.

———, ed. *Voices and Visions. The Poet in America.* New York: Random House, 1987.

Vestal, Stanley. *Sitting Bull, Champion of the Sioux: A Biography.* 1932. Reprint. Norman: University of Oklahoma Press, 1956.

———. "The Works of Sitting Bull, Real and Imaginary." *Southwest Review* 19 (April 1934): 265–278.

Warren, Robert Penn. *Chief Joseph of the Nez Perce, Who Called Themselves the Nimupu—* *"The Real People."* New York: Random House, 1982.

Weatherford, Jack. *Savages and Civilization: Who Will Survive?* New York: Ballantine, 1994.

Weinberger, Eliot. Review of *The Country Between Us,* by Carolyn Forché. In *Sulfur 6: A Literary Tri-Quarterly of the Whole Art,* 2 (1983): 158–164.

Welch, James. *The Death of Jim Loney.* New York: Harper & Row, 1979.

———. *Fools Crow.* New York: Viking, 1986.

———. Interview, April 1985. Columbia, Mo: American Audio Prose Library. Audiocassette.

———. *Killing Custer: The Battle of the Little Bighorn and the Fate of the Plains Indians.* With Paul Stekler. New York: Norton, 1994.

———. *Riding the Earthboy 40.* New York: World, 1971. Reprint, New York: Harper & Row, 1976.

———. *Winter in the Blood.* New York: Harper & Row, 1974.

Welsh, Andrew. *Roots of Lyric: Primitive Poetry and Modern Poetics.* Princeton: Princeton University Press, 1978.

Wesling, Donald. *The Chances of Rhyme: Device and Modernity.* Berkeley and Los Angeles: University of California Press, 1980.

White, Hayden. "The Wild Man Within." In *The Wild Man Within,* edited by Edward J. Dudley and Maximillian E. Novak. Pittsburgh: University of Pittsburgh Press, 1973.

Whiteman, Roberta J. Hill. "Immersed in Words." In *Speaking for the Generations: Native Writers on Writing.* Edited by Simon J. Ortiz. Tucson: University of Arizona Press, 1998.

———. (Published under Roberta J. Hill). *Philadelphia Flowers.* Minneapolis: Holy Cow! Press, 1997.

———. *Star Quilt.* Minneapolis: Holy Cow! Press, 1984.

Williams, William Carlos. *The Autobiography of William Carlos Williams.* New York: New Directions, 1967.

———. *The Desert Music.* New York: New Directions, 1954.

———. *Imaginations.* New York: New Directions, 1970.

———. *In the American Grain.* New York: New Directions, 1925.

———. *Kora in Hell.* New York: New Directions, 1920.

———. *Paterson.* New York: New Directions, 1946–58.

———. *Pictures from Brueghel.* New York: New Directions, 1962.

———. *The Selected Letters of William Carlos Williams.* Edited by John C. Thirlwall. New York: New Directions, 1984.

———. *Selected Poems.* Introduction by Randall Jarrell. New York: New Directions, 1949.

———. *Spring and All.* New York: New Directions, 1921.

Winn, James Anderson. *Unsuspected Eloquence: A History of the Relation Between Poetry and Music.* New Haven: Yale University Press, 1981.

Winters, Yvor. *Forms of Discovery: Critical and Historical Essays on the Form of the Short Poem in English.* Chicago: Swallow, 1967.

———. *In Defence of Reason: Primitivism and Decadence; a Study of American Experimental Poetry.* Denver: University of Denver Press, 1947.

————. *Maude's Curse*. Norfolk, Conn.: New Directions, 1938.

Witherspoon, Gary. *Language and Art in the Navajo Universe*. Ann Arbor: University of Michigan Press, 1977.

Witt, Shirley Hill, and Stan Steiner. *The Way: An Anthology of American Indian Literature*. New York: Knopf, 1972.

Woodard, Charles L. *Ancestral Voices: Conversations with N. Scott Momaday*. Lincoln: University of Nebraska Press, 1989.

Zolbrod, Paul. *Reading the Voice: Native American Oral Poetry on the Written Page*. Salt Lake City: University of Utah Press, 1995.

INDEX

Text: 10/12 Baskerville
Display: New Baskerville
Composition: Binghamton Valley Composition
Printing and binding: Maple-Vail Book Mfg. Group